The Finance Act 2011

The Finance Act 2011

Contributors

Graham Airs
Mohammed Amin
MA, FCA, AMCT, CTA (Fellow)
Tom Aston
Tony Austin
Lynnette Bober ACA, CTA, TEP
Sarah Bradford BA,
ACA, CTA (Fellow)
Stuart Chalcraft
Mark Downey BA
Steve Edge
Phil Greatrex FCA, ATII
John Hayward,
Pension Consultant
Andrew Hubbard BMus, PhD,
CTA (Fellow) ATT

Zigurds Kronbergs MA, BSc,
ARCS, ACA, FCCA
Michael Lane
John Lindsay BA, FCA, FTII
David O'Keeffe
Anne Redston, FCA, CTA (Fellow)
Gary Richards MA, LLB,
ATII, Solicitor
Mark Schofield
Dana Ward
Neil Warren
Andrew Watt
Jeremy White LLB, FIIT, Barrister
Martin Wilson MA, FCA

LexisNexis®

Members of the LexisNexis Group worldwide

United Kingdom	LexisNexis, a Division of Reed Elsevier (UK) Ltd, Halsbury House, 35 Chancery Lane, London, WC2A 1EL, and London House, 20–22 East London Street, Edinburgh EH7 4BQ
Australia	LexisNexis Butterworths, Chatswood, New South Wales
Austria	LexisNexis Verlag ARD Orac GmbH & Co KG, Vienna
Benelux	LexisNexis Benelux, Amsterdam
Canada	LexisNexis Canada, Markham, Ontario
China	LexisNexis China, Beijing and Shanghai
France	LexisNexis SA, Paris
Germany	LexisNexis Deutschland GmbH, Munster
Hong Kong	LexisNexis Hong Kong, Hong Kong
India	LexisNexis India, New Delhi
Italy	Giuffrè Editore, Milan
Japan	LexisNexis Japan, Tokyo
Malaysia	Malayan Law Journal Sdn Bhd, Kuala Lumpur
New Zealand	LexisNexis NZ Ltd, Wellington
Poland	Wydawnictwo Prawnicze LexisNexis Sp, Warsaw
Singapore	LexisNexis Singapore, Singapore
South Africa	LexisNexis Butterworths, Durban
USA	LexisNexis, Dayton, Ohio

Published by LexisNexis

This is a Tolley title

A CIP Catalogue record for this book is available from the British Library.

ISBN 9781405755368 (LNB)

Typeset by Letterpart Ltd, Reigate, Surrey

Printed in the UK by CPI William Clowes Ltd, Beccles, NR34 7TL

Visit LexisNexis at www.lexisnexis.co.uk

FINANCE ACT 2011
FOREWORD

For the fourth time now I am grateful to LexisNexis for giving me the opportunity to write a brief foreword to the Annotated Copy of the annual Finance Act (or Acts, as it turned out to be last year). This year's Act is, as Zigurd Kronbergs observes at the beginning of his Introduction, 'by no means as long as the blockbusting Acts of recent years.' But, as he immediately adds, the Act 'nevertheless weighs in at 93 sections, 26 Schedules and 381 pages.'

For a statute of that nature this volume, with its full introduction and detailed annotations on the contents, seems to me to be an indispensable boon to practitioners. Thinking back to 40 years or so ago, when I was a fairly recently established practitioner in revenue law, Finance Bills were more modest in size. It was possible to read a current Bill as a whole – admittedly with care and concentration, and taking quite some time to do it – and emerge feeling that one had a sufficient basis to be able to research and deal with the detailed questions which might arise in practice. It is hard to imagine a practitioner being able to do that now, so many are the different topics covered by a contemporary Act and so intricate and lengthy are the provisions on any particular topic likely to be.

But in this volume the provisions on each topic have been carefully studied and researched by distinguished specialists who have been able to concentrate on particular topics and to prepare full annotations about them. The annotations will be of great value to practitioners confronted by questions from clients who (to quote from Forewords of mine relating to Acts of 2009 and 2010) 'expect him or her to know all about the latest Finance Acts and to be able to provide quick and informed advice on all sorts of different matters which, for all that the clients know, may be fundamentally affected by some small print provision tucked away somewhere'.

As in the last three years, I warmly recommend this 2011 volume to tax practitioners and other users for whom it has been prepared.

Andrew Park

(Sir Andrew Park, formerly Andrew Park QC, and later, from 1997 to 2006, Mr Justice Park)
July 2011

CONTENTS

		Page
	Relevant Dates and Abbreviations	
	About the Authors	
	Introduction	*i*
	Finance Act 2011	
	Arrangement of sections	**1**
Sections		
	Charges, Rates, Allowances etc	**5**
1–3	Income tax	5
4–7	Corporation tax	6
8–9	Capital gains tax	8
10–12	Capital allowances	11
13–15	Alcohol duties	15
16	Tobacco duties	17
17–18	Gambling duties	18
19–20	Fuel duties	20
21–22	Vehicle excise duty	22
23–25	Environmental taxes	26
	Income Tax, Corporation Tax and Capital Gains Tax	**27**
26–34	Anti-avoidance provisions	27
35–43	Exemptions and reliefs	31
44–46	Chargeable gains	38
47–48	Foreign profits	39
49–50	Investment trusts	39
51–60	Miscellaneous	42
61–64	*Oil*	**49**
65–72	*Pensions*	**51**
73	*Bank Levy*	**57**
	Other Taxes	**57**
74–77	Value added tax	57
78–80	Climate change levy	60
81	Aggregates levy	61
82–83	Stamp duty land tax	62
84	Stamp duty reserve tax	62
85–87	*Administration etc*	**63**
88–91	*Miscellaneous Provisions*	**65**
92–93	*Final Provisions*	**68**
Sch 1	New high strength beer duty	69
Sch 2	Employment income provided through third parties	70
Sch 3	Tainted charity donations	138
Sch 4	Amounts not fully recognised for accounting purposes	152
Sch 5	Group mismatch schemes	156
Sch 6	Leasing businesses	164
Sch 7	Investment companies	170
Sch 8	Reduction in childcare relief for higher earners	174
Sch 9	Value shifting	178
Sch 10	Company ceasing to be member of group	180
Sch 11	Pre-entry losses	189
Sch 12	Controlled foreign companies	192
Sch 13	Profits of foreign permanent establishments etc	209

Sch 14	Furnished holiday lettings	235
Sch 15	Chargeable gains: oil activities	247
Sch 16	Benefits under pension schemes	250
Sch 17	Annual allowance charge	288
Sch 18	Lifetime allowance charge	304
Sch 19	The bank levy	309
Sch 20	Supplies of commodities to be used in producing electricity	350
Sch 21	Prevention of SDLT avoidance	353
Sch 22	Transfers involving multiple dwellings	355
Sch 23	Data-gathering powers	360
Sch 24	Amendments of Schedule 36 to FA 2008	379
Sch 25	Mutual assistance for recovery of taxes etc	382
Sch 26	Redundant reliefs	386
	Finance Bill Debates	389
	Index	399

RELEVANT DATES AND ABBREVIATIONS

Budget statement	23 March 2011
Finance Bill	31 March 2011
Royal Assent	19 July 2011

ALDA	=	Alcoholic Liquor Duties Act 1979
BGDA	=	Betting and Gaming Duties Act
CA	=	Companies Act
CAA	=	Capital Allowances Act
CEMA	=	Customs and Excise Management Act 1979
CFC	=	Controlled Foreign Company
CGT	=	Capital Gains Tax
Ch	=	Chapter (of a part of an Act)
CRCA	=	Commissioners for Revenue and Customs Act 2005
CTA	=	Corporation Tax Act
CTSA	=	Corporation Tax Self-Assessment
CTTA	=	Capital Transfer Tax Act
ECJ	=	European Court of Justice
EIS	=	Enterprise Investment Scheme
FA	=	Finance Act
F(No 2)A	=	Finance (No 2) Act
F(No 3)A	=	Finance (No 3) Act
FISMA	=	Financial Services and Markets Act 2000
HMRC	=	Her Majesty's Revenue and Customs
HODA	=	Hydrocarbon Oil Duties Act
ICTA	=	Income and Corporation Taxes Act
IHTA	=	Inheritance Tax Act
ITA	=	Income Tax Act
ITEPA	=	Income Tax (Earnings and Pensions) Act 2003
ITMA	=	Income Tax Management Act
ITTOIA	=	Income Tax (Trading and Other Income) Act 2005
OTA	=	Oil Taxation Act
para	=	paragraph (of a Schedule to an Act)
PRTA	=	Petroleum Revenue Tax Act
reg	=	regulation (of an SI)
s	=	section (of an Act)
SAYE	=	Save as you Earn
Sch	=	Schedule (to an Act)
SDTS	=	Simon's Direct Tax Service
SI	=	Statutory Instrument (since 1948)
ss	=	sections
sub-para	=	sub-paragraph
sub-s	=	subsection
SWTI	=	Simon's Weekly Tax Intelligence
TA	=	Income and Corporation Taxes Act 1988
TCGA	=	Taxation of Chargeable Gains Act 1992
TMA	=	Taxes Management Act 1970
TIOPA	=	Taxation (International and Other Provisions) Act 2010
TPDA	=	Tobacco Products Duty Act
VATA	=	Value Added Tax Act 1994
VCT	=	Venture Capital Trust
VERA	=	Vehicle Excise and Registration Act

ABOUT THE AUTHORS

Graham Airs

Graham Airs is a Tax Partner at Slaughter and May. He is also a member of the Law Society's Tax Law Committee and of its International Tax Sub-Committee.

Mohammed Amin MA FCA AMCT CTA (Fellow)

Mohammed Amin is an Islamic finance consultant and was previously UK head of Islamic finance at PricewaterhouseCoopers LLP. He is also a Council Member of the Chartered Institute of Taxation.

Tom Aston

Tom Aston is a tax partner with KPMG in the UK and an adviser to banking and insurance groups on a range of corporate and international tax issues. His direct line is 020-7311-5811 and his e-mail address is tom.aston@kpmg.co.uk

Tony Austin FCA

Tony Austin is a qualified accountant and tax consultant with many years' experience advising individuals and companies on their tax affairs. For the last 15 years he has been heavily involved in the charity sector advising on direct taxation matters affecting charities and donors. Formerly a tax partner with BDO and Mazars, he now operates as an independent consultant.

Lynnette Bober ACA CTA TEP

Lynnette Bober is a private client tax director at the London office of Rawlinson & Hunter.

Lynnette is a chartered accountant, a chartered tax adviser, and a member of the Society of Trust and Estate Practitioners. Specialising in the field of personal taxation and trusts (including remittance basis issues and offshore trust planning), she contributes to various technical publications and journals. Lynnette is a member of the ICAEW Tax Faculty Committee and serves in various capacities on a number of the Tax Faculty's technical subcommittees and working parties.

Sarah Bradford, BA (Hons), ACA, CTA (Fellow)

Sarah Bradford is the director of Writetax Ltd, a company providing technical writing services on tax and National Insurance contributions. She writes extensively and has contributed to a range of products and services, including various editions of the Finance Act Handbook and Simon's Direct Tax Service. She can be contacted by email at sarah.bradford@writetax.co.uk.

Stuart Chalcraft

Stuart Chalcraft is an Associate Partner at Ernst & Young LLP, specialising in asset management. He has 15 years experience in advising a wide range of clients from global asset managers and their funds through to private equity houses and hedge fund managers. He is a member of the IMA tax committee and a frequent speaker at a number of industry events.

Mark Downey, BA
Mark Downey is a Senior Tax Manager at a major listed UK insurance group where he specialises in all aspects of the taxation of life insurance companies. He also has experience in the taxation of policyholder benefits and life insurance product design.
Before taking on his current role, Mark spent four years as a senior consultant in the insurance tax group of a Big Four accountancy firm.
Mark began his tax career in the Inland Revenue as was, spending fourteen years as an inspector of taxes. He specialised in the taxation of insurance companies, both life and general, for the final five years of his Revenue career.
Mark is a regular writer and conference speaker on tax issues affecting life insurance companies.

Steve Edge, Solicitor
Steve Edge is a partner in Slaughter and May's tax department with a broad tax practice. Steve is a frequent contributor to a variety of tax publications and a regular speaker at conferences.

Phil Greatrex, FCA, ATII
Phil qualified as a Chartered Accountant with Arthur Young in London. After four years auditing a wide spread of industrial, service industry, and financial clients he spent two years advising on accounting and UK company law issues before transferring into corporate tax in 1982.
Since then, Phil has been providing advice to a wide range of clients, mainly in the international field, on issues from cross-border corporate re-organisations, acquisitions and disposals and the raising of capital.
Phil is the consulting editor for the Oil and Gas Tax section of Halsbury's Laws of England. He has been a member and secretary of the Brindex tax committee since the late 1980's and has also been an active member of the UKOITC industry tax committee for a number of years. In these capacities he has extensive experience of dealing with Treasury and HMRC personnel on lobbying for tax changes.

John Hayward
John Hayward is a self-employed pension consultant, well-known author and conference speaker. He has written for Pensions World and Tax Journal and is a member of the latter's Editorial Board. He has contributed to Butterworth's Tax Planning Service, Robin Ellison's Pensions Law and Practice, Simon's Direct Tax Service, Tolley's Finance and Law for the Older Client, the Finance Act Handbook 2004–2007 and to the ICAEW's TAXline. He is a past chairman of the former Association of Pensioner Trustees and its first honorary life member.

Andrew Hubbard, BMus, PhD, CTA (Fellow), ATT
Andrew Hubbard is National Tax Policy Director at Tenon and President of the Chartered Institute of Taxation. He is a regular speaker and writer on taxation matters and won the Tax Writer of the Year award at the Taxation Awards in 2006. He is a member of the Administrative Burdens Advisory Board and The Powers Implementation Oversight Board

Zigurds Kronbergs, MA, BSc, ARCS, ACA, FCCA
Zigurds G Kronbergs is International Tax Services Coordinator with BDO Global Coordination BV in Brussels. He is an experienced tax author and has contributed to professional and general publications on UK and international tax for over 20 years. He also reports regularly on Latvian tax developments for the International Bureau for Fiscal Documentation (IBFD) in Amsterdam and has been a member of a team of IBFD consultants advising the Latvian State Revenue Service.

Michael Lane
Mike Lane is a tax partner at Slaughter and May. Mike's practice covers all direct taxes, stamp duties, VAT and, in particular, corporation tax. He has extensive experience in advising on mergers and acquisitions, capital markets transactions, group reorganisations and structured finance.

John Lindsay, BA FCA FTII
John Lindsay is a consultant in the tax department of Linklaters LLP. He specialises in advising on the tax aspects of financing and treasury transactions. John is a contributor to Simons Taxes and is a co-author of the 'Taxation of Companies and Company Reconstructions' (Sweet & Maxwell 2009). He is a member of the CIOT Corporate Tax Sub-committee.

David O'Keeffe

Ann Redston, FCA, CTA (Fellow)
Anne is the visiting professor of tax law at King's College and a barrister at Temple Tax Chambers"

Gary Richards, MA, LLB, ATII, Solicitor
Gary Richards is a partner at Berwin Leighton Paisner LLP, advising on a wide range of international and domestic transactions. Gary is a member of the Law Society's Tax Law Committee, chairing the VAT & Duties sub-committee and participating in the Stamp Taxes working group. He is also a member of the editorial team for the British Tax Review. He was actively involved in HMRC's consultation on the reform of foreign profits and participates in the Joint VAT Consultative Committee. He is a member of the Stamp Taxes Practitioners Group.

Mark Schofield
Mark Schofield is a senior partner in the UK Firm and the global leader of PricewaterhouseCoopers Sustainability and Climate Change Tax network. In addition to mainstream client work, Mark leads a team of advisers providing businesses with advice and support on tax issues arising from both the governmental response (such as the introduction of carbon, environmental taxes and other regulation), and from the business response (such as reorganisation or acquisition), to the sustainability and climate change agenda. Mark is the lead author of the PwC Appetite for Change report, published in 2010, which examines the attitude of businesses in 15 countries to the role that tax, regulation and incentives can play in the shift to a low carbon economy.

Dana Ward

Dana Ward is a tax partner in Grant Thornton and leads their financial services tax practice.

She advises both fund managers and funds including Investment Trusts, Authorised Unit Trusts, Open Ended Investment Companies, Hedge Funds, Pension Schemes, Venture Capital Trusts, Private Equity Funds and Partnerships on a wide range of tax issues.

Dana is a member of the IMA tax committee and was also a member of AIMA's tax committee from 2005 to 2007.

Neil Warren

Neil Warren is an independent VAT consultant, lecturer and author and was the Taxation Awards Tax Writer of the Year in 2008. He is the author of Tolley's annual VAT Planning book and writes extensively on VAT for most of the leading tax publications in the UK. He also acts as a technical expert on VAT for a number of publishers and is a member of both the ATT Council and ATT's VAT Technical Committee.

Andrew Watt

Watt is a Managing Director at international tax consultants Alvarez & Marsal, where he heads the Tax Investigations and Disputes team. Andrew used to be a fraud investigator in what is now HMRC Specialist Investigations and is co-chairman of the ICAEW's Tax Investigation Practitioners' Group.

Jeremy White, LLB, FIIT, Barrister

Jeremy White is a barrister practicing in Pump Court Tax Chambers at 16 Bedford Row, London specialising in tax advice and advocacy. He is the consultant editor of Tolley's Customs Duties Handbook, Tolley's Excise Duties Handbook and Halsbury's Laws of England Customs and Excise volumes.

Martin Wilson, MA, FCA

Martin Wilson is Chairman of the Capital Allowances Partnership Limited (www.cap-allow.com), specialists in all aspects of capital allowances and related reliefs. He is the author of numerous published works on the subject, including Tottel's Capital Allowances: Transactions & Planning.

FINANCE ACT 2011

INTRODUCTION

This year's Finance Act, although by no means as long as some of the blockbusting Acts of recent years, nevertheless weighs in at 93 sections, 26 Schedules and 398 pages. The added pages far exceed those that can be deleted from tax legislation as a result of the repeal of redundant reliefs under s 91 and Sch 26, even if one were to include the further 36 repeals on which the Government is consulting. Schedule 2 (disguised remuneration) alone adds 69 pages, and the bank levy (Sch 19) adds 52 pages.

PART 1
CHARGES, RATES, ALLOWANCES ETC

Income tax. Income tax is reimposed for the tax year 2011 12 at the same rates (20 per cent, 40 per cent and 50 per cent) as applied in 2010–11, but the basic rate limit is reduced from £37,400 to £35,000 and the indexation clause under ITA 2007 s 21 disapplied (ss 1 and 2). The personal allowance for those aged under 65 is increased by £1,000 to £7,475 and the indexation clause under ITA 2007 s 57 disapplied in respect of that allowance (s 3).

Corporation tax. The main rate of corporation tax for the financial year 2011 (the year ending 31 March 2012) is set at 26 per cent, overriding FA 2010 s 2(2)(a) (as amended by F(No 2)A 2010 s 1), which had set it at 27 per cent, with retroactive effect to 1 April 2011 (s 4). The main rate of corporation tax for the financial year 2012 (the year ending 31 March 2013) is set at 25 per cent, but the rate on ring-fence profits remains at 30 per cent (s 5). The small profits rate for the financial year 2011 is set at 20 per cent on profits other than ring-fence profits and at 19 per cent for ring-fence profits. The standard fraction for marginal relief is 3/200ths and the ring-fence fraction 11/400ths (s 6). The supplementary charge to corporation tax in respect of ring-fence trades under CTA 2010 s 330 is increased from 20 per cent to 32 per cent, in relation to accounting periods beginning after 23 March 2011. Where an accounting period (a 'straddling period') begins before 24 March 2011 and ends on or after that date, it is to be treated as if it were two separate accounting periods, the first ending on 23 March 2011 and the second what remains, and the company's adjusted ring-fence profits are to be apportioned pro rata temporis (counting in days) between the two. Where a strict time apportionment would lead to an unjust or unreasonable result, the company may elect for another basis. The application of the Instalment Payments Regulations (SI 1998/3175) is modified accordingly (s 7).

Capital gains tax. The annual exempt amount for the tax year 2011 12 (and future years, subject to indexation) is set at £10,600 (an increase of £400 over 2010 11) and the indexation clause under TCGA 1992 s 3(3) is disapplied. In a year where there is no increase in the retail prices index in the 12 months to the September immediately preceding the tax year in question, the Treasury need no longer make an indexation order (effectively a 'nil order') under TCGA 1992 s 3 as amended (s 8). The 'lifetime allowance' for entrepreneurs' relief under TCGA 1992 s 169N is doubled from £5 million to £10 million, with effect for disposals occurring after 5 April 2011 (s 9).

Capital allowances. As previously announced, the rate of the writing-down allowance for expenditure on plant and machinery under CAA 2001 Part 2, is reduced from 20 per cent to 18 per cent, and the rate for special-rate expenditure under CAA 2001 s 104D is reduced from 10 per cent to 8 per cent, with effect for chargeable periods beginning after 31 March 2012 (for the purposes of corporation tax) or 5 April 2012 (for the purposes of income tax). For chargeable periods straddling 1 or 6 April 2012 ('the relevant day'), as the case may be, the rate to be applied is a hybrid rate calculated according to the number of days in the chargeable period falling on either side of the relevant day, counting the relevant day itself as a day in which the new lower rate applies (s 10). Also as previously announced (in the 'Emergency Budget Speech' of 23 June 2010), the amount of the annual investment allowance under CAA 2001 s 51A is reduced from £100,000 to £25,000, with effect for chargeable periods beginning after 31 March 2012 (for the purposes of corporation tax) or 5 April 2012 (for the purposes of income tax). For chargeable periods straddling 1 or 6 April 2012 ('the relevant day'), as the case may be, the maximum amount is the sum of the maximum amounts that apply in respect of two deemed chargeable periods, the first ending on the day before the relevant day and the second consisting of the remainder of the actual chargeable period (s 11). The cut-off period for short-life assets (the period for which expenditure on such assets qualifies for short-life treatment under

CAA 2001 s 86) is doubled from four years to eight years in respect of qualifying expenditure incurred after 31 March 2012 (for the purposes of corporation tax) or 5 April 2012 (for the purposes of income tax) (s 12).

Alcohol duties. The rates of excise duty under ALDA 1979 on all types of alcoholic liquor are increased by 7.2 per cent (2 per cent above the relevant rate of inflation), with effect from 28 March 2011 (s 13). A new reduced rate of duty on 'lower-strength beer', under new ALDA 1979 s 36(1AA)(za), is to be charged at a rate of £9.29 per hectolitre per cent of alcohol content (c.f. the standard rate of beer duty, set at £18.57 per hectolitre per cent of alcohol content by s 13). The new rate is to apply equally to lower-strength beer from small breweries, and the reduced rates applicable to small-brewery beer under ALDA 1979 ss 36A–36H are accordingly not to apply to lower-strength beer. Lower-strength beer is defined as beer that exceeds 1.2 per cent but does not exceed 2.8 per cent of alcohol by volume, and the new rate has effect from 1 October 2011 (s 14). A new, additional rate of excise duty on 'high-strength beer' is to be charged under ALDA 1979 s 37, as inserted by Sch 1 para 1, with effect from 1 October 2011. The rate of the duty is £4.64 per hectolitre per cent of alcohol content. Consequential amendments are made to other provisions of ALDA 1979 (s 15 and Sch 1).

Tobacco duties. There is a change in the rates and the balance of excise duty on cigarettes under TPDA 1979. The ad valorem rate is decreased from 24 per cent to 16 per cent, but the specific duty per 1000 cigarettes is increased by £36.92 to £154.95 (an increase of 31 per cent). The overall effect is to increase the retail price of 20 economy cigarettes by £0.50 and that of premium cigarettes by £0.33. The rate of duty on cigars is increased by £13.01 (7.2 per cent) per kilogram, duty on hand-rolling tobacco by £22.31 (17.2 per cent) per kilogram, and on chewing tobacco and other smoking tobacco by £5.72 (7.2 per cent) per kilogram. These increases had effect from 18:00 on 23 March 2011 (s 16).

Gambling duties. The gross gaming-yield bands for gaming duty under FA 1997 s 11(2) are revalorised to take account of the increase in the retail price index for the 12 months to December 2010 (4.66 per cent). There is no change in the rates of duty. The new bands have effect for accounting periods beginning after 31 March 2011 (s 17). A new table of rates of amusement machine licence duty under BGDA 1981 is introduced with effect for licence applications received after 16:00 on 25 March 2011. The rates are generally increased, but by different percentage rates and not in all cases (s 18).

Fuel duties. The rates of excise duty under HODA 1979 are decreased. On the main road fuels (unleaded petrol, heavy oil and light oil other than unleaded petrol or aviation gasoline) the decrease is £0.01 per litre. The duty on other fuels is reduced so as to maintain differentials. The decreases have effect from 18:00 on 23 March 2011 (s 19). The duty increases originally scheduled to take effect on 1 April 2011 are now to take effect from 1 January 2012. The increase on the main road fuels is 3.02p per litre (s 20).

Vehicle excise duty. The general rate of duty under VERA 1994 on vehicles taxed by engine size (generally those registered before February 2001) is increased by £10 to £215 for engine sizes above 1549 cc and by £5 to £130 in respect of smaller engines. Rates dependent on CO2 emissions are also increased, but by no more than the rate of inflation. There are also increases in respect of motor cycles and motor tricycles, but rates on heavy goods vehicles and buses are in general left unchanged. The new rates have effect for licences taken out after 31 March 2011 (s 21). Increased rates of duty under VERA 1994 are set for certain goods vehicles without 'road-friendly suspension', with effect for licences taken out after 31 March 2011 (s 22).

Environmental taxes. The rates of climate change levy as charged in FA 2000 Sch 6 para 42(1) are increased by approximately 5 per cent across the board, with effect for supplies taking place after 31 March 2012. Revalorisation for inflation has been a feature of climate change levy rates since 2007 (s 23). The 5 per cent increase in the rate of aggregates levy to £2.10 per tonne, due to take effect on 1 April 2011 under FA 2010 s 16, has been deferred by repealing the section. The rate remains £2.00 per tonne (FA 2001 s 16(4) as amended by FA 2008 s 20). The deferment has been introduced pending agreement with the European Commission on the reintroduction of the aggregates levy credits scheme in Northern Ireland; see also s 81 below (s 24). The standard rate of landfill tax under FA 1996 s 42 is increased by £8 (14.3 per cent) to £64 per tonne as from 1 April 2012 (s 25).

PART 2
INCOME TAX, CORPORATION TAX AND CAPITAL GAINS TAX

Anti-avoidance provisions. Section 26 introduces Sch 2, which introduces a charge to income tax in certain cases where remuneration is provided to an employee by the agency of a third party. The intention is that the charge should apply to (a) certain loans of money or assets by third parties to the employee; (b) the earmarking of money or assets for the employee by a third party and in some (limited) cases by the employer and (c) the outright payments of money or transfers of assets to the employee by a third party.

Schedule 2 para 1 inserts new ITEPA 2003 Part 7A, headed 'Employment income provided through third parties', and consisting of new ss 554A–554Z21. Chapter 1 (ss 554A–554Z1) provides for the application of the charge; Chapter 2 (ss 554Z2–554Z15) imposes the charge, and Chapter 3 (ss 554Z16–554Z21) applies where there is an undertaking to pay certain pension contributions. Throughout these provisions, A refers to an employee, former employee or prospective employee of another person ('B'), B is that employer and P is the person taking the relevant step.

New s 554A provides that the charge under ITEPA 2003 Part 7A Chapter 2 is to apply where (a) a 'relevant arrangement' exists to which A or any person linked with A is a party and a 'relevant step' is taken by a 'relevant third person' in connection with that arrangement, and (b) it is reasonable to suppose that the relevant arrangement insofar as it relates to A or any person linked with A is wholly or partly concerned with the provision of 'rewards or recognition or loans' in connection with A's prospective, current or former employment with B. The charge is not to apply, however, where the relevant step is taken after A's death. A 'relevant third person' is A or B when acting as a trustee or any person other than A or B. Except where there is a direct or indirect connection between the relevant step and a tax-avoidance arrangement, references in that definition to B where B is a company include references to any other company in a group of which B is a member at the time of the relevant step, and include references to any wholly owned subsidiary of B where B is a limited-liability partnership.

New ss 554B–554D specify what the 'relevant steps' are that must be taken for there to be a charge to income tax under these provisions. New s 554B describes the circumstances in which a relevant step consisting of the earmarking of a sum of money or of an asset is considered to have been taken. This occurs where either (a) a person, P, earmarks (however informally) a sum of money or an asset with a view to the taking of a later relevant step in relation to that sum of money or asset or to any sum of money or asset directly or indirectly deriving or arising therefrom or (b) a sum of money or an asset otherwise starts to be held with such a view. New s 554C addresses relevant steps consisting of the payment of a sum of money or the transfer of an asset. Such a step is taken where a person, P, pays a sum of money, transfers an asset or grants a lease with an effective duration likely to exceed 21 years to a 'relevant person'. A relevant step within this section is also taken where P takes a step by virtue of which a relevant person acquires securities, interests in securities or securities options, or where P makes available a sum of money or asset for use as security for a loan to a relevant person or as security for the meeting of any liability or the performance of any undertaking by a relevant person. A 'relevant person' is A, a person chosen by A or one of a class of persons chosen by A. It also includes any other person where P is taking such a step on A's behalf or at A's direction or request. New s 554D defines a relevant step involving making an asset available without transferring it. A relevant step within this section is taken where P makes an asset available for a relevant person enabling that person to benefit from it in a way substantially similar to that which ownership (transfer) would have conferred. Also included is a situation where P makes an asset available for the benefit of a relevant person two years or more after A's employment with B has ceased. It does not matter that the relevant person may not actually benefit from the asset at all. As in new s 554C, a relevant person is A, a person chosen by A or one of a class of persons chosen by A. It also includes any other person where P is taking such a step on A's behalf or at A's direction or request.

New ss 554E–554Y set out a whole raft of exclusions disapplying the charge in certain specific situations. New s 554E excludes relevant steps under approved share incentive plans, approved SAYE option schemes, approved company share-option plans, registered pension schemes and similar arrangements. New s 554F excludes relevant steps that are part of an ordinary commercial transaction. New s 554G excludes steps under certain employee-benefit packages other than pension schemes. Such benefits must be available to a substantial proportion of B's employees and not be limited to directors, senior employees, the highest-earning employees etc. New s 554H excludes certain deferred-remuneration arrangements. New s 554I introduces the exclusions defined in new ss 554J–554M. These exclusions refer to employee share schemes, i.e. awards of shares, securities or money or grants of rights to acquire shares or securities or receive money determined by reference to the market value of certain shares or securities. New s 554J applies to employee share schemes under deferred-award terms, under which the award of shares or money is deferred until a vesting date that is no later than 10 years after the award date, subject to specified conditions, and there is a reasonable chance that not all those conditions will be met at the vesting date, and thus that the award will not be made. There is no charge under these provisions where the relevant step otherwise falling within new s 554B is the earmarking etc of shares for the purposes of the deferred award and there is no connection with a tax-avoidance arrangement. Exceptions to the exclusion are also made. New s 554K applies to employee share schemes under which a sum of money is to be awarded solely on the occurrence of a specified 'exit event', and there is a reasonable chance when the award is made that the exit event will occur. That exit event (as defined in new s 554I) is (a) the listing of relevant shares on a stock exchange; (b) the disposal of all or a substantial proportion of the relevant shares to an unconnected person; (c) where the relevant shares are shares in a trading company, where all or a substantial part of that company's trade is transferred to a person who is not a 'relevant connected person'; (d) where all or a substantial part of the company's assets are transferred to a person who is not a 'relevant connected person'; (e) when the company begins to be wound up or (f) control of the company passes to an unconnected person or persons. There is no charge under these provisions where the relevant step otherwise falling within new s 554B is the earmarking etc of relevant shares for the purposes of the award and there is no connection with a tax-avoidance arrangement. Exceptions to the exclusion are also made. New s 554L applies to employee share schemes under deferred-grant terms, under which a share option is granted, to be exercised no earlier than a later vesting date that is no later than 10 years after the date of the grant, subject to certain specified conditions, and there is a reasonable chance that not all the specified conditions will be met by the vesting date, thus preventing the exercise of the option. There is no charge under these provisions where the relevant step otherwise falling within new s 554B is the earmarking etc of relevant shares for the purposes of the award and there is no connection with a tax-avoidance arrangement. Exceptions to the exclusion are also made. New s 554M is the equivalent, as regards share options, to new s 554K. It applies to employee share schemes under deferred grant terms, under which a share option is to be awarded solely on the occurrence of a specified 'exit event', and there is a reasonable chance when the award is made that the exit event will occur. As in new s 554K, the exit event is (a) the listing of relevant shares on a stock exchange; (b) the disposal of all or a substantial proportion of the relevant shares to an unconnected person; (c) where the relevant shares are shares in a trading company, where all or a substantial part of that company's trade is transferred to a person who is not a 'relevant connected person'; (d) where all or a substantial part of the company's assets are transferred to a person who is not a 'relevant connected person'; (e) when the company begins to be wound up or (f) control of the company passes to an unconnected person or persons. Again, there is no charge where the relevant step otherwise falling within new s 554B is the earmarking etc of relevant shares for the purposes of the award and there is no connection with a tax-avoidance arrangement. Exceptions to the exclusion are also made. New s 554N excludes certain other events in connection with employment-related securities. There is no charge under these provisions where there is a relevant step (a) the subject of which are employment-related securities and the acquisition of the securities is an exempt acquisition of restricted securities under ITEPA 2003 s 425 or (b) the subject of which is an employment-related securities option and the acquisition of that option is exempt under ITEPA 2003 s 475. There are further exclusions where certain events occur by virtue of which A receives employment income in respect of his employment with B. The events in question are (a) chargeable events under ITEPA 2003 ss 426 (charge on post-acquisition chargeable events relating to restricted securities, 438 (charge on post-acquisition chargeable events relating to convertible securities) or 476 (charge on post-acquisition chargeable event relating to securities options); (b) an event giving rise to the discharge of a notional loan for the purposes of ITEPA 2003 s 446U (securities acquired for less than market value) or (c) a disposal of an employment-related security for more than its market value to which ITEPA 2003 Part 7 Chapter 3D applies. Certain other events giving rise to the receipt of employment income are also excluded. New s 554O excludes steps under certain employee car-ownership schemes. These schemes are ones that provide for employees to purchase a new car from a third party by means of a car loan repayable after no more than four years and enable them to sell the car back to the third party for a price based on an estimate of the likely amount outstanding on the loan on the repayment date. The charge under these provisions will not then apply to a relevant step taken for the sole purpose of the purchase or sale-back of the car or for the making of the car loan. If the loan is not fully repaid, the exclusion will not apply to that part of the loan that remains unpaid. New s 554P provides that there is no charge under these provisions where the relevant step is one to the subject of which an employment exemption under ITEPA 2003 Part 4 Chapter 2 (approved mileage allowance and passenger payments) applies. New s 554Q excludes a charge under these provisions on income arising from an earmarked asset or sum of money to which the charge has already applied, if the income is the subject in its own right of a relevant step to which s 554B would otherwise apply. New s 554R excludes a relevant step the subject of which is a sum of money or asset wholly acquired out of another sum of money or asset that has already given rise to a charge under these provisions by virtue of the fact that a relevant step within new s 554B was taken with the original money or asset as its subject, or would have given rise to such a charge had it not been for this section, or new s 554Q (see above) or new s 554T (see below). New ss 554S–554X exclude certain retirement benefits. New s 554S provides that a relevant step that consists of the provision of pension income chargeable to tax under ITEPA 2003 Part 9 is not also to give rise to a charge under these provisions. It also provides that new ss 554T–554X are to be applied sequentially where applicable. New s 554T provides that a relevant step within new s 554B is not to give rise to a charge under these provisions where the money or asset or part thereof is derived directly or indirectly from an 'excluded pension contribution' paid by A after 5 April 2011. It also provides an exclusion in respect of relevant steps within new ss 554B or 554D where the money or asset represents relevant benefits and arises directly or indirectly from an excluded pension contribution by A. An excluded pension contribution is one that is neither relievable nor tax-relieved, is made by A so as to secure rights to receive relevant benefits and has nothing to do with a loan or money or asset that has been the subject of a relevant step under new s 554C. Where the money or asset in question derives only partly from an excluded pension contribution, the relevant step is excluded to the extent that it so derives. New s 554U provides that a relevant step does not give rise to a charge under these provisions where it relates to money or an asset that is directly or indirectly derived from money that was paid by B before 6 April 2006 under an employer-financed retirement benefits scheme and on which A was taxed. Again, where the money or asset derives only partly from the taxed sum, the relevant step is excluded to the extent that it so derives. The exclusion under new s 554V applies where an annuity contract is purchased from an insurance company wholly out of A's rights under a pension scheme, and those rights are annuity rights arising wholly or partly before 6 April 2011. No charge is to arise under these provisions either where the purchaser or the insurance company takes a relevant step as specified. There is no exclusion to the extent that the rights derive only partly from pre-6 April 2011 annuity rights. The exclusion under new s 554W applies where a relevant benefit is provided under a relevant scheme by the payment (which constitutes a relevant step under new s 554C) of a lump sum wholly out of rights under the scheme that A has and those rights are lump-sum rights arising wholly or partly before 6 April 2011. There is no exclusion to the extent that the rights derive only partly from pre-6 April 2011 lump-sum rights. New s 554X excludes certain transfers between foreign pension schemes. It applies where A has rights under a 'section 390 scheme' (a foreign scheme corresponding to a non-approved retirement benefits scheme, payments to which were exempt from a charge to tax under former ITEPA 2003 s 386 where made on behalf of a non-domiciled employee employed by a foreign employer). Section 390 (ITEPA 2003 s 390) was repealed with effect from 6 April 2006. New s 554Y confers on HMRC the power to exclude certain other relevant steps by regulation. New ss 554Z and 554Z1 are interpretation sections; new s 554Z1 defines who or what is meant by a person 'linked with' A.

Part 7A Chapter 2 (consisting of new ss 554Z2–554Z15) imposes the charge to tax. New s 554Z2 contains the basic rule, namely that it is the value of a non-excluded relevant step that constitutes employment income of A in respect of his employment with B. Where the relevant step is taken before A's employment begins, it is attributed to the tax year in which the employment begins; otherwise, it is income of the tax year in which it is taken. Where the relevant step also gives rise to an amount that would be treated as A's earnings under the benefits code (the provisions of ITEPA 2003 charging benefits to tax) or to income that would otherwise be dealt with under

ITTOIA 2005 Part 4 Chapter 3 (dividends and tax credit from UK-resident companies), these provisions apply instead of those provisions. New s 554Z3 defines the value of a relevant step. Where a relevant step involves a sum of money, its value is the amount of that sum. In any other case, the value is the greater of (a) the market value of the asset involved when the step is taken and (b) the cost of the step. The cost of the step is, however, not to be taken into account in certain circumstances, and the value as defined by this section is subject to the rules in new ss 554Z4–554Z8, applied, if necessary, in that order. New s 554Z4 provides that where the value of the relevant step counts as earnings for a year in which A is non-resident, it is to be reduced to the extent that it is not in respect of duties performed in the United Kingdom. Otherwise, the rules in ITEPA 2003 ss 16(1)–(4) and 17(1)–(3) apply as if the value of the relevant step were general earnings. Where there is an overlap between a sum of money or an asset that is the subject of a relevant step and a sum of money or an asset that was the subject of an earlier relevant step giving rise to a charge under these provisions, new s 554Z5 provides that the value of the later relevant step is to be reduced by the value of the earlier step (but not below nil). Where the overlap is partial, the reduction is by that part of the value of the earlier step that corresponds to the part of the money or asset involved in the earlier step that is covered by the overlap. An overlap is regarded as existing where the earlier and later sums of money or assets are the same sum or asset or where the later sum or asset essentially replaces the earlier sum or asset. Where the relevant step also gives rise to earnings that are chargeable to tax as earnings from employment under ITEPA 2003 Part 3 Chapter 1 or treated as earnings under ITEPA 2003 Part 3 Chapter 12 or constitute a deemed employment payment under ITEPA 2003 s 50 (intermediaries — the 'IR35' legislation), new s 554Z6 provides that the charge under these provisions is reduced by the amount of the earnings charged under the enumerated provisions. New s 554Z7 provides that in certain circumstances, where A would have to pay an amount ('the exercise price') to exercise an option under an employee share scheme, the exercise price may be deducted from the value chargeable under these provisions. New s 554Z8 provides for a reduction in the value of a relevant step within new s 554C where the relevant step is taken in return for consideration consisting of the transfer of an asset from A to P, provided that there is no connection with a tax-avoidance arrangement. Where the section applies, the value of the relevant step is reduced by the market value of the asset transferred by A. It also applies where there is a relevant step under new ss 554C or 554D but not involving money, and the consideration is money consideration, in which case the value of the relevant step is reduced by the amount paid. New ss 554Z9–554Z11 address the situation where the remittance basis applies to A. Where A is ordinarily resident in the United Kingdom, A's employment with B is employment with a foreign employer and A's duties in the relevant tax year are carried out wholly outside the United Kingdom, new s 554Z9 provides that the employment income treated as accruing to A as a result of these provisions is 'taxable specific income' to the extent only that it is remitted to the United Kingdom. New s 554Z10 makes similar provision in respect of a year in which A is not ordinarily resident and the value of the relevant step is not in respect of duties performed in the United Kingdom. New s 554Z11 supplements the two previous sections. New s 554Z12 provides who is liable to the tax arising under these provisions if the relevant step is taken or any of A's employment income is remitted to the United Kingdom on or after A's death. New s 554Z13 applies where a later event occurs after a relevant step is taken and that later event would otherwise give rise to an income tax liability for A or any other person, except by virtue of these provisions, ITEPA 2003 Part 7 Chapters 2 to 5 (charge in respect of employment-related securities) or ITEPA 2003 Part 9 (pension income). Where in these circumstances it would be just and reasonable to avoid a double charge to income tax, then to that extent there is to be no charge in respect of the later event. New s 554Z14 provides for a claim to relief to be made where there has been a charge to tax under these provisions and a later event occurs that is not itself a relevant step and makes it impossible for a further relevant step to be taken in respect of the money or asset that was the subject of the original relevant step or directly or indirectly derives or arises or may derive or arise from that money or asset. On the making of such a justified claim (which must be done no later than four years from the occurrence of the later event), HMRC must give such relief as they consider to be just and reasonable in respect of the income tax previously paid. New s 554Z15 applies certain provisions of ITEPA 2003 to determine where employment duties are located for the purposes of these provisions.

Part 7A Chapter 3 (consisting of new ss 554Z16–554Z21) applies where undertakings are given to pay contributions to pension arrangements other than registered pension schemes. New s 554Z16 provides that Chapter 3 applies where such an undertaking is given, and, as a direct or indirect result, relevant benefits are directly or indirectly provided out of that contribution by a 'relevant third person' (as defined in new s 554A above), and the provision of those benefits would be a relevant step for the purposes of these provisions. Chapter 3 does not apply where the contribution benefits from either tax relief or tax exemption. New s 554Z17 provides that where B takes a step (otherwise than when acting as a trustee) that involves earmarking (as defined in new s 554Z18) or provides security (as defined in new s 554Z19), Part 7 Chapters 1 and 2 are to apply, with prescribed modifications, to impose a charge to tax under Part 7 Chapter 2 on the value of the step. References to B in Chapter 3 include references to any member of B's group where B is a company and to any company that is a wholly owned subsidiary where B is a limited-liability partnership. New s 554Z18 sets out the circumstances in which a step involving earmarking gives rise to a charge under these provisions. It is drafted analogously to new s 554B. Thus, earmarking for these purposes occurs where either (a) the employer, B, earmarks (however informally) a sum of money or an asset with a view to later performing the relevant undertaking wholly or partly out of that sum of money or asset or out of any sum of money or asset directly or indirectly deriving or arising therefrom or (b) a sum of money or an asset otherwise starts to be held by or on behalf of B with such a view. New s 554Z19 deals with the situation in which security is provided, and applies where B provides security for the performance of the relevant undertaking (except where acting as a trustee).New s 554Z20 sets out how the value of a step taken within new s 554Z19 is to be valued for the purposes of the charge. Essentially, the value of the step is the lower of (a) the amount payable as a contribution under the relevant undertaking determined justly and reasonably at the time the step is taken and (b) the value of the security. New s 554Z21 provides for a measure of relief where the step of earmarking or providing security is not followed by a contribution or relevant benefit. It does so by modifying the effect of new s 554Z14 appropriately.

Schedule 2 (paras 2–51) makes consequential amendments to ITEPA 2003 (paras 2–34), ITTOIA 2005 (paras 35–39), ITA 2007 (paras 40–43), CTA 2009 (paras 44–48) and other statutes. In particular, para 27 inserts new ITEPA 2003 s 567A, which provides relief where there is an amount of taxable pension income arising or accruing from rights that have arisen or derived from a sum or money or an asset involved in a relevant step in respect of which there has been a charge to income tax under these provisions. The relief takes the form of a deduction from the taxable pension income equal in amount to the income that was charged to tax under these provisions. Where that amount is greater than the taxable pension income, the excess may be carried forward indefinitely. Paragraph 29 inserts new ITEPA 2003 s 687A. This provides that where the value of a relevant step that is the payment of a sum of money counts as employment income under these provisions, B (the employer) is normally to be treated as making a payment of PAYE income to A of an amount that is the best estimate of that employment income. Similar provision is made in respect of a relevant step that is not the payment of a sum of money, by new ITEPA 2003 s 695A, inserted by para 31. For the purposes of the PAYE regulations, B is treated in these circumstances as making a payment of PAYE income that is the best estimate of the employment income. Paragraph 49 inserts new TCGA 1992 s 119C. TCGA 1992 s 119A provides that where there is a disposal of an asset consisting of employment-related securities which gives rise to an income tax charge under certain provisions of ITEPA 2003 relating to employment-related securities, expenditure on the asset for the purposes of capital gains tax is increased by the amount charged to income tax. New TCGA 1992 s 119C provides that the amount treated as employment income and treated as expenditure does not include any unremitted income under these provisions.

Schedule 2 paras 52 to 63 are commencement and transitional provisions. Paragraph 52 provides that these provisions (ITEPA 2003 Part 7A) apply to relevant steps taken after 5 April 2011. However, paras 53 and 54 make anti-forestalling provisions in respect of certain relevant steps taken after 8 December 2010 and before 6 April 2011. Finally, para 64 confers powers on the Treasury to make provision by statutory instrument for the interaction between new Part 7A and any other provision of the Tax Acts or enactments relating to capital gains tax or inheritance tax (s 26 and Sch 2).

Section 27 introduces Sch 3, which contains a new anti-avoidance code to prevent the abuse of tax reliefs available in respect of charitable donations. It also repeals the substantial donors legislation in ITA 2007 ss 549–557 and CTA 2010 ss 502–510.

Sch 3 Part 1 (para 1) contains the new income tax legislation in respect of what are called 'tainted charity donations'. It inserts ITA 2007 Part 13 Chapter 8, consisting of new ss 809ZH to 809ZR. New s 809ZH gives an overview of the Chapter, stating that it makes provision for removing entitlement to income tax reliefs and countering income tax advantages where a person makes a 'relievable charity donation' that is a 'tainted donation'. New s 809ZI defines a 'relievable charity donation'. This is a gift or other disposal, eligible for tax relief, made by a person to a charity. Such a donation is eligible for tax relief if tax relief would be available for it were it not a 'tainted charity donation' and/or the charity is entitled to claim a repayment of tax in respect of that donation. The tax relief in question is that under ITEPA 2003 Part 12 (payroll giving); ITTOIA 2005 s 108 and CTA 2009 s 105 (gifts of trading stock); ITA 2007 Part 8 Chapters 2 and 3 (gift aid, gifts of shares); CAA 2001 s 63(2) (gifts of plant and machinery); CTA 2010 Part 6 (charitable donations relief for corporation tax); or TCGA 1992 s 257 (gifts of chargeable assets). New s 809ZJ defines the concept of a 'tainted donation'. A donation is a tainted donation if each of three conditions (A, B and C) is met. Condition A describes the situation where a 'linked person' enters into arrangements and it is reasonable to assume whether from the likely effects of the donation and the arrangements or from the circumstances in which the donation is made and in which the arrangements are entered into or from both that the donation would not have been made and the arrangements not entered into independently of one another. A 'linked person' is either the donor or a person connected with the donor during a specified period. Condition B applies where the main purpose or one of the main purposes for which the linked person enters into the arrangement is to obtain a financial advantage directly or indirectly from the charity concerned or from a connected charity for one or more linked persons who are not charities ('potentially advantaged persons'). Condition C is that the donor is neither a 'qualifying charity-owned company' (as defined in new s 809ZJ(8)) nor a 'relevant housing provider' linked with the charity to which the donation is made (as defined in new s 809ZJ(7)). Certain financial advantages, specified by new s 809ZL, are to be ignored for these purposes, however. New s 809ZK prescribes circumstances in which a financial advantage is deemed to be obtained for the purposes of Condition B, but is not exclusive. New s 809ZL defines what financial advantages are to be ignored for these purposes. New ss 809ZM to 809ZO contain the provisions removing income tax relief and imposing a charge to tax in respect of tainted donations. New s 809ZM removes the income tax relief that would otherwise be available in respect of a tainted donation. Where one or more 'associated donations' are involved with a tainted donation, relief is removed from all such donations. However, a donation made by a qualifying charity-owned company or by a relevant housing provider linked with the charity to which the donation is made is not an associated donation. A tainted donation remains a qualifying donation in the hands of a charity for certain purposes, allowing a charity to reclaim a repayment of tax under Gift Aid, for example, so that it is the donor rather than the charity that is penalised under these provisions. New s 809ZN imposes a charge to income tax where a person makes a tainted donation in respect of which Gift Aid relief would otherwise have been available and the charity concerned is entitled to claim a repayment of tax in respect of the donation. The tax charged is equal to the amount of the repayment to which the charity is or would be entitled on making a claim. New s 809ZO makes parallel provisions in respect of a tainted donation made by trustees from the income of a settlement. New s 809ZP defines when charities are connected; new s 809ZQ applies the definition of 'connected person' from ITA 2007 s 993, with modifications; and new s 809ZR contains minor definitions.

Schedule 3 Part 2 (para 2) inserts new CTA 2010 Part 21C (consisting of new ss 939A to 939I), which contains provisions parallel to those of Part 1 but applicable for corporation tax purposes. Thus new s 939A is an overview of the Part; new s 939B defines 'relievable charity donation'; new s 939C defines tainted donations; new s 939D defines circumstances in which a financial advantage is deemed to be obtained; new s 939E specifies which financial advantages are to be ignored; new s 939F removes corporation tax relief in respect of tainted donations; new s 939G defines when charities are connected; new s 939H applies the definition of 'connected person' in CTA 2010 s 1122, with modifications; and new s 939I contains minor definitions.

Schedule 3 Part 3 (para 3) inserts new TCGA 1992 s 257A, which disapplies TCGA 1992 s 257. The latter section provides relief from capital gains tax to gains arising on a donation made to a charity. There is to be no relief where the donation is a tainted donation or an associated donation.

Schedule 3 Part 4 (paras 4–26) makes consequential amendments. Schedule 3 Part 5 contains commencement and transitional provisions. The new legislation is to have effect in respect of relievable charity donations made after 31 March 2011. However, the repeals of the substantial donors legislation have effect from 1 April 2013. Transitional provisions provide for continuation of the substantial donors legislation after 31 March 2013 in some cases and for the new legislation to apply in some cases to arrangements made before 1 April 2011 (s 27 and Sch 3).

Section 28 introduces Sch 4, which addresses amounts that are 'derecognised' (or not fully recognised) for accounting purposes. Sch 4 introduces a new general rule that, for the purposes of the loan-relationships and derivative-contracts legislation, loans and derivative contracts that are not recognised for accounting purposes under generally accepted accounting principles (GAAP) will nevertheless be brought into account for tax purposes where tax-avoidance arrangements are involved. The rule posits a motive test in place of a detailed description of the circumstances as a trigger for the anti-avoidance legislation to apply.

Sch 4 paras 1–5 amend the loan-relationships legislation (CTA 2009 Part 5), paras 7 11 amend the derivative-contracts legislation (CTA 2009 Part 7), and para 12 makes consequential repeals and para 13 provides for commencement. Paragraph 1 is introductory. Paragraphs 2 and 3 amend CTA 2009 ss 311 and 312 respectively. Currently, CTA 2009 s 311 and 312 provide that, in the case of a company that is or is treated as a party to a creditor relationship, and an amount is not fully recognised for the purposes of GAAP in respect of the creditor relationship and the corresponding debtor relationship, it is nevertheless to be recognised for determining the credits and debits that need to be taken into account for tax purposes where one of four conditions is satisfied. CTA 2009 s 311 sets out the conditions and CTA 2009 s 312 prescribes the tax consequences where one or more of those conditions is satisfied. Paragraph 2 amends CTA 2009 s 311 so as to remove the four conditions and instead substitute a single condition, namely that CTA 2009 s 312 is to apply where a company is or is treated as a party to a creditor relationship and an amount is, in accordance with GAAP, not fully recognised in respect of the creditor relationship, as a result of tax-avoidance arrangements to which the company is a party. 'Tax-avoidance arrangements' and 'arrangements' are defined in the customary way. A company is to be treated as a party to a creditor relationship for these purposes even where it has disposed of its rights under the relationship to another person under either a repo or stock-lending relationship or a transaction, being the creation of a mortgage or charge, that is treated under TCGA 1992 s 26 as not involving a disposal. The definition of when an amount is not fully recognised is amended so as to remove references to contributions and securities, which refer back to the conditions that are now repealed. Paragraph 3 amends CTA 2009 s 312. It now provides that where (a) a company is a party to tax-avoidance arrangements; (b) it becomes or is treated as becoming party to a debtor relationship; and (c) an amount is in accordance with GAAP not fully recognised in respect of the debtor relationship, then credits are taken into account as if the whole of the relationship had been taken into account for accounting purposes but that no debits (hence no losses) are to be recognised on the creditor relationship. As before, any debits to be brought into account on the debtor relationship may not exceed the credits taken into account in respect of the creditor relationship. Paragraphs 4 and 5 amend CTA 2009 Part 5 Chapter 15, which provides for the consequences for the loan-relationships legislation of the existence of tax-avoidance arrangements. Paragraph 4 makes a consequential amendment to CTA 2009 s 440. Paragraph 5 inserts new CTA 2009 s 455A, which provides for the consequences of the derecognition of a creditor relationship as the result of tax-avoidance arrangements. Where a company is a party to tax-avoidance arrangements, as a result of which all or part of a creditor relationship to which the company is a party is derecognised by that company in accordance with GAAP, but the company continues to be a party to the relationship immediately after the event giving rise to the derecognition, then no debit that would otherwise have been brought into account by the company as a result of the derecognition is to be brought into account either for the purposes of the loan-relationships legislation nor for any other corporation tax purposes. Paragraph 6 makes a consequential amendment to CTA 2009 s 464.

Paragraphs 7 to 11 make analogous amendments to the derivative-contracts legislation in CTA 2009 Part 7. Paragraph 7 is introductory. Paragraph 8 amends CTA 2009 s 599A, which is the analogous provision to CTA 2009 s 311. It currently provides that where a company is or is treated as a party to a derivative contract, and an amount is not fully recognised in respect of the contract as result of the application of GAAP, then CTA 2009 s 599B is to apply where any one of three conditions is met. The amendments made by para 8 remove mention of the three conditions and replace them by a single new condition, to the effect that CTA 2009 s 599B is to apply where a company is or is treated as a party to a derivative contract and an amount is in accordance with GAAP not fully recognised in respect of the contract as a result of tax-avoidance arrangements to which the company is a party. 'Tax avoidance arrangements' and 'arrangements' are defined in the customary way. A company is to be treated as a party to a derivative contract for these purposes even where it has disposed of its rights and liabilities under the contract to another person under either a repo or stock-lending relationship or a transaction, being the creation of a mortgage or charge, that is treated under TCGA 1992 s 26 as not involving a disposal. The definition of when an amount is not fully recognised is amended so as to remove references to contributions and securities, which refer back to the conditions that are now repealed. Paragraph 9 amends CTA 2009 s 599B, which provides for the consequences where CTA 2009 s 599A applies. As amended, CTA 2009 s 599B now provides that in determining the credits and debits that a company is to bring into account in respect of a derivative contract falling within CTA 2009 s 599A, credits are to be taken into account as if the whole of the contract were recognised (as previously) but that, in addition, no debits are to be brought into account in respect of that contract. Furthermore, where the company is or is treated as being a party to the contract at the beginning of the period in question, and the fair value of the contract at that time is greater than its carrying value, a credit equal to the difference is to be brought into account in respect of the contract.

Paragraphs 10 and 11 amend CTA 2009 Part 7 Chapter 11, which provides for the consequences for the derivative-contracts legislation of the existence of tax avoidance arrangements. Paragraph 10 makes a consequential amendment to CTA 2009 s 689. Paragraph 11 inserts new CTA 2009 s 698A, which provides for the consequences of the derecognition of a derivative contract as the result of tax avoidance arrangements. Where a company is a party to tax-avoidance arrangements, as a result of which all or part of a derivative contract to which the company is a party is derecognised by that company in accordance with GAAP, but the company continues to be a party to the contract immediately after the event giving rise to the derecognition, then no debit that would otherwise have been brought into account by the company as a result of the derecognition is to be brought into account either for the purposes of the derivative-contracts legislation nor for any other corporation tax purposes. Paragraph 12 makes consequential repeals. Paragraph 13 provides that the amendments made by Sch 4 have effect for periods of account beginning after 5 December 2010 and for straddling periods to be divided. Certain provisions of CTA 2009 are not to apply where the company becomes party to tax-avoidance arrangements before 23 March 2011 (s 28 and Sch 4).

Section 29 makes further amendments to the loan-relationships legislation, where debtors and creditors are connected. These are by way of a response to specific schemes that have sought to circumvent existing anti-avoidance legislation in CTA 2009 ss 418 and 419. Those sections apply to the provision of intra-group finance by means of convertible securities. Currently, CTA 2009 s 418 applies where two connected companies are party to a loan relationship, one as creditor and the other as debtor and two further conditions are met. Condition A is that rights under the relationship include provision for the creditor company to be or become entitled or required to acquire shares in any company. Condition B is that the debits to be brought into account by the debtor company exceed the credits to be brought into account by the creditor company. In such a case, the creditor company is required to bring into account additional credits equal to the excess. CTA 2009 s 418 is now amended to extend Condition A to circumstances where any company connected with the creditor company may be the one entitled or required to acquire shares. CTA 2009 s 419 is amended to bring controlled foreign companies (CFCs) expressly into the ambit of CTA 2009 s 418. The amendments have effect in relation to loan relationships to which a company is or is treated as being a party after 5 December 2010, but amounts relating to a time on or before that day are to continue to be brought into account as if the amendments had not been made (s 29). However, CTA 2009 ss 418 and 419, even as amended, are themselves to be abolished with effect from 19 July 2011 as a result of the amendments made by Sch 5.

Section 30 introduces Sch 5, which contains provisions relating to so-called 'group mismatch schemes'. These are avoidance schemes that seek to exploit accounting or tax asymmetries in the way in which loan relationships and derivative contracts are treated within a group of companies so as to bring debits into account without also bringing into accounts the corresponding credits.

Schedule 5 inserts new CTA 2010 Part 21B, comprising new ss 938A to 938N and makes consequential amendments. Paragraph 1 makes a consequential amendment. Paragraph 2 inserts new Part 21B. New s 938A sets out the basic rule. It provides that where a company is a party to a 'group mismatch scheme' and is a member of the 'scheme group', no 'scheme loss or profit' made by the company in any accounting period in relation to the scheme is to be brought into account for the purposes of either the loan-relationships legislation (CTA 2009 Part 5), the derivative-contracts legislation (CTA 2009 Part 7) or any other purpose of corporation tax. New s 938B defines 'group mismatch scheme' and 'scheme group'. A scheme is a group mismatch scheme where the parties to the scheme are, or include, members of the same group and one of two conditions (A or B) is met. Condition A is that when the scheme is entered into, there is no practical likelihood that the scheme will fail to secure a 'relevant tax advantage' of £2 million or more. It thus sets a de minimis test. Condition B is that the purpose or one of the main purposes that any member of the scheme group has for entering into the scheme is to obtain the chance of securing a 'relevant tax advantage' of any amount and that at the time of entry into the scheme there is either no chance that the scheme will secure a 'relevant tax disadvantage' or, if there is such a chance, the scheme is nevertheless expected to produced a positive value. Both conditions therefore refer to likelihoods or expectations as perceived or had at the outset, not subsequently. The 'scheme group' is simply the group that includes the companies that are parties to the scheme. New s 938C defines 'scheme loss' and 'scheme profit'. A scheme loss or scheme profit is one that (a) arises from a transaction or series of transactions forming part of the scheme; (b) is or is comprised in an amount brought into account as a debit or credit under the loan relationships or derivative contracts legislation and (c) meets one of two 'asymmetry conditions'. The first asymmetry condition is that the loss or profit affects the amount of any relevant tax advantage secured by the scheme. In the case of uncertainty at the end of any accounting period as to whether any relevant tax advantage will be secured or as to its amount, the first asymmetry condition is treated as satisfied if, in effect, a chance exists that it may be. The second asymmetry condition is that the loss or profit, while not meeting the first asymmetry condition, arises from a transaction or series of transactions that might have given rise to a loss or profit that would have done so. This ensures that any profits from the scheme will escape taxation whether or not earlier losses have been disregarded. New s 938D defines 'relevant tax advantage' and 'relevant tax disadvantage'. A relevant tax advantage is a non-negligible economic profit made by the scheme group over the scheme period (the period over which the scheme has effect) and arising from asymmetries in the way in which different members of the scheme group bring into account or disregard debits and credits for the purposes of the legislation. A relevant tax disadvantage is similarly a non-negligible economic loss made by the scheme group over the scheme period and arising from asymmetries in the way in which different members of the scheme group bring into account or disregard debits and credits for the purposes of the legislation. Asymmetries may relate to quantity as well as timing, or be of some other nature. New s 938E defines a group for these purposes as a company and any other company associated with it which is also a party to the scheme. Any one of five conditions defines association. New s 938F provides that an economic profit or loss is to be computed taking into account in particular profits and losses arising from the operations of the Corporation Tax Acts and any adjustments for the time value of money. New s 938G provides that when determining whether a scheme will or might secure a relevant tax advantage, it is to be assumed that each company that is a party to the scheme obtains the full tax benefit of any loss made by it in relation to a loan relationship or derivative contract and incurs the full tax cost of any profit made by it in such a connection. 'Full tax benefit' and 'full tax cost' are defined. New s 938H defines a scheme as including any scheme, arrangement or understanding of any kind, whether or not legally enforceable, involving a single transaction or a number of transactions. New s 938I provides that where one party to the scheme has a debtor repo or quasi-repo (as defined in CTA 2009 ss 548 and 549) and the advance under the arrangement is received directly or indirectly from another member of the scheme group, amounts brought into or left out of account as respects the corporation tax charge on the repayment of the advance are to be treated as if they were references to debits and credits brought into or left out of account for the purposes of these provisions. Amounts brought into or left out of account in respect of the repayment of the advance under a type 1, 2 or 3 structured finance arrangement (as defined in CTA 2010 ss 758, 763 and 767) are similarly brought within the ambit of these provisions by new s 938J. References to amounts brought into or left out of account for the purposes of these provisions are to include amounts brought into or left out of account under CTA 2009 ss 297 or 573 as expenses or receipts of a trade (new s 938K). New s 938L ensures that amounts that a company does not bring into account because it is non-resident or has made an election under CTA 2009 s 18A (inserted by s 48 and Sch 13) to exclude the profits of its foreign permanent establishments from UK tax are not treated as debits or credits left out of account for the purposes of these provisions. New s 938M ensures that controlled foreign companies are brought within the scope of these provisions. New s 938N provides that these provisions have priority over CTA 2009 s 441 (loan relationships for unallowable purposes); CTA 2009 s 690 (derivative contracts for unallowable purposes); TIOPA 2010 Part 4 (transfer pricing); TIOPA 2010 Part 6 (tax arbitrage) and TIOPA 2010 Part 7 (tax treatment of financing costs and income). Paragraphs 3 and 4 make consequential amendments, including the renumbering of CTA 2010 ss 938–940 as ss 940A–940C. Paragraph 6 provides for commencement. In general, these provisions are to have effect in relation to schemes whenever entered into, but new s 938A, the operative rule itself, is not to apply to scheme losses or profits relating to a time before 19 July 2011 or scheme profits that relate to a time after 18 July 2011 but made in relation to a scheme entered into on or before that date. Paragraph 7 repeals CTA 2009 ss 418 and 419, themselves amended by s 29, presumably because they are considered redundant following the enactment of Part 21B, and certain other provisions in consequence, including s 29 (of FA 2011). The repeals have effect for loan relationships to which a company is or is treated as being a party before 19 July 2011, subject to transitional provisions. Repealed from the same date, and subject to identical transitional provisions, is CTA 2009 s 453, which seeks to counter advantages enjoyed by connected parties deriving a benefit from creditor relationships (s 30 and Sch 5).

Section 31 extends the scope of TCGA 1992 s 179, which imposes a charge to capital gains tax ('the degrouping charge') when a company leaves a group in certain circumstances. The degrouping charge to tax is imposed, broadly, where a company leaving the group had acquired an asset from another group member within the previous six years, and deems that asset to have been subject to a disposal and reacquisition immediately after its acquisition, at its market value at that time. TCGA 1992 s 179(2) provides that where two or more associated companies leave the group at the same time, the degrouping charge does not apply in respect of an asset acquired by one such company from another such company. However, this rule is modified by TCGA 1992 s 179(2A), which reimposes the degrouping charge where s 179(2) has previously applied, and the acquiring company subsequently leaves a second, connected, group. The test of connection is applied at the time the acquiring company leaves the second group. Section 179(2A) is now amended to act as an introductory subsection to new TCGA 1992 s 179(2AA). The latter subsection is to apply whenever a company that has acquired an asset from another company in its group leaves that group at the same time as the company from which it acquired that asset so that the acquisition is not subject to the degrouping charge, and the following events happen: (1) on leaving the first group, the acquiring company becomes a member of a second group; (2) at that time, there is a connection between the first group and the second group; and subsequently (3) the acquiring company leaves the second group or before it leaves the second group, the two groups cease to be connected. Thus the test of connection is now applied at the time, which is the same, when the acquiring company leaves the first group and becomes a member of the second group. Furthermore, the degrouping charge will also be imposed when the connection ceases without the need for the acquiring company to leave the second group. However, the degrouping charge under new TCGA 1992 s 179(2AA) will not apply where the fact that the companies leave the first group at the same time is not part of a tax-avoidance arrangement. A consequential amendment is made to TCGA 1992 s 179(2B), which defines when a connection is regarded as existing between the two groups. The amendments have effect in relation to any case in which the acquiring company ceases to be a member of the first group after 22 March 2011 (s 31). TCGA 1992 s 179 is further amended by s 45 (see below).

Section 32 introduces Sch 6, which makes yet another amendment to the anti avoidance provisions concerning the sale of leasing companies and partnerships. Paragraphs 1 to 9 amend CTA 2010 Part 9 Chapter 3, which contains the existing anti-avoidance provisions addressing the sale of a leasing business carried on by a company alone. Broadly speaking, those provisions apply where there is a 'qualifying change of ownership' in relation to a company carrying on a business of leasing plant or machinery, and they deem the company to have received an amount of taxable income on the day of the change and to have incurred a deductible expense of an equal amount on the subsequent day. Paragraph 1 is introductory. Paragraph 2 amends CTA 2010 s 387, which defines when a company is considered to carry on a business of leasing plant or machinery. Broadly, it does so where at least half by value of its plant and machinery is represented by 'qualifying plant and machinery' or at least half of its income in the previous 12 months derives from qualifying plant and machinery. CTA 2010 s 387(7) and (8) define 'qualifying plant and machinery'. These subsections are replaced by new sub ss (7)–(10), which substitute a significantly new definition. The plant and machinery in question (no longer referred to as 'qualifying plant and machinery') is now plant and machinery that has at any time in the previous 12 months been 'leased out' by the company or a 'qualifying associate' of that company under a plant or machinery lease other than an excluded lease of background plant or machinery for a building, excluding leases from a qualifying associate to the company (sub s (7)). 'Leased out', 'associate' and 'qualifying associate' are defined (sub s (8)). Where the company is owned by a consortium or is a qualifying 75 per cent subsidiary of a consortium-owned company, 'associate' includes any member of the consortium and any person connected with a member (sub s (9)). Paragraphs 3, 4 and 5 make consequential amendments. CTA 2010 s 398A allows companies to elect out of the deeming provisions in certain circumstances, in return for accepting restrictions on the use of losses etc. CTA 2010 s 398G prevents the successor from 'stepping into the shoes' of the predecessor as regards the predecessor's capital allowances on the transfer of a trade (it disapplies CTA 2010 s 948) where such an election has been made by the predecessor or the successor. On such an occasion, the disposal value has been market value, or market value as determined for the sales of lessors provisions under CTA 2010 s 437(9). Paragraph 6 amends CTA 2010 s 398G such that the 'ascribed value' of the plant and machinery is substituted for the market value if greater than the latter. 'Ascribed value' is defined in new CTA 2010 ss 437A–437C, inserted by para 22. Paragraphs 7 and 8 make consequential adjustments. Paragraph 9 amends CTA 2010 s 403, which defines 'TWDV' (tax written-down value), one of the elements in calculating the amount of the income attributed to the company that undergoes the qualifying change of ownership under these provisions. TWDV is the sum of various elements of unrelieved qualifying expenditure. The amendment provides that any part of unrelieved qualifying expenditure that consists of 'relevant new expenditure' is to be left of account, and defines 'relevant new expenditure'.

Paragraphs 10 to 15 make analogous provisions for cases where the leasing business is carried on by a company in partnership. Paragraph 10 is introductory. Paragraph 11 amends CTA 2010 s 410, which is the equivalent in CTA 2010 Part 9 Chapter 4 of CTA 2010 s 387, replacing the definition of 'qualifying plant and machinery'. Paragraphs 12 to 14 make consequential amendments. Paragraph 15 amends CTA 2010 s 421 to provide that 'relevant new expenditure' is not to be taken into account when calculating TWDV, and defines 'relevant new expenditure'. Paragraphs 16 to 19 amend the anti-avoidance provisions in CTA 2010 Part 9 Chapter 5, which are common to both leasing businesses carried on by a company alone and to those carried on by a company in partnership. Paragraph 16 is introductory. Paragraph 17 amends CTA 2010 s 434, which sets the conditions for the application of CTA 2010 ss 435 and 436. These require adjustments to be made, where, broadly, the balance-sheet values of plant and machinery have been manipulated to secure a tax advantage. Previously, these sections have applied if either of two questions (A and B) applies as to the application of CTA 2010 Part 9 Chapters 3 or 4. The amendment adds a third question, question C, which is a question as to the amount of any disposal value to be substituted by CTA 2010 s 398G(3) (inserted by para 6), which substitutes the higher of market value and ascribed value on a disposal caused by the transfer of a trade. Consequent upon the addition of Question C, para 18 amends CTA 2010 s 435 to add other adjustments that may be made in a case where manipulation is considered to be present. Paragraph 19 amends CTA 2010 s 436, which requires balance-sheet amounts to be determined on the assumption that the company has no liabilities (where the balance-sheet value of plant and machinery would otherwise be nil or lower than it would be if the assumption is made) to refer also to partnerships, where appropriate. Paragraphs 20 and 21 make consequential amendments. Paragraph 22 inserts new CTA 2010 ss 437A–437C, which define 'ascribed value'. Ascribed value is to be substituted for market value, it will be recalled, in appropriate cases. New CTA 2010 s 437A defines ascribed value in one of three ways, depending on whether or not the plant or machinery is subject to a lease, an equipment lease of fixtures under CAA 2001 s 177, or is not currently under lease. Where the lease is not an equipment lease, the ascribed value is the higher of market value and the present value of the lease. Where, on the other hand, the lease is an equipment lease in respect of which an election has been made under CAA 2001 s 177 to treat the equipment lessor as the owner, the ascribed value is the present value of the lease. In any other circumstance, the ascribed value is the market value. New CTA 2010 s 437B prescribes how market value is to be determined and new CTA 2010 s 437C how the present value of a lease is to be determined for these purposes. Paragraphs 23 to 26 make consequential amendments. Paragraph 27 provides for commencement. As the case may be, the amendments made by Sch 6 have effect in relation to qualifying changes of ownership, disposal events or transfers of trade occurring after 22 March 2011 (s 32 and Sch 6).

Section 33 makes amendments to the calculation of the lessee's qualifying expenditure under a long funding finance lease, in order to counter an avoidance scheme disclosed to HMRC, involving the use of what purports to be a guarantee but also results in acquisition of the plant or machinery by the lessee at the end of the lease. CAA 2001 s 70C provides that the lessee's qualifying expenditure under such a lease is normally the sum of the present value at the appropriate time of the minimum lease payments plus any 'unrelievable pre-commencement rentals'. It is now amended to the effect that any 'relievable amounts' must be excluded from the minimum lease payments in calculating their present value. An amount is a relievable amount where three conditions are satisfied: (1) there is an arrangement in place under which all or part of the residual amount under the lease (so much of the fair value of the plant or machinery as the lessor cannot reasonably expect to recover from the lease payments) is guaranteed by the lessee or a connected person; (2) the amount so guaranteed falls within the minimum lease payments because of the arrangement; and (3) it is reasonable to assume that were that amount to be incurred under the arrangement, relief would be available for it in addition to any relief under CAA 2001 s 70C or CAA 2001 s 70E (determination of disposal value). CAA 2001 s 70D provides additional allowances for the lessee where the present value of the minimum lease payments is increased as a result of expenditure incurred by the lessee on the plant or machinery. The section is amended to exclude any relievable amounts from being considered as eligible for additional allowances. In determining the disposal value of plant and machinery under a long funding finance lease, CAA 2001 s 70E(2C) provides that the qualifying amount that is deductible in computing the disposal value is the aggregate of the lessor's payments under the lease and any payments made under a guarantee for any residual amount. This provision is amended to exclude any 'relievable payments' from the qualifying amounts. Relievable payments are defined analogously to relievable amounts under CAA 2001 s 70C. The amendments to CAA 2001 ss 70C and 70D have effect for arrangements entered into after 8 March 2011 and the amendments to CAA 2001 s 70E have effect to payments made after 8 March 2011 (s 33).

Section 34 introduces Sch 7, which is intended to prevent the generation by investment companies of deductible foreign-exchange losses by virtue of a change in their functional currency. Paragraph 1 amends CTA 2010 s 6. That section provides that where a UK-resident company prepares its accounts in a currency other than sterling but identifies sterling as its functional currency, its profits and losses must be calculated in sterling for the purposes of corporation tax as if the company prepared its accounts in sterling. It is now amended so as to apply to a UK resident investment company only where it has not elected under new CTA 2010 s 9A (inserted by para 3) to have a currency other than sterling as its 'designated currency'. A similar amendment is made to CTA 2010 s 7. This section provides that where a UK-resident company prepares its accounts in one foreign currency but identifies another foreign currency as its functional currency, its profits and losses must be calculated for the purposes of corporation tax first in the functional currency and then translated into their sterling equivalent. As amended by para 2, this section is to apply to a UK-resident investment company only where it has not elected to have sterling or the currency in which it prepares its accounts as its designated currency. Paragraph 3 inserts new CTA 2010 ss 9A and 9B. New CTA 2010 s 9A provides that a UK-resident investment company may elect to have a designated currency. The election may be made without restriction in the period beginning with the company's incorporation and ending immediately before its first accounting period, but may not be retroactive. At any other time, it may make the election only if one of two conditions (A or B) is met. Condition A is that a significant proportion of the company's assets and liabilities are denominated in that currency. Condition B is that the currency is the functional currency of another company with which, broadly, the first company's accounts are or would need to be consolidated. However, an election made before the company's first accounting period is void if neither Condition A nor B is met when that first period begins. New CTA 2010 s 9B defines the period for which an election under CTA 2010 s 9B is valid and provides for the treatment of periods straddling either the day on which the election takes effect or the date on which the election is treated as revoked. Paragraph 4 inserts a definition of 'investment company' in CTA 2010 s 17. Paragraph 5 amends the CFC (controlled foreign company) provisions in TA 1988 Sch 24, of which Sch 24 para 4 provides that when calculating the hypothetical UK corporation tax charge on a controlled foreign company, all elections on which relief under the UK Corporation Tax Acts is dependent are assumed to have been made. New TA 1988 Sch 24 para 4(2B) provides that a designated-currency election under new CTA 2010 s 9A is not to be such an election. New TA 1988 Sch 24 para 4(2C) provides, however, that a UK company or companies having a majority interest in a

CFC may by notice require the assumption to be made that the CFC has made a designated-currency election under new CTA 2010 s 9A. Paragraph 6 amends CTA 2009 s 328, which deals with the treatment of exchange gains and losses under loan relationships. The amendment has the effect that an exchange gain or loss is not to be brought into account as a debit or credit under the loan relationship where it has arisen only because of a change in the company's functional currency as between the period of account in which the gain or loss arises and a period of account ending within the 12 months immediately preceding that period. An equivalent amendment is made by para 7 to the analogous provision (CTA 2010 s 606) in the derivative-contracts legislation. Paragraph 8 provides that the amendments made by Sch 7 have effect in relation to periods of account beginning after 31 March 2011, but an election made under new CTA 2010 s 9A may be made or revoked at any time after 8 December 2010. Where an election made before 27 June 2011 does not specify the date on which it is to take effect, it is to have effect on the first day of the first period of account beginning after the election is made (s 34 and Sch 7).

Exemptions and reliefs. Section 35 introduces Sch 8, which reduces childcare relief for 'higher earners'. Paragraph 1 is introductory. Under ITEPA 2003 s 270A, qualifying childcare vouchers are up to a certain maximum amount exempt from the charge to tax on benefits-in-kind, subject to certain conditions (A to C). Paragraph 2 introduces a further condition (Condition D), which is that, at the required time, the employer must have made an estimate of the employee's 'relevant earnings amount' for the tax year concerned. The maximum amount qualifying for relief, which has hitherto been £55 per qualifying week, is reduced to £22 per week where the employee's estimated relevant earnings amount exceeds the higher rate limit and to £28 per qualifying week where it exceeds the basic rate limit but not the higher rate limit. ITEPA 2003 s 270A is further amended by s 36 (see below). Paragraph 3 inserts new ITEPA 2003 s 270B, which defines 'relevant earnings amount' and 'required time'. The relevant earnings amount is the aggregate of the amount of the employee's relevant earnings for the tax year from employment with that employer and the employee's taxable benefits under the Benefits Code (ITEPA 2003 Part 3 Chapters 2–12), less any excluded amounts. Where the employee's employment began during the course of the tax year, the aggregate is reduced pro rata by reference to the number of days of the employment. Relevant earnings are salary, wages and fees and any other earnings specified in regulations. Excluded amounts are also to be specified in regulations. The 'required time' is the beginning of the tax year or, if later, the time at which the employee joins the scheme. Amendments equivalent to those made to ITEPA 2003 s 270A are made by para 4 to ITEPA 2003 s 318A, which provides the analogous relief for employer-provided childcare at premises other than workplace nurseries. ITEPA 2003 s 318A is further amended by s 36 (see below). Para 5 inserts new ITEPA 2003 s 318AA, which contains the identical definitions to those in new ITEPA 2003 s 270B. Paragraph 6 makes consequential amendments to ITEPA 2003 s 318D. Subject to transitional provisions in paras 8 to 10, Sch 8 has effect from the tax year 2011 12 (s 35 and Sch 8).

Further amendments are made to ITEPA 2003 ss 270A and 318A to permit the exclusion of 'relevant low-paid employees' from childcare voucher schemes and employer provided childcare schemes run on the basis of salary-sacrifice or flexible-remuneration arrangements without endangering the requirement for the schemes to be generally available. 'Relevant low-paid employees are those whose remuneration would fall below the national minimum wage if the salary sacrifice or flexible remuneration arrangements were to be applied to them. These amendments have retroactive effect from the tax year 2005 06 (s 36). Payments made to MPs for overnight accommodation under section 5(1) of the Parliamentary Standards Act 2009 are exempt from tax under ITEPA 2003 s 292. The exemption is now extended to qualifying payments made after 31 October 2010 to other persons at the Member's discretion under section 6(7) of the Parliamentary Standards Act 2009 (s 37). There is to be no charge to income tax on subsistence allowances paid by a 'relevant EU body' to experts seconded to that body by their employers, under new ITEPA 2003 s 304A. The bodies concerned are the European Medicines Agency, the European Police College, the European Banking Authority (all of which are based or to be based in the United Kingdom) and any other body so designated by Treasury order. The exemption has effect for allowances paid for periods beginning after 31 December 2010 (s 38). There is to be no charge to income tax in respect of the payment or reimbursement by an employer of the employee's application fee to join a Protection of Vulnerable Groups Scheme in Scotland (under the Protection of Vulnerable Groups (Scotland) Act 1997), with effect from the tax year 2010 11, under new ITEPA 2003 s 326A. The Treasury may by order extend the exemption to fees paid to equivalent schemes in England and Wales or Northern Ireland, which do not currently exist (s 39). Additional provision is made in respect of individual investment plans (IIP), to pave the way for the Government's stated intention to introduce other such plans, such as Junior ISAs for example, alongside the single existing example, the ISA. ITTOIA 2005 s 694, which gives the Treasury power to exempt income from IIPs from income tax by order, is amended to include in its scope income paid to a child which is deemed under ITTOIA 2005 s 629 to be income of the parent settlor. New ITTOIA 2005 s 695A is inserted to provide further regulation-making power in respect of investment plans for children, and consequential amendments are made to other related provisions of ITTOIA 2005 and TCGA 1992 (s 40).

The maximum benefits that donors may derive from the charity or Community Amateur Sports Club that they support under the Gift Aid scheme without losing entitlement to tax relief for their donations is increased from £500 to £2,500, with effect from gifts made after 5 April 2011 or in accounting periods beginning after 31 March 2011, as the case may be. The appropriate amendments are made to ITA 2007 s 418 (individual donors) and CTA 2010 s 197 (corporate donors). The limits per individual gift, based on the size of the gift, remain unchanged (s 41).

The rate at which relief under the Enterprise Investment Scheme (EIS) is given is increased from 20 per cent to 30 per cent, with effect from the tax year 2011 12. The rate at which EIS relief is withdrawn is to be the rate ('the original rate') in force for the tax year in which the relief was obtained, except that for 2007 08 and previous tax years, this is deemed to be 20 per cent. However, these amendments have effect from a day yet to be appointed, pending state-aid approval from the European Commission (s 42). The additional deduction that small and medium sized enterprises (SMEs) may make in respect of qualifying expenditure on research and development is increased from 75 per cent to 100 per cent, and the deemed trading loss that they may claim in respect of qualifying pre-trading expenditure and the surrenderable loss is correspondingly increased from 175 per cent to 200 per cent of the expenditure. However, the amount that may be claimed under CTA 2009 s 1058 as a tax credit is reduced from 14 per cent to 12.5 per cent of the surrenderable loss. The additional deduction that a company, whether an SME or not, may claim in respect of vaccine or medicine research is reduced from 40 per cent to 20 per cent, with a corresponding reduction in the deemed trading loss and surrenderable loss. The amendments are to have effect for expenditure incurred after 31 March 2011, but as with the changes to EIS relief, they have effect from a day yet to be appointed, pending state-aid approval from the European Commission (s 43).

Chargeable gains. The three sections under this rubric, and the two under the next rubric, with their accompanying Schedules, can genuinely be considered as tax-reforming measures, which considerably simplify, and in the case of the provisions under this rubric, target existing anti-avoidance provisions more closely.

Section 44 introduces Sch 9, which amends the value-shifting provisions of TCGA 1992. It is intended to simplify this complex anti-avoidance legislation, and its enactment follows considerable consultation. The value-shifting provisions are currently found in TCGA 1992 ss 29–34. The basic rule is contained in TCGA 1992 s 30, which provides that where a scheme has been effected or arrangements made whereby the value of an asset that is the subject of a disposal or that of a 'relevant asset' has been materially reduced such that a tax-free benefit is or will be conferred on the disponer, a person connected with the disponer or in some circumstances, any other person, any allowable loss or chargeable gain on the disposal is calculated as if the consideration for the disposal were increased by a just and reasonable amount with regard to the scheme or arrangement. A 'relevant asset' is an asset owned at the time of the disposal by a company associated with the disposing company, where the disposal is made by a company. Where transactions within a group are involved, the basic rule is made subject to the provisions of TCGA 1992 ss 31–34.

Paragraph 1 amends TCGA 1992 s 30, which disapplies that section for the purposes of corporation tax if the disposal is one of shares or securities in another company. Instead, new TCGA 1992 s 31 is to apply. Paragraph 2 repeals the existing TCGA 1992 ss 31–34 and replaces them with a single new TCG 1992 s 31. The new section is to apply where (a) arrangements have been made whereby the value of those shares or securities (or of any relevant asset) has been materially reduced (or in the case where the disposal precedes the acquisition, materially increased); (b) the main purpose or one of the main purposes of the arrangements is to obtain a tax advantage; and (c) the arrangements consist of something other than or additional to the making of an exempt distribution. Where the section applies, any allowable loss or chargeable gain on the disposal is calculated as if the consideration for the disposal were increased by a just and reasonable amount with regard to the arrangements and any charge to or relief from corporation tax that would otherwise arise as a result of the disposal or the arrangements. A relevant asset is now defined as an asset owned at the time of the disposal by a fellow member of the disposing company's group. Where arrangements to obtain a tax advantage exist, they are not to override TCGA 1992 s 29(2), which deems a disposal of certain shares or rights to occur where a person controlling a company exercises his control so that value passes out of those shares or rights. 'Arrangements', 'exempt distribution', 'group;, 'securities' and 'tax advantage' are defined. Paragraph 3 introduces a six-year limitation on the anti-avoidance provisions of TCGA 1992 s 176 relating to depreciatory transactions. Hitherto, it has been possible to refer back to depreciatory transactions dating back all the way to 31 March 1982. Paragraph 4 makes a consequential amendment and para 5 makes consequential repeals. These amendments generally have effect in relation to disposals made after 18 July 2011, but nothing is to prevent the continuing effect of TCGA 1992 s 31A (asset-holding companies leaving the group) if the related disposal takes place before 19 July 2011 (s 44 and Sch 9).

Section 45 introduces Sch 10, which significantly amends the legislation on the degrouping charge where a company leaves a group. The relevant legislation is TCGA 1992 ss 179, 179A, 179B and 181. Paragraph 1 makes a consequential amendment to TCGA 1992 s 139. Paragraph 2 removes the prohibition preventing the election under TCGA 1992 s 171A to allocate a gain arising from the degrouping charge to another member of the group, to pave the way for repeal of TCGA 1992 s 179A, which serves the same function in respect of the degrouping charge. Paragraph 3 amends TCGA 1992 s 179, which is the substantive provision imposing the degrouping charge. The degrouping charge to tax is imposed, broadly, where a company leaving the group had acquired an asset from another group member within the previous six years and deems that asset to have been subject to a disposal and reacquisition immediately after its acquisition, at its market value at that time, provided that the company leaving the group still owns the asset or an associated company also leaving the group holds the replacement property to which the gain on the original asset has been rolled over. The wording of s 179(1) and s 179(2A)(a) is amended to clarify that the degrouping charge is imposed only where the acquiring and disposing companies were members of the same group at the time of the acquisition. Section 179(2) currently provides that where two or more associated companies leave the group at the same time, the degrouping charge does not apply in respect of an asset acquired by one such company from another such company. Companies are associated for this purpose if by themselves they would form a group (s 179(10)(a)).This exclusion is replaced by a new exclusion, which provides that when two companies cease to be members of the group at the same time, there is to be no degrouping charge in respect of an asset acquired by one company from the other only if one or other of two conditions (A and B) is met. Condition A is that both companies are both 75 per cent subsidiaries and effective 51 per cent subsidiaries of another company at the time of the acquisition and remain both 75 per cent subsidiaries and effective 51 per cent subsidiaries of that same company until immediately after they cease to be members of the group. Condition B is that one of the companies is both a 75 per cent subsidiary and effective 51 per cent subsidiary of the other company at the time of the acquisition and remains both a 75 per cent subsidiary and effective 51 per cent subsidiary of the other company until immediately after they cease to be members of the group. New rules are introduced, by virtue of new s 179 (3A) (3H), to deal with the situation where a company leaves a group as a result of one or more share disposals by a group company. The disposals in question are of shares in the company itself or in another group company. It is important here to distinguish between the company making the disposal (here called 'the disposing company') as a result of which another company leaves the group, and that other company (here called 'the departing company'), which is deemed to make the disposal and reacquisition. New sub ss (3A) and (3B) provide that the chargeable gain or allowable loss on the deemed disposal that would otherwise accrue to the departing company will not do so where (a) the disposing company in respect of at least one disposal is UK-resident and the shares were chargeable assets in relation to that company before their disposal (i.e. the company is chargeable to UK corporation tax on chargeable gains on the disposal); or (b) the disposing company is non-resident and any part of the chargeable gain or allowable loss accruing to it is attributed to its UK shareholders under TCGA 1992 s 13; or (c) any gain arising on each of the disposals would, had the disposing company been UK-resident and had it been disposing of the shares as chargeable assets, have been exempt under TCGA 1992 Sch 7AC as gains from the disposal of substantial shareholdings. The degrouping charge will continue to apply as before where none of the situations (a) to (c) applies or where the departing company is a REIT and the chargeable gain or allowable loss accruing to it would not have been an exempt gain under CTA 2010 s 535. For these purposes, new sub s (3C) provides that a disposal is nevertheless a disposal even where it occurs on a reorganisation and would otherwise not be treated as a disposal under TCGA 1992 s 127. In the event that the normal operation of the degrouping charge is prevented by sub s (3A), sub s (3D) provides that the chargeable gain or allowable loss that accrues to the disposing company on the disposal is to be calculated as if (a) the gain that would have accrued to the departing company were added to the consideration received for the disposal by the disposing company or (b) the loss that would have accrued to the departing company were added to the allowable expenditure on the disposal, but not in the event that the disposal by the disposing company is one to which TCGA 1992 s 127 applies. Sub s (3E) deals with the situation where the disposal is one to which TCGA 1992 s 127 applies, so that there is no immediate disposal for the purposes of tax on capital gains. It provides that on the subsequent disposal of the new holding by the disposing company, the gain that would have accrued to the departing company is deducted from the allowable expenditure on the disposal of the new holding. If that gain exceeds the allowable expenditure, it is instead to be treated as an additional gain to any actual gain or loss accruing on the disposal of the new holding. In the event that a loss would have accrued to the departing company, that loss is to be treated as additional allowable expenditure of the disposing company on the disposal of the new holding. New sub s (3F) provides that where there is more than one disposal of shares causing the departing company to leave the group, the disposing companies may allocate the gain or loss that would have accrued to the departing company in any proportion they elect. In the absence of an election, the gain or loss is allocated between the disposing companies equally. New sub s (3G) provides that the election must be made no later than two years after the end of the first accounting period in which the gain or loss is deemed to accrue. Sub s (3H) allows for the increase or deduction under sub ss (3D) or (3E) to be apportioned between different classes of shares. TCGA 1992 s 179(5)–(8) deal with the situation where a departing company leaves a group by virtue only of the fact that its principal company becomes a member of another group. Broadly, they provide that there is no immediate deemed disposal and reacquisition, but if within the following six years, the departing company ceases to be both a 75 per cent subsidiary and effective 51 per cent subsidiary of the new group, there is a deemed disposal and reacquisition at that point if either the departing company or a member of its group holds the replacement asset to which the gain on the original asset has been rolled over. These provisions are now also amended to apply the same mechanism as applies on a group disposal, as provided by new TCGA 1992 s 179(3A)–(3H). The definition of when companies are associated is also amended such that two companies are associated with one another if one is a 75 per cent subsidiary of the other or both are 75 per cent subsidiaries of a third company. Paragraph 4 inserts new TCGA 1992 s 179ZA. This allows the departing company or, where the effect of the degrouping charge is transferred to the disposing company or companies, the disposing company or companies, to make a claim to HMRC for the amount of the gain to be reduced by an amount that is just and reasonable. In determining what is just and reasonable, regard will be had in particular to the transaction as a direct or indirect result of which the asset to which the gain relates was acquired. Paragraph 5 repeals TCGA 1992 s 179A, which allows the degrouping-charge gain to be allocated to another group member (this can now be done by virtue of an election under TCGA 1992 s 171A); TCGA 1992 s 179B, which provided for the degrouping charge to be rolled over to a replacement asset; and TCGA 1992 Sch 7AB, which contains modifications to enactments enabling the degrouping charge to be rolled over. Under TCGA 1992 Sch 7AC, a gain made by a trading company or a member of a trading group ('the investing company') on the disposal of a substantial shareholding is not a chargeable gain provided, inter alia, that the shareholding has been a substantial shareholding for at least 12 months in the two year period immediately preceding the disposal. Paragraph 6 inserts new TCGA 1992 Sch 7AC para 15A, which provides, subject to certain conditions, for an extension to the period in which a substantial shareholding is held in certain circumstances where, a trading asset has been transferred to the company in which the substantial shareholding exists (here called 'the investee company' from now on). The conditions are that (a) a substantial shareholding is actually held by the investing company in the investee company immediately before the disposal; (b) the investee company holds the transferred asset as a trading asset at the time of the disposal; (c) that the asset was transferred by the investing company or another company at a time when both the investing company, the investee company and, if different, the transferor company, were all members of the same group; and (d) the asset was a trading asset of a member company of the group at a time when the company was a member of that group. If these conditions are met, the investing company is to be treated as having held the substantial shareholding at any time in the final 12 months preceding the disposal when the asset was used in the trade of the transferor, if it did not already do so at that time. An amendment is also made to TCGA 1992 Sch 7AC para 19, which sets out conditions the investee company must meet. One of those conditions is that it have been a trading company or the holding company of a trading group or subgroup throughout a period beginning with the latest 12-month period in which the substantial shareholding persists and ending with the time of the disposal. This condition is amended so that where the conditions in new TCGA 1992 Sch 7AC para 15A for the transferred trading asset are met, the investee company is to be treated as a trading company at any time during the final 12 months preceding the disposal when the transferor company used the asset in its trade, if it was not already a trading company. Paragraph 7 amends CTA 2009 Part 7 to provide for the consequences of the new degrouping rules for the treatment of intangible fixed assets. CTA 2009 s 780 imposes a deemed realisation and reacquisition of a chargeable intangible fixed asset when a company leaves a group within six years of the transfer to it of such an asset. CTA 2009 s 783 makes an exception from the deemed realisation and reacquisition in certain circumstances where two or more associated companies leave the group at the same time, unless the transferee company subsequently leaves a second group and there is a 'relevant connection' (defined in CTA 2009 s 784) between the two groups. This exception is amended to impose additional conditions, identical to those added to TCGA 1992 s 179(2) by para 3 above. Consequential amendments are made to CTA 2009 ss 780 and 788. Paragraph 8 makes consequential repeals. Paragraph 9 provides for commencement. Essentially, the provisions apply to events occurring after 18 July 2011. However, where the principal company of a group makes an 'early commencement election', the provisions are to apply as from 1 April 2011. Such an early commencement election must receive the consent of any company that left the group between 1 April and 19 July 2011. The election must be made or if already made, revoked, before 1 April 2012 (s 45 and Sch 10).

Section 46 introduces Sch 11, which relaxes the rules on the use of pre entry losses — brought forward capital losses that a company has incurred prior to its entry into a group. The legislation relating to these losses is found in TCGA 1992 s 177A and Sch 7A. TCGA 1992 s 177A, introducing TCGA 1992 Sch 7A, provides that it applies not only to losses accruing to a company before it becomes a member of a group of companies but also to losses accruing on assets held by any company at such a time. The existing legislation thus also applies to restrict the use of losses incurred by any group member on assets held before the entry of the relevant company into the group (losses on 'pre-entry assets').

Paragraph 1 deletes the reference in TCGA 1992 s 177A to losses accruing to any company on pre-entry assets. The legislation is thus to apply solely to losses accruing to a company before the time when it becomes a member of a group of companies ('pre entry losses'). Paragraph 2 provides that amendments are to be made to TCGA 1992 Sch 7A. Paragraph 3 amends Sch 7A para 1 to delete references to losses on pre entry assets. Thus, in particular, Sch 7A para 1(2) as amended clarifies that the pre entry losses the set-off of which the provisions of the Schedule restrict are solely the allowable losses that have accrued to a company that becomes a member of a group of companies at a time before it became a member of that group. Paragraph 4 provides for the omission of Sch 7A paras 2 to 5, all of which deal with losses on pre entry assets and are hence redundant. Sch 7A para 6 determines the order in which pre entry losses are to be treated as deducted from chargeable gains. Except for gains accruing in accounting periods ending before 16 March 1993 (when the pre entry legislation was first introduced), where a set order is prescribed, companies may elect for the order they choose. Paragraph 5 omits the provisions relating to pre 16 March 1993 periods, which are clearly now spent. Sch 7A para 7(1) sets out the gains from which pre entry losses may be deducted. These are (a) gains on pre entry disposals; (b) gains on post entry disposals of pre entry assets and (c) gains on disposals of certain post entry assets. As far as post entry gains on post entry assets are concerned, these are limited to gains from the disposal of any post entry asset acquired by the company from outside the group which has been used or held for the purposes of a trade carried on by the company immediately before entry and which it still carries on up to the time of the disposal. Paragraph 6 amends these rules so that the pre entry loss may now be set off against a gain on the disposal of any post entry asset acquired from outside the group either by the company with the pre entry loss or by any other company that was a member of that company's group at the time of the acquisition. Furthermore, whereas that asset must have been used by the company with the pre entry loss for the purposes of a trade or business it carried on immediately before entry, post-entry, that trade or business may have been carried on by another member of the group. Where the company with the pre entry loss subsequently becomes a member of another group, these provisions continue to apply to the loss by reference to the original group. It also deletes references to losses on pre entry assets and substitutes a new definition of what constitutes a pre entry asset, since the original definition has been deleted from Sch 7A para 1 by para 3 (see above). Sch 7A para 8 provides that where there has been a major change in the nature or conduct of a trade carried on by the company with the pre entry loss, that trade is to be disregarded for the purposes of determining whether it was carried on by the company pre entry. Paragraph 7 adds references to a business as well as a trade and a specific reference to a company with investment business. Paragraphs 8 to 10 make consequential amendments and repeals. Paragraph 11 provides that the amendments made by Sch 11 have effect in relation to the deduction of pre entry losses at any time after 18 July 2011, regardless of when the loss was incurred and when the company became a member of the relevant group, subject to transitional provisions in para 12 (s 46 and Sch 11).

Foreign profits. Section 47 introduces Sch 12, which makes detailed but interim amendments to the CFC (controlled foreign company) regime, pending the full reform to be enacted in FA 2012. Sch 12 Part 1 (paras 1 to 3) introduces two new exemptions from the CFC regime. Sch 12 Part 2 (paras 4 and 5) amends the small chargeable profits exemption. Sch 12 Part 3 (paras 6 to 8) introduces a temporary exemption following reorganisation. Sch 12 Part 4 (para 9) extends the transitional provision for holding companies. Sch 12 Part 5 (paras 10 to 13) makes minor and consequential amendments, whereas Sch 12 Part 6 (para 14) provides for commencement. Pending complete reform, the CFC provisions have remained in TA 1988, in Part XVII Chapter IV (ss 747–756 and Schs 25 and 26) to be precise.

Paragraph 1 amends TA 1988 s 748, which specifies cases where the CFC rules do not apply. Two further exemptions are now added: an exemption for trading companies with limited UK connection, as defined in new TA 1988 Sch 25 Part 2A and an exemption for companies exploiting intellectual property with limited UK connection, as defined in new TA 1988 Sch 25 Part 2B. Paragraph 2 inserts new TA 1988 s 751AB, which provides for a reduction in the CFC charge in cases where the conditions for the new exemptions are not fully satisfied. Where there is a 'relevant failure', a UK-resident company to which the chargeable profits of the CFC are to be apportioned may apply to HMRC for the apportionable amount to be reduced, to nil where appropriate. To the extent that the claim is granted, the CFC's creditable tax is reduced correspondingly. Before granting the claim, HMRC must be satisfied that the profits left in charge are not less than the 'relevant amount' and that they have not granted a previous application under either TA 1988 s 751A (reduction for certain activities of EEA business establishments) or new TA 1988 s 751AC (reduction following an exempt period), inserted by para 7, in respect of the same accounting period. A 'relevant failure' is either (a) one in which the CFC's UK connection is greater than the 10 per cent limit for the new exemption for a trading company with limited UK connection to apply but less than 50 per cent or (b) one in which the CFC's financial income and income from intellectual property ('IP income') together exceed the stipulated 5 per cent for the new exemption for a trading company with limited UK connection to apply but the IP income property taken on its own does not exceed 5 per cent or (c) one in which the CFC's finance income exceeds the maximum 5 per cent for the new intellectual property exemption to apply. The 'relevant amount' — the amount of CFC profits that must remain in charge — is defined as follows. In the case of failures (a) and/or (b) above, it is the excess of the CFC's finance and IP income over the 5 per cent limit, plus, broadly, profits other than those representing the net economic value arising in the CFC's territory from work done there by individuals working there for the CFC and any profits attributable directly or indirectly to transactions with persons chargeable to UK tax. In the case of failure (c) above, the relevant amount is the excess of the CFC's finance income over the 5 per cent limit. Paragraph 3 inserts new TA 1988 Sch 25 Parts 2A and 2B, which contain the two new exemptions. Sch 25 Part 2A, consisting of paras 12B to 12N, contains the exemption for trading companies with limited UK connection. Paragraph 12B provides that a CFC qualifies for this exemption if it satisfies requirements as to (1) its business establishment; (2) its business activities; (3) its UK connection and (4) its finance income and relevant IP income. Requirement (1), defined in para 12C, is that throughout the accounting period concerned it have a business establishment in the territory in which it is resident. Requirement (2), defined in para 12D, is satisfied where the CFC's business does not at any time in the accounting period include non-exempt activities to a substantial extent or, where it is wholly engaged in banking and similar businesses, that its business does not at any time in the period include non-exempt activities other than investment business. Non-exempt activities are defined, being activities of a largely passive or investment character. Requirement (3), defined in para 12E, is satisfied where the CFC does not have a significant connection with the United Kingdom. Such a significant connection exists where one of two further conditions is satisfied. Those are that either (A) its UK-connected gross income exceeds 10 per cent of its gross business income and it fails to satisfy further conditions requiring it to have sufficient individuals working for it outside the United Kingdom to undertake all or substantially all of its business, its EBIT (profits before deductions for interest and tax) not to exceed 10 per cent of its operating expenses, and its UK-connected gross income not to exceed 50 per cent of its total gross income or (B) the CFC's UK-connected related-party business expenditure exceeds 50 per cent of its total related-party business expenditure and it has been involved in a (UK) tax-reduction scheme. Various relevant terms are defined. Requirement (4), relating to finance and IP income, is defined in para 12F. Simply put, this requirement is that the CFC's 'finance income' and 'relevant IP income' not exceed 5 per cent of its gross income for the relevant accounting period. Finance income is defined as income arising from a financial asset, according to GAAP, and any return economically equivalent to interest arising from an arrangement to which the CFC is party. 'Relevant IP income' is royalties and receipts of a similar nature arising from intellectual property. Gross income is defined in para 12G. Part 2B, comprising paras 12H to 12N, introduces the exemption for companies exploiting intellectual property with limited UK connection. Paragraph 12H provides that the exemption applies to a CFC that satisfies requirements as to its (1) business establishment; (2) intellectual property business; (3) other business activities; (4) UK connection and (5) finance income. Requirement (1), contained in para 12I, is that throughout the accounting period concerned, the CFC have its business establishment in the territory in which it is resident. Requirement (2), contained in para 12J, is that its main business throughout that accounting period consist of the exploitation of intellectual property that does not have a 'relevant UK connection'. A relevant UK connection exists where at any time in the accounting period or the six immediately preceding years, the intellectual property has been held by a UK resident person or where activities relating to its creation, maintenance or enhancement have been carried on by a person related to the company and within the charge to UK tax. Requirement (3), contained in para 12K, is that the CFC either not carry on any activities outside its main business or that, where such secondary activities are carried on, they not be substantial or that taken on their own they would qualify for the trading-activities exemption or the exempt-activities condition in new Part 2A. Requirement (4), contained in para 12L, is that the CFC not have a significant connection with the United Kingdom during the accounting period. A significant connection with the United Kingdom exists where either (a) all or a substantial proportion of the CFC's gross income consists of income from the exploitation of intellectual property deriving from persons within the charge to UK tax or (b) it incurs expenditure on payments to R&D subcontractors or the creation, development or maintenance of intellectual property without a relevant UK connection and that expenditure or those payments are income of a person related to the CFC and within the charge to UK tax. Requirement (5), contained in para 12M, is that no more than 5 per cent of the CFC's gross income consist of finance income. Paragraph 12N provides for interpretation.

Schedule 12 Part 2 introduces amendments to the existing small chargeable profits (de minimis) exemption. TA 1988 s 748(1)(d) currently provides that a CFC's chargeable profits will not be attributed under the CFC rules where they do not exceed £50,000 (or the equivalent proportion where the accounting period is less than 12 months). Paragraph 4 amends this exemption to extend the exemption to profits of up to £200,000 (or the equivalent proportion) but the exemption now refers to 'relevant profits', which are the company's accounting profits, as calculated in accordance with GAAP (disregarding exempt distributions and capital gains and losses), and including income of a trust of which the company is either a beneficiary or settlor, and the company's share of the income of any partnership of which it is a partner. Paragraph 5 inserts new TA 1988 s 748ZA, which establishes exclusions from the small profits exemption. It provides that the exemption is not to apply where any of three conditions (A, B or C) is met. Condition A is that there exists a scheme to ensure that the new exemption apply. Condition B is that there exists a scheme to shift profits from the CFC to another company in order that the exemption apply to one or more CFCs. Condition C is that in determining the CFC's chargeable profits, either CTA 2009 s 418(5) has effect to treat the CFC as bringing into account credits where its debits from loan relationships exceed its credits from those relationships or new CTA 2010 Part 21B (group mismatch schemes — see above under s 30) has effect to exclude a debit or a credit from being taken into account. Schedule 12 Part 3 introduces a temporary exemption following a reorganisation. The exemption excludes the chargeable profits of companies that have newly entered the CFC regime from attribution for a set period, referred to as the 'exempt period'. It further allows claims to be made to reduce any apportionment in respect of accounting periods that would have ended during the exempt period if that period had not been terminated prematurely in certain circumstances. The provisions relating to the exempt period are contained in new TA 1988 Sch 25 Part 3A, inserted by para 8, for which see below. Paragraph 6 adds a new exemption to TA 1988 s 748, namely in respect of the chargeable profits of an accounting period that ends during an exempt period. Para 7 inserts new TA 1988 s 751AC, which provides for claims to reduce an apportionment following early termination of an exempt period. Such a claim may be made where a CFC's exempt period has ended following an 'early termination event' in respect of an accounting period that would have ended in the exempt period had it not been for the early termination. The claim must specify the amount to which the attributable profits are to be reduced, which may be nil. To the extent that the claim is granted, the CFC's creditable tax is reduced correspondingly. Before granting the claim, HMRC must be satisfied that the profits left in charge are not less than the 'relevant amount' and that they have not granted a previous application under either TA 1988 s 751A (reduction for certain activities of EEA business establishments) or new TA 1988 s 751AB (failure to qualify for exemptions), inserted by para 2, for which see above, in respect of the same accounting period. The 'relevant amount' — the amount of CFC profits that must remain in charge — is the amount of profits that it is just and reasonable to regard as referable to the transaction that caused the early termination or any later relevant transaction occurring before the exempt period would otherwise have ended. Paragraph 8 inserts new TA 1988 Sch 25 Part 3A, comprising paras 15A to 15G, which contains the provisions relating to exempt periods. Paragraph 15A is introductory. Paragraph 15B provides that an exempt period begins at the time ('the relevant time') when the company in question (X) (being a non resident company under the control of UK resident persons) has at least one 'relevant UK corporate investor' (broadly a company to which X's profits could be apportioned under the CFC rules) and either of two sets of conditions is met. Paragraph 15C contains the first set of conditions. They are that (a) X had a 'relevant UK corporate investor at any time before the relevant time; (b) no asset owned or business carried on by X at the relevant time was previously owned or carried on by another company related to X and under the control of UK resident persons; (c) a 'disqualifying relevant transaction' has not taken place and (d) any one of four further conditions (A, B, C and D) is satisfied. Condition A is that X existed before the relevant time but was not a member of the same group as any UK resident person who alone or with other UK resident persons controls X. Condition B is that at the relevant time X was controlled by a UK resident company and was immediately previously controlled by the same company, which was not then UK resident. Condition C is that at the relevant time X was controlled by a UK resident intermediate parent that was itself controlled by a non resident parent, but that immediately previously, X was controlled by the parent but not by the intermediate parent. Condition D is that X was a CFC when it was incorporated by one or more persons for the purpose of controlling one or more other companies in the expectation that an exempt period would begin when X began to control those other companies. The alternative set of conditions is contained in para 15D, namely that (a) the relevant time falls after 23 March 2011; (b) X has an accounting period encompassing that date; (c) X did not at any time during that period have a relevant UK corporate investor; (d) X had no relevant UK corporate investor immediately before the relevant time; (e) X was at the relevant time controlled by a UK resident company and not under the control of any one or more other bodies corporate and (f) no 'disqualifying relevant transaction' occurs. Paragraph 15E defines a 'disqualifying relevant transaction' as either a 'relevant transaction' that occurs at the relevant time or a 'relevant transaction' occurring as part of an avoidance scheme after 8 December 2010 but before the relevant time. A 'relevant transaction' is, broadly, one involving the making, or increase in a loan made, by X to a related person within the charge to UK tax or a prescribed change in the terms and conditions of such a loan (an upstream loan). A 'relevant transaction' may also be one referable to non-exempt activities carried on by X, which are reflected in its profits and achieve a reduction in UK tax. Paragraph 15F specifies how and when an exempt period may end. An exempt period normally ends 24 months after the end of X's first accounting period to end after the relevant time. However, a number of events, referred to as 'early termination events', may cause the exempt period to end prematurely. Such an event is either the occurrence of a 'relevant transaction' as defined in para 15E or (in the case where Condition D immediately above was satisfied in order to cause the exempt period to begin), an event whereby X's business no longer consists wholly in holding shares in its subsidiaries. Para 15G provides for interpretation.

Schedule 12 Part 4 (to wit, para 9) extends the transitional exemption for holding companies contained in FA 2009 Sch 16 Part 2. The commencement date of the abolition of the exemption in respect of qualifying holding companies is deferred by one year to 1 July 2012, and consequential amendments made. Schedule 12 Part 5 (paras 10 to 13) make minor and consequential amendments. Schedule 12 Part 6, comprising para 14, provides for commencement. The extension by para 9 of the transitional holding-company exemption is deemed always to have had effect. The remaining amendments have effect for CFC accounting periods beginning after 31 December 2010 (s 47 and Sch 12).

Section 48 introduces Sch 13, which contains provision for an elective exemption from UK corporation tax on the profits of a UK company's foreign permanent establishments. Schedule 13 Part 1, comprising paras 1 to 11, amends CTA 2009 to add the substantive provisions relating to the exemption. Schedule 13 Part 2 (paras 12 to 30) makes the necessary amendments to other enactments, while Sch 13 Part 3 (paras 31 to 37) contains commencement and transitional provisions. Paragraph 1 is introductory. Paragraphs 2 and 3 make consequential amendments. Paragraph 4 inserts new CTA 2009 Part 2 Chapter 3A, comprising new CTA 2009 ss 18A to 18S. New s 18A contains the exemption for the profits or losses of foreign permanent establishments (from now on, 'PEs'). A UK resident company may make an election for 'exemption adjustments' to be made in computing its total taxable profits for an accounting period. These adjustments have the effect of leaving out of account any profits or losses attributable to that company's foreign PEs, referred to as the 'foreign permanent establishments amount' (from now on, 'the FPEA'). The FPEA is the aggregate of the UK company's profits (its 'relevant profits amount') from each foreign territory in which it has or has had a PE less the aggregate of its losses from each such foreign territory (its 'relevant losses amount'). The relevant profits amount is the profits which, in a territory with which the United Kingdom has a full treaty, would be those defined by reference to the treaty; in any other case, they are the profits or losses as defined by reference to the OECD Model Treaty. A full treaty for these purposes is a double taxation arrangement that contains a relevant non-discrimination provision. In either case, the profits are those taken into account for determining the foreign tax credit available to the UK company in respect of those profits. The relevant losses amount is similarly defined. New s 18B provides for the treatment of capital gains for the purposes of the exemption. Adjustment is to be made to remove the effect of including any capital gain or loss taken into account in computing the FPEA. Gains on the disposal of immovable property used for the purposes of the foreign PE's business are to be included in the profits by reference to which the foreign tax credits are computed, however. Foreign gains and losses arising on the disposal of any asset before the election has effect are not so included. New s 18C provides for the treatment of capital allowances. Any allowances for plant or machinery under CAA 2001 Part 2 which could have been made in respect of assets provided for a foreign PE by a company that has made the exemption election are to be made notionally and reflected in any calculation of the profits or losses attributable to that foreign PE. Disposal and acquisition values for the notional disposal caused by an exemption election are to be set at the tax written-down value at the time the election takes effect. Any profits or losses arising from a lease of plant or machinery are to be left out of account in computing any relevant profits amount or relevant losses amount. In calculating those amounts it is to be assumed that all claims and allowances other than those under CAA 2001 Part 2 have been made. New s 18D provides that where a UK resident person would be obliged under ITA 2007 Part 15 to deduct non-repayable income tax from a payment to a company resident in a foreign territory, any profits or losses referable to any transaction between that person and a foreign PE are to be left out of account in calculating the relevant profits amount or the relevant losses amount under new CTA 2009 s 18A. The exclusion does not apply to a bank unless the transaction is part of an arrangement to avoid application of ITA 2007 Part 15. New s 18E provides that any relief given to a company under CTA 2009 Part 12 Chapter 2 or 3 (shares or options acquired by employees etc) is to be taken into account in calculating the relevant profits amount or the relevant losses amount to the extent that it is linked to the business carried on through the relevant PE. New s 18F provides that an election made under new s 18A is normally irrevocable and applies to all accounting periods beginning on or after the 'relevant day'. That day is the day on which the accounting period following that in which the election is made is expected to begin. Where an accounting period straddles the relevant day, it is to be treated as if it were two distinct periods: the first ending immediately before the relevant day and the second beginning on the relevant day. Any apportionment of profits is to be made on a just and reasonable basis. However, an election under new s 18A may be revoked, if revocation takes place at any time before the relevant day. New ss 18G to 18I contain an anti-avoidance rule. New s 18G provides that, where the 'lower level of tax test' is met in relation to any foreign PE, any 'adjusted relevant profits amount' is taken to be nil, i.e. those relevant profits do not qualify for the exemption. The adjusted relevant profits amount (from now on, 'ARPA') is the relevant profits amount before taking into account any chargeable gains or allowable losses. The lower level of tax test is met where the amount of tax paid under the law of the territory in which the particular PE is located in respect of the ARPA under the relevant treaty is less than 75 per cent of the amount of UK corporation tax that would be payable if the PE were subject in full to that tax, ignoring any foreign tax credit and taking an average rate of corporation tax where that changes during the relevant accounting period. Two exceptions to the rule are provided. It will not apply where either the ARPA is less than £200,000 (reduced proportionally for accounting periods shorter than 12 months) or the 'motive test' is satisfied. The motive test is set out in new s 18H, and consists of two conditions, A and B, which must both be met. Condition A is that any reduction in UK tax achieved by means of a relevant transaction is either minimal or was not the purpose or one of the main purposes of the transaction or transactions. A relevant transaction is one the results of which are reflected in the profits attributable to the PE. Condition B is that the achievement of a reduction in UK tax by diverting profits abroad was not the main reason or one of the main reasons for carrying on business through the PE. A test is provided for establishing whether or not the PE achieves a reduction in UK tax by diverting profits from the United Kingdom. New s 18I provides that where Condition A in new s 18H is not met (i.e. the reduction in UK tax is not minimal or is purposive) but Condition B is met, the ARPA will be adjusted only to the extent that is just and reasonable to correct for the effect of those transactions intended to achieve and which have achieved a reduction in UK tax. New ss 18J to 18O provide for a recapture of previously allowed losses to the extent prescribed. New s 18J provides that these sections will apply where a company that has made the election has a 'total opening negative amount' (from now on, 'TONA') at the beginning of the first accounting period for which the election has effect. The TONA is established by a three-step process. Step 1 is to find the 'adjusted foreign permanent establishments amount' (from now on, 'the adjusted FPEA') in relation to the earliest affected period for which it is negative. The adjusted FPEA is the FPEA (as defined in new s 18A) adjusted by excluding chargeable gains and allowable losses. The affected periods are the accounting period in which the election is made plus all previous accounting periods ending less than six years before the end of that period. Step 2 adds to the Step 1 amount the adjusted FPEA for the next prior period. However, if that adjusted FPEA is positive, only so much of it is added as to reduce the result to zero. Step 3 repeats this process period by period starting with the earliest and ending with the adjusted FPEA for the accounting period in which the election is made. If this amount is negative, there is a TONA. New s 18K provides the mechanism for recapturing the losses that the TONA represents. Beginning with the first accounting period for which the election is effective, the TONA is reduced by the amount (if any) of the company's aggregate relevant profits amount (from now on, 'AGRPA') for that period, but not to below nil. The AGRPA is the aggregate of the relevant profits amount for each foreign territory for which there is a relevant profits amount in that period. To the extent that the AGRPA is used to reduce the TONA, it is not exempt (not available under new s 18A to adjust the company's taxable total profits). In the accounting period in which the AGRPA exceeds the balance of the TONA, the excess is available for the exemption adjustment, and the company may in its company tax return for that period indicate to which part of the AGRPA the exemption is to apply. The mechanism prescribed in new s 18K is the default mechanism, which can be displaced, if the company so elects, by a 'streaming election' under new s 18L. A streaming election, which must be made at the same time as the exemption election under new s 18A, is made under new s 18L, and allows the company to specify one or more foreign territories for which the TONA is to be calculated and reduced separately by the relevant profits amount for that territory. As with the exemption election under new s 18A, a streaming election under new s 18L is irrevocable, except before it takes effect. The company may specify an amount to be streamed that is less than the total amount eligible to be streamed. New s 18M prescribes the matching mechanism that is to apply in respect of each streamed territory. It is identical in respect of each such territory to the default 'global' matching mechanism under new s 18K. New s 18N prescribes the matching mechanism for any residual opening negative amount, which is that part of the TONA that is not subject to a streaming election under new s 18L. New s 18O addresses the case where a company transfers a business it carries on in a foreign PE to a connected company that is or later becomes UK resident, and there is a 'transferred total opening negative amount' ('transferred TONA'). Where an election under new s 18A had not been made by the transferor or had not taken effect before the transfer, the transferred TONA is the amount that would have been the TONA for the transferor at the beginning of its first relevant accounting period on the assumption that the transferred business was its only business, the transfer had not taken place and an election under new s 18A had effect from the day following the transfer. If the transferor had, however, made an election under new s 18A and it was already in effect before the transfer, the transferred TONA is the amount that would have been the TONA for the transferor on the transfer day if the accounting period in which the transfer took place had ended on that day, less what that amount would have been if the transferor had never carried on the business transferred. It cannot be less than nil, however. Where the transferee makes an election under new s 18A to apply on a date after the transfer, in calculating its adjusted FPEA (for which see under new s 18J above) only so much of the transferred TONA is taken into account as is attributable to profits or losses arising after the beginning of its earliest affected prior accounting period (for which see Step 1 under new s 18J above). Where an election has effect, streaming and matching under new ss 18K to 18N have effect as if references to the TONA were references to the transferred TONA and certain other modifications are made. New ss 18P and 18Q deal with special cases. If the company is a 'small company' (defined in new s 18S as a small or microenterprise within the meaning of Commission Recommendation 2003/361/EC of 6 May 2003), then for any accounting period in which it is a small company, new s 18P provides that the exemption election under new s 18A is to apply in respect of territories with which the United Kingdom has a full (double tax) treaty. New s 18Q provides how these provisions are to apply to insurance companies. New ss 18R and 18S provide for interpretation. Paragraph 5 amends CTA 2009 s 775 so as to prevent the transfer of an intangible fixed asset from one group company to another qualifying for tax neutrality where the transferor has made an exemption election under new s 18A and the asset in question has at any time been held by the transferor wholly or partly for the purposes of a foreign PE through which the transferor carries on its business. Paragraph 6 makes a minor amendment to CTA 2009 s 803(b). Paragraph 7 paves the way for para 8, which inserts new CTA 2009 s 848A. This amends the rule in CTA 2009 s 845 that transfers of an intangible asset between related parties are to be at market value. New s 848A applies where CTA 2009 s 775 as amended by para 5 above prevents a tax-neutral transfer of the asset and that asset had not at all times been held by the transferor wholly for the purposes of a foreign PE. In such a case, the transfer is treated as being made at a value of WDV + FPEA, where WDV is the tax written-down value of the asset and FPEA is what the transferor's foreign permanent establishments amount would be if the transfer were at market value. The effect is that the transferor has a gain or loss equal to that FPEA. Paragraphs 9 to 11 make consequential amendments.

Schedule 13 Part 2, consisting of paras 12 to 30 makes amendments to other enactments. The following are worthy of note. Paragraph 13 inserts TCGA 1992 s 276A, which provides that where a no gain/no loss disposal is made by a company that has made an exemption election under new s 18A, the amount of the disposal value is to be determined taking account of these provisions, so that it includes the amount that would have been the company's FPEA if the disposal were not at no gain/no loss. CAA 2001 s 15(2A), inserted by para 15, provides that a business carried on through one or more foreign PEs by a company that has made an exemption election is to be treated as an activity separate from any other activity of the company and as one none of the profits or gains of which are chargeable to tax.CAA 2001 s 62A, inserted by para 17, provides that on the occasion of a deemed disposal of plant and machinery when a company makes an exemption election, the disposal value is to be the 'transition value'. The transition value is the amount that gives rise to neither a balancing allowance nor a balancing charge (i.e. it is equal to the tax written-down value). By way of exception, if the qualifying expenditure in respect of the plant or machinery or of the group of assets of which it is a part, exceeds £5 million, and the company has used the plant or machinery otherwise than for the purposes of a foreign PE at any time during the loss-recapture period (the accounting period in which the election is made and any previous accounting periods ending less than six years before the end of that period), the disposal value is to be determined under the normal rules, i.e. it will be the market value. New CAA 2001 s 62A is subject to the transitional provision contained in para 36. Paragraph 26 inserts TIOPA 2010 s 18(3A), which provides that the foreign tax in respect of which a foreign tax credit may be claimed is not to include tax paid in respect of a relevant profits amount or relevant loss amount by a company that has made an exemption election under new s 18A. TIOPA 2010 s 43 currently provides that in determining how much of a UK company's chargeable profits is attributable to a foreign PE of the company in order to compute the maximum foreign tax credit available, all of the 'permanent-establishment provisions' of CTA 2009 Part 2 Chapter 4 apply. Paragraph 27 substitutes a new TIOPA 2010 s 43. This substantially repeats the 'separate enterprise principle' provisions of CTA 2009 s 21, but as regards the allocation of equity and loan capital to the PE, it now provides that this is to be done on a just and reasonable basis between the foreign PEs and the entity that the company would consist of if each foreign PE were a distinct and separate entity. If the PE is located in a territory with which the United Kingdom has a full treaty, this rule is subject to the provisions of that treaty. These allocations prevail over any allocation that the company itself may have made. Separate provision is made for insurance companies. New TIOPA 2010 s 317A, inserted by para 30, provides that in calculating the worldwide debt cap for the purposes of TIOPA 2010 Part 7, any financing expense amount or financing income amount of a company that has made an exemption election under new s 18A is to be left of account to the extent that it is taken into account in calculating the exempt profit or loss. Schedule 13 Part 3 provides for commencement and makes transitional provisions. The amendments made by Sch 13 are to apply from 19 July 2011 (para 31). Paragraphs 32 and 33 provide for an assumption that Condition B of the motive test under new s 18H is met during the initial phases of an exemption election if certain conditions are satisfied. Paragraph 32 applies in an accounting period that is the first accounting period in which the election has effect and in any other accounting period beginning within 12 months of the beginning of the first accounting period, provided only that the company carried on its business through the foreign PE in question for at least the 12 months preceding 19 July 2011. The three other conditions that must be satisfied so that Condition B is deemed to have been met are (a) that the foreign PE's gross income for the period in question does not exceed its gross income for the 12 month period ending immediately before the beginning of the first accounting period to which the election applies; (b) that there has been no major change in the nature or conduct of the business carried on through the PE in the period beginning with the 12 months before 19 July 2011 and ending with the end of the last period affected by this transitional provision and (c) no asset attributable to the PE and no part of the business carried on through that PE was previously owned or previously carried on by a CFC whose chargeable profits and creditable tax would have been apportioned to a UK resident person. Paragraph 33 makes parallel provision for cases where the business was carried on by a non-resident company controlled by the company in question, except that in this case there are four other conditions that must be satisfied. The first two are the same as under (a) and (b) above in respect of para 32 above. The third condition is that the controlled company carrying on the business not be a CFC whose chargeable profits would be apportionable, and the fourth condition is that no asset attributable to the PE and no part of the business carried on through that PE was previously owned or previously carried on by such a company. Where there was an exceptionally large relevant loss amount in the six years preceding 19 July 2011, the periods over which the loss may be recaptured are extended. Under new s 18J, it will be recalled, the periods affected were the accounting period in which the election is made and all other accounting periods ending less than six years before the end of that period. Under para 34, where there is a relevant loss amount exceeding £50 million in relation to any foreign territory for any accounting period beginning within the period of six years and ending on 18 July 2011, the loss-recapture period begins with that accounting period and every later accounting period that would not otherwise fall into the loss-recapture period. Where the business of a foreign PE is transferred and new s 18O applies (so that there is a transferred TONA), and following a post-transfer election under new s 18A, the effect of new s 18O(4) would be to ignore a relevant loss exceeding £50 million in the three-step calculation of TONA under new s 18J(2), para 35 effectively overrides that effect by adding back the relevant loss to the adjusted FPEA of the transferee for the accounting period in which the transfer takes place. Paragraph 36 amends the operation of new CAA 2001 s 62A, inserted by para 17. Where the qualifying expenditure in respect of the plant and machinery or of the group of assets of which it is part does not exceed £50 million, the earliest accounting period to which the exception to the rule in that section may look back is a period ending no more than 12 months before 19 July 2011. Where the qualifying expenditure does exceed £50 million, the exception may look back to any accounting period beginning no earlier than six years before 18 July 2011 (s 48 and Sch 13).

Investment trust. Section 49 substitutes new versions of CTA 2010 ss 1158 and 1159, which define an investment trust and prescribe how it shall be approved. Hitherto, an investment trust has been defined simply as a company that is not a close company and is approved as an investment trust by HMRC. CTA 2010 s 1159 sets out six conditions for approval. New CTA 2010 s 1158 takes a different approach. It provides that a company is an investment trust in any accounting period when it is approved as such by HMRC and meets three conditions (A, B and C) throughout that period. Condition A is that the business of the company consists of investing in shares, land or other assets with the aim of spreading risk and giving its members the benefit of the results of managing its funds. Condition B is that the shares making up its ordinary share capital must be listed for trading on a regulated market. Condition C is that the company is not a venture capital trust or a company UK REIT. The Treasury may make regulations varying some details of these conditions. New CTA 2010 s 1159 sweeps away the previous conditions for approval and replaces them by a power vested in HM Treasury to make regulations concerning approval, in particular as to applications for approval, the determination of those applications, requirements to be met by the trust while it is approved, the withdrawal of approval and the consequences of such a withdrawal. CTA 2010 ss 1160–1165, which supplement the former CTA 2010 s 1159, are repealed. These amendments have effect in relation to accounting periods beginning on or after a day yet to be appointed (s 49). Section 50 inserts new CTA 2010 s 622A, which gives HM Treasury the power to make regulations prescribing that certain specified transactions carried out by an investment trust are not to be trading transactions (s 50).

Miscellaneous. ITEPA 2003 s 139 specifies the appropriate percentage to be used in the calculation of the benefit-in-kind for employer-provided cars. As from 6 April 2012, it provides (as amended by FA 2010 s 59) that the appropriate percentage will be zero for zero-emission cars; 5 per cent for cars with emissions of between 1 and 75g CO_2 per kilometre; 10 per cent for cars with emissions from 76g to 100g CO_2 per kilometre; and a 1 per cent increase thereafter for every 5g step, subject to a maximum of 35 per cent. The amendment made by s 51 is to reduce the ceiling for the 10 per cent band from 100g to 95g, with effect from 6 April 2013 (s 51).

Section 52 introduces Sch 14, which makes new provisions for the treatment of furnished holiday lettings. These provisions are the result of a compromise between the previous government's intention, which was to extend the scope of the legislation temporarily to properties in the rest of the European Economic Area (as it was obliged to do under European law) but then abolish the special treatment entirely, and letting the extended rules continue with no other modification. This government has instead chosen to let the rules continue but to restrict the reliefs they confer. Schedule 14 Part 1 (paras 1 to 6) contains the new rules for income tax; Part 2 (paras 7 to 11) contains the rules for corporation tax; Part 3 (paras 12 and 13) contains the rules for capital allowances; and Part 4 (paras 14 to 17) the rules for chargeable gains.

Paragraph 1 amends FA 2004 s 189, which defines 'relevant UK individual' for the purposes of tax relief on contributions to registered pension schemes, to the effect that 'relevant UK earnings' are now to include income chargeable under ITTOIA 2005 Part 3 and immediately derived from the carrying-on of an 'EEA furnished holiday lettings business'. The income tax rules on the commercial letting of furnished holiday accommodation are found in ITTOIA 2005 Part 3 Chapter 6 (ss 322 to 328). ITTOIA 2005 s 322(2) currently lists the provisions in which special treatment of furnished UK lettings occurs. The amendments made by para 2 have the effect of including a similar list of the provisions in which special treatment of holiday lettings in other EEA states is to occur. Paragraph 2 also increases the minimum period for which the accommodation must be available for letting to the general public (the availability condition) from 140 days to 210 days, and the minimum period for which the accommodation must actually be so let (the letting condition) from 70 days to 105 days. New ITTOIA 2005 s 326A, inserted by para 2(5), provides alternative relief for under-used holiday accommodation (accommodation failing solely the letting test). Where a person lets qualifying holiday accommodation in any tax year, and continues to let the holiday accommodation over the next tax year or the next two tax years, and the accommodation fails the letting condition (but only the letting condition) in the next tax year or the next two tax years, the person may elect to have the accommodation treated as qualifying holiday accommodation for that year or years. The election may not be made if the averaging election under ITTOIA 2005 s 326 has been made in respect of the same tax year and must be made no later than the first anniversary of the 31 January following the end of the tax year in respect of which the election is made. If it is not made for the first of the two tax years, it cannot be made in respect of the second. New ITTOIA 2005 s 328A, inserted by para 2(8), deals with capital allowances and loss relief for an overseas property business. It provides that where an overseas property business consists partly of the commercial letting of furnished holiday accommodation in one or more EEA states and partly of other transactions, separate calculations are to be made of the profits from the letting business and of the profits from the remainder of the business if effect is to be given under CAA 2001 ss 250 or 250A to capital allowances and charges or to loss relief under ITA 2007 Part 4 with respect to either part. Similarly, where profits of the EEA furnished business form part of UK relevant earnings under FA 2004 s 189 (ITTOIA 2005 s 328B). Paragraph 3 amends ITA 2007. New ITA 2007 s 127ZA makes provision for an EEA furnished holiday lettings business to be treated as a trade. However, losses of that trade will no longer be eligible for either relief against general income (under ITA 2007 ss 64–82) or terminal loss relief (under ITA 2007 ss 89–95). This is so for the deemed UK trade also. Subject to exceptions, the amendments made by Sch 14 Part 1 have effect from the tax year 2011 12.

Schedule 14 Part 2 makes similar provision for corporation tax. Accordingly, CTA 2009 s 264 is amended to include a list of the provisions in which special treatment of holiday lettings in other EEA states is to occur. CTA 2009 ss 267 and 268 increase the minimum period for which the accommodation must be available for letting to the general public (the availability condition) from 140 days to 210 days, and the minimum period for which the accommodation must actually be so let (the letting condition) from 70 days to 105 days. New CTA 2009 s 268A, inserted by para 7(5), provides alternative relief for under-used holiday accommodation (accommodation failing solely the letting test). Where a company lets qualifying holiday accommodation in any accounting period, and continues to let the holiday accommodation over the next accounting period or the next two accounting periods, and the accommodation fails the letting condition (but only the letting condition) in the next accounting period or the next two accounting periods, the company may elect to have the accommodation treated as qualifying holiday accommodation for that period or periods. The election may not be made if the averaging election under CTA 2009 s 268 has been made in respect of the same tax year and must be made no later than two years after the end of the accounting period in respect of which the election is made. If it is not made for the first of the two accounting periods, it cannot be made in respect of the second. New CTA 2009 s 269A, inserted by para 7(7), deals with capital allowances and loss relief for an overseas property business. It provides that where an overseas property business consists partly of the commercial letting of furnished holiday accommodation in one or more EEA states and partly of other transactions, separate calculations are to be made of the profits from the letting business and of the profits from the remainder of the business if effect is to be given under CAA 2001 ss 250 or 250A to capital allowances and charges or to loss relief under CTA 2009 Part 4 Chapters 2, 4 or 6 with respect to either part. Paragraph 8 amends CTA 2010. In particular, it inserts new CTA 2010 s 67A, which provides that an EEA furnished holiday lettings business carried on by a company is to be treated as a single trade, but that relief for losses of that trade is not available against total profits (under CTA 2010 ss 37 44). This is so for a UK furnished holiday lettings business also. Subject to transitional provisions, the amendments made by Sch 14 Part 2 have effect in relation to accounting periods beginning after 31 March 2011.

Schedule 14 Part 3 amends CAA 2001. New CAA 2001 s 13B, inserted by para 12(2), provides that where a person has been using plant or machinery for the purposes of (a) an ordinary UK property business; (b) a UK furnished holiday lettings business; (c) an ordinary overseas property business or (d) an EEA furnished holiday lettings business and ceases to use it for one of those relevant qualifying activities without also ceasing to use it for another such activity, for the purposes of which he incurred capital expenditure on it, the person is to be treated as having incurred qualifying expenditure on the day after the cessation of an amount equal to the market value of the plant or machinery at the date of cessation but the plant or machinery is to be treated as if it were different plant or machinery. However, if the actual expenditure was lower than the market value, the deemed expenditure is the actual expenditure. In other words, the original expenditure is replaced for capital-allowance purposes by the market value, if lower. New CTA 2001 s 17A (inserted by para 12(6)) defines 'ordinary overseas property business' as an overseas property business to the extent that it is not an EEA furnished holiday lettings business. New CTA 2001 s 17B (also inserted by para 12(6)) defines 'EEA furnished holiday lettings business'. New CAA 2001 s 250A (inserted by para 12(14)) provides that allowances and charges in respect of an EEA furnished holiday lettings business are to be given effect by treating the allowances as expenses of the business and the charges as receipts of that business. Various consequential amendments are made. The amendments made by Sch 14 Part 3 have effect for chargeable periods beginning after 31 March 2011 for the purposes of corporation tax and for chargeable periods beginning after 5 April 2011 for the purposes of income tax.

Schedule 14 Part 4 amends TCGA 1992. New TCGA 1992 s 241A (inserted by para 14(3)) provides for the treatment of chargeable gains arising from the commercial letting of furnished holiday accommodation in EEA states other than the United Kingdom. Such letting is to be treated as a trade for the purposes of (a) TCGA 1992 ss 152–157 (rollover relief on the replacement of business assets); (b) TCGA 1992 s 165 (gifts relief); (c) TCGA 1992 s 169S (entrepreneurs' relief); (d) TCGA 1992 s 253 (relief for loans to traders) and (e) TCGA 1992 Sch 7AC (the substantial shareholdings exemption). The amendments made by Sch 14 Part 4 generally apply in relation to disposals made in accounting periods beginning after 31 March 2011 for the purposes of corporation tax and to disposals made after 5 April 2011 for the purposes of capital gains tax. However, for the purpose of determining whether a trade was carried on in any period beginning after 31 December 1993, in relation to disposals and claims for which Sch 14 Part 4 has effect, new TCGA 1992 s 241A(5) (the provisions for the purposes of which an EEA furnished holiday lettings business is treated as a trade) is deemed to have had effect after 31 December 1993 (s 52 and Sch 14).

Section 53 makes provision for likely forthcoming changes in the treatment of leasing under accounting standards. Except insofar as there is a change to UK GAAP equivalent to that provided in the IFRS for small and medium sized enterprises issued by the IASB, any change in the way in which accounting for leases needs to be carried out occurring after 31 December 2010 is to be ignored for any purpose under the Taxes Acts relating to the taxation of leases (s 53). CTA 2010 s 398A allows companies that would otherwise be subject to the deemed receipt and expense on a qualifying change of ownership of a company carrying on a leasing business to elect not to incur the deemed receipt and expense in return for accepting further restrictions on the use of losses etc. No such elections may be made after 22 March 2011 (s 54). CTA 2010 s 27 contains the familiar tests of association between companies for the purpose of determining the limits for the small profits and marginal rates of corporation tax. A new CTA 2010 s 27 is substituted with effect for accounting periods ending after 31 March 2011. It provides that when it is necessary to determine whether one company is associated with another for that purpose, any person to whom the rights and duties of his associates fall to be attributed under CTA 2010 s 451(4) and (5) in its application to this section is deemed to have no associates, unless there is substantial commercial interdependence between the two companies. The Treasury may prescribe factors to be taken into account in determining whether a relationship between two companies is one of substantial commercial interdependence (s 55).TA 1988 s 432C specifies how an insurance company's gains are to be attributed between its life-assurance business and its gross roll-up business. The definition of 'D' (in the relevant fraction referred to in TA 1988 s 432C(9)) is amended in order to correct an unintentional error when the section was rewritten by FA 2007 s 38 and Sch 7 para 17, with effect for accounting periods beginning after 31 December 2010 (s 56).

Amendments are made to the treatment under tonnage tax of capital allowances on ships leased to companies. FA 2000 Sch 22 para 94 currently provides that where the lessor of the ship to a company under the tonnage tax regime is entitled to capital allowances in respect of the ship, those allowances are restricted to a writing-down allowance of 20 per cent on the first £40 million and of 10 per cent on the next £40 million of expenditure, both under the reducing-balance method, and to no further allowances on any balance of expenditure over £80 million. As amended, it will now provide that the rate of allowance on the first £40 million will be the main rate as specified in CAA 2001 s 56(1) (currently 20 per cent) if the ship is not a long-life asset and will be the special rate (currently 10 per cent) if the ship is a long-life asset, and the expenditure is to be allocated to separate pools accordingly. Allowances on the next £40 million will be at the special rate, regardless of whether the ship is or is not a long-life asset. Consequential amendments are made. All amendments have effect for chargeable periods ending after 31 December 2010 but have no effect on expenditure incurred before 1 January 2011 (s 57). TIOPA 2010 s 164 provides that TIOPA 2010 Part 4 (the transfer-pricing provisions) is to be read in a way that best secures consistency with the transfer-pricing guidelines of the OECD, in cases where the relevant double tax treaty incorporates the whole or part of the OECD Model Tax Convention. The transfer-pricing guidelines are defined as all the documents published by the OECD prior to 1 May 1998 as part of its Transfer Pricing Guidelines for

Multinational Enterprises and Tax Administrations and such documents as the OECD has published subsequently as are designated by the Treasury. This definition is now amended to refer to the version of the Transfer Pricing Guidelines for Multinational Enterprises and Tax Administrations approved by the OECD on 22 July 2010 and other documents published subsequently as are designated by the Treasury, including updates and supplements. This amendment has effect in relation to accounting periods beginning after 31 March 2011 for the purposes of corporation tax and from the tax year 2011 12 for the purposes of income tax (s 58).An offshore fund that is an undertaking for collective investment in transferable securities (UCITS) for the purposes of the UCITS Directive (Directive 2009/65/EC of the European Parliament and of the Council) and is authorised under Article 5 of that Directive in a Member State other than the United Kingdom that would otherwise be treated as resident in the United Kingdom for the purposes of income tax, corporation tax or capital gains tax is not to be so treated where it is a body corporate and, under the law of the Member State where it is authorised, is treated as resident for the purposes of any tax on income. Where TCGA 1992 applies to the fund as if it were a company by virtue of TCGA 1992 ss 99 (application to unit-trust schemes) or 103A (application to certain offshore funds) the fund is to be treated as if it were a non-resident company (new TCGA 1992 s 363A, inserted by s 59).CTA 2009 s 399(4) defines an index-linked gilt-edged security as a gilt-edged security the payments on which are wholly or partly determined by reference to the Retail Prices Index. This definition is amended to refer instead to an index of prices published by the Statistics Board. The amendment has effect in relation to securities issued after 18 July 2011 (s 60).

PART 3
OIL

OTA 1975 Sch 1 para 7(4) currently provides that in determining whether qualifying assets in an area of an oil field have been decommissioned, HMRC must, in the absence of a UK offshore decommissioning regime, have regard to the law applicable to the relevant area. The reference to the 'relevant area' is considered inappropriate and is replaced by reference to [the law of] "those qualifying assets". The amendment has effect for chargeable periods beginning after 30 June 2009 (s 61).CTA 2009 s 809 provides that an oil licence is not considered to be an intangible fixed asset for the purposes of CTA 2009 Part 8 (the '2002 regime' for intangible fixed assets). The section is amended to provide that references to an oil licence or an interest in an oil licence are to include all goodwill and any intangible asset relating to, deriving from or connected with an oil licence or an interest in an oil licence. The amendments are made to prevent the amortisation under the 2002 regime of goodwill recognised on the acquisition of an oil licence, and have effect for accounting periods beginning after 22 March 2011. Straddling periods are to be split at 23 March 2011 (s 62).A field allowance under CTA 2010 Part 8 Chapter 7 reduces an oil company's ring-fence profits subject to the supplementary charge under CTA 2010 s 330. CTA 2010 s 337(1) provides that the initial licensee in a new field is to hold a field allowance for that field from the beginning of the authorisation day (the day on which development of the field is authorised). This provision is amended so that the allowance is now considered to be held from the beginning of the accounting period in which the authorisation day falls. CTA 2010 s 350 currently defines a new oil field as a qualifying oil field the development of which is authorised at any time after 21 April 2009. A new CTA 2010 s 350 is substituted by s 63(2). It now provides that a new oil field is a qualifying oil field authorised in whole or in part after 21 April 2009 and adds provisions concerning decommissioning. Where all the relevant assets of an oil field have been decommissioned, any authorisations in respect of that oil field that were given before the decommissioning are left out of account. The provisions of OTA 1975 Sch 1 para 7(2)–(9) are to apply to determine whether a relevant asset has been decommissioned as they apply to the decommissioning of a relevant area. These amendments have effect for accounting periods ending after 31 March 2011 and corresponding amendments having effect for accounting periods ending after 21 April 2009 are deemed to have been made in FA 2009 Sch 44 (s 63). Section 64 introduces Sch 15, which concerns capital gains relating to oil activities. Schedule 15 Part 1, comprising paras 1 to 4 relates to licence swaps. Paragraph 1 makes a consequential amendment. Paragraph 2 inserts new TCGA 1992 s 195F, which makes provision for reimbursed expenditure. Where (a) expenditure is incurred before the disposal by a disposing or acquiring company on a licence of which it has disposed under a licence-consideration swap or a mixed-consideration swap; (b) the expenditure is allowable enhancement expenditure under TCGA 1992 s 38(1)(b); and (c) that expenditure is reimbursed or effectively reimbursed by the company to which the disposal is made, that expenditure is to be treated as allowable enhancement expenditure incurred on the licence by that other company immediately after the disposal. TCGA 1992 s 196 is amended to provide additionally that any determination of the consideration given for exchanges of licences at arm's length prices, of the non-licence consideration element in a mixed-consideration swap, or of the value of a licence comprised in a licence swap, are to be made at the time the swap arrangements are entered into. However, where the economic benefits and liabilities under the licences concerned in the swap arrangements are treated as passing at an effective time before or after the arrangements are entered into, the rule is that those determinations are to be made at that effective time. Furthermore, if the swap arrangements provide for an increase in the non-licence consideration to reflect the passage of time between the effective time and the time when the consideration is payable, a corresponding increase in the amount determined as at the effective time is made. The amendments in Sch 15 Part 1 have effect in relation to disposals made after 22 March 2011.Schedule 15 Part 2, comprising paras 5 and 6 relate to the reinvestment of ring-fence assets. TCGA 1992 ss 198A 198H make provision for the capital gains treatment of the replacement of oil assets. New TCGA 1992 s 198I, inserted by para 5, provides that for the purposes of these reinvestment provisions, expenditure incurred on exploration, appraisal and development in the course of a ring-fence trade is to be treated as the acquisition of replacement assets that are oil assets taken into use and used solely for the ring-fence trade and qualifying for rollover treatment. These amendments have effect for disposals made after 23 March 2010 (s 64 and Sch 15).

PART 4
PENSIONS

The provisions in this Part (ss 65–72) enact the pension reforms consisting of the removal of the requirement to purchase an annuity by the age of 75, and anticipate the reduction of the annual allowance to £50,000 and of the lifetime allowance to £1.5 million, both with effect from 2012 13. They also make changes in connection with the establishment of NEST (the National Employment Savings Trust).

Section 65 introduces Sch 16, which makes the changes consequent on the removal of the annuity requirement. It comprises no less than 109 paragraphs. Schedule 16 Part 1 (paras 1 to 48) makes the substantive changes to the pensions regime in FA 2004 Part 4 and to certain provisions of ITEPA 2003. Part 2 (paras 49 to 84) makes consequential amendments to FA 2004 and other enactments. Part 3 (paras 85 to 109) provides for commencement and transitional provisions).

The essential features of the reform are that the requirement to buy an annuity by the age of 75 is removed and the rules relating to alternatively secured pensions are repealed. Members will be able to leave the fund invested and once they reach minimum pension age make an annual withdrawal by way of a drawdown pension, subject to an annual cap, equal to 100 per cent of a 'basis amount', which is, broadly, the equivalent annuity that could have been bought with the fund value. Before the member reaches the age of 75, this amount will be evaluated at regular intervals of no more than three years, and annually once the member is 75 or over. Members who satisfy the 'minimum income requirement' and certain other 'flexible-drawdown conditions' will not be subject to the cap. Broadly, the minimum income requirement is satisfied if the member can demonstrate to the scheme administrator that he or she has a secure pension income for life of at least £20,000 per annum. The main income tax consequences of the new regime are simple to summarise. All drawdown amounts are to be taxable as pension income. Liability to income tax on withdrawals from UK schemes by a person who was previously UK resident while he or she is temporarily non resident may be taxed in the United Kingdom if the member again becomes UK resident after a period of less than five full tax years. Similar rules apply to payments from certain non UK schemes. Additional pension savings by members who benefit from flexible (uncapped) drawdown will be subject to the annual allowance charge on 'pension input amounts'. Lump-sum death benefits to a member who dies before the age of 75 without having drawn a pension will be free of tax. Once the member reaches 75 or begins to draw a pension, the lump-sum death benefit is to be taxable at 55 per cent.

The amendments made by para 1 replace the concepts of unsecured and alternatively secured pensions by the drawdown pension. New Pension Rule 5, states that the total drawdown pension that may be paid in respect of a money purchase arrangement in each drawdown pension year may not exceed 100 per cent of the 'basis amount' for that year. However, that limit is not to apply to an arrangement if the member meets the flexible-drawdown conditions and makes a valid declaration that is acceptable to the scheme administrator. New FA 2004 s 165(3B) defines the flexible-drawdown conditions, which include, inter alia, that the member satisfy the 'minimum income requirement'. Paragraphs 2 to 5 define 'drawdown pension'. Paragraph 6 replaces the concept of the 'member's unsecured pension fund' by that of the 'member's drawdown pension fund'. Paragraphs 7 to 9 define 'drawdown pension year' and the basis amount for a drawdown pension year. Paragraph 10 sets out the minimum income requirement and other provisions relating to flexible drawdown. A member satisfies the minimum income requirement if, broadly, the amount of all pension payments, including social security pensions, is not less than the minimum income threshold, which is £20,000. Paragraphs 11 to 15 define the dependants' drawdown pension on the death of the member. Paragraph 16 defines the 'dependant's drawdown pension fund' on the basis of the existing 'dependant's unsecured pension fund'. Paragraphs 17 to 19 define the dependant's drawdown pension year and the basis amount for a dependant's drawdown pension year. Paragraph 20 sets out the minimum income requirement and other provisions relating to flexible drawdown for dependants. A dependant satisfies the minimum income requirement if, broadly, the amount of all pension payments, including social security pensions, payable to the dependant is not less than the minimum income threshold, which is £20,000. Paragraph 21 amends the rules in ITEPA 2003 Part 9 relating to the taxation of foreign pensions. Under new ITEPA 2003 s 576A, a person returning to the United Kingdom after a period of temporary non-residence may become liable to UK income tax on certain withdrawals from certain non UK schemes made while he or she was non resident. An income withdrawal from a relevant non UK scheme paid to a person under a flexible drawdown arrangement during a year of non residence not otherwise chargeable to UK income tax will be so chargeable in the first tax year in which the person again becomes resident, provided that the person was UK resident in at least four of the seven tax years immediately before the tax year of departure and there are fewer than five tax years between the tax year when the person was last UK resident and the tax year in which he or she again becomes UK resident, subject to certain exceptions. Nothing in a double tax treaty is to prevent such a charge. Under new ITEPA 2003 s 579CA, inserted by para 22, a similar rule is enacted in respect of withdrawals from UK schemes. Any income withdrawal or dependant's income withdrawal under a registered pension scheme paid to a person in respect of a flexible drawdown arrangement relating to that person under the scheme during a year of non residence and not otherwise chargeable to UK income tax will be so chargeable in the first tax year in which the person again becomes UK resident, provided that the person was UK resident in at least four of the seven tax years immediately before the tax year of departure and there are fewer than five tax years between the tax year when the person was last UK resident and the tax year in which he or she again becomes UK resident. Nothing in a double tax treaty is to prevent such a charge. A substituted new ITEPA 2003 s 579D provides for interpretation. Paragraphs 23 to 31 amend FA 2004 Sch 29 Part 1 (the lump-sum rule) with respect to lump sums payable to persons aged 75 or over. Paragraphs 32 to 39 amend FA 2004 Sch 29 Part 2 (the lump-sum death-benefit rule) with respect to lump-sum death benefits payable to persons aged 75 or over. Paragraph 40 inserts FA 2004 s 205A, which provides for a charge to income tax on serious ill-health lump sums. A charge to income tax, to be known as the serious ill-health lump-sum charge, is to arise where a serious ill-health lump sum is paid by a registered pension scheme to a member who has reached the age of 75. The rate of the charge is 55 per cent, and the person liable is the scheme administrator. It is of no consequence whether or not the scheme administrator and the person to whom the sum is paid are resident, ordinarily resident or domiciled in the United Kingdom. A serious ill-health lump-sum charge paid to a member who has reached the age of 75 is not to be treated as income for any purpose of the Tax Acts. Paragraph 41 amends FA 2004 s 206, which imposes the special lump-sum death-benefits charge. The reference to an unsecured pension fund lump-sum death benefit, on the payment of which the charge arises, is replaced by a reference to a drawdown pension fund lump-sum death benefit. The charge is also to arise when a defined-benefits lump-sum death benefit or an uncrystallised funds lump-sum death benefit is paid. The person liable is the scheme administrator and it is of no consequence whether or not the scheme administrator and the person to whom the sum is paid are resident, ordinarily resident or domiciled in the United Kingdom. The rate of the charge is increased from 35 per cent to 55 per cent. Neither a pension-protection lump-sum death benefit nor an annuity-protection lump-sum death benefit is to be treated as income for any purpose of the Tax Acts, nor are a defined benefits lump-sum death benefit or an uncrystallised funds lump-sum death benefit to be so treated, if paid in respect of a member who had reached the age of 75 at the time of death. Paragraph 42 amends ITEPA 2003 s 636A, which confers exemption from income tax on certain lump sums and lump-sum death benefits. The exemption for serious ill-health lump sums is limited to those paid to members who have not reached the age of 75. Similarly, a defined benefits lump-sum death benefit and an uncrystallised funds lump-sum death benefit are now to be exempt only where paid in respect of a member who had not reached the age of 75 at the time of death. A serious ill-health lump sum paid under a registered pension scheme to a member who has reached the age of 75 is to be subject to income tax on the scheme administrator under new FA 2004 s 205A (inserted by para 40, for which see above) but not otherwise. Defined benefits lump-sum death benefits and uncrystallised funds lump-sum death benefits paid in respect of a member who had reached the age of 75 at the time of death are to be subject to income tax on the scheme administrator under FA 2004 s 206 but not otherwise. Paragraph 43 amends FA 2004 s 216 so as to provide that the amount crystallised on a benefit crystallisation event that is triggered when the individual relating to whom there is a money-purchase arrangement reaches the age of 75 is the amount of any remaining unused funds. This amount is defined in new FA 2004 Sch 32 para 14A, inserted by para 44. Paragraph 45 inserts new FA 2004 s 227A, which applies the annual allowance charge in certain circumstances on individuals who meet flexible drawdown conditions. For each tax year after the first tax year in which there is a flexible drawdown arrangement in relation to an individual, the annual allowance charge under FA 2004 s 227 is to apply on the amount by which the individual's total pension input amount for the tax year (TPIA) exceeds so much of the aggregate pension input amounts in respect of each defined-benefits or cash-balance arrangement relating to the individual under any registered pension scheme of which the individual is not an active member as does not exceed the annual allowance. Paragraphs 46 to 48 remove certain charges to inheritance tax in respect of pension schemes. Paragraph 46 is introductory. Paragraph 47 amends IHTA 1984 s 12 to provide that the non-exercise of pension rights under a registered pension scheme, a qualifying non-UK pension scheme or a section 615(3) scheme by a person who is a member of the scheme is not to be a transfer of value by virtue of IHTA 1984 s 3(3). Further provisions relating to pension schemes, namely IHTA 1984 s 12(2A)–(2E) are omitted. IHTA 1984 s 12 is further amended by para 50. Paragraph 48 repeals the following provisions of IHTA 1984: (a) s 151A (person dying with alternatively secured pension fund); (b) s 151B (relevant dependant with pension fund inherited from member over 75); (c) s 151BA (rate or rates of charge under IHTA 1984 s 151B); (d) s 151C (dependant dying with other pension fund); (e) s 151D (unauthorised payment where person dies over 75 with pension or annuity; and (f) s 151E (rate or rates of charge under IHTA 1984 s 151D).

Schedule 16 Part 2 makes consequential amendments to FA 2004 and other enactments. Paragraphs 49 to 57 amend IHTA 1984. Paragraph 58 amends the Pension Schemes Act 1993 and para 59 amends the Pension Schemes (Northern Ireland) Act 1993. Paragraphs 60 and 61 make minor amendments to ITEPA 2003. Paragraphs 62 to 82 amend FA 2004. Paragraph 83 amends ITA 2007 and para 84 makes consequential repeals.

Schedule 16 Part 3 provides for commencement and transition. Paragraph 85 provides that subject to transitional provisions, amendments made by Sch 16 are to have effect from the tax year 2011 12. Paragraphs 86 to 109 make transitional provisions.

Section 66 introduces Sch 17, which amends provisions relating to the annual allowance charge, consequent on the reduction of the annual allowance to £50,000 and the introduction of carry forward facilities for any unused annual allowance. Schedule 17 Part 1 (paras 1 to 26) makes the substantive amendments to FA 2004 and other enactments. Schedule 17 Part 2 (paras 27 to 34) provides for commencement and transition. Paragraph 1 is introductory and para 2 makes a minor consequential amendment. Paragraph 3 amends FA 2004 s 227, which applies the annual allowance charge on the excess of the total pension input amount for the tax year over the amount of the annual allowance. The provision imposing liability on the individual is deleted, as is the provision that this liability is regardless of the residence or domicile status of the individual or the scheme administrator. The rate of the charge is now not to be 40 per cent, but the 'appropriate rate'. This is defined as the basic rate (of income tax) on so much of the excess as when added to the individual's 'reduced net income' for the tax year does not exceed the basic-rate limit for the year, the higher rate on so much of that excess as when so added exceeds the basic-rate limit but not the higher-rate limit, and the additional rate on that part of the excess which exceeds the higher-rate limit. It is thus to be charged at the individual's marginal rate of income tax. The 'reduced net income' is the amount found after taking Steps 1, 2 and 3 in ITA 2007 s 23, i.e. net income less personal allowances. Paragraph 4 substitutes a new FA 2004 s 228, which now provides that the annual allowance for the tax year 2011 12 and subsequent years is to be £50,000, subject to any uprating order for tax years after 2011 12. In 2010 11, the annual allowance was £255,000. Paragraph 5 inserts new FA 2004 s 228A, which provides for excess annual allowance to be carried-forward. Where in any tax year, the annual allowance exceeds an individual's total pension input amount for that year, the excess may be carried forward for addition to the annual allowance of the following tax year, for a maximum of three further tax years, so that, for example, where there is an excess in year 0, that excess may be carried forward up to but not beyond year 3. Each year's excess (the 'unused annual allowance') is calculated before increasing the current year's annual allowance by any excess brought forward. Unused allowance in respect of a year may be carried forward only if the individual was a member of a registered pension scheme at some time in that year. Paragraph 6 amends FA 2004 s 229 so that the total pension input amount in a tax year in which the individual satisfies the 'severe ill-health condition' is to be nil. An individual satisfies the severe ill-health condition where any one of three further conditions is satisfied. Those further conditions are that the individual (a) is a member of the armed forces who becomes entitled under to a tax-free wounds and disability pension under ITEPA 2003 s 641; or (b) becomes entitled to a serious ill-health lump sum or (c) becomes entitled to all the benefits to which he or she is entitled under the scheme once the administrator receives medical evidence that the individual is unlikely to be able to undertake gainful work before reaching pensionable age. Paragraph 7 amends FA 2004 s 230, which provides for the calculation of the pension input amount in respect of a cash-balance arrangement. Paragraph 8 amends FA 2004 s 231, which provides for uprating of the opening value of an individual's rights under a cash-balance arrangement. Paragraph 9 amends FA 2004 s 232, which provides for adjustments to the closing value under a cash-balance arrangement. Paragraph 10 amends FA 2004 s 234, which prescribes how the pension input amount is to be calculated for a defined-benefits arrangement. Among the amendments is an increase from 10 to 16 in the factor by which the opening and closing values of an individual's assumed pension payments are uprated when computing the opening and closing value of the individual's rights under the arrangement. Paragraph 11 amends FA 2004 s 235, which provides for an uprating of the opening value of an individual's rights, to substitute references to the consumer price index for references to the retail price index. Paragraph 12 amends FA 2004 s 236, which provides for adjustments of the closing value of an individual's rights under a defined-benefits arrangement. Adjustments are now to be made under the section not to the closing value as such but to its two components, PE (the annual pension that would be payable to the individual if he or she became entitled to payment at the end of the pension input period) and LSE (the amount of the lump sum to which the individual would become entitled (otherwise than by commutation) at the end of the pension input period. Paragraph 13 inserts new FA 2004 s 236A, concerning post-entitlement enhancements. It applies where during a pension input period, the individual enters into a scheme which involves an increase in the annual rate of a scheme pension at a time after the member has become entitled to the pension, and where the main purpose or one of the main purposes in entering into the scheme was to avoid or reduce a liability to the annual allowance charge. In such an event, the opening value of the individual's rights is deemed to be the expected cost, calculated according to normal actuarial practice, of giving effect to the individual's rights at the end of the immediately preceding pension input period. Similarly, the closing value of the individual's rights is deemed to be the expected cost, calculated according to normal actuarial practice, of giving effect to the individual's rights at the end of the pension input period. Paragraph 14 makes a minor consequential amendment. Paragraph 15 inserts new FA 2004 ss 237A–237F, which prescribe who is to be liable to the annual allowance charge under FA 2004 s 227. New FA 2004 s 237A provides that the liability is the individual's and that this is the case regardless of whether or not the individual or the scheme administrator are resident, ordinarily resident or domiciled in the United Kingdom. This principle is, however, subject to the provisions of new FA 2004 ss 237B to 237F. Under new FA 2004 s 237B, an individual whose liability to the annual allowance charge in any tax year is above £2,000 and whose pension scheme input amount in relation to a registered pension scheme for the tax year exceeds the annual allowance may give notice to the scheme administrator specifying that the individual and the scheme administrator are to be jointly and severally liable in respect of so much of the annual allowance charge as the notice specifies. This amount is, however, subject to a maximum, calculated by reference to the individual's marginal rate of income tax. Such a notice must be given no later than 31 July in the calendar year following that in which the tax year ends. New FA 2004 s 237C provides for exceptions. The scheme administrator does not become liable under new FA 2004 s 237B during an assessment period for the scheme. If he is already so liable when an assessment period begins, his liability ceases at that point. Neither is the scheme administrator liable under new FA 2004 s 237B in respect of any amount if there is no power to make a consequential adjustment of the individual's entitlement to benefits in respect of that amount as a result of new FA 2004 s 237E(2). Under new FA 2004 s 237D, the scheme administrator may apply to HMRC for a discharge of the liability on the grounds that either (a) paying the amount for which the administrator is liable would be to the substantial detriment of the members' interests or (b) it would not be just and reasonable for the administrator to be liable. Under new FA 2004 s 237E, any consequential adjustment a scheme administrator makes after discharging liability under new FA 2004 s 237B to the individual's entitlement to benefits under the scheme must be just and reasonable and cannot come into conflict with the individual's rights to a guaranteed minimum pension etc. New FA 2004 s 237F gives HMRC the power to vary the rules of registered pension schemes in order to facilitate the working of new FA 2004 ss 237A-237E. Paragraph 16 amends FA 2004 s 238, which defines the pension input period. Paragraph 17 inserts new FA 2004 s 238A, which gives the Treasury the power to make provisions concerning the annual allowance charge by order. Paragraph 18 amends FA 2004 s 254, which prescribes how scheme administrators account for tax. Paragraphs 19 and 20 make minor consequential amendments. Paragraphs 21 and 22 insert definitions; para 23 amends FA 2004 s 282 to provide that no order may be made under FA 2004 s 228 to vary the annual allowance to an amount less than that of the immediately preceding tax year and no order may be made under new FA 2004 s 238A concerning the annual allowance charge which increases any person's liability to tax. Paragraph 24 amends FA 2004 Sch 34, concerning the application of certain charges to non-UK schemes. The amendments allow members of registered pension schemes to bring forward any unused annual allowance from years in which they were currently relieved members of a currently relieved non UK pension scheme and currently relieved members of such schemes to bring forward unused annual allowance from years in which they were members but not currently relieved members. Paragraphs 25 and 26 make consequential amendments.

Sch 17 Part 2 (paras 27–34) makes provision for commencement and transitional matters. With the exception of two amendments made by para 16 with respect to the pension input period, the amendments made by Part 1 have effect from the tax year 2011 12. Transitional provisions are made for pension input periods that end in 2011 12 but begin before 14 October 2010.

Section 67 introduces Sch 18, which amends the provisions relating to the lifetime allowance consequent on its reduction to £1.5 million. Schedule 18 Part 1 (paras 1 to 12) makes the substantive amendments; Part 2 (paras 13 and 14) provides for commencement and makes transitional provisions. Paragraph 1 is introductory. Paragraph 2 amends FA 2004 s 218 to provide that from the tax year 2012 13, the lifetime allowance is to be £1,500,000 (down from £1,800,000 in previous years), and that the amount may be varied by Treasury order at any time after 2012 13. Further amendments give some measure of relief to individuals who have accrued pension rights in the belief that the lifetime allowance would remain at the higher figure. Where individuals are entitled to a lifetime-allowance enhancement factor under any of FA 2004 ss 220 (pension credits from previously crystallised rights), 222 (non residence: money purchase arrangements), 223 (non residence: other arrangements) or 224 (transfers from recognised overseas pension schemes) the amount of standard lifetime allowance (SLA)multiplied by the lifetime-allowance enhancement factor (LAEF) in the formula in FA 2004 s 218(4) for calculating the enhanced allowance is to be taken as £1.8 million if in any of the relevant sections, SLA is defined with reference to a time before 6 April 2012. Similarly, where an individual is entitled to primary protection under FA 2004 Sch 36 para 7, SLA in both places where it appears in the formula in FA 2004 s 218(4) is taken to be £1.8 million. Paragraphs 3 to 7 make amendments to FA 2004 Sch 29 paras 7 (trivial commutation lump sum), 10 (winding up lump sum), 20 (trivial commutation lump sum death benefit) and 21 (winding up lump sum death benefit). In each case, where the benefit in question would otherwise be 1 per cent of the standard lifetime allowance, it is instead to be £18,000 or a higher amount to be set by Treasury order. Paragraphs 8 to 11 amend FA 2004 Sch 36 (transitional provisions on the enactment of the new pensions regime under FA 2004). Paragraph 12 makes a consequential amendment. Paragraph 13 provides that the amendments made by Sch 18 Part 1 have effect from the tax year 2012 13. Detailed transitional provisions are made by para 14 for individuals under a registered pension scheme who are not entitled to a lifetime-allowance enhancement factor under either primary protection or enhanced protection (s 67 and Sch 18).

FA 2004 s 182 imposes a charge on unauthorised borrowing by a registered pension scheme. Section 68 removes the unauthorised borrowing charge on a so called 'section 67 pension scheme'. These are schemes established under Pensions Act 2008 s 67. Specifically, the new National Employment Savings Trust (NEST) is such a scheme. This section has effect from 6 April 2011 (s 68). New ITTOIA 2005 s 753A is inserted to exempt from tax any interest that the Pension Regulator requires an employer to pay to an employee's pension account in respect of late-paid pension contributions, with effect from 19 July 2011 (s 69). Section 70 entitles the Treasury to make regulations imposing or providing relief from income tax, corporation tax, capital gains tax and inheritance tax on section 67 pension schemes (s 70). Similarly, s 71 gives the Treasury power to make regulations imposing or providing relief from income tax, corporation tax, capital gains tax and inheritance tax, value added tax, stamp duty land tax, stamp duty and stamp duty reserve tax to an event arising as a consequence of Pensions Act 2008 Part 1 (s 71). Section 72 is designed to override certain cases where a provision in a double tax treaty may prevent a charge to UK tax on a foreign pension or lump sum paid to a UK resident individual and derived from pension savings transferred from a UK scheme to a foreign scheme precisely in order to take advantage of the treaty exemption. It does so by inserting new TIOPA 2010 s 130A. Where a double taxation arrangement provides in any way for a pension or other similar remuneration (as defined in the OECD Model Treaty) arising outside the United Kingdom and paid to a person resident in the United Kingdom to be exempt from UK tax, such a provision is not to have effect where two conditions are satisfied. The first is that the pension etc is paid out of sums or assets that were the subject of a 'relevant transfer' or out of related sums or assets. The second is that the transfer was or was associated with a tax-avoidance scheme. A 'relevant transfer' is a transaction or series of transactions as a result of which sums or assets are transferred out of a (UK) pension scheme and into the (foreign) scheme out of which the pension or other similar remuneration is paid. Significantly, it does not matter for these purposes whether the relevant double tax treaty was actually in existence at the time that the arrangement is entered into. These provisions have effect from the tax year 2011 2012, regardless of when the avoidance arrangement was entered into (s 72).

PART 5
BANK LEVY

Section 73 introduces Sch 19, which contains the provisions on bank levy. Schedule 19 comprises nine Parts. Part 1 (paras 1 to 3) is introductory. Part 2 (paras 4 to 7) imposes the levy. Part 3 (paras 8 to 13) defines the incidence of the tax. Part 4 (paras 14 to 39) defines chargeable equity and liabilities. Part 5 (paras 40 to 48) makes supplementary provisions. Part 6 (paras 49 to 65) provides for collection and management. Part 7 (paras 66 to 69) provides for double taxation relief; Part 8 (paras 70 to 80) contains definitions and Part 9 (para 81) provides for regulations to be made.

There is to be a tax known as 'bank levy' to be charged on certain types of equity and liabilities of certain groups of entities and individual entities (paras 1 and 2). Paragraph 3 sets out how the remainder of the Schedule is organised. The bank levy is to be charged at the end of a chargeable period on the parent entity of (a) a UK banking group; (b) a building society group; (c) a foreign banking group; or (d) of a relevant non banking group, provided that the parent entity in question is not itself the subsidiary of any other entity. The levy applies in respect of periods of account ending after 31 December 2010 (para 4). The levy will also apply to certain UK resident banks, building societies, or relevant foreign banks that are not members of a group (para 5). Paragraph 6 prescribes how the amount of the levy is to be calculated. Where the relevant group's or entity's chargeable equity and liabilities (from now on, 'CEL') total no more than £20 million, the levy is nil for that period. Where they exceed £20 million, they are to be classified as short term or long term. The amount of short term CEL is then to be reduced by that percentage of £20 million that is equal to the percentage of total CEL that is short term, and the amount of long-term CEL by that percentage of total CEL that is long term. Where the chargeable period is not 12 months, these reduced amounts are decreased or increased pro rata temporis by reference to the number of days in the period compared to 365. The rate of the levy charged on the short term CEL (adjusted as necessary for the length of the chargeable period) is to be 0.078 per cent, and the rate on the long term CEL (similarly adjusted where necessary) 0.039 per cent. The total bank levy due is the sum of the two parts. Different rates apply in 2011. From 1 January to 28 February, the rates were 0.025 per cent (long term) and 0.05 per cent (short term). From 1 March to 30 April, the rates were 0.05 per cent and 0.10 per cent respectively, while in the period 1 May to 31 December 2011, they are 0.0375 per cent and 0.075 per cent respectively (para 7). Paragraphs 8 to 11 contain the definitions of 'UK banking group', 'building society group', 'foreign banking group' and 'relevant non banking group'. The term 'banking group' is defined in para 12. A banking group is a group satisfying any one of four conditions and not satisfying the 'exempt-activities condition'. Paragraph 13 provides that the exempt-activities condition is satisfied where at least 90 per cent of the relevant group's trading income derives from exempt activities or where at least 50 per cent of such a group's trading income derives from 'non-financial trading activities'. 'Exempt activities' are insurance activities, asset-management activities and related activities and 'non-financial trading activities'. 'Non financial trading activities' are activities other than lending activities and dealing on own account (except for certain hedging activities) carried on by an entity that is not a financial trading entity. Other definitions of terms necessary to interpret the above are also set out.

Paragraph 14 defines 'assets', 'equity' and 'liabilities' by reference to their meaning in international accounting standards, subject to any provision in this Schedule that requires anything to be done by reference to UK GAAP. Paragraph 15 defines 'chargeable equity and liabilities' for a UK banking group or a building society group. These are the group's non excluded equity and liabilities at the end of the chargeable period, (a) adjusted as necessary for assets and liabilities as against third parties that may be netted off under para 16 and/or under para 44 for the avoidance of a double charge in the case of a joint venture and (b) minus certain of the group's 'high-quality liquid assets' and amounts in respect of certain financial assets in respect of intra-group cash advances, underlying which as collateral is an asset owned by the lender and which would be a high-quality liquid asset were it owned by the group. Excluded equity and liabilities are defined in paras 28 to 39. Paragraph 16 allows for adjustments to be made in determining the group's chargeable equity and liabilities (CEL) where (a) a group member (M) has liabilities to a third party (N) (i.e. not a group member) and that third party has assets corresponding to M's liabilities, and where M or another member of M's group has assets corresponding to liabilities that N or another third party has to M or that other member of M's group; and (b) there is a legally binding netting off agreement between the respective parties covering all of their liabilities to each other. Paragraph 17 defines CEL for a foreign banking group. These are the sums of its 'type A', 'type B', 'type C' and 'type D' equity and liabilities. The group's type A equity and liabilities are the CEL of any relevant UK sub group. The group's type B equity and liabilities are the CEL of any UK resident entity that is a member of the relevant group but not a member of a relevant UK sub group. The group's type C equity and liabilities are the CEL of any non UK resident entity that is a member of the relevant group and is a member of a UK sub group but not a member of a relevant UK sub group. The group's type D equity and liabilities are the UK allocated equity and liabilities (as defined by para 24) as at the end of the chargeable period of any relevant foreign bank that is a member of the relevant group but not a member of a UK sub group. The terms 'UK sub group' and 'relevant UK sub group' are defined. Paragraph 18 contains further provisions to supplement the calculation of the various amounts defined in para 17. Paragraph 19 defines CEL for a relevant non banking group. As for a foreign banking group, these comprise the sum of its type A, type B, type C and type D equity and liabilities. The group's type A equity and liabilities are the CEL of any relevant UK sub group, as for a foreign banking group. The group's type B equity and liabilities are the CEL of any UK resident bank that is a member of the relevant group but not a member of a relevant UK banking sub group. The group's type C equity and liabilities are the CEL of any entity (apart from a UK resident bank) that is a member of the relevant group and is a member of a UK banking sub group but not a member of a relevant UK banking sub group. The group's type D equity and liabilities are the UK allocated equity and liabilities (as defined by para 24) as at the end of the chargeable period of any relevant foreign bank that is a member of the relevant group but not a member of a UK banking sub group. The terms 'UK banking sub group' and 'relevant UK banking sub group' are defined. Paragraph 20 contains parallel provisions to those in para 18, to supplement the calculation of the various amounts defined in para 19. Paragraphs 21 and 22 define the CEL of 'stand alone' UK entities — those UK resident banks and building societies liable to the bank levy but which are not members of a group. Paragraph 23 defines the CEL of a relevant foreign bank that is not a member of a group. These are its 'UK allocated equity and liabilities as at the end of the chargeable period. Paragraphs 24 to 27 define 'UK allocated equity and liabilities' for the purposes of paras 19 and 23. Paragraphs 28 to 39 define what equity and liabilities are excluded equity and liabilities. Broadly, these are liabilities representing protected deposits, tier one capital equity and liabilities, sovereign repo liabilities, sovereign stock-lending liabilities, relevant insurance liabilities, relevant property, plant and equipment reserves, relevant tax liabilities, relevant retirement-benefit liabilities, financial services compensation-scheme liabilities, liabilities representing clients' money held by an authorised person, and currency liabilities. Paragraph 40 allows the Treasury to add, repeal or otherwise amend by order the provisions relating to netting off agreements in paras 16, 18(8)–(17), 20(8)–(17), 22 and 25. Paragraph 41 defines the chargeable period for an entity that does not prepare financial statements for a relevant period. Paragraph 42 defines what is meant for the purposes of these provisions by 'financial statements' and 'consolidated financial statements' and how amounts not stated in sterling are to be translated. Paragraphs 43 and 44 provide for how adjustments are to be made where a member of the relevant group has an interest in a joint venture. Paragraph 45 provides that 'residence' is to be understood as it is for the purposes of corporation tax and that a partnership is to be considered resident where the control and management of its trade and investment activities takes place. Paragraph 46 provides that no deduction is to be allowed in respect of the bank levy when calculating profits or losses for the purposes of income tax or corporation tax, and no account is to be taken of intra-group payments for meeting or reimbursing the cost of the bank levy. Paragraph 47 is an anti avoidance provision. Where one or more entities enter into arrangements, and the main purpose or one of the main purposes of any of the entities concerned is to avoid or reduce a charge or assessment to the bank levy, and as a result, the bank levy is not charged or assessed as it would have been in the absence of the arrangements, the effect of the arrangements is to be negated. A number of arrangements are to be ignored in this respect. Paragraph 48 makes consequential amendments.

Schedule 19 Part 6 deals with collection and management. This is to be the responsibility of HMRC (para 49). Bank levy is to be payable as if it were an amount of corporation tax chargeable on the 'responsible member' of the group, or in the case of standalone entities, on that entity. Where the responsible member's accounting period ends at the same time as the bank-levy chargeable period, it is payable for that accounting period; otherwise, for the accounting period in which the chargeable period ends. The bank levy payable for a chargeable period may be apportioned over two or more accounting periods (paras 50 and 51). All enactments applying generally to corporation tax, modified where appropriate, are to apply to the bank levy also (para 52). Where bank levy is payable in respect of a group, all members of the relevant group that are chargeable to UK corporation tax are to be jointly and severally liable for the tax; in the case of a relevant non banking group, it is all relevant members chargeable to UK corporation tax that are so liable (para 53). The responsible member may be a member of the group nominated by the group and satisfying certain conditions, the parent entity or some other entity as prescribed (para 54). Nominations may be made only once during the chargeable period; HMRC may from time to time publish related information requirements, and may, within 30 days of receipt, reject a nomination on grounds that are specified (para 55). Paragraph 56 makes a consequential amendment to PCTA 1968. Paragraphs 57 to 59 amend TMA 1970, allowing regulations under TMA 1970 s 59E to be made in respect of bank levy and for bank levy to be included in group payment arrangements under TMA 1970 s 59F. Paragraphs 60 to 64 amend the provisions relating to company tax returns in FA 1998 Sch 18. Paragraph 65 makes transitional provisions for chargeable periods beginning before 19 July 2011. Paragraphs 66 to 69 (Part 7) provide for double tax relief in relation to the bank levy and equivalent foreign levies. Part 8 (paras 70 to 80) contains definitions. Paragraph 70(1) is an indexing provision for definitions elsewhere in Sch 19; para 70(2) refers to definitions in the FSA Handbook. There follow definitions of 'asset management activities' (para 71); 'capital resources condition' (para 72); 'excluded entity' (para 73); 'long term equity and liabilities' (paras 74 to 77); 'relevant foreign bank' (para 78); 'relevant regulated activity' (para 79); and 'UK resident bank' (para 80). Paragraph 81 confers on the Treasury the power to amend Sch 19 by order (s 73 and Sch 19).

PART 6
OTHER TAXES

Value added tax. Article 16 of the VAT Directive (2006/112/EC), (formerly Article 5(6) of the Sixth VAT Directive (77/388/EEC), provides that applications by a taxable person of goods forming part of his business for the giving of samples or the making of gifts of small value for the purposes of the taxable person's business are not to be treated as supplies made for consideration. In the United Kingdom, VATA 1994 Sch 4 para 5 has hitherto provided that a transfer or disposal (whether or not for a consideration) of goods forming part of the goods of a business is a supply of those goods. An exception is made for gifts of small value and, in the case of a gift to any person of a sample of any goods, where a number of identical or practically identical goods are given as samples to the same person, in respect only of the first or one such sample. In EMI Group Ltd v The Commissioners for Her Majesty's Revenue and Customs (Case C 581/08), the European Court of Justice held that this blanket exclusion of all but one sample was not compatible with the VAT Directive. VATA 1994 Sch 4 para 5 is accordingly amended to replace the reference to a gift of any samples by a reference to "the provision to a person, otherwise than for a consideration, of a sample of goods" and remove the restriction to one sample. The amendments have effect from 19 July 2011 (s 74). Section 75 is an anti avoidance provision intended to prevent the artificial splitting of what is essentially a single supply of printed matter. VATA 1994 Sch 8 Part 2 Group 3 provides for zero rating of books and other printed matter. A Note 2 is inserted, providing that where a supply of goods is connected with a supply of services and those connected supplies are made by different suppliers, the goods concerned are not to qualify for zero rating. The amendments have effect for supplies made after 18 July 2011 (s 75). The supply of free education is outside the scope of VAT as a non business activity, and thus input VAT incurred in relation to those supplies would not be recoverable. Schools under local-authority control are, however, entitled to recovery of this input VAT by virtue of the special refund scheme for local authorities under VATA 1994 s 33A. A new VATA 1994 s 33B is now inserted to provide that the proprietor of an academy (a school designated as such by the Secretary of State for Education and not under local authority control) may apply for a refund of VAT incurred otherwise than for the purposes of the proprietor's business on (a) the supply of goods and services; (b) the acquisition of goods from any other Member State; or (c) the importation of any goods from outside the European Union. Such claims must be made within four years of the date on which the input VAT is incurred. The amendments have effect in relation to supplies, acquisitions and importations taking place after 31 March 2011 (s 76). The VAT (Imported Goods) Relief Order 1984 (SI 1984/746) is amended to reduce the value of goods that may be imported free of VAT from outside the European Union (the Channel Islands being outside the European Union for this purpose) from £18 to £15, with effect from 1 November 2011 (s 77).

Climate change levy. Section 78 introduces Sch 20, which makes amendments to FA 2000 Sch 6, which contains the provisions relating to climate change levy. The amendments remove the exemption for supplies of fossil fuels for the generation of electricity, which are to be subject to new rates, known as carbon-price support rates. Paragraph 1 is introductory. Paragraph 2 amends FA 2000 Sch 6 para 6, which imposes the charge on supplies of gas made by a gas utility, but exempts supplies made to other gas utilities or to the utility itself. The amendments extend the charge to supplies made by an unregulated gas supplier to a person to be used by that person in producing electricity. However, a supply of gas made by an unregulated gas supplier to any person who intends to use it in an output of a fully or partly exempt combined heat and power station is to be exempt. FA 2000 Sch 6 para 14 exempts supplies of a taxable commodity to a person to be used by that person in producing electricity in a generating station that is neither a fully exempt nor partly exempt combined heat and power station. Paragraph 3 amends that paragraph so that it applies not to taxable commodities in general but solely to electricity. Paragraph 4 amends FA 2000 Sch 6 para 21, which provides for HMRC to make regulations to avoid a double charge to climate change levy, so that it does not apply in respect of a taxable supply subject to the new carbon-price support rates. Paragraph 5 amends FA 2000 Sch 6 para 42 so that the rates of levy charged by that paragraph are not to apply to taxable supplies subject to the new carbon-price support rates. Paragraph 6 inserts new FA 2000 Sch 6 para 42A, which provides for the new rates. The carbon-price support rate is to apply to the supply of a taxable commodity other than electricity to a person for use by that person in producing electricity. However, such supplies made to a person who intends to use them in a fully or partly exempt combined heat and power station in producing outputs of that station are excluded from the new rates. The carbon-price support rate varies according to the nature of the taxable commodity. Paragraph 7 amends FA 2000 Sch 6 para 101 so that a penalty may be charged where a person incorrectly claims to have received a supply charged at the carbon-price support rate. Paragraph 8 provides that, subject to transitional provisions in para 9, the amendments made by Sch 20 are to apply to supplies treated as taking place after 31 March 2013. Paragraph 9 contains those transitional provisions (s 78 and Sch 20). FA 2000 Sch 6 para 11A exempts supplies made by gas utilities of gas that is to be burned in Northern Ireland. This exemption constitutes a State aid for which approval by way of a derogation from EC Directive 2003/96 was obtained. That approval expired on 31 March 2011, and the UK Government concluded that a further full exemption was unlikely to be approved. Accordingly, FA 2000 Sch 6 para 11A is now repealed. Instead, for supplies made by a gas utility to a person intending to cause the gas to be burned in Northern Ireland, a lower rate of levy is to apply. For supplies treated as taking place after 31 March 2011 but before 1 April 2012, the rate is to be £0.00059 per KWh, and for supplies treated as taking place after 31 March 2012 and before 1 November 2013 (when the derogation expires), the rate is to be £0.00062 per KWh (s 79). FA 2000 Sch 6 para 18A exempts supplies for use in recycling processes from climate change levy. This exemption is a State aid, approval for which from the European Commission expired on 31 March 2011. HM Treasury is accordingly given the power to suspend this provision by order to the extent specified in the order, pending negotiations on further approval (s 80).

Aggregates levy. Under FA 2001 s 30A, a transitional credit of 80 per cent was available in respect of aggregates levy on aggregates subject to commercial exploitation in Northern Ireland. State aid approval from the European Commission was received for the period from 1 April 2004 to 31 March 2011, and the credit accordingly was also set to be available no later than that date. However, on 9 September 2010, the European General Court annulled the Commission's decision that the credit scheme was an approvable State aid, and the scheme was suspended with effect from 1 December 2010 by the Aggregates Levy (Northern Ireland Tax Credit) (Revocation) Regulations 2010 (SI 2010/2598). The UK Government intends to negotiate a new approval for a further 10 years. In the meantime, the section is amended to apply in respect of a prescribed time (s 81).

Stamp duty land tax. Section 82 introduces Sch 21, which amends existing anti avoidance provisions relating to stamp duty land tax. Paragraph 1 is introductory. FA 2003 s 45(3) makes an exception from the sub sales rules for instances where the secondary contract gives rise to a transaction exempt from charge under FA 2003 s 73(3) by virtue of its being land sold to a financial institution and resold to an individual in an alternative property finance transaction). The effect of the exception is to ensure that a charge to stamp duty land tax applies in that situation. Paragraph 2 amends this provision so that exception now applies to any alternative property finance transaction within FA 2003 ss 71A to 73. Paragraph 3 inserts new FA 2003 s 73BA, which defines a financial institution for the purposes of the alternative property finance provisions, and deletes the definitions currently appearing in FA 2003 ss 71A(8), 72(7), 72A(8) and 73(5)(a). The new definition introduces the definition in ITA 2007 s 564B, with the omission of ITA 2007 s 564B(1)(d), so that persons authorised under Consumer Credit Act 1974 Part 3 to carry on a consumer-credit business or a consumer-hire business do not come within the definition for these purposes. FA 2003 Sch 4 para 5 provides how the chargeable consideration is to be determined on a land exchange. Broadly speaking, where the exchange involves a major interest in land, the chargeable consideration is deemed to be the market value of that interest or (in the case of a grant of a lease at a rent, that rent). Paragraph 4 amends these rules to provide that the chargeable consideration is to be the higher of (a) the market value or the rent, as the case may be and (b) what the value would be in the absence of the market-value rule in FA 2003 Sch 4 para 5. Paragraph 5 provides for commencement. Subject to transitional provisions, the amendments to FA 2003 s 45 and FA 2003 Sch 4 para 5 (the amendments made by paras 2 and 4) apply to transactions the effective date of which is after 23 March 2011. The amended definition of 'financial institution' (the amendment made by para 3) is to have effect from 24 March 2011 (s 82 and Sch 21). Section 83 introduces Sch 22, which is a relieving measure, intended to reduce the amount of stamp duty land tax payable on a purchase of multiple dwellings. Paragraph 1 is introductory. Paragraph 2 inserts new FA 2003 s 58D, which provides that new FA 2003 Sch 6B is to have effect to provide relief in the case of transfers involving multiple dwellings. Paragraph 3 inserts the new Schedule. Schedule 6B para 1 outlines the structure of the Schedule. Schedule 6B para 2 provides that it applies to a chargeable transaction (a) the main subject-matter of which consists of an interest in at least two dwellings or an interest in at least two dwellings and other property or (b) that is one of a number of linked transactions having as its main subject-matter an interest in a single dwelling or in a single dwelling and other property, provided that the main subject-matter of at least one of the other linked transactions is an interest in some other dwelling or dwellings or an interest in some other dwelling or dwellings and other property. However, transactions consisting of an exercise of collective rights by tenants of flats within FA 2003 s 74 or of a crofting community's right to buy within FA 2003 s 75 are excluded, as are transactions in respect of which relief under FA 2003 Sch 7 (group relief and relief on acquisitions and reconstructions) or FA 2003 Sch 8 (charities relief) would be available. Superior interests in a lease granted for an initial term of more than 21 years are to be ignored in determining whether a transaction qualifies for relief under these provisions. A transaction to which relief applies under new Sch 6B is referred to as a 'relevant transaction' (Sch 6B para 3). Where relief is claimed under these provisions, the tax chargeable on a relevant transaction is to be a percentage of the consideration attributable to the dwelling or dwellings concerned plus a percentage of the remaining consideration, if any (Sch 6B para 4). The percentage chargeable in respect of the dwellings and referred to in Sch 6B para 4 is determined by reference to the table of rates in FA 2003 s 55, on the assumption that the relevant land consists entirely of residential property and the consideration were the amount arrived at by dividing the total consideration for the dwellings by the number of dwellings. However, if the result is 0 per cent, it is instead taken to be 1 per cent. The percentage applicable to any other consideration is the rate that would be applied to the transaction in the absence of these provisions (Sch 6B para 5). Schedule 6B para 6 provides for an adjustment and a further return to be made where an event occurs within three years of the effective date of the relevant transaction, or if shorter, prior to disposal of the dwelling(s) by the purchaser to an unconnected person, which would, if it had occurred immediately before the relevant transaction, have caused more tax to be payable. Schedule 6B para 7 defines what is to be considered as a dwelling for the purpose of these provisions. Schedule 22 paras 4 to 8 make consequential amendments. Schedule 22 para 9 provides that the amendments made by Sch 22 are to have effect with respect to relevant transactions the effective date of which is after 18 July 2011 and that are not linked to land transactions with an effective date before 19 July 2011 (s 83 and Sch 22).

Stamp duty reserve tax. FA 1986 s 99(5B)(b) provides that exemption from stamp duty reserve tax for an interest under a collective investment scheme applies if and only if the scheme is an authorised unit trust scheme or an open-ended investment company and the property subject to the scheme can only be invested in such a way that any income arising to the trustees or the company is chargeable to tax under the former Schedule D Case III and can only be invested in exempt investments. This restrictive exemption is replaced by one that confers exemption on any collective investment scheme unless more than 20 per cent of the market value of the scheme investments is attributable to investments that are not exempt investments. This amendment has effect from 24 July 2011 (s 84).

PART 7
ADMINISTRATION ETC

ITEPA 2003 s 684 is to be amended so as to give HMRC power to make regulations requiring security or further security to be given for amounts due to HMRC in respect of PAYE deductions. Failure to comply is to constitute an offence punishable on summary conviction to a fine not exceeding level 5 on the standard scale. The amendment is to have effect from 19 July 2011 but HMRC has made it known that the relevant regulations will not have effect until 6 April 2012 (s 85).

Section 86 introduces Schs 23 and 24, which bring about a comprehensive reform of HMRC's information-gathering powers vis à vis third parties. Schedule 23 contains the new provisions and Sch 24 contains consequential amendments to the existing information and inspection powers in FA 2008 Sch 36.

Schedule 23 Part 1 (paras 1 to 7) provides for the power to obtain 'data'; Part 2 (paras 8 to 27) defines who are 'relevant data-holders'; Part 3 (paras 28 and 29) provides for appeals; Part 4 (paras 30 to 42) provides for penalties; Part 5 (paras 43 to 50) contains miscellaneous other provisions; Part 6 (paras 51 to 64) makes consequential provisions; and Part 7 (para 65) provides for commencement. Paragraph 1 provides that a 'relevant data-holder' (as defined in Part 2) may be required, by a notice in writing from an officer of HMRC to provide 'relevant data', which may be general data or data relating to particular persons or matters and may include personal data such as names or addresses of individuals. 'Relevant data' are data of a kind specified in respect of that particular data-holder in regulations. These notices are to be referred to as 'data-holder notices'. Paragraph 2 prescribes for which purposes the power may be exercised. Relevant data may only be specified in a data-holder notice if the officer of HMRC has reason to believe they could have a bearing on chargeable periods ending within the period of four years before the date of the notice (para 3). Paragraph 4 specifies the means by which and the form in which the data must be provided. Officers need not obtain the approval of the tribunal before issuing a notice but may do so. The hearing may be ex parte. A decision by the tribunal is to be final (para 5). HMRC may take copies of documents provided under a notice (para 6) and may retain documents for a reasonable period (para 7). Paragraph 8 introduces Part 2. Paragraph 9 is the equivalent provision to the existing TMA 1970 ss 15 (returns by employers and others) and 16 (fees, commissions etc). It provides that a relevant data-holder for the purposes of this paragraph are each of (a) an employer; (b) a person concerned in making payments to or in respect of another person's employees in respect of their employment with that person; (c) an approved payroll-giving agent under ITEPA 2003 s 714; and (d) a person carrying on a business in connection with which relevant payments are or are likely to be made. These relevant payments are payments for or in connection with services provided by persons who are not employees of that business or periodical or lump sum payments in respect of certain intellectual-property rights. Paragraph 10 is the equivalent provision to the existing TMA 1970 s 16A (returns in respect of agency employees). It extends the provisions of para 9 to services provided under an agency contract treated under ITEPA 2003 s 44(2) as duties of an employment with the agency and remuneration receivable under arrangements within ITEPA 2003 s 45 treated as earnings from an employment with the agency. Paragraph 12 is the equivalent provision to the existing TMA 1970 s 15A (formerly FA 1974 s 24), and extends the provisions of para 9 to earnings for duties performed in the United Kingdom under an employment with a non resident employer and for the benefit of a UK resident person or a person carrying on a trade, profession or vocation in the United Kingdom. The only information that may be requested in this circumstance is the employee's name and place of residence. Paragraph 12 is the equivalent provision to the existing TMA 1970 ss 17 and 18 (payments of interest etc without deduction of income tax). A relevant data-holder in respect of this paragraph is a person by or through whom interest is paid or credited. 'Interest' includes building-society dividends, redemption payments to the holder of a deeply discounted security, foreign dividends, and alternative finance returns. 'Alternative finance return' is defined. Paragraph 13 is the equivalent provision to the existing TMA 1970 s 13 (return by persons in receipt of taxable income belonging to others). It provides that a person who is in receipt of money or value belonging to another person is a relevant data-holder for these purposes. Paragraph 14 is the equivalent provision to the existing TMA 1970 ss 21 (in part), 24 and 26 (information in respect of securities) and CTA 2010 ss 31(1), 465(1), 728, 1046(5)–(7), 1097, 1102(2) and 1109(4). It provides, with respect to payments derived from securities that each of the following is a relevant data-holder: (a) the registered or inscribed holder; (b) a person who receives or would be entitled to receive a payment derived from securities; (c) a person who receives a payment treated by an unquoted trading company as a purchase of its own shares and (d) a person who receives a chargeable payment on a demerger. The information that may be required from data-holders under this paragraph is restricted and defined. No exception for banks such as currently provided in TMA 1970 s 24(3), (3ZA) and (3ZB), is reproduced in the new provision. Paragraph 15 is the equivalent provision to the existing TMA 1970 s 21(4A) and defined as a relevant data-holder any person who makes a payment derived from securities which has been received from or is paid on behalf of another person. Paragraph 16 is the equivalent provision to the existing TMA 1970 s 18A (in part). It provides that a person making a payment out of public funds by way of grant or subsidy is a relevant data-holder. Paragraph 17 is the equivalent provision to the existing TMA 1970 s 18A(2). It provides that a person issuing or maintaining a register of licences or approvals is a relevant data-holder. Paragraph 18 is the equivalent provision to the existing TMA 1970 s 19. With respect to rents and other payments arising from land each of the following is a relevant data-holder: (a) a lessee or successor in title of a lessee); (b) an occupier of land; (c) a person having the use of land; and (d) an agent who manages land or is in receipt of rents and other payments in respect of land. Paragraph 19 is the equivalent provision to TMA 1970 ss 21, 24 and 25 (all in part) and 26 and FA 2008 Sch 36 para 61A, Table, No 8. It provides with respect to dealing etc in securities that a data-holder is to be (a) a person who effects or is a party to securities transactions wholly or partly on behalf of others; (b) a person acting as registrar or administrator in respect of securities transactions as part of his business; (c) a person who makes a payment derived from securities to anyone other than their registered or inscribed holder; (d) a person making a payment derived from bearer securities; and (e) an accountable person under the Stamp Duty Reserve Tax Regulations (SI 1986/1711). Taken together, paras 14, 15 and 19 are intended to simplify and clarify the provisions they replace. Paragraph 20 is the equivalent provision to the existing TMA 1970 s 25(6), (7). It includes data-holders for its purposes as (a) clearing houses; (b) auctioneers; (c) dealers in tangible movable property; and (d) agents or intermediaries in dealings with tangible movable property. Paragraph 21 is the equivalent provision to the existing FA 2008 Sch 36 para 61A, Table, No 4. Lloyd's managing agents are to be data-holders. Paragraph 22 is the equivalent provision to FA 2008 Sch 36 para 61A, Table, Nos 2 and 3. It defines plan managers of an individual investment plan under ITTOIA 2005 s 696 and account providers in relation to a child trust under Child Trust Funds Act 2004 s 3 as data-holders. Paragraph 23 is the equivalent provision to the existing FA 2008 Sch 36 para 61A, Table, No 9, and defines holders of licences granted under Petroleum Act 1998 Part 1 and responsible persons in relation to an oil field within the meaning of OTA 1975 Part 1 as data-holders. Paragraph 24 is the equivalent provision to the existing FA 2008 Sch 36 para 61A, Table, Nos 5–7. In relation to insurance activities, it defines persons involved in an insurance business, persons who make arrangements for persons to enter into contracts of insurance (e.g. brokers and financial advisers) and persons in a business other than an insurance business involved in entering into an insurance contract providing cover associated with the business as data-holders. Paragraph 25 is the equivalent provision to the existing FA 2008 Sch 36 para 61A, Table, Nos 10–12. In relation to environmental activities, it defines certain persons liable to aggregates levy, climate change levy and landfill tax as data-holders. Paragraph 26 is the equivalent provision to the existing TMA 1970 s 27 and ITTOIA 2005 s 647. It defines settlors, trustees, beneficiaries and any other persons to whom income is payable under a settlement as data-holders. Finally in this Part, para 27 defines charities as data-holders.

Schedule 23 Part 3 provides for appeals. Data-holders may appeal against a data holder notice as such or against any requirement in such a notice on the grounds that (a) compliance is unduly onerous; (b) that they are not relevant data-holders with respect to the information required; or (c) the data specified in the notice are not relevant data. There is no appeal, however, against a notice that has been approved by the tribunal under Sch 23 para 5 (para 28). The notice of appeal must be in writing and given within 30 days of the date of the data holder notice. Where the appeal is referred to the tribunal, the tribunal's decision is final. The tribunal may confirm, vary or set aside the notice. The provisions of TMA 1970 Part V concerning appeals are generally to apply (para 29). Schedule 23 Part 4 provides for penalties. Failure to comply with a data holder notice incurs a fixed penalty of £300. Failure to comply is further defined (para 30). Once that penalty has been assessed, continued failure to comply incurs a daily penalty of up to £60 per day (para 31). The provision of inaccurate information may incur a penalty of up to £3,000 (para 32). Failure to comply with a time limit will not give rise to a penalty if the required action is taken within a further period specified by an officer of HMRC (para 33). A penalty under either para 30 or para 31 will not be imposed if the data-holder has a reasonable excuse (para 34). The procedure for HMRC to assess a penalty is provided in para 35, and the right to appeal against the imposition of a penalty or its amount is provided in para 36. Notices of appeal under para 36 must be given within 30 days of the notice of assessment to the penalty. Where the appeal is referred to a tribunal, the tribunal may confirm or cancel the penalty or confirm or vary the amount, as the case may be. The provisions of TMA 1970 Part V concerning appeals are generally to apply (para 37). Data-holders assessed to a penalty under para 30 who continue to be in default for more than 30 days after the notice of assessment has been issued may be charged with an increased daily default penalty, which must, however, be approved by the tribunal, which is to determine the amount. The increased penalty replaces the continued default penalty under para 31 and may not exceed £1,000 per day (para 38). The procedure for charging that penalty is prescribed by para 39. Penalties are generally payable within 30 days and may be enforced as if they were income tax charged under an assessment and due and payable (para 40). The Treasury may vary the penalty amounts chargeable under Sch 23 Part 4 by order (para 41). A data-holder who has been convicted of an offence may not also be charged a penalty under Sch 23 Part 4 in respect of the same act or omission (para 42). Subject to any contrary provision in Sch 23, TMA 1970 ss 108, 114 and 115 are to apply (para 43). Regulations under Sch 23 are to be made by statutory instrument (para 44). The taxes in respect of which Sch 23 applies are income tax, capital gains tax, corporation tax, VAT, insurance premium tax, inheritance tax, stamp duty land tax, stamp duty reserve tax, petroleum revenue tax, aggregates levy, climate change levy, landfill tax and 'relevant foreign tax'. Not included are stamp duty, excise and customs duties, and the various gaming etc duties (para 45). Paras 46 to 49 provide for interpretation. Schedule 23 applies to the Crown but not to the Queen in her private capacity (para 50). Schedule 23 Part 6 (paras 51–64) makes consequential provisions, including in particular the repeal of TMA 1970 ss 13, 14, 15, 15A, 16, 16A, 17, 18, 18A, 19, 21, 23, 24, 25, 26, 27, 76 and 77I (para 51).TMA 1970 ss 18B–18E (which contain information powers relating to the EU Savings Directive) remain in force. Schedule 23 is to come into force on 1 April 2012 (para 65).

Schedule 24 amends FA 2008 Sch 36, which contains HMRC's new information and inspection powers, which came into effect on 1 April 2009. Certain amendments extend the powers to cover certain foreign taxes and others are consequential on the introduction of Sch 23. Paragraph 1 is introductory. Paragraph 2 amends FA 2008 Sch 36 to extend the power to obtain information and documents concerning persons whose identity is unknown to foreign taxes. These amendments have effect from 1 April 2012. FA 2008 Sch 36 para 40A provides for a penalty in cases where a person provides inaccurate information or inaccurate documents and either of two conditions (A and B) is met. The paragraph is amended to add a third condition (C) that is identical in effect to condition B in Sch 23 para 32, namely that the person concerned knew of the inaccuracy when providing the information or document but did not at that time inform HMRC of that fact. This amendment also has effect from 1 April 2012 (para 3). Paragraph 4 inserts new FA 2008 Sch 36 paras 49A and 49B, which provide for an increased daily default penalty in circumstances analogous to those in which the same penalty is to be charged under Sch 23 para 38. Paragraph 5 amends FA 2008 Sch 36 para 50 in order to clarify the relevant date for charging a tax-related penalty. Paragraph 6 makes a minor amendment to FA 2008 Sch 36 para 61A (s 86 and Schs 23 and 24).

Section 87 introduces Sch 25, which gives effect to the United Kingdom's obligations under Council Directive 2010/24/EU concerning mutual assistance for the recovery of claims relating to taxes, duties and other measures ('MARD'), and provides for regulations to be made by the Treasury to give effect to future amendments to the Directive and other related instruments. Schedule 25 para 1 is introductory. Paragraph 2 provides that HMRC is a competent authority and the central liaison office for all purposes under MARD. No obligation of secrecy is to preclude a public authority from disclosing information required in relation to MARD or to a related instrument (para 3). Onward disclosure of information received by HMRC in this connection is, however, an offence if not specifically permitted as mentioned (para 4). Paragraph 5 provides for a defence against a charge brought under para 4 and for prosecutions and punishment. Paragraph 6 provides for the method of enforcing foreign claims in the United Kingdom. Paragraph 7 defines the relevant UK authority for foreign claims and para 8 defines what is a corresponding UK claim in relation to enforcement under para 6. The relevant UK authority may by regulation adapt, apply or refrain from applying any rule of law or enactment relating to corresponding UK claims (para 9). Paragraph 10 gives the Treasury the power to make further regulations. Paragraph 11 provides for proceedings on a foreign claim to be suspended in certain circumstances where proceedings in a foreign court or other competent body may be pending. Where a final decision is given by a foreign court or other competent body in favour of the person against whom a claim has been made, steps against that person under para 6 are not to be taken or continued in the United Kingdom (para 12). No question as to the relevant person's liability may be raised except under para 12 (para 13). Requests made by foreign applicant authorities are to be presumed valid, unless the contrary is proved (para 14). Paragraph 15 provides for regulations to be made. Paragraph 16 provides for interpretation. Paragraphs 17 and 18 make consequential amendments. Paragraph 19 provides that Sch 25 is to have effect from 19 July 2011 in respect of sums becoming due at any time (s 87 and Sch 25).

PART 8
MISCELLANEOUS PROVISIONS

Section 88 makes amendments to PCTA 1968 as a result of changes to the Parliamentary timetable, under which sessions are to end in the spring rather than in the autumn as at present. This will normally entail that a session ends while the Finance Bill for a particular year is still undergoing its passage through Parliament. The maximum period for which a resolution under PCTA 1968 may have effect is to be seven months. Where proceedings under a Finance Bill have been commenced but not completed when a session ends, the resolution will continue to have effect provided that the Bill is reintroduced within 30 days of the opening of the new session (s 88). Section 89 rectifies the unintended consequences of the FISMA 2000 (Regulated Activities) (Amendment) Order 2010 (SI 2010/86), relating to sharia-compliant securities. A second order under FISMA 2000 rectified matters as from

16 February 2011, but could not have retroactive effect. This section provides that the second order is to have had effect from 24 February 2010, which was the date on which the original order took effect (s 89). Section 90 gives HMRC the authority to incur expenditure in preparation for the introduction of gaming-machine duty, which is intended to replace amusement-machine licence duty (s 90). Section 91 introduces Sch 26, which repeals redundant reliefs. This represents the Government's response to the report 'Review of Tax Reliefs' by the Office of Tax Simplification, published on 8 March 2011. Schedule 26 repeals seven reliefs, and the Government is consulting on the repeal of a further 36. The reliefs to be repealed are: (a) the transitional relief for charities etc on the abolition of payment for tax credits on distributions (F(No 2)A 1997 s 35 and Sch 5; ITA 2007 Sch 1 para 379; FA 2010 Sch 6 para 14); (b) Millennium Gift Aid (FA 1998 s 48; FA 1999 ss 56 and 57; FA 2000 s 42; ITA 2007 Sch 2 para 98); (c) payroll deduction scheme supplement (FA 2000 s 38; ITEPA 2003 Sch 6 para 243; FA 2003 s 146; ITA 2007 Sch 1 para 390); (d) the exemption for the first £70 of National Savings Bank ordinary-account interest (ITTOIA 2005 s 691); (e) exemption from stamp duty for certain assignments by seamen (FA 1944 s 45); (f) exemption from stamp duty for instruments relating to National Savings (FA 1953 s 31); and (g) exemption from stamp duty for instruments for the sale etc of ships or vessels (FA 1999 Sch 13 para 24(b)). These repeals have effect from 19 July 2011 (s 91 and Sch 26). Section 92 provides for interpretation and s 93 provides the short title of the Act.

Zigurds G Kronbergs
2 August 2011

FINANCE ACT 2011

2011 CHAPTER 11

CONTENTS

PART 1

CHARGES, RATES, ALLOWANCES ETC

Income tax

1 Charge and main rates for 2011–12
2 Basic rate limit for 2011–12
3 Personal allowance for 2011–12 for those aged under 65

Corporation tax

4 Main rate for financial year 2011
5 Charge and main rate for financial year 2012
6 Small profits rate and fractions for financial year 2011
7 Increase in rate of supplementary charge

Capital gains tax

8 Annual exempt amount
9 Entrepreneurs' relief

Capital allowances

10 Plant and machinery writing-down allowances
11 Annual investment allowance
12 Short-life assets

Alcohol duties

13 Rates of alcoholic liquor duties
14 General beer duty: reduced rate for lower strength beer
15 New high strength beer duty

Tobacco duties

16 Rates of tobacco products duty

Gambling duties

17 Rates of gaming duty
18 Amusement machine licence duty

Fuel duties

19 Fuel duties: rates of duty and rebates from 23 March 2011
20 Fuel duties: rates of duty and rebates from 1 January 2012

Vehicle excise duty

21 VED rates for light passenger vehicles, light goods vehicles, motorcycles etc
22 VED rates for certain goods vehicles without road-friendly suspension

Environmental taxes

23 Rates of climate change levy
24 Rate of aggregates levy
25 Standard rate of landfill tax

PART 2

INCOME TAX, CORPORATION TAX AND CAPITAL GAINS TAX

Anti-avoidance provisions

26 Employment income provided through third parties

27 Tainted charity donations
28 Amounts not fully recognised for accounting purposes
29 Loan relationships involving connected debtor and creditor
30 Group mismatch schemes
31 Company ceasing to be member of group: availability of relief
32 Leasing businesses
33 Long funding finance leases
34 Investment companies

Exemptions and reliefs

35 Reduction in childcare relief for higher earners
36 Childcare: salary sacrifice etc and the national minimum wage
37 Accommodation expenses of MPs
38 Experts seconded to European Union bodies
39 Employment income: exemption for fees relating to monitoring schemes
40 Individual investment plans for children
41 Gift aid: increase of limits on total value of benefits associated with gifts
42 Enterprise investment scheme: amount of relief
43 Relief for expenditure on R&D by SMEs

Chargeable gains

44 Value shifting
45 Company ceasing to be member of a group
46 Pre-entry losses

Foreign profits

47 Controlled foreign companies
48 Profits of foreign permanent establishments etc

Investment trusts

49 Meaning of "investment trust"
50 Power to make provision about treatment of transactions

Miscellaneous

51 Taxable benefits: calculating the appropriate percentage for cars
52 Furnished holiday lettings
53 Leases and changes to accounting standards
54 Leasing companies: withdrawal of election
55 Companies with small profits: associated companies
56 Insurance companies: apportionment of amounts brought into account
57 Tonnage tax: capital allowances in respect of ship leasing
58 Transfer pricing: application of OECD principles
59 Offshore funds
60 Index-linked gilt-edged securities

PART 3

OIL

61 PRT: areas treated as continuing to be oil fields
62 Intangible fixed assets: oil licences
63 Reduction of supplementary charge for certain new oil fields
64 Chargeable gains: oil activities

PART 4

PENSIONS

65 Benefits under pension schemes
66 Annual allowance charge
67 Lifetime allowance charge
68 Borrowing by section 67 pension scheme
69 Exemption from tax on interest on unpaid relevant contributions
70 Power to make further provision about section 67 pension scheme
71 Tax provision consequential on Part 1 of Pensions Act 2008 etc
72 Foreign pensions of UK residents

3 *Stamp duty reserve tax*

PART 5

BANK LEVY

73 The bank levy

PART 6

OTHER TAXES

Value added tax

74 Business samples
75 Zero-rating: splitting of supplies
76 Academies
77 Relief from VAT on imported goods of low value

Climate change levy

78 Supplies of commodities to be used in producing electricity
79 Northern Ireland gas supplies
80 Power to suspend exemption for supplies used in recycling processes

Aggregates levy

81 Transitional tax credit

Stamp duty land tax

82 Prevention of avoidance
83 Transfers involving multiple dwellings

Stamp duty reserve tax

84 Interests in collective investment schemes

PART 7

ADMINISTRATION ETC

85 Security for payment of PAYE
86 Data-gathering powers
87 Mutual assistance for recovery of taxes etc

PART 8

MISCELLANEOUS PROVISIONS

88 Amendments of section 1 of the Provisional Collection of Taxes Act 1968
89 Specified investments
90 Machine games duty
91 Redundant reliefs

PART 9

FINAL PROVISIONS

92 Interpretation
93 Short title

SCHEDULES

Schedule 1—New high strength beer duty
Schedule 2—Employment income provided through third parties
Schedule 3—Tainted charity donations
Part 1—Income tax
Part 2—Corporation tax
Part 3—Capital gains tax
Part 4—Consequential amendments
Part 5—Commencement and transitional provision
Schedule 4—Amounts not fully recognised for accounting purposes
Schedule 5—Group mismatch schemes
Schedule 6—Leasing businesses
Schedule 7—Investment companies

Schedule 8—Reduction in childcare relief for higher earners
Schedule 9—Value shifting
Schedule 10—Company ceasing to be member of group
Schedule 11—Pre-entry losses
Schedule 12—Controlled foreign companies
Part 1—Exemptions for companies with limited UK connection
Part 2—Amendment of small chargeable profits exemption
Part 3—Temporary exemption following reorganisation etc
Part 4—Holding companies: extension of transitional provision
Part 5—Minor and consequential amendments
Part 6—Commencement and transitional provision
Schedule 13—Profits of foreign permanent establishments etc
Part 1—Amendments of CTA 2009
Part 2—Amendments of other Acts
Part 3—Commencement and transitional provision
Schedule 14—Furnished holiday lettings
Part 1—Income tax
Part 2—Corporation tax
Part 3—Capital allowances
Part 4—Chargeable gains
Schedule 15—Chargeable gains: oil activities
Part 1—Licence swaps
Part 2—Reinvestment of ring fence assets
Schedule 16—Benefits under pension schemes
Part 1—Changes to benefits available under pension schemes etc
Part 2—Consequential amendments
Part 3—Commencement and transitional provision
Schedule 17—Annual allowance charge
Part 1—Amendments
Part 2—Commencement and transitional provision
Schedule 18—Lifetime allowance charge
Part 1—Amendments
Part 2—Commencement and transitional provision
Schedule 19—The bank levy
Part 1—Introduction
Part 2—Charging of bank levy
Part 3—Groups covered by the bank levy
Part 4—Chargeable equity and liabilities
Part 5—Supplementary provision
Part 6—Collection and management
Part 7—Double taxation relief
Part 8—Definitions
Part 9—Power to make consequential changes
Schedule 20—Supplies of commodities to be used in producing electricity
Schedule 21—Prevention of SDLT avoidance
Schedule 22—Transfers involving multiple dwellings
Schedule 23—Data-gathering powers
Part 1—Power to obtain data
Part 2—Relevant data-holders
Part 3—Appeals against data-holder notices
Part 4—Penalties
Part 5—Miscellaneous provision and interpretation
Part 6—Consequential provisions
Part 7—Application of this Schedule
Schedule 24—Amendments of Schedule 36 to FA 2008
Schedule 25—Mutual assistance for recovery of taxes etc
Schedule 26—Redundant reliefs
Part 1—Income tax and corporation tax
Part 2—Stamp duty

AN ACT TO grant certain duties, to alter other duties, and to amend the law relating to the National Debt and the Public Revenue, and to make further provision in connection with finance.

PART 1
CHARGES, RATES, ALLOWANCES ETC

Income tax

1 Charge and main rates for 2011–12

(1) Income tax is charged for the tax year 2011–12.

(2) For that tax year—

(a) the basic rate is 20%,
(b) the higher rate is 40%, and
(c) the additional rate is 50%.

GENERAL NOTE

Section 1 sets out the income tax rates for 2011–12. There is no change from the rates which applied in the previous year.

In his Budget Speech the Chancellor said that the 50% rate was not intended to be a permanent measure, although he did not give any timescale for its abolition. He did, however, announce that he had asked HMRC to review the effectiveness of the 50% rate because of concerns that it was not bringing in as much tax as was predicted. It may be that when the outcome of this review is known we will have more idea of the timescale for any changes to the 50% rate.

2 Basic rate limit for 2011–12

(1) For the tax year 2011–12 the amount specified in section 10(5) of ITA 2007 (basic rate limit) is replaced with "£35,000".

(2) Accordingly section 21 of that Act (indexation of limits), so far as relating to the basic rate limit, does not apply for that tax year.

GENERAL NOTE

One effect of the increase in the personal allowance (see s 3 below) is that without any adjusting mechanism all higher-rate taxpayers (other than those whose income level means that they are no longer entitled to a personal allowance) would obtain a greater benefit from the increase than would basic rate taxpayers. In order to prevent this, the basic rate limit for 2011–12 will be reduced to £35,000. In the 2011 Budget the Chancellor also announced that the basic rate limit for 2012–13 will be £34,370: this is to remove the higher rate benefit on the planned increase in the personal allowance for 2012–13.

3 Personal allowance for 2011–12 for those aged under 65

(1) For the tax year 2011–12 the amount specified in section 35(1) of ITA 2007 (personal allowance for those aged under 65) is replaced with "£7,475".

(2) Accordingly section 57 of that Act (indexation of allowances), so far as relating to the amount specified in section 35(1) of that Act, does not apply for that tax year.

GENERAL NOTE

The personal allowance for those under 65 for 2011–12 will be £7,475. The automatic uprating of personal allowances under s57 ITA 2007 is disapplied.

The Chancellor also announced that the personal allowance for 2012–13 will be £8,105. This is all part of the coalition's long-term plan to increase the personal allowance to £10,000.

Corporation tax

4 Main rate for financial year 2011

(1) In section 2(2)(a) of FA 2010 (main corporation tax rate for financial year 2011 on profits other than ring fence profits), for "27%" substitute "26%".

(2) The amendment made by this section is treated as having come into force on 1 April 2011.

GENERAL NOTE

The main rate of corporation tax (other than for ring fence profits) is set at 26% for the financial year 2011. The new rate is treated as coming into force on 1 April 2011 (the start of financial year 2011).

The rate change is given legislative effect by amending FA 2010 s 2(2)(a), thereby implementing the Budget announcement that the main rate or corporation tax would be reduced by a further one per cent on top of the one per cent reduction already announced. Legislation introduced by FA 2010 s 2(2)(a) had previously reduced the rate to 27 per cent for the financial year 2011. This provision further reduces the rate by one per cent to 26 per cent.

5 Charge and main rate for financial year 2012

(1) Corporation tax is charged for the financial year 2012.

(2) For that year the rate of corporation tax is—

(a) 25% on profits of companies other than ring fence profits, and
(b) 30% on ring fence profits of companies.

(3) In subsection (2) "ring fence profits" has the same meaning as in Part 8 of CTA 2010 (see section 276 of that Act).

GENERAL NOTE

In his Emergency Budget in June 2010, the Chancellor announced that the main rate of corporation tax would fall by a further one per cent in the financial years 2012, 2013 and 2014. Giving effect to the measure for the financial year 2012, and reflecting the additional one per cent reduction in the main rate introduced by s 4, the main rate of corporation tax for the financial year 2012 (commencing on 1 April 2012) is set at 25 per cent.

Profits from oil extraction and oil rights in the UK and the UK continental shelf (ring fence profits) are subject to a separate main rate of corporation tax. This will continue to be the case for the financial year 2011, for which the rate of corporation tax on ring fence profits remains at 30 per cent.

Ring fence profits are as defined in CTA 2010 s 276.

6 Small profits rate and fractions for financial year 2011

(1) For the financial year 2011 the small profits rate is—

(a) 20% on profits of companies other than ring fence profits, and
(b) 19% on ring fence profits of companies.

(2) For the purposes of Part 3 of CTA 2010, for that year—

(a) the standard fraction is 3/200ths, and
(b) the ring fence fraction is 11/400ths.

(3) In subsection (1) "ring fence profits" has the same meaning as in Part 8 of that Act (see section 276 of that Act).

GENERAL NOTE

Section 6 reduces the small profits rate of corporation tax for all non-ring fence profits from 21 per cent to 20 per cent for the financial year beginning 1 April 2011. The small profits rate for ring fence profits will remain at 19 per cent.

7 Increase in rate of supplementary charge

(1) In section 330 of CTA 2010 (supplementary charge in respect of ring fence trades), in subsection (1), for "20%" substitute "32%".

(2) The amendment made by subsection (1) has effect in relation to accounting periods beginning on or after 24 March 2011 (but see also subsection (3)).

(3) Subsections (4) to (10) apply where a company has an accounting period beginning before 24 March 2011 and ending on or after that date ("the straddling period").

(4) For the purpose of calculating the amount of the supplementary charge on the company for the straddling period—

(a) so much of that period as falls before 24 March 2011, and so much of that period as falls on or after that date, are treated as separate accounting periods, and

(b) the company's adjusted ring fence profits for the straddling period are apportioned to the two separate accounting periods in proportion to the number of days in those periods.

(5) But if the basis of apportionment in subsection (4)(b) would work unjustly or unreasonably in the company's case, the company may elect for its profits to be apportioned on another basis that is just and reasonable and specified in the election.

(6) The amount of the supplementary charge on the company for the straddling period is the sum of the amounts of supplementary charge that would, in accordance with subsections (4) and (5), be chargeable on the company for those separate accounting periods.

(7) In relation to the straddling period—

(a) the Instalment Payments Regulations apply as if the amendment made by subsection (1) had not been made, but

(b) those Regulations also apply separately, in accordance with subsection (8), in relation to the increase in the amount of any supplementary charge on the company for that period that arises as a result of that amendment.

(8) In the separate application of those Regulations under subsection (7)(b), those Regulations have effect as if, for the purposes of those Regulations—

(a) the straddling period were an accounting period beginning on 24 March 2011,

(b) supplementary charge were chargeable on the company for that period, and

(c) the amount of that charge were equal to the increase in the amount of the supplementary charge for the straddling period that arises as a result of the amendment made by subsection (1).

(9) Any reference in the Instalment Payment Regulations to the total liability of a company is, accordingly, to be read—

(a) in their application as a result of subsection (7)(a), as a reference to the amount that would be the company's total liability for the straddling period if the amendment made by subsection (1) had not been made, and

(b) in their application as a result of subsection (7)(b), as a reference to the amount of the supplementary charge on the company for the deemed accounting period under subsection (8)(a).

(10) For the purposes of the Instalment Payment Regulations—

(a) a company is to be regarded as a large company as respects the deemed accounting period under subsection (8)(a) if (and only if) it is a large company for those purposes as respects the straddling period, and

(b) any question whether a company is a large company as respects the straddling period is to be determined as it would have been determined if the amendment made by subsection (1) had not been made.

(11) In this section—

"adjusted ring fence profits" has the same meaning as in section 330 of CTA 2010;

"the Instalment Payments Regulations" means the Corporation Tax (Instalment Payments) Regulations 1998 (SI 1998/3175);

"supplementary charge" means any sum chargeable under section 330(1) of CTA 2010 as if it were an amount of corporation tax.

GENERAL NOTE

The rate of supplementary charge (SCT), which applies to oil and gas related ring fence profits (as adjusted), is increased from 20% to 32% with effect from March 24th 2011.

Where any accounting period straddles March 24th the profits are to be apportioned, on a time basis, to a deemed accounting period commencing on March 24th, unless the taxpayer, by election, seeks to apportion on a, different, just and reasonable basis.

For any accounting period which straddles March 24th instalment payments have to be made as usual in respect of the original 20% rate, but additional payments have to be made in respect of the 12% increase as if a new accounting period had commenced on March 24th. For a December year end company it will therefore need to make additional instalment payments in respect of the SCT increase on October 7th 2011, January 7th 2012 and January 14th 2012 (on which date it will also be making a "normal" instalment payment).

Capital gains tax

8 Annual exempt amount

(1) Section 3 of TCGA 1992 (annual exempt amount) is amended as follows.

(2) For subsection (2) substitute—

"(2) The exempt amount for a tax year is £10,600."

(3) For subsections (3) and (4) substitute—

"(3) If there is a relevant increase in RPI in relation to a tax year—

(a) the exempt amount is to be increased in accordance with Steps 1 and 2, and

(b) subsection (2) has effect from then on (for that and subsequent tax years) as if it referred to the increased amount,

unless Parliament otherwise determines.

(3A) There is a relevant increase in RPI in relation to a tax year if the retail prices index for the September before the start of the tax year is higher than it was for the previous September.

(3B) Steps 1 and 2 are—

Step 1

Increase the exempt amount for the previous tax year by the same percentage as the percentage of the relevant increase in RPI.

Step 2

If the result of Step 1 is not a multiple of £100, round it up to the nearest multiple of £100.

(4) If there is a relevant increase in RPI in relation to a tax year, the Treasury must before the start of that tax year make an order showing the amount arrived at as a result of Steps 1 and 2."

(4) The amendment made by subsection (2) has effect for the tax year 2011–12 and subsequent tax years.

(5) For the tax year 2011–12, section 3(3) of TCGA 1992 (indexation) does not apply.

(6) The amendment made by subsection (3) has effect for the tax year 2012–13 and subsequent tax years.

GENERAL NOTE

Section 8 does two things. Firstly, in sub-sections two and four it fixes the Capital Gains Tax annual exemption for 2011/12 at £10,600 by adjusting TCGA 1992 s 3(2) accordingly. As the annual exempt amount for 2011/12 has been fixed at £10,600 sub-section five specifies that the indexation calculation at TCGA 1992 s 3 should not apply for the tax year.

The fixing of the individual's Capital Gains Tax annual exempt amount at £10,600 means that the standard trustees' Capital Gains Tax annual exemption is £5,300 (which will be reduced if the anti-fragmentation provisions at TCGA 1992 Sch 1 para 1(3) apply).

The second change is with respect to the default TCGA 1992 s 3 indexation mechanism which sets the Capital Gains Tax annual exempt amount where Parliament has not determined otherwise for the tax year. The current s 3(3) and s 3(4) are replaced by a new sub-ss 3(3), 3(3A), 3(3B) and 3(4). This was felt necessary as there was some concern that the wording of the current sub-section was not sufficiently clear where there is zero or negative inflation (as was the case in the twelve months to September 2009). The revised wording makes it clear that if inflation is zero or negative the annual exempt amount for the previous year is carried forward automatically.

In summary new sub-s 3 provides that:

- there is only an increase to the annual exempt amount where there is a relevant increase in the retail price index (RPI) in relation to the relevant tax year;
- where there is an increase, unless Parliament determines otherwise:
  - the two step process in sub-s 3B should be followed; and
  - the annual exempt amount determined should for that and subsequent years be taken to override the £10,600 amount at TCGA 1992 s 3(2).

New sub-s 3A establishes when there will be a "relevant increase in the retail price index in relation to the relevant tax year". It states that in determining whether there is a relevant increase for a tax year one looks to see whether the retail price index for the September before the start of the relevant tax year is higher than it was for the previous September.

The two step process in new sub-s 3B is in line with the pre FA 2011 legislation (though, as discussed below, we know that there will be a major change in Finance Bill 2012). The relevant steps being:

1 Calculate the RPI increase (that is the increase when comparing the RPI figure for the September before the relevant tax year to the figure for the previous September) and apply that to the exempt amount specified at TCGA 1992 s 3(2).
2 Round the result up to the nearest multiple of £100.

The new sub-s 4 inserted into TCGA 1992 s 3 is different. The pre FA 2011 sub-s 4 provides that where the TCG 1992 s 3 provisions establishes what the annual exempt amount is (as opposed to it being fixed by Parliament) the Treasury must make an order, prior to the start of the relevant tax year, specifying the annual exempt amount so determined. The new sub-section 4 relaxes this requirement so that a Treasury order is only necessary where there has been a relevant increase in RPI. This means that from 2012/13 no Treasury order will be required where (i) the TCGA 1992 s 3 default annual exempt amount computation provisions apply; and (ii) as a result of there being no RPI increase (that is either the two September RPI amounts compared are the same or there has been a decrease in the RPI figure), the annual exempt amount from the previous tax year is carried forward.

It was announced in the 2011 Budget and confirmed in the Finance Bill Committee debates that from April 2012 there will be a move from calculating inflationary increases in line with the retail price index to using the consumer price index. As such TCGA 1992 s 3 will have to be amended again in Finance Act 2012. As was confirmed in the Finance Bill Committee exchanges the consumer price index is generally lower than the retail price index so (unless overridden by Parliament) the anticipated change will result in lower ongoing increases in the annual exempt amount.

9 Entrepreneurs' relief

(1) In section 169N of TCGA 1992 (amount of relief: general)—

(a) in subsection (4) for "£5 million" substitute "£10 million", and

(b) in subsection (4A) for "£5 million" substitute "£10 million".

(2) The amendments made by this section have effect in relation to qualifying business disposals occurring on or after 6 April 2011.

GENERAL NOTE

Entrepreneurs' Relief (ER) was enacted by FA 2008 Sch 3. The main provisions were inserted as TCGA 1992 ss 169H–169S, with the incidental, commencement and transitional provisions contained in FA 2008 Sch 3 paras 3–8.

For a valid ER claim to be made there must have been a 'qualifying business disposal'. The legislation (TCGA 1992 s 169H(2)) sets down three main categories of qualifying disposal:

1 A material disposal of business assets (TCGA 1992 s 169I).
2 A disposal of trust business assets (TCGA 1992 s 169J).
3 A disposal associated with a relevant material disposal (TCGA 1992 s 169K).

Where a valid ER claim is made, provided the qualifying gain does not exceed the available lifetime ER allowance, for disposals effected on or after 23 June 2010 ER relief is provided by taxing the ER gain at a special 10% rate of tax. Where there is insufficient available ER lifetime allowance to cover the entire gain the gain is split with the excess amount being subject to tax at the individual's marginal Capital Gains Tax rate (as illustrated in the example below).

FA 2011 s 9 increases the ER lifetime limit to £10 million for disposals occurring on or after 6 April 2011. As the table below shows this is the third increase to the ER lifetime limit in the last four Finance Acts.

Disposal Period	*ER lifetime limit*
Prior to 6 April 2010	£1 million
From 6 April 2010 to 22 June 2010	£2 million
From 23 June 2011 to 5 April 2011	£5 million
From 6 April 2011	£10 million

In very simple terms with effect from 6 April 2011 relief can be claimed on a further £5 million of qualifying business gains:

— Where the lifetime allowance had been entirely utilised prior to that date the individual in effect has a further £5 million of allowance.

— Where the individual has surplus lifetime allowance immediately prior to 6 April 2011 this amount will be increased by £5 million.

Miss Fruit claimed ER relief on the following qualifying business disposals:

Date	*Disposal*	*ER gain*
14 July 2009	Shares in her personal company Banana Ltd	£750,000
17 May 2010	Shares in her personal company Blueberry Ltd	£2 million
25 February 2011	Shares in her personal company Watermelon Ltd	£2.5 million
27 August 2011	Shares in her personal company Strawberry Ltd	£7.5 million

2009/10 disposal

The £750,000 ER gain realised in 2009/10 is within the £1 million lifetime allowance. Full ER relief would be due such that the effective rate of tax on the gain would be 10% (at this time the mechanism for relief was a 4/9 reduction in the gain which when combined with a fixed 18% tax rate resulted in an effective 10% tax rate on the full ER gain).

2010/11 – disposal 1

The £2 million ER gain in 2010/11 has to be added to the 2009/10 gain so as to test the aggregate ER gains amount against the lifetime allowance. This gives an aggregate ER gains amount of £2,750,000 and a lifetime allowance at the time of £2 million. As such £750,000 is not covered by the lifetime allowance. £1,250,000 of the gain is covered by ER relief (so an effective rate of tax of 10%) and £750,000 is not (so a fixed rate of tax of 18%).

2010/11 – disposal 2

The £2.5 million ER gain in 2010/11 has to be added to the prior aggregate amount with respect to which ER was given so as to test the aggregate ER gains amount against the lifetime allowance. This gives an aggregate ER gains amount of £4.5 million (the maximum £2 million as at 22 June 2010 plus the current £2.5 million gain) and a lifetime allowance at the time of £5 million. The entire gain is within the ER lifetime allowance so the £2.5 million is taxed at the special 10% ER rate.

2011/12 disposal

The £7.5 million ER gain in 2011/12 has to be added to the prior aggregate amount with respect to which ER was given so as to test the aggregate ER gains amount against the lifetime allowance. This gives an aggregate ER gains amount of £12 million (the maximum £2 million as at 22 June 2010 plus the 2010/11 post 22 June

£2.5 million and the £7.5 million current year gain)) and a lifetime allowance of £10 million. Only £5.5 million of the £7.5 million gain can be covered by ER relief. As such £5.5 million will be subject to tax at the special ER rate of 10% with the excess £2 million being taxed at 28%.

Tax rate changes and optimising relief through tax efficient claims

Note that Miss Fruit's policy of making an ER claim for all qualifying disposals is not optimal in terms of tax efficiency. ER does not have to be claimed just because the qualifying conditions are met. This means that she did not have to claim ER on the £750,000 disposal effected in 2009/10 and the £2 million disposal effected on 17 May 2010 claim. If she had not claimed relief those gains would have been subject to tax in full at the fixed 18% rate prevailing at the time of the disposal (£750,000 of the £2 million gain was anyway as it was not covered by the lifetime allowance).

Assuming these two earlier claims were not made her ER aggregate claim amount would have only been £2.5 million immediately prior to 2011/12. This would have meant that in 2011/12 she would have been able to claim the special 10% ER rate on the entire £7.5 gain rather than having to pay tax at 28% on £2 million of that gain. Overall, therefore, not making the claims for the first two qualifying ER gains will reduce the tax liability as the ER claim saves tax at 18% in 2011/12 as opposed to a saving of only 8% (the saving if ER had been claimed on the first two qualifying gains).

Capital allowances

10 Plant and machinery writing-down allowances

(1) Part 2 of CAA 2001 (plant and machinery allowances) is amended as follows.

(2) In section 56 (amount of allowances and charges), in subsection (1) for "20%" substitute "18%".

(3) In section 104D (writing-down allowances: special rate expenditure)—

(a) in subsection (1) for "10%" substitute "8%", and
(b) after that subsection insert—

"(1A) But, in relation to special rate expenditure incurred wholly for the purposes of a ring fence trade in respect of which tax is chargeable under section 330(1) of CTA 2010 (supplementary charge in respect of ring fence trades), the amount of the writing-down allowance to which a person is entitled for a chargeable period is 10% of the amount by which AQE exceeds TDR."

(4) Accordingly—

(a) in the heading for section 104D, after "**at**" insert "**8% or**", and
(b) in sections 56(2)(a) and 104E(1)(a), before "10%" insert "8% or".

(5) Part 10 of Schedule 22 to FA 2000 (companies within tonnage tax: capital allowances in respect of ship leasing), as it has effect (by virtue of section 57(9) of this Act) in relation to expenditure incurred before 1 January 2011, is amended as follows.

(6) In each of the following provisions, for "20%" (in each place) substitute "18%"—

(a) paragraph 94(3)(a) and (4),
(b) paragraph 95(4),
(c) paragraph 97(2) and (3),
(d) paragraph 98(8), and
(e) paragraph 99(2) and (5).

(7) In each of the following provisions, for "10%" substitute "8%"—

(a) paragraph 94(3)(b) and (4),
(b) paragraph 95(4),
(c) paragraph 97(2), (3) and (4),
(d) paragraph 98(8), and
(e) paragraph 99(2).

(8) The amendments made by this section have effect in relation to—

(a) chargeable periods beginning on or after the relevant day, and
(b) chargeable periods beginning before, and ending on or after, the relevant day.

(9) But in respect of a chargeable period within subsection (8)(b), they have effect as if—

(a) in section 56(1) of CAA 2001 and the provisions of Schedule 22 to FA 2000 mentioned in subsection (6), references to 18% were references to X%, and

(b) in section 104D(1) of CAA 2001 and the provisions of Schedule 22 to FA 2000 mentioned in subsection (7), references to 8% were references to Y%.

(10) For the purposes of subsection (9)—

X=(20× (BRD / CP))+(18 × (ARD / CP))

Y=(10× (BRD / CP))+(8 × (ARD / CP))

(11) Where X or Y would be a figure with more than 2 decimal places, it is to be rounded up to the nearest second decimal place.

(12) In subsection (10)—

BRD is the number of days in the chargeable period before the relevant day,
ARD is the number of days in the chargeable period on and after the relevant day, and
CP is the number of days in the chargeable period.

(13) The relevant day is—

(a) for corporation tax purposes, 1 April 2012, and
(b) for income tax purposes, 6 April 2012.

GENERAL NOTE

Section 10 amends CAA 2001 s 56 and provides for the main rate of writing-down allowance on plant and machinery to reduce from 20 per cent per annum to 18 per cent per annum.

It additionally amends s 104D to provide for the rate of writing-down allowance on 'special rate expenditure' (including integral features) to reduce from 10 per cent per annum to 8 per cent per annum.

In each case, the change takes effect for accounting periods ending on or after 6 April 2012 (income tax) or 1 April 2012 (corporation tax).

The change does not affect expenditure incurred by ring fence trades (ie, those within the definition of 'oil-related activities') taxable under CTA s 330.

Where an accounting period overlaps the date of the change, the rate of allowance will be a hybrid rate (rounded up to the nearest second decimal place), calculated as a time-apportioned rate, based on the number of days in the accounting period falling after the date of the change, and the number of days in the accounting period falling before that date.

ABC Limited makes up accounts for the year to 30 September 2012. For that year, the rate of writing down allowance will be 19 per cent (183/366 x 20 per cent plus 183/366 x 18 per cent).

11 Annual investment allowance

(1) Section 51A of CAA 2001 (entitlement to annual investment allowance) is amended as follows.

(2) In subsection (5) (maximum allowance), for "£100,000" substitute "£25,000".

(3) In subsection (8) (power to amend maximum allowance), for "other" substitute "greater".

(4) The amendment made by subsection (2) has effect in relation to expenditure incurred on or after the relevant day.

(5) Subsections (6) and (7) apply in relation to a chargeable period ("the actual chargeable period") which—

(a) begins before the relevant day, and
(b) ends on or after that day.

(6) The maximum allowance under section 51A of CAA 2001 for the actual chargeable period is the sum of each maximum allowance that would be found if—

(a) the period beginning with the first day of the chargeable period and ending with the day before the relevant day, and
(b) the period beginning with the relevant day and ending with the last day of the chargeable period,

were treated as separate chargeable periods.

(7) But, so far as concerns expenditure incurred on or after the relevant day, the maximum allowance under section 51A of CAA 2001 for the actual chargeable period is the maximum allowance, calculated in accordance with subsection (6), for the period mentioned in paragraph (b) of that subsection.

(8) Subsections (6) and (7) are also to apply for the purpose of determining the maximum allowance under section 51K of CAA 2001 (operation of annual investment allowance where restrictions apply) in a case where one or more chargeable periods in which the relevant AIA qualifying expenditure is incurred are chargeable periods within subsection (5), but the modifications in subsections (9) to (11) are to apply.

(9) There is to be taken into account for the purpose mentioned in subsection (8) only chargeable periods of one year or less (whether or not they are chargeable periods within subsection (5)), and if there is more than one such period, only that period which gives rise to the greatest maximum allowance.

(10) For the purposes of subsection (9) any chargeable period—

(a) which is longer than a year, and
(b) which ends in the tax year 2012–13,

is to be treated as being a chargeable period of one year ending at the same time as it actually ends.

(11) The limit in section 51K(6) of CAA 2001 in relation to a chargeable period ("the chargeable period concerned") is to be treated as reduced (but not below nil) by the amount of the annual investment allowance allocated to relevant AIA qualifying expenditure incurred in any other chargeable period which ends on or after the last day of the chargeable period concerned.

(12) Nothing in subsections (8) to (11) affects the operation of sections 51M and 51N of that Act.

(13) In this section "the relevant day" means—

(a) for corporation tax purposes, 1 April 2012, and
(b) for income tax purposes, 6 April 2012.

GENERAL NOTE

Expenditure on most types of plant and machinery has, since 6 April 2008 (income tax) or 1 April 2008 (corporation tax) qualified for an annual investment allowance ('AIA') to an annual maximum of £50,000. With effect from 6 April 2010 (income tax) or 1 April 2010 (corporation tax), the maximum AIA was increased to £100,000.

Section 11 provides legislation to reduce the amount of the entitlement to annual investment allowance (AIA) from £100,000 to £25,000. The reduction is effective for expenditure incurred on or after 1 April 2012 for persons within the charge to corporation tax and on or after 6 April 2012 for persons within the charge to income tax.

For a chargeable period straddling the relevant date, the maximum AIA is effectively time-apportioned, by considering how much of the chargeable period falls before the relevant date, and how much after (s 11(6)).

However, so far as concerns expenditure actually incurred after the relevant date, the maximum is restricted to the time-apportioned amount of the AIA relating to the part of the chargeable period falling after the change (s 11(7)).

A company with a calendar year chargeable period from 1 January 2012 to 31 December 2012 would calculate its maximum AIA entitlement based on:

(a) the proportion of a year from 1 January 2012 to 31 March 2012, that is, 91/366 x £100,000 = £24,863; and
(b) the proportion of a year from 1 April 2012 to 31 December 2012, that is 275/366 x £25,000 = £18,784.

The company's maximum AIA for this transitional chargeable period would therefore be the total of (a) + (b) = £24,863 + £18,784 = £43,647.

However, the restriction in s11(7) would then apply to expenditure incurred after 31 March 2012 – if £10,000 was incurred before that date, and £30,000 thereafter, the maximum AIA would be £28,784:

(a) £18,784 for the 'later' expenditure (limited as above), plus
(b) £10,000 for the 'early' expenditure.

It is not possible to claim the full £43,647 AIA because of the restriction imposed by s 11(7) and the fact that there is insufficient expenditure pre-31 March 2012. If the expenditure incurred after the relevant date had been £10,000 rather than £30,000, and the expenditure before that date had been £300,000 rather than £10,000, the AIA would be the full permitted £43,647, effectively:

(a) £10,000 for the 'later' expenditure plus

(b) £33,647 (the balance up to the £43,647 maximum) for the 'earlier' expenditure.

This calculation merely establishes the maximum AIA–there is no requirement to calculate separate 'pre' and 'post' AIAs and allocate each to the relevant expenditure. Consequently the apparent anomaly in the above example, where an 'early' AIA of £33,647 is calculated, even though only £30,000 was incurred in the 'early' period, is perfectly possible.

In certain circumstances, the AIA is to be shared between related businesses, i e those under common control. Subsection 11 ensures that where more than two businesses with different chargeable periods share an AIA, the maximum AIA that a business can claim is reduced (but not below nil) by any amounts allocated to another business or businesses with the same or later (ending) chargeable period(s).

If four companies in a company group with different chargeable periods ending in the financial year 2012—2013 were required to share a single AIA their individual maximum amounts might look like this:

Company	CP ending on	Maximum time-apportioned AIA £
A	30 April 2012	93,750
B	31 December 2012	43,750
C	31 March 2013	25,000
D	31 March 2013	25,000

The rule in sub-s (9) provides that the absolute maximum AIA that the companies can share is £93,750. However, sub-s (11) provides that companies C & D cannot each claim £25,000 AIA and if between them companies C & D did claim amounts totalling £25,000 then companies A & B's maximum claim would be reduced by £25,000. Similarly if company B did claim the reduced maximum of £18,750 following claim(s) by companies C & D, then company A could only claim the reduced balance of £50,100.

Subsection 3 restricts HM Treasury's power to amend the amount of the maximum AIA by way of secondary legislation to a power to increase the maximum amount (s 11(3)).

12 Short-life assets

(1) Part 2 of CAA 2001 (plant and machinery allowances) is amended as follows.

(2) In section 86 (short-life asset pool)—

(a) in subsection (2), for "four-year" (in each place) substitute "relevant",

(b) for subsection (3) substitute—

"(3) In this Chapter "the relevant cut-off" means—

(a) if any of the qualifying expenditure incurred on the provision of the short-life asset was incurred before the designated day, the fourth anniversary of the end of the relevant chargeable period, and

(b) in any other case, the eighth anniversary of the end of the relevant chargeable period.

(3A) In subsection (3)—

"the designated day" means—

(a) for corporation tax purposes, 1 April 2011, and

(b) for income tax purposes, 6 April 2011;

"the relevant chargeable period" means—

(a) the chargeable period in which the qualifying expenditure was incurred on the provision of the short-life asset, or

(b) if the qualifying expenditure was incurred in different chargeable periods, the first chargeable period in which any of the qualifying expenditure was incurred.", and

(c) in subsection (4), for "four-year" substitute "relevant".

(3) In section 65 (the final chargeable period), in subsection (3), for "four-year" substitute "relevant".

(4) In section 87 (short-life assets provided for leasing), in subsection (1)—

(a) in paragraph (b), for "four-year" substitute "relevant", and
(b) in paragraph (c), for "4 years" substitute "8 years".

(5) In section 89 (disposal to connected person), in subsections (1) and (5), for "four-year" (in each place) substitute "relevant".

(6) In Schedule 1 (defined expressions)—

(a) at the appropriate place insert—

"relevant cut-off (in Chapter 9 of Part 2)   section 86(3)",

and

(b) omit the entry for "four-year cut-off (in Chapter 9 of Part 2)".

GENERAL NOTE

Since 1985, it has been possible to elect for 'short life asset' ('SLA') treatment for most items of plant and machinery. The intention is to enable tax allowances to be brought into line with the actual depreciation of plant or machinery when an item is scrapped or sold within a specified cut-off period from its acquisition. The term 'short life' is something of a misnomer – it would be more accurate to refer to a 'short period of ownership'.

The current cut-off point is four years from the end of the chargeable period in which the asset is acquired. This is now being extended by s 12 to eight years from the end of that chargeable period. The change takes effect for expenditure incurred on or after 1 April 2011 (corporation tax) or 6 April 2011 (income tax).

A business investing in plant or machinery (subject to certain exceptions, see below) can elect for SLA treatment. The expenditure is then allocated to a 'single asset pool'. Writing-down allowances are given on the reducing balance each year, currently at 20 per cent (set to reduce to 18 per cent from April 2012). If the item is scrapped or sold within the cut-off period, the remaining balance of expenditure in the pool is compared with the disposal proceeds. A further allowance, or charge, is made for the difference. According to HM Treasury Explanatory Notes, 'this ensures that allowances given to this point match the actual net cost to the business of the SLA'.

One should note, however, that CAA 2001 s 84 precludes short life treatment for a range of assets, including, notably, integral features and plant and machinery provided for leasing (which includes fixtures in a let property).

ABC Limited acquires a property and immediately scraps the existing heating system. An election for short life asset treatment is not possible, even though the asset has been owned only briefly, because the heating system is an integral feature. Tax relief on the heating system will be obtained only over many years, long after the asset has been disposed of.

HM Treasury's claim that 'this ensures that allowances given match the actual net cost to the business of the SLA' is largely misleading so far as landlords and property owners are concerned.

Alcohol duties

13 Rates of alcoholic liquor duties

(1) ALDA 1979 is amended as follows.

(2) In section 5 (rate of duty on spirits), for "£23.80" substitute "£25.52".

(3) In section 36(1AA)(a) (standard rate of duty on beer), for "£17.32" substitute "£18.57".

(4) In section 62(1A) (rates of duty on cider)—

(a) in paragraph (a) (rate of duty per hectolitre in the case of sparkling cider of a strength exceeding 5.5 per cent), for "£217.83" substitute "£233.55",
(b) in paragraph (b) (rate of duty per hectolitre in the case of cider of a strength exceeding 7.5 per cent which is not sparkling cider), for "£50.22" substitute "£53.84", and
(c) in paragraph (c) (rate of duty per hectolitre in any other case), for "£33.46" substitute "£35.87".

(5) For the table in Schedule 1 substitute—

"TABLE OF RATES OF DUTY ON WINE AND MADE-WINE

"PART 1
WINE OR MADE-WINE OF A STRENGTH NOT EXCEEDING 22 PER CENT

Description of wine or made-wine	*Rates of duty per hectolitre £*
Wine or made-wine of a strength not exceeding 4 per cent	74.32
Wine or made-wine of a strength exceeding 4 per cent but not exceeding 5.5 per cent	102.21
Wine or made-wine of a strength exceeding 5.5 per cent but not exceeding 15 per cent and not being sparkling	241.23
Sparkling wine or sparkling made-wine of a strength exceeding 5.5 per cent but less than 8.5 per cent	233.55
Sparkling wine or sparkling made-wine of a strength of 8.5 per cent or of a strength exceeding 8.5 per cent but not exceeding 15 per cent	308.99
Wine or made-wine of a strength exceeding 15 per cent but not exceeding 22 per cent	321.61

PART 2
WINE OR MADE-WINE OF A STRENGTH EXCEEDING 22 PER CENT

Description of wine or made-wine	*Rates of duty per litre of alcohol in wine or made-wine £*
Wine or made-wine of a strength exceeding 22 per cent	25.52".

(6) The amendments made by this section are treated as having come into force on 28 March 2011.

GENERAL NOTE

The rates of excise duty under ALDA 1979 on all types of alcoholic liquor are increased by 7.2 per cent (2 per cent above the relevant rate of inflation) with effect from 28 March 2011.

The rate of duty on spirits is set at £25.52 per litre of alcohol.

The standard rate of duty on beer is set at £18.57 per hectolitre per cent of alcohol.

The rate of duty on sparkling cider of a strength exceeding 5.5 per cent of alcohol by volume is set at £233.55 per hectolitre.

The rate of duty on cider that is not sparkling cider and is of a strength exceeding 7.5 per cent of alcohol by volume is set at £53.84 per hectolitre.

The rate of duty on all other ciders is set at £35.87 per hectolitre.

The rates of duty on wine or made-wine are as set out in the Tables.

14 General beer duty: reduced rate for lower strength beer

(1) Part 3 of ALDA 1979 (beer) is amended as follows.

(2) In section 36 (general beer duty), in subsection (1AA) (rates of duty)—

(a) before paragraph (a) insert—

"(za) in the case of beer that is of a strength which exceeds 1.2 per cent but does not exceed 2.8 per cent, £9.29 per hectolitre per cent of alcohol in the beer;",

(b) in paragraph (a), after "that" insert "is of a strength which exceeds 2.8 per cent and",

(c) in paragraph (b), after "small brewery beer" insert "that is of a strength which exceeds 2.8 per cent and is", and

(d) in paragraph (c), after "small brewery beer" insert "that is of a strength which exceeds 2.8 per cent and is".

(3) For the italic heading immediately preceding section 36A substitute "*Beer from small breweries*".

(4) In section 36D (rate of general beer duty for small brewery beer from singleton breweries)—

(a) in subsection (2), after "section" insert ", unless the beer is within section 36(1AA)(za) (rate for lower strength beer)", and

(b) in the heading after "**beer**" insert "**(other than lower strength beer)**".

(5) In section 36F (rate of general beer duty for small brewery beer from co-operated breweries)—

(a) in subsection (2), after "section" insert ", unless the beer is within section 36(1AA)(za) (rate for lower strength beer)", and

(b) in the heading after "**beer**" insert "**(other than lower strength beer)**".

(6) Immediately above section 36H (power to vary reduced rate provisions) insert as an italic heading "*Power to vary rates*".

(7) The amendments made by this section come into force on 1 October 2011.

GENERAL NOTE

A new reduced rate of duty on 'lower-strength beer', under new ALDA 1979 s 36(1AA)(za), is to be charged at a rate of £9.29 per hectolitre per cent of alcohol content (c.f. the standard rate of beer duty, set at £18.57 per hectolitre per cent of alcohol content by s 13). The new rate is to apply equally to lower-strength beer from small breweries, and the reduced rates applicable to small-brewery beer under ALDA 1979 ss 36A–36H are accordingly not to apply to lower-strength beer. Lower-strength beer is defined as beer that exceeds 1.2 per cent but does not exceed 2.8 per cent of alcohol by volume, and the new rate has effect from 1 October 2011.

15 New high strength beer duty

(1) Schedule 1 contains provision for and in connection with a duty of excise on high strength beer.

(2) The Commissioners for Her Majesty's Revenue and Customs are responsible for the collection and management of that duty.

GENERAL NOTE

A new, additional rate of excise duty on 'high-strength beer' is to be charged under ALDA 1979 s 37, as inserted by Schedule 1 para 1, with effect from 1 October 2011.

Excise duty, to be known as 'high-strength beer duty' is to be charged on high-strength beer imported into or produced in the United Kingdom after 30 September 2011. The rate of the duty is £4.64 per hectolitre per cent of alcohol content. The duty is to be charged and paid and the amount payable determined and becomes due under the Beer Regulations 1993 (SI 1993/1228). ALDA 1979 s 36, which is the general charging section for excise duty on beer, is amended so that it charges 'general beer duty'. Beer that is subject to high-strength beer duty is also subject to general beer duty. Consequential amendments are made to other provisions of ALDA 1979.

Tobacco duties

16 Rates of tobacco products duty

(1) For the table in Schedule 1 to TPDA 1979 substitute—

"TABLE

1Cigarettes	An amount equal to 16.5 per cent of the retail price plus £154.95 per thousand cigarettes
2Cigars	£193.29 per kilogram
3Hand-rolling tobacco	£151.90 per kilogram
4Other smoking tobacco and chewing tobacco	£84.98 per kilogram".

(2) The amendment made by this section is treated as having come into force at 6 pm on 23 March 2011.

GENERAL NOTE

Section 16 increases the rates of excise duty on tobacco products (cigarettes, cigars, hand-rolling tobacco, other smoking tobacco and chewing tobacco) with effect from 6 pm on 23 March 2011.

Subsection (1) substitutes a new table of rates of duty into TPDA Sch 1. The duty rates on tobacco products are changed as follows:

1 Cigarettes – the ad valorem element is reduced from 24 per cent to 16.5 per cent; the specific duty is increased from £119.03 to £154.95 per 1000 cigarettes;
2 Cigars – increased from £180.28 to £193.29 per kilogram;
3 Hand-rolling tobacco – increased from £129.59 to £151.90 per kilogram; and
4 Other smoking tobacco and chewing tobacco – increased from £79.26 to £84.98 per kilogram.

Subsection (2) provides for the new table of duty rates to have effect from 6pm on 23 March 2011.

Section 16 increases excise duty on all tobacco products by at least 2 per cent in real terms, thereby helping to provide a further deterrent to smoking, as well as maintaining a contribution to government revenues. This is in accordance with the March 2010 announcement of increases of two per cent above retail price inflation in 2011 for all tobacco duty rates.

The composition of excise duty on cigarettes has been adjusted so that a greater proportion of the tax is based on the quantity and a smaller proportion on the recommended price. This will support health objectives by targeting the duty increase on cheaper cigarettes.

A further increase of 10 per cent in duty on hand rolling tobacco will reduce the difference between the duty on hand-rolling tobacco and cigarettes, thereby supporting health objectives.

The duty increase, together with consequential VAT, will on average increase the price of a packet of 20 economy cigarettes by 50p, a packet of 20 premium cigarettes by 33p, a pack of 5 small cigars by 10p, a 25 gram pack of hand-rolling tobacco by 67p; and a 25 gram pack of pipe tobacco by 17p.

Gambling duties

17 Rates of gaming duty

(1) In section 11(2) of FA 1997 (rates of gaming duty), for the table substitute—

"TABLE	
Part of gross gaming yield	*Rate*
The first £2,067,000	15 per cent
The next £1,425,000	20 per cent
The next £2,496,000	30 per cent

The next £5,268,000	40 per cent
The remainder	50 per cent".

(2) The amendment made by this section has effect in relation to accounting periods beginning on or after 1 April 2011.

GENERAL NOTE

Section 17 increases the gross gaming yield (GGY) bands for gaming duty in line with inflation for accounting periods starting on or after 1 April 2011.

Subsection (1) substitutes a new table for the existing table in FA 1997 s 11(2).

Subsection (2) provides for this change to have effect for accounting periods beginning on or after 1 April 2011.

Gaming duty is charged on any premises in the UK where dutiable gaming takes place (FA 1997 s 11(1)). Dutiable gaming includes the playing of casino games such as roulette, baccarat, and blackjack (FA 1997 s 15). The amount of duty is calculated by reference to bands of gross gaming yield (ie . gross profits) for that accounting period (FA 1997 s 11). Duty is paid at a rate of 15 per cent on the first £2,067,000 of GGY, then 20 per cent for the next £1,425,000 of GGY, and so on. Gaming duty is charged on premises in respect of accounting periods of six months, normally beginning on 1 April and 1 October, with an interim payment after three months (FA 1997 ss 11 & 15 and Sch 1).

Section 17 increases the GGY bands but does not increase the rates. The basis of revalorisation of the bands is the Retail Price Index change for the year ended 31 December 2010 which was calculated at 4.66 per cent.

18 Amusement machine licence duty

(1) In section 23(2) of BGDA 1981 (amount of duty payable on amusement machine licence), for the table substitute—

"TABLE						
Months for which licence granted	*Category A* £	*Category B1* £	*Category B2* £	*Category B3* £	*Category B4* £	*Category C* £
1	535	270	215	215	195	85
2	1070	535	425	425	385	160
3	1605	805	635	635	575	240
4	2140	1070	845	845	765	320
5	2675	1340	1055	1055	960	400
6	3210	1605	1265	1265	1150	480
7	3745	1875	1475	1475	1340	555
8	4280	2140	1685	1685	1530	635
9	4815	2410	1895	1895	1725	715
10	5350	2675	2105	2105	1915	795

11	5885	2945	2315	2315	2105	875
12	6110	3055	2405	2405	2185	905".

(2) The amendment made by this section has effect in relation to cases where the application for the amusement machine licence is received by the Commissioners for Her Majesty's Revenue and Customs after 4 pm on 25 March 2011.

GENERAL NOTE

Section 18 increases the amounts of amusement machine licence duty (AMLD) payable in respect of licence applications that are received by HMRC after 4pm on 25 March 2011.

Subsection (1) substitutes a new table for the existing table of amounts of AMLD in BGDA s 23(2) thereby increasing the amount of duty payable on licences.

Subsection (2) provides that the increase in duty will have effect for any application for an amusement machine licence that is received by HMRC after 4pm on 25 March 2011.

AMLD is a duty of excise charged on a licence allowing gaming machines to be provided for play (BGDA s 22). Other than specific exemptions from the requirement for a licence (BGDA Sch 4 Part I) and certain specific classes of "excepted machines" (BGDA s 21(5)), all gaming machines fall within the scope of AMLD. The amount of duty that is payable is determined by the licence period, between one and 12 months, and the numbers and categories of machines (BGDA s 23). Machine categories are defined by reference to their maximum prize values and cost to play (BGDA s 23(3)).

The Government intends to replace AMLD with a new machine games duty (see s 90 paving provision below).

Fuel duties

19 Fuel duties: rates of duty and rebates from 23 March 2011

(1) HODA 1979 is amended as follows.

(2) In section 6(1A) (main rates)—

(a) in paragraph (a) (unleaded petrol), for "£0.5895" substitute "£0.5795",
(b) in paragraph (aa) (aviation gasoline), for "£0.3835" substitute "£0.3770",
(c) in paragraph (b) (light oil other than unleaded petrol or aviation gasoline), for "£0.6867" substitute "£0.6767", and
(d) in paragraph (c) (heavy oil), for "£0.5895" substitute "£0.5795".

(3) In section 8(3) (road fuel gas)—

(a) in paragraph (a) (natural road fuel gas), for "£0.2615" substitute "£0.2470", and
(b) in paragraph (b) (other road fuel gas), for "£0.3304" substitute "£0.3161".

(4) In section 11(1) (rebate on heavy oil)—

(a) in paragraph (a) (fuel oil), for "£0.1088" substitute "£0.1070", and
(b) in paragraph (b) (gas oil), for "£0.1133" substitute "£0.1114".

(5) In section 14(1) (rebate on light oil for use as furnace fuel), for "£0.1088" substitute "£0.1070".

(6) In section 14A(2) (rebate on certain biodiesel), for "£0.1133" substitute "£0.1114".

(7) The amendments made by this section are treated as having come into force at 6 pm on 23 March 2011.

GENERAL NOTE

Section 19 changes the rates of duty and the rates of rebate on products charged to duty under HODA. Duty rates on the main road fuels are decreased by 1 penny per litre (ppl) and effective rates of duty on non-road fuels are decreased by the same proportion. The duty rates on natural gas and road fuel other than natural gas are decreased to maintain the differential with the main road fuels. Duty on leaded petrol is decreased by 1 ppl and on aviation gasoline by 0.65 ppl. These changes came into effect from 6pm on 23 March 2011.

Subsection (2) amends the rates of duty on unleaded petrol, aviation gasoline, light oil other than unleaded petrol or aviation gasoline and heavy oil in HODA.

Subsection (3) amends the rate of duty on road fuel gases.

Subsections (4)–(6) amend the effective rate of duty on fuel oil, gas oil, light oil for use as furnace fuel and biodiesel for off-road use.

In the Budget 2011 the Government announced that the fuel duty escalator was being abolished and replaced with a fair fuel stabiliser. As part of the fair fuel stabiliser fuel duty will increase by RPI only when oil prices are high. However, if the oil price falls below a set trigger price on a sustainable basis, fuel duty will increase by RPI plus 1 ppl in each such year. The Government will set a final trigger price and mechanism after seeking views from oil and gas companies and motoring groups.

In the Budget 2011 the Government declared that it wanted to ease the burden on motorists at a time of record pump prices, and the Government announced that the 1 April 2011 increase would be deferred and implemented on 1 January 2012. Until then, duty on the main rates is being cut by 1 ppl.

The effect of ss 19 and 20 is set out in a table after s 20.

20 Fuel duties: rates of duty and rebates from 1 January 2012

(1) HODA 1979 is amended as follows.

(2) In section 6(1A) (main rates)—

(a) in paragraph (a) (unleaded petrol), for "£0.5795" substitute "£0.6097",
(b) in paragraph (aa) (aviation gasoline), for "£0.3770" substitute "£0.3966",
(c) in paragraph (b) (light oil other than unleaded petrol or aviation gasoline), for "£0.6767" substitute "£0.7069", and
(d) in paragraph (c) (heavy oil), for "£0.5795" substitute "£0.6097".

(3) In section 8(3) (road fuel gas)—

(a) in paragraph (a) (natural road fuel gas), for "£0.2470" substitute "£0.2907", and
(b) in paragraph (b) (other road fuel gas), for "£0.3161" substitute "£0.3734".

(4) In section 11(1) (rebate on heavy oil)—

(a) in paragraph (a) (fuel oil), for "£0.1070" substitute "£0.1126", and
(b) in paragraph (b) (gas oil), for "£0.1114" substitute "£0.1172".

(5) In section 14(1) (rebate on light oil for use as furnace fuel), for "£0.1070" substitute "£0.1126".

(6) In section 14A(2) (rebate on certain biodiesel), for "£0.1114" substitute "£0.1172".

(7) The amendments made by this section come into force on 1 January 2012.

GENERAL NOTE

Section 20 changes the rates of duty and the rates of rebate on products charged to duty under HODA. Duty rates on the main road fuels are increased by 3.02 pence per litre (ppl) and effective rates of duty on non-road fuels are increased by the same proportion. The duty on natural gas maintains the differential with the main road fuels, while the differential for road fuel gas other than natural gas is reduced by the equivalent of 1 ppl. Duty on leaded petrol is increased by 3.02 ppl and on aviation gasoline by 1.96ppl. These changes come into effect on 1 January 2012.

Subsection (2) amends the rates of duty on unleaded petrol, aviation gasoline, light oil other than unleaded petrol or aviation gasoline and heavy oil in HODA.

Subsection (3) amends the rate of duty on road fuel gases.

Subsections (4)–(6) amend the effective rate of duty on fuel oil, gas oil, light oil for use as furnace fuel and biodiesel for off-road use.

Table of Effect of Sections 19 & 20

Fuel duty–Pence per litre (unless stated)			
	Before 6pm 23 March 2011	After 6pm 23 March 2011	On and after 1 January 2012
Light oils			
Unleaded petrol	58.95	57.95	60.97

Light oil (other than unleaded petrol or aviation gasoline)	68.67	67.67	70.69
Aviation gasoline (Avgas)	38.35	37.70	39.66
Light oil delivered to an approved person for use as furnace fuel	10.88	10.70	11.26
Heavy oils			
Heavy oil (Diesel)	58.95	57.95	60.97
Marked gas oil	11.33	11.14	11.72
Fuel oil	10.88	10.70	11.26
Heavy oil other than fuel oil, gas oil or kerosene used as fuel	10.88	10.70	11.26
Kerosene to be used as motor fuel off road or in an excepted vehicle	11.33	11.14	11.72
Biofuels			
Bio-ethanol	58.95	57.95	60.97
Biodiesel	58.95	57.95	60.97
Biodiesel for non road use	11.33	11.14	11.72
Biodiesel blended with gas oil not for road fuel use for non road use	11.33	11.14	11.72
Road fuel gases			
Road fuel Natural gas including biogas	26.15/kg	24.70/kg	29.07/kg
Liquefied petroleum gas(LPG)	33.04/kg	31.61/kg	37.34/kg

Vehicle excise duty

21 VED rates for light passenger vehicles, light goods vehicles, motorcycles etc

(1) Schedule 1 to VERA 1994 (annual rates of duty) is amended as follows.

(2) In paragraph 1 (general)—

(a) in sub-paragraph (2) (vehicle not covered elsewhere in Schedule otherwise than with engine cylinder not exceeding 1,549cc), for "£205" substitute "£215", and
(b) in sub-paragraph (2A) (vehicle not covered elsewhere in Schedule with engine cylinder capacity not exceeding 1,549cc), for "£125" substitute "£130".

(3) In paragraph 1B (graduated rates of duty for light passenger vehicles)—

(a) for the tables substitute—

Table 1 Rates Payable on First Vehicle Licence for Vehicle			
CO_2 emissions figure		*Rate*	
(1)	*(2)*	*(3)*	*(4)*
Exceeding	*Not exceeding*	*Reduced rate*	*Standard rate*
g/km	*g/km*	£	£
130	140	105	115

140	150	120	130
150	165	155	165
165	175	255	265
175	185	305	315
185	200	435	445
200	225	570	580
225	255	780	790
255	—	990	1000

Table 2 Rates Payable on any other Vehicle Licence for Vehicle			
CO_2 emissions figure		Rate	
(1)	*(2)*	*(3)*	*(4)*
Exceeding	*Not exceeding*	*Reduced rate*	*Standard rate*
g/km	*g/km*	*£*	*£*
100	110	10	20
110	120	20	30
120	130	85	95
130	140	105	115
140	150	120	130
150	165	155	165
165	175	180	190
175	185	200	210
185	200	235	245
200	225	250	260
225	255	435	445
255	—	450	460";

(b) in the sentence immediately following the tables, for paragraphs (a) and (b) substitute—

"(a) in column (3), in the last two rows, "250" were substituted for "435" and "450", and

(b) in column (4), in the last two rows, "260" were substituted for "445" and "460"."

(4) In paragraph 1J (VED rates for light goods vehicles)—

(a) in paragraph (a), for "£200" substitute "£210", and
(b) in paragraph (b), for "£125" substitute "£130".

(5) In paragraph 2(1) (VED rates for motorcycles)—

(a) in paragraph (a), for "£15" substitute "£16",
(b) in paragraph (b), for "£33" substitute "£35",

(c) in paragraph (c), for "£50" substitute "£53", and
(d) in paragraph (d), for "£70" substitute "£74".

(6) The amendments made by this section have effect in relation to licences taken out on or after 1 April 2011.

GENERAL NOTE

The general rate of duty under VERA 1994 Sch 1 para 1 on vehicles taxed by engine size (generally those registered before February 2001) is increased by £10 to £215 for engine sizes above 1549 cc and by £5 to £130 in respect of smaller engines. The graduated rates of duty on light passenger vehicles under VERA 1994 Sch 1 para 1B Table 1 on the first licence are increased by between £5 (the lowest two bands) and £50 (the highest band). Rates on second and further licences (those in Table 2) are also generally increased, except for the lowest two bands. The rates for light goods vehicles in VERA 1994 Sch 1 para 1J are increased by £5. Smaller increases apply to the rates for motorcycles under VERA 1994 Sch 1 para 2(1).

Rates on heavy goods vehicles and buses are left unchanged.

The new rates have effect for licences taken out after 31 March 2011.

22 VED rates for certain goods vehicles without road-friendly suspension

(1) Part 8 of Schedule 1 to VERA 1994 (rates for goods vehicles) is amended as follows.

(2) In—

(a) paragraph 9(1) (rigid vehicles exceeding 3,500 kilograms revenue weight in case of which pollution requirements are not satisfied), and
(b) paragraph 9A(2) (rigid vehicles exceeding that weight in case of which pollution requirements are satisfied),

after "(3)" insert "and paragraph 11D".

(3) In—

(a) paragraph 11(1) (tractive units exceeding 3,500 kilograms revenue weight in case of which pollution requirements are not satisfied), and
(b) paragraph 11A(2) (tractive units exceeding that weight in case of which pollution requirements are satisfied),

for "paragraph 11C" substitute "paragraphs 11C and 11D".

(4) In paragraph 11C(2) (tractive units between 41,000 and 44,000 kilograms revenue weight, with 3 or more axles and used for conveyance of semi-trailers with 3 or more axles and usable on public road in accordance with law immediately before 21 March 2000), for "The" substitute "Subject to paragraph 11D, the".

(5) After paragraph 11C insert—

"Certain vehicles without road-friendly suspension

11D (1) This paragraph applies to goods vehicles which do not have road-friendly suspension.

(2) A goods vehicle does not have road-friendly suspension if any driving axle of the vehicle has neither—

(a) an air suspension (that is, a suspension system in which at least 75 per cent of the spring effect is caused by an air spring), nor
(b) a suspension which is regarded as being equivalent to an air suspension for the purposes under Annex II of Council Directive 96/53/EC.

(3) The annual rate of vehicle excise duty applicable to a rigid goods vehicle to which this paragraph applies and which has—

(a) a revenue weight of 15,000 kilograms, and
(b) two axles,

is £238.

(4) The annual rate of vehicle excise duty applicable to a rigid goods vehicle to which this paragraph applies and which—

(a) is a vehicle with respect to which the reduced pollution requirements are satisfied,
(b) has a revenue weight of 21,000 kilograms, and
(c) has three axles,

is £193.

(5) The annual rate of vehicle excise duty applicable to a rigid goods vehicle to which this paragraph applies and which—

(a) is a vehicle with respect to which the reduced pollution requirements are satisfied,

(b) has a revenue weight of not less than 23,000 kilograms but less than 26,000 kilograms, and

(c) has three axles,

is £299.

(6) The annual rate of vehicle excise duty applicable to a rigid goods vehicle to which this paragraph applies and which—

(a) is a vehicle with respect to which the reduced pollution requirements are satisfied,

(b) has a revenue weight of 27,000 kilograms, and

(c) has four or more axles,

is £314.

(7) The annual rate of vehicle excise duty applicable to a tractive unit to which this paragraph applies and which has two axles and either—

(a) has a revenue weight of 25,000 kilograms, or

(b) is a vehicle with respect to which the reduced pollution requirements are satisfied and has a revenue weight exceeding 25,000 kilograms but less than 28,000 kilograms,

is £266.

(8) The annual rate of vehicle excise duty applicable to a tractive unit to which this paragraph applies and which—

(a) has a revenue weight of 28,000 kilograms,

(b) has two axles, and

(c) is to draw semi-trailers with two or more axles,

is £177.

(9) The annual rate of vehicle excise duty applicable to a tractive unit to which this paragraph applies and which—

(a) is a vehicle with respect to which the reduced pollution requirements are satisfied,

(b) has a revenue weight of 31,000 kilograms,

(c) has two axles, and

(d) is to draw semi-trailers with two or more axles,

is £403.

(10) The annual rate of vehicle excise duty applicable to a tractive unit to which this paragraph applies and which—

(a) is a vehicle with respect to which the reduced pollution requirements are satisfied,

(b) has a revenue weight of 36,000 kilograms,

(c) has three axles, and

(d) is to draw semi-trailers with two or more axles,

is £394.

(11) The annual rate of vehicle excise duty applicable to a vehicle to which paragraph 11C and this paragraph apply and which—

(a) is a vehicle with respect to which the reduced pollution requirements are satisfied, and

(b) has a revenue weight less than 44,000 kilograms,

is £464.

(12) This paragraph does not apply to a vehicle for which the annual rate of duty is determined under paragraph 9(2) or 11(2)."

(6) The amendments made by this section have effect in relation to licences taken out on or after 1 April 2011.

GENERAL NOTE

Increased rates of duty under VERA 1994 are set for certain goods vehicles without 'road-friendly suspension', with effect for licences taken out after 31 March 2011.

A new VERA 1984 Sch 1 para 11D is inserted, to charge special rates of duty for goods vehicles with driving axles that have neither an air suspension nor a suspension that is considered to be equivalent to an air suspension under Annex II of Directive 96/53/EC laying down for certain road vehicles circulating within the Community the maximum authorised dimensions in national and international traffic and the maximum authorised weights in international traffic. Annex II prescribes conditions relating to equivalence between certain non-air suspension systems and air suspension for vehicle driving axles. Vehicles lacking such axles are referred to as not having 'road-friendly suspension'.

Nine rates of duty are charged in respect of these vehicles, depending on their revenue weight (as defined by VERA 1994 s 60A) and number of axles, on whether the vehicle is a rigid goods vehicle or a tractive unit, and on whether or not the reduced pollution requirements (for the grant of a reduced pollution certificate under the Road Vehicles (Registration and Licensing) Regulations 2002 (SI 2002/2742) Sch 2) are satisfied. The rates range from £177 to £464.

Environmental taxes

23 Rates of climate change levy

(1) In Schedule 6 to FA 2000 (climate change levy), for the table in paragraph 42(1) substitute—

"TABLE	
Taxable commodity supplied	*Rate at which levy payable if supply is not a reduced-rate supply*
Electricity	£0.00509 per kilowatt hour
Gas supplied by a gas utility or any gas supplied in a gaseous state that is of a kind supplied by a gas utility	£0.00177 per kilowatt hour
Any petroleum gas, or other gaseous hydrocarbon, supplied in a liquid state	£0.01137 per kilogram
Any other taxable commodity	£0.01387 per kilogram".

(2) The amendment made by this section has effect in relation to supplies treated as taking place on or after 1 April 2012.

GENERAL NOTE

Climate change levy (CCL) is a tax on the supply of certain energy products for business or public sector use. The rates of CCL increase in line with inflation for supplies treated as taking place from 1 April 2012.

From that date, the rate of CCL charged on the supply of electricity is increased from £0.00485 to £0.00509 per kilowatt hour. The rate of CCL on gas supplied by a gas utility, or any other gas in a gaseous state of a kind supplied by a gas utility, is increased from £0.00169 to £0.00177 per kilowatt hour. The rate of CCL charged on any petroleum gas or other gaseous hydrocarbon supplied in a liquid state is increased from £0.01083 per kilogram to £0.01137 per kilogram. The rate of CCL on any other taxable commodity is increased from £0.01321 to £0.01387 per kilogram (FA 2000 Sch 6 para 42(1) Table, as substituted by FA 2011 s 23(1)).

24 Rate of aggregates levy

(1) Section 16 of FA 2010 (increase in rate of aggregates levy from 1 April 2011) is repealed.

(2) Accordingly, the amendment made by section 20 of FA 2008 (increase in rate of aggregates levy from 1 April 2009) continues to have effect in relation to aggregate subjected to commercial exploitation on or after 1 April 2011.

(3) This section is treated as having come into force on 31 March 2011.

GENERAL NOTE

Aggregates levy is charged on virgin aggregates subjected to commercial exploitation. This tax was due to increase from £2 to £2.10 per tonne from 1 April 2011 (FA 2001 s 16(4)) as amended by FA 2010 s 15(1)). But Budget 2011 announced the intention to defer this increase until 1 April 2012.

25 Standard rate of landfill tax

(1) In section 42(1)(a) and (2) of FA 1996 (amount of landfill tax), for "£56" substitute "£64".

(2) The amendments made by this section have effect in relation to disposals made (or treated as made) on or after 1 April 2012.

GENERAL NOTE

Landfill tax is charged on the disposal of active and inactive waste material at authorised landfill sites, or on the use of material in certain specified activities at authorised landfill sites. The standard rate of tax applies to active material. Qualifying material (as specified by Treasury Order) attracts a lower rate of £2.50 per tonne.

The standard rate of landfill tax for disposals made or treated as made from 1 April 2012 has increased from £56 per tonne to £64 per tonne (FA 1996 ss 42(1)(a), (2) as amended by FA 2011 s 25(1)). The rate increased from £48 per tonne to £56 per tonne from 1 April 2011 by virtue of FA 2010 s 15(1). The Government's intention is to increase the standard rate by £8 per year up to and including 2014, when it will reach £80 per tonne. The lower rate will remain at £2.50 from 1 April 2012.

PART 2

INCOME TAX, CORPORATION TAX AND CAPITAL GAINS TAX

Anti-avoidance provisions

26 Employment income provided through third parties

Schedule 2 contains provision about steps which are taken in pursuance of, or which have some other connection with, arrangements concerned with the provision of rewards or recognition or loans in connection with current, former or prospective employments.

FGENERAL NOTE

This introduces Schedule 2, which is intended to tackle what the government calls disguised remuneration, i e . arrangements which seek to provide what is essentially employment income without triggering a PAYE and NIC charge.

27 Tainted charity donations

Schedule 3 contains provision about gifts and other disposals to charities and community amateur sports clubs.

GENERAL NOTE

Section 27 introduces Schedule 3

28 Amounts not fully recognised for accounting purposes

Schedule 4 contains amendments of Parts 5 and 7 of CTA 2009 (loan relationships and derivative contracts) relating to cases where amounts are not fully recognised for accounting purposes.

GENERAL NOTE

Section 28 introduces Schedule 4.

29 Loan relationships involving connected debtor and creditor

(1) In section 418 of CTA 2009 (loan relationships involving connected debtor and creditor where debits exceed credits), in subsection (2), after "creditor company" insert "or any company connected with it".

(2) In section 419 of that Act (section 418: supplementary), after subsection (6) insert—

"(6A) References in section 418 to a company bringing debits or credits into account under or for the purposes of this Part include bringing debits or credits into account under or for the purposes of this Part in determining the chargeable profits of the company (or in determining that there were no such profits) for the purposes of Chapter 4 of Part 17 of ICTA (controlled foreign companies)."

(3) The amendments made by this section have effect in relation to loan relationships to which a company is a party (or to which it is treated as a party under section 418(6A) of CTA 2009) on or after 6 December 2010.

(4) But amounts are to continue to be brought into account for the purposes of Part 5 of CTA 2009 disregarding those amendments if the amounts relate to a time before that day.

GENERAL NOTE

This section made changes to CTA 2009 ss 418–419. These sections were originally introduced to counteract arrangements that sought to exploit asymmetries in accounting treatment where convertible securities were issued between group companies. Broadly, these sections applied where the loan relationship debits that the debtor company recognised in its accounts in respect of the debtor relationship exceeded the credits that the creditor company recognised in respect of the corresponding creditor relationship. In such cases the creditor was required to recognise additional credits equal to the difference in computing its loan relationship profits.

These provisions were introduced by FA 2008 and were amended in FA 2009 and FA 2010. The amendments made by s 29 extended the scope of CTA 2009 s 418 so that it applied where a person connected with the holder of the security had rights to acquire, or could be required to acquire, shares in any company under the terms of the loan relationship. At the same time the amendments provided that the debits and credits that were to be taken into account for the purposes of CTA 2009 s 418 should include debits or credits that were taken into account in computing the chargeable profits of a CFC.

The amendments had effect for times on after 6 December 2010 up to Royal Assent of FA 2011 when CTA 2009 ss 418–419 were repealed by Sch 5 para 7.

30 Group mismatch schemes

Schedule 5 contains provision about group mismatch schemes.

GENERAL NOTE

Section 30 introduces Schedule 5.

31 Company ceasing to be member of group: availability of relief

(1) Section 179 of TCGA 1992 (company ceasing to be member of group: post-appointed day cases) is amended as follows.

(2) In subsection (2A)—

(a) for "Where" substitute "Subsection (2AA) applies where", and

(b) for paragraphs (c) and (d) and the words following those paragraphs substitute—

"(c) at the time company A ceases to be a member of the first group there is a connection between that group and the group of companies of which company A becomes a member on leaving the first group ("the second group"), and

(d) subsequently—

(i) company A ceases to be a member of the second group, or

(ii) (before sub-paragraph (i) applies) there ceases to be a connection between the two groups."

(3) After that subsection insert—

"(2AA) Where this subsection applies—

(a) in a case within subsection (2A)(d)(ii), for the purposes of this section (other than subsection (2A)) as it applies as respects the acquisition, company A and any associated company are to be treated as having ceased to be members of the second group at the time the connection between the two groups ceases,

(b) subsection (1) has effect in relation to company A's ceasing to be a member of the second group as if it had been the second group of which both companies had been members at the time of the acquisition, and

(c) subsection (2) may operate to prevent subsection (1) applying by virtue of paragraph (b), unless subsection (2AB) applies.

(2AB) This subsection applies if company A's ceasing to be a member of the first group at the same time as one or more associated companies forms part of arrangements the main purpose, or one of the main purposes, of which is the avoidance of a liability to corporation tax."

(4) In subsection (2B) for "if, at the time when company A ceases to be a member of the second group" substitute "at a particular time if, at that time,".

(5) The amendments made by this section have effect in relation to a company in any case in which the time of the company's ceasing to be a member of the first group is on or after 23 March 2011.

GENERAL NOTE

This is a new provision to bolster the anti-avoidance rules in respect of the degrouping charge. The target is the avoidance of corporation tax by a series of transactions within a group prior to a disposal intended to avoid a degrouping charge by use of the associated companies exception at TCGA 1992 s 179(2). The existing anti-avoidance rule imposes the degrouping charge if the relevant company ceases to be a member of another group of companies which is connected to the first group (using a control test for connection).

Under the new rules, the degrouping charge is imposed either if the company ceases to be a member of the connected group of companies or if the two groups cease to be connected. The associated companies exception can still apply to this subsequent degrouping charge unless the availability of this exception is part of arrangements the main purpose, or one of the main purposes, of which is the avoidance of a liability to corporation tax. In essence, therefore, the associated companies exception can only apply to a de-grouping charge under s 179(2A) if the availability of that exception was not a main purpose of the arrangements under which the de-grouping event has occurred.

32 Leasing businesses

Schedule 6 contains provision about leasing businesses carried on by companies alone or in partnership.

GENERAL NOTE

Section 32 introduces Schedule 6, which modifies the sale of lessor rules contained in CTA 2010 Part 9.

33 Long funding finance leases

(1) Chapter 6 of Part 2 of CAA 2001 (which includes provision about lessees under long funding leases) is amended as follows.

(2) In section 70C (long funding finance lease: amount of capital expenditure), after subsection (4) insert—

"(4A) But where the minimum lease payments include a relievable amount, the present value of that amount must be excluded in determining the commencement PVMLP.

(4B) An amount ("amount X") is a relievable amount if—

(a) an arrangement is in place under which all or part of any residual amount (as defined in section 70YE) is guaranteed by the lessee or a person connected with the lessee,

(b) amount X is within the minimum lease payments because of that arrangement (see subsection (1)(a) of that section), and

(c) it is reasonable to assume that, were amount X to be incurred under the arrangement, relief would be available as a result (beyond relief, by virtue of this section and section 70E, because amount X is within those minimum lease payments).

(4C) In deciding for the purposes of subsection (4B)(c) whether relief would be available as a result, no account is to be taken of—

(a) any part of the arrangement other than the part by virtue of which all or part of the residual amount is guaranteed, or

(b) any other arrangement connected with the arrangement or forming part of a set of arrangements that includes the arrangement."

(3) In section 70D (long funding finance lease: additional expenditure: allowances for lessee), after subsection (1) insert—

"(1A) Any increase attributable to a relievable amount is to be ignored for the purposes of subsection (1)(d).

(1B) Subsections (4B) and (4C) of section 70C apply (with any necessary modifications) for the purposes of this section as for the purposes of that section."

(4) In section 70E (disposal events and disposal values), in subsection (2C)(b), after "section 70YE)" insert "other than any relievable payment".

(5) In that section, after subsection (2D) insert—

"(2DA) A payment ("payment X") is a relievable payment if—

(a) an arrangement is in place under which all or part of any residual amount (as defined in section 70YE) is guaranteed by the lessee or a person connected with the lessee,

(b) payment X is within the minimum lease payments because of that arrangement (see subsection (1)(a) of that section), and

(c) it is reasonable to assume that relief would be available as a result of making payment X (beyond relief, by virtue of section 70C or 70D and this section, because payment X is within those minimum lease payments).

(2DB) For the purposes of subsection (2DA)(c)—

(a) "relief" has the meaning given in section 70C, and

(b) subsection (4C) of that section applies as it applies for the purposes of subsection (4B)(c) of that section."

(6) The amendments made by subsections (2) and (3) have effect in cases where the arrangement is entered into on or after 9 March 2011.

(7) The amendments made by subsections (4) and (5) have effect in relation to payments made on or after 9 March 2011 (regardless of when the arrangement was entered into).

GENERAL NOTE

This section targets a disclosed tax avoidance scheme which purports to give a lessee of plant or machinery tax relief of up to twice the actual cost. The new provision is intended to prevent relief being available for more than the actual amount of the expenditure incurred on plant and machinery.

Under the long funding finance lease rules, a guarantee that is given by the lessee (or a person connected with the lessee) of all or any part of the expected residual value of the leased asset at the end of the lease is included in the calculation of the lessee's capital expenditure. The disclosed scheme involved arrangements which claimed to have the effect not only of ensuring that the guaranteed amount was taken into account in calculating the lessee's capital expenditure for capital allowance purposes but also gave rise to tax relief when paid. The changes made by section 33 are intended to ensure that where arrangements are in place for a residual amount to be guaranteed by the lessee or a connected person, a payment is included in the minimum lease payments calculation as a consequence and it is reasonable to assume that relief would otherwise be available for the payment if it were made, the amount of that payment is excluded in calculating capital expenditure under CAA 2001 s 70C and additional capital expenditure under s 70D. It is also not a "qualifying amount" for the purposes of s 70E.

These changes have effect in relation to any payment made on or after 9 March, 2011.

34 Investment companies
Schedule 7 contains provision about investment companies.

GENERAL NOTE
Section 34 introduces Schedule 7.

Exemptions and reliefs

35 Reduction in childcare relief for higher earners
Schedule 8 contains provision for reducing childcare relief for higher earners.

GENERAL NOTE
Section 35 introduces Schedule 8.

36 Childcare: salary sacrifice etc and the national minimum wage
(1) In section 270A of ITEPA 2003 (limited exemption for qualifying childcare vouchers), after subsection (5) insert—

"(5A) Where the scheme under which the vouchers are provided involves—

(a) relevant salary sacrifice arrangements, or
(b) relevant flexible remuneration arrangements,

Condition C is not prevented from being met by reason only that the scheme is not open to relevant low-paid employees.

(5B) In subsection (5A)—

"relevant salary sacrifice arrangements" means arrangements (whenever made) under which the employees for whom the vouchers are provided give up the right to receive an amount of general earnings or specific employment income in return for the provision of the vouchers;

"relevant flexible remuneration arrangements" means arrangements (whenever made) under which the employees for whom the vouchers are provided agree with the employer that they are to be provided with the vouchers rather than receive some other description of employment income;

"relevant low-paid employees" means any of the employer's employees who are remunerated by the employer at a rate such that, if the relevant salary sacrifice arrangements or relevant flexible remuneration arrangements applied to them, the rate at which they would then be so remunerated would be likely to be lower than the national minimum wage."

(2) In section 318A of that Act (exemption for childcare other than employer-provided care), after subsection (5) insert—

"(5A) Where the scheme under which the care is provided involves—

(a) relevant salary sacrifice arrangements, or
(b) relevant flexible remuneration arrangements,

Condition C is not prevented from being met by reason only that the scheme is not open to relevant low-paid employees.

(5B) In subsection (5A)—

"relevant salary sacrifice arrangements" means arrangements (whenever made) under which the employees for whom the care is provided give up the right to receive an amount of general earnings or specific employment income in return for the provision of the care;

"relevant flexible remuneration arrangements" means arrangements (whenever made) under which the employees for whom the care is provided agree with the employer that they are to be provided with the care rather than receive some other description of employment income;

"relevant low-paid employees" means any of the employer's employees who are remunerated by the employer at a rate such that, if the relevant salary sacrifice arrangements or relevant flexible remuneration arrangements applied to them, the rate at which they would then be so remunerated would be likely to be lower than the national minimum wage."

(3) The amendments made by this section have effect for the tax year 2005–06 and subsequent tax years.

GENERAL NOTE

Salary sacrifice arrangements, under which an employee gives up part of his or her cash salary in return for a non-cash benefit, are frequently used to enable employees to benefit from the exemptions available in respect of the provision of childcare vouchers and employer-supported childcare other that on the employer's premises. The employer also benefits from the arrangement saving the secondary Class 1 National Insurance contributions that would have been payable on the foregone salary.

In common with many other tax exemptions, the exemptions for childcare vouchers and employer-supported childcare are dependent on the scheme being available to employees generally or to those employees at a particular location.

A potential conflict arises in meeting this requirement in relation to low paid employees whose earnings would fall below the level of the national minimum wage were they to participate in a salary sacrifice scheme of this nature. Most employees with children whose earnings are at or near the national minimum wage receive financial assistance towards childcare costs in the form of the childcare element of the working tax credit.

To enable employers to exclude workers at or near the national minimum wage from salary sacrifice schemes (thereby ensuring that the employee is paid at least the national minimum wage) without jeopardising the exemption for employer supported childcare and childcare vouchers, the qualifying conditions for both the childcare voucher and employer-supported childcare exemptions have been amended.

In relation to childcare vouchers amendments are made to ITEPA 2003 s 270A. New ITEPA 2003 s 270A(5A) (inserted by s 36(1)) provides that where the scheme under which the vouchers are provided involves relevant salary sacrifice arrangements or relevant flexible remuneration arrangements, condition C (which requires that the scheme is open to the employer's employees generally or to those at a particular location) is not prevented from applying by reason that the scheme is not open to relevant low-paid employees.

The terms 'relevant salary sacrifice arrangements', relevant flexible remuneration arrangements' and 'relevant low-paid employees' are defined by new ITEPA 2003 s 270A(5B) (as inserted by s 36(1)).

Corresponding changes are made to ITEPA 2003 s 318A in relation to employer-supported childcare provided other than at the employer's premises (s 36(2)).

The relaxation of the qualifying conditions so as to allow employers to exclude employees whose earnings would be likely to fall to below the national minimum wage were they to participate in a salary sacrifice or flexible remuneration arrangements from employer supported childcare or childcare vouchers schemes is backdated to take effect for 2005/06 and subsequent tax years (s 36(3)). This ensures that any outstanding tax liability for schemes that did not meet the conditions for exemption only by virtue of excluding employees at or near the national minimum wage is removed.

37 Accommodation expenses of MPs

(1) In section 292 of ITEPA 2003 (accommodation expenses of MPs), after subsection (4) insert—

> "(5) The reference in subsection (1) to a payment made to a member of the House of Commons under section 5(1) of the Parliamentary Standards Act 2009 includes a payment made under that section to another person at the direction of a member (see section 6(7) of that Act)."

(2) The amendment made by this section has effect in relation to payments made under section 5(1) of the Parliamentary Standards Act 2009 on or after 1 November 2010.

GENERAL NOTE

A new scheme for the paying of MPs expenses was introduced by the Independent Parliamentary Standards Authority (IPSA) under which MPs expenses have been paid since the election on 6 May 2010. Prior to that date MPs expenses were paid by the House of Commons authorities.

The payment of MPs expenses was simplified from 1 November 2010. Since that date IPSA make payment of MPs rental charges direct to the landlord where authorised to do so by the claimant MP.

By virtue of ITEPA 2003 s 292, accommodation expenses paid to MPs are exempt from tax if certain conditions are met. The provision is amended to reflect the changes to the rules from 1 November 2010 and to extend the exemption so that it applies to payments made under the Parliamentary Standards Act 2009 s 5(1) to another person at the direction of a member (new ITEPA 2003 s 292(5), as inserted by s 37(1)).

The amendment applies with effect in relation to payments made under the Parliamentary Standards Act 2009 s 5(1) on or after 1 November 2010.

38 Experts seconded to European Union bodies

(1) In Chapter 8 of Part 4 of ITEPA 2003 (employment income: special kinds of employment), after section 304 insert—

"304A Experts seconded to other European Union bodies

(1) No liability to income tax arises in respect of any subsistence allowances paid by a relevant EU body to persons who, because of their expertise in matters relating to the subject matter of the functions of the relevant EU body, have been seconded to the body by their employers.

(2) Each of the following is a "relevant EU body"—

(a) the European Medicines Agency, established as the European Agency for the Evaluation of Medicinal Products by Council Regulation (EEC) No 2309/93 of 22 July 1993,

(b) the European Police College, established by Council Decision of 20 September 2005 (2005/681/JHA),

(c) the European Banking Authority, established by Regulation (EU) No 1093/2010 of 24 November 2010, and

(d) any other body established by an EU instrument which is designated as a relevant EU body for the purposes of this section by an order made by the Treasury."

(2) The amendment made by this section has effect in relation to subsistence allowances paid in respect of periods beginning on or after 1 January 2011.

GENERAL NOTE

Under current law, subsistence allowances paid to experts seconded to an EU body located in the UK are subject to income tax and National Insurance contributions. If the secondment last less than two years, relief may be available under the temporary workplace rules. However, as most such secondments last more than two years, the relief is not usually in point.

Following concerns about a possible disparity in tax treatment between workers seconded to an EU body located in the UK and workers seconded to an EU body based in another member State in which tax relief for subsistence allowances may be available, a tax exemption is introduced in respect of any subsistence allowances paid by a relevant EU body to a person who, because of his or her expertise in the subject matter of the functions of the relevant EU body, has been seconded to that by body by his or her employer (new ITEPA 2003 s 304A, as inserted by s 38(1)). Relevant EU bodies for these purposes are listed in new ITEPA 2003 s 304A(2).

The exemption introduced by new ITEPA 2003 s 304A applies in relation to subsistence allowances paid in respect of periods beginning on or after 1 January 2011 (s 38(2)).

39 Employment income: exemption for fees relating to monitoring schemes

(1) In Chapter 11 of Part 4 of ITEPA 2003 (employment income: miscellaneous exemptions), after section 326 insert—

"Monitoring schemes

326A Fees relating to monitoring schemes relating to vulnerable persons

(1) No liability to income tax arises by virtue of the payment or reimbursement of a fee in respect of an application to join the scheme administered under section 44 of the Protection of Vulnerable Groups (Scotland) Act 2007 (asp 14) (scheme to collate and disclose information about individuals working with vulnerable persons).

(2) The Treasury may by order amend subsection (1) so as—

(a) to add to the fees covered by that subsection a fee of a specified kind payable in connection with a scheme for England and Wales or Northern Ireland which corresponds to the scheme administered under section 44 of the Protection of Vulnerable Groups (Scotland) Act 2007, or

(b) to amend or remove a reference to a fee added under paragraph (a)."

(2) The amendment made by this section has effect for the tax year 2010–11 and subsequent tax years.

GENERAL NOTE

This inserts a new ITEPA 2003 Part 4 Chapter 11 s 326A, which is the chapter dealing with miscellaneous exemptions from the employment income charge.

Background

It will become an offence in Scotland for an employer to hire a person who is barred from working with children or vulnerable adults to undertake regulated work. In most cases where employers employ individuals to undertake such work this will mean that prospective and current employees are required to be registered under the PVGS.

New s 326A(1) This provides that where fees are paid in respect of an application under a scheme to collate and disclose information about individuals working with vulnerable people under the Protection of Vulnerable Groups (Scotland) Act 2007 s 44 no liability to income tax arises. There is also no liability where an individual pays such a fee and it is reimbursed to him or her.

New s 326A(2) This give the Treasury power to amend s 1 above to extend it to payments and reimbursement of similar fees paid to corresponding schemes in the rest of the UK.

This section applies for tax year 2010–11 and subsequent years. This is because the scheme is intended to operate in Scotland from February 2011 and thus early payments of fees may fall into the 2010–11 tax year.

The Budget Day press release indicated that a similar exemption will be introduced for National Insurance purposes.

40 Individual investment plans for children

(1) Chapter 3 of Part 6 of ITTOIA 2005 (income from individual investment plans) is amended in accordance with subsections (2) to (5).

(2) In section 694 (income from individual investment plans), after subsection (1) insert—

"(1A) In subsection (1) "income of an individual from investments under a plan" includes income from investments which is treated as the individual's income by virtue of section 629 (income paid to relevant children of settlor)."

(3) After section 695 insert—

"695A Investment plans for children

(1) This section applies where investment plan regulations provide that income of a child from investments under a plan (a "child plan") is exempt from income tax (either wholly or to such extent as is specified in the regulations).

(2) In addition to any provision which may be made by virtue of any other provision of this Chapter, investment plan regulations may—

(a) specify descriptions of persons by whom investments may be made for a child,

(b) provide that withdrawals may be made only in the circumstances specified in the regulations, and

(c) provide that, in the case of a child who is under 16, the plan managers may act only on the direction of a person of a description specified in the regulations.

(3) They may also provide—

(a) that any assignment of, or agreement to assign, investments under a child plan, and any charge on or agreement to charge any such investments, is void,

(b) that, on the bankruptcy of a child with investments under a child plan, the entitlement to those investments does not pass to any trustee or other person acting on behalf of the child's creditors, and

(c) that, where a contract is entered into by or on behalf of a child who is 16 or over in connection with a child plan under which investments are held—

(i) by the child, or

(ii) by another child in relation to whom the child has parental responsibility,

the contract has effect as if the child had been 18 or over when it was entered into.

(4) Where, by virtue of provision made in investment plan regulations under subsection (2)(a), investments are made for a child under a child plan, for the purposes of this Chapter the child is treated as having made those investments.

(5) In this section—

"assignment" includes assignation, and "assign" is to be construed accordingly;

"bankruptcy", in relation to a child, includes the sequestration of the child's estate;

"charge on or agreement to charge" includes a right in security over or an agreement to create a right in security over;

"child" means an individual under 18;

"parental responsibility" means—

(a) parental responsibility within the meaning of the Children Act 1989 or the Children (Northern Ireland) Order 1995, or

(b) parental responsibilities within the meaning of the Children (Scotland) Act 1995;

and any reference to investments being held by a child includes a reference to investments being held by plan managers on behalf of the child by virtue of section 696(1)."

(4) In section 699 (non-entitlement to exemption), at the end insert—

"(9) In this section references to an investor include an individual entitled to an exemption given by investment plan regulations by virtue of section 694(1A)."

(5) In section 701 (general and supplementary powers), at the end insert—

"(6) In this section references to an investor include an individual entitled to an exemption given by investment plan regulations by virtue of section 694(1A)."

(6) In section 151 of TCGA 1992 (personal equity plans), in subsection (2)—

(a) for "section 694(1) and (2)" substitute "section 694(1) to (2)", and

(b) for the words from "but with" to the end substitute

"but with the following modifications—

(a) any reference to income tax is to be read as a reference to capital gains tax,

(b) the reference in section 695A(1) to the case where regulations provide that income of a child from investments under a plan is exempt from income tax is to be read as a reference to the case where regulations provide that a child who invests under a plan is entitled to relief from capital gains tax in respect of the investments,

(c) the reference in section 695A(4) to that Chapter is to be read as a reference to this section, and

(d) that Chapter has effect as if sections 699(9) and 701(6) were omitted."

GENERAL NOTE

On 26 October 2010 the Government announced plans to introduce Junior ISAs, tax-free savings accounts for children. It is expected that Junior ISAs will be made available from autumn 2011. Draft junior ISA regulations were published on 31 March 2011.

To facilitate the introduction of regulations setting out the detailed account rules and processes for Junior ISAs, the Treasury are provided with additional regulation-making powers by new ITTOIA 2005 s 695A (as introduced by s 40(3)).

The new section applies where investment plan regulations provided that income of a child from investments under a plan (referred to as a 'child plan') are exempt from tax to the extent specified in the regulations (new ITTOIA 2005 s 695A(1)).

Regulations made under new ITTTOIA 2005 may specify the descriptions of persons by whom investments may be made for a child, the circumstances in which withdrawals may be made, and in the case of a child under 16, that managers may only act on the direction of a person specified in the regulations (new ITTOIA 2005 s 695A(2)).

Such regulations may also prevent child plan investments from being used as security or being passed to a trustee or person acting on behalf on the child's creditors on the bankruptcy of the creditor. The regulations may also provide that contracts in relation to the plan entered into by a child age 16 to 18 have effect as if the child were 18 or over at the time that the contract was made (new ITTOIA 2005 s 695A(3)).

Where investment are made for a child under a child plan by another person, for example a parent or grandparent, the investments are treated for the purposes of investment plan regulations as having been made by the child (new ITTOIA 2005 s 695(4)).

Various terms applying for the purposes of new ITTOIA 2005 s 695A are set out in new ITTOIA 2005 s 695A(5).

As a result of the introduction of new ITTOIS 2005 s 695A consequential changes are made to ITTOIA 2005 s 699, 701, which enable investment plan regulations made under these provisions to apply in relation to a parent who has paid amounts into their child's Junior ISA (s 40(5), (6)).

An amendment is also made to ITTOIA 2005 s 694 (by s 40(1)) to provide that an individual's income from investment under a plan includes investments treated as the individual's by virtue of ITTOIA 2005 s 629 (which deems income paid to children of the settlor to be that of the settlor) (s 40(2)). The government intends to provide in investment plan regulations that income arising from any sum paid by a parent into a child's Junior ISAS will not be taxed as income of the parent under ITTIA 2005 s 629.

Amendments made to TCGA 1992 s 151 (by s 40(6)) enable the Treasury to make regulations to provide exemption from capital gains tax on gains made on investments held within a Junior ISA.

41 Gift aid: increase of limits on total value of benefits associated with gifts

(1) In section 418 of ITA 2007 (gifts to charities by individuals: restrictions on associated benefits), in subsection (3), for "£500" substitute "£2,500".

(2) In section 197 of CTA 2010 (gifts to charities by companies: restrictions on associated benefits), in subsection (3), for "£500" substitute "£2,500".

(3) Accordingly, omit section 60(1)(b) of FA 2007.

(4) The amendments made by subsections (1) and (3) have effect in relation to gifts made on or after 6 April 2011.

(5) The amendment made by subsection (2) has effect in relation to gifts made in an accounting period ending on or after 1 April 2011.

GENERAL NOTE

The gift aid rules for donations by individuals and companies to charities and Community Amateur Sports Clubs allow the donor to receive a low level of benefit in consequence of their donation, usually used by charities as a gesture of thanks for the donation, although the reason is irrelevant. In addition to limits relative to the amount of the donation, there is an overall limit on the aggregate value of benefits that any individual or company can receive in any one year from the same charity or CASC, irrespective of the number or size of the donations made in that period.

This overall limit has been increased from £500 to £2,500 by this section. The limits for single donations still also apply being 25% of the gross value of the donation for donations under £100, £25 for donations between £100 and £1,000 and 5% of the gross value for donations of £1,000 or more. This change means that the 5% limit applies to donations of up to £50,000.

42 Enterprise investment scheme: amount of relief

(1) Part 5 of ITA 2007 (enterprise investment scheme) is amended in accordance with subsections (2) to (4).

(2) In section 158 (form and amount of EIS relief), in subsection (2A) for "20%" substitute "30%".

(3) In the following provisions for "EIS rate" substitute "EIS original rate"—

(a) section 209(3);
(b) section 210(1)(b);
(c) section 213(2);
(d) section 220(1)(b);
(e) section 224(2);
(f) section 229(1)(b).

(4) After section 256 insert—

"256A Meaning of "the EIS original rate"

In this Part "the EIS original rate", in relation to EIS relief, means the EIS rate for the tax year for which the EIS relief was obtained."

(5) In Schedule 4 to that Act (index of defined expressions), at the appropriate place insert—

"EIS original rate (in Part 5)	section 256A"

(6) This section comes into force on such day as the Treasury may by order appoint.

(7) The amendments made by this section have effect in relation to the tax year 2011–12 and subsequent tax years.

(8) But where the EIS relief attributable to shares was obtained for the tax year 2007–08 or an earlier tax year, the references to the EIS original rate in the provisions mentioned in paragraph (a) to (f) of subsection (3) are to be read as references to 20%.

GENERAL NOTE

The Government announced various amendments to the Enterprise Investment Scheme (EIS) at Budget 2011 in the hope of increasing the incentive for individuals to invest in small, higher risk trading companies. A significant change sees the rate of income tax relief available to individual investors increasing upon qualifying share subscriptions on or after 6 April 2011.

Enterprise Investment Scheme

ITA 2007 Part 5 outlines the qualifying conditions for EIS approved companies, and the qualifying investor conditions. Section 158(2)(a) has been updated to show the increased rate of income tax relief available to qualifying investors, denoting a rise from 20 percent to 30 percent.

It is proposed that the increased rate of relief will apply to the 2011/12 tax year and subsequent years, that is, qualifying share issues made on or after 6 April 2011.However, as changes to the EIS are subject to European State aid approval, subsection (6) provides for the Treasury to appoint, by order, when the section comes into force.

As a result of the proposed increased rate of income tax relief, consequential legislative amendments have been made to ensure that any withdrawal of relief from qualifying subscriptions prior to 6 April 2011 is done at the 'EIS original rate'. Here, 'EIS original rate', refers to the 20 percent rate of income tax relief received for the tax year in which relief was obtained (inserted s 256A).

Income tax relief, where claimed, is withdrawn or reduced upon the occurrence of certain events within three years of either the issue of the shares, or the issuing company commencing trading, if later. The most common events that would trigger a withdrawal of relief include a sale of shares by the individual and the issuing company failing to meet the qualifying EIS conditions, within the three year period.

Where a claim is made to carry back an investment made in the 2011/12 tax year to the 2010/11 tax year under s 158(4), income tax relief at 20 percent only would be received on the amount so carried back.

The increase in the rate of income tax relief is likely to be viewed as consistent with the Government's aim of supporting smaller enterprises, and in particular, its eagerness for the private sector to drive the recovery and growth of the UK economy.

43 Relief for expenditure on R&D by SMEs

(1) Part 13 of CTA 2009 (additional relief for expenditure on research and development) is amended as follows.

(2) Chapter 2 (relief for small or medium-sized enterprises ("SMEs")) is amended in accordance with subsections (3) to (6).

(3) In section 1044 (additional deduction in calculating profits of trade), in subsection (8), for "75%" substitute "100%".

(4) In section 1045 (alternative treatment for pre-trading expenditure: deemed trading loss), in subsection (7), for "175%" substitute "200%".

(5) In section 1055 (tax credit: meaning of "Chapter 2 surrenderable loss"), in subsection (2)(b), for "175%" substitute "200%".

(6) In section 1058 (amount of tax credit), in subsection (1)(a), for "14%" substitute "12.5%".

(7) Chapter 7 (relief for SMEs and large companies: vaccine research etc) is amended in accordance with subsections (8) to (11).

(8) In section 1089 (SMEs: amount of deduction), in subsection (2), for "40%" substitute "20%".

(9) In section 1090 (modification of section 1089 for larger SMEs), in subsection (2), for "40%" substitute "20%".

(10) In section 1092 (SMEs: deemed trading loss for pre-trading expenditure), in subsection (8)—

(a) in paragraph (a), for "40%" substitute "20%", and
(b) in paragraph (b), for "140%" substitute "120%".

(11) In section 1104 (tax credit: meaning of "Chapter 7 surrenderable loss"), in subsection (5), for "140%" substitute "120%".

(12) This section comes into force on such day as the Treasury may by order appoint.

(13) The amendments made by this section have effect in relation to expenditure incurred on or after 1 April 2011.

GENERAL NOTE

This section will increase the additional deduction for qualifying R&D expenditure given to SMEs in computing business profits or losses for corporation tax purposes. Subject to state aid approval, for expenditure incurred on or after 1 April 2011 the additional deduction will increase from 75 per cent to 100 per cent of the qualifying R&D expenditure, a total deduction of 200 per cent. As a consequence, the amount of the tax credit for SMEs is reduced from 14 per cent to 12.5 per cent and the deduction available under vaccine research relief for SMEs is reduced to 20 per cent of qualifying R&D expenditure on vaccines research from 1 April 2011. Subject to state aid approval, legislation will be introduced in Finance Bill 2012 to increase the additional deduction for R&D expenditure by a further 25 per cent giving a total deduction of 225 per cent from 1 April 2012. However, the deduction available for vaccine research for SMEs will be withdrawn. Subject to consultation, the following changes will be made to simplify the relief for SMEs for expenditure incurred on or after 1 April 2012—

(a) the rule limiting a SME company's payable R&D tax credit to the amount of PAYE and national insurance contributions it pays will be abolished;
(b) the £10,000 minimum expenditure condition will be abolished for all companies; and,
(c) changes will also be made to the rules governing the provision of relief for work done by subcontractors under the large company scheme.

Further details were set out in Tax Information and Impact Note (TIIN) "Research and Development Tax Credits for SMEs", 23 March 2011; see Simon's Weekly Tax Intelligence 2011, Issue 12, p 1050.

Chargeable gains

44 Value shifting

Schedule 9 contains provision about value shifting.

GENERAL NOTE

Section 44 introduces Schedule 9.

45 Company ceasing to be member of a group

Schedule 10 contains provision about the consequences, for the purposes of corporation tax on chargeable gains, of a company ceasing to be a member of a group.

GENERAL NOTE

Section 45 introduces Schedule 10.

46 Pre-entry losses

Schedule 11 contains provision about losses accruing to a company before the time when it becomes a member of a group of companies and losses accruing on assets held by a company at such a time.

GENERAL NOTE

Section 46 introduces Schedule 11.

Foreign profits

47 Controlled foreign companies

Schedule 12 contains provision in relation to controlled foreign companies.

GENERAL NOTE

The Controlled Foreign Company (CFC) rules are designed to prevent UK companies from avoiding UK corporation tax by diverting income to subsidiaries in lower tax jurisdictions. Where the CFC provisions are applied they impose a tax charge on the UK company, broadly equating to the difference between the tax due on apportioned profits in the UK and foreign tax jurisdictions.

Following several rounds of consultation, Sch 12 introduces some interim improvements to the CFC regime with the main reform to the CFC rules due for inclusion in Finance Bill 2012.

48 Profits of foreign permanent establishments etc

Schedule 13 contains provision about the profits of foreign permanent establishments of UK resident companies etc

GENERAL NOTE

Section 48 introduces Schedule 13.

Investment trusts

49 Meaning of "investment trust"

(1) Chapter 4 of Part 24 of CTA 2010 (investment trusts) is amended as follows.

(2) For section 1158 (meaning of "investment trust" in the Corporation Tax Acts) substitute—

"1158 Meaning of "investment trust"

(1) For the purposes of the Corporation Tax Acts a company is an "investment trust" with respect to an accounting period if—

(a) conditions A to C are met throughout the period, and

(b) the company is approved for the period by the Commissioners for Her Majesty's Revenue and Customs (see section 1159).

(2) Condition A is that the business of the company consists of investing its funds in shares, land or other assets with the aim of spreading investment risk and giving members of the company the benefit of the results of the management of its funds.

(3) Condition B is that the shares making up the company's ordinary share capital (or, if there are such shares of more than one class, those of each class) are admitted to trading on a regulated market.

(4) For this purpose "regulated market" has the same meaning as in Directive 2004/39/EC of the European Parliament and of the Council on markets in financial instruments (see Article 4.1(14)).

(5) Condition C is that the company is not—

(a) a venture capital trust (within the meaning of Part 6 of ITA 2007), or
(b) a company UK REIT (within the meaning of Part 12 of this Act).

(6) The Treasury may by regulations provide—

(a) for one or both of conditions A and B to be treated as met in the cases, and subject to any conditions, specified in the regulations, and
(b) for the period for which the condition or conditions are treated as met.

(7) The Treasury may also by regulations amend subsection (3) or (4).

(8) A statutory instrument containing the first regulations under subsection (6) may not be made unless a draft of the instrument has been laid before and approved by a resolution of the House of Commons.

(9) Any other statutory instrument containing regulations under this section is subject to annulment in pursuance of a resolution of the House of Commons."

(3) For section 1159 (conditions for approval) substitute—

"1159 Approval

(1) The Treasury may by regulations make provision about the approval of a company for an accounting period for the purposes of section 1158(1)(b), including provision about—

(a) applications for approval,
(b) the determination of applications for approval,
(c) requirements to be met by the company while approved,
(d) the withdrawal of approval by notice, or
(e) the consequences of the withdrawal of approval.

(2) The regulations may, in particular—

(a) include provision under which an application for approval—

(i) is to be made by reference to the accounting period in which the application is made or such earlier or later accounting period as may be specified in the application, and
(ii) is to constitute an application for approval for that and all subsequent accounting periods,

(b) specify the form and content of, and information to accompany, an application,
(c) permit or require the Commissioners to grant or refuse an application where conditions specified in the regulations are met (or appear to the Commissioners to be met) in relation to the company,
(d) permit or require the Commissioners to withdraw approval where—

(i) conditions specified in the regulations are met (or appear to the Commissioners to be met) in relation to the company, or
(ii) the company has failed to comply with requirements imposed by the regulations,

(e) include provision prohibiting a company from which approval has been withdrawn from reapplying, or
(f) include provision under which approval may or must be withdrawn in relation to an accounting period that ends before the notice withdrawing approval is given.

(3) Regulations under this section—

(a) may make different provision for different cases or purposes, and
(b) may make incidental, consequential, supplementary or transitional provision.

(4) A statutory instrument containing the first regulations under this section may not be made unless a draft of the instrument has been laid before and approved by a resolution of the House of Commons.

(5) Any other statutory instrument containing regulations under this section is subject to annulment in pursuance of a resolution of the House of Commons.

(6) In this section "the Commissioners" means the Commissioners for Her Majesty's Revenue and Customs."

(4) Omit sections 1160 to 1165 (which relate to the interpretation of the provisions replaced by this section).

(5) In Schedule 4 (index of defined expressions), omit the following entries—

"company (in Chapter 4 of Part 24)"
"scheme of reconstruction (in Chapter 4 of Part 24)"
"shares (in Chapter 4 of Part 24)".

(6) The amendments made by this section have effect in relation to accounting periods beginning on or after such day as the Treasury may by order appoint.

GENERAL NOTE

Investment trusts are listed investment companies that, providing they meet certain requirements, are exempt from corporation tax on chargeable gains. The current legislation governing investment trusts is contained in CTA 2010 Part 24 Chapter 4. This legislation has remained largely unchanged since its introduction in 1965, and the investment trust industry has long been calling for its modernisation and simplification. Following a Consultation Document published by HM Treasury in July 2010, FA 2011 implements legislation to update the rules.

This section inserts new CTA 2010 ss 1158 and 1159.

New section 1158 provides for a new definition of "investment trust". For a company to be an investment trust it must meet conditions A to C and also be approved by HM Revenue and Customs under the terms of s 1159.

Condition A requires the business of the company to be investing in shares, land or other assets with the aim of spreading investment risk and giving the members of the company the benefit of the results of the management of the funds. This is a relaxation of the previous rules which required an investment trusts income to be "wholly or mainly from shares and securities" (s 1159(1) Condition C) and that a holding in an investee company could not exceed 15% by value of the investment trust's assets (s 1159(1) Condition E).

Condition B requires that the ordinary share capital of the company is admitted to trading on a regulated market. This is another relaxation of the previous rules which required the ordinary share capital to be admitted to the UK official list (s 1159(1) Condition B).

Condition C prevents venture capital trusts or UK REITs from being an investment trust.

New s 1159 gives HM Treasury the power to make regulations setting out the process and conditions required for approval as an investment trust.

50 Power to make provision about treatment of transactions

In Part 13 of CTA 2010 (special types of company etc), after Chapter 3 insert—

"CHAPTER 3A

INVESTMENT TRUSTS

622A Power to make provision about treatment of transactions

(1) The Treasury may by regulations provide that a transaction of a specified kind entered into by an investment trust is to be treated for the purposes of the Corporation Tax Acts as entered into by it otherwise than in the course of a trade.

(2) Regulations under this section—

(a) may make different provision for different cases or purposes, and

(b) may make incidental, consequential, supplementary or transitional provision.

(3) A statutory instrument containing the first regulations under this section may not be made unless a draft of the instrument has been laid before and approved by a resolution of the House of Commons.

(4) Any other statutory instrument containing regulations under this section is subject to annulment in pursuance of a resolution of the House of Commons.

(5) In this section "specified" means specified in regulations under this section."

GENERAL NOTE

This inserts a new CTA 2010 s 622A. The new section gives HM Treasury the power to make regulations to provide that certain transactions carried out by an investment trust will be treated for the purposes of corporation tax as non-trading transactions.

There has historically been a concern in the investment trust industry that certain transactions, especially those using derivatives, could be considered to be trading for tax purposes. If this is the case the profits made on such transactions would be taxable as trading income rather than fall to be treated as exempt chargeable gains. Similar regulations have already been passed that apply to authorised investment funds (Part 2B of the Authorised Investment Funds (Tax) Regulations 2006, SI 2006/964) and this will allow the similar regulations to be made for investment trusts.

Miscellaneous

51 Taxable benefits: calculating the appropriate percentage for cars

(1) In section 139 of ITEPA 2003 (cars with a CO_2 emissions figure: the appropriate percentage), as substituted by section 59 of FA 2010 with effect for the tax year 2012–13 and subsequent tax years, in subsection (5) for "100 grams" substitute "95 grams".

(2) The amendment made by this section has effect for the tax year 2013–14 and subsequent tax years.

GENERAL NOTE

This amends the car benefit rules by substituting 95 grams for 100 grams. The effect of this is that the car scale charge for petrol cars with emissions between 95 and 219 g/km will increase by one percentage points. There is a similar increase for diesel cars up to 204 g/km.

This increase applies for 2013–14 onwards.

52 Furnished holiday lettings

Schedule 14 contains provisions about furnished holiday lettings.

GENERAL NOTE

Section 52 introduces Schedule 14.

53 Leases and changes to accounting standards

(1) This section applies where there is a change in a leasing accounting standard which—

(a) occurs on or after 1 January 2011, and

(b) is not within subsection (3),

(in this section referred to as a "leasing change").

(2) "Leasing accounting standard" means—

(a) International Accounting Standard 17 (leases) issued by the International Accounting Standards Board,

(b) Statement of Standard Accounting Practice 21 (accounting for leases and hire purchase contracts) recognised by the Accounting Standards Board,

(c) the part of the International Financial Reporting Standard for Small and Medium-sized Entities issued by the International Accounting Standards Board which relates specifically to leases,

(d) the part of the Financial Reporting Standard for Smaller Entities issued by the Accounting Standards Board which relates specifically to leases, or

(e) any accounting standard, or part of an accounting standard, which replaces (wholly or in part) a standard or part mentioned in paragraphs (a) to (d).

(3) A change is within this subsection if, and to the extent that, it is one which permits or requires persons, when preparing accounts in accordance with UK GAAP, to account for a lease, or a transaction accounted for as a lease, in a manner equivalent to that provided for by the International Financial Reporting Standard for Small and Medium-sized Entities issued by the International Accounting Standards Board (disregarding any leasing change which may be made to that Standard).

(4) Changes within subsection (1) include those which may or must be adopted for periods of account which fall wholly or partly before the time the change occurs or before the day on which this Act is passed.

(5) For the purposes of the Taxes Acts any reference in those Acts (other than this section)—

(a) to a thing being determined or done in accordance with or by reference to generally accepted accounting practice, or

(b) to accounts prepared (or not prepared) in accordance with international accounting standards or UK GAAP,

is to be construed as if any leasing change had not occurred.

(6) Section 997 of ITA 2007 and section 1127 of CTA 2010 (meaning of "generally accepted accounting practice" and related expressions in the Tax Acts) have effect subject to subsection (5).

(7) Where a person prepares or is required to prepare accounts in accordance with new standards for a period of account, the Taxes Acts (other than this section) have effect as

if the person prepared or was required to prepare accounts, for that period, in accordance with the corresponding old standards.

(8) For the purposes of subsection (7)—

(a) if the new standards are international accounting standards, the corresponding old standards are international accounting standards disregarding any leasing change, and

(b) if the new standards are UK GAAP, the corresponding old standards are UK GAAP disregarding any leasing change.

(9) In this section—

"accounting body" means the International Accounting Standards Board or the Accounting Standards Board, or a successor body to either of those Boards;

"accounting standard" includes any statement of practice, guidance or other similar document issued or recognised by an accounting body;

"change", in relation to a leasing accounting standard, means the issue, revocation, amendment or recognition of, or withdrawal of recognition from, the standard by an accounting body;

"international accounting standards" has the same meaning as in section 1127 of CTA 2010;

"new standards" means accounting standards which reflect one or more leasing changes;

"Taxes Acts" means—

(a) the Tax Acts, and

(b) TCGA 1992 and all other enactments relating to capital gains tax;

"UK GAAP" means UK generally accepted accounting practice as defined in section 997(2) of ITA 2007 and section 1127(2) of CTA 2010.

(10) This section has effect in relation to any period (including any period falling wholly or partly before the day on which this Act is passed) in respect of which a change to a leasing accounting standard which occurs on or after 1 January 2011 may or must be adopted by any person for accounting purposes.

GENERAL NOTE

This section has been introduced in response to changes that are anticipated in 2011 to lease accounting under international financial reporting standards (IFRS), including in particular the proposal to remove the distinction between finance leases and operating leases. It is also anticipated that similar changes might be adopted for UK generally accepted accounting practice (UK GAAP) during 2013.

A significant part of the corporation tax and income tax code for leases is based on accounting definitions, in particular the distinction between a finance lease and an operating lease and the resulting entries prepared in accordance with either IFRS or UK GAAP. In order to allow time to work out what changes may be required to tax legislation to accommodate the new accounting treatment, s 53 provides that for a transitional period where there is a change to the relevant leasing accounting standard (see s 53(2)), which occurs on or after 1 January 2011, the taxable profits of a company or business will be computed as if the old standard continued to apply.

This transitional measure does not apply in a case where a company or business begins to prepare its accounts in accordance with the Financial Reporting Standard for Small and Medium-size Enterprises unless there is a change to the way in which that standard applies to leases.

54 Leasing companies: withdrawal of election

(1) In section 398A(1)(a) of CTA 2010 (election out of qualifying change of ownership), after "day")" insert "before 23 March 2011".

(2) The amendment made by this section is to be treated as having come into force on 23 March 2011.

GENERAL NOTE

This section withdraws, with effect from 23 March 2011, the option to ring fence a leasing business as an alternative to incurring deemed income and expense amounts under the sale of lessors rules in CTA 2010 Part 9. This option was only introduced in FA 2010 as a response to claims that the sale of lessor rules, which do not contain a motive test, were deterring genuine commercial transactions. However, it is being withdrawn as HMRC perceive it as having been abused.

55 Companies with small profits: associated companies

(1) For section 27 of CTA 2010 (meaning of "associated company": attribution to persons of rights and powers of their partners) substitute—

"27 Attribution to persons of rights and powers of their associates

(1) This section applies if—

(a) it is necessary to determine in accordance with section 25(4) and (5) whether a company is an associated company of another company, and

(b) the relationship between the two companies is not one of substantial commercial interdependence.

(2) In the application of section 451 (meaning of "control": rights to be attributed) for the purposes of the determination, any person to whom rights and duties fall to be attributed under subsections (4) and (5) of that section is to be treated, for the purposes of those subsections, as having no associates.

(3) The Treasury may by order prescribe factors that are to be taken into account in determining whether a relationship between two companies amounts to substantial commercial interdependence for the purposes of this section."

(2) The amendment made by this section has effect in relation to accounting periods ending on or after 1 April 2011.

(3) But a company may elect that the amendment made by this section is of no effect in relation to an accounting period that begins before that date.

(4) An election under subsection (3) must be made within one year from the end of the accounting period to which it relates.

(5) The first order under section 27(3) of CTA 2010 (as substituted by subsection (1) of this section) may be made so as to have effect in relation to accounting periods ending on or after 1 April 2011.

GENERAL NOTE

The "associated companies" rule in CTA 2010 s 25 is designed to prevent the fragmentation of profits between a number of companies to exploit the corporation tax small companies' relief provisions. Where a company has one or more associated companies, the lower and upper limits for small companies' relief are proportionately reduced.

The "control" tests in CTA 2010 s 450 are applied for the purpose of determining whether a company is "associated" with another company. Before the enactment of FA 2011 s 55, CTA 2010 s 451 automatically applied to attribute to an individual to whom the "control" test was being applied the rights and powers of his or her associates. However, Extra-Statutory Concession C9 ("ESC C9") limited such attribution between relatives (apart from spouses and minor children) solely to circumstances where substantial commercial interdependence existed between the companies.

Following a two year consultation on the simplification of the "associated companies" rule, s 55 essentially puts the treatment currently afforded by ESC C9 onto a statutory footing and extends it to all associates.

In practice, this change is unlikely to affect many companies. According to the related Tax Information and Impact Note, some 3000 companies may benefit by finding that they are no longer deemed to be "associated" with other companies.

Section 55(1) inserts a new CTA 2010 s 27. New sub-s (1) provides that s 27 applies where the relationship between the companies is not one of substantial commercial interdependence.

New sub-s (2) provides essentially that where new s 27, there will be no attribution to a person of rights and powers of associates under CTA 2010 sub-ss 451(4) and (5).

New sub-s (3) confers on the Treasury a power to prescribe, by order, factors to be taken into account in determining whether a relationship between two companies amounts to a substantial commercial interdependence for the purpose of CTA 2010 s 27. The Corporation Tax Act 2010 (Factors Determining Substantial Commercial Interdependence) Order 2011 (the "Order") is the first order to be made under this sub-section.

The Order provides that, in determining whether a relationship between two companies amounts to substantial commercial interdependence, the degree to which companies are financially interdependent, economically interdependent, or organisationally interdependent, should be taken into account.

The draft guidance to be inserted into the Company Taxation Manual as CTM03750 to CTM03800 (the "Guidance") states that the period of time (during the relevant accounting period) for which the interdependence exists will be relevant to the degree of interdependence. The Guidance states, by way of example, that a loan between companies existing for only one week is unlikely to indicate a substantial commercial interdependence, regardless of its size.

Two companies will be treated as financially interdependent if, in particular, one gives financial support (directly or indirectly) to the other or each has a financial interest in the affairs of the same business (para 3 of the Order).

Two companies will be treated as economically interdependent if, in particular, the companies seek to realise the same economic objective, the activities of one benefit the other, or the companies have common customers (paragraph 4 of the Order).

Two companies will be treated as organisationally interdependent if, in particular, the businesses of the companies have or use common management, common employees, common premises or common equipment (para 5 of the Order).

The Guidance emphasises that it is not necessary for all three types of link to exist and that each case will depend on its specific circumstances. HMRC do not consider substantial commercial interdependence to be present where there is an "accident of circumstance" but only where there is "in a real sense" interdependence between the parties (CTM03800).

Section 55(2) provides that s 27 will apply in relation to accounting periods ending on or after 1 April 2011.

Section 55(3) allows a company to make an election such that s 27 will apply to it only in relation to accounting periods beginning after 1 April 2011.

Section 55(4) provides that an election under s 55(3) must be made within one year after the end of the accounting period to which it relates.

Section 55(5) provides that the first order under s 27(3) may be made so as to have effect in relation to accounting periods ending on or after 1 April 2011.

56 Insurance companies: apportionment of amounts brought into account

(1) In section 432C of ICTA (section 432B apportionment: non-participating funds), in subsection (9), for the words from "D is" to the end substitute—

"D is the sum of—

(a) the mean of the opening and closing liabilities of the relevant business so far as referable to basic life assurance and general annuity business (but taking that mean to be nil if it would otherwise be below nil), reduced (but not below nil) by the mean of the opening and closing net values of any assets linked to that category of business, and

(b) the mean of the opening and closing liabilities of the relevant business so far as referable to PHI business (but taking that mean to be nil if it would otherwise be below nil), reduced (but not below nil) by the mean of the opening and closing net values of any assets linked to that category of business."

(2) The amendment made by this section has effect in relation to periods of account beginning on or after 1 January 2011.

(3) For the purposes of section 432CA of ICTA, where the current period of account begins on or after 1 January 2011, the reference in subsection (4) to section 432C is a reference to that section as amended by this section even if the applicable appropriate period of account began before that date.

(4) In subsection (3), "current period of account", "appropriate period of account" and "applicable" have the meaning given by section 432CA of ICTA.

GENERAL NOTE

Section 56 amends the rules in TA 1988 s 432C for apportioning the income and gains of a non-profit fund. The change introduced by s 56 corrects an inadvertent alteration to the mechanics of TA 1988 s 432C made when it was substantially amended by FA 2007.

The change made by s 56 is to the definition of "D" in the denominator of the fraction set out in TA 1988 s 432C(9). Before amendment that definition could be read in a way that resulted in the apportionment of the amount brought into account in the gross roll up business computation exceeding the total amount brought into account in respect of life assurance business which was clearly nonsensical. It appears that some affected companies have interpreted the original legislation in a way that gave a sensible result but HMRC felt obliged to apply the law as enacted even when it gave rise to inappropriate results. There was some debate between the industry and HMRC as to whether it was possible to deal with the anomalous situation through guidance but a statutory fix was seen as the preferred option, hence s 56.

In essence the amendment provides that in calculating "D" the total mean linked asset values referable to BLAGAB and PHI are to be deducted from the total of the BLAGAB and PHI liabilities rather than the mean liabilities of those two categories being separately reduced by the mean linked asset values referable to them. Although a relatively subtle change this ensures that it is far more unlikely, although not theoretically impossible, to have the over-apportionment allowed by the unamended legislation.

This change has effect for periods of account beginning on or after 1 January 2011. It remains to be seen how HMRC will deal with the issue for prior periods.

As a consequence should TA 1988 s 432CA apply to fix the apportionment percentages for a period of account beginning on or after 1 January 2011 then any references in that section to TA 1988 s 432C are to be read as applying to the amended version of that section.

57 Tonnage tax: capital allowances in respect of ship leasing

(1) Part 10 of Schedule 22 to FA 2000 (companies within tonnage tax: capital allowances in respect of ship leasing) is amended as follows.

(2) In paragraph 94 (quantitative restrictions on allowances)—

(a) in sub-paragraph (3)(a), for "a rate of 20% per annum" substitute "the rate determined under sub-paragraph (3A)",

(b) in sub-paragraph (3)(b), for "a rate of 10% per annum" substitute "the rate specified in section 104D(1) of the Capital Allowances Act 2001",

(c) after sub-paragraph (3) insert—

"(3A) The rate mentioned in sub-paragraph (3)(a) is—

(a) if the rate of the writing down allowance to which the lessor would be entitled in respect of the expenditure apart from this paragraph is that specified in section 56(1) of the Capital Allowances Act 2001, that rate, and

(b) otherwise, the rate specified in section 104D(1) of that Act.",

(d) in sub-paragraph (4)—

(i) omit the words "within each of those bands",

(ii) after "separate pools" insert "in accordance with sub-paragraph (4A)", and

(iii) omit the second sentence, and

(e) after that sub-paragraph insert—

"(4A) The expenditure is to be allocated to the following pools—

(a) to the extent that it is expenditure in respect of which the lessor is entitled to writing down allowance at the rate specified in section 56(1) of the Capital Allowances Act 2001, a pool to be known as "the tonnage tax (main rate) pool", and

(b) to the extent that it is expenditure in respect of which the lessor is entitled to writing down allowance at the rate specified in section 104D(1) of that Act, a pool to be known as "the tonnage tax (special rate) pool"."

(3) In paragraph 95(4)—

(a) for "(4)" substitute "(4A)", and

(b) for "20%" substitute "tonnage tax (main rate)" and for "10%" substitute "tonnage tax (special rate)".

(4) In paragraph 97—

(a) in sub-paragraphs (2) and (3), for "20%" substitute "tonnage tax (main rate)" and for "10%" substitute "tonnage tax (special rate)", and

(b) in sub-paragraph (4), for "10%" substitute "tonnage tax (special rate)".

(5) In paragraph 98(8), for "20%" substitute "tonnage tax (main rate)" and for "10%" substitute "tonnage tax (special rate)".

(6) In paragraph 99 (quantitative restrictions: change of circumstances taking case out of restrictions)—

(a) in sub-paragraph (2), for "20%" substitute "tonnage tax (main rate)" and for "10%" substitute "tonnage tax (special rate)",

(b) in sub-paragraph (4), for the words from "the whole of" to the end substitute "the amount that the tax written down value of the ship would have been, at the time the change of circumstances occurs, had paragraph 94 never applied.", and

(c) omit sub-paragraph (5).

(7) In consequence of the amendments made by this section, omit section 80(5) to (7) of FA 2008.

(8) The amendments made by this section have effect in relation to chargeable periods ending on or after 1 January 2011.

(9) But the amendments made by this section are of no effect in relation to expenditure incurred before that date.

GENERAL NOTE

FA 2000 Sch 22 para 94 currently provides that where the lessor of the ship to a company under the tonnage tax régime is entitled to capital allowances in respect of the ship (which will generally not be the case where the lease is a long funding lease), those allowances are restricted to a writing-down allowance of 20 per cent on the first £40 million and of 10 per cent on the next £40 million of expenditure, both under the reducing-balance method, and to no further allowances on any balance of expenditure over £80 million.

With the general reduction in the rates of allowance on plant and machinery both already enacted and to come in 2012, these 'restrictions' would in fact have become more generous, with respect to the first £80 million of expenditure, than the general allowances.

As amended by this section, the rate of writing-down allowance on the first £40 million will be the main rate as specified in CAA 2001 s 56(1) (currently 20 per cent, but to be reduced to 18 per cent) if the ship is not a long-life asset and will be the special rate (currently 10 per cent but to be reduced to 8 per cent) if the ship is a long-life asset. The expenditure is to be allocated to separate pools ('the tonnage tax main-rate pool' and the 'tonnage tax special-rate pool') accordingly. Allowances on the next £40 million will be at the special rate, regardless of whether the ship is or is not a long-life asset.

Consequential amendments are made.

All amendments have effect for chargeable periods ending after 31 December 2010 but have no effect on expenditure incurred before 1 January 2011.

58 Transfer pricing: application of OECD principles

(1) In section 164 of TIOPA 2010 (Part to be interpreted in accordance with OECD principles), for subsection (4) substitute—

"(4) In this section "the transfer pricing guidelines" means—

(a) the version of the Transfer Pricing Guidelines for Multinational Enterprises and Tax Administrations approved by the Organisation for Economic Co-operation and Development (OECD) on 22 July 2010, or

(b) such other document approved and published by the OECD in place of that (or a later) version or in place of those Guidelines as is designated for the time being by order made by the Treasury,

including, in either case, such material published by the OECD as part of (or by way of update or supplement to) the version or other document concerned as may be so designated."

(2) The amendment made by this section has effect (in relation to provision made or imposed at any time)—

(a) for corporation tax purposes, for accounting periods beginning on or after 1 April 2011, and

(b) for income tax purposes, for the tax year 2011–12 and subsequent tax years.

GENERAL NOTE

Section 58 updates the definition of "transfer pricing guidelines" to refer to the Organisation for Economic Co-operation and Development (OECD) Transfer Pricing Guidelines for Multinational Enterprises and Tax Administrations approved by OECD for publication in July 2010. The measure makes clear that, for accounting periods beginning on or after 1 April 2011 (corporation tax) and for the tax year 2011–12 and subsequent years (income tax) this version of the OECD guidelines is to be referred to. The amended power will also allow changes to the definition of "transfer pricing guidelines", whether supplementing or replacing the 2010 Guidelines, to be made by secondary legislation.

59 Offshore funds

In Part 8 of TIOPA 2010 (offshore funds), after section 363 insert—

"363A Residence of offshore funds which are undertakings for collective investment in transferable securities

(1) This section applies to an offshore fund (within the meaning of section 355) which—

(a) is, for the purposes of the UCITS Directive, an undertaking for collective investment in transferable securities, and

(b) is authorised pursuant to Article 5 of the UCITS Directive in a Member State other than the United Kingdom.

(2) If—

(a) the offshore fund is a body corporate which, under the law of the Member State in which it is authorised pursuant to Article 5 of the UCITS Directive, is treated as resident in that State for the purposes of any tax imposed under that law on income, and

(b) (apart from this section) the body corporate would be treated as resident in the United Kingdom for the purposes of any enactment (within the meaning of section 354) relating to income tax, corporation tax or capital gains tax,

the body corporate is instead to be treated as if it were not resident in the United Kingdom.

(3) If, by virtue of section 99 or 103A of TCGA 1992, that Act applies in relation to the offshore fund as if it were a company, that Act applies as if the company were neither resident nor ordinarily resident in the United Kingdom (if it would not otherwise do so).

(4) In this section "the UCITS Directive" means Directive 2009/65/EC of the European Parliament and of the Council."

GENERAL NOTE

This section inserts a new TIOPA 2010 s 363A. This section provides that offshore funds constituted as bodies corporate resident in another Member State of the EU and authorised as a UCITS fund in that Member State will not be treated as resident in the UK.

In addition s 363A(3) provides that where TCGA 1992 ss 99 or 103A apply to treat an offshore fund as if it was a company, that company will be treated as neither resident nor ordinarily resident in the UK.

Under the latest version of the UCITS Directive (Directive 2009/65/EC, also known as UCITS IV) certain management functions of UCITS funds can be carried out by entities resident in a different EU Member State than the fund. There was a concern that if these functions were carried on in the UK they could constitute the central management and control of the fund and hence bring the fund within the charge to UK corporation tax. This new section prevents that from occurring.

60 Index-linked gilt-edged securities

(1) In section 399 of CTA 2009 (index-linked gilt-edged securities: basic rules), for subsection (4) substitute—

"(4) In this section and sections 400 to 400C—

"index-linked gilt-edged securities" means any gilt-edged securities under which the amounts of the payments are determined wholly or partly by reference to an index of prices published by the Statistics Board;

"relevant prices index", in relation to an index-linked gilt-edged security, means the index of prices by reference to which the amounts of the payments under the security are wholly or partly determined."

(2) In the following provisions of that Act, for "retail" substitute "relevant"—

(a) section 400(1)(b), (2), (3) and (6);

(b) section 400A(3) and (7)(b).

(3) Accordingly, in Schedule 14 to FA 2010, omit paragraph 4(4).

(4) The amendments made by this section have effect in relation to securities issued on or after the day on which this Act is passed.

GENERAL NOTE

The definition of an index-linked gilt edged security applying for corporation tax purposes is amended in relation to securities issued on or after the date of Royal Assent to the Finance (No. 3) Bill.

From that date, an index-linked gilt-edged security is a gilt-edged security under which the amount of the payments is determined by a reference to an index of prices published by the Statistics Board (CTA 2009 s 399(4) as substituted by s 60(1)). Prior to Royal Assent, the definition refers to payments being determined by reference to the Retail Prices Index (RPI) (CTA 2009 s 399(4) prior to substitution).

Consequential amendments are made to CTA 2009 s 400, 400A and FA 2010 Sch 14.

PART 3

OIL

61 PRT: areas treated as continuing to be oil fields

(1) In Schedule 1 to OTA 1975 (determination of oil fields), in paragraph 7(4), for "the relevant area" substitute "those qualifying assets".

(2) The amendment made by this section has effect in relation to chargeable periods that begin after 30 June 2009.

GENERAL NOTE

This section amends the provision that was introduced in FA 2009 to deem oil field status to continue after the relevant licence ceases to exist, until such time as the decommissioning of all relevant field assets is complete. The change arises as a result of industry lobbying as it was thought the original words did not deal adequately with the situation where the assets were situated outside the field boundary. The change is deemed to have applied since the legislation was originally introduced.

62 Intangible fixed assets: oil licences

(1) Section 809 of CTA 2009 (oil licences) is amended as follows.

(2) After subsection (1) insert—

"(1A) The reference in subsection (1) to an oil licence or an interest in an oil licence includes all goodwill, and any intangible asset, which relates to, derives from or is connected with an oil licence or an interest in an oil licence."

(3) In subsection (2), for "subsection (1)" substitute "this section".

(4) In subsection (4), for "subsection (1)" substitute "this section".

(5) The amendments made by this section have effect in relation to accounting periods beginning on or after 23 March 2011 (and, in relation to those accounting periods, are to be treated as always having had effect).

(6) For the purposes of subsection (5), an accounting period beginning before, and ending on or after, 23 March 2011 is to be treated as if so much of the period as falls before that date, and so much of the period as falls on or after that date, were separate accounting periods.

GENERAL NOTE

The cost of acquiring oil and gas licences is specifically prohibited from falling within the intangible fixed asset (IFA) rules. When such assets are acquired it is possible that goodwill would be recognised as part of the acquisition in the accounts of the purchaser, particularly where the acquirer accounts under IFRS. Such goodwill would appear to have been allowable under the IFA rules, even if it related to an oil and gas licence. The change prevents relief being claimed under the IFA rules for any costs associated with the acquisition of an oil and gas licence.

The change is effective for accounting periods beginning on or after March 23rd 2011 such that no claim for a deduction can be made under the IFA rules in such a period (notwithstanding the goodwill may have been recognised in the accounts in an earlier accounting period). In respect of an accounting period straddling March 23rd 2011 relief could still be available for the first part of the year.

63 Reduction of supplementary charge for certain new oil fields

(1) In section 337 of CTA 2010 (initial licensee to hold a field allowance), in subsection (1), for "authorisation day" substitute "accounting period in which the authorisation day falls".

(2) For section 350 of that Act (meaning of "new oil field") substitute—

"350 New oil field"

(1) In this Chapter "new oil field" means an oil field—

(a) which is a qualifying oil field, and

(b) whose development (in whole or in part) is authorised for the first time on or after 22 April 2009.

(2) If all assets of an oil field which are relevant assets have been decommissioned, there is to be ignored for the purposes of subsection (1)(b) any authorisation in respect of that oil field which occurs before that decommissioning.

(3) Sub-paragraphs (2) to (9) of paragraph 7 of Schedule 1 to OTA 1975 apply for the purpose of determining whether relevant assets of an oil field are decommissioned as they apply for the purpose of determining whether qualifying assets of a relevant area are decommissioned.

(4) For the purposes of this section, an asset is a relevant asset of an oil field if—

(a) it has at any time been a qualifying asset (within the meaning of the Oil Taxation Act 1983) in relation to any participator in the field, and

(b) it has at any time been used for the purpose of winning oil from the field."

(3) In section 357 of that Act (other definitions), in the definition of "authorisation day", after "authorised" insert "as mentioned in section 350(1)(b)".

(4) The amendments made by this section have effect in relation to accounting periods ending on or after 1 April 2010.

(5) Corresponding amendments, having effect in relation to accounting periods ending on or after 22 April 2009, are to be treated as having been made in Schedule 44 to FA 2009.

GENERAL NOTE

A relief against supplementary charge, known as field allowance, is given in respect of certain fields given development consent after 22 April 2009 if they meet certain criteria (see CTA 2010 s 352 et seq.). When these rules were first introduced in 2009 there were two anomalies which are now being corrected.

Under sub-s 1, the field allowance can be activated once the field starts producing. However the relief available is restricted, inter alia, to the total pool of allowance available at the start of the accounting period. Under the original wording the allowance only first became available from the date of the field's development consent. If there was income from the field in that first accounting period it would not therefore activate any allowance. The change provides that an amount first becomes available from the first day of the accounting period in which the field's development consent is obtained, such that any income in that first accounting period can activate some of the allowance.

Subsection 2 introduces a revised CTA 2010 s 350, sub-s (2), which provides that were an original field development has been fully decommissioned, and a second development of the field takes place, the original development decision date is ignored in determining whether the field is a "new field" for the purposes of the field allowance. This will enable so-called re-commissioned fields to qualify for field allowance if they receive a development consent after 22 April 2009.

Subsection 3 of new s 350 imports the rules for determining the period up until when fields, where the relevant licence expires, continue to exist, to determine whether the original field development has been fully decommissioned.

These amendments apply to accounting periods beginning on or after 22 April 2009.

64 Chargeable gains: oil activities

Schedule 15 contains provisions about chargeable gains in relation to oil activities.

GENERAL NOTE

Schedule 15 contains provisions about chargeable gains in relation to oil activities.

PART 4
PENSIONS

GENERAL NOTE

There are three major items of pensions legislation in FA 2011 stemming from announcements made by the Chancellor in his Emergency Budget of 22 June 2010. These concern the requirement to purchase an annuity by age 75 and the measures to restrict tax relief given at above the basic rate of tax on pension contributions from 6 April 2011.

Firstly, in the Emergency Budget the Chancellor announced that he would end the effective requirement for members of registered pension schemes to purchase an annuity by age 75 with effect from 2011–12. Before then the Government would consult on the detail of the change which commenced on 15 July 2010 with the publication of its consultation document, Removing the requirement to annuitise by age 75. Meanwhile, as an interim measure the age limit was increased to 77 by FA 2010 s 6 and Sch 3 which contained appropriate amendments to the current legislation. The consultation was completed on 10 September 2010 and FA 2011 s 65 and Sch 16 contain provisions to amend the original legislation in FA 2004 Part 4 as it relates to registered pension schemes and to individuals reaching the age of 75.

Secondly, in the Emergency Budget the Chancellor announced that the widely criticised, complicated and cumbersome measures in FA 2010 s 23 and Sch 2 to restrict tax relief given at above the basic rate on pension contributions paid in 2011–12 et seq by high income individuals would be reviewed. The review was carried out in consultation with employers, pension schemes, experts and other interested parties to determine the best design of a regime for raising the same tax revenue by simpler means. FA 2010 s 5 contained provisions to repeal the legislation in FA 2010 Sch 2 should it later be considered appropriate following the review. The review was completed with definitive proposals made on 14 October 2010 and with draft legislation published thereafter which, following further refinement, now appears in FA 2011 s 66 and Sch 17 relating to the annual allowance charge that will restrict tax relief. The legislation in FA 2010 Sch 2 was repealed by Treasury Order on 10 December 2010.

Thirdly, consultations also took place during 2010 following the change of Government on reducing the lifetime allowance. Consultations were concluded on 27 August 2010 and formed part of the Summary of Responses document on the Restriction of pensions tax relief: a discussion document published on 14 October 2010. This document announced the reduction and the legislation now appears in FA 2011 s 67 and Sch 18 relating to the restrictions on tax relief as a result of the reduction to the lifetime allowance charge.

FA 2011 also contains some minor measures regarding pension schemes and one major piece of legislation which was introduced as an amendment during the passage of the Finance Bill through Parliament. Clarification is provided in s 68 so that a tax charge does not arise in respect of borrowing by the National Employment Savings Trust and s 69 provides for an exemption from income tax on any interest that the Pensions Regulator requires an employer to pay on pension contributions paid late. In addition power is provided in ss 70 and 71 to HM Treasury to make regulations regarding respectively, the application of tax to the National Employment Savings Trust and in a situation where a tax issue arises in consequence of anything in the Pensions Act 2008 Part 1 or the Pensions (No. 2) Act (Northern Ireland) 2008 Part 1.

The major Amendment is contained in s 72 preventing UK residents from transferring their pensions to a qualifying registered overseas pension scheme and then taking an income in the UK as a tax avoidance ploy.

65 Benefits under pension schemes

Schedule 16 contains provision about the benefits available under pension schemes and related matters.

GENERAL NOTE

Section 65 introduces Schedule 16 containing detailed provisions for the removal of the long standing requirement for members of registered pension schemes to purchase an annuity by the age of 75.

66 Annual allowance charge

Schedule 17 contains provision about the annual allowance charge.

GENERAL NOTE

Section 66 introduces Schedule 17, which amends FA 2004 Part 4 in relation to the annual allowance tax charge.

67 Lifetime allowance charge

Schedule 18 contains provision about the lifetime allowance charge.

GENERAL NOTE

Section 67 introduces Sch 18, which amends FA 2004 Part 4 in relation to the lifetime allowance tax charge in consequence of the amendments being made to the annual allowance tax charge by Sch 17.

68 Borrowing by section 67 pension scheme

(1) Section 182 of FA 2004 (unauthorised borrowing) does not cause a section 67 pension scheme to be not authorised to borrow an amount for the purposes of meeting costs of establishing, administering or managing the pension scheme.

(2) Accordingly, in the case of a section 67 pension scheme, references in sections 182 and 183 of FA 2004 to amounts previously borrowed do not include any amount previously borrowed for those purposes.

(3) For the purposes of this section neither—

(a) borrowing an amount for making investments for the purposes of a pension scheme, nor

(b) borrowing an amount for making deposits with a view to deriving income for the purposes of a pension scheme (otherwise than prior to applying the amount for meeting costs of establishing, administering or managing the pension scheme),

is to be taken to be borrowing the amount for the purposes of meeting costs of establishing, administering or managing the pension scheme.

(4) In this section "section 67 pension scheme" means a pension scheme which is established under section 67 of the Pensions Act 2008.

(5) Section 163(2) of FA 2004 (meaning of "borrowing") applies for the interpretation of this section.

(6) This section is treated as having come into force on 6 April 2011.

GENERAL NOTE

Under FA 2004 s 182 a registered pension scheme is not authorised to borrow more than half of the value of the fund otherwise a tax charge arises on the scheme administrator on the excess borrowing. The National Employment Savings Trust (NEST) is a registered pension scheme that is self-financing, but its initial cost of setting up is to be funded by loans. An unintended tax charge would arise on the borrowing used to finance its initial cost, so the legislation in this s ensures that the tax charge is removed. This puts the cost of funding NEST on the same footing as other pension schemes where the cost of establishment has been funded by the sponsoring employer or pension provider and obviates any unauthorised borrowing.

Subsection 1 provides that FA 2004 s 182 does not make any borrowing unauthorised if the borrowing is used to fund the costs of establishing, administering or managing a pension scheme established under Pensions Act 2008 s 67 such as NEST. Subsection 2 goes on to state that any calculation of the amount of borrowing by NEST for the purposes of FA 2004 ss 182 and 183 should not include any amounts previously borrowed to fund the costs of establishing, administering or managing NEST. Subsection 3 ensures that the definition of establishing, administering and managing does not include investment. Section 68 comes into force on 6 April 2011 by virtue of subsection 6.

69 Exemption from tax on interest on unpaid relevant contributions

(1) ITTOIA 2005 is amended as follows.

(2) In section 369(3)(e) (exemptions from income tax charge on income), after "loans," insert "unpaid relevant contributions,".

(3) After section 753 insert—

"753A Interest on unpaid relevant contributions

(1) No liability to income tax arises in respect of interest paid in compliance with a requirement in a compliance notice or an unpaid contributions notice to pay interest in respect of unpaid relevant contributions.

(2) In this section—

"compliance notice" means a notice under section 35 of the Pensions Act;

"the Pensions Act" means the Pensions Act 2008 or the Pensions (No2) Act (Northern Ireland) 2008;

"unpaid contributions notice" means a notice under section 37 of the Pensions Act;

"unpaid relevant contributions" has the same meaning as in section 38(2)(a) of the Pensions Act."

GENERAL NOTE

When employers deduct pension contributions from their employees' remuneration they are obliged to pay the contributions to the pension scheme concerned by a certain date otherwise the Pension Regulator has to be informed. In these circumstances the Pensions Regulator may require an employer to pay interest from which tax would be deductible to the employees' pension account on the contributions paid late. The interest compensates the employee for lost investment growth. As the investment growth in the pension scheme would be tax-free, an amendment to legislation is necessary to exempt the tax charge on the interest. So ITTOIA 2005 s 369(3)(c) is being amended by subsection 2 by adding relevant unpaid contributions to the list of exemptions from the income tax charge on interest on such contributions. Subsection 3 amends ITTOIA 2005 s 753 to provide there is no liability to income tax on interest that is paid to comply with a compliance notice issued under Pensions Act 2008 s 35 or an unpaid contributions notice issued under Pensions Act 2008 s 37 by the Pensions Regulator. The amendments in subsection 3 also cover compliance notices issued under Northern Ireland legislation.

70 Power to make further provision about section 67 pension scheme

(1) The Treasury may by regulations make provision for and in connection with—

(a) the application of the relevant taxes in relation to a pension scheme established under section 67 of the Pensions Act 2008, and

(b) the application of the relevant taxes in relation to any person in connection with such a pension scheme.

(2) The provision that may be made by regulations under this section includes provision imposing any of the relevant taxes (as well as provisions for exemptions or reliefs).

(3) The relevant taxes are—

(a) income tax,
(b) capital gains tax,
(c) corporation tax, and
(d) inheritance tax.

(4) Regulations under this section may include provision having effect in relation to any time before they are made if the provision does not increase any person's liability to tax.

(5) Regulations under this section may include—

(a) provision amending any enactment or instrument, and
(b) consequential, supplementary and transitional provision.

(6) Regulations under this section are to be made by statutory instrument.

(7) A statutory instrument containing regulations under this section is subject to annulment in pursuance of a resolution of the House of Commons.

GENERAL NOTE

The National Employment Savings Trust (NEST) is a registered pension scheme and like all other registered pension schemes would qualify for generous tax reliefs and could be subject to tax charges where the rules are not followed. However, when the pension tax rules were introduced a pension scheme like NEST had not been envisaged, so NEST or its members could be subject to unintended tax charges. So regulations containing tax provisions may be needed to prevent these unintended tax charges from arising. Section 70 therefore gives HM Treasury the power to make regulations regarding the application of tax to a pension scheme established under Pensions Act 2008 s 67, such as NEST, and any person in connection with such a scheme.

Subsection 2 provides that the provision made by the regulations may impose the relevant taxes as well as providing exemptions or reliefs. The relevant taxes are set out in sub-s 3. There is provision in sub-s 4 for the regulations to have retrospective effect provided they do not increase a person's liability to tax. Subsection 5 states that the regulations can amend any primary or secondary legislation and make consequential, supplementary and transitional provision. Subsection 7 makes it clear that the regulations made under s 70 are made under the negative resolution procedure of the House of Commons.

71 Tax provision consequential on Part 1 of Pensions Act 2008 etc

(1) The Treasury may by regulations make provision in relation to any of the relevant taxes in consequence of Part 1 of the Pensions Act 2008 or Part 1 of the Pensions (No 2) Act (Northern Ireland) 2008.

(2) The provision that may be made by regulations under this section includes provision imposing any of the relevant taxes (as well as provisions for exemptions or reliefs).

(3) The relevant taxes are—

(a) income tax,
(b) capital gains tax,
(c) corporation tax,
(d) inheritance tax,
(e) value added tax,
(f) stamp duty land tax,
(g) stamp duty, and
(h) stamp duty reserve tax.

(4) Regulations under this section may include provision having effect in relation to any time before they are made if the provision does not increase any person's liability to tax.

(5) Regulations under this section may make different provision for different cases.

(6) Regulations under this section may include—

(a) provision amending any enactment or instrument, and

(b) consequential, supplementary and transitional provision.

(7) Regulations under this section are to be made by statutory instrument.

(8) A statutory instrument containing regulations under this section is subject to annulment in pursuance of a resolution of the House of Commons.

GENERAL NOTE

Pension schemes that meet the employer duty provisions of Pensions Act 2008 Part 1 or Pensions (No. 2) Act (Northern Ireland) 2008 Part 1 must be registered for tax purposes from 2012. Like all other registered pension schemes this type of pension scheme would qualify for generous tax reliefs and could be subject to tax charges where the rules are not followed. So tax provisions may be needed to prevent unintended tax charges arising in consequence of the interaction of the tax rules for registered pension schemes and the provisions of Part 1 Pensions Act 2008 and its Northern Ireland counterpart legislation. Some changes to tax legislation have already been made and so the power in s 71 to make regulations enables any further necessary changes to be made to the tax rules once the provisions of those Pensions Acts take effect. However, the power is also contained in s 71 to make any tax provision required in consequence of the interaction of the tax rules and the Pensions Acts provisions. This ensures that all registered pension schemes fit within the existing pensions tax framework.

Subsection 1 gives power to HM Treasury to make regulations in respect of the taxes listed in sub-s 3. Subsection 2 provides that the provision made by the regulations may impose the relevant taxes as well as provide exemptions or reliefs from them. There is provision in sub-s 4 for the regulations to have retrospective effect provided they do not increase a person's liability to tax. Subsection 5 states that the regulations can amend any primary or secondary legislation and make consequential, supplementary and transitional provision. Subsection 8 makes it clear that the regulations made under s 71 are made under the negative resolution procedure of the House of Commons.

72 Foreign pensions of UK residents

(1) In Part 2 of TIOPA 2010 (double taxation relief), in Chapter 3 (miscellaneous provisions), after section 130 insert—

"130A Interpreting provision about UK taxation of pensions etc

(1) Subsection (3) applies if double taxation arrangements make the provision, however expressed, mentioned in subsection (2).

(2) The provision is that pensions and other similar remuneration which—

(a) arise outside the United Kingdom, and

(b) are paid to persons who are resident in the United Kingdom,

are not to be subject to United Kingdom tax.

(3) That provision does not prevent a pension or other similar remuneration of a person resident in the United Kingdom being chargeable to income tax if—

(a) the pension or other similar remuneration is paid out of sums or assets that were the subject of a relevant transfer or related sums or assets, and

(b) the relevant transfer or any transaction forming part of that transfer was, or formed part of, a tax avoidance scheme.

(4) But nothing in subsection (3) prevents credit being allowed under Chapter 2 of this Part (double taxation relief by way of credit) against any tax so charged.

(5) In determining whether a pension or other similar remuneration is paid out of sums or assets within subsection (3)(a), it is to be assumed that it is paid out of such sums or assets in priority to any other sums or assets.

(6) A "relevant transfer", in respect of any sums or assets, is a transaction or series of transactions as a result of which—

(a) the sums or assets are transferred out of a pension scheme, and

(b) the sums or assets or related sums or assets (or both) are transferred into the pension scheme under which the pension or other similar remuneration is paid.

(7) A scheme is a "tax avoidance scheme" if the main purpose, or one of the main purposes, of any party to the scheme in entering into the scheme is to secure an

income tax advantage for any person under this Part by virtue of provision mentioned in subsection (2) made by double taxation arrangements.

(8) For the purposes of subsection (7)—

(a) "scheme" includes any scheme, arrangements or understanding of any kind whatever, whether or not legally enforceable, involving a single transaction or two or more transactions,
(b) it does not matter whether or not the double taxation arrangements were in existence at the time the tax avoidance scheme was entered into or given effect to, and
(c) "income tax advantage" is to be construed in accordance with section 572A(3) to (5) of ITA 2007.

(9) In this section—

"pension" and "other similar remuneration" have the same meaning as in the Model Tax Convention on Income and on Capital published (from time to time) by the Organisation for Economic Co-operation and Development;
"pension scheme" has the same meaning as in Part 4 of FA 2004 (see section 150 of that Act);
"related sums or assets", in relation to other sums or assets ("the original sums or assets"), means sums or assets which arise, or (directly or indirectly) derive, from the original sums or assets or from sums or assets which so arise or derive."

(2) The amendment made by this section has effect in relation to the tax year 2011–12 and subsequent tax years (and it does not matter whether the tax avoidance scheme was entered into or effected before, or on or after, 6 April 2011).

GENERAL NOTE

Under most of the UK's double taxation agreements (DTAs) a pension paid to a UK resident is taxable in the UK. In a limited number of cases where the UK and the other country tax pensions differently the DTA provides that a pension or lump sum is taxed solely in the country or territory where the pension arises. On 6 April 2011 the Government announced that legislation would be introduced in the Finance Bill to prevent DTAs being used to avoid taxation of foreign pensions paid to UK residents where pensions savings have been transferred to a pension scheme outside the UK. This measure apparently arises from a DTA that came into effect on 6 April 2011 where there is a specific issue with qualifying registered overseas pension schemes (QROPS) registered in Hong Kong. This was followed up by a written ministerial statement on 24 May 2011. When using a QROPS income tax is paid on pensions income at the rate which applies in the jurisdiction in which the QROPS is registered rather than at the rate under which the assets were accumulated. A UK resident who retires overseas to a territory with a lower income tax rate would receive tax relief on their UK contributions, but receive their pension as income with a lower rate of tax. It is believed that HMRC is closing this loophole as a result of the operation of the early trigger point for disclosure of marketed tax schemes under the disclosure of tax avoidance schemes legislation in FA 2004 Part 7.

Sub-section 1 inserts TIOPA 2010 s 130A to ensure that a provision in a DTA cannot prevent foreign pensions or lump sums paid to UK residents being taxable in the UK in certain circumstances. Thus, if a DTA provides that a foreign pension of lump sum paid to a UK resident is not subject to UK tax, then this legislation applies. It provides for UK income tax to be levied on payments from a QROPS where a payment that arises in another territory is received by a UK resident and the pension savings in respect of which the pension or other similar remuneration is paid have been transferred to a pension scheme in another territory and the main purpose, or one of the main purposes, of any person concerned with the transfer of pension savings is respect of which the payment is made was to take advantage of the DTA in respect of that payment by means of that transfer. In the event that tax is paid in the other jurisdiction appropriate credit will be available against the UK tax chargeable. If the pension savings used to pay the foreign pension or lump sum are only partly formed of transferred pension savings, then the pension or lump sum paid to a UK resident is assumed to be paid from the transferred pension first. The legislation confirms that the DTA does not have to be in place when the tax avoidance scheme is entered into.

Sub-section 2 provides for the provisions of TIOPA s 130A to take effect for 2011–12 et seq regardless of whether the tax avoidance scheme was entered into before, or on or after, 6 April 2011.

PART 5
BANK LEVY

73 The bank levy

Schedule 19 contains provision for and in connection with the bank levy.

GENERAL NOTE

The Chancellor of the Exchequer announced in the June 2010 Budget the introduction of a bank levy to UK banks, UK building society groups, foreign banks operating in the UK and UK banks in non-banking groups. The levy will apply for periods of account ending on or after 1 January 2011. In addition to the legislation in the FA there are also regulations for the Collection and Management of the bank levy, with guidance provided by HMRC's bank levy manual.

Section 73 introduces Schedule 19, which contains the detailed provisions governing the bank levy.

The legislation is lengthy and complex, containing no fewer than 80 paragraphs. However, many of these are duplicative in that they aim to apply similar sets of rules to the various different group structures to which the bank levy will be applied.

PART 6
OTHER TAXES

Value added tax

74 Business samples

(1) In Schedule 4 to VATA 1994 (matters to be treated as supply of goods or services), paragraph 5 (transfer or disposal of goods forming part of the assets of a business) is amended as follows.

(2) For sub-paragraph (2)(b) substitute—

> "(b) the provision to a person, otherwise than for a consideration, of a sample of goods."

(3) Omit sub-paragraph (3).

GENERAL NOTE

When goods on which input tax has been reclaimed are disposed of for no consideration, VAT normally becomes due. An exception to this situation is if the goods are classed as 'gifts of small value' or 'samples' – the UK parameter for 'small gifts' is £50 (cost) – either as a single gift or combination of gifts to any one 'person' over any 12-month period.

With regard to samples, UK legislation has always placed a restriction on the number of VAT free samples of a product that can be given away by a business. Only the first sample has been disregarded in the past for output tax purposes – more than one identical sample given to the same person creates an output tax liability.

Following a recent ECJ case concerning the VAT treatment of DVDs given away to retailers by a music publisher (case taken by EMI – ref: C581/08) the UK restriction was confirmed to be incorrect within EU VAT law. There should be no limit to the number of VAT free samples that can be given away by a UK business as long as they are given away for business purposes eg as in the case of EMI which is clearly providing free samples in order to promote its music sales.

75 Zero-rating: splitting of supplies

(1) In Part 2 of Schedule 8 to VATA 1994 (zero-rating: groups), Group 3 (books, etc) is amended as follows.

(2) For "*Note*: Items 1 to 6—" substitute—

> *Notes*
>
> (1) Items 1 to 6—".

(3) At the end insert—

"(2) Items 1 to 6 do not include goods in circumstances where—

(a) the supply of the goods is connected with a supply of services, and

(b) those connected supplies are made by different suppliers.

(3) For the purposes of Note (2) a supply of goods is connected with a supply of services if, had those two supplies been made by a single supplier—

(a) they would have been treated as a single supply of services, and

(b) that single supply would have been a taxable supply (other than a zero-rated supply) or an exempt supply."

(4) The amendments made by this section have effect in relation to supplies made on or after the day on which this Act is passed.

GENERAL NOTE

This section is an anti-avoidance measure that will prevent a business splitting supplies of services and printed matter to gain a VAT advantage through the zero-rating of the printed matter. This is intended to prevent eg an exempt business such as a bank acquiring an input tax gain. It will only be relevant to a very limited number of businesses, and will not affect a business that sells printed matter and services separately, and where the customer is not contractually obliged to buy both the printed matter and the services at the same time.

To give a practical example of how the legislation will block a previous input tax gain for an exempt business, let us consider a company called Computer Services Ltd (CSL) that has agreed to carry out a major computer upgrade job for ABC Bank (the latter is exempt and cannot claim input tax). The job quote is £50m. This fee will be entirely standard rated, even if part of the work of CSL is to produce computer manuals (zero-rated) to enable bank staff to understand the computer system. This is because the manuals are classed as an incidental supply to the computer services ie . a single standard rated supply is evident under the 'mixed supply' rules of VAT.

However, if it is agreed that a separate company Computer Books Ltd (CBL) will supply the manuals to the bank as a separate supply, so that the £50m fee will be split on a £45m/£5m basis ie . so that the £5m charge by CBL is zero-rated as relevant to printed matter, this would have saved the bank £1m of irrecoverable input tax under previous rules. But the revised legislation blocks this gain by applying the same VAT outcome as if only one company had jointly supplied the services and manuals ie . the whole fee is standard rated.

As a final comment, the legislation is not intended to capture normal trading situations where printed matter is supplied in its own right. For example, if an accountant forms a new company for a client, and uses a company that charges £30 plus VAT for the formation service, with extra zero-rated supplies of eg paper copies of articles of association/memorandum of association available to be purchased at a separate price, then the split in the VAT liability if fine. The key point with this arrangement is that there is no contractual obligation for the printed matter and the formation service to be bought at the same time as a connected purchase – the buyer has the choice.

76 Academies

(1) In Part 2 of VATA 1994 (reliefs, exemptions and repayments), after section 33A insert—

"33B Refunds of VAT to Academies

(1) This section applies where—

(a) VAT is chargeable on—

(i) the supply of goods or services to the proprietor of an Academy,

(ii) the acquisition of any goods from another member State by the proprietor of an Academy, or

(iii) the importation of any goods from a place outside the member States by the proprietor of an Academy, and

(b) the supply, acquisition or importation is not for the purposes of any business carried on by the proprietor of the Academy.

(2) The Commissioners shall, on a claim made by the proprietor of the Academy at such time and in such form and manner as the Commissioners may determine, refund to that proprietor the amount of VAT so chargeable.

(3) Subject to subsection (4), the claim must be made before the end of the period of 4 years beginning with the day on which the supply is made or the acquisition or importation takes place.

(4) If the Commissioners so determine, the claim period is such shorter period beginning with that day as the Commissioners may determine.

(5) Subsection (6) applies where goods or services supplied to, or acquired or imported by, the proprietor of the Academy cannot be conveniently distinguished from goods or services supplied to, or acquired or imported by, it for the purpose of a business carried on by that proprietor.

(6) The amount to be refunded under this section is such amount as remains after deducting from the whole of the VAT chargeable on any supply to, or acquisition or importation by, the proprietor of the Academy such proportion of that VAT as appears to the Commissioners to be attributable to the carrying on of the business.

(7) References in this section to VAT do not include any VAT which, by virtue of an order under section 25(7), is excluded from credit under section 25.

(8) In this section—

(a) references to the proprietor of an Academy are to the proprietor of the Academy acting in that capacity, and

(b) "Academy" and "proprietor" have the same meaning as in the Education Act 1996 (see section 579 of that Act)."

(2) In section 79 of that Act (repayment supplement in respect of certain delayed payments or refunds)—

(a) in subsection (1), after paragraph (c) insert

", or

(d) the proprietor of an Academy who is registered is entitled to a refund under section 33B,",

(b) in subsection (5), after paragraph (c) insert

", and

(d) a supplement paid to the proprietor of an Academy under subsection (1)(d) shall be treated as an amount due to that proprietor by way of refund under section 33B.", and

(c) in subsection (6)(b) after "33A" insert "or 33B".

(3) In section 90 of that Act (failure of resolution under the Provisional Collection of Taxes Act 1968), in subsection (3) after "33A," insert "33B,".

(4) In Part 2 of Schedule 9 to that Act (exemptions: groups), in Group 14 (supplies of goods where input tax cannot be recovered), in Note (9) after "33A," insert "33B,".

(5) The amendments made by this section have effect in relation to supplies made, and acquisitions and importations taking place, on or after 1 April 2011.

GENERAL NOTE

A new s 33B is being inserted into VATA 1994, in order that academies will be able to reclaim VAT paid on expenses relevant to their non-business activities ie . free education. The purpose of the legislation is simple, namely to ensure that academies are in the same position as local authorities as far as VAT recovery on expenses is concerned. Local authorities have always been able to reclaim VAT paid on their non-business activities through what is known as a 's 33' claim.

The legislation gives an academy a four-year window to claim VAT on its non-business expenditure and claims can also be made in relation to VAT paid on imported goods or acquisitions from other EU countries.

77 Relief from VAT on imported goods of low value

(1) In Schedule 2 to the Value Added Tax (Imported Goods) Relief Order 1984 (SI 1984/746) (reliefs for goods of certain descriptions), in item 8 of Group 8 (consignments of goods not exceeding a certain value), for "£18" substitute "£15".

(2) The amendment of that Schedule by this section is without prejudice to any power to amend that Schedule by subordinate legislation.

(3) The amendment made by this section has effect in relation to goods imported on or after 1 November 2011.

GENERAL NOTE

Goods can currently be imported into the UK from outside the EU without VAT being payable if they have a value of £18 or less. This figure will reduce to £15 on 1 November 2011, with further reductions possibly on the cards in future years. The £18 concession, known as Low Value Consignment Relief, was originally intended to serve as an administrative measure to reduce the costs to businesses, Royal Mail and HMRC, but has in reality become a very effective way for some big retailers to import VAT free goods from the Channel Islands, particularly DVDs and similar computer related products.

In effect, the 'importers' wishing to avoid VAT after November must now suffer a £3 reduction in their profit margins for those items they were selling at the top price of £18, or instead deflect such sales back to their UK branches and pay 20% VAT i e £15 plus £3 = £18. The measure is good news for smaller UK retailers having to compete with these imports.

Note – the £15/£18 import limit does not apply to 'alcoholic beverages, tobacco products, toilets waters or perfumes'. A zero threshold applies to these goods because they are specifically excluded from the legislation that relates to Low Value Consignment Relief.

Climate change levy

78 Supplies of commodities to be used in producing electricity

Schedule 20 contains provision for and in connection with the charging of climate change levy on supplies of commodities to be used in producing electricity.

GENERAL NOTE

Section 78 introduces Schedule 20.

79 Northern Ireland gas supplies

(1) In Schedule 6 to FA 2000 (climate change levy), omit paragraph 11A (exemption for Northern Ireland gas supplies).

(2) Subsection (3) applies to a supply of gas if—

(a) the supply is made by a gas utility (within the meaning of that Schedule (see paragraph 147)),

(b) the person to whom the supply is made intends to cause the gas to be burned in Northern Ireland, and

(c) the supply is treated as taking place on or after 1 April 2011 but before 1 November 2013.

(3) Paragraph 42 of that Schedule (amount payable by way of levy) has effect as if—

(a) for sub-paragraphs (1) and (1A) there were substituted—

"(1) The amount payable by way of levy on a taxable supply is—

(a) if the supply is treated as taking place before 1 April 2012, £0.00059 per kilowatt hour, and

(b) if the supply is treated as taking place on or after that date, £0.00062 per kilowatt hour.", and

(b) in sub-paragraph (3) the reference to a reduced-rate supply were a reference to a supply in relation to which this subsection applies.

(4) In FA 2001, omit section 105(2) (which inserted paragraph 11A of that Schedule).

(5) The amendments made by subsections (1) and (4) have effect in relation to a supply of gas to a person if the gas is actually supplied to the person on or after 1 April 2011.

(6) Subsections (2) and (3) are treated as having come into force on 1 April 2011.

GENERAL NOTE

Climate change levy (CCL) is a tax on the supply of certain energy products for business and public sector use. Supplies by a gas utility of gas to be burned in Northern Ireland are exempt from CCL under FA 2000 Sch 6 para 11A. State Aid approval for the exemption expired on 31 March 2011 and the Government decided not to seek an extension. Accordingly, s 78 cancels this exemption with effect from 1 April 2011 by removing Sch 6 para 11A.The exemption is being replaced by a reduced rate of CCL 65% lower than the normal CCL rate for gas. The rate is set at £0.00059 per kilowatt hour from 1 April 2011 and £0.00062 per kilowatt hour from 1 April 2012. Applying a lower rate is still a State Aid, but as the lower rate meets the minimum rate of taxation for gas as prescribed by Council Directive 2003/96/EC, simplified State Aid clearance is available under Commission Regulation (EC) No 800/2008.

80 Power to suspend exemption for supplies used in recycling processes

(1) The Treasury may by order provide that Schedule 6 to FA 2000 (climate change levy) is to have effect in relation to any supply of a taxable commodity made on or after 1 April 2011 as if—

(a) paragraph 18A (exemption: supply for use in recycling processes), and
(b) any reference to that paragraph,

were omitted.

(2) An order made under this section may apply—

(a) generally, or
(b) only in relation to supplies of a description specified in the order.

(3) Any revocation order made under this section may provide for the revocation to have effect in relation to supplies made on or after a day which is earlier than the day on which the revocation order is made.

(4) In this section a "revocation order" is an order revoking the whole or any part of an order containing the provision mentioned in subsection (1).

(5) The power to make an order under this section, other than a revocation order, may not be exercised after 31 March 2012.

(6) The power to make an order under this section is exercisable by statutory instrument.

(7) A statutory instrument containing an order under this section is subject to annulment in pursuance of a resolution of the House of Commons.

(8) Any reference in this section to the time at which a supply of a taxable commodity is made is to be read as a reference to the time at which the taxable commodity is actually supplied.

GENERAL NOTE

Climate change levy (CCL) is a tax on the supply of certain energy products for business and public sector use. FA 2000 Sch 6 para 18A provides for exemption from CCL for taxable products to be used in a prescribed recycling process. The exemption is restricted by regulation SI 2005/1715 to recycling of aluminium and steel. Exemption for lead recycling was revoked with effect from 1 April 2011 (SI2011/616).

State aid approval for this exemption expired on 31 March 2011 and the European Commission hasn't yet made a final decision on its renewal.

Section 80 provides the power to suspend all or part of the exemption, up to 31 March 2012, and to revoke either or both parts of that suspension with retrospective effect. This will allow the exemption to be restored back to 1 April 2011, as appropriate following State Aid approval.

Aggregates levy

81 Transitional tax credit

(1) Section 30A of FA 2001 (transitional tax credit in Northern Ireland) is amended as follows.

(2) For subsection (2) substitute—

"(2) The cases are those where a charge to aggregates levy has arisen on a quantity of aggregate which has been subjected to commercial exploitation during a prescribed period."

(3) Omit subsection (3).

(4) In subsection (5), for paragraph (a) substitute—

"(a) for a person to be entitled to a tax credit under the regulations in respect of aggregate originating from a site in respect of which any person holds an aggregates levy credit certificate which has not been withdrawn;".

GENERAL NOTE

Aggregates levy is charged on virgin aggregates subjected to commercial exploitation. FA 2001 s 30A provides for regulations to make provision for a tax credit of up to 80%, where the charge to aggregates levy has arisen in Northern Ireland, up to 31 March 2011. SI 2004/1959 established an 80% tax credit available in Northern Ireland (Aggregates Levy Credit Scheme (ALCS)) subject to meeting various conditions. State Aid approval originally granted for the ALCS was annulled by the European General Court in September 2010 and the ALCS was suspended with effect from 1 December 2010 (SI2010/2598). The Government has announced its intention to apply for State Aid approval to reintroduce the scheme at the earliest date possible.

Section 81 amends FA 2001 s 30A to leave open the period available to make regulations and restricts any tax credit to be no earlier than the date when s 30A came into force. It also removes previous restrictions on the persons to be granted relief, pending any required amendments to ALCS to comply with European law.

Stamp duty land tax

82 Prevention of avoidance

Schedule 21 contains provision preventing avoidance of stamp duty land tax.

GENERAL NOTE

Although the SDLT legislation contains what is in effect an anti-avoidance provision, FA 2003 s 75A, HMRC continues to make changes to the legislation to limit the use of SDLT reliefs where it perceives avoidance. The changes made by Sch 21 limit the scope of the alternative finance relief and change the way in which SDLT is calculated where there is an exchange.

83 Transfers involving multiple dwellings

Schedule 22 contains provision about the amount of stamp duty land tax chargeable in respect of a transaction or set of transactions involving the acquisition of an interest in more than one dwelling.

GENERAL NOTE

The SDLT legislation currently applies the concept of linked transactions when calculating the tax payable on individual transactions. In effect SDLT is calculated on each transaction at the highest rate applicable as a result of aggregating the consideration for each transaction: see FA 2003 ss 55 and 108. Section 83 introduces Sch 22 which provides, via the insertion of a new FA 2003 Sch 6B, for a new relief which can be claimed on multiple acquisitions of dwellings to calculate tax at a rate determined by averaging the aggregate consideration over the dwellings concerned.

Stamp duty reserve tax

84 Interests in collective investment schemes

(1) Section 99 of FA 1986 (stamp duty reserve tax: interpretation) is amended as follows.

(2) In subsection (5B)—

(a) in paragraph (b), for the words after "exempt investment" substitute ", unless subsection (5C) applies to the scheme;", and

(b) omit the sentence after paragraph (d).

(3) After subsection (5B) insert—

"(5C) This subsection applies to a collective investment scheme if more than 20% of the market value of the investments in which the property subject to the scheme is invested is attributable to investments which are not exempt investments for the purposes of subsection (5A)(b).

(5D) In subsections (5B) and (5C) "collective investment scheme" has the same meaning as in Part 17 of the Financial Services and Markets Act 2000."

(4) This section comes into force on the first Sunday after the day on which this Act is passed.

GENERAL NOTE

Background Note

FA 1999 Sch 19 provides for the circumstances in which Stamp Duty Reserve Tax ("SDRT") is charged on dealings in unit trusts, replacing the charges that used to apply under the stamp duty legislation. SDRT is charged when an interest in a unit trust which is a chargeable security is sold or surrendered: see para 2. The basic rate of SDRT (i e ½%) can be reduced where, and to the extent that, in the relevant two week period the manager creates units – see para 4 – and in addition the amount of SDRT is reduced by reference to the proportion of exempt to total assets (exempt and non-exempt) held by the managers – see para 5 – in that period. Exempt investments are defined in FA 1986 s 99(5A)(b). As a result of concerns over competitiveness there had been a consultation over the scope and operation of Sch 19.

Section 84 amends and extends the definition of exempt investments applicable to unit trusts in FA 1986 s 99(5B). It does that by providing that where a unit trust invests in an underlying scheme that investment is itself exempt (see FA 1986 s 99(5B)(b) as amended by s 84(2)) unless that underlying scheme itself has greater than 20% of its assets invested in securities that are themselves not exempt investments within ss 99(5A(b)): see new s 99(5C) inserted into FA 1986 by s 84(3)(a). Section 84(3)(b) inserts an identical definition of "collective investment scheme" to that previously set out at the end of s 99(5B)(b), which sentence was removed by s 84(2)(b) in consequence of the amendments made by s 84(2)(a).

Commencement

The amendments apply to relevant periods which commence on or after the first Sunday after Royal Assent (see s 84(4)).

PART 7
ADMINISTRATION ETC

85 Security for payment of PAYE

(1) Section 684 of ITEPA 2003 (PAYE regulations) is amended as follows.

(2) In subsection (2), after item 4A insert—

> "**4B** Provision for and in connection with requiring the giving, in specified circumstances, of security (or further security) for the payment of amounts in respect of which a person is or may be accountable to the Commissioners under the regulations."

(3) After subsection (4) insert—

> "(4A) A person who fails to comply with a requirement imposed under PAYE regulations to give security, or further security, for the payment of any amount commits an offence if the failure continues for such period as is specified; and a person guilty of an offence under this subsection is liable on summary conviction to a fine not exceeding level 5 on the standard scale."

GENERAL NOTE

Background note

HMRC has been increasingly concerned that there is a serious loss of PAYE and NIC in cases where employers deduct tax from wages and salaries but do not pay it over to HMRC. There are existing power to enforce the payment of such liabilities but these can be cumbersome and if the employer has disappeared can be of little practical assistance. The government is therefore intending to give HMRC power to require certain employers to give security before they are permitted to operate a PAYE scheme. There is already such a power in respect of VAT.

s 85(1) This introduces an amendment to ITEPA 2003 s 684, which is the section which sets out the power under which PAYE regulations are made.

s 85(2) This inserts a new item 4B into s 684(2). This gives the Treasury power to introduce regulations under which, in specified circumstances, an employer can be required to give security in respect of PAYE matters.

It also inserts a new s 4A into s 684. This treats failures to comply with the above security regulations as an offence to which a person is liable, on summary conviction, to a fine not exceeding level 5 on the standard scale, ie £5,000.

Draft regulations under this section were published in December 2010. In the debate on this section during the committee stage the minister made the following comments:

> "The Government are clearly committed to making sure that everyone pays their fair share. This activity performed by a small minority of employers damages the ability of the tax system to deliver its objectives, imposes additional costs on all taxpayers and undermines the tax system. This power is restricted by regulations to the seriously non-compliant. These are employers who are determined not to pay, those involved in "phoenixism" or contrived liquidations, and those who build up significant PAYE and NICs debt with little or no response to contact by HMRC. The changes made by the clause will ensure that HMRC secures these PAYE and NIC debts. While it is estimated that £5 million additional yield would be gained from using PAYE security, simply having the power is expected to protect in the region of £150 million per year. "

A consultation document, with draft regulations, was published in December last year. HMRC held six meetings with representative bodies who were generally supportive of this measure and the criminal sanction attached to this power. It felt that the sanction was needed to target the seriously non-compliant segment of taxpayers who would not pay their PAYE. The Chartered Institute of Taxation said:

> "HMRC should come down hard on those employers who deliberately refuse to pay over PAYE and NICs that is properly due and in breach of their obligations as an employer."

The draft regulations exclude employers who employ personal employees, and those who are care and support employers. These safeguards were welcomed. To ensure that the power remained strictly focused on the seriously non-compliant, HMRC was asked to take all reasonable steps to ensure that taxpayers were aware of time-to-pay arrangements. The Government made it clear at the Budget that time-to-pay arrangements would continue to be available to help taxpayers who genuinely and temporarily could not pay their tax bills, and further changes have been made to the regulations to provide that protection.

There was some concern that HMRC might automate the security process and thereby go beyond the seriously non-compliant. This does not occur for VAT securities, which are given case-by-case consideration, and this will continue for PAYE. I hope that this reassures Members that the vast majority of employers will be unaffected by this measure and addresses the concern expressed by the right hon. Member for Delyn about the width of the measures. Only a small number of employers who have been passing their tax liabilities on to the taxpaying population will be negatively affected. HMRC will also expose draft guidance for consultation in good time before the power comes in.

86 Data-gathering powers

(1) Schedule 23 contains provision for officers of Revenue and Customs to obtain data from data-holders.

(2) Schedule 24 contains amendments of Schedule 36 to FA 2008 (information and inspection powers).

GENERAL NOTE

This section and Schedules 23 and 24 introduce provisions to enhance HM Revenue & Customs' (HMRC) information gathering powers for use in carrying out risk assessment and compliance checks. Schedule 23 empowers HMRC to obtain data from data-holders and Schedule 24 contains amendments to FA 2008 Sch 36. The changes are part of an ongoing process initiated by the Review of Powers, Deterrents and Safeguards set up to review legislation following the creation of the single Department of HMRC. The changes also reflect HMRC's commitment to its international obligations arising out of increasing cooperation between tax authorities worldwide.

87 Mutual assistance for recovery of taxes etc

(1) Schedule 25 contains provision for the purpose of giving effect to Council Directive 2010/24/EU (which concerns mutual assistance for the recovery of claims relating to taxes, duties and other measures).

(2) The Treasury may by regulations make provision for the purpose of giving effect to—

(a) any amendments or extensions of Council Directive 2010/24/EU,

(b) any EU instrument that—

(i) wholly or partly replaces that Directive or a replacement of it, or

(ii) otherwise makes provision for or in connection with mutual assistance between member States in the recovery of claims relating to taxes, duties and other measures, and

(c) any amendments or extensions of any such EU instrument.

(3) Regulations under subsection (2) may amend, replace or repeal Schedule 25 and any other enactment (whenever passed).

(4) Regulations under subsection (2) are to be made by statutory instrument.

(5) An instrument containing regulations under subsection (2) is subject to annulment in pursuance of a resolution of the House of Commons.

GENERAL NOTE

Section 87 introduces Schedule 25 and sets out the power to make regulations for the purpose of giving effect to amendments or extensions of the new Directive.

PART 8

MISCELLANEOUS PROVISIONS

88 Amendments of section 1 of the Provisional Collection of Taxes Act 1968

(1) Section 1 of the Provisional Collection of Taxes Act 1968 (temporary statutory effect of House of Commons resolutions relating to certain taxes) is amended in accordance with subsections (2) to (7).

(2) In subsection (2) for "(8)" substitute "(9)".

(3) For subsection (3) substitute—

"(3) The period is one expiring at the end of seven months after the date on which the resolution is expressed to take effect or, if no such date is expressed, after the date on which the resolution is passed."

(4) In subsection (5)—

(a) in paragraph (c) omit "or prorogued", and

(b) after paragraph (c) insert

", or

(d) Parliament is prorogued."

(5) After subsection (5) insert—

"(5A) Subsection (5B) applies in relation to a resolution instead of subsection (5)(d) where Parliament is prorogued at the end of a session if—

(a) one of the following happens during the session—

(i) a Bill renewing, varying or, as the case may be, abolishing the tax is read a first time by the House, or

(ii) a Bill is amended by the House in Committee or on Report or by any Public Bill Committee of the House so as to include provision for the renewal, variation or, as the case may be, abolition of the tax,

(b) the Standing Orders or Sessional Orders of the House provide, or during the session the House orders, that proceedings on the Bill not completed before the end of the session shall be resumed in the next session, and

(c) proceedings on the Bill are not completed during the session.

(5B) The resolution shall cease to have statutory effect under this section if, during the period of thirty sitting days beginning with the first sitting day of the next session, no Bill renewing, varying or, as the case may be, abolishing the tax is presented to the House.

(5C) In subsection (5B) "sitting day" means a day on which the House sits.

(5D) Where a Bill is amended as mentioned in subsection (5A)(a)(ii), it does not matter for the purposes of subsection (5A)(b) if the House orders as mentioned in subsection (5A)(b) before the amendment to the Bill is made."

(6) In subsection (6) for "(4) or (5)" substitute "(4), (5) or (5B)".

(7) After subsection (8) insert—

"(9) Subsection (8) does not apply where the later resolution is passed in a different calendar year from that in which the earlier resolution is passed."

(8) Accordingly, the following provisions are repealed—

(a) section 205(4) of FA 1993;
(b) section 50(1) and (3) of F(No2)A 1997.

(9) The amendments made by this section come into force on such day as the Treasury may by order made by statutory instrument appoint.

(10) Subject to subsection (11), the amendments do not apply in relation to any resolution passed before the day appointed under subsection (9).

(11) The cases covered by section 1(9) of the Provisional Collection of Taxes Act 1968 (as inserted by subsection (7)) include cases where the earlier resolution (but not the later resolution) is passed before the day appointed under subsection (9).

GENERAL NOTE

This section amends PCTA 1968. A little background on the PCTA is helpful in understanding the function of s 88.

The position before FA 2011

When the government announces an income or corporation tax provision has been abolished or varied from a date, usually Budget day, it is the PCTA which allows that change to have effect, even though the relevant Finance Act is not yet law–provided a parliamentary resolution has been passed to that effect,

However, in order not to undermine parliamentary sovereignty, the PCTA operates within strict controls. Firstly, resolutions are time-limited. Those passed in October or November expire on 5 May of the following year, and those passed in March or April run out on 5 August. These time limits are intended to cover resolutions passed in the autumn and spring budgets respectively. Until FA 2011, 'other' resolutions had a maximum lifespan of four months.

Secondly, the matter contained within the resolution must:

(a) have been included in a Bill which has been given its second reading before the House of Commons, and this second reading must have happened within the 30 days on which the House sits after the resolution was passed; or
(b) have been included as an amendment to a Bill within the same period (PCTA s 4).

Finally, until FA 2011, all resolutions ceased to have effect when parliament is prorogued (ie, when a parliamentary session comes to an end), see PCTA s 5(c).

The effect of FA2011

The coalition government decided to change the parliamentary timetable, so that sessions end in the spring rather than the autumn. As a result, parliament will normally be prorogued after the spring Budget. If the PCTA were not amended, Budgetary and other PCTA resolutions would fall away.

Section 88 therefore amends the PCTA to allow resolutions to continue to have effect after prorogation, providing that, when parliament is prorogued:

— a Bill containing a clause corresponding to the resolution has already had its first reading, or a Bill has been amended to include this material (PCTA s 1(5A)(a));
— the Standing or Sessional Orders of the House provide that proceedings are to be resumed in the next session (PCTA s 1(5A)(b)); and
— a Bill including the relevant material is presented to the House within the first thirty sitting days (PCTA s 1(5B)).

The Act also extends the maximum period for 'other' resolutions from four to seven months, and makes other minor amendments.

In the view of this commentator, it is surprising that no provision has been introduced to give the thirty day rule in new s1(5A) priority over that in s 1(4). As a result, the clause corresponding to the resolution has not only to be introduced within 30 sitting days of prorogation, but to have reached its second reading by that date. This failure to give priority to the new section may be an oversight.

89 Specified investments

(1) The amendments made by the second order are to be treated, for all tax purposes, as having come into force on 24 February 2010 immediately after the coming into force of the first order.

(2) A person may elect that subsection (1) is not to have effect in relation to that person.

(3) An election under subsection (2)—

(a) is to be made by notice in writing to an officer of Revenue and Customs,
(b) may not be made after the end of the period of 30 days beginning with the day on which this Act is passed, and
(c) is irrevocable.

(4) In this section—

"the first order" means the Financial Services and Markets Act 2000 (Regulated Activities) (Amendment) Order 2010 (SI 2010/86);
"the second order" means the Financial Services and Markets Act 2000 (Regulated Activities) (Amendment) Order 2011 (SI 2011/133);
"tax" means any tax or duty.

(5) Nothing in this section affects the commencement of the second order otherwise than as provided for by this section.

GENERAL NOTE

Sukuk are a type of Islamic financial instrument, as illustrated by the diagram below.

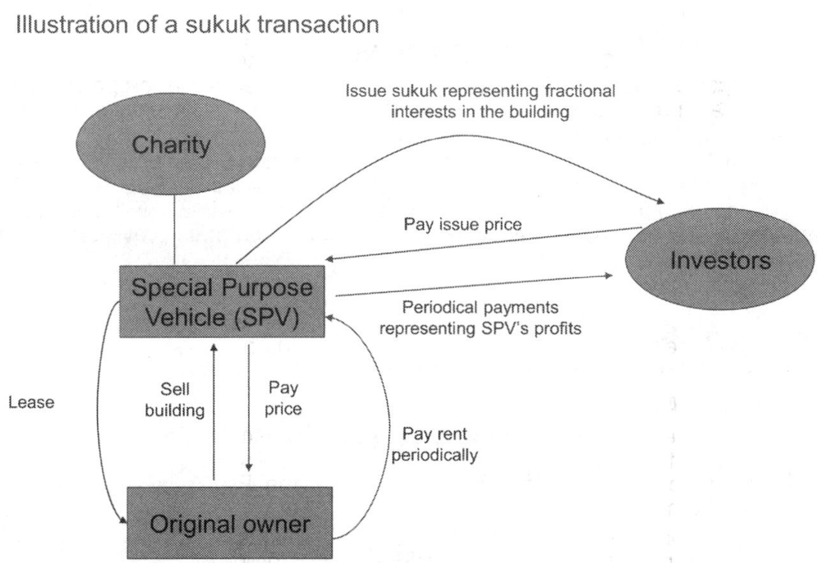

In order to comply with the requirements of Islamic law the SPV will own the property on behalf of the investors collectively, with each of them having a fractional interest in the asset. Accordingly there has long been concern that sukuk might constitute a collective investment scheme with onerous regulatory consequences.

To eliminate such concerns, the first order which took effect on 24 February 2010 put beyond doubt that sukuk (provided they fall within the provisions legislated) are not a collective investment scheme. It accomplished this by inserting into SI 2001/544 a new article 77A defining an "alternative finance investment bond" (in such a way that most sukuk should fall within the definition) and then amending SI 2001/1062 (which deals with collective investment schemes) to provide that instruments falling within the new art 77A do not constitute a collective investment scheme.

Unfortunately due to a drafting error the first order also amended art 77. The effect of the amendment to art 77 was that some conventional (i e non-Islamic) financial instruments arguably failed to fall within the new art 77A or within art 77 (which would have applied to them prior to its amendment). The consequence was that the affected conventional financial instruments were no longer eligible for the loan capital exemption from stamp duty. Also in certain cases the issuing companies became ineligible for the special tax regime for securitisation companies.

The second order corrected this error prospectively with effect from 16 February 2011. However the powers under which it was made did not allow retrospective correction of the tax status of the affected instruments between 24 February 2010 and 16 February 2011. That is achieved by this section. As the provision has retrospective effect, any person may elect out of its effect, should the provision have an adverse impact upon them.

90 Machine games duty

The Commissioners for Her Majesty's Revenue and Customs may incur expenditure in preparing for the introduction of a new duty to be charged in respect of games played on machines.

GENERAL NOTE

Section 90 paves the way for HMRC to incur expenditure in preparing for the introduction of a new machine games duty (MGD) before it is formally enacted.

The Government intends to replace amusement machine licence duty (payable in respect of each machine according to category and period under BGDA s 22) with a new duty payable on the profits from games played on machines. Supplies in relation to the playing of games on machines which are liable to MGD will also become exempt from VAT. The Government intends to introduce the main provisions for MGD in Finance Bill 2012.

91 Redundant reliefs

Schedule 26 contains provision repealing redundant reliefs.

GENERAL NOTE

This section introduces Schedule 26.

PART 9

FINAL PROVISIONS

92 Interpretation

(1) In this Act—

"ALDA 1979" means the Alcoholic Liquor Duties Act 1979,
"BGDA 1981" means the Betting and Gaming Duties Act 1981,
"CAA 2001" means the Capital Allowances Act 2001,
"CRCA 2005" means the Commissioners for Revenue and Customs Act 2005,
"CTA 2009" means the Corporation Tax Act 2009,
"CTA 2010" means the Corporation Tax Act 2010,
"FISMA 2000" means the Financial Services and Markets Act 2000,

"HODA 1979" means the Hydrocarbon Oil Duties Act 1979,
"ICTA" means the Income and Corporation Taxes Act 1988,
"IHTA 1984" means the Inheritance Tax Act 1984,
"ITA 2007" means the Income Tax Act 2007,
"ITEPA 2003" means the Income Tax (Earnings and Pensions) Act 2003,
"ITTOIA 2005" means the Income Tax (Trading and Other Income) Act 2005,
"OTA 1975" means the Oil Taxation Act 1975,
"PRTA 1980" means the Petroleum Revenue Tax Act 1980,
"TCGA 1992" means the Taxation of Chargeable Gains Act 1992,
"TIOPA 2010" means the Taxation (International and Other Provisions) Act 2010,
"TMA 1970" means the Taxes Management Act 1970,
"TPDA 1979" means the Tobacco Products Duty Act 1979,
"VATA 1994" means the Value Added Tax Act 1994, and
"VERA 1994" means the Vehicle Excise and Registration Act 1994.

(2) In this Act—

"FA", followed by a year, means the Finance Act of that year;
"F(No 2)A", followed by a year, means the Finance (No 2) Act of that year.

93 Short title

This Act may be cited as the Finance Act 2011.

SCHEDULE 1

NEW HIGH STRENGTH BEER DUTY

Section 15

1 In Part 3 of ALDA 1979 (beer), after section 36H insert—

"Charge of excise duty: high strength beer

37 High strength beer duty

(1) A duty of excise is charged on high strength beer—

(a) imported into the United Kingdom, or
(b) produced in the United Kingdom,

on or after 1 October 2011.

(2) "High strength beer" means beer which is of a strength exceeding 7.5 per cent.

(3) The duty charged by subsection (1) is referred to in this Act as "high strength beer duty".

(4) High strength beer duty is charged at £4.64 per hectolitre per cent of alcohol in the beer.

(5) Subject to the provisions of this Act—

(a) the high strength beer duty on beer produced in, or imported into, the United Kingdom is to be charged and paid, and
(b) the amount chargeable in respect of any such duty is to be determined and becomes due,

in accordance with regulations under section 49 and with any regulations under section 1 of the Finance (No 2) Act 1992."

Consequential amendments in ALDA 1979

2 ALDA 1979 is amended as follows.

3 In section 4 (interpretation), in subsection (1) insert at the appropriate places—

""general beer duty" has the meaning given by section 36(1ZAA);", and
""high strength beer duty" has the meaning given by section 37(3);".

4 (1) Section 36 (beer: charge of excise duty) is amended as follows.

(2) After subsection (1) insert—

"(1ZAA) The duty charged by subsection (1) is referred to in this Act as "general beer duty"."

(3) In subsection (1AA), for "the duty" substitute "general beer duty".

(4) In subsection (1A), after "No" insert "general beer".

(5) In subsection (2)(a), for "the duty" substitute "general beer duty".

(6) For the heading substitute "**General beer duty**".

5 In section 36B (interpretation of provisions relating to small brewery beer), in subsection (5), after "rate of" insert "general beer".

6 (1) Section 36D (rate of duty for small brewery beer from singleton breweries) is amended as follows.

(2) In subsection (2), after "rate of" insert "general beer".

(3) In the heading, after "**Rate of**" insert "**general beer**".

7 (1) Section 36F (rate of duty for small brewery beer from co-operated breweries) is amended as follows.

(2) In subsection (2), after "rate of" insert "general beer".

(3) In the heading, after "**Rate of**" insert "**general beer**".

8 (1) Section 36G (assessments where incorrectly low rate of duty applied) is amended as follows.

(2) In subsection (1)(a), for "duty is charged by section 36 above" substitute "general beer duty is charged".

(3) In subsection (2)(a), for "duty is charged by section 36 above" substitute "general beer duty is charged".

(4) In subsection (3)(a), for "duty charged on the beer by section 36 above" (in both places) substitute "general beer duty charged on the beer".

(5) In subsection (4)—

(a) for "duty charged" substitute "general beer duty charged", and

(b) in paragraph (a), for "the duty" substitute "that duty".

9 In section 36H (power to vary reduced rate provisions), in subsection (1) for "excise duty" substitute "general beer duty".

10 In section 41 (exemption from duty of beer produced for private consumption), for "The duty on beer produced in the United Kingdom shall not be" substitute "Neither general beer duty on beer produced in the United Kingdom, nor high strength beer duty on beer so produced, is".

11 In section 49 (beer regulations), in subsection (1)—

(a) for "the duty" (in the first place it occurs) substitute "general beer duty or high strength beer duty", and

(b) for "the duty" (in the second place it occurs) substitute "any duty".

12 In section 49A (drawback allowable to registered brewer), in subsection (2) for "the excise" substitute "any excise".

GENERAL NOTE

This Schedule is dealt with in the commentary for s 15.

SCHEDULE 2

EMPLOYMENT INCOME PROVIDED THROUGH THIRD PARTIES

Section 26

Main provision

1 After Part 7 of ITEPA 2003 insert—

"PART 7A

EMPLOYMENT INCOME PROVIDED THROUGH THIRD PARTIES

CHAPTER 1

APPLICATION ETC

Application

554A Application of Chapter 2

(1) Chapter 2 applies if—

(a) a person ("A") is an employee, or a former or prospective employee, of another person ("B"),

(b) there is an arrangement ("the relevant arrangement") to which A is a party or which otherwise (wholly or partly) covers or relates to A,

(c) it is reasonable to suppose that, in essence—

(i) the relevant arrangement, or

(ii) the relevant arrangement so far as it covers or relates to A,

is (wholly or partly) a means of providing, or is otherwise concerned (wholly or partly) with the provision of, rewards or recognition or loans in connection with A's employment, or former or prospective employment, with B,

(d) a relevant step is taken by a relevant third person, and

(e) it is reasonable to suppose that, in essence—

(i) the relevant step is taken (wholly or partly) in pursuance of the relevant arrangement, or

(ii) there is some other connection (direct or indirect) between the relevant step and the relevant arrangement.

(2) In this Part "relevant step" means a step within section 554B, 554C or 554D.

(3) Subsection (1) is subject to subsection (4) and sections 554E to 554Y.

(4) Chapter 2 does not apply by reason of a relevant step within section 554B taken on or after A's death.

(5) In subsection (1)(b) and (c)(ii) references to A include references to any person linked with A.

(6) For the purposes of subsection (1)(c) it does not matter if the relevant arrangement does not include details of the steps which will or may be taken in connection with providing, in essence, rewards or recognition or loans as mentioned (for example, details of any sums of money or assets which will or may be involved or details of how or when or by whom or in whose favour any step will or may be taken).

(7) In subsection (1)(d) "relevant third person" means—

(a) A acting as a trustee,

(b) B acting as a trustee, or

(c) any person other than A and B.

(8) If B is a company and is a member of a group of companies at the time the relevant step is taken, in subsection (7) references to B are to be read as including references to any other company which is a member of that group at that time.

(9) If B is a limited liability partnership, in subsection (7) references to B are to be read as including references to any company which is a wholly-owned subsidiary (as defined in section 1159(2) of the Companies Act 2006) of B at the time the relevant step is taken.

(10) Neither subsection (8) nor subsection (9) applies if there is a connection (direct or indirect) between the relevant step and a tax avoidance arrangement.

(11) For the purposes of subsection (1)(e)—

(a) the relevant step is connected with the relevant arrangement if (for example) the relevant step is taken (wholly or partly) in pursuance of an arrangement at one end of a series of arrangements with the relevant arrangement being at the other end, and

(b) it does not matter if the person taking the relevant step is unaware of the relevant arrangement.

(12) For the purposes of subsection (1)(c) and (e) in particular, all relevant circumstances are to be taken into account in order to get to the essence of the matter.

Relevant steps

554B Relevant steps: earmarking etc of sum of money or asset

(1) A person ("P") takes a step within this section if—

(a) a sum of money or asset held by or on behalf of P is earmarked (however informally) by P with a view to a later relevant step being taken by P or any other person (on or following the meeting of any condition or otherwise) in relation to—

(i) that sum of money or asset, or

(ii) any sum of money or asset which may arise or derive (directly or indirectly) from it, or

(b) a sum of money or asset otherwise starts being held by or on behalf of P, specifically with a view, so far as P is concerned, to a later relevant step being taken by P or any other person (on or following the meeting of any condition or otherwise) in relation to—

(i) that sum of money or asset, or

(ii) any sum of money or asset which may arise or derive (directly or indirectly) from it.

(2) For the purposes of subsection (1)(a) and (b) it does not matter—

(a) if details of the later relevant step have not been worked out (for example, details of the sum of money or asset which will or may be the subject of the step or details of how or when or by whom or in whose favour the step will or may be taken),

(b) if any condition which would have to be met before the later relevant step is taken might never be met, or

(c) if A, or any person linked with A, has no legal right to have a relevant step taken in relation to any sum of money or asset mentioned in subsection (1)(a)(i) or (ii) or (b)(i) or (ii) (as the case may be).

(3) For the purposes of subsection (1)(b) it does not matter whether or not the sum of money or asset in question has previously been held by or on behalf of P on a basis which is different to that mentioned in subsection (1)(b).

554C Relevant steps: payment of sum, transfer of asset etc

(1) A person ("P") takes a step within this section if P—

(a) pays a sum of money to a relevant person,

(b) transfers an asset to a relevant person,

(c) takes a step by virtue of which a relevant person acquires an asset within subsection (4),

(d) makes available a sum of money or asset for use, or makes it available under an arrangement which permits its use—

(i) as security for a loan made or to be made to a relevant person, or

(ii) otherwise as security for the meeting of any liability, or the performance of any undertaking, which a relevant person has or will have, or

(e) grants to a relevant person a lease of any premises the effective duration of which is likely to exceed 21 years.

(2) In subsection (1) "relevant person"—

(a) means A or a person chosen by A or within a class of person chosen by A, and

(b) includes, if P is taking a step on A's behalf or otherwise at A's direction or request, any other person.

(3) In subsection (2) references to A include references to any person linked with A.

(4) The following assets are within this subsection—

(a) securities,

(b) interests in securities, and

(c) securities options,

as defined in section 420 for the purposes of Chapters 1 to 5 of Part 7; and in subsection (1)(c) "acquires" is to be read in accordance with section 421B(2)(a).

(5) For the purposes of subsection (1)(d)—

(a) references to making a sum of money or asset available are references to making it available in any way, however informal,

(b) it does not matter if the relevant person has no legal right to have the sum of money or asset used as mentioned, and

(c) it does not matter if the sum of money or asset is not actually used as mentioned.

(6) Subsections (7) and (8) apply for the purpose of determining the likely effective duration of a lease of any premises granted to a relevant person ("the original lease") for the purposes of subsection (1)(e).

(7) If there are circumstances which make it likely that the original lease will be extended for any period, the effective duration of the original lease is to be determined on the assumption that the original lease will be so extended.

(8) Further, if—

(a) A is, or is likely to become, entitled to a later lease, or the grant of a later lease, of the same premises, or

(b) it is otherwise likely that A will be granted a later lease of the same premises,

the original lease is to be treated as continuing until the end of the later lease (and subsection (7) also applies for the purpose of determining the duration of the later lease).

(9) In subsection (8)—

(a) references to A include references to—

(i) any person linked with A, and

(ii) the person to whom the original lease was granted where the original lease was not granted to A or any person linked with A, and

(b) references to the same premises include references to any premises which include the whole or part of the same premises.

(10) In this section "lease" and "premises" have the same meaning as they have in Chapter 4 of Part 3 of ITTOIA 2005.

554D Relevant steps: making asset available

(1) A person ("P") takes a step within this section if, without transferring the asset to the relevant person, P—

(a) at any time, makes an asset available for a relevant person to benefit from in a way which is substantially similar to the way in which the relevant person would have been able to benefit from the asset had the asset been transferred to the relevant person at that time, or

(b) at or after the end of the relevant period, makes an asset available for a relevant person to benefit from.

(2) If—

(a) before the end of the relevant period, P makes available an asset for a relevant person to benefit from, and

(b) at the end of the relevant period, P continues to make the asset available for the relevant person to benefit from,

P is treated as taking a step within this section by virtue of subsection (1)(b) at the end of the relevant period.

(3) For the purposes of subsections (1) and (2)—

(a) references to making an asset available are references to making it available in any way, however informal,

(b) it does not matter if the relevant person has no legal right to benefit from the asset, and

(c) it does not matter if the relevant person does not actually benefit from the asset.

(4) In subsections (1) and (2) "the relevant period" means the period of two years starting with the day on which A's employment with B ceases.

(5) In subsections (1) and (2) "relevant person"—

(a) means A or a person chosen by A or within a class of person chosen by A, and

(b) includes, if P is taking a step on A's behalf or otherwise at A's direction or request, any other person.

(6) In subsection (5) references to A include references to any person linked with A.

(7) The following factors (among others) may be taken into account in determining whether a step within this section is taken by virtue of subsection (1)(a)—

(a) any limitations on the way in which the relevant person may benefit from the asset,

(b) the period over which the asset is being made available and (if relevant) the extent to which that period covers the expected remaining useful life of the asset,

(c) the extent to which the relevant person has, or is to have, a say over the disposal of the asset, and

(d) the extent to which the relevant person may benefit from any proceeds arising from the disposal of the asset or otherwise have a say in the way the proceeds are used.

Exclusions

554E Exclusions: steps under certain schemes etc

(1) Chapter 2 does not apply by reason of a relevant step if the step is taken under any of the following—

(a) an approved SIP (within the meaning of Chapter 6 of Part 7),

(b) an approved SAYE option scheme (within the meaning of Chapter 7 of Part 7),

(c) an approved CSOP scheme (within the meaning of Chapter 8 of Part 7),

(d) an arrangement the sole purpose of which is the provision of excluded benefits (as defined in section 393B(3)),

(e) an arrangement the sole purpose of which is the making of payments which are to be disregarded in the calculation mentioned in regulation 25 of the Social Security (Contributions) Regulations 2001 (SI 2001/1004) by virtue of paragraph 12 of Part 10 of Schedule 3 to those Regulations (as that paragraph has effect by virtue of regulation 2(3) of the Social Security (Contributions) (Amendment No 9) Regulations 2007 (SI 2007/2905)),

(f) a pension scheme set up by a government outside the United Kingdom for the benefit of its employees or primarily for their benefit,

(g) a registered pension scheme, or

(h) an arrangement the sole purpose of which is the making of payments (within the meaning of Chapter 3 of Part 4 of FA 2004 (see section 161(2) of that Act))—

(i) to which section 161(4) of FA 2004 applies in relation to a registered pension scheme (or a registered pension scheme which has been wound up), and

(ii) which are authorised in relation to that scheme by section 160(1) of FA 2004.

(2) Subject to subsection (4), subsection (3) applies to a relevant step taken by a person ("P") if—

(a) the relevant step is not taken under an arrangement mentioned in subsection (1)(a) to (c), and

(b) there is no connection (direct or indirect) between the relevant step and a tax avoidance arrangement.

(3) Chapter 2 does not apply by reason of the relevant step if the step is taken solely for the purpose of—

(a) acquiring or holding shares—

(i) to be awarded under an approved SIP, or

(ii) to be provided pursuant to options granted under an approved SAYE option scheme or an approved CSOP scheme, or

(b) providing shares pursuant to—

(i) an award of shares under an approved SIP, or

(ii) an option granted under an approved SAYE option scheme or an approved CSOP scheme.

(4) Subsection (3) does not apply to the relevant step if, immediately before or after the step is taken—

(a) the total number of shares of any type held, in relation to the approved SIP, the approved SAYE option scheme or the approved CSOP scheme, by P and any other persons for purposes within subsection (3)(a) and (b), exceeds

(b) the maximum number of shares of that type which might reasonably be expected to be required, in relation to the approved SIP, the approved SAYE option scheme or the approved CSOP scheme, for those purposes over the period of ten years starting with the day on which the relevant step is taken.

(5) Terms used in subsections (2) to (4) have the same meaning as they have in Chapter 6, 7 or 8 of Part 7 (as the case may be).

(6) Chapter 2 does not apply by reason of a relevant step taken by a person ("P") if—

(a) the relevant step is taken for the sole purpose of—

(i) granting qualifying options under an EMI arrangement,

(ii) acquiring or holding shares to be provided pursuant to qualifying options granted under an EMI arrangement, or

(iii) providing shares pursuant to qualifying options granted under an EMI arrangement, and

(b) there is no connection (direct or indirect) between the relevant step and a tax avoidance arrangement.

(7) But subsection (6) does not apply to the relevant step if, immediately before or after the step is taken—

(a) the total number of shares of any type held, in relation to the EMI arrangement, by P and any other persons for purposes within subsection (6)(a)(i) to (iii), exceeds

(b) the maximum number of shares of that type which might reasonably be expected to be required, in relation to the EMI arrangement, for those purposes over the period of ten years starting with the day on which the relevant step is taken.

(8) In subsections (6) and (7) "EMI arrangement" means an arrangement under which qualifying options are granted.

(9) Terms used in subsections (6) to (8) have the same meaning as in Chapter 9 of Part 7.

(10) Subsection (11) applies if—

(a) a person ("P") takes a relevant step within section 554B by reason of which Chapter 2 would apply apart from subsection (3) or (6), and

(b) at any time ("the relevant time") the sum of money or asset (or any part of it) which is the subject of the relevant step—

(i) ceases to be held by or on behalf of P solely for purposes within subsection (3)(a) and (b) or (6)(a)(i) to (iii), but

(ii) continues to be held by or on behalf of P on the basis mentioned in section 554B(1)(a) or (b).

(11) This Part has effect as if a relevant step within section 554B were taken at the relevant time—

(a) the subject of which is the sum of money or asset (or the part of it) mentioned in subsection (10)(b), and

(b) by reason of which Chapter 2 is to apply (subject only to section 554A(4)).

(12) Chapter 2 does not apply by reason of a relevant step taken by the Independent Parliamentary Standards Authority in relation to a member of the House of Commons.

554F Exclusions: commercial transactions

(1) Chapter 2 does not apply by reason of a relevant step which is the payment of a sum of money by way of a loan if—

(a) the loan is a loan on ordinary commercial terms within the meaning of section 176, ignoring conditions B and C in that section, and

(b) there is no connection (direct or indirect) between the relevant step and a tax avoidance arrangement.

(2) Chapter 2 does not apply by reason of a relevant step taken by a person ("P"), which is not the payment of a sum of money by way of a loan, if—

(a) the step is taken for the sole purpose of a transaction which P has with A and which P entered into in the ordinary course of P's business,

(b) a substantial proportion of P's business involves similar transactions with members of the public,

(c) the terms on which P entered into the transaction with A are substantially the same as the terms on which P normally enters into similar transactions with members of the public, and

(d) there is no connection (direct or indirect) between the relevant step and a tax avoidance arrangement.

(3) For the purposes of subsection (2)(b) and (c) a transaction is "similar" if it is of the same or a similar type to the transaction which P has with A.

(4) In subsection (2)(b) and (c) "members of the public" means members of the public at large with whom P deals at arm's length.

(5) In this section references to A include references to any person linked with A.

554G Exclusions: transactions under employee benefit packages

(1) Chapter 2 does not apply by reason of a relevant step taken by a person ("P") if—

(a) the step is not taken under a pension scheme,

(b) the step is taken for the sole purpose of a transaction which P has with A and which P entered into in the ordinary course of P's business,

(c) if the step is the payment of a sum of money by way of a loan—

(i) a substantial proportion of P's business involves making similar loans to members of the public,

(ii) the transaction with A is part of a package of benefits which is available to a substantial proportion of B's employees, and

(iii) subsection (3) does not apply,

(d) if the step is not the payment of a sum of money by way of a loan, the transaction with A is part of a package of benefits which is available—

(i) to a substantial proportion of B's employees, or

(ii) to a substantial proportion of those employees of B whose status as employees of B is comparable with A's status as an employee of B (taking into account (for example) levels of seniority, types of duties and levels of remuneration),

(e) the terms on which similar transactions are offered by P under the package of benefits mentioned in paragraph (c)(ii) or (d) (as the case may be) are generous enough to enable substantially all of the employees of B to whom the package is available to take advantage of what is offered (if they want to),

(f) the terms on which P entered into the transaction with A are substantially the same as the terms on which P normally enters into similar transactions with employees of B under the package of benefits,

(g) if B is a company, a majority of B's employees to whom the package of benefits is available do not have a material interest (as defined in section 68) in B, and

(h) there is no connection (direct or indirect) between the relevant step and a tax avoidance arrangement.

(2) For the purposes of subsection (1)(c)(i)—

(a) a loan is "similar" if it is made for the same or similar purposes as the loan which is the subject of the relevant step, and

(b) "members of the public" means members of the public at large with whom P deals at arm's length.

(3) This subsection applies if any feature of the package of benefits mentioned in subsection (1)(c)(ii) has or is likely to have the effect that, of the employees of B to whom the package is available, it is employees within subsection (4) on whom benefits under the package will be wholly or mainly conferred.

(4) The employees within this subsection are—

(a) directors,

(b) senior employees,

(c) employees who receive, or as a result of the package of benefits are likely to receive, the higher or highest levels of remuneration, and

(d) if B is a company and is a member of a group of companies, any employees not within paragraph (b) or (c) who—

(i) are senior employees in the group, or

(ii) receive, or as a result of the package of benefits are likely to receive, the higher or highest levels of remuneration in the group.

(5) For the purposes of subsection (1)(e) and (f) a transaction is "similar" if it is of the same or a similar type to the transaction which P has with A.

(6) If the relevant step is not the payment of a sum of money by way of a loan, in this section references to employees of B are references to those employees of B whose duties of employment are performed in the United Kingdom; and for this purpose duties performed outside the United Kingdom the performance of which is merely incidental to the performance of duties in the United Kingdom are to be treated as performed in the United Kingdom.

(7) In this section (apart from subsection (1)(d)(ii)) references to A include references to any person linked with A.

554H Exclusions: earmarking of deferred remuneration

(1) This section applies if—

(a) on a date ("the award date") A is awarded remuneration ("the deferred remuneration") in respect of A's employment with B,

(b) the main purpose of the award is not the provision of relevant benefits (within the meaning of Chapter 2 of Part 6, but ignoring section 393B(2)(a)),

(c) the deferred remuneration is awarded on terms ("the deferred remuneration terms") the main purpose of which is to defer the provision to A of the deferred remuneration to a specified date ("the vesting date") which is after the award date, while providing that the award of the deferred remuneration is revoked if specified conditions are not met on or before the vesting date,

(d) the vesting date is not more than five years after the award date,

(e) as at the award date, there is a reasonable chance that the award of the deferred remuneration will be revoked because not all the specified conditions will be met on or before the vesting date,

(f) if the deferred remuneration were to be provided to A by any person on the award date, that action would, for the purposes of Part 11, be a payment of PAYE employment income of A in respect of A's employment with B,

(g) before the end of the vesting date, a person ("P") takes a relevant step within section 554B by reason of which Chapter 2 would apply apart from this section,

(h) on the taking of the relevant step, the sum of money or asset which is the subject of the step represents the deferred remuneration or any part of it (and nothing else), and

(i) there is no connection (direct or indirect) between the relevant step and a tax avoidance arrangement.

(2) In addition to the provision relating to revocation required by subsection (1)(c) (which must be included), the deferred remuneration terms may also provide that the award of the deferred remuneration is partly revoked if specified conditions are not met on or before the vesting date.

(3) Chapter 2 does not apply by reason of the relevant step mentioned in subsection (1)(g).

(4) In the following subsections "the earmarked deferred remuneration" means the deferred remuneration so far as, on the taking of the relevant step mentioned in subsection (1)(g), it is represented by the sum of money or asset which is the subject of the step as mentioned in subsection (1)(h).

(5) Subsection (6) applies if, at any time ("the relevant time")—

(a) any sum of money or asset held by or on behalf of P on the basis mentioned in section 554B(1)(a) or (b) which represents any of the earmarked deferred remuneration ceases to represent that earmarked deferred remuneration or a part of it (because the remuneration is to be provided to A in another way or its award has been revoked or for any other reason), but

(b) the sum of money or asset continues to be held by or on behalf of P on the basis mentioned in section 554B(1)(a) or (b).

(6) This Part has effect as if a relevant step within section 554B were taken at the relevant time—

(a) the subject of which is—

(i) the sum of money or asset mentioned in subsection (5), and

(ii) a just and reasonable proportion of any relevant income (see subsection (12)), and

(b) by reason of which Chapter 2 is to apply (subject only to section 554A(4)).

(7) Subsection (8) applies if neither subsection (10) nor subsection (11) applies to the earmarked deferred remuneration or to a part of it.

(8) This Part has effect as if a relevant step within section 554B were taken at the end of the vesting date—

(a) the subject of which is—

(i) a sum of money of the notional PAYE amount, and

(ii) a just and reasonable proportion of any relevant income (see subsection (12)), and

(b) by reason of which Chapter 2 is to apply (subject only to section 554A(4)).

(9) In subsection (8)(a) "the notional PAYE amount" means the amount which the payment of PAYE employment income would have been had, as the case may be—

(a) the earmarked deferred remuneration, or

(b) the part of it to which neither subsection (10) nor subsection (11) applies,

been provided to A at the end of the vesting date in a way which is, for the purposes of Part 11, a payment of PAYE employment income of A in respect of A's employment with B.

(10) This subsection applies to the earmarked deferred remuneration so far as it is provided to A before the end of the vesting date in a way which is, for the purposes of Part 11, a payment of PAYE employment income of A in respect of A's employment with B.

(11) This subsection applies to the earmarked deferred remuneration so far as, before the end of the vesting date, the award of the earmarked deferred remuneration is revoked in accordance with the deferred remuneration terms.

(12) In subsections (6)(a)(ii) and (8)(a)(ii) "relevant income" means any income—

(a) which, before the relevant time or the end of the vesting date (as the case may be)—

(i) arises (directly or indirectly) from a sum of money or asset held by or on behalf of P representing any of the earmarked deferred remuneration, and

(ii) is the subject of a relevant step within section 554B taken by P by reason of which Chapter 2 would apply apart from section 554Q, and

(b) which, at the relevant time or the end of the vesting date (as the case may be), continues to be held by or on behalf of P on the basis mentioned in section 554B(1)(a) or (b).

554I Exclusions: introduction to sections 554J to 554M

(1) Sections 554J and 554K are about steps within section 554B taken in relation to awards of certain shares or securities or of sums of money determined by reference to the market value of certain shares or securities.

(2) Sections 554L and 554M are about steps within section 554B taken in relation to grants of rights to acquire certain shares or securities or to receive sums of money determined by reference to the market value of certain shares or securities.

(3) Sections 554J to 554M apply only if B is a company.

(4) In those sections—

"relevant benefits" has the same meaning as in Chapter 2 of Part 6, but ignoring section 393B(2)(a),

"relevant shares" means—

(a) shares (including stock) in B,

(b) instruments issued by B which are securities for the purposes of Chapters 1 to 5 of Part 7 within section 420(1)(b), or

(c) units in a collective investment scheme (as defined in section 420(2)) managed by B which are securities for the purposes of Chapters 1 to 5 of Part 7 within section 420(1)(e), and

"trading company" means a company the business of which consists wholly or mainly in the carrying on of a trade.

(5) If B is a member of a group of companies, in the definition of "relevant shares" in subsection (4) references to B are to be read as including references to any other company which is a member of that group.

(6) For the purposes of sections 554K and 554M an exit event occurs if—

(a) shares in the relevant company are admitted to trading on a stock exchange,

(b) all the shares in the relevant company, or a substantial proportion of them, are disposed of to persons none of whom is connected with any of the persons making any disposal,

(c) if the relevant company is a trading company (as defined in subsection (4)), the company's trade, or a substantial proportion of it, is transferred to a person who is not a relevant connected person,

(d) the relevant company's assets, or a substantial proportion of them, are disposed of to a person who is not a relevant connected person,

(e) the winding up of the relevant company starts, or

(f) a person ("P") who controls the relevant company ceases to control it, so long as no person connected with P starts to control it.

(7) For the purposes of subsection (6)—

(a) "the relevant company" means—

(i) if the relevant shares mentioned in section 554K(1)(a)(i) or (ii) or 554M(1)(a)(i) or (ii) are shares (including stock), the company in which they are shares, or

(ii) if the relevant shares so mentioned are instruments within paragraph (b) of the definition of "relevant shares" in subsection (4), the company by which those instruments are issued,

(b) "relevant connected person" means a person who—

(i) is connected with the relevant company, or

(ii) is a shareholder in the relevant company or is connected with a shareholder in the relevant company,

(c) the relevant company's trade, or a substantial proportion of it, is transferred to another person if—

(i) the relevant company ceases to carry on the trade or the proportion of it, and

(ii) on that occurring, the other person starts to carry on the trade or the proportion of it, and

(d) section 12(7) of CTA 2009 applies for the purpose of determining when the winding up of the relevant company starts.

554J Exclusions: earmarking for employee share schemes (1)

(1) This section applies if—

(a) there is an arrangement ("B's employee share scheme") under which, in respect of A's employment with B, an award may be made to A of—

(i) relevant shares, or

(ii) a sum of money the amount of which is to be determined by reference to the market value of any relevant shares at the time the sum is to be paid,

(b) the main purpose of the award of the relevant shares or sum of money would not be the provision of relevant benefits,

(c) the award of the relevant shares or sum of money would be on terms ("the deferred award terms") the main purpose of which is to defer the receipt of the shares by A, or the payment of the sum of money to A, to a specified date ("the vesting date") which is after the date ("the award date") on which the award is made, while providing that the award is revoked if specified conditions are not met on or before the vesting date,

(d) the vesting date would not be more than ten years after the award date, and

(e) as at the award date, there would be a reasonable chance that the award of the relevant shares or sum of money will be revoked because not all the specified conditions will be met on or before the vesting date.

(2) In addition to the provision relating to revocation required by subsection (1)(c) (which must be included), the deferred award terms may also provide that the award of the relevant shares or sum of money is partly revoked if specified conditions are not met on or before the vesting date.

(3) Chapter 2 does not apply by reason of a relevant step within section 554B (by reason of which it would otherwise apply) taken by a person ("P") if—

(a) the subject of the relevant step is relevant shares ("earmarked shares") which are earmarked, or otherwise start being held, solely with a view to the meeting of—

(i) an award of relevant shares or a sum of money made to A under B's employee share scheme as mentioned in subsection (1)(a) in relation to which the requirements of subsection (1)(b) to (e) are met, or

(ii) an award of relevant shares or a sum of money which is expected to be made to A under B's employee share scheme as mentioned in subsection (1)(a) and in relation to which the requirements of subsection (1)(b) to (e) would be met,

(b) the number of relevant shares of any type which are earmarked shares does not exceed the maximum number of relevant shares of that type which might reasonably be expected to be needed for meeting the award or expected award, and

(c) there is no connection (direct or indirect) between the relevant step and a tax avoidance arrangement.

(4) If the relevant step mentioned in subsection (3) is taken in relation to an expected award as mentioned in subsection (3)(a)(ii), subsection (5) applies if—

(a) the award is not made before the end of the date ("the final award date") falling immediately after the period of three months starting with the date on which P takes the relevant step, and

(b) as at the end of the final award date, any of the earmarked shares continue to be held by or on behalf of P solely on the basis mentioned in subsection (3)(a).

(5) This Part has effect as if a relevant step within section 554B were taken at the end of the final award date—

(a) the subject of which is—

(i) the shares which continue to be held as mentioned in subsection (4)(b), and

(ii) any relevant income in relation to those shares (see subsection (13)), and

(b) by reason of which Chapter 2 is to apply (subject only to section 554A(4)).

(6) Subsection (7) applies if, at any time ("the relevant time")—

(a) any of the earmarked shares cease to be held by or on behalf of P solely on the basis mentioned in subsection (3)(a), but

(b) the shares continue to be held by or on behalf of P on the basis mentioned in section 554B(1)(a) or (b).

(7) This Part has effect as if a relevant step within section 554B were taken at the relevant time—

(a) the subject of which is—

(i) the shares mentioned in subsection (6), and

(ii) any relevant income in relation to those shares (see subsection (13)), and

(b) by reason of which Chapter 2 is to apply (subject only to section 554A(4)).

(8) Subsection (9) applies if—

(a) the relevant step mentioned in subsection (3) is taken in relation to an award which has been made as mentioned in subsection (3)(a)(i), or

(b) the relevant step mentioned in subsection (3) is taken in relation to an expected award as mentioned in subsection (3)(a)(ii) and the award is made before the end of the final award date.

(9) This Part has effect as if a relevant step within section 554B were taken at the end of the vesting date—

(a) the subject of which is—

(i) any of the earmarked shares to which none of subsections (10) to (12) applies, and

(ii) any relevant income in relation to any of the earmarked shares mentioned in sub-paragraph (i) (see subsection (13)), and

(b) by reason of which Chapter 2 is to apply (subject only to section 554A(4)).

(10) This subsection applies to any earmarked shares if—

(a) A receives the shares before the end of the vesting date, and

(b) the receipt of the shares by A gives rise to employment income of A which is chargeable to income tax or which is exempt income.

(11) This subsection applies to any earmarked shares if—

(a) the sum of money mentioned in subsection (1)(a)(ii) (or a part of it) is paid to A before the end of the vesting date,

(b) the payment of the sum to A gives rise to employment income of A which is chargeable to income tax or which is exempt income, and

(c) the payment represents the proceeds of the disposal of the shares, or the payment is made from another source and, correspondingly, the shares are no longer held by any person in relation to the award.

(12) This subsection applies to any earmarked shares if—

(a) before the end of the vesting date, the award (or any part of it) is revoked in accordance with the deferred award terms, and

(b) correspondingly, the shares are no longer held by any person in relation to the award.

(13) In subsections (5)(a)(ii), (7)(a)(ii) and (9)(a)(ii) "relevant income", in relation to any earmarked shares, means any income—

(a) which, before the relevant step is treated as being taken by subsection (5), (7) or (9) (as the case may be)—

(i) arises (directly or indirectly) from the shares, and

(ii) is the subject of a relevant step within section 554B taken by P by reason of which Chapter 2 would apply apart from section 554Q, and

(b) which, at the time the relevant step is treated as being taken, continues to be held by or on behalf of P on the basis mentioned in section 554B(1)(a) or (b).

554K Exclusions: earmarking for employee share schemes (2)

(1) This section applies if—

(a) there is an arrangement ("B's employee share scheme") under which, in respect of A's employment with B, an award may be made to A of—

(i) relevant shares, or

(ii) a sum of money the amount of which is to be determined by reference to the market value of any relevant shares at the time the sum is to be paid,

(b) the main purpose of the award would not be the provision of relevant benefits,

(c) the relevant shares would be—

(i) shares (including stock) in, or

(ii) instruments within paragraph (b) of the definition of "relevant shares" in section 554I(4) issued by,

a trading company or a company which controls a trading company,

(d) the award would be on terms the main purpose of which is to ensure—

(i) that the relevant shares are received, or

(ii) that the sum of money is paid,

only if a specified exit event, or an exit event within a specified description, occurs, and

(e) as at the time the award is made, there would be a reasonable chance that the specified exit event, or an exit event within the specified description, will occur.

(2) Chapter 2 does not apply by reason of a relevant step within section 554B (by reason of which it would otherwise apply) taken by a person ("P") if—

(a) the subject of the relevant step is relevant shares ("earmarked shares") which are earmarked, or otherwise start being held, solely with a view to the meeting of—

(i) an award of relevant shares or a sum of money made to A under B's employee share scheme as mentioned in subsection (1)(a) in relation to which the requirements of subsection (1)(b) to (e) are met, or

(ii) an award of relevant shares or a sum of money which is expected to be made to A under B's employee share scheme as mentioned in subsection (1)(a) and in relation to which the requirements of subsection (1)(b) to (e) would be met,

(b) the number of relevant shares of any type which are earmarked shares does not exceed the maximum number of relevant shares of that type which might reasonably be expected to be needed for meeting the award or expected award, and

(c) there is no connection (direct or indirect) between the relevant step and a tax avoidance arrangement.

(3) If the relevant step mentioned in subsection (2) is taken in relation to an expected award as mentioned in subsection (2)(a)(ii), subsection (4) applies if—

(a) the award is not made before the end of the date ("the final award date") falling immediately after the period of three months starting with the date on which P takes the relevant step, and

(b) as at the end of the final award date, any of the earmarked shares continue to be held by or on behalf of P solely on the basis mentioned in subsection (2)(a).

(4) This Part has effect as if a relevant step within section 554B were taken at the end of the final award date—

(a) the subject of which is—

(i) the shares which continue to be held as mentioned in subsection (3)(b), and

(ii) any relevant income in relation to those shares (see subsection (12)), and

(b) by reason of which Chapter 2 is to apply (subject only to section 554A(4)).

(5) Subsection (6) applies if, at any time ("the relevant time")—

(a) any of the earmarked shares cease to be held by or on behalf of P solely on the basis mentioned in subsection (2)(a), but

(b) the shares continue to be held by or on behalf of P on the basis mentioned in section 554B(1)(a) or (b).

(6) This Part has effect as if a relevant step within section 554B were taken at the relevant time—

(a) the subject of which is—

(i) the shares mentioned in subsection (5), and

(ii) any relevant income in relation to those shares (see subsection (12)), and

(b) by reason of which Chapter 2 is to apply (subject only to section 554A(4)).

(7) Subsection (8) applies if—

(a) the relevant step mentioned in subsection (2) is taken in relation to an award which has been made as mentioned in subsection (2)(a)(i), or

(b) the relevant step mentioned in subsection (2) is taken in relation to an expected award as mentioned in subsection (2)(a)(ii) and the award is made before the end of the final award date,

and the specified exit event, or an exit event within the specified description, occurs.

(8) This Part has effect as if a relevant step within section 554B were taken at the end of the exit period—

(a) the subject of which is—

(i) any of the earmarked shares to which neither subsection (9) nor subsection (10) applies, and

(ii) any relevant income in relation to any of the earmarked shares mentioned in sub-paragraph (i) (see subsection (12)), and

(b) by reason of which Chapter 2 is to apply (subject only to section 554A(4)).

(9) This subsection applies to any earmarked shares if—

(a) A receives the shares before the end of the exit period, and

(b) the receipt of the shares by A gives rise to employment income of A which is chargeable to income tax or which is exempt income.

(10) This subsection applies to any earmarked shares if—

(a) the sum of money mentioned in subsection (1)(a)(ii) (or a part of it) is paid to A before the end of the exit period,

(b) the payment of the sum to A gives rise to employment income of A which is chargeable to income tax or which is exempt income, and

(c) the payment represents the proceeds of the disposal of the shares, or the payment is made from another source and, correspondingly, the shares are no longer held by any person in relation to the award.

(11) In subsections (8), (9)(a) and (10)(a) "the exit period" means the period of six months starting with the date on which the exit event occurs.

(12) In subsections (4)(a)(ii), (6)(a)(ii) and (8)(a)(ii) "relevant income", in relation to any earmarked shares, means any income—

(a) which, before the relevant step is treated as being taken by subsection (4), (6) or (8) (as the case may be)—

(i) arises (directly or indirectly) from the shares, and

(ii) is the subject of a relevant step within section 554B taken by P by reason of which Chapter 2 would apply apart from section 554Q, and

(b) which, at the time the relevant step is treated as being taken, continues to be held by or on behalf of P on the basis mentioned in section 554B(1)(a) or (b).

554L Exclusions: earmarking for employee share schemes (3)

(1) This section applies if—

(a) there is an arrangement ("B's employee share scheme") under which, in respect of A's employment with B, a right ("a relevant share option") may be granted to A—

(i) to acquire relevant shares, or

(ii) to receive a sum of money the amount of which is to be determined by reference to the market value of any relevant shares at the time the sum is to be paid,

(b) the main purpose of the grant of the relevant share option would not be the provision of relevant benefits,

(c) the grant would be made on terms ("the deferred grant terms") the main purpose of which is to ensure that the relevant share option is not exercisable by A before a specified date ("the vesting date") which is after the date ("the grant date") on which the grant is made, while providing that the relevant share option is not to be exercisable at all by A if specified conditions are not met on or before the vesting date,

(d) the vesting date would not be more than ten years after the grant date, and

(e) as at the grant date, there would be a reasonable chance that the relevant share option will not be exercisable at all by A because not all the specified conditions will be met on or before the vesting date.

(2) In addition to the provision relating to revocation required by subsection (1)(c) (which must be included), the deferred grant terms may also provide that the relevant share option may be exercised by A only in part if specified conditions are not met on or before the vesting date.

(3) Chapter 2 does not apply by reason of a relevant step within section 554B (by reason of which it would otherwise apply) taken by a person ("P") if—

(a) the subject of the relevant step is relevant shares ("earmarked shares") which are earmarked, or otherwise start being held, solely with a view to providing relevant shares, or paying a sum of money, pursuant to—

(i) a relevant share option granted to A under B's employee share scheme as mentioned in subsection (1)(a) in relation to which the requirements of subsection (1)(b) to (e) are met, or

(ii) a relevant share option which is expected to be granted to A under B's employee share scheme as mentioned in subsection (1)(a) and in relation to which the requirements of subsection (1)(b) to (e) would be met,

(b) the number of relevant shares of any type which are earmarked shares does not exceed the maximum number of relevant shares of that type which might reasonably be expected to be needed for providing shares, or paying a sum of money, pursuant to the relevant share option which is granted or expected to be granted, and

(c) there is no connection (direct or indirect) between the relevant step and a tax avoidance arrangement.

(4) If the relevant step mentioned in subsection (3) is taken in relation to an expected grant of a relevant share option as mentioned in subsection (3)(a)(ii), subsection (5) applies if—

(a) the grant is not made before the end of the date ("the final grant date") falling immediately after the period of three months starting with the date on which P takes the relevant step, and

(b) as at the end of the final grant date, any of the earmarked shares continue to be held by or on behalf of P solely on the basis mentioned in subsection (3)(a).

(5) This Part has effect as if a relevant step within section 554B were taken at the end of the final grant date—

(a) the subject of which is—

(i) the shares which continue to be held as mentioned in subsection (4)(b), and
(ii) any relevant income in relation to those shares (see subsection (15)), and

(b) by reason of which Chapter 2 is to apply (subject only to section 554A(4)).

(6) Subsection (7) applies if, at any time ("the relevant time")—

(a) any of the earmarked shares cease to be held by or on behalf of P solely on the basis mentioned in subsection (3)(a), but
(b) the shares continue to be held by or on behalf of P on the basis mentioned in section 554B(1)(a) or (b).

(7) This Part has effect as if a relevant step within section 554B were taken at the relevant time—

(a) the subject of which is—

(i) the shares mentioned in subsection (6), and
(ii) any relevant income in relation to those shares (see subsection (15)), and

(b) by reason of which Chapter 2 is to apply (subject only to section 554A(4)).

(8) Subsection (9) applies if—

(a) the relevant step mentioned in subsection (3) is taken in relation to a grant of a relevant share option made as mentioned in subsection (3)(a)(i), or
(b) the relevant step mentioned in subsection (3) is taken in relation to an expected grant of a relevant share option as mentioned in subsection (3)(a)(ii) and the grant is made before the end of the final grant date.

(9) This Part has effect as if a relevant step within section 554B were taken at the end of the final exercise date—

(a) the subject of which is—

(i) any of the earmarked shares to which none of subsections (10) to (13) applies, and
(ii) any relevant income in relation to any of the earmarked shares mentioned in sub-paragraph (i) (see subsection (15)), and

(b) by reason of which Chapter 2 is to apply (subject only to section 554A(4)).

(10) This subsection applies to any earmarked shares if—

(a) the relevant share option becomes exercisable (in whole or in part) by A before the end of the vesting date,
(b) A exercises the option (wholly or partly) before the end of the final exercise date and, as a result, receives the shares, and
(c) the receipt of the shares gives rise to employment income of A—

(i) which is chargeable to income tax or would be chargeable apart from section 474, or
(ii) which is exempt income.

(11) This subsection applies to any earmarked shares if—

(a) the relevant share option becomes exercisable (in whole or in part) by A before the end of the vesting date,
(b) A exercises the option (wholly or partly) before the end of the final exercise date and, as a result, a sum of money is paid to A as mentioned in subsection (1)(a)(ii),
(c) the payment of the sum gives rise to employment income of A—

(i) which is chargeable to income tax or would be chargeable apart from section 474, or
(ii) which is exempt income, and

(d) the payment represents the proceeds of the disposal of the shares, or the payment is made from another source and, correspondingly, the shares are no longer held by any person in relation to the relevant share option.

(12) This subsection applies to any earmarked shares if—

(a) in accordance with the deferred grant terms, before the end of the vesting date, the relevant share option ceases to be exercisable by A (in whole or in part), and
(b) correspondingly, the shares are no longer held by any person in relation to the relevant share option.

(13) This subsection applies to any earmarked shares if—

(a) the relevant share option becomes exercisable by A (in whole or in part) before the end of the vesting date but the option lapses (in whole or in part) before the end of the final exercise date, and

(b) correspondingly, the shares are no longer held by any person in relation to the relevant share option.

(14) In subsections (9) to (13) "the final exercise date" means the date which is ten years after the grant date.

(15) In subsections (5)(a)(ii), (7)(a)(ii) and (9)(a)(ii) "relevant income", in relation to any earmarked shares, means any income—

(a) which, before the relevant step is treated as being taken by subsection (5), (7) or (9) (as the case may be)—

(i) arises (directly or indirectly) from the shares, and

(ii) is the subject of a relevant step within section 554B taken by P by reason of which Chapter 2 would apply apart from section 554Q, and

(b) which, at the time the relevant step is treated as being taken, continues to be held by or on behalf of P on the basis mentioned in section 554B(1)(a) or (b).

554M Exclusions: earmarking for employee share schemes (4)

(1) This section applies if—

(a) there is an arrangement ("B's employee share scheme") under which, in respect of A's employment with B, a right ("a relevant share option") may be granted to A—

(i) to acquire relevant shares, or

(ii) to receive a sum of money the amount of which is to be determined by reference to the market value of any relevant shares at the time the sum is to be paid,

(b) the main purpose of the grant of the relevant share option would not be the provision of relevant benefits,

(c) the relevant shares would be—

(i) shares (including stock) in, or

(ii) instruments within paragraph (b) of the definition of "relevant shares" in section 554I(4) issued by,

a trading company or a company which controls a trading company,

(d) the grant would be made on terms ("the deferred grant terms") the main purpose of which is to ensure that the relevant share option is exercisable by A only if a specified exit event, or an exit event within a specified description, occurs, and

(e) as at the time the grant is made, there would be a reasonable chance that the specified exit event, or an exit event within the specified description, will occur.

(2) Chapter 2 does not apply by reason of a relevant step within section 554B (by reason of which it would otherwise apply) taken by a person ("P") if—

(a) the subject of the relevant step is relevant shares ("earmarked shares") which are earmarked, or otherwise start being held, solely with a view to providing relevant shares, or paying a sum of money, pursuant to—

(i) a relevant share option granted to A under B's employee share scheme as mentioned in subsection (1)(a) in relation to which the requirements of subsection (1)(b) to (e) are met, or

(ii) a relevant share option which is expected to be granted to A under B's employee share scheme as mentioned in subsection (1)(a) and in relation to which the requirements of subsection (1)(b) to (e) would be met,

(b) the number of relevant shares of any type which are earmarked shares does not exceed the maximum number of relevant shares of that type which might reasonably be expected to be needed for providing shares, or paying a sum of money, pursuant to the relevant share option which is granted or expected to be granted, and

(c) there is no connection (direct or indirect) between the relevant step and a tax avoidance arrangement.

(3) If the relevant step mentioned in subsection (2) is taken in relation to an expected grant of a relevant share option as mentioned in subsection (2)(a)(ii), subsection (4) applies if—

(a) the grant is not made before the end of the date ("the final grant date") falling immediately after the period of three months starting with the date on which P takes the relevant step, and

(b) as at the end of the final grant date, any of the earmarked shares continue to be held by or on behalf of P solely on the basis mentioned in subsection (2)(a).

(4) This Part has effect as if a relevant step within section 554B were taken at the end of the final grant date—

(a) the subject of which is—

(i) the shares which continue to be held as mentioned in subsection (3)(b), and

(ii) any relevant income in relation to those shares (see subsection (14)), and

(b) by reason of which Chapter 2 is to apply (subject only to section 554A(4)).

(5) Subsection (6) applies if, at any time ("the relevant time")—

(a) any of the earmarked shares cease to be held by or on behalf of P solely on the basis mentioned in subsection (2)(a), but

(b) the shares continue to be held by or on behalf of P on the basis mentioned in section 554B(1)(a) or (b).

(6) This Part has effect as if a relevant step within section 554B were taken at the relevant time—

(a) the subject of which is—

(i) the shares mentioned in subsection (5), and

(ii) any relevant income in relation to those shares (see subsection (14)), and

(b) by reason of which Chapter 2 is to apply (subject only to section 554A(4)).

(7) Subsection (8) applies if—

(a) the relevant step mentioned in subsection (2) is taken in relation to a grant of a relevant share option made as mentioned in subsection (2)(a)(i), or

(b) the relevant step mentioned in subsection (2) is taken in relation to an expected grant of a relevant share option as mentioned in subsection (2)(a)(ii) and the grant is made before the end of the final grant date,

and the specified exit event, or an exit event within the specified description, occurs.

(8) This Part has effect as if a relevant step within section 554B were taken at the end of the exit period—

(a) the subject of which is—

(i) any of the earmarked shares to which none of subsections (9) to (11) applies, and

(ii) any relevant income in relation to any of the earmarked shares mentioned in sub-paragraph (i) (see subsection (14)), and

(b) by reason of which Chapter 2 is to apply (subject only to section 554A(4)).

(9) This subsection applies to any earmarked shares if—

(a) A exercises the relevant share option (wholly or partly) before the end of the exit period and, as a result, receives the shares, and

(b) the receipt of the shares gives rise to employment income of A—

(i) which is chargeable to income tax or would be chargeable apart from section 474, or

(ii) which is exempt income.

(10) This subsection applies to any earmarked shares if—

(a) A exercises the relevant share option (wholly or partly) before the end of the exit period and, as a result, a sum of money is paid to A as mentioned in subsection (1)(a)(ii),

(b) the payment of the sum gives rise to employment income of A—

(i) which is chargeable to income tax or would be chargeable apart from section 474, or

(ii) which is exempt income, and

(c) the payment represents the proceeds of the disposal of the shares, or the payment is made from another source and, correspondingly, the shares are no longer held by any person in relation to the relevant share option.

(11) This subsection applies to any earmarked shares if—

(a) the relevant share option becomes exercisable by A before the end of the exit period but the option lapses (in whole or in part) at or before the end of that period, and

(b) correspondingly, the shares are no longer held by any person in relation to the relevant share option.

(12) In subsections (8), (9)(a), (10)(a) and (11)(a) "the exit period" means—

(a) the period of six months starting with the date on which the exit event occurs, or

(b) if it ends earlier, the period during which the relevant share option is exercisable by A in accordance with the deferred grant terms.

(13) If the exit event is an event within section 554I(6)(a), in subsection (12)(a) the reference to six months is to be read as a reference to five years.

(14) In subsections (4)(a)(ii), (6)(a)(ii) and (8)(a)(ii) "relevant income", in relation to any earmarked shares, means any income—

(a) which, before the relevant step is treated as being taken by subsection (4), (6) or (8) (as the case may be)—

(i) arises (directly or indirectly) from the shares, and

(ii) is the subject of a relevant step within section 554B taken by P by reason of which Chapter 2 would apply apart from section 554Q, and

(b) which, at the time the relevant step is treated as being taken, continues to be held by or on behalf of P on the basis mentioned in section 554B(1)(a) or (b).

554N Exclusions: other cases involving employment-related securities etc

(1) Chapter 2 does not apply by reason of a relevant step the subject of which is employment-related securities if—

(a) by virtue of the step, the securities are acquired by a person, and

(b) section 425(2) applies, or would apply apart from section 421E(1), to the acquisition.

(2) Chapter 2 does not apply by reason of a relevant step the subject of which is an employment-related securities option if—

(a) by virtue of the step, the option is acquired by a person, and

(b) section 475(1) applies, or would apply apart from section 474(1), to the acquisition.

(3) Terms used in subsection (1) or (2) have the same meaning as they have in Chapter 2 or 5 of Part 7 (as the case may be).

(4) Chapter 2 does not apply by reason of an event within subsection (5) if by virtue of the event an amount counts as employment income of A in respect of A's employment with B.

(5) The events within this subsection are—

(a) a chargeable event for the purposes of section 426, 438 or 476,

(b) an event which gives rise to the discharge of a notional loan for the purposes of section 446U, or

(c) a disposal to which Chapter 3D of Part 7 applies.

(6) Chapter 2 does not apply by reason of an event to which subsection (4) would apply apart from section 421B(6), 421E(1), 429, 443, 474(1) or 477(2) or apart from an election under section 430 or 431.

(7) Subsection (11) applies if there is an acquisition of an asset within section 554C(4)(a) or (b) ("the relevant asset") and—

(a) relevant consideration is given by A for the relevant asset of an amount equal to or greater than the market value of the relevant asset at the time of the acquisition, or

(b) ignoring any relevant consideration given for the relevant asset, the acquisition gives rise (or would give rise) to earnings of A within Chapter 1 of Part 3 from A's employment with B—

(i) the amount of which is equal to or greater than the market value of the relevant asset at the time of the acquisition, and

(ii) which are not exempt income.

(8) In subsection (7) "relevant consideration"—

(a) means consideration—

(i) which is given before, or at or about, the time of the acquisition, and

(ii) which is money or money's worth, but

(b) does not include—

(i) a promise to do anything, or

(ii) the performance of any duties of, or in connection with, an employment.

(9) If section 437(1) or 452(1) applies in relation to the acquisition, or would apply if Chapter 3 or 4A of Part 7 (as the case may be) applied in relation to the acquisition, in subsection (7) references to the market value of the relevant asset are to be read as references to that value determined on the basis mentioned in section 437(1) or 452(1) (as the case may be).

(10) Subsection (11) also applies if—

(a) there is an acquisition of an asset within section 554C(4)(a) or (b) ("the relevant asset"),

(b) the acquisition is pursuant to an employment-related securities option (within the meaning of Chapter 5 of Part 7, but ignoring section 474(1)) acquired by reason of A's employment, or former or prospective employment, with B, and

(c) the acquisition is a chargeable event for the purposes of section 476 or would be a chargeable event apart from section 474(1).

(11) Chapter 2 does not apply by reason of a relevant step taken after the acquisition if—

(a) the subject of the relevant step is the relevant asset, and

(b) there is no connection (direct or indirect) between the relevant step and a tax avoidance arrangement.

(12) In subsections (7) to (11) "acquisition" is to be read in accordance with section 421B(2)(a).

(13) Chapter 2 does not apply by reason of a relevant step within section 554C(1)(a) taken by a person if—

(a) the payment of the sum of money is by way of a loan ("the relevant loan"),

(b) the relevant loan is made and used solely for the purpose of enabling A to exercise an employment-related securities option (within the meaning of Chapter 5 of Part 7),

(c) the exercise of the option by A gives rise to employment income of A in respect of A's employment with B—

(i) which is chargeable to income tax or would be chargeable apart from section 474, or

(ii) which is exempt income, and

(d) there is no connection (direct or indirect) between the relevant step and a tax avoidance arrangement.

(14) Subsection (15) applies if—

(a) apart from subsection (13), Chapter 2 would apply by reason of the relevant step mentioned in that subsection, and

(b) by the end of the relevant period, the relevant loan has not been fully repaid.

(15) This Part has effect as if a relevant step within section 554C(1)(a) were taken at the end of the relevant period—

(a) the subject of which is a sum of money of an amount equal to the outstanding amount of the relevant loan as at the end of the relevant period,

(b) in relation to which the relevant person (within the meaning of section 554C(1)) is the person to whom the relevant loan is made, and

(c) by reason of which Chapter 2 is to apply.

(16) In subsections (14) and (15) "the relevant period" means the period of 40 days starting with the day on which the relevant step mentioned in subsection (13) is taken.

554O Exclusions: employee car ownership schemes

(1) This section applies if—

(a) there is an arrangement ("the car ownership arrangement") which—

(i) provides for A to purchase a new car from another person ("P") using a loan ("the car loan") to be made to A by a licensed lender,

(ii) specifies the date ("the repayment date") by which the car loan must be fully repaid which must be no later than four years after the date on which the car loan is made, and

(iii) permits A, in order to obtain funds to repay the car loan, to sell the car back to P on a specified date at a specified price based on an estimate (made at the time the car ownership arrangement is made) of the likely outstanding amount of the car loan on the specified date, and

(b) as provided for by the car ownership arrangement, A purchases the car using the car loan.

(2) Chapter 2 does not apply by reason of a relevant step taken for the sole purpose of—

(a) the purchase of the car or its sale-back as provided for by the car ownership arrangement, or

(b) the making of the car loan as so provided,

so long as the car ownership arrangement is not a tax avoidance arrangement and there is no other connection (direct or indirect) between the relevant step and a tax avoidance arrangement.

(3) Subsection (4) applies if—

(a) apart from subsection (2), Chapter 2 would apply by reason of the making of the car loan, and

(b) by the end of the repayment date, the car loan has not been fully repaid.

(4) This Part has effect as if a relevant step within section 554C(1)(a) were taken at the end of the repayment date—

(a) the subject of which is a sum of money of an amount equal to the outstanding amount of the car loan as at the end of the repayment date,

(b) in relation to which the relevant person (within the meaning of section 554C(1)) is A, and

(c) by reason of which Chapter 2 is to apply.

(5) In this section—

"car" has the meaning given by section 235(2), and

"licensed lender" means a person—

(a) who is a licensee under the Consumer Credit Act 1974 acting within the terms of the person's licence, and

(b) who is not acting as a trustee.

554P Exclusions: employment income exemptions under Part 4

(1) Chapter 2 does not apply by reason of a relevant step if an employment income exemption under Part 4 applies to the subject of the relevant step.

(2) If the employment income exemption applies to the subject of the relevant step in part only, the relevant step is to be treated for the purposes of this Part as being two separate relevant steps—

(a) one in relation to the subject of the step so far as the exemption applies to it, and

(b) one in relation to the subject of the step so far as the exemption does not apply to it,

with subsection (1) applying only in relation to the separate relevant step mentioned in paragraph (a).

(3) In order to give effect to subsection (2), the sum of money or asset which is the subject of the relevant step is to be apportioned between the two separate relevant steps on a just and reasonable basis.

(4) In this section "employment income exemption" includes the exemption under section 271.

554Q Exclusions: income arising from earmarked sum or asset

(1) This section applies if—

(a) a sum of money or asset ("sum or asset R") is held by or on behalf of a person ("P"),

(b) income arises from sum or asset R, and

(c) when the income arises, it—

(i) is received by or on behalf of P, and

(ii) is the subject of a relevant step within section 554B taken by P.

(2) Chapter 2 does not apply by reason of the relevant step mentioned in subsection (1)(c)(ii) if—

(a) before the income arises, sum or asset R was the subject of a relevant step within section 554B taken by P,

(b) Chapter 2 applied by reason of the relevant step mentioned in paragraph (a) in respect of A's employment with B or would have so applied apart from this section or section 554R or any of sections 554H to 554M or section 554T,

(c) immediately before the income arises, sum or asset R is still earmarked or otherwise held on the basis mentioned in section 554B(1)(a) or (b), and

(d) subsection (3) does not apply.

(3) This subsection applies if it is reasonable to suppose that, taking into account the type of investments from which the income derives (directly or indirectly), in essence, the income represents a return from sum or asset R which exceeds the return which might be expected applying the assumption that all relevant connected persons are acting at arm's length of each other.

(4) In subsection (3) "relevant connected person" means a person with a connection (direct or indirect) to the arrangement under which the income arises.

554R Exclusions: acquisitions out of sums or assets

(1) This section applies if—

(a) a sum of money or asset ("sum or asset S") is held by or on behalf of a person ("P"),

(b) a sum of money or asset ("sum or asset T") is acquired by or on behalf of P wholly out of sum or asset S,

(c) sum or asset T is not acquired (directly or indirectly) from A or any person linked with A, and

(d) subsection (2) does not apply.

(2) This subsection applies if it is reasonable to suppose that, in essence—

(a) at the time of the acquisition of sum or asset T, the value of sum or asset T is greater or less than the value of sum or asset S, and

(b) the difference (or any part of the difference) in the values might not have been expected applying the assumption that all relevant connected persons are acting at arm's length of each other.

(3) In subsection (2)—

(a) the reference to sum or asset S is to sum or asset S so far as sum or asset T is acquired out of it, and

(b) "relevant connected person" means a person with a connection (direct or indirect) to the arrangement under which sum or asset T is acquired.

(4) The cases covered by subsection (1)(b) include (in particular) cases in which sum or asset T represents the proceeds of the disposal of sum or asset S.

(5) Subsection (6) applies if, on its acquisition, sum or asset T is the subject of a relevant step within section 554B taken by P.

(6) Chapter 2 does not apply by reason of the relevant step if—

(a) before the acquisition, sum or asset S was the subject of a relevant step within section 554B taken by P,

(b) Chapter 2 applied by reason of the relevant step mentioned in paragraph (a) in respect of A's employment with B or would have applied apart from this section or section 554Q or 554T, and

(c) immediately before the acquisition, sum or asset S is still earmarked or otherwise held on the basis mentioned in section 554B(1)(a) or (b).

(7) Subsection (8) applies if—

(a) on its acquisition, sum or asset T—

(i) is the subject of a relevant step within section 554B taken by P by reason of which Chapter 2 applies or would apply apart from subsection (6) above or any of sections 554H to 554M, 554Q or 554T, or

(ii) if sub-paragraph (i) does not apply, is held by or on behalf of P on the same basis as that on which sum or asset S was held by or on behalf of P immediately before the acquisition, and

(b) for the sole purpose of the acquisition, sum or asset S or sum or asset T is the subject of a relevant step within section 554C(1)(a) to (c).

(8) Chapter 2 does not apply by reason of the relevant step mentioned in subsection (7)(b).

554S Exclusions: pension income chargeable under Part 9 etc

(1) Chapter 2 does not apply by reason of a relevant step within section 554C or 554D if the step is the provision of pension income which is chargeable to income tax under Part 9 or is exempt income (within the meaning of that Part).

(2) Sections 554T, 554U, 554V, 554W and 554X contain further provision relating to retirement benefits etc and are to be applied, so far as applicable, in that order.

554T Exclusions: employee pension contributions

(1) Chapter 2 does not apply by reason of a relevant step within section 554B if the sum of money or asset which is the subject of the step arises or derives (whether wholly or partly or directly or indirectly) from an excluded pension contribution paid by A on or after 6 April 2011.

(2) If the sum of money or asset arises or derives from the excluded pension contribution only partly, the relevant step is to be treated for the purposes of this Part as being two separate relevant steps—

(a) one in relation to the sum of money or asset so far as it arises or derives from the excluded pension contribution, and

(b) one in relation to the sum of money or asset so far as it does not arise or derive from the excluded pension contribution, with subsection (1) applying only in relation to the separate relevant step mentioned in paragraph (a).

(3) Chapter 2 does not apply by reason of a relevant step within section 554C or 554D if the sum of money or asset which is the subject of the step—

(a) represents relevant benefits, and

(b) arises or derives (whether wholly or partly or directly or indirectly) from an excluded pension contribution paid by A.

(4) If the sum of money or asset arises or derives from the excluded pension contribution only partly, the relevant step is to be treated for the purposes of this Part as being two separate relevant steps—

(a) one in relation to the sum of money or asset so far as it arises or derives from the excluded pension contribution, and

(b) one in relation to the sum of money or asset so far as it does not arise or derive from the excluded pension contribution,

with subsection (3) applying only in relation to the separate relevant step mentioned in paragraph (a).

(5) In order to give effect to subsection (2) or (4), the sum of money or asset which is the subject of the relevant step is to be apportioned between the two separate relevant steps on a just and reasonable basis.

(6) For the purposes of this section an excluded pension contribution is a contribution—

(a) which is made to an arrangement by A by way of a payment of a sum of money,

(b) by virtue of which A acquires rights to receive relevant benefits under the arrangement (and nothing else),

(c) which is neither a relievable pension contribution nor a tax-relieved contribution, and

(d) which is not a repayment of any loan and otherwise has nothing to do with any loan and has nothing to do with a sum of money or asset which has been the subject of a relevant step within section 554C(1)(d).

(7) In this section—

"relevant benefits" has the same meaning as in Chapter 2 of Part 6, but ignoring section 393B(2)(a),

"relievable pension contribution" means a contribution in respect of which an individual is entitled to relief under section 188 of FA 2004, and

"tax-relieved contribution" has the meaning given by paragraph 3(3) of Schedule 34 to FA 2004.

554U Exclusions: pre-6 April 2006 contributions to employer-financed retirement benefit schemes

(1) This section applies if the subject of a relevant step is a sum of money or asset which has (wholly or partly) arisen or derived (directly or indirectly) from a sum of money ("the taxed sum")—

(a) which was paid by B in accordance with an employer-financed retirement benefits scheme (within the meaning of Chapter 2 of Part 6) with a view to the provision of benefits under the scheme, and

(b) in respect of which A is taxed.

(2) For the purpose of determining whether A is taxed in respect of a sum of money, paragraph 53(3) of Schedule 36 to FA 2004 applies as it applies for the purpose of determining whether an employee is taxed for the purposes of paragraph 53(1)(b) of that Schedule.

(3) Chapter 2 does not apply by reason of the relevant step.

(4) Subsection (5) applies if the sum of money or asset which is the subject of the relevant step only partly arises or derives from the taxed sum.

(5) The relevant step is to be treated for the purposes of this Part as being two separate relevant steps—

(a) one in relation to the sum of money or asset so far as it arises or derives from the taxed sum, and

(b) one in relation to the sum of money or asset so far as it does not arise or derive from the taxed sum,

with subsection (3) applying only in relation to the separate relevant step mentioned in paragraph (a).

(6) In order to give effect to subsection (5), the sum of money or asset which is the subject of the relevant step is to be apportioned between the two separate relevant steps on a just and reasonable basis.

(7) If B is a company and is a member of a group of companies at any time ("the relevant time"), in subsection (1)(a), in relation to any sum of money paid at the relevant time, the reference to B is to be read as including a reference to any other company which is a member of that group at the relevant time.

554V Exclusions: purchases of annuities out of pension scheme rights

(1) This section applies if—

(a) an annuity contract is purchased from an insurance company wholly out of rights which A has under a pension scheme, and

(b) A's rights out of which the annuity contract is purchased are, wholly or partly, pre-6 April 2011 annuity rights.

(2) If the purchaser—

(a) takes a relevant step for the sole purpose of purchasing the annuity contract or transferring the beneficiary's rights under the annuity contract to A or a person linked with A, or

(b) on the purchase of the annuity contract, otherwise takes a relevant step within section 554B the subject of which is the beneficiary's rights under the annuity contract,

Chapter 2 does not apply by reason of the relevant step.

(3) If the insurance company—

(a) takes a relevant step for the sole purpose of selling the annuity contract, or

(b) on the sale of the annuity contract, otherwise takes a relevant step within section 554B the subject of which is a sum of money or asset representing the purchase price received for the annuity contract,

Chapter 2 does not apply by reason of the relevant step.

(4) If A's rights out of which the annuity contract is purchased are only partly pre-6 April 2011 annuity rights, any relevant step mentioned in subsection (2)(a) or (b) or (3)(a) or (b) is to be treated for the purposes of this Part as being two separate relevant steps—

(a) one in relation to the annuity contract so far as it is purchased out of rights which are pre-6 April 2011 annuity rights, and

(b) one in relation to the annuity contract so far as it is purchased out of rights which are not pre-6 April 2011 annuity rights,

with subsection (2) or (3) (as the case may be) applying only in relation to the separate relevant step mentioned in paragraph (a) of this subsection.

(5) In order to give effect to subsection (4), the sum of money or asset which is the subject of the relevant step mentioned in subsection (2)(a) or (b) or (3)(a) or (b) is to be apportioned between the two separate relevant steps on a just and reasonable basis.

(6) In this section—

"annuity contract" means a contract for the provision of an annuity—

(a) granted for consideration in money or money's worth in the ordinary course of a business of granting annuities on human life, and

(b) payable for a term ending at a time ascertainable only by reference to the end of a human life,

although for this purpose it does not matter that the annuity may in some circumstances end before or after the life,

"insurance company" means—

(a) a person or EEA firm within section 275(1)(a) or (b) of FA 2004, or

(b) a person resident in a territory outside the European Economic Area—

(i) whose normal business includes the provision of annuities, and

(ii) who is regulated in the conduct of that business by the government of that territory or by a body established under the law of that territory for the purpose of regulating such business, and

"pre-6 April 2011 annuity rights" means rights, which accrued before 6 April 2011, specifically to receive an annuity.

554W Exclusions: certain retirement benefits etc

(1) This section applies if—

(a) a relevant benefit is provided under a relevant scheme by way of a payment of a lump sum wholly out of rights which A has under the scheme,

(b) A's rights out of which the lump sum is paid are, wholly or partly, pre-6 April 2011 lump sum rights, and

(c) the payment of the lump sum is a relevant step within section 554C.

(2) Chapter 2 does not apply by reason of the relevant step.

(3) If A's rights out of which the lump sum is paid are only partly pre-6 April 2011 lump sum rights, the relevant step is to be treated for the purposes of this Part as being two separate relevant steps—

(a) one in relation to the lump sum so far as it is paid out of rights which are pre-6 April 2011 lump sum rights, and

(b) one in relation to the lump sum so far as it is paid out of rights which are not pre-6 April 2011 lump sum rights,

with subsection (2) applying only in relation to the separate relevant step mentioned in paragraph (a).

(4) In order to give effect to subsection (3), the lump sum is to be apportioned between the two separate relevant steps on a just and reasonable basis.

(5) In this section—

"pre-6 April 2011 lump sum rights" means rights, which accrued before 6 April 2011, specifically to receive relevant benefits by way of lump sum payments,

"relevant benefit" has the same meaning as in Chapter 2 of Part 6, and

"relevant scheme" means an employer-financed retirement benefits scheme (within the meaning of that Chapter) or a superannuation fund to which section 615(3) of ICTA applies.

554X Exclusions: transfers between certain foreign pension schemes

(1) This section applies if rights which A has under a section 390 scheme are transferred to another section 390 scheme or to an overseas pension scheme.

(2) This section also applies if—

(a) rights which A has under an overseas pension scheme are transferred to another overseas pension scheme, and

(b) some or all of the rights transferred are section 390 scheme rights.

(3) Chapter 2 does not apply by reason of—

(a) a relevant step within section 554C taken for the sole purpose of transferring the rights, or

(b) a relevant step within section 554B taken by the transferee in relation to the transferred rights on their transfer.

(4) Subsection (5) applies in relation to a transfer within subsection (2) if not all the transferred rights are section 390 scheme rights.

(5) Any relevant step mentioned in subsection (3) is to be treated for the purposes of this Part as being two separate relevant steps—

(a) one in relation to the section 390 scheme rights, and

(b) one in relation to the rest of the transferred rights,

with subsection (3) applying only in relation to the separate relevant step mentioned in paragraph (a) of this subsection.

(6) In order to give effect to subsection (5), the sum of money or asset which is the subject of the relevant step mentioned in subsection (3) is to be apportioned between the two separate relevant steps on a just and reasonable basis.

(7) Subsection (8) applies if any of the transferred rights arise or derive (directly or indirectly) from contributions to any scheme which—

(a) are paid by B on or after 6 April 2006, and

(b) are neither tax-relieved contributions nor tax-exempt provision.

(8) Any relevant step mentioned in subsection (3) is to be treated for the purposes of this Part as being two separate relevant steps—

(a) one in relation to the rights mentioned in subsection (7), and

(b) one in relation to the rest of the transferred rights,

with subsection (3) applying only in relation to the separate relevant step mentioned in paragraph (b) of this subsection.

(9) In order to give effect to subsection (8), the sum of money or asset which is the subject of the relevant step mentioned in subsection (3) is to be apportioned between the two separate relevant steps on a just and reasonable basis.

(10) If subsection (5) applies in relation to a transfer—

(a) in subsection (7) the reference to the transferred rights is to be read as a reference to the transferred section 390 scheme rights only, and

(b) in subsections (8) and (9) references to any relevant step mentioned in subsection (3) are to be read as references to the separate relevant step mentioned in subsection (5)(a).

(11) If B is a company and is a member of a group of companies at any time ("the relevant time"), in subsection (7)(a), in relation to any contribution paid at the relevant time, the reference to B is to be read as including a reference to any other company which is a member of that group at the relevant time.

(12) In this section—

"overseas pension scheme" has the same meaning as in Part 4 of FA 2004 (see section 150(7) of that Act),

"section 390 scheme" means a scheme in relation to which a claim was accepted under section 390,

"section 390 scheme rights" means rights which A has under an overseas pension scheme and which—

(a) have been transferred to the scheme (directly or indirectly) from a section 390 scheme, or

(b) have arisen or derived (directly or indirectly) from rights that have been so transferred, and

"tax-exempt provision" and "tax-relieved contribution" have the meaning given by paragraph 3(3) and (4) of Schedule 34 to FA 2004.

554Y Power to exclude other relevant steps

(1) The Commissioners for Her Majesty's Revenue and Customs may by regulations provide for Chapter 2 not to apply—

(a) by reason of a relevant step falling within a specified description, or

(b) in the cases otherwise specified in the regulations.

(2) Regulations under this section may, in consequence of provision within subsection (1)—

(a) provide—

(i) for a relevant step to be treated for the purposes of this Part as if it were two or more separate relevant steps,

(ii) for the provision within subsection (1) to apply only to one or some of the separate relevant steps, and

(iii) for the sum of money or asset which is the subject of the relevant step to be apportioned between the separate relevant steps on a just and reasonable basis,

(b) make provision, in relation to cases in which Chapter 2 does not apply by reason of a relevant step by virtue of the provision within subsection (1)—

(i) for a relevant step to be treated as taking place if, subsequently, specified conditions are met or not met, and

(ii) for Chapter 2 to apply by reason of the relevant step treated as taking place, and

(c) make other provision modifying the application of any provision of this Part.

(3) Regulations under this section may contain incidental, supplemental, consequential and transitional provision and savings.

(4) Regulations under this section may have retrospective effect.

Interpretation

554Z Interpretation: general

(1) This section applies for the purposes of this Part.

(2) "A" and "B" are defined in section 554A(1)(a).

(3) "Arrangement" includes any agreement, scheme, settlement, transaction, trust or understanding (whether or not it is legally enforceable).

(4) "Market value" has the same meaning as it has for the purposes of TCGA 1992 by virtue of Part 8 of that Act.

(5) Section 170(2) to (11) of TCGA 1992 applies for the purpose of determining whether a company is a member of a group of companies.

(6) And for that purpose, section 170(2) to (11) is to be read as if for "75 per cent" (wherever occurring) there were substituted "51 per cent" (with section 1154(2) of CTA 2010 applying accordingly).

(7) References to the payment of a sum of money include (in particular) references to the payment of a sum of money by way of a loan.

(8) "Pension scheme" has the same meaning as in Part 4 of FA 2004 (see section 150(1) of that Act).

(9) "Relevant step" is defined in section 554A(2).

(10) References to a relevant step which involves a sum of money are references to—

(a) a step within section 554B where the subject of the relevant step is a sum of money,

(b) a step within section 554C(1)(a), or

(c) a step within section 554C(1)(d) where the subject of the relevant step is a sum of money.

(11) References to the asset which is the subject of a relevant step are, in the case of a step within section 554C(1)(e), references to the lease granted.

(12) For this purpose, the lease granted is to be treated as including any extensions of the lease, or any later lease, which by virtue of section 554C(7) or (8) is taken into account in determining the likely effective duration of the lease for the purposes of section 554C(1)(e).

(13) "Tax avoidance arrangement" means an arrangement which has a tax avoidance purpose.

(14) For the purposes of subsection (13) an arrangement has a tax avoidance purpose if subsection (15) applies to a person who is a party to the arrangement.

(15) This subsection applies to a person if the main purpose, or one of the main purposes, of the person in entering into the arrangement is the avoidance of tax or national insurance contributions.

(16) The following paragraphs apply for the purpose of determining whether any relevant step or any other step is connected with a tax avoidance arrangement—

(a) the step is connected with a tax avoidance arrangement if (for example) the step is taken (wholly or partly) in pursuance of—

(i) the tax avoidance arrangement, or

(ii) an arrangement at one end of a series of arrangements with the tax avoidance arrangement being at the other end, and

(b) it does not matter if the person taking the step is unaware of the tax avoidance arrangement.

554Z1 Interpretation: persons linked with A

(1) In this Part references to any person linked with A are references to—

(a) any person who is or has been connected with A,

(b) a close company in which A or a person within any other paragraph of this subsection is or has been a participator,

(c) a company in which A or a person within any other paragraph of this subsection is or has been a participator and which would be a close company if it were a UK resident company, or

(d) a company which is a 51% subsidiary of a company within paragraph (b) or (c).

(2) In applying section 993 of ITA 2007 for the purposes of subsection (1)—

(a) a man and woman living together as if they were spouses of each other are treated as if they were spouses of each other, and

(b) two people of the same sex living together as if they were civil partners of each other are treated as if they were civil partners of each other.

(3) In subsection (1) "participator"—

(a) in relation to a close company, means a person who is a participator in relation to the company for the purposes of section 455 of CTA 2010 (see sections 454 and 455(5) of that Act), and

(b) in relation to a company which would be a close company if it were a UK resident company, means a person who would be such a participator if the company were a close company.

CHAPTER 2

TREATMENT OF RELEVANT STEP FOR INCOME TAX PURPOSES

Employment income

554Z2 Value of relevant step to count as employment income

(1) If this Chapter applies by reason of a relevant step, the value of the relevant step (see section 554Z3) counts as employment income of A in respect of A's employment with B—

(a) if the relevant step is taken before A's employment with B starts, for the tax year in which the employment starts, or

(b) otherwise, for the tax year in which the relevant step is taken.

(2) If the relevant step gives rise to—

(a) an amount which (apart from this subsection) would be treated as earnings of A under a provision of the benefits code, or

(b) any income of A which (apart from this subsection) would be dealt with under Chapter 3 of Part 4 of ITTOIA 2005,

subsection (1) applies instead of that provision of the benefits code or Chapter 3 of Part 4 of ITTOIA 2005 (as the case may be).

(3) In particular, in a case in which the relevant step is the making of an employment-related loan (within the meaning of Chapter 7 of Part 3), the effect of subsection (2)(a) is that the loan is not to be treated for any tax year as a taxable cheap loan for the purposes of that Chapter.

554Z3 Value of relevant step

(1) If the relevant step involves a sum of money, its value is the amount of the sum.

(2) In any other case, the value of the relevant step is—

(a) the market value when the relevant step is taken of the asset which is the subject of the step, or

(b) if higher, the cost of the relevant step.

(3) Subsection (2)(a) is subject to sections 437 and 452.

(4) Subsection (2)(b) is to be ignored if—

(a) the relevant step is within section 554C(1)(c), and

(b) any of Chapters 2 to 4A of Part 7 apply by virtue of the acquisition.

(5) Subsection (2)(b) is also to be ignored if section 554Z7 applies.

(6) In subsection (2)(b) the reference to the cost of the relevant step is to the expense incurred in connection with the relevant step (including a proper proportion of any expense relating partly to the relevant step and partly to other matters) by the person or persons at whose cost the relevant step is taken.

(7) Subsections (1) and (2) are subject to sections 554Z4, 554Z5, 554Z6, 554Z7 and 554Z8, which, so far as applicable, are to be applied in that order.

554Z4 Residence issues

(1) After the value of the relevant step is determined under section 554Z3, the particular tax year or years which the value of the relevant step is "for" are to be determined.

(2) For this purpose, apply sections 16(1) to (4) and 17(1) to (3) as if the value of the relevant step were general earnings.

(3) Subsection (4) applies if the value of the relevant step, or a part of it, is "for" a tax year in which A is non-UK resident.

(4) The value, or the part of it, is to be reduced so far as it is not in respect of duties performed in the United Kingdom.

(5) The question of the extent to which the value, or the part of it, is not in respect of duties performed in the United Kingdom is to be determined on a just and reasonable basis.

(6) This section does not change the tax year for which the value of the relevant step counts as employment income under section 554Z2(1).

554Z5 Overlap with earlier relevant step

(1) This section applies if there is overlap between—

(a) the sum of money or asset ("sum or asset P") which is the subject of the relevant step, and

(b) the sum of money or asset ("sum or asset Q") which was the subject of an earlier relevant step ("the earlier relevant step") by reason of which this Chapter applied in respect of A's employment with B.

(2) The value of the relevant step (after any reductions under section 554Z4) is reduced (but not below nil)—

(a) if the overlap covers the whole of sum or asset Q, by the value of the earlier relevant step, or

(b) if the overlap covers only part of sum or asset Q, by the part of the value of the earlier relevant step which corresponds to the part of sum or asset Q covered by the overlap as determined on a just and reasonable basis.

(3) In subsection (2) references to the value of the earlier relevant step are to that value—

(a) after any reductions made to it under section 554Z4 or this section or section 554Z7, but

(b) before any reductions made to it under section 554Z6 or 554Z8.

(4) For the purposes of this section there is overlap between sum or asset P and sum or asset Q so far as—

(a) they are the same sum of money or asset, or

(b) sum or asset P, essentially, replaces sum or asset Q.

(5) Further, if any reductions were made under this section to the value of the earlier relevant step, sum or asset P is treated as overlapping with any other sum of money or asset so far as the other sum of money or asset was treated as overlapping with sum or asset Q for the purposes of this section.

554Z6 Overlap with certain earnings

(1) This section applies if the relevant step gives rise to relevant earnings of A from A's employment with B—

(a) which are, in accordance with section 16 and (if applicable) section 17, "for" a tax year in which A is UK resident, or

(b) which are, in accordance with section 29 and (if applicable) section 30, "for" a tax year in which A is non-UK resident but which are in respect of duties performed in the United Kingdom for the purposes of section 27(1)(a).

(2) The value of the relevant step (after any reductions under section 554Z4 or 554Z5) is reduced (but not below nil) by the amount of the relevant earnings.

(3) For the purposes of this section the following are "relevant" earnings—

(a) earnings within Chapter 1 of Part 3,

(b) amounts treated as earnings under Chapter 12 of Part 3, and

(c) a deemed employment payment under section 50 or any part of such a payment.

(4) But anything which is exempt income, or which falls within Chapter 3 of Part 4 of ITTOIA 2005, is not "relevant".

554Z7 Exercise price of share options

(1) Subsection (3) applies if—

(a) the relevant step is a step within section 554B (other than one treated as being taken by section 554L(5), (7) or (9) or 554M(4), (6) or (8)),

(b) B is a company,

(c) there is an arrangement ("B's employee share scheme") under which, in respect of A's employment with B, a right ("a relevant share option") may be granted to A—

(i) to acquire relevant shares, or

(ii) to receive a sum of money the amount of which is to be determined by reference to the market value of any relevant shares at the time the sum is to be paid,

(d) in order to exercise the relevant share option so as—

(i) to acquire the relevant shares, or

(ii) to receive the sum of money,

A would, under the terms of the option, have to pay a sum of money the amount of which can be determined at the time of the grant of the option,

(e) the subject of the relevant step is relevant shares ("earmarked shares") which are earmarked, or otherwise start being held, solely with a view to providing shares, or paying a sum of money, pursuant to—

(i) a relevant share option granted to A under B's employee share scheme as mentioned in paragraph (c) in relation to which the requirements of paragraph (d) are met, or

(ii) a relevant share option which is expected to be granted to A under B's employee share scheme as mentioned in paragraph (c) and in relation to which the requirements of paragraph (d) would be met,

(f) the number of relevant shares of any type which are earmarked shares does not exceed the maximum number of relevant shares of that type which might reasonably be expected to be needed for providing shares, or paying a sum of money, pursuant to the relevant share option which is granted or expected to be granted, and

(g) there is no connection (direct or indirect) between the relevant step and a tax avoidance arrangement.

(2) Subsection (3) also applies if—

(a) the relevant step is a step treated as being taken by section 554L(9) or 554M(8), and

(b) in order to exercise the relevant share option to which the step relates so as—

(i) to acquire the shares which are the subject of the relevant step, or

(ii) to receive the sum of money determined by reference to the market value of those shares,

A would, under the terms of the option, have to pay a sum of money the amount of which can be determined at the time the option is granted.

(3) The value of the relevant step (after any reductions under sections 554Z4 to 554Z6) is to be reduced (but not below nil) by—

(a) the amount of the sum of money which A would have to pay as mentioned in subsection (1)(d) or (2)(b), or

(b) if the value of the relevant step was reduced under section 554Z4, X% of the amount of that sum of money.

(4) In subsection (3)(b) "X%" means the proportion of the value of the relevant step (as determined under section 554Z3) left after the reduction under section 554Z4.

(5) If subsection (3) applies by virtue of subsection (1) and the relevant step is taken in relation to an expected grant of a relevant share option as mentioned in subsection (1)(e)(ii), subsection (7) applies if—

(a) the grant is not made before the end of the date ("the final grant date") falling immediately after the period of three months starting with the date on which the relevant step is taken, and

(b) as at the end of the final grant date, any of the earmarked shares continue to be held by or on behalf of P solely on the basis mentioned in subsection (1)(e).

(6) If subsection (3) applies by virtue of subsection (1), subsection (7) also applies if at any time after the taking of the relevant step—

(a) any of the earmarked shares cease to be held by or on behalf of P solely on the basis mentioned in subsection (1)(e), but

(b) the shares continue to be held by or on behalf of P on the basis mentioned in section 554B(1)(a) or (b).

(7) This Part has effect as if a relevant step within section 554B were taken at the end of the final grant date or when the shares cease to be held as mentioned in subsection (6)—

(a) the subject of which is the earmarked shares mentioned in subsection (5)(b) or (6), and

(b) by reason of which this Chapter is to apply (subject only to section 554A(4)).

(8) In this section "relevant shares" has the meaning given by section 554I(4).

554Z8 Cases where consideration given for relevant step

(1) Subsection (2) applies if—

(a) the relevant step is a step within section 554C(1)(a) to (c),

(b) the relevant step is for consideration given by A in the form of the transfer of an asset to P from A,

(c) the transfer by A of the asset is made before, or at or about, the time the relevant step is taken and is not by way of a loan, and

(d) there is no connection (direct or indirect) between the transfer by A of the asset and a tax avoidance arrangement.

(2) The value of the relevant step (after any reductions under sections 554Z4 to 554Z6) is reduced (but not below nil) by—

(a) the market value of the asset transferred by A at the time of its transfer, or

(b) if the value of the relevant step was reduced under section 554Z4, X% of that market value.

(3) For the purposes of subsection (1)(d) it is (in particular) to be assumed that the transfer by A of the asset is connected with a tax avoidance arrangement if—

(a) before the transfer, the asset was transferred to A by another person by way of a loan, or

(b) the asset is, or carries with it, any rights or interests under the relevant arrangement or any arrangement which is connected (directly or indirectly) with the relevant arrangement.

(4) In subsection (3)(b) "the relevant arrangement" has the meaning given by section 554A(1)(b).

(5) Subsection (6) applies if—

(a) the relevant step is a step within section 554C(1)(b) or (c) or (e) or 554D and does not also involve a sum of money,

(b) the relevant step is for consideration given by A in the form of the payment of a sum of money to P by A, and

(c) the payment is made before, or at or about, the time the relevant step is taken.

(6) The value of the relevant step (after any reductions under sections 554Z4 to 554Z6) is reduced (but not below nil) by—

(a) the amount of the consideration given, or

(b) if the value of the relevant step was reduced under section 554Z4, X% of the amount of that consideration.

(7) In subsections (2)(b) and (6)(b) "X%" means the proportion of the value of the relevant step (as determined under section 554Z3) left after the reduction under section 554Z4.

(8) In this section references to A include references to any person linked with A.

Remittance basis

554Z9 Remittance basis: A is ordinarily UK resident

(1) Subsection (2) applies if—

(a) the value of the relevant step, or a part of it, is "for" a tax year ("the relevant tax year") as determined under section 554Z4,

(b) section 809B, 809D or 809E of ITA 2007 (remittance basis) applies to A for the relevant tax year,

(c) A is ordinarily UK resident in the relevant tax year,

(d) A's employment with B in the relevant tax year is employment with a foreign employer, and

(e) the duties of A's employment with B in the relevant tax year are performed wholly outside the United Kingdom.

(2) A's employment income by virtue of section 554Z2(1), or the relevant part of it, is "taxable specific income" in a tax year so far as it is remitted to the United Kingdom in that year.

(3) For this purpose, any income which is remitted before A's employment with B starts is treated as being remitted in the tax year in which the employment starts.

(4) Subsection (5) applies if in the relevant tax year—

(a) A has associated employments, and

(b) the duties of the associated employments are not performed wholly outside the United Kingdom.

(5) The amount of A's employment income to which subsection (2) applies is limited to such amount as is just and reasonable, having regard to—

(a) A's employment income for the relevant tax year from all associated employments, together with A's employment with B,

(b) the proportion of that income which is general earnings to which section 22 applies or is employment income to which section 41A applies,

(c) the nature of and time devoted to the duties performed outside the United Kingdom, and those performed in the United Kingdom, in the relevant tax year, and

(d) all other relevant circumstances,

and, if the amount of A's employment income to which subsection (2) would otherwise apply exceeds that limit, the amount of A's employment income to which that subsection applies is instead to be such amount as is just and reasonable.

(6) In this section "associated employments" means employments with B or with employers associated with B; and section 24(5) and (6) applies for the purposes of this subsection.

554Z10 Remittance basis: A is not ordinarily resident

(1) Subsection (2) applies if—

(a) the value of the relevant step, or a part of it—

(i) is "for" a tax year ("the relevant tax year") as determined under section 554Z4, and

(ii) is not in respect of duties performed in the United Kingdom,

(b) section 809B, 809D or 809E of ITA 2007 (remittance basis) applies to A for the relevant tax year, and

(c) A is not ordinarily UK resident in the relevant tax year.

(2) A's employment income by virtue of section 554Z2(1), or the relevant part of it, is "taxable specific income" in a tax year so far as it is remitted to the United Kingdom in that year.

(3) For this purpose, any income which is remitted before A's employment with B starts is treated as being remitted in the tax year in which the employment starts.

(4) The question of the extent to which the value of the relevant step, or any part of it, is not in respect of duties performed in the United Kingdom is to be determined on a just and reasonable basis.

554Z11 Remittance basis: supplementary

(1) Subsection (2) applies if section 554Z9(1)(a) or 554Z10(1)(a) applies to a part ("the relevant part") of the value of the relevant step.

(2) Any reduction to the value of the relevant step to be made under any of sections 554Z5 to 554Z8 is to be made so that X% of the reduction is made by way of reducing the relevant part.

(3) In subsection (2) "X%" means the proportion of the value of the relevant step represented by the relevant part before any reductions under any of sections 554Z5 to 554Z8.

(4) For the purpose of applying section 554Z9(2) or 554Z10(2), see Chapter A1 of Part 14 of ITA 2007 for the meaning of "remitted to the United Kingdom" etc

(5) If the relevant step involves a sum of money, for the purposes of that Chapter the sum of money is treated as deriving from A's employment income (or the relevant part of it) to which section 554Z9(2) or 554Z10(2) applies.

(6) In any other case, for the purposes of that Chapter the asset which is the subject of the relevant step is treated as deriving from A's employment income (or the relevant part of it) to which section 554Z9(2) or 554Z10(2) applies.

(7) Subsection (8) applies if—

(a) after the relevant step is taken, there is another relevant step ("the later relevant step") by reason of which this Chapter applies in respect of A's employment with B, and

(b) within the meaning of section 554Z5, there is overlap between the sum of money or asset ("sum or asset R") which is the subject of the relevant step and the sum of money or asset ("sum or asset S") which is the subject of the later relevant step.

(8) Except so far as, in any event—

(a) sum or asset S and sum or asset R are the same sum of money or asset, or

(b) sum or asset S derives from sum or asset R,

for the purposes of Chapter A1 of Part 14 of ITA 2007 sum or asset S is treated, to the extent of the overlap, as deriving from sum or asset R.

(9) Subsections (10) and (11) apply if—

(a) the relevant tax year within the meaning of section 554Z9 or 554Z10 is the tax year 2007–08 or any earlier tax year, and

(b) A—

(i) was UK resident in that year, but

(ii) was not domiciled in the United Kingdom, or was not ordinarily UK resident, in that year.

(10) Section 554Z9 or 554Z10 (as the case may be) applies as if section 809B of ITA 2007 applied to A for the relevant tax year.

(11) In section 554Z9(1)(d) the reference to a foreign employer is to be read as not including a person resident in the Republic of Ireland.

Supplementary

554Z12 Relevant step taken after A's death etc

(1) Subsection (3), (4) or (5) (as the case may be) applies if the relevant step is a step within section 554C or 554D and—

(a) the relevant step is taken on or after A's death, or

(b) if relevant, any of A's employment income by virtue of section 554Z2(1) is remitted to the United Kingdom on or after A's death.

But none of those subsections applies if A's employment with B never started before A's death.

(2) In subsections (3) to (5) "the relevant person" means the relevant person (within the meaning of section 554C(1) or 554D(1) or (2)) in relation to the relevant step.

(3) If the relevant person is A, A's personal representatives are liable for, as the case may be, the income tax on—

(a) A's employment income by virtue of section 554Z2(1), or

(b) so much of that income as is remitted.

(4) If the relevant person is an individual other than A, the amount which, as the case may be—

(a) counts as employment income of A, or

(b) is remitted,

is to count as an amount of employment income of the relevant person for the tax year in which the relevant step is taken or the income is remitted.

(5) If the relevant person is not an individual, the relevant taxable person is chargeable to income tax on the amount which, as the case may be—

(a) counts as employment income of A, or

(b) is remitted.

(6) In subsection (5) "the relevant taxable person" is to be read as follows—

(a) if the person (or any of the persons) who took the relevant step is UK resident, "the relevant taxable person" is the person (or each of the UK resident persons) who took the relevant step,

(b) if paragraph (a) does not apply and B is still alive or in existence when the relevant step is taken, "the relevant taxable person" is B, or

(c) if neither paragraph (a) nor paragraph (b) applies, "the relevant taxable person" is the non-UK resident person (or each of the non-UK resident persons) who took the relevant step.

(7) For the purposes of subsection (5)—

(a) the rate of tax is the rate applying for the purposes of section 394(2) (see section 394(4)) at the time of the relevant step or remittance of income, and

(b) the tax is charged for the tax year in which the relevant step is taken or the income is remitted.

(8) If there is more than one relevant person in relation to the relevant step, the amount which, as the case may be—

(a) counts as employment income of A, or

(b) is remitted,

is to be apportioned between the relevant persons on a just and reasonable basis with subsections (3) to (5) applying accordingly.

554Z13 Subsequent income tax liability

(1) This section applies if—

(a) after the relevant step is taken, another event ("the later event") occurs,

(b) other than by virtue of—

(i) this Chapter,

(ii) Chapters 2 to 5 of Part 7, or

(iii) Part 9,

the later event would (apart from this section) give rise to a liability for income tax of A or any other person on an amount ("the later amount"), and

(c) it is just and reasonable for this section to apply in order to avoid a double charge to income tax in respect of the sum of money or asset which is the subject of the relevant step.

(2) So far as it is just and reasonable in order to avoid a double charge to income tax as mentioned in subsection (1)(c), there is to be no liability to income tax on the later amount by virtue of the later event.

554Z14 Relief where earmarking not followed by further relevant step

(1) An application for relief may be made by A (or, if A has died, A's personal representatives) to an officer of Revenue and Customs if—

(a) this Chapter has applied by reason of a relevant step ("the original relevant step") within section 554B taken by a person ("P"),

(b) there occurs an event ("the relevant event") which is not a relevant step in relation to a relevant sum or asset,

(c) by reason of the relevant event no further relevant step is or will be taken by P or any other person in relation to any relevant sum or asset, and

(d) there is no connection (direct or indirect) between the relevant event and a tax avoidance arrangement.

(2) In section 554Z(15) the reference to the avoidance of tax includes (in particular) a reference to the avoidance of tax by way of obtaining relief under this section.

(3) In subsection (1) "relevant sum or asset" means—

(a) the sum of money or asset which is the subject of the original relevant step, or

(b) a sum of money or asset which (directly or indirectly) has arisen or derived, or may arise or derive, from the sum of money or asset mentioned in paragraph (a).

(4) The application for relief must be made within four years from the time when the relevant event occurs.

(5) If an officer of Revenue and Customs is satisfied that the requirements in subsection (1) are met, the officer must give such relief as the officer considers just and reasonable (if any) in respect of income tax paid on any previously charged amount.

(6) In subsection (5) "previously charged amount" means—

(a) the amount which counted as employment income of A under this Chapter as a result of this Chapter applying by reason of the original relevant step, or

(b) any amount treated by section 222 as earnings of A in relation to the notional payment (within the meaning of that section) which B is treated as having made by virtue of the original relevant step.

(7) Subsection (8) applies if, by virtue of this Chapter having applied by reason of the original relevant step, any tax liability of A or any other person arising from another event is reduced (including to nil) by virtue of section 554Z5 or 554Z13 or otherwise.

(8) In determining what is a just and reasonable amount of relief, the officer of Revenue and Customs must have regard (in particular) to the reduction in the tax liability and reduce the amount of relief which would otherwise have been given accordingly (including to nil).

(9) The relief is to be given by repayment or otherwise as appropriate.

(10) In relation to times after the relief is given, the Tax Acts have effect as if this Chapter had never applied by reason of the original relevant step.

554Z15 Location of employment duties

The following provisions apply for the purposes of this Chapter—

(a) section 38 (but as if references to general earnings were to the value of the relevant step or a part of it),

(b) section 39(1) and (2),

(c) section 40 (but as if in subsections (3) and (4) references to section 24(1)(b) were to section 554Z9(4)(b)), and

(d) section 41 (but as if references to general earnings were to the value of the relevant step or a part of it).

CHAPTER 3

UNDERTAKINGS GIVEN BY EMPLOYERS ETC IN RELATION TO RETIREMENT BENEFITS ETC

554Z16 Application etc

(1) This Chapter applies if there is an undertaking ("the relevant undertaking") that a contribution to which subsection (2) would apply will be paid.

(2) This subsection applies to a contribution if—

(a) the contribution is paid to an arrangement which is not a registered pension scheme,

(b) in connection with that arrangement (directly or indirectly), relevant benefits are to be provided (directly or indirectly) out of the contribution by a relevant third person,

(c) the provision of the relevant benefits would be a relevant step, and
(d) the contribution is neither a tax-relieved contribution nor tax-exempt provision.

(3) In subsection (2)—

"relevant benefits" has the same meaning as in Chapter 2 of Part 6, but ignoring section 393B(2)(a),
"relevant third person" means a person within section 554A(7)(a) to (c) (ignoring this Chapter), and
"tax-exempt provision" and "tax-relieved contribution" have the meaning given by paragraph 3(3) and (4) of Schedule 34 to FA 2004.

(4) In this Chapter references to an undertaking include references to—

(a) an undertaking which is not legally enforceable, and
(b) an undertaking which is to be performed only on or following the meeting of a condition (including a condition which might never be met).

554Z17 Employer etc to be treated as relevant third person etc

(1) If B takes a step within section 554Z18 or 554Z19, Chapters 1 and 2 have effect in relation to the step—

(a) as if B were a relevant third person for the purposes of section 554A(1)(d), and
(b) as if the step were a relevant step within section 554B (if it would not otherwise be).

(2) For the purpose of determining whether Chapter 2 applies by reason of the step, Chapter 1 has effect—

(a) as if sections 554F to 554O, 554S to 554U, 554W and 554X were omitted,
(b) if the step is within section 554Z18, as if sections 554Q(2)(d), (3) and (4) and 554R(1)(c) and (d), (2) and (3) were omitted, and
(c) if the step is within section 554Z19, as if sections 554Q and 554R were omitted.

(3) If Chapter 2 applies by reason of the step, Chapter 2 has effect as if sections 554Z7 to 554Z12 were omitted.

(4) If Chapter 2 does not apply by reason of the step by virtue of section 554E(3) or (6), section 554E(10) and (11) does not apply in relation to the step.

(5) For further modifications of Chapters 1 and 2, see sections 554Z18(3) and (4), 554Z19(5) and (6), 554Z20 and 554Z21.

(6) Regulations under section 554Y may (in particular) make provision covering cases in which Chapters 1 and 2 have effect as provided for by this section.

(7) In this Chapter—

(a) references to B do not include references to B acting as a trustee,
(b) if B is a company and is a member of a group of companies, references to B are to be read as including references to any other company which is a member of that group, and
(c) if B is a limited liability partnership, references to B are to be read as including references to any company which is a wholly-owned subsidiary (as defined in section 1159(2) of the Companies Act 2006) of B.

554Z18 Earmarking etc

(1) B takes a step within this section if—

(a) a sum of money or asset held by or on behalf of B is earmarked (however informally) by B with a view to the relevant undertaking being performed at a later time (wholly or partly) out of—

(i) that sum of money or asset, or
(ii) any sum of money or asset which may arise or derive (directly or indirectly) from it, or

(b) a sum of money or asset otherwise starts being held by or on behalf of B, specifically with a view, so far as B is concerned, to the relevant undertaking being performed at a later time (wholly or partly) out of—

(i) that sum of money or asset, or
(ii) any sum of money or asset which may arise or derive (directly or indirectly) from it.

(2) For the purposes of subsection (1)(b) it does not matter whether or not the sum of money or asset in question has previously been held by or on behalf of B on a basis which is different to that mentioned in subsection (1)(b).

(3) Subsection (4) applies if, in the application of section 554Q or 554R in any case, the relevant step mentioned in section 554Q(2)(a) or 554R(6)(a) is a step within this section taken by B.

(4) In section 554Q(2)(c) or 554R(6)(c) (as the case may be) the reference to section 554B(1)(a) or (b) is to be read as a reference to subsection (1)(a) or (b) above.

554Z19 Provision of security

(1) B takes a step within this section if B provides security for the performance of the relevant undertaking.

(2) For the purposes of this Part, the sum of money or asset which is the subject of the step is to be taken to be—

(a) any sums of money which, as at the time the step is taken, are the subject of the security, and

(b) any assets which, as at that time, are the subject of the security,

and references to the sum of money or asset which is the subject of a relevant step are to be read accordingly.

(3) If, when the step is taken, the security covers other undertakings as well as the relevant undertaking, the sums of money and assets within subsection (2)(a) and (b) are to be apportioned between the relevant undertaking and the other undertakings on a just and reasonable basis.

(4) Subsections (2) and (3) are subject to section 554Z20(7).

(5) Section 554Q does not apply in any case in which the relevant step mentioned in section 554Q(2)(a) would be a step within this section taken by B.

(6) Section 554R(6) does not apply in any case in which the relevant step mentioned in section 554R(6)(a) would be a step within this section taken by B.

(7) In this Chapter references to providing security for the performance of an undertaking are references to providing such security in any way, however informal.

554Z20 Valuation of step within section 554Z19

(1) This section applies if, by virtue of section 554Z17, Chapter 2 applies by reason of a step taken by B within section 554Z19.

(2) Section 554Z3 has effect as if subsections (3) and (4) below were substituted for subsections (1) to (6) of that section.

(3) The value of the relevant step is—

(a) the amount to be paid as a contribution under the relevant undertaking determined, as at the time the step is taken, on a just and reasonable basis assuming that any condition to be met before any payment is made will be met, or

(b) if lower, the value of the security.

(4) For the purposes of subsection (3)(b) the value of the security—

(a) consists of—

(i) the total amount of the sums of money included in the subject of the step (see section 554Z19(2)(a)), and

(ii) the total market value, as at the time the step is taken, of the assets included in the subject of the step (see section 554Z19(2)(b)), but

(b) is to be subject to a just and reasonable reduction to take account of any term of the security which limits the total amount which may be made available under the security for the performance of the relevant undertaking to an amount which is lower than the amount determined under paragraph (a).

(5) The following subsections apply if, as at the end of the day of an anniversary of the taking of the step ("the anniversary day"), B continues to provide the security for the performance of the relevant undertaking.

(6) This Part has effect as if B's continuing to provide the security were a new step ("the anniversary step") within section 554Z19—

(a) which is taken by B at the end of the anniversary day, and

(b) by reason of which Chapter 2 is to apply by virtue of section 554Z17 (subject only to section 554A(4)).

(7) If the total amount of the sums of money which are the subject of the security ("the security sums") varies from time to time, for the purpose of determining the sums of money included in the subject of the anniversary step, in section 554Z19(2)(a) the reference to the time the step is taken is to be read as a reference to the time during the preceding year at which the total amount of the security sums is at its highest.

(8) For the purposes of subsection (4)(a)(ii) the market value of any asset included in the subject of the anniversary step may be determined as at any time during the preceding year (so long as the asset is the subject of the security, or one of the assets which is the subject of the security, as at that time).

(9) In subsections (7) and (8) "the preceding year" means the year ending with the anniversary day.

554Z21 Relief for earmarking or security not followed by contribution or relevant benefit

(1) This section applies if, by virtue of section 554Z17, Chapter 2 applies by reason of a step taken by B within section 554Z18 or 554Z19.

(2) Section 554Z14 has effect in relation to the step with the following modifications.

(3) Subsection (1)(b) has effect as if for "not a relevant step in relation to a relevant sum or asset" there were substituted "neither the payment of the relevant contribution (or any part of it) nor the provision of any relevant benefit".

(4) Subsection (1)(c) has effect as if for the words from "no further relevant step" to "any relevant sum or asset" there were substituted "the relevant contribution (or any part of it) will not be paid or a relevant benefit will not be provided".

(5) Subsection (1) has effect as if subsection (6) below were substituted for subsection (3).

(6) In subsection (1)—

(a) "the relevant contribution" means the contribution to be paid under the relevant undertaking (within the meaning of Chapter 3), and

(b) "relevant benefit" means a relevant benefit to be provided out of the relevant contribution as mentioned in section 554Z16(2)(b) and (c)."

Other amendments to ITEPA 2003

2 ITEPA 2003 is amended as follows.

3 In section 1(1)(a) (overview of contents of Act) for "7" substitute "7A".

4 (1) Amend section 3 (structure of employment income Parts) as follows.

(2) At the end of subsection (1) insert—

"Part 7A deals with employment income provided through third parties."

(3) In subsection (2) for "7" substitute "7A".

5 For the "or" after section 7(6)(b) (meaning of "specific employment income") substitute—

"(ba) Part 7A (employment income provided through third parties), or".

6 (1) Amend section 10 (provision relating to "taxable specific income") as follows.

(2) In subsection (3) for "or 7" substitute ", 7 or 7A".

(3) After subsection (4) insert—

"(5) Subsection (3) is also subject to sections 554Z9 to 554Z11 (employment income under Part 7A: remittance basis)."

7 (1) Amend section 13 (person liable for tax) as follows.

(2) In subsection (3) for "or 7" substitute ", 7 or 7A".

(3) After subsection (4A) insert—

"(4B) Subject to section 554Z12, if—

(a) the tax is on specific employment income under Chapter 2 of Part 7A, and

(b) the relevant step is taken, or (if relevant) the income is remitted to the United Kingdom, after the death of A,

A's personal representatives are liable for the tax.

(4C) Terms used in subsection (4B) have the same meaning as in Part 7A."

(4) In subsection (5) for "or (4A)" substitute ", (4A) or (4B) or section 554Z12(3)".

8 After section 63(4) (the benefits code) insert—

"(5) The benefits code has effect subject to section 554Z2(2)."

9 Under Step 1 in section 218(1) (exclusion of lower-paid employments from benefits code: calculation of earnings rate for tax year)—

(a) omit the "and" after paragraphs (c) and (d), and

(b) after paragraph (e) insert

", and

(f) the total amount which counts as employment income in respect of the employment for the year under Chapter 2 of Part 7A."

10 In section 222(1)(a) and (3) (payments treated as earnings: payments by employer on account of tax where deduction not possible) after "687," insert "687A,".

11 After section 227(4) (scope of exemptions to income tax under Part 4) insert—

"(5) In relation to the interaction between this Part and Part 7A, see section 554P(1)."

12 (1) Amend section 271 (income tax exemptions: removal benefits and expenses) as follows.

(2) In subsection (1) after "earnings" insert "or by virtue of Part 7A".

(3) In subsection (2) for "Subsection" substitute "In relation to earnings, subsection".

(4) After subsection (2) insert—

"(2A) In relation to Part 7A, subsection (1) does not apply to any amount so far as the amount (disregarding this section and section 554P) would count as employment income to which section 554Z9 or 554Z10 would apply."

13 (1) Amend section 287 (income tax exemptions: limit on exemption for removal benefits and expenses) as follows.

(2) In subsection (2)—

(a) omit the "and" after paragraph (a), and

(b) after paragraph (b) insert

", and

(c) the Part 7A employment income".

(3) After subsection (5) insert—

"(6) In this section "the Part 7A employment income" means the amount in respect of which section 271 (when read with section 554P) would prevent liability to income tax arising if this section were to be disregarded."

14 (1) Amend section 394 (employer-financed retirement benefits: charge on benefit received) as follows.

(2) After subsection (4) insert—

"(4A) Subsection (4B) applies if the receipt of a benefit to which this Chapter applies gives rise to other relevant income of the employee, or the former employee, to or in respect of whom the benefit is provided.

(4B) Subsection (1) or (2) (as the case may be) applies to the amount of the benefit only so far as that amount exceeds the other relevant income.

(4C) In subsections (4A) and (4B) "other relevant income" means—

(a) general earnings of the employee or former employee which are chargeable to income tax,

(b) an amount which counts as employment income of the employee or former employee under Chapter 2 of Part 7A, or

(c) an amount which would be within paragraph (a) or (b) apart from the employee or former employee having been non-UK resident for any tax year."

(3) After subsection (5) insert—

"(6) Subsection (5) does not affect—

(a) any liability to income tax on general earnings, or

(b) any liability to income tax on an amount which counts as employment income under Chapter 2 of Part 7A."

15 After section 428(6) (restricted employment-related securities: amount of charge) insert—

"(6A) CE also includes any amount that has counted as employment income of the employee in respect of the employment under Chapter 2 of Part 7A in relation to the employment-related securities where the relevant step (within the meaning of that Part) was taken before the chargeable event occurred."

16 In section 431(3) (restricted employment-related securities; election for disapplication of Chapter 2 of Part 7)—

(a) omit the "and" after paragraph (c), and

(b) after paragraph (d) insert

", and

(e) determining any amount that counts as employment income of the employee in respect of the employment under Chapter 2 of Part 7A (employment income provided through third parties)".

17 In section 437(1)(a) (convertible employment-related securities: market value) after "option)" insert "or Chapter 2 of Part 7A (employment income provided through third parties)".

18 After section 441(9) (convertible employment-related securities: amount of gain realised) insert—

"(10) Subsection (11) applies for the purposes of subsection (2) or (3) if—

(a) prior to the acquisition, the employment-related securities were the subject of a relevant step within the meaning of Part 7A by reason of which Chapter 2 of that Part applied in respect of the employment, and

(b) the amount mentioned in subsection (11)(a) is higher than the amount mentioned in subsection (11)(b).

(11) The amount of the gain realised is reduced (but not below nil) by the amount equal to—

(a) the amount that counted as employment income of the employee in respect of the employment under Chapter 2 of Part 7A, less

(b) the market value of the employment-related securities when the relevant step was taken determined as if they were not convertible securities or an interest in convertible securities."

19 In section 446B(4) (employment-related securities with artificially depressed market value: charge on acquisition)—

(a) omit the "or" after paragraph (d), and

(b) after paragraph (e) insert

", or

(f) Chapter 2 of Part 7A (employment income provided through third parties)".

20 After section 446C(4) (employment-related securities with artificially depressed market value: amount of charge) insert—

"(4A) Subsection (4B) applies if, prior to the acquisition, the employment-related securities were the subject of a relevant step within the meaning of Part 7A by reason of which Chapter 2 of that Part applied in respect of the employment.

(4B) If what would be MV in accordance with subsection (3) or (4) (as the case may be) is less than the amount that counted as employment income of the employee in respect of the employment under Chapter 2 of Part 7A, MV is the amount of that employment income instead of the amount determined in accordance with subsection (3) or (4)."

21 After section 446S(3) (employment-related securities acquired for less than market value: notional loan) insert—

"(4) This section is not affected by section 554Z2(2)."

22 In section 446T(3) (employment-related securities acquired for less than market value: amount of notional loan)—

(a) omit the "and" after paragraph (d), and

(b) after paragraph (e) insert

", and

(f) any amount that has counted as employment income of the employee in respect of the employment under Chapter 2 of Part 7A in relation to the employment-related securities."

23 In section 446V (employment-related securities acquired for less than market value: charges under Chapter 3C of Part 4 to be additional to other charges)—

(a) omit the "or" after paragraph (d), and

(b) after paragraph (e) insert

", or

(f) Chapter 2 of Part 7A (employment income provided through third parties)".

24 In section 452(2) (shares in research institution spin-out companies: market value on acquisition)—

(a) omit the "and" after paragraph (c), and

(b) after paragraph (d) insert

", and

(e) determining any amount that counts as employment income of the employee in respect of the employment under Chapter 2 of Part 7A (employment income provided through third parties)".

25 In section 480(5) (employment-related securities options: deductible amounts)—

(a) omit the "and" after paragraph (b), and

(b) after paragraph (c) insert

", and

(d) any amount that has counted as employment income of the employee in respect of the employment under Chapter 2 of Part 7A in relation to the employment-related securities option or to any sum of money or asset held solely for the purposes of the option."

26 In section 567(5) (pension income: amount charged to tax) before "section 617" insert—

"section 567A (deduction to avoid double taxation where Part 7A has applied to the source of the pension income);".

27 After section 567 insert—

"567A Cases in which Part 7A has applied to source of pension income

(1) This section applies if—

(a) for a tax year there is an amount ("amount TPI") of taxable pension income for a pension, annuity or other item of pension income,

(b) the pension, annuity or other item of pension income accrues or arises out of rights ("the relevant rights") which represent, or have arisen or derived (directly or indirectly) from, a sum of money or asset which was the subject of a relevant step within the meaning of Part 7A, and

(c) Chapter 2 of that Part applied by reason of the relevant step.

(2) A deduction is allowed from amount TPI.

(3) The amount of the deduction allowed is the amount ("amount EI") which counted as employment income of A under Chapter 2 of Part 7A in relation to the relevant step (see section 554Z2(1)).

(4) If amount EI exceeds amount TPI, the excess is to be carried forward to future tax years to be deducted under this section (when applicable) until all of amount EI has been deducted.

(5) Subsection (6) applies if it is determined on a just and reasonable basis that the relevant rights represent, or have arisen or derived from, only part of the sum of money or asset which was the subject of the relevant step.

(6) In subsection (3) the reference to the amount which counted as employment income is to be read as a reference to the corresponding proportion of that amount."

28 After section 687(4) (PAYE: payments by intermediary) insert—

"(5) This section does not apply in relation to a payment so far as the sum paid is employment income under Chapter 2 of Part 7A."

29 After section 687 insert—

"687A Payment of employment income under Part 7A

(1) This section applies if—

(a) the value of a relevant step counts as employment income under Chapter 2 of Part 7A, and

(b) the relevant step is the payment of a sum of money,

and references to A and B are to be read accordingly.

(2) For the purposes of PAYE regulations B is treated as making a payment of PAYE income of A of an amount which, on the basis of the best estimate which can reasonably be made, is the amount of the employment income.

(3) The payment is treated as made on the latest of the following days—

(a) the day on which the relevant step is taken,

(b) the day on which A's employment with B starts, and

(c) the day which is 30 days after the day on which FA 2011 is passed.

(4) Subsection (2) does not apply if the person who takes the relevant step (whether or not a person to whom PAYE regulations apply) deducts income tax from the payment, and accounts for it, in accordance with PAYE regulations."

30 (1) Amend section 689 (PAYE: employee of non-UK employer) as follows.

(2) After subsection (1) insert—

"(1A) Subject to subsection (4), subsection (1)(b) does not apply in relation to a payment so far as the sum paid is employment income under Chapter 2 of Part 7A."

(3) In subsection (4) after "sections" insert "687A and".

31 Before section 696 insert—

"695A Employment income under Part 7A

(1) This section applies if—

(a) the value of a relevant step counts as employment income under Chapter 2 of Part 7A, and

(b) the relevant step is not the payment of a sum of money,

and references to A and B are to be read accordingly.

(2) For the purposes of PAYE regulations B is treated as making a payment of PAYE income of A of an amount which, on the basis of the best estimate which can reasonably be made, is—

(a) the amount of the employment income, less

(b) so much of that amount (if any) to which section 554Z9(2) or 554Z10(2) applies.

(3) The payment is treated as made on the latest of the following days—

(a) the day on which the relevant step is taken,

(b) the day on which A'semployment with B starts, and

(c) the day which is 30 days after the day on which FA 2011 is passed.

(4) Subsection (2) does not apply if the person who takes the relevant step (whether or not a person to whom PAYE regulations apply) accounts for income tax on the relevant step in accordance with PAYE regulations."

32 After section 696(2) (PAYE: readily convertible assets) insert—

"(3) This section does not apply to any PAYE income so far as it is employment income under Chapter 2 of Part 7A."

33 In section 710(2)(a) (PAYE: accounting for tax on notional payments) after "687," insert "687A,".

34 (1) Amend section 716A (priority rule in relation to certain dividend income) as follows.

(2) Make the existing text subsection (1).

(3) After subsection (1) insert—

"(2) Subsection (1) is subject to section 554Z2(2)."

Amendments to ITTOIA 2005

35 ITTOIA 2005 is amended as follows.

36 (1) Amend section 39 (employee benefit contributions: meaning of "employee benefit scheme" etc) as follows.

(2) In subsection (2) after "employer" insert "or persons linked with present or former employees of the employer".

(3) After subsection (2) insert—

"(3) Section 554Z1 of ITEPA 2003 applies for the purposes of subsection (2) but as if references to A were to a present or former employee of the employer.

(4) So far as it is not covered by subsection (2), "employee benefit scheme" also means—

(a) an arrangement ("the relevant arrangement") within subsection (1)(b) of section 554A of ITEPA 2003 to which subsection (1)(c) of that section applies, or

(b) any other arrangement connected (directly or indirectly) with the relevant arrangement."

37 (1) Amend section 40 (employee benefit contributions: provision of qualifying benefits) as follows.

(2) In subsection (5) after "scheme" insert

"and the payment or transfer—

(a) gives rise to an employment income tax charge under Chapter 2 of Part 6 of ITEPA 2003 or under Part 9 of that Act, or

(b) is an excluded benefit as defined in section 393B(3) of that Act."

(3) After subsection (6) insert—

"(6A) For the purposes of section 38 qualifying benefits are also provided if—

(a) a relevant step within the meaning of Part 7A of ITEPA 2003 is taken, and

(b) Chapter 2 of that Part applies by reason of the step."

38 (1) Amend section 41 (employee benefit contributions: timing of qualifying benefits etc) as follows.

(2) For subsection (1) substitute—

"(1) If the provision of a qualifying benefit takes the form of a payment of money, the benefit, so far as Chapter 4 of Part 2 of ITEPA 2003 applies to the money, is provided for the purposes of section 38 when the money is treated as received for the purposes of that Chapter (applying the rules in section 18 of that Act (receipt of money earnings))."

(3) After subsection (1) insert—

"(1A) Except so far as subsection (1) applies to the provision of the qualifying benefit, if the provision of a qualifying benefit is a chargeable relevant step, for the purposes of section 38—

(a) the benefit is provided when A's employment with B starts if the chargeable relevant step is taken before then, or

(b) otherwise, the benefit is provided when the chargeable relevant step is taken."

(4) In subsection (2)—

(a) after "an asset" insert "which meets condition A, B, C or D in section 40",

(b) omit the "and" after paragraph (a), and

(c) after paragraph (b) insert

", and

(c) if the transfer is a chargeable relevant step, the cost of the relevant step so far as not covered by paragraph (a) or (b)".

(5) After subsection (3) insert—

"(4) If the provision of a qualifying benefit is a chargeable relevant step which does not involve a sum of money (see section 554Z(10) of ITEPA 2003) and is not covered by subsection (2), the amount provided for the purposes of section 38 is the cost of the relevant step (subject to subsection (5)).

(5) If the provision of a qualifying benefit is a chargeable relevant step which is not covered by subsection (2) (whether or not it involves a sum of money), the amount provided for the purposes of section 38 is not to exceed the amount that—

(a) is charged to tax under ITEPA 2003 in relation to the relevant step (whether under Part 7A of that Act or otherwise), or

(b) would be charged had not A been non-UK resident in any tax year.

(6) In this section—

(a) "chargeable relevant step" means a relevant step within the meaning of Part 7A of ITEPA 2003 by reason of which Chapter 2 of that Part applies (and references to A and B are to be read accordingly), and

(b) references to the cost of a chargeable relevant step are to be read in accordance with section 554Z3(6) of that Act."

39 In section 44(1) (employee benefit contributions: interpretation)—

(a) in the definition of "employee benefit scheme" for "39(2)" substitute "39(2) to (4)", and

(b) in the definition of "employer-financed retirement benefits scheme" after "Act)" insert "but ignoring section 393B(2)(a) and (c) of that Act".

Amendments to ITA 2007

40 ITA 2007 is amended as follows.

41 After section 809F(5) (remittance basis: effect) insert—

"(5A) For the effect on amounts which count as employment income under Chapter 2 of Part 7A of ITEPA 2003, see sections 554Z9 to 554Z11 of that Act."

42 After section 809K(1)(c) (remittance basis: application of sections 809L to 809Z6) insert—

"(ca) sections 554Z9 to 554Z11 of that Act (employment income provided through third parties charged on remittance basis),".

43 For section 809Z7(4) (remittance basis: meaning of "foreign specific employment income") substitute—

"(4) An individual's "foreign specific employment income" for a tax year ("the relevant tax year") consists of the income (if any) within subsections (4A) and (4B).

(4A) The income within this subsection is the individual's specific employment income for the relevant tax year so far as it consists of foreign securities income for the purposes of section 41A of ITEPA 2003.

(4B) The income within this subsection is any income, or any part of any income, of the individual—

(a) to which section 554Z9(2) or 554Z10(2) of ITEPA 2003 applies, and

(b) which consists of the value of a relevant step, or a part of the value of a relevant step, which is "for" the relevant tax year as determined under section 554Z4 of ITEPA 2003."

Amendments to CTA 2009

44 CTA 2009 is amended as follows.

45 (1) Amend section 1291 (employee benefit contributions: meaning of "employee benefit scheme" etc) as follows.

(2) In subsection (2) after "employer" insert "or persons linked with present or former employees of the employer".

(3) After subsection (2) insert—

"(3) Section 554Z1 of ITEPA 2003 applies for the purposes of subsection (2) but as if references to A were to a present or former employee of the employer.

(4) So far as it is not covered by subsection (2), "employee benefit scheme" also means—

(a) an arrangement ("the relevant arrangement") within subsection (1)(b) of section 554A of ITEPA 2003 to which subsection (1)(c) of that section applies, or

(b) any other arrangement connected (directly or indirectly) with the relevant arrangement."

46 (1) Amend section 1292 (employee benefit contributions: provision of qualifying benefits) as follows.

(2) In subsection (5) after "scheme" insert

"and the payment or transfer—

(a) gives rise to an employment income tax charge under Chapter 2 of Part 6 of ITEPA 2003 or under Part 9 of that Act, or

(b) is an excluded benefit as defined in section 393B(3) of that Act."

(3) After subsection (6) insert—

"(6A) For the purposes of section 1290 qualifying benefits are also provided if—

(a) a relevant step within the meaning of Part 7A of ITEPA 2003 is taken, and

(b) Chapter 2 of that Part applies by reason of the step."

47 (1) Amend section 1293 (employee benefit contributions: timing of qualifying benefits etc) as follows.

(2) For subsection (1) substitute—

"(1) If the provision of a qualifying benefit takes the form of a payment of money, the benefit, so far as Chapter 4 of Part 2 of ITEPA 2003 applies to the money, is provided for the purposes of section 1290 when the money is treated as received for the purposes of that Chapter (applying the rules in section 18 of that Act (receipt of money earnings))."

(3) After subsection (1) insert—

"(1A) Except so far as subsection (1) applies to the provision of the qualifying benefit, if the provision of a qualifying benefit is a chargeable relevant step, for the purposes of section 1290—

(a) the benefit is provided when A's employment with B starts if the chargeable relevant step is taken before then, or

(b) otherwise, the benefit is provided when the chargeable relevant step is taken."

(4) In subsection (2)—

(a) after "an asset" insert "which meets condition A, B, C or D in section 1292",

(b) omit the "and" after paragraph (a), and

(c) after paragraph (b) insert

", and

(c) if the transfer is a chargeable relevant step, the cost of the relevant step so far as not covered by paragraph (a) or (b)".

(5) After subsection (3) insert—

"(4) If the provision of a qualifying benefit is a chargeable relevant step which does not involve a sum of money (see section 554Z(10) of ITEPA 2003) and is not covered by subsection (2), the amount provided for the purposes of section 1290 is the cost of the relevant step (subject to subsection (5)).

(5) If the provision of a qualifying benefit is a chargeable relevant step which is not covered by subsection (2) (whether or not it involves a sum of money), the amount provided for the purposes of section 1290 is not to exceed the amount that—

(a) is charged to tax under ITEPA 2003 in relation to the relevant step (whether under Part 7A of that Act or otherwise), or

(b) would be charged had not A been non-UK resident in any tax year.

(6) In this section—

(a) "chargeable relevant step" means a relevant step within the meaning of Part 7A of ITEPA 2003 by reason of which Chapter 2 of that Part applies (and references to A and B are to be read accordingly), and

(b) references to the cost of a chargeable relevant step are to be read in accordance with section 554Z3(6) of that Act."

48 In section 1296(1) (employee benefit contributions: interpretation)—

(a) in the definition of "employee benefit scheme" for "1291(2)" substitute "1291(2) to (4)", and

(b) in the definition of "employer-financed retirement benefits scheme" after "Act)" insert "but ignoring section 393B(2)(a) and (c) of that Act".

Other amendments

49 (1) TCGA 1992 is amended as follows.

(2) In section 119A (increase in expenditure by reference to tax charged in relation to employment-related securities)—

(a) in subsection (5)(a) for "or (b)" substitute ", (b) or (d)", and

(b) at the end of subsection (5A) insert "and section 119C (unremitted Part 7A income)".

(3) After section 119B insert—

"119C Section 119A: unremitted Part 7A income

(1) This section applies for the purposes of section 119A if an amount deducted under section 480(5)(d) of ITEPA 2003, which (apart from this section) would by virtue of section 119A(5)(a) be added back to an amount counting as employment income, is or includes unremitted Part 7A income.

(2) So much of the amount deducted as is unremitted Part 7A income is not to be added back.

(3) In this section "unremitted Part 7A income" means an amount counting as employment income under Chapter 2 of Part 7A of ITEPA 2003—

(a) to which section 554Z9(2) or 554Z10(2) of that Act applies, and

(b) which has not been remitted to the United Kingdom by the end of the tax year in which the disposal mentioned in section 119A(1) occurs.

(4) Section 119B(4) to (6) applies if any of the unremitted Part 7A income is remitted to the United Kingdom after the end of the tax year referred to in subsection (3)(b)."

50 In the following provisions, in the definition of "the employment income Parts of ITEPA 2003", for "7" substitute "7A"—

(a) section 122(1) of the Social Security Contributions and Benefits Act 1992, and

(b) section 121(1) of the Social Security Contributions and Benefits (Northern Ireland) Act 1992.

51 In Schedule 34 to FA 2004 (non-UK pension schemes) after paragraph 3(6) insert—

"(7) The provision which may be made under sub-paragraph (6) includes (in particular) provision in consequence of Part 7A of ITEPA 2003."

Commencement and transitional provision relating to Part 7A of ITEPA 2003

52 (1) Part 7A of ITEPA 2003 (as inserted by paragraph 1 of this Schedule) has effect in relation to relevant steps taken on or after 6 April 2011; and the other amendments made by this Schedule have effect accordingly.

(2) Sub-paragraph (1) is subject to the following paragraphs.

53 (1) This paragraph applies if—

(a) on or after 9 December 2010 but before 6 April 2011 a relevant step ("the early step") within section 554C(1)(a) of ITEPA 2003 is taken,

(b) Chapter 2 of Part 7A of ITEPA 2003 would have applied by reason of the early step had the reference in paragraph 52(1) of this Schedule to 6 April 2011 been a reference to 9 December 2010, and

(c) the early step is not chargeable to income tax by virtue of Schedule 34 to FA 2004 in whole or in part.

(2) Subject to what follows, Chapter 2 of Part 7A of ITEPA 2003 is to apply by reason of the early step; and the amendments made by this Schedule have effect accordingly.

(3) In determining the tax year for which the employment income of A counts for the purposes of section 554Z2(1) of ITEPA 2003, the early step is treated as having been taken on 6 April 2012; but otherwise Chapter 2 of Part 7A of that Act applies by reference to when the early step was actually taken.

(4) The amount which (apart from this sub-paragraph) would count as employment income of A is to be reduced by an amount to reflect so much of the sum paid as has been repaid to P before 6 April 2012 by the person to whom the payment was made; and the Tax Acts are to apply in relation to the sum paid so far as repaid to P before that date by that person as if Chapter 2 of Part 7A of ITEPA 2003 had never applied by reason of the early step, with any adjustments that need to be made to any assessment to tax being made accordingly.

(5) The amount of the reduction (if any) under sub-paragraph (4)—

(a) is to be determined on a just and reasonable basis, and

(b) may be the full amount of the employment income or nil or an amount in between (depending on the circumstances).

(6) Section 554Z5 of ITEPA 2003 does not apply in relation to the early step and, in the application of that section in relation to any other relevant step (whenever taken), the early step is to be ignored.

(7) Section 554Z12 of ITEPA 2003 does not apply in relation to the early step.

(8) For the purposes of section 687A(3)(a) of ITEPA 2003 (as inserted by paragraph 29 of this Schedule), the early step is treated as having been taken on 6 April 2012.

(9) For the purposes of section 41(1A) of ITTOIA 2005 (as inserted by paragraph 38(3) of this Schedule), the early step is treated as having been taken on 6 April 2012; and for the purpose of determining whether section 41(1A) of that Act applies, section 41(1) is to be read as substituted by paragraph 38(2) of this Schedule.

(10) For the purposes of section 1293(1A) of CTA 2009 (as inserted by paragraph 47(3) of this Schedule), the early step is treated as having been taken on 6 April 2012; and for the purpose of determining whether section 1293(1A) of that Act applies, section 1293(1) is to be read as substituted by paragraph 47(2) of this Schedule.

54 (1) This paragraph applies if—

(a) on or after 9 December 2010 but before 6 April 2011 a relevant step ("the early step") within section 554C(1)(d) of ITEPA 2003 is taken,

(b) the relevant step does not involve a sum of money within the meaning of section 554Z(10) of ITEPA 2003,

(c) the asset which is the subject of the early step is a readily convertible asset which P makes available to secure the payment of a sum of money,

(d) Chapter 2 of Part 7A of ITEPA 2003 would have applied by reason of the early step had the reference in paragraph 52(1) of this Schedule to 6 April 2011 been a reference to 9 December 2010, and

(e) the early step is not chargeable to income tax by virtue of Schedule 34 to FA 2004 in whole or in part.

(2) For the purposes of sub-paragraph (1)(a) section 554C(1)(d) of ITEPA 2003 is to be read as if the words "or makes it available under an arrangement which permits its use" were omitted.

(3) In this paragraph "readily convertible asset" means anything mentioned in section 702(1)(a) to (c) of ITEPA 2003 (ignoring section 702(3)).

(4) Subject to what follows, Chapter 2 of Part 7A of ITEPA 2003 is to apply by reason of the early step; and the amendments made by this Schedule have effect accordingly.

(5) In determining the tax year for which the employment income of A counts for the purposes of section 554Z2(1) of ITEPA 2003, the early step is treated as having been taken on 6 April 2012; but otherwise Chapter 2 of Part 7A of that Act applies by reference to when the early step was actually taken.

(6) The amount which (apart from this sub-paragraph) would count as employment income of A is to be reduced to nil if—

(a) before 6 April 2012 the readily convertible asset has been returned to P, and

(b) as at that date the asset is not being used to secure the payment of the sum of money (or any part of it),

and the Tax Acts are to apply in relation to the early step as if Chapter 2 of Part 7A of ITEPA 2003 had never applied by reason of it, with any adjustments that need to be made to any assessment to tax being made accordingly.

(7) Section 554Z5 of ITEPA 2003 does not apply in relation to the early step and, in the application of that section in relation to any other relevant step (whenever taken), the early step is to be ignored.

(8) Section 554Z8 of ITEPA 2003 applies in relation to the early step as if subsection (6)(b) were omitted.

(9) Section 554Z12 of ITEPA 2003 does not apply in relation to the early step.

(10) For the purposes of section 695A(3)(a) of ITEPA 2003 (as inserted by paragraph 31 of this Schedule), the early step is treated as having been taken on 6 April 2012.

(11) For the purposes of section 41(1A) of ITTOIA 2005 (as inserted by paragraph 38(3) of this Schedule), the early step is treated as having been taken on 6 April 2012; and for the purpose of determining whether section 41(1A) of that Act applies, section 41(1) is to be read as substituted by paragraph 38(2) of this Schedule.

(12) For the purposes of section 1293(1A) of CTA 2009 (as inserted by paragraph 47(3) of this Schedule), the early step is treated as having been taken on 6 April 2012; and for the purpose of determining whether section 1293(1A) of that Act applies, section 1293(1) is to be read as substituted by paragraph 47(2) of this Schedule.

55 (1) For the purpose of determining whether Chapter 2 of Part 7A of ITEPA 2003 would have applied by reason of the early step as mentioned in paragraph 53(1)(b) or 54(1)(d), section 554G of ITEPA 2003 is to be read—

(a) as if subsection (1)(a) were omitted, and

(b) as if the definition contained in sub-paragraph (2) applied for the purposes of the reference to a group of companies in subsection (4)(d) instead of section 554Z(5) of ITEPA 2003.

(2) The definition referred to in sub-paragraph (1)(b) is—

> “”group of companies” means a company and any other companies of which it has control (as defined in section 995 of ITA 2007)”.

(3) For the purpose of determining whether Chapter 2 of Part 7A of ITEPA 2003 would have applied by reason of the early step, Chapter 1 of that Part is to be read as if section 554N(13) to (16) were omitted.

(4) If, by virtue of section 554O of ITEPA 2003, Chapter 2 of Part 7A of that Act would not have applied by reason of the early step, section 554O(3) and (4) have effect in relation to the car loan.

(5) But, for this purpose, if the repayment date is before 6 April 2012, in section section 554O(3) and (4) references to the repayment date are to be read as references to 6 April 2012.

56 (1) This paragraph applies for the purposes of section 554Q of ITEPA 2003 in a case in which—

(a) the relevant step mentioned in subsection (2)(a) of that section was taken before 6 April 2011, and

(b) the requirement of subsection (2)(b) of that section would have been met had Part 7A of ITEPA 2003 had effect in relation to relevant steps within section 554B of that Act taken before that date.

(2) The requirement of subsection (2)(b) of that section is to be treated as met in that case.

57 (1) This paragraph applies for the purposes of section 554R of ITEPA 2003 in a case in which—

(a) the relevant step mentioned in subsection (6)(a) of that section was taken before 6 April 2011, and

(b) the requirement of subsection (6)(b) of that section would have been met had Part 7A of ITEPA 2003 had effect in relation to relevant steps within section 554B of that Act taken before that date.

(2) The requirement of subsection (6)(b) of that section is to be treated as met in that case.

58 (1) This paragraph applies if—

(a) B takes a step within section 554Z19 of ITEPA 2003 before 6 April 2011 by providing security (“the early security”) for the performance of an undertaking (“the early undertaking”),

(b) on or after 6 April 2011 at a time when B is continuing to provide the early security, there is a change in the terms of the early undertaking which does not amount to the giving of a new undertaking, and

(c) as a result of the change, the amount to be paid as a contribution (“the early contribution”) under the early undertaking increases, or will increase.

(2) Chapter 3 of Part 7A of ITEPA 2003 has effect—

(a) as if the change in the terms of the early undertaking were a new undertaking to pay a contribution covering the increase in the amount of the early contribution as determined on a just and reasonable basis, and

(b) as if B, in continuing to provide the early security, provides security for the performance of the new undertaking at the time of the change in the terms.

(3) Section 554Z17(7) of ITEPA 2003 applies for the purposes of this paragraph as it applies for the purposes of Chapter 3 of Part 7A of that Act.

59 (1) This paragraph applies if—

(a) a relevant step within section 554C or 554D of ITEPA 2003 ("the chargeable step") is taken,

(b) Chapter 2 of Part 7A of ITEPA 2003 applies by reason of the chargeable step,

(c) in a tax year before 6 April 2011 ("the pre-6 April 2011 tax year") a relevant step ("the pre-6 April 2011 step") within section 554B of ITEPA 2003 was taken,

(d) before the chargeable step is taken—

(i) an agreement was made between Her Majesty's Revenue and Customs and either A or B (or both) under which it was agreed that the pre-6 April 2011 step was to be treated as giving rise to earnings of A from A's employment with B within Chapter 1 of Part 3 of ITEPA 2003 for the pre-6 April 2011 tax year, or

(ii) the tax payable by A for the pre-6 April 2011 tax year was otherwise decided on the basis that the pre-6 April 2011 step was to be treated as giving rise to earnings of A from A's employment with B within Chapter 1 of Part 3 of ITEPA 2003 for that tax year,

(e) before the chargeable step is taken, A or B has paid, or otherwise accounted for, any tax which A or B is required to pay or otherwise account for as a consequence of—

(i) the agreement mentioned in paragraph (d)(i), or

(ii) the tax payable by A for the pre-6 April 2011 tax year having otherwise been decided on the basis mentioned in paragraph (d)(ii), and

(f) after any reductions under sections 554Z4 to 554Z8 of ITEPA 2003, it is determined on a just and reasonable basis that the value of the chargeable step represents (or still represents after any such reductions) to any extent—

(i) the earnings treated as arising from the pre-6 April 2011 step as mentioned in paragraph (d)(i) or (ii), or

(ii) any return on those earnings since the taking of the pre-6 April 2011 step (whether income or capital, direct or indirect or realised or unrealised).

(2) After any reductions under sections 554Z4 to 554Z8 of ITEPA 2003, the value of the chargeable step is to be reduced (but not below nil) by an amount reflecting the extent to which, as determined under sub-paragraph (1)(f), that value represents (or still represents) the earnings mentioned in subparagraph (1)(f)(i) or any return on those earnings mentioned in subparagraph (1)(f)(ii).

(3) In sub-paragraph (1)(f)(ii) "return" does not include any return so far as, it is reasonable to suppose, the return exceeds the return which might have been expected applying the assumption that all relevant connected persons are acting at arm's length of each other.

(4) In sub-paragraph (3) "relevant connected person" means a person with a connection (direct or indirect) to an arrangement (within the meaning of Part 7A of ITEPA 2003) by virtue of which the return arises.

Other commencement provision

60 The amendments made by paragraph 14 of this Schedule, so far as relating to general earnings, have effect in relation to benefits to which Chapter 2 of Part 6 of ITEPA 2003 applies received on or after 6 April 2011.

61 The amendments made by paragraphs 36, 39(a), 45 and 48(a) of this Schedule have effect in relation to acts or omissions occurring on or after 6 April 2011.

62 The amendments made by paragraphs 37(2), 39(b), 46(2) and 48(b) of this Schedule have effect in relation to payments or transfers made on or after 6 April 2011.

63 The amendments made by paragraphs 38(2) and 47(2) of this Schedule have effect in relation to money treated as received on or after 6 April 2011 (subject to paragraphs 53(9) and (10) and 54(11) and (12) of this Schedule).

Power to make provision dealing with interactions etc

64 (1) The Treasury may by order made by statutory instrument make such provision as the Treasury consider appropriate dealing with the interaction between Part 7A of ITEPA 2003 (as inserted by paragraph 1 of this Schedule) and any other provision of the Tax Acts or any enactment relating to capital gains tax or inheritance tax.

(2) The Treasury may by order made by statutory instrument make such provision as the Treasury consider appropriate in consequence of this Schedule.

(3) An order under this paragraph may contain provision having retrospective effect, so long as it does not increase any person's liability to any tax.

(4) An order under this paragraph may amend, repeal or revoke any provision made by or under an Act, including, in the case of an order under sub-paragraph (1), Part 7A of ITEPA 2003.

(5) An order under this paragraph may contain incidental, supplemental, consequential and transitional provision and savings.

(6) The powers conferred by this paragraph may not be exercised after 5 April 2015.

(7) A statutory instrument containing an order under this paragraph is subject to annulment in pursuance of a resolution of the House of Commons.

GENERAL NOTE

Schedule 2 introduces a new ITEPA 2003 Part 7A.

Part 7A is the latest in a long line of attacks by the government on the use of Employee Benefit Trusts (EBTs) and similar structures to avoid PAYE and NIC on what – at least in the eyes of HMRC – is in reality employment income.

EBTs have been a feature of remuneration planning for at least a generation. One of their earliest uses was to exploit a defect in the NIC legislation, which did not impose an NIC charge on payments of certain earnings out of EBTs. That loophole has long been closed, but tax advisors have found increasingly inventive ways in which EBTs can be used.

For a number of years EBTs tended to be used primarily as a mechanism for creating a corporate tax deduction without triggering a corresponding PAYE and NIC charge. HMRC were successful in litigation on the CT point in the Dextra and Sempra cases, and in any event FA 2003 Sch 23 was introduced to create a new statutory regime for the deductibility of EBT contributions – in broad terms the effect of this was to link a CT deduction to a PAYE and NIC charge. Attention then shifted to ways of enabling companies to pass value to employees without such a PAYE charge – in some cases accepting that there would be no CT relief in doing so. Many of these arrangements involved the making of loans.

In HMRC's view many of these loans were in fact remuneration because there appeared to be no intention that they would ever be repaid. However HMRC has not currently been able to persuade a tribunal of this in any particular case, although at the time of writing a number of other cases on the point are known to be proceeding towards litigation.

The government has therefore been looking at alternative approaches to this problem, in particular at ways of objectively defining which payments and benefits provided by EBTs should be taxed as earnings. In the Spring 2010 Budget the previous government announced its intention to bring forward proposals to block the uses of EBTs. Those proposals led to the publication of draft legislation in December 2010. This draft legislation was widely criticised as being too wide in its scope and of bringing within its ambit many perfectly straightforward and non-contentious remuneration arrangements, in particular employee share schemes and benefit packages.

To its credit the government listened to these concerns and when the legislation was published in the Finance Bill many of these straightforward arrangements were taken out of charge. While this is to be welcomed it has meant that what was already very complex legislation has become even more complicated: one indication of this is that the schedule expanded from 30 to 60 pages. Over 80 further amendments were introduced at committee stage although, perhaps mercifully, no further amendments were introduced at Report or Third Reading.

The end result of this is that Part 7A has become one of the most complicated pieces of tax legislation ever introduced and it has been very widely criticised as almost incomprehensible – see, for example, the comments from the House of Lords at the end of this commentary.

In view of its length and complexity some signposting of the contents of the new Schedule will be helpful.

Chapter 1 (s 554A–s 554Z1) defines what is within the scope of the charge. It can be further broken down as follows:

— s 554A sets out the basic conditions for Part 7A to apply;
— s 554B–D set out the relevant steps which are necessary to trigger a charge;
— s 554E–H set out the main exclusions from the charge;
— s 554I–N set out exclusions for employee share schemes;

— s 554O–R set out further exclusions;
— s 554S–X set out exclusions relating to pension schemes;
— s 554Y–Z deals with definitions.

Chapter 2 (ss 554Z2–Z15) deals with how relevant steps are to be treated for income tax purposes. It can be further broken down as follows:

— s 554Z2–Z8 set out the basic charging and valuation provisions;
— s 554Z9–Z11 deal with remittance basis;
— s 554Z12–Z15 deal with supplementary issues.

Chapter 3 (ss 554Z16–Z21) deals with undertakings given by employers in relation to retirement benefits

The rest of Sch 2 (paras 2–64) is mainly concerned with consequential amendments to ITEPA 2003 and other legislation.

The commencement provisions are set out at paras 52–64.

With this basic framework set out we can now commence a detailed review of the provisions. We should note, however, that as is the convention the Finance Act only deals with income tax issues. The parallel NIC provisions are expected to be enacted soon after Royal Assent.

Chapter One – Application etc

Para 1 inserts new ITEPA 2003 Part 7A. The commentary will look at each section of this new Part 7A in turn.

S554A – Application of chapter 2

This sets out the conditions necessary for a charge to arise. There is a five-part test.

(a) A person (A) is an employee of another person (B). In this context employee includes a former or prospective employee;
(b) There is an relevant arrangement to which A is a party or which relates to A;
(c) It is reasonable to suppose that the relevant arrangement is in essence concerned with providing reward, recognition or loans in connection with A's employment with B;
(d) A relevant step is taken by a relevant third person;
(e) It is reasonable to suppose that the relevant step is taken in pursuance of the relevant arrangement, or that there is some connection between the relevant step and the relevant arrangement.

Each of these five conditions has to be satisfied in order for a charge to arise. There are detailed definitions of the key terms in this test in the succeeding sections.

s 554A(4) There is an exclusion for relevant steps under s 554B (earmarking) taken on or after A's death. Note that this is the only exclusion for death: in all other cases the taking of a relevant step on or after death will trigger a charge.

s 554A(5) References to A include references to any person linked with A. It will be seen that this is defined widely.

s 554A(6) A very broad definition of arrangement is used – it is not necessary for all of the details of the steps in any arrangement to be set out. This is deliberate: throughout this legislation the draftsman has wanted to give the provisions the widest possible scope so that the possibilities for avoidance are minimised.

s 554A(7) Relevant third person is any person other than A or B – in other words any person anywhere in the world: there does not have to be a connection between A or B and the third person. In addition if either A or B themselves are acting as a trustee of an arrangement they will be a relevant third person. This is to defeat schemes under which, for example, no separate EBT is set up but where the employer himself holds funds on trust for employees.

s 554A(8–10) When the original draft legislation was issued there were problems with the way in which it applied to groups of companies. For example if one company in a group provided benefits to employees of another group company those benefits would potentially have been caught by a Part 7A charge. Section 554A8 solves this by treating all of the companies in a group as being B (the employer). Section 554A9 does the same for companies which are subsidiaries of an LLP. Subsections 554A8 and 9 are however disapplied in tax avoidance contexts

s 554B(11–12) A very wide definition of relevant arrangements and in connection with a relevant arrangement is adopted – again to ensure that avoidance opportunities are minimised.

Relevant steps

In order for a charge to arise under Part 7A s 554A requires there to be a relevant step. Subsections 554B–D define what constitutes a relevant step.

s 554B – earmarking

s 554B(1) A person (P) takes a relevant step if a sum of money is earmarked by P with a view to a later relevant step being taken by P or any other person, or a sum of money starts to be held by P with a view to a later relevant step being taken.

s 554B(2) Earmarking is a very loose concept and the definition makes it clear that earmarking can be done informally and does not entail the existence of legal obligations. There is also no requirement that all of the details of any later relevant step have been worked out and it does not matter that there may be conditions which have to be met before a later relevant step can be carried out. Again the draftsman has gone out of his way to give as wide as possible a definition to earmarking to ensure that it will not be possible to design arrangement which do not technically amount to earmarking but which would still give the benefit of funds to an employee.

This section is designed to catch situations where a fund is set aside for an employee (perhaps via a sub fund of an EBT) and, it will be seen, it imposes a charge at that point, ie . before the employee has necessarily had a benefit from that fund. The mere fact of earmarking is sufficient to create a relevant step.

s 554B(3) It does not matter for the purposes of s 554B(2) whether or not funds were previously held on behalf of P on a non-earmarked basis. This is again to prevent avoidance.

s 554C – payment of sums, transfer of assets etc

There are five circumstances in which there can be a relevant step under s 554C:

(a) The payment of a sum of money to a relevant person;

(b) The transfer of an asset to a relevant person;

(c) The taking a step by virtue in which a relevant person acquires a class of asset specified in s 554C(4)

(d) The making available a sum of money or asset for use as security for a loan or otherwise as security for the meeting of a liability

(e) The grant to a relevant person of a lease of premises for an effective duration likely to exceed 21 years.

The key point here is that (a) applies to loans as well as absolute payments of money. In other words the making of a loan will (subject to any of the limited exceptions below) will trigger a PAYE charge. As will be seen later there is, other than in very specific circumstances, no relief if the loan is subsequently repaid.

s 554C(2 and 3) The definition of relevant person is wide. The basic rules is A or person or class of person chosen by A are relevant persons. But this is extended, if P is taking a step on A's behalf or at his direction, to include any other person. That person does not have to be connected to A or to B. So if A asks trustees to make a payment to, say, Marks and Spencer's, Marks and Spencer's will be a relevant persons and the payment will be a relevant step. References to A include a person linked with A.

s 4554C(4) The defined assets are securities, interests in securities and securities options.

s 445C(5) Making available including informal ways of making available and does not require any legal obligations. It does not matter if the asset is not actually used as mentioned in sub(1)(d) (security); all that matters is that it was made available for that purpose.

s 445C(7–9) In determining the duration of a lease it is to be assumed that any rights to extend the duration of a lease will be exercised and that if it is likely that A will become entitled to a successor lease on the same premises the duration of the lease is to include the duration of the successor lease. For these purposes references to A include persons linked with A or to any person to whom an original lease was granted.

s 554D Relevant steps: making asset available

s 554D(1) There is a relevant step where a person (P) makes available an asset to relevant person, without transfer of ownership, on terms which are substantially similar to those under which the person would have been able to benefit from the asset had there actually been a transfer of the asset. There is also a relevant step where a person makes an asset available for a relevant person to benefit from.

So, for example, if trustees buy a house for an employee to live in there will be a relevant step when the house is made available, even if trustees retain the ownership of the property.

s 554D(*2*) If before the end of the relevant period P makes an asset available to a relevant person and at the end of the relevant period P continues to make the asset available to the relevant person, P is treated as taking a relevant step at the end of the relevant period.

s 554D(*3*) As in the previous section there is a very wide definition of making an asset available: informal arrangements are included and it is not necessary for there to be any legal obligation or for the relevant person actually to benefit from the asset.

s 554D(*4*) The relevant period is the two-year period starting with the date on which A's employment with B ceases

s 554D (*5 and 6*) A relevant person includes a person chosen by A or within a class of persons chosen by A . Where P is taking a step on A's behalf or at his direction or request, any other person is a relevant person. References to A include reference to any person linked with A

s 554D(*7*) This lists a number of factors which may be taken into account in determining whether or not an asset is made available: it is not an exhaustive list and other factors may also be taken into account when relevant.

s 554D is intended to stop trusts etc allowing beneficiaries to have the use of an asset on terms which for all practical purpose amount to a transfer of ownership of the asset but which technically do not involve a change of ownership.

There are likely to be practical difficulties in determining whether or not there is a relevant step where an asset is made available on a non-exclusive basis – for example where trustees make a holiday home available to an employee but where there is the possibility that other people may also use it. Much will depend on the facts of any particular case.

Exclusions

Subsections 554B–D are in themselves a fairly compact code to determine what is a relevant step. To that extent the legislation so far is relatively straightforward. The rest of this chapter (ss 554E–554Z1) is all concerned with exemption to the basic tests. Those exemptions are of huge importance. The definition of relevant steps within ss 554B–D is very widely drawn and without relieving provisions would catch many situations which would not on any judgement constitute tax avoidance. These relieving provisions are much more complex and extensive than the charging provisions themselves. Much of the debate about the drafting of the legislation has therefore been centred upon the exclusions, and the extent to which they are in fact effective in preventing charges arising in straightforward circumstances.

s 554E Exclusions: steps under certain schemes

s 554E(*1*) This gives a list of exclusions. There is an exclusion from Chapter two for relevant steps taken under approved share schemes;

— Registered pension schemes or equivalent overseas pension schemes;

— Holiday pay schemes.

In principle these are straightforward exclusions but they have in fact created many problem because of the way that they are drafted. For example, although the exclusions as originally drafted would have covered steps directly associated with share schemes, such as the grant of share options, they would not have covered associated steps, such as the use by a company of an EBT to warehouse shares used as part of a share scheme or a loan made for the purposes of allowing employees to exercise options. Additional measures have had to be introduced to deal with these knock-on problems.

s 554(*2–11*)

These provisions seek to deal with these problems by extending the exemption to incidental steps associated with approved share schemes, particularly steps taken to acquire shares which are to be used for the purpose of share option schemes.

There are separate but parallel provisions for SAYE, SIPs and CSOPs, and for EMI options. These give relief where shares are acquired for the purposes of these types of approved share schemes. But the relief is disapplied where there is a tax avoidance arrangement or where the total number of shares involved in the step exceeds the number of shares which may reasonably be required under the scheme for the 10 year period (this limit was increased from five years during the Committee stage) starting with the date on which the relevant step is first taken. This is clearly designed to stop companies accumulating large numbers of shares under the guise of their being needed for an employee share scheme but which in reality are intended for avoidance purposes.

s 554E(12)

This is a curious measure in this context. It exempts from charge a relevant step taken by the Independent Parliamentary Authority in relation to members of the House of Commons. The existence of this subsection led to much press speculation because it appeared to show that there was one rule for MPs and one for everybody else. In fact the explanation is much more prosaic. After the furore over MP's expenses the systems of payment was changed and expenses are now paid by an independent authority. That authority would be a third party under Part 7A and thus all expenses would have been subject to a charge under these provisions. This would have meant that, without that relief, normal reimbursement of expenses would have been charged to income tax. The fact that such a relief had to be introduced is however indicative of the complexity of the legislation and the huge number of unintended consequences which have had to be guarded against. The various iterations of the legislation have certainly ironed out many of these, but it would be a very confident (or naïve) commentator who could say that none remain.

s 554F – Exclusions: commercial transactions

One of the main concerns with the original drafting of these provisions was the number of situations in which ordinary commercial transactions between employers, trustees and employees would be caught. The various amendments to the original draft have attempted to remedy this defect but the legislation dealing with it does not constitute a coherent code but is scattered throughout Part 7A. In later parts of this legislation the draftsman solves the problem by the way in which the computation of the chargeable amount is to be calculated: here the draftsman wholly exempts certain transactions from charge.

s 554F(1) This gives an exemption for loans made on ordinary commercial terms provided that there is no connection between the making of the loan and a tax avoidance arrangement. For this purpose the existing definition of ordinary commercial loan in ITEPA 2003 s 176 is adopted except that conditions B and C of that section (which deal with alterations to existing loans) are not to be taken into account.

s 554F(2–5) This gives a more limited relief for relevant steps which are not loans. There is an exemption for steps taken by P which are entered into in the ordinary part of P's business. But the exemption only applies where a substantial proportion of P's business involves similar transactions with members of the public, P enters into the transaction with A (or a person linked with A) on terms which are similar to those which apply to similar transactions with members of the public and there is not a direct or indirect connection between the relevant step and a tax avoidance arrangement.

s 554G exclusions for transactions under employee benefit packages

One of the major concerns about the original draft legislation was that it would have created additional tax charges in many straightforward employee benefit arrangements. In any situation where benefits were provided by somebody other than the employer – for example a company contracted to supply, say, nursery vouchers – a charge would have arisen under Part 7A in circumstances where they may not have been a charge under the normal benefit in kind rules or where that charge was on a lower amount – ie . cost to the employer rather than the full market value of the benefit. Section 554G is intended to remove these sorts of situations from a Part 7A charge.

s 554G(1) The exclusion does not apply to steps taken under pension schemes (these are dealt with later in Part 7A) but otherwise applies where a step is taken by P (ie the third party) in the ordinary course of P's business.

If the step is the making of a loan it is necessary that a substantial part of P's business involved making of similar loans to members of the pubic and that the loan to A (the individual) is part of a package of benefits is available to a substantial proportion of B's (the employer) employees. It is also necessary that the package of benefits will not, or is unlikely to, be conferred wholly or mainly on directors or senior employees. That term is explained later.

If the step is not a loan then there is a similar type of test, although this is potentially more restrictive. The transaction with A must be part of package of benefits which is available to a substantial proportion of B's employees or a substantial proportion of B's employees who have the same status level (measured by such things as seniority, duties and remuneration level) as A. The terms of the package must be sufficiently generous to enable substantially all of B's employees who want to take advantage of the package to do so, and the terms under which A enters into the transaction must be substantially similar to those on which other employees enter into the transaction. If B is a company a majority of employees to whom the package of benefits is offered must not have a material interest (as defined in ITEPA s 68) in the company. Finally there must be no connection, direct or indirect, between the relevant step and a tax avoidance arrangement.

s 554G(2) defines similar terms and members of the public.

s 554G(3 and 4) defines senior employees as directors, senior employees, and employees who receive or are likely to receive the highest level of remuneration. Where B is a company which is a member of a group the definition extends to employees in the group as a whole.

s 554G(5) defines a similar transaction

s 554G(6) Where the relevant step is not a loan the reference to employees of B is limited to those employees whose duties are performed in the UK. This would meant that a group of UK employees would not be able to take advantage of the exemption because their pay, although high in relation to other UK employees, was low compared to employees in group companies in other parts of the world.

As in other sections references to A include any person linked with A.

s 554H –earmarking of deferred remuneration

One of the other criticisms of the original draft legislation was that it would have brought into charge the deferred element of many remuneration packages. This was seen as running directly counter to the government's policy of encouraging senior executives to take part of their reward on deferred terms. Section 554H was therefore introduced to ensure that in genuine cases of deferred remuneration there is no unintended upfront charge.

There is clearly a tension here between wanting not to penalise genuine deferred arrangements and opening the door to complex avoidance schemes. As a result the conditions under which the exemption applies are far from straightforward: there are nine separate conditions which have to be satisfied. These can be broadly summarized as follows:

- There has to be an award of deferred remuneration in respect of A's employment with B which is not for the purpose of the provision of retirement benefits;
- The deferred remuneration must be awarded on terms which defer the provision of remuneration until a vesting date within five years of the date of the award ;
- The receipt of the deferred remuneration could be revoked if conditions are not met by the vesting date;
- There must also be a reasonable chance that the reward will be revoked because the conditions will not all be met. In other words the conditions must be real and not merely a theoretical possibility;
- The deferred remuneration when it is actually provided has to be something which would be PAYEable income. (i e deferred remuneration which would not be subject to PAYE when it is paid is not within the exclusion.)
- P must earmark an amount before vesting day which represents the deferred remuneration and nothing else.
- Finally there must be no connection with a tax avoidance arrangement.

s 554H(2) allows for partial revocation. It is an absolute condition that there must be the possibility of full revocation if performance conditions are not met. Provided that that term is included in a scheme it is also possible to provide for partial revocation if specified conditions are not met i e provided that there is a risk that all of the award could fail then it is permissible to set conditions under which only part of the award would fail.

s 554H(3) This is the main exemption. It states that the charge on earmarking which would otherwise arise will not apply.

s 554H(4–12) set out the mechanics under which a PAYE charge will actually arise.

If an amount ceases to be earmarked under the deferred remuneration conditions but continues to be earmarked under any other circumstances there will be a relevant step at the point that the earmarking specifically for deferred remuneration purposes ceases.

There will be a relevant step on the vesting date of the amount of income which is payable under the deferred arrangement – i e after taking account of any amounts actually paid out previously (that is sums which were never earmarked) or sums which have been revoked. The key point here is that the charge arises once the amount has vested, not when it is actually paid out.

ss 554I–554M Earmarking for Employee Share schemes

The next five sections are a series of extremely complex provisions to deal with some of the problems that the original draft legislation created for employee share schemes. It is important to understand that these provisions are relieving provisions – they are intended to ensure that genuine share schemes remain taxable under the existing provisions of ITEPA (themselves of course highly complex) and are not brought within the even more draconian charge under Part 7A.

s 554I(1 and 2) This sets outs the structure of these five sections. Section 554I introduces the provisions and gives some key definitions. Sections 554J and K deal with direct awards of shares (or of cash amounts related to the value of shares); Sections 554L and M deal with awards of options to acquire shares (or of cash amounts related to the value of shares).

s 554I(3) These provisions only apply if B is a company.

s 554I(4) Defines relevant benefits, relevant shares and trading companies .

s 554I(5) Where the issuing company is a member of a group the definition of relevant shares is to extend to all of the companies in the group

s 554I(6) This defines an exit event – a concept which is integral to the way in which ss 554K and M operate. An exit event is the listing of the company's shares on a stock exchange, the disposal of the shares in the company (or a substantial proportion of them) to unconnected persons, the transfer of a trading company's trade to a non connected person, the disposal of the company's assets to an unconnected person, the winding up of the company or a change of control of the company.

s 554(7) This defines the key terms used in sub-s (6).

s 554J – exclusions – earmarking for employee share schemes)

This is the first of the four substantive sections dealing with employee share schemes. Full commentary will be provided on this section. For the other three sections, which embody many of the same concepts, briefer commentary will be provided which will concentrate on the points which are specific to that particular section.

s 554J(1) This sets out the basic conditions. There must be an arrangement (which the draftsman calls "B's employee share scheme") relating to A's employment with B under which there will be an award of shares or of a sum of money which is determined by the market value of the shares at the time of vesting (often called an phantom share arrangement). The main purpose of the award must not be the provision of relevant benefits (ie . pension). The key here is that there is not an immediate award of shares – instead the terms of the share scheme are that shares will be awarded a later date, subject to performance conditions. There terms under which the award is made must provide that the award can be revoked if performance conditions are not met before the vesting date, which cannot be more than 10 years after the date of the award. Finally there must be a reasonable chance that the award could be revoked. This last is a condition which has been met elsewhere in this legislation (see s 554H(1)(e)).

Provided that there is reasonable chance that the award could be revoked in full it is possible to include a condition which allows for partial revocation.

s 554J(3) This is the main relieving section. There would normally be a relevant step under s 554B when shares or cash are earmarked for an award, or prospective award, of shares under B's employee share scheme. However, provided that there is no connection with a tax avoidance arrangement and that the number of shares which are earmarked does not exceed the maximum number which are reasonably required for the purpose of satisfying the share scheme award, there is no relevant step at that point and thus no earmarking charge.

s 554J(4–13) set out the way of determining, in various circumstances, when a relevant step does actually occur in relation to the employee share scheme.

s 554J(4 and 5) These sections apply where the earmarking is of shares which are expected to be made to A (rather than definitely to be made to A). Provided that the award is not made within 3 months of the date of the earmarking and that the shares are then held definitely for award to A (ie . no longer provisionally), there is a relevant step three months after the date of the earmarking – the subject of that earmarking charge will be the shares which are now definitely held for award to A and any relevant income relating to those shares (this term is defined later). This charge does not arise if the employee has died. In other words once it has been determined which shares are to go to A after the performance conditions have been satisfied there will be a relevant step if they are still earmarked after three months have elapsed. (If they are distributed before the end of the three months the charge arises under the provisions discussed below.)

s 554J(6 and 7) These sections apply if shares which have been specifically earmarked for the purpose of B's employee share scheme ceased to be earmarked for that purpose but remain earmarked (ie no longer in connection with the share scheme). There is a relevant step in respect of the shares themselves and any relevant income relating to those shares, at the point that the earmarking for the purposes of the employee share scheme ceases.

s 554J(8 and 9) These apply where shares have been specifically allocated or there has been an expected award made within three months of the vesting date. In these circumstances there is a charge under s 554B on the vesting date in respect of the earmarked shares or on any relevant income in relation to the earmarked shares. This is subject to the rules in sub-ss (10)–(12) below. Again no charge arises after death.

s 554J (10–12)

These set out priority rules – the effect is that if an employment income charge would arise on the actual award that charge takes precedence over the charge in s 554J. Subsection 10 states that where there is an award of shares before the vesting date which would be chargeable as employment income at that point then there is no Part 7A charge. Subsection 11 applies the same principle to sums of money received by A under a phantom arrangement which are subject to an employment income charge.

Subsection 12 deals with cases where the award is revoked in accordance with the terms of the share award and as a consequence the shares are no longer held by any person. In such a case there is no charge under Part 7A (or of course under any other provision).

Subsection 13 defines relevant income as income which arises directly or indirectly from the shares, which would have been the subject of a earmarking charge under s 554B but for s 554Q (which will be discussed later), and which continues to be earmarked. This is a very complex definition but it seems to be saying that where income derived from shares is included within the share scheme then that income is the subject of a Part 7A charge at the same time as the underlying shares.

Section 554J is, as can be seen, very complex. The important point to understand is that it is a relieving provision. What it is trying to do is to ensure that in straightforward share scheme arrangements Part 7A does not apply when shares are earmarked by trustees and the existing rules continue to operate so that (broadly) tax arises when an employee gets the benefit of the shares. The intention is therefore to restrict the Part 7A charge to avoidance cases. Given the complexity of the legislation, however, it is far from clear at this stage whether the draftsman has succeeded in his aim.

s 554K Earmarking for employee share schemes

s 554K is designed to deal with share awards which are specifically linked to an exit event.

s 554K(1) This applies in a similar was to s 445J to awards of shares, or sums of money representing shares, as part of B's share scheme. Again the section does not apply to the provision of relevant benefits. The definition of shares is wider, to include shares and securities issued by a trading company or a company which controls a trading company. The key feature is s 554(1)(d). This says that the main purpose of the award is that the shares (or a sum of money representing the shares) are to be received by the employee on the occurrence of a specified exit event (as defined above) and that there is a reasonable chance that the specified exit event will occur.

s 554K(2) This disapplies Chapter 2 if the shares are earmarked solely with a view to meeting an aware of shares under B's share scheme provided that the conditions in s 554K(1) are met: it also applies where there is expected to be an award under the scheme. As in the previous section the relief only applies if the number of earmarked shares does not exceed the maximum which are reasonably expected to be awarded and that there is no connection between the award and a tax avoidance arrangement.

The remaining subsections set out circumstances where a charge may arise. They mirror almost precisely the rules in s 554J, except that references to the vesting date are replaced with references to the exit event. The exit period is defined as the period of 6 months starting with the date of the exit event.

S554L Earmarking for employee share schemes

This set out a similar exemption for shares which are earmarked for the purpose of an employee share option scheme. Again very similar conditions apply to the previous sections. Note that the options have to have a vesting date which is not more than 10 years following the date of grant

S554M Earmarking for employee share schemes

This sets out an exemption for employee share option schemes where the exercise of the option is linked to an exit event. Again very similar conditions apply to those in s 445K.

The fact that the draftsman has had to introduce 12 pages of highly repetitious legislation just to ensure that most share incentives continue to be taxed under the current rules is an indication of just how complex and unwieldy these provisions have become. I doubt that anybody could say with any confidence that these provisions have the precise effect which is intended, simply because of their complexity, and I would think it highly likely that anomalies and uncertainties will arise over the ensuing months which will require further amendments or, at the very least, additional guidance.

s 554N Other cases involving employment-related securities

Employment related securities are already subject to a highly complex income tax regime (see ITEPA 2003 part 7). Section 545N seeks to ensure that charges under that code take priority over any potential charges under the disguised remuneration regime.

s 554N (*1 and 2*) set out the scope. Part 7A does not apply to acquisitions of employment related securities if they are acquired by a person (i e not subscribed for) and the exemption in ITEPA s 425(2) applies. That is the exemption which exempts from charge post employment acquisitions if the acquisition would not have been taxable in the final year in which the employment was held. Part 7A also does not apply to employment related securities options which are exercisable more than ten years after grant.

The exemptions within s 554N(1 and 2) are very narrow in their scope and are unlikely to apply in many situations. The substantive exemptions are contained within the rest of the section.

s 554N(*3*) This is a definition section

s 554N (*4 and 5*) This sets out the main category of exemption. There is no Part 7A charge where there is a chargeable event under s 426 (conditional interests in shares), s 438 (conversion of shares); s 476 (exercise etc of share options); s 446A (discharges of notional loans) or disposals under Chapter 3D of Part 7 (disposals at greater than market value).

s 554N6 This extends the relief from the Part 7A charge by preserving the existing exemptions within Part 7. If it were not for this provision the elaborate scheme of exemptions with Part 7 would be rendered wholly ineffective. Those exemptions are s 421B6 (Death), s 421E(1) (non residence), s 429 (restrictions apply to all classes of shares), s443 (conversions applying to all classes of shares) , s474(1) (non residence) and s477(2) (death). The exemption also applies where an election has been made under ss 430 or 431 to take an upfront tax charge on the value of securities. Again, there would be little point in making such an election if it did not also remove a taxpayer from the possibility of a Part 7A charge.

s 554N (*7–12*) set out a further exemption. The key subsection here is 11, which states that Part 7A does not apply to relevant steps taken after certain share acquisitions, provided that the subject of the relevant step is a relevant asset and there is no connection between the step and a tax avoidance arrangement. Subsection 7 defines which assets are with the scope of the exemption. The acquisition of the asset has to be within s 554C(4)(a) or (b) and the consideration given for the asset must be greater or equal to the value of the asset, or the acquisition must give rise to an earnings charge on acquisition. Subsection 8 defines consideration given for the asset: this can include money's worth but cannot include a promise to do anything or the value of the performance of duties in connection with the employment. In other words there must be real valuable consideration passing. These are complex provisions but again the intention is to ensure that there are no double charges and that Part 7 remains the relevant charging provision,

s 554N(*9*) extends references to market value to references to value determined under s 437(1) or 452(1).

s 554N(*10*) extends sub-s 11 to employment related securities options where the acquisition is a chargeable event under s 476 or would be apart from s 474(1).

s 554N(*12*) is a further definitional section.

s 55N(13–16) set out a further exemption. This applies to loans. It will be recalled that the making of a loan will generally constitute a relevant step under s 554C(1)(a). This measure gives relief from that charge where the making of a loan is solely for the purposes of enabling a person to exercise a securities option which is chargeable on exercise (or would be apart from s 474) or is exempt income, and there is no connection between the loan and a tax avoidance arrangement. This is a very necessary provision. In many employee share schemes employees are lent money to fund the exercise price of their share options and the loan is repaid out of the proceeds of the sale of those shares. Without such a relief the advance of the loan could have given rise to a tax charge had it been made by a third party, such as a bank or an EBT.

This is subject to the condition that the loan is repaid. If the loan is not repaid within 40 days of the date it was advanced there will be a charge under s 554C(1)(a) on the amount outstanding after 40 days. This is obviously to stop avoidance via loans which are nominally linked to the exercise of share options but where the loan is made many months before it is actually needed for the purpose of making the exercise.

s 554N is, as anybody who has read this far will agree, extremely complex. Again it is worth stressing that it is a relieving section. It seeks to ensure that in straightforward non-avoidance cases the existing charges under the employment-related securities apply rather than charges under Part 7A. The intention is clearly to restrict the Part 7A charge to avoidance cases.

s 5540 Employee car ownership schemes

When the original legislation was first published in December 2010 it was, as has been said, widely criticised as being far too wide in its scope. Many perfectly straightforward remuneration and benefit arrangements would have been brought within the charge. One of those was car ownership schemes. Many employers involve third parties in their car ownership plans to provide finance and these arrangements would have been subject to unexpected and penal tax charges. s 554O takes most of these arrangements out of charge.

s 5540(1) This sets out the scope of the exemption. There must be an arrangement which provides for a person to acquire a new car by means of a car loan from a licensed lender, on terms which specify the date on which the car loan is to be repaid (which cannot be more than 4 years after the loan is taken out) and which permits the person to sell the car back to the provider at a price which is estimated at the time at which the loan is taken out. In other words a commercial car loan under which the car is sold back to the dealer at the end of the finance period for an agreed value which will depend, typically, on mileage and condition. The individual must actually use the loan to purchase the car!

s 554O(2) Such loan arrangements are outside the scope of Part 7A provided that there is no tax avoidance connection.

s 554(3–4) If any part of the loan is not repaid by the specified repayment date a charge under s 554C(1)(a) arises at that point.

s 554(5) defines a car and a licensed lender.

s 554P Employment income exemptions under Part 4

Part 4 of ITEPA includes a number of exemptions from the employment income charge for such things as mileage payments, training, recreational facilities etc. These exemptions also apply for the purposes of Part 7A, so that these existing tax benefits are preserved. The exemption under s 271 for certain removal expenses is also included within this exemption. Where a relevant step is only partly related to an exemption in Part 4 the amounts involved are to be apportioned on a just and reasonable basis and Part 7A will apply to the proportion not exempted under Part 4.

s 554Q Income arising from earmarked sums or assets

One of the most serious objections to the original legislation was the fact that it would have imposed PAYE liabilities on income arising within EBTs etc as it was received. This would have created many practical problems (not least because the connection with the original employer might have been severed years previously, but the liability to account for PAYE would still have fallen on that employer). Section 554Q is an important measure, because it gives relief from such income – although the scope of the relief has been criticized as being incomplete.

s 554Q(1) This sets out the terms of the exclusions. It applies where a sum of money or asset is held by or on behalf of a person "P", income arises from that income or asset and when the income arises it is received and is earmarked by P.

These is no earmarking charge if the sum or money or asset from which the income arises was itself the subject of an earmarking charge (or would have been apart from the listed exemption) and immediately before the income arises the original sum or asset is still held on an earmarked basis. There is also an arms length test: the exemption only applies if it is reasonable to suppose that the income represents a return which might have been derived from the original sum/asset on an arm's length basis. This is to prevent schemes being set up where the original transfer into the EBT etc is of a nominal sum, but circumstances are then contrived to produce high levels of what appears to be income in order to avoid the earmarking charge.

Essentially, therefore, s 445Q is saying that if the original funds were subject to an earmarking charge the income derived from those funds will not be itself subject to an earmarking charge. See the note to para 57 below, which sets out an important proviso in relation to the commencement provisions for this section – essentially it extends the relief to sums derived from pre 6 April 2011 amounts which would have been subject to an earmarking charge had the provisions been in effect at the date on which the original sums were earmarked. This means that, broadly, income arising from funds in existing EBTs will not be the subject of an earmarking charge.

s 554S Pensions income chargeable under Part 9 etc

Pension benefits are almost always provided by a third party and thus could potentially be within the scope of Part 7A. S554S introduces an exemption for pension income chargeable under Part 9 or which is exempt. There are however then five further sections (ss 554T–554W) which set out in more detail the precise extent to which pensions income is outside the scope of Part 7A.

s 554T Employee pension contributions

This is the main exemption for pension contributions.

s 554T(1) There is no charge under the earmarking provisions for a sum of money or asset arising from excluded pension contributions paid by A after 6 April 2011. Excluded pension contribution is defined below

s 554T(2) This provided for an apportionment where what is earmarked derives partly from an excluded pension contribution and partly from something else.

s 554T(3) The first two subsections prevent a charge when funds are earmarked within a pension scheme (which in practice is likely to be as soon as the they are received by the pension provider). Section 554T(3) provides relief from Part 7A for payment of pensions. The exemption applies to payments or provision of assets where those payments/assets would constitute relevant benefits (ie . pension income) and which derive wholly or partly from excluded pension contributions.

s 554T(4) This allows for apportionment for payments/assets which partly derive from excluded pensions and partly from some other source.

s 554T(5) This specifies that any apportionment for the purposes of s 554T(2) or (4) should be made on a just and reasonable basis.

s 554T(6) This defines an excluded pension contribution.

s 554T(7) This defines terms for the purposes of this section

s 554U Pre-6 April 2006 contributions to employer-financed retirement benefit schemes

s 554U(1–3) The gives relies for sums which derive from pre-6 April 2006 employer financed retirement benefit schemes. That date is important because (broadly speaking) payment into FURBS were, up to that date, taxable when the contribution was made and not when funds were paid out: after that date contributions are generally non taxable but payments out are taxable.

The exclusion applies where the relevant step is the payment of a sum of money or transfer of an asset which is derived from a sum of money which was paid under an employer financed retirement benefits scheme (as defined in Chapter 2 of Part 6) and in respect of which the employee was taxed. The test in FA 2004 Sch 36 para 53(3) applies for this purpose. This is a sensible measure to prevent a double charge. If funds have been taxed when they are contributed it would be wrong also to tax them when they are paid out.

s 554U(5–6) This provide for apportionment where sums derive partly from a FURBS and partly from another source.

s 554U(7) This treats all of the companies in the paying company's group as a single company for the purposes of this section.

s 554V Purchases of annuities out of pension scheme rights

s 554V(1) This sets out the basic conditions for this section. It applies to annuities purchased by an employee out of rights which he has under a pension scheme, provided that they are, wholly or partly, pre-6 April 2011 annuity rights.

s 554V(2) This gives relief from a Part 7A charge where the purchaser purchases an annuity contract or transfers annuity rights to an employee, or earmarks funds which represent the beneficiary's right under the annuity contract. Again this to prevent a double charge.

s 554V(3) This gives similar relief for relevant steps taken by the insurance company in providing the annuity.

s 554V(4 and 5) This allows for apportionment where relevant steps are taken partly in relation to pre 6-April 2011 annuity rights and partly in relation to something else.

s 554V(6) This defines terms for the purposes of this section

s 554W Certain retirement benefits

This section ensures that sums derived from pension lumps sums are not brought within the Part 7A charge.

s 554W(1) The section applies where the relevant benefit consists of the payment of a lump sum to an employee out of pre-6 April 2011 lump sum rights.

s 554W(2) Where sub (1) applies there is no Part 7A charge.

s 554W (3 and 4) This allows for apportionment along similar lines to that in the previous sections.

s 554W(5) This defines certain terms for the purposes of this section.

s 554X transfers between certain foreign pension schemes

s 554X(1) The section applies where a person has rights under a s 390 scheme and those rights are transferred to another s 390 scheme or to an overseas pension scheme. A s 390 scheme is a scheme for non domiciled employees of non resident employers.

s 554X(2) The section also applies if A transfers rights in an overseas pension scheme to another overseas pension scheme and some or all of those rights are s 390 scheme rights.

s 554X(3) This is the operative section. There is an exemption where a relevant step within s 554C is taken for the sole purpose of transferring the rights (i e by payments or transfers of assets) or sums are earmarked by the transferee in relation to the transferred rights.

s 5544X(4–6) This allows for apportionment where not all of the rights which are transferred are s390 rights.

s 554X(7–9) This applies if any of the transferred rights derive from contributions by B after 6 April 2006 and are neither tax-relieved contributions or tax-exempt provision. There is an apportionment between rights under sub-s 7 and sums under sub-s 3.

s 554X(10) Is a definition section.

s 554X(11) This treats all of the companies in B's group as a single company.

s 554X(12) This gives definitions for the purposes of this section.

s 554Y Power to exclude other relevant steps

s 554Y This gives the Commissioners of HMRC the power to introduce regulations to exempt steps from the Part 7A charge. Regulations may have retrospective effect.

Note that the regulation are only for the purposes of exempting steps from the s 7A charge. There is no power to bring items within the charge which are not otherwise within it. Thus any retrospective regulations cannot be used to create a retrospective tax charge.

s 554Z Interpretation – general

This sets out a large number of interpretations which apply for the purpose of Part 7A. It is not necessary to go through each of them but attention is drawn to the following.

Subsection (7)—References to the payment of a sum or money includes the payment of a sum of money by way of loan.

Subsection (16)—This defines whether a step is connected with a tax avoidance arrangement. It is very widely drawn, and includes a series of arrangements with the tax avoidance arrangement only at one end of the arrangement. Note it is does not matter whether or not the person taking the step is unaware of the tax avoidance arrangement.

s 554Z1 Person's linked with A

This defines a person linked with A.

A person is linked with A if he/it is connected with A, is a close company in which A is or has been a participator, is a company in which A is or has been a participator in a company which would be close if were UK resident, or is a 51% subsidiary of a such a company.

Note that for these purposes references to A is to a person within any other paragraph of this subsection.

For the purposes of the connection test a man and woman living together as if they were spouses are treated as if they were spouses, and persons of the same sex living together as if they were in a civil partnership are treated as a civil partners.

Participator takes the definition in CTA 2010 s 455 but is extended to a person who would be a participator if the non-resident company would be close if it were UK resident.

Chapter 2 Treatment of relevant step for income tax purposes

All that has gone before has been for the purposes of defining what is and what is not a relevant step. Those sections (ss 554A–554Z1) are so extensive and complex that readers could be forgiven for being rather perplexed by what they are trying to achieve. It is therefore perhaps worth giving a reminder before we look at the next chapter that in fact there are really only three types of relevant steps:

— Earmarking (s 554B)

— Payment of a sum of money (s 554C)

— Transfer of assets (s 554D)

Chapter 2 now sets out how relevant steps are to be taxed.

s 554Z2 Value of relevant step to count as employment income

s 554Z2(1) This set out the basic principle. The value of the relevant step counts as employment income of A in respect of A's employment with B. Where, as will usually be the case, the relevant step is taken after the commencement of employment the value of the step will be taken as employment income of the year in which the step is taken. Where the step is taken before A's employment starts the relevant step is employment income of the year in which the employment starts.

s 554Z2(2) This sets out an order of priority. If the amount which is treated as earnings would also be treated as earnings under the benefits code the Part 7A charge takes priority. Similarly any income which would dealt with under ITTOIA 2005 part 4 Ch 3 (i e distributions) is to be dealt with under Part 7A. This does not of course meant that all dividends are now to be taxed under Part 7A. But it does mean that in the very limited circumstances where a dividend could be a relevant step under Part 7A and was not within any of the exemptions, the Part 7A charge on the relevant step would displace the normal charge under the distribution rules.

s 554Z2(3) This makes it clear that where the relevant step would also constitute an employment related loan the charge under Part 7A (which would be on the entire amount of the loan) displaces any charge on the interest benefit under the normal cheap loan provisions.

s 554Z3 Value of relevant step

s 554Z3(1)(2) If the relevant step is a sum of money its value is the amount of the sum itself. In other cases the value is the higher of the market value of the relevant step or the cost of the relevant step.

s 554Z3(3) The market value test is subject to s 437 and s 542.

s 554Z3(4) The cost of the relevant step is ignored if the relevant step is within s 554C(1)(c) – taking a relevant step by virtue of which a person acquires a security or interest in a security – and the acquisition is chargeable under Chapters 2 to 4A of Part 7 (i e the normal employment securities rules).

s 554Z3(5) The cost is also to be ignored if s 554Z7–share options – applies.

s 554Z3(6) The cost of a relevant step includes the expenses incurred in connection with the relevant step (including an appropriate proportion of costs which are partly attributable to the cost of the relevant step and partly for some other purpose).

s 554Z3(7) The rules about the value of the benefit are subject to the specific rules in s 554Z(4) to s 554Z(8), which are discussed below.

s 554Z4 Residence issues

s 554Z4(1) sub-ss 554Z 2 and 3 have determined the value of the relevant step and established that the relevant step counts as employment income. It is now necessary to determine which year the relevant step is "for". In reality this only applies when dealing with non residents.

s 554Z4(2) The basic rule is that the steps in ITEPA 2003 ss16(1–4) and 17(1–3) are to apply as if the value of the relevant step were general earnings.

s 554Z4(3–5) If the value of a relevant step (or part of it) is for a tax year in which the individual was not UK resident the value is to be reduced, on a just and reasonable basis, to the extent that the relevant step was not in respect of duties performed in the UK.

s 554Z2(1) Nothing in this section, however, changes the tax year for which the value of the relevant step counts as employment income – the section is purely for the purpose of dealing with periods of non-residence.

s 554Z5 Overlap with earlier relevant step

There is considerable potential for double charges within Part 7A. The most obvious is when a sum is earmarked (thus triggering a charge under s 554B) and there is then a payment of a sum of money out of those earmarked funds. In the absence of any relieving measure this would also create a charge under s 554C on potentially the same amount. Section 554Z5 deal with this problem.

s 554Z5(1) The section applies where there is an overlap between (a) the sum of money or relevant asset which is the subject of a relevant step and (b)a sum of money or asset which was the subject of an earlier relevant step that gave rise to a charge under Part 7A.

s 554Z5(2) Where this is the case the value of the relevant step is reduced by the value of the earlier relevant step – or proportional part thereof where there is only partial overlap. In applying this test any adjustments under s 554Z4 – residence – are to be made first.

s 5544Z5(3) In applying this section the value of the earlier step is the value after applying reductions under s 554A45 or 7, but not after s 554Z 6 or 8. (The significance of those later sections is explained below).

s 554Z5(4) This defines where there is an overlap. There is an overlap where the sum or money or asset used in each step is the same, or where the money/asset used in the second step has essentially replaced the first sum/asset.

s 554Z(5) This section also applies to any further relevant steps which are taken with that sum or asset. Essentially this provision ensures that there will only be one charge on the amount or value of the asset regardless of the number of relevant steps subsequently taken in respect of that amount or value.

s 554Z6 Overlap with certain earnings

This is another section to deal with potential overlaps with existing charges.

s 554Z6(1) This section applies where the relevant step gives rise to relevant earnings which are taxable in accordance with s 16 or (where relevant) s 17 for a tax year in which the individual is resident; or are taxable in accordance with s 29 or (where relevant) s 30 for a tax year in which the individual is not resident but which are in respect of duties performed in the UK.

s 554Z6(2) The value of the relevant step is to be reduced by the amount of the relevant earnings (though not to below Nil).

s 554Z6 (3 and 4) These sections define relevant earnings.

This section would apply for example to cash payments from an EBT. Most cash payments from an EBT would be earnings under general principles and thus are already within the charge. Those payments would also be a relevant step under s 554ZC – payment of a sum of money – but the effect of this section is to reduce any charge under s 554ZC by the amount which is charged to income tax as earnings. Thus in practice no charge under Part 7A would arise.

s 554Z7 Exercise price of share options

This is a highly complex piece of drafting to ensure that if a charge under Part 7A arises in respect of share options (which is in fact unlikely to be the case in most cases because of the relieving provisions in s 554L) the amount of the charge is reduced by the amount which the employee has to pay to acquire the shares.

s 554Z7((1–4) The essence of this section is that if a sum is earmarked for the purposes of an employee share scheme (or a bonus scheme which is related to the value of shares) and the employee must pay a sum of money, determined in advance, to acquire the shares or to participate in the bonus scheme, then provided that the earmarking is not for a greater number of shares which might be reasonably required for the purpose of the scheme and there is no tax avoidance arrangement, the value of the relevant step is to be reduced by the amount which the employee will have to pay.

s 554Z7(5) This allows for an apportionment where the value of the relevant step was reduced under s554Z4–Z6 (ie if the value of the relevant step is apportioned the exercise price is similarly apportioned).

s 554Z7(5 and 6) If the options are not actually granted within three months of the date of the relevant step and an amount remains earmarked there is an earmarking charge at that point and there is no deduction for the amount payable for the options.

s 554Z7(8) This defines relevant shares.

s 554Z8 Cases where consideration given for relevant step

One of the major criticisms of the original draft was the fact that it did not adequately deal with transactions between an employee and the third party. If for example an employee sells an asset to an EBT for market value there is no economic change in either party's position. But because this would constitute the payment of a sum of money by the EBT to the employee a charge would arise under s 554C. Charges would also arise where the transaction was in the other direction (ie the employee buys the asset), because this would have been the transfer of an asset by the EBT.

s 554Z8 attempts to deal with this, by, in broad terms, exempting market value transactions between employees and third parties.

s 554Z8(1) This sets out the basic relief. It applies where the relevant step is within s 554C(1)(a)–(c) – ie payments of a sum of money or transfers of assets. The relevant step must be for consideration by the employee in the form of a transfer of assets to the 3rd party by the employee. The transfer must be made before, at or about the time that the relevant step is taken and must not be by way of loan. There must not be a tax avoidance connection.

s 554Z8(2) The value of the relevant step is reduced – again not to below nil – by the market value of the asset transferred by A , or where the value of the relevant step was reduced under s 554Z4 (reduction for non residence) a proportionate part of the market value.

s 554Z8(3) For the purposes of the tax avoidance test it is to be assumed that there was a tax avoidance connection if before the transfer the asset was loaned to the employee or any other person, or the relevant asset carries with it rights connected with the relevant arrangement. Again the draftsman's concern to see that the relief is not exploited for avoidance purposes can be clearly seen.

s 554Z8(5–6) apply where the relevant step is within s 554C(1)(b) or (c) – ie transfers of assets, does not also involve a sum of money, the employee gives consideration in the form of a sum of money and the payment is made before, on or about the time of the relevant step. In such a case the value of the relevant step is reduced by the amount of the consideration given (with the usual apportionment if there is a reduction in the value of the relevant step under s 554Z4).

s 554Z(8)(7 and 8) These are definition sections.

In the normal case, therefore, employees can buy and sell assets to an EBT or other third party at market value without triggering a Part 7A charge.

s 554Z9 Remittance basis: A is ordinarily UK resident

This is the first of three sections dealing with the interaction of the remittance basis with the new Part 7A.

s 554Z9(1) This sets out five basic conditions. The value of the relevant step is "for" a particularly tax year (s 554Z4 applies); the remittance basis applies to the employee for the relevant tax year (by virtue of ITA 2007 ss 809B, D or E); the employee is ordinary resident in the tax year; the employees' employment is employment with a foreign employer and the duties of A's employment are performed wholly outside the UK.

s 554Z9(2) Where the conditions in (1) above apply the employee's employment income (as defined in s 554Z2(1)) is taxable specific income for the year in which it is remitted.

s 554Z9(3) Any income which is remitted before A's employment with B starts is treated as remitted in the year in which the employment starts.

s 554Z9(4–6) These allow for an apportionment where the individual has associated employments which are not performed wholly outside the UK.

s 554Z10 Remittance basis: A is not ordinarily resident

s 554Z10(1) This sets out three basic conditions which must be met for s 554Z10 to apply. The value of the relevant step is not in respect of duties performed in the UK; the employee (A) is taxable on the remittance basis under the same sections as mentioned above; and the employee is not ordinarily resident in the UK.

s 554Z10(2) The employment income is taxable specific income of the tax year in which it remitted.

s 554Z10(3) Any income which is remitted before A's employment with B starts is treated as remitted in the year in which the employment starts.

s 554Z10(4) Apportionments are to be done on a just and reasonable basis if the value of the relevant step is not wholly in respect of duties performed outside the UK.

s 554Z10 Remittance basis: supplementary

These provisions supplement the basic rules set out in the two previous sections.

s 554Z11(1–3) These clarify how certain apportionments are to be made

s 554Z11(4–6) This uses the definition in ITA 2007 Part 14 Ch A1 for the purposes of the expression remitted to the UK and links the definitions in Part 7A back to that chapter.

s 554Z11(7 and 8) These sections ensure that there is no double counting where a further relevant step is taken. They mirror similar provisions in s 554Z(4).

s 554Z11(9–11) These are technical amendments to ensure that the rules work consistently with earlier definitions of residence and domicile. They apply where the relevant year for the purposes of s 554Z9 or Z10 was 2007–8 or earlier.

s 554Z12 Relevant step taken after A's death

s 554Z12–15 are a final series of sections within Chapter 2 supplementing the earlier material.

s 554Z12(1) deals with the mechanics of certain relevant steps taken after an employee's death. If you are still with me at this point – and there is a long way to go yet! – you will recall that there is no general exemption on death: the only exemption is for earmarking after a person's death. Section 554Z12 applies where there is relevant step under s 554C or D – broadly payments of a sum of money or making an asset available – and the step is taken after the employee's death (or ,where the remittance basis applies, is remitted after his death.)

In one of the most bizarre parts of this very bizarre legislation the ensuing subsections are not to apply "if A's employment with B never started before A's death". This does not, I believe, refer to ghostly employments from the afterlife but to situations where a person died before he could take up employment but benefits were still provided even though he was never employed.

s 554Z12(2) defines the relevant person for the purposes of this section. It means the relevant person in relation to the particular step under s 554C or D as appropriate.

s 554Z12(3) If the relevant person is A, i e the employee, his personal representatives are liable for the income tax.

s 554Z12 (4) If the relevant person is an individual other than A the amount is to be taken as employment income of the relevant person

s 554Z12(5) If the relevant person is not an individual the amount is taxable on the relevant taxable person at the applicable rate defined below.

s 554Z12(6) Defines who is the relevant taxable person. It specifies three categories and sets out an order of priority. The first is any UK resident person who took the relevant step; the second is the employer, if he is still alive, or if a corporate employer, is still in existence when the relevant step was taken; the third is the non-UK resident person who took the relevant step.

s 554Z12(7) The applicable rate of tax is the rate which applies for the purposes of s 394(4) – i e the rate specified by treasury order, which is currently 50% .

s 554Z12(8) Where there is one or more person who could be the relevant person there is to be an apportionment of that income on a just and reasonable basis.

s 554Z13 Subsequent income tax liability

This is a catch all section. Where after a relevant step is taken there is another event which gives rise to an income tax liability to the employee, other than a charge under Part7A, chapters 2 to 5 of Part 7 (employment related securities) or Part 9 (pensions income), a just and reasonable basis can be used to prevent a double charge.

Given the complexity of both this part and the employment related securities legislation it is difficult to see circumstances in which such a double charge could arise, but the draftsman is undoubtedly giving himself some room for manoeuvre just in case some odd situation arises in which there could potentially be double taxation.

s 554Z14 Relief where earmarking not followed by a further relevant step

This is a relieving section. It can normally be expected that once a sum has been earmarked it will subsequently be paid out to the employee in some form or another. To that extent the earmarking charge simply brings forward the point at which the tax charge would other arise (albeit that this could be by many years). There could however be situations where funds are earmarked, and thus subject to a tax charge, but the individual never actually enjoys any benefit from those funds. This section gives a limited form of relief in such case.

s 554Z14(1) sets out the main conditions which apply. There has to have been a relevant step under s554B (earmarking); an relevant event occurs in relation to the earmarked sum or asset which is not a relevant step; by virtue of the relevant event no further relevant step will be taken by P or any other person in relation to that asset, and there is no tax avoidance connection.

s 554Z14(2) A tax avoidance connection includes avoidance by taking relief under this section (It appears that the draftsman has made an error here in the statutory cross reference – the reference to S554Z(15) does not make any sense and presumably should be to s 554Z(14)(d)

s 554Z14(3) This defines relevant sum or asset.

s 554Z14(4) Application for relief must be made within four years of the date of the relevant event.

s 554Z14(5) If relief is due it is to be given on a just and reasonable basis by reference to income tax paid on any previously charged amount.

s 554Z14(6) This defines a previously charged amount.

s 554Z14(7 and 8) If the amount chargeable was reduced by reference to s 554Z5 or s 554Z13 (ie overlap with previously charged amounts) the relief which is given under this section is to be reduced on a just and reasonable basis.

s 554Z14(9) Relief is to be given by repayment or otherwise

s 554Z 14(10) Once relief has been given under this section Part 7A is deemed never to have applied by reason of the original relevant step.

s 554Z15 Location of employment duties

This section cross refers to the various tests which already apply to define where employment duties are carried out.

CHAPTER 3 – Undertakings given by employers in relation to retirement benefits etc.

It is a measure of just how much the original draft of the legislation has been amended that this entirely new chapter was inserted into the legislation at committee stage, ie after the Bill had already doubled in size between publication of the draft Bill in December and the publication of the Bill proper in March.

It deals again with the potential interaction between the pensions legislation and the new disguised remuneration rules. The explanatory note issued with these sections state that its purpose is to provide for employment income tax charges to arise when an employer gives an undertaking to pay a contribution to an unregistered pension scheme, and subsequently assures that the contribution will be paid by either earmarking property for this purpose or otherwise providing security. I state that in full here because it is almost impossible, without that explanation, to make sense of what this new chapter is trying to achieve.

s 554Z16 Application etc

s 554Z16(1) This sets out the scope of the chapter. It applies where there is an undertaking (as defined) that certain specified contributions will be paid.

s 554Z16(2) This sets out what is a specified contribution. There are four conditions. The contribution must be to an arrangement which is not a registered pension scheme; relevant benefits are to be provided out of the contribution by a relevant third person; the provision of the benefits would be a relevant step; and the contribution is neither tax relieved or tax exempt.

s 554Z16(3) This defines the terms used in sub-s (2)

s 554Z16(4) This defines an undertaking. It is widely drawn and includes references to undertakings which are not legally enforceable and undertakings which are dependent on performance conditions.

s 554Z17 Employer to be treated as relevant third person

This is one of the most tortuously drafted of all of the sections within Part 7A. Its purpose is to treat certain actions by the employer as if they were made by a third party and thus bring them within the scope of Part 7A. It will be recalled that one of the fundamental principles of Part 7A is that there must be the involvement of a third party. This section breaches that fundamental principle by imposing a Part 7A charge on certain actions taken by the employer him or herself.

s 554Z17(1) This sets out the basic test. If the employer takes a step within s 554Z18 or 19 (these, as will be discussed below, are essentially concerned with earmarking and the provision of security) the disguised remuneration legislation is to apply as if the employer was a relevant third person and as if the step triggered an earmarking charge. NB the step may trigger an earmarking charge in any event without the need for this specific rule, but if there would not otherwise be an earmarking charge one is deemed to arise.

s 554Z17(2) In determining whether a step would create a charge under Chapter 2 many of the relieving sections within Chapter 1 are to be ignored. In fact the only exclusions which are still to be taken into account are s 554E (approved share schemes); s 554P (employment income); s 554Q (income arising from earmarked sums); s 554R (acquisitions out of sums or assets); and s 554V(Annuity purchases). In other words for the purposes of this test the full very wide extent of the definition of relevant step is to be used, subject only to these limited exemptions.

Subs 2b and c then impose further restrictions as to the sections which can be taken into account as relieving provisions. If the step is under s 554Z18 (earmarking) certain specified sections of s 554Q and R are to be disregarded. If the step is under s 554Z19 (security), s 554Q and R are to be disregarded in their entirety.

s 554Z17(3) The test in (2) is for the purposes of determining whether Chapter 2 applies to a step. If it is concluded that Chapter 2 does indeed apply then in working out how Chapter 2 is to apply ss 554Z7–12 are to be disregarded.

s 554Z17(4) If the only reason that Chapter 2 does not apply to the step is because of s 554E(3) or (6) – those are the sections dealing with earmarking for the purposes of employee share schemes – ss 554E(10 and 11) do not apply. Those are the sections which give an earmarking charge where funds cease to be held for the purposes of an employee share scheme.

s 554Z17(5) This is a signpost to the fact that there are yet further modifications to Chapters one and two in the following sections.

s 554Z17(6) This makes provision for any regulations made under s 554Y also to make provisions relating to cases where Chapters one and two have effect under this section.

s 554Z17(7) This defines certain terms used in this section

At this point the reader may well be completely baffled: the author admits that though he has read these provisions many times he is still far from clear exactly what they are intended to achieve. It is therefore appropriate to insert here what the official explanatory note says about this section.

New section 554Z17(1) to (4) provide that Chapters 1 and 2 of Part 7A are to have effect with prescribed modifications if there is a step within new ss 554Z16 or 554Z17 taken by the employer ("B"). As a result, the value of the step gives rise to employment income tax charges under Chapter 2 of Part 7A. The effect of the modifications is explicitly to disapply certain provisions in Chapters 1 and 2, including anti-avoidance provisions, which it is not appropriate should apply when steps are treated as taken by virtue of Chapter 3 of Part 7A.

s 554Z18 Earmarking

s 554Z18(1) This sets out the first circumstance in which B (the employer) is treated as taking a relevant step for the purposes of Chapter 3 (and only for that purpose: generally relevant steps taken by an employer are not, as we have discussed before, relevant for Part 7A) He takes a step if he earmarks money with a view to its being used for the performance of a relevant undertaking, i e an undertaking within s 554Z16 to contribute to a pension arrangement. Apart from the reference to an undertaking rather than to a relevant step the wording here follows that in s 554B, the main section dealing with earmarking.

s 5544Z18(2) This mirrors the provision in s 554B which states that it does not matter whether or not a sum of money or asset has been previously held on a different basis.

s 554Z18(3 and 4) Under s554Q and R there is relief if income arises, or assets are acquired, out of sums which have been subject to an earmarking charge. s 554Z18(3 and 4) extend this to situations where there has been an earmarking charge under s 554Z18. They thus preserve the principle that there should not be double taxation of what is essentially the same amount.

s 554Z19 Provision of security

s 554Z19(1) This section applies if B provides security for the performance of the relevant undertaking.

s 554Z19(2) This states that for this purpose the sum of money or asset is that which applies at the time that the security is given.

s 554Z19(3) This allows for apportionment where the security is partly in respect of relevant undertakings and partly for some other purpose.

s 554Z19(4) This states that the above sections are subject to s 554Z20(7) – valuation

s 554Z19(5) Section 554Q, which is the section which gives relief for income arising from earmarked sums – is disapplied for the purpose of this section. This is because that income is taken into account for valuation purposes in s 554Z20, as discussed below.

s 554Z19(6) This disapplies s 554R(6) – acquisitions out of sums or assets – for the same reason as above.

s 554Z19(7) Reference to the provision of security include the provision of security in any way, however informal.

s 554Z20 Valuation of steps within s 554Z19

s 554Z20(1) This explains that the section applies to steps within s 554Z19, i e the provision of security.

s 554Z20(2) This disapplies the normal basis for determining the value of a relevant step (i e those set out in s 554Z3) and substitutes a set of rules specifically for this purpose.

s 554Z20(3) The value of the relevant step is to be taken as the lower of (a) the amount to be paid under the relevant undertaking , as determined at the time the security is given and assuming that any performance conditions are to be met; and (b) the value of the security

s 554Z20(4) The value of the security is to be taken as the total amount of the sums that were given as security and the total market value of the assets given as security (taking the value at the time that the security was given). These amounts are however subject to a just and reasonable reduction to take account of any term of the security which limits the total amount available as security for the undertaking.

s 554Z20(5) This introduces an annual test for the determination of the value of the relevant step. It applies where a sum or asset is still held as security one year after it was originally applied, and on each successive annual anniversary.

s 554Z20(6) A relevant step is deemed to arise on each anniversary day (other than in cases where the individual has died before the anniversary day).

s 554Z20(7) Where the sum of money which is used as security varies the value to be used in determining the value of the anniversary step is the highest value in the year before the anniversary step.

s 554Z20(8) Where an asset is used for security the value of the asset for the purposes of determining the value of the anniversary step can be determined at any time in the anniversary year. This is an important distinction compared with sub-s (7) above.

s 554Z20(9) This defines anniversary year.

s 554Z21 Relief for earmarking or security not followed by contribution or relevant benefit

This extends the principle in s 554Z14, i e that where earmarking is not followed by another relevant step any tax paid at the point of earmarking is repayable on a just and reasonable basis, to tax payable as a result of an earmarking charge under s 554Z18 or 19.

Note that para 58 below deals with commencement provisions for these particular sections of the new Chapter 3.

A pause for breath

At this point we have reached the end of the new Part 7A. However there are still some 17 pages of the Schedule to deal with. These introduce modifications to others parts of ITEPA and to various other acts. They also contain the commencement provisions and certain anti-forestalling provision.

Fortunately we will not have to deal with each of the 63 remaining paragraphs of the schedule (everything so far as been part of para 1!). We will, however, comment on the substantive paragraphs in the remainder of the schedule.

Paras 2 to 26

These are all consequential drafting amendments to ITEPA 2003.

Para 27

This introduces a new s 567A to allow for relief against a pensions income charge if there has been a prior charge under Part 7A

New s 567A(1) This applies where there an amount of taxable pension income which has derived directly or indirectly from rights which represent or have arisen from a sum of money or asset which was the subject of a relevant step under Part 7A and on which a charge arose.

New s 567A(2) This allows for a deduction against the amount of taxable pensions income.

New s 567A(3) The amount of the deduction is the amount which counted as employment income under Part 7A.

New s 567A(4) If the amount of deduction exceeds the amount of taxable pension income the balance is carried forward against future taxable pension income until it has been exhausted.

New s 567A(5 and 6) This allows for a just and reasonable apportionment if the pensions income arises partly from the relevant step and partly from something else.

Para 28 This ensures that any PAYE charges which could arise under both the intermediaries legislation and the disguised remuneration legislation are only to be subject to PAYE under the latter. This is an important practical point, as there will be many circumstances – such as cash payments out of an EBT – which could potentially be taxable under both sets of legislation. As will be seen below this priority rule will be critical in determining where the obligation to account for the PAYE lies.

Para 29 This introduces a new s 687A, which brings charges under Part 7A within the PAYE regime. This is an important section – without it there would be no machinery for the collection of any tax charges arising under Part 7A.

New s 687A(1) This sets out the scope of the provision. It applies where the value of relevant step which counts as employment income is the payment of a sum of money.

New s 687A(2) For the purposes of the PAYE regulations the employer is treated as making a payment of PAYEable income on an amount which is the best estimate of the amount of employment income. In the vast majority of cases this will simply be the amount of the sum of money itself. Note that the obligation falls very clearly on the employer. As a practical point it will be important to ensure that arrangements are put in place to ensure that employers are aware of this obligation. Ordinarily there is no obligation, for example, on trustees of an EBT to inform the employer of payments made to beneficiaries. Those payments will almost certainly now trigger a PAYE liability on the employer.

New s 687A(3) This states the date on which the payment is treated as being made. Normally it will be the date on which the relevant step is taken. However where it takes place before A's employment with B commences the payment will be treated as being made at the date of commencement of employment. This is subject to a rule that the earliest date on which the payment is deemed to arise is 30 days after Royal Assent to the Finance Bill. This last proviso would therefore apply to relevant steps taken in the early months of tax year 2011–12.

New s 687A(4) The obligation on the employer to account for PAYE is displaced where the person who actually takes the relevant step deducts income tax and accounts for it under PAYE regulations. Note that this does not mean that there is any obligation on the third party actually to account for PAYE. But if the third party does meet the liability then the employer is absolved from responsibility.

Para 30 This is drafting amendment to deal with non-UK employers

Para 31 This introduces a new s 695A, which deals with relevant steps which are not the payment of money. The section closely mirrors the new s 687A, except that the amount on which PAYE is to be applied is the best estimate of the employment income less any amounts dealt with on the remittance basis under s 554Z9(2) or s 554A10(2).

Para 32 This is another important section. It states that where there is a charge under Part 7A there is no PAYE charge under the readily convertible assets legislation. This is important. Although the quantum of any charge might be the same under both sets of legislation responsibility for payment of the PAYE might not be. In particular the readily convertible assets legislation can impose the obligation to account for PAYE on the third party, whereas the obligation under Part 7A falls on the employer. This priority rules ensures that it is always the employer who has the obligation to account to for PAYE.

Paras 33–34 These are further drafting amendments to ITEPA 2003

Paras 35–39 These are consequential drafting amendments to ITTOIA 2005

Paras 40–43 These are consequential drafting amendments to ITA 2007

Paras 44–48 These are consequential drafting amendments to CTA 2009. Their effect is to give corporation tax relief under the employee benefit contribution rules to amounts which are chargeable under Part 7A.

Paras 49–51 These are consequential drafting amendments to TCGA 1992.

Commencement

Paras 52–63 These set out the commencement provisions for the new Part 7A. They are extremely complex and need to be considered on a paragraph by paragraph basis. The complexity is caused by the fact that the draftsman has had to deal not only with structures which are set up ab initio after the legislation become law but also situations where structures were already in place, but where steps were taken in respect of those structures after the introduction of these new rules. Finally the draftsman has also had to introduce anti-forestalling provisions to ensure that certain transactions were caught immediately from the date of the publication of the draft legislation in order to prevent taxpayers and their advisers planning to avoid the impact of the new rules.

Para 52(1) The basic rule is, mercifully, very straightforward. Part 7A applies to relevant steps taken on or after 6 April 2011.

Para 54(2) This basic rule is however modified in the situations set out in the following paragraphs.

Para 53(1)(2) This is the first of the anti-forestalling provisions. It applies where a relevant step within s554C(1)(a) is taken on or after 9 December 2010 and before 6 April 2011. The legislation calls such a step "the early step". 9 December 2010 was the date of the publication of the first draft of these provisions. Section 554C(1)(a) deals with steps which are the payment of a sum of money and it is important to note that this particular anti-forestalling provision is thus restricted to payments of a sum of money: it does not apply to any other relevant step within s 554C(1)(a) , for example it does not apply to transfers of assets.

If the payment of a sum of money would have given rise to Part 7A charge had Part 7A been in force from 9 December 2010 (and the step was not chargeable to income tax under FA 2004 Sch 34 (non UK pension schemes)) then a charge under Part 7A arises on the payment of that sum of money.

So, for example, a cash payment from an EBT to an employee, whether by way of absolute payment or by way of loan, made on, say, 1 January 2011 would give rise to a Part 7A charge.

Para 53(3) Although the early step will by definition have actually taken place in tax year 2010–11 it is deemed to have taken place on 6 April 2012 for the purpose of determining the year in which the employment income arises. This means that for PAYE purposes it is income for the month 6 April to 5 May 2012 and PAYE will consequently need to be accounted for on 19 May 2012. This might seem a very generous provision – the reason for it is to give effect to the relief in para 53(4).

Para 53(4) This is an important relieving provision. The amount which would otherwise be the subject of the anti-forestalling charge is reduced by the amount which has been repaid to P (ie the third party such as the EBT) by 5 April 2012. The effect of this is that the amount so repaid is treated as never having given rise to a Part 7A charge. Any adjustments to any assessment to tax which need to be made in order to give effect to this relief are to be made accordingly.

The principal situation in which this will arise in practice is where loans were made between 9 December 2010 and 5 April 2011. Provided that those loans are repaid by 5 April 2012 no liability will arise under Part 7A. It is important to note that this is the only circumstance in which repayment of a loan will extinguish a Part 7A charge. Loans made on or after 6 April 2011 will attract a charge which will NOT be reduced if the loan is subsequently repaid.

Para 53(5) If not all of the amount which was paid has been repaid the reduction in para 54(4) is to be made on a just and reasonable basis.

Para 53(6) s 554Z5 – which is the section which gives relief where there is an overlap with an earlier relevant step – does not apply to this anti-forestalling rule. The reason for this is that otherwise a taxpayer could say that the payment of the sum of money was out of funds which had been earmarked before 9 December 2010. There would not have been a charge on the earmarking, but if s 554Z5 had applied if would have given relief to the charge on the payment because of the prior earmarking.

Para 53(7) s 554Z12 (which is the section dealing with the incidence of tax if a step is taken after a person's death) does not apply in relation to the early step. It does not however prevent the charge itself arising.

Para 53(8–10) These are drafting amendments

Para 54(1) This is the second of the anti-forestalling provisions.

It applies where a relevant step under s 554C(1)(d) is taken. That is the section which deals with making a sum of money or assets available as security for a loan or liability. It only applies where the step does not involve a sum of money within s 554Z(10) (i e the definition used throughout Part 7A),and where is that the asset is a readily convertible asset which P (the third party) makes available to secure the payment of a sum of money. Finally it is a condition is that the step would have been within Part 7A had the legislation been in force from 9 December and that the early step is not chargeable under FA2004 Sch 24, i e the same test as above.

Para 54(2) For this purpose the scope of s 554C(1)(d) is restricted to sums of money or assets which are actually made available for use – the wider alternative test within s 554C(1)(d) , which is concerned making available under an arrangement which permits the use ,does not apply to the anti-forestalling provision.

Para 54(3) Readily convertible asset takes its normal meaning except that the provisions under which PAYE regulations excluding certain description of arrangements from the definition are to be disregarded.

Para 54(4–12) These sections mirror the provisions in para 53 i e the step is deemed to have taken place on 6 April 2011 and is reduced if the asset is returned to P by 5 April 2012 (or if the sum of money is not being used as security at that date)

Para 55 contains additional rules which are to apply in determining whether or not a Part 7A charge would have arisen when considering the anti-forestalling provisions.

Para 55(1 and 2) make modifications to s 554G for the purposes of the anti forestalling rules. Section 1(a) is to be omitted – i e steps taken under pension schemes are to be included – and a different definition of a group of companies is used, based on the control test in ITA 2007 s 995.

Para 55(3) This states that for anti-forestalling purposes s 554N(13)–(16) are not to apply. Those are the sections dealing with loans related to share schemes. In other words, such loans ARE within the anti-forestalling rules

Para 55(4) This deals with car loans. Car loans made before 6 April 2011 are not caught by the anti-forestalling provisions, but if such a loan is outstanding on 6 April 2012 there is a charge at that point.

These three preceding paragraphs, 53–55, are the extent of the anti-forestalling provision. It will be seen therefore that they are essentially restricted to cash, or to quasi cash in the form of readily convertible assets. No other assets are within the anti-forestalling rules and, crucially, earmarking before 6 April 2012 is not subject to an anti-forestalling charge.

Para 56 This is the first of a group of provisions which deal with structures which were already in place before the new provisions took effect. The relief in para 56 is particularly important. It will be recalled – if you are still awake – that under s 554Q if income arising from an earmarked sum or asset is itself earmarked there is no charge at the point of that latter earmarking. There was no concept in tax law of a relevant step before the introduction of this legislation, and therefore income which arose from assets which had been earmarked before 9 December 2011 would have been within Part 7A : in other words each time income was received within a trust it would have been subject to an earmarking charge. This was one of the most criticized features of the original legislation. Para 56(1) therefore allows relief where the earmarking took place before 9 December 2011. There is no retrospective charge on the earmarking itself, but income arising out of those earmarked funds will not itself be subject to an earmarking charge. Of course if that income is subsequently paid to an employee there will be a charge under s 554B(1)(a) at that point.

Para 57 This introduces a parallel rule for acquisitions out of sums or assets which were earmarked before 6 April 2011.

Para 58 This deals with steps within s 554A19 – provision of security for undertakings in connection with retirement – taken before 6 April 2011. If there is a change in the terms of an undertaking which in law does not amount to a new undertaking and the amount which is to be paid under the undertaking increases or will increase, Chapter 3 applies as if there were a new undertaking at the point when the terms change. The amount of that new undertaking is the increase in the amount which is to be paid under the undertaking following the change in its terms. This paragraph is clearly intended to prevent employers increasing the amounts of pre-existing undertakings and claiming that there is no charge because there is in law no new undertaking and that the original undertaking was not caught because it was given before 6 April 2011.

Para 59 This paragraph was not in the original draft legislation. It is an important addition which need to be considered in the light of HMRC's overall approach to EBTs and EFRBS. As stated at the beginning of this commentary, HMRC's view is that many if not all existing EBT and EFRBs arrangements do not work in the way that their promoters claim and that in fact they give rise to PAYE and NIC charges at the point, broadly speaking, at which they are set up. HMRC's have therefore been seeking to persuade companies which have established EBTs etc to settle the PAYE and NIC liabilities which HMRC believes are due rather than seek to prolong what can often be very protracted disputes via litigation. See http://www.hmrc.gov.uk/employers/employee-benefit-trusts.htm

Any company which did settle on the basis that there was a PAYE and NIC charge on creation of the scheme would be faced with a potential double charge under Part 7A on the unwinding of the EBT structure, because that unwinding would almost certainly create a charge under s 554C(1)(a) – payment of a sum of money. There was, in the original draft of Part 7A, no relief for payments out an EBT if the funds used to settle the EBT had been the subject of a PAYE and NIC charge on entry.

Para 59 seeks to alleviate this. It applies where a relevant step is taken within s 554C or D to which a Part 7A charge arises. If there had been a previous relevant step under s 554B – i e earmarking – before 6 April 2011 and there is either an agreement between HMRC and the employer and/or the employee that that earmarking was to be treated as giving rise to an earnings charge, or A is taxed on the basis that there is an earnings charge, the amount which would otherwise be chargeable under Part 7A on the subsequent relevant step (e g the payment of the money out of the trust) is reduced by the amount on which A is charged as employment income. This is subject to a proviso that the tax on the earnings charge is paid or accounted for in advance of EBT being unwound. There are provisions for agreement on a just and reasonable basis if the amount of the payment is greater than the amount of the earmarked funds plus with the amount which represents a reasonable investment return on those earmarked funds.

This is a complicated way of saying something very straightforward: HMRC only wants to tax the amount in the EBT once. If it accepted that there is an upfront earnings charge then there will no additional earnings charge when the arrangement is unwound.

It remains to be seen how attractive this proposition will be to companies which set up EBTs many years ago and where the liability is still in dispute.

Paras 60–63 These are consequential drafting amendments.

Para 64 This provision allows the Treasury to introduce statutory instruments to deal with the interaction of Part 7A with any other provision of the taxes acts, including those relating to capital gains tax and inheritance tax. The power is very widely drafted but it is subject to two provisos: firstly that it cannot be used in increase any person's liability to tax retrospectively and secondly that it cannot be used after 5 April 2015.

Concluding remarks

The fact that such a power had to be given to the Treasury is indicative of just how complex these provisions have become. However skilfully the draftsman may have done his work, and however carefully thought through the policy intention may have been, it is virtually axiomatic that such complex legislation, which at times almost defies comprehension, is bound to contain unexpected problems and will give rise to charges where there is no avoidance intent or mischief intended.

One has a lot of sympathy with HMRC, who have been faced with a major logistical problem dealing with the proliferation of EBT schemes over the years, to say nothing of the very complex technical problems that such schemes bring. One can also see why HMRC wanted a set of objective rules which would determine what was and was not within the charge – they did not want to be faced with arguments about motive or to have to investigate the circumstances of every loan to see whether in fact it was a genuine loan or simply a smokescreen to disguise what was in reality an emolument. But the resulting legislation has become so complex that it is grave danger of collapsing under its own weight: indeed many would argue that it has already collapsed.

Perhaps the last words should go to the House of Lords. In their report on the Finance Bill their lordships said:

> The legislation to address disguised remuneration avoidance is extremely complex and beyond the scope of most business people to decide whether or not it applies to them. One witness called it 'the worst legislation he had ever seen'. There was clearly a very wide and deep unhappiness with this draft legislation.
>
> Many of our private sector witnesses said that 'they would not have started from here' if they had been constructing this legislation. Notwithstanding the justifications put forward by the Exchequer Secretary in the Commons Public Bill Committee and by officials to us, we remain unpersuaded that there was no alternative to this complexity.
>
> Although it is clearly too late to change the legislative approach at this stage in the Finance Bill cycle, we recommend that HMRC should carry out an in-depth examination of the alternative approaches that would have been open to them in framing the disguised remuneration legislation. This could be part of the review that we recommended earlier. The lessons learned should help HMRC to avoid similar pitfalls when tackling other avoidance schemes (House of Lords Finance Bill report paras 174–176).

This author confidently expects to be writing commentary in next year's Finance Act handbook on amendments to Part 7A occasioned by problems which will emerge over the coming months.

This is not the end of the story.

SCHEDULE 3

TAINTED CHARITY DONATIONS

Section 27

PART 1

INCOME TAX

1 In Part 13 of ITA 2007 (tax avoidance), after Chapter 7 insert—

"CHAPTER 8

TAINTED CHARITY DONATIONS

Introduction

809ZH Overview of Chapter

(1) This Chapter makes provision for removing entitlement to income tax reliefs, and counteracting income tax advantages, where a person makes a relievable charity donation which is a tainted donation.

(2) See section 257A of TCGA 1992 and Part 21C of CTA 2010 for the removal of entitlement to other reliefs where a person makes a relievable charity donation which is a tainted donation.

809ZI Relievable charity donations

(1) In this Chapter "relievable charity donation" means a gift or other disposal which—

(a) is made by a person to a charity, and
(b) is eligible for tax relief.

(2) A gift or other disposal is eligible for tax relief if one or both of the following apply—

(a) (ignoring the tainted donation provisions) tax relief would be available in respect of it under a relevant relieving provision;
(b) the charity is entitled to claim a repayment of tax in respect of it.

(3) "The tainted donation provisions" are—

(a) this Chapter,
(b) section 257A of TCGA 1992 (tainted charity donations: disapplication of section 257), and

(c) Part 21C of CTA 2010 (tainted charity donations: removal of corporation tax reliefs).

(4) The following are "relevant relieving provisions"—

(a) section 257 of TCGA 1992 (gifts of chargeable assets),
(b) section 63(2)(a), (aa) and (ab) of CAA 2001 (gifts of plant and machinery),
(c) Part 12 of ITEPA 2003 (payroll giving),
(d) section 108 of ITTOIA 2005 (gifts of trading stock),
(e) Chapters 2 and 3 of Part 8 of this Act (gift aid and gifts of shares),
(f) section 105 of CTA 2009 (gifts of trading stock), and
(g) Part 6 of CTA 2010 (charitable donations relief).

(5) For the purposes of this Chapter, an amount of income which arises under a UK settlement and to which a charity is entitled under the terms of the settlement is to be regarded as an amount gifted to the charity by the trustees of the settlement.

"UK settlement" has the same meaning as in section 628 of ITTOIA 2005.

Tainted donations

809ZJ Tainted donations

(1) For the purposes of this Chapter, a relievable charity donation is a tainted donation if (and only if) Conditions A, B and C are met.

(2) Condition A is that—

(a) a linked person enters into arrangements (whether before or after the donation is made), and
(b) it is reasonable to assume from either or both of—
   (i) the likely effects of the donation and the arrangements, and
   (ii) the circumstances in which the donation is made and the circumstances in which the arrangements are entered into,

that the donation would not have been made and the arrangements would not have been entered into independently of one another.

(3) "Linked person" means—

(a) the person who made the donation ("the donor"), or
(b) a person connected with the donor at a relevant time.

(4) In subsection (3) "relevant time" means a time during the period which begins with the earliest, and ends with the latest, of the following times—

(a) the time when the arrangements are entered into as mentioned in subsection (2);
(b) the time when the relievable charity donation is made;
(c) the time when the arrangements are first materially implemented.

(5) Condition B is that the main purpose, or one of the main purposes, of the linked person in entering into the arrangements is to obtain a financial advantage—

(a) directly or indirectly from the charity to which the donation is made or a connected charity,
(b) for one or more linked persons who are not charities (each of whom is referred to in this Chapter as "a potentially advantaged person").

(6) Condition C is that the donor is not—

(a) a qualifying charity-owned company, or
(b) a relevant housing provider linked with the charity to which the donation is made.

(7) For the purposes of subsection (6)(b) a relevant housing provider is linked with the charity if (and only if)—

(a) one is wholly owned, or subject to control, by the other, or
(b) both are wholly owned, or subject to control, by the same person.

(8) In this section—

"qualifying charity-owned company", in relation to a relievable charity donation, means a company which—

(a) is wholly owned by one or more charities, at least one of which is the charity to which the donation is made or a connected charity, and
(b) has not previously been under the control of, and does not carry on a trade or business previously carried on by, one or more of the following—
   (i) a potentially advantaged person;

(ii) a person (other than a charity) who, at any time within the period of 4 years ending with the day on which paragraph (a) was first satisfied, was connected with a person who is a potentially advantaged person;

"relevant housing provider" means a body which is—

(a) a non-profit registered provider of social housing, or

(b) entered on a register maintained under section 1 of the Housing Act 1996, section 20 of the Housing (Scotland) Act 2010 (asp 17) or Article 14 of the Housing (Northern Ireland) Order 1992 (SI 1992/1725 (NI 15)).

(9) Section 200 of CTA 2010 (company wholly owned by a charity) applies for the purposes of subsection (8), and for those purposes references in that section to "charity" include a registered club within the meaning of section 658(6) of that Act.

(10) This section is subject to section 809ZL (certain financial advantages to be ignored).

809ZK Circumstances in which financial advantage deemed to be obtained

(1) This section applies for the purposes of Condition B.

(2) Subsection (3) applies where the arrangements entered into by the linked person (as mentioned in Condition A) involve a transaction to which—

(a) that or any other linked person ("X"), and

(b) another person ("Y"),

are parties.

(3) X obtains a financial advantage from the charity to which the donation is made or a connected charity if—

(a) the terms of the transaction are less beneficial to Y or more beneficial to X (or both) than those which might reasonably be expected in a transaction concluded between parties dealing at arm's length, or

(b) the transaction is not of a kind which a person dealing at arm's length and in place of Y might reasonably be expected to make.

(4) Nothing in this section is intended to limit the circumstances in which a linked person may be regarded as obtaining a financial advantage for the purposes of section 809ZJ.

(5) In this section—

"Condition A" and "Condition B" have the same meaning as in section 809ZJ;

"linked person" has the meaning given by section 809ZJ(3);

"transaction" includes (for example)—

(a) the sale or letting of property,

(b) the provision of services,

(c) the exchange of property,

(d) the provision of a loan or any other form of financial assistance, and

(e) investment in a business.

809ZL Certain financial advantages to be ignored

(1) When determining whether a relievable charity donation is a tainted donation, a financial advantage within subsection (2), (3), (4) or (5) is to be ignored.

(2) A financial advantage is within this subsection if the person for whom it is obtained applies the advantage for charitable purposes only.

(3) A financial advantage is within this subsection if (ignoring the tainted donation provisions) it is—

(a) a benefit associated with a gift which is a qualifying donation for the purposes of Chapter 2 of Part 8 (gift aid), or

(b) a benefit associated with a payment which is a qualifying payment for the purposes of Chapter 2 of Part 6 of CTA 2010 (charitable donations relief: payments to charity).

(4) A financial advantage is within this subsection if (ignoring the tainted donation provisions)—

(a) the relievable charity donation is a disposal in respect of which tax relief would be available under Chapter 3 of Part 8 of this Act (gifts of shares, securities and real property to charities etc) or Chapter 3 of Part 6 of CTA 2010 (charitable donations: certain disposals to charity), and

(b) the advantage is a benefit the value of which would be taken into account in determining the relievable amount in respect of the disposal for the purposes of the Chapter in question.

(5) A financial advantage is within this subsection if (ignoring the tainted donation provisions)—

(a) the relievable charity donation is a gift in respect of which tax relief would be available under section 108 of ITTOIA 2005 or section 105 of CTA 2009 (gifts of trading stock to charities etc), and

(b) the advantage is a benefit attributable to the making of the gift in respect of which an amount would be brought into account under section 109 of ITTOIA 2005 or section 108 of CTA 2009 (receipt of benefits by donor or connected person).

(6) In this section—

"benefit associated with a gift" has the meaning given by section 417;

"benefit associated with a payment" has the meaning given by section 196 of CTA 2010;

"the tainted donation provisions" has the meaning given by section 809ZI(3).

Removal of reliefs and imposition of charge to tax

809ZM Removal of income tax relief in respect of tainted donations etc

(1) This section applies where a tainted donation is made by a person.

(2) Where (ignoring this Chapter) income tax relief would be available in respect of the tainted donation, that relief is not available.

(3) Where—

(a) (ignoring this Chapter) income tax relief would be available in respect of an associated donation, and

(b) entitlement to that relief is not withdrawn by subsection (2),

that relief is not available.

(4) In this section—

"associated donation", in relation to a tainted donation, means a relievable charity donation made—

(a) in accordance with the relevant arrangements, and

(b) by a person, other than—

(i) a qualifying charity-owned company in relation to that relievable charity donation, or

(ii) a relevant housing provider linked (within the meaning of section 809ZJ(7)) with the charity to which that donation is made;

"income tax relief" means relief under—

(a) section 63(2)(a), (aa) or (ab) of CAA 2001 (gifts of plant and machinery), so far as it applies in relation to income tax,

(b) Part 12 of ITEPA 2003 (payroll giving),

(c) section 108 of ITTOIA 2005 (gifts of trading stock),

(d) Chapter 2 of Part 8 of this Act (gift aid), or

(e) Chapter 3 of that Part (gifts of shares etc);

"qualifying charity-owned company" has the meaning given by section 809ZJ(8) (except that paragraph (b) of that definition does not apply);

"relevant housing provider" has the meaning given by section 809ZJ(8);

"the relevant arrangements", in relation to a tainted donation, means the arrangements by reference to which Conditions A and B in section 809ZJ are met.

(5) Where entitlement to relief is withdrawn under this section in respect of a donation—

(a) subsections (6) and (7) apply if the relief is under Chapter 2 of Part 8 (gift aid), and

(b) subsection (8) applies if the relief is under Part 12 of ITEPA 2003 (payroll giving).

(6) For the purposes of Step 2 in section 58(1), the donation is not a qualifying donation for the purposes of Chapter 2 of Part 8.

(7) But—

(a) the donation remains a qualifying donation for the purposes of—

(i) Part 10 (special rules about charitable trusts etc),

(ii) section 899(5) (meaning of "qualifying annual payment"),

(iii) Chapter 2 of Part 11 of CTA 2010 (charitable companies: gifts and other payments),

(iv) section 664 of that Act (community amateur sports clubs: exemption for interest and gift aid income), and

(b) accordingly, section 414(2)(a) (donation treated as made after deduction of basic rate income tax) applies for the purposes of section 520(4) (income tax treated as deducted to be treated as income tax paid by charitable trust).

(8) The donation remains a donation for the purposes of Part 12 of ITEPA 2003 for the purposes of—

(a) section 521A (gifts under payroll deduction scheme: income tax liability and exemption), and

(b) section 472A of CTA 2010 (gifts under payroll reduction scheme: corporation tax liability and exemption).

809ZN Income tax charge where gift aid is withdrawn

(1) Income tax is charged under this section if—

(a) a person makes a tainted donation in a tax year,

(b) (ignoring this Chapter) relief would have been available under Chapter 2 of Part 8 in respect of the tainted donation or an associated donation ("the gift aid donation"), and

(c) the charity to which the gift aid donation is made is entitled to claim a repayment of tax in respect of that donation.

(2) The amount of the tax charged under this section is equal to the amount of the repayment of tax which the charity is entitled to claim in respect of the gift aid donation (whether or not such a claim is made).

(3) Each of the persons mentioned in subsection (4) is liable for any tax charged under this section, and the liability of those persons is joint and several.

(4) The persons are—

(a) the donor in respect of the gift aid donation,

(b) if different, the donor in respect of the tainted donation,

(c) each potentially advantaged person under the relevant arrangements relating to the tainted donation, and

(d) any charity to which the gift aid donation or (if different) the tainted donation is made, or any connected charity, which falls within subsection (5).

(5) A charity falls within this subsection if the charity—

(a) is or was party to the relevant arrangements relating to the tainted donation, and

(b) was aware, at the time it entered into those arrangements, that a linked person was entering (or had entered or was likely to enter) into the arrangements in circumstances falling within Condition B in section 809ZJ.

(6) No liability to income tax arises under this section in respect of a repayment of tax, if (and to the extent that) the repayment is itself repaid to the Commissioners for Her Majesty's Revenue and Customs under any other provision of the Tax Acts.

(7) In this section—

"associated donation" has the same meaning as in section 809ZM;

"linked person" has the same meaning as in section 809ZJ;

"the relevant arrangements" has the same meaning as in section 809ZM.

809ZO Income tax charge where payment of trust income to charity

(1) Income tax is charged under this section if—

(a) a person makes a tainted donation in a tax year,

(b) the tainted donation or an associated donation is a payment by the trustees of a settlement of income arising under the settlement ("the trust donation"), and

(c) the charity to which the trust donation is made is entitled to claim a repayment of tax in respect of that donation.

(2) The amount of the tax charged under this section is equal to the amount of the repayment of tax which the charity is entitled to claim in respect of the trust donation (whether or not such a claim is made).

(3) Each of the persons mentioned in subsection (4) is liable for any tax charged under this section, and the liability of those persons is joint and several.

(4) The persons are—

(a) the trustees of the settlement who made the trust donation,

(b) if different, the donor in respect of the tainted donation,

(c) if section 628 or 630 of ITTOIA 2005 (gifts from settlor-interested trusts etc) applies in relation to the income out of which the trust donation is made, the settlor in relation to the settlement,

(d) each potentially advantaged person under the relevant arrangements relating to the tainted donation,
(e) any beneficiary of the settlement who is party to those arrangements, and
(f) any charity to which the trust donation or (if different) the tainted donation is made, or any connected charity, which falls within subsection (5).

(5) A charity falls within this subsection if—

(a) the charity is or was party to the relevant arrangements relating to the tainted donation, and
(b) the charity was aware, at the time it entered into those arrangements, that a linked person was entering (or had entered or was likely to enter) into the arrangements in circumstances falling within Condition B in section 809ZJ.

(6) No liability to income tax arises under this section in respect of a repayment of tax if that repayment is itself repaid to the Commissioners for Her Majesty's Revenue and Customs under any other provision of the Tax Acts.

(7) In this section—

"associated donation" has the same meaning as in section 809ZM;
"linked person" has the same meaning as in section 809ZJ;
"the relevant arrangements" has the same meaning as in section 809ZM;
"settlement" and "settlor" have the same meaning as in Chapter 5 of Part 5 of ITTOIA 2005 (see section 620 of that Act).

Supplementary

809ZP Connected charities

For the purposes of this Chapter, a "connected charity" in relation to another charity means a charity which is connected with that other charity in a matter relating to the structure, administration or control of either charity.

809ZQ Connected persons (1) Section 993 (meaning of "connected" persons) applies for the purposes of this Chapter—

(a) subject to section 809ZP, and
(b) as if, after subsection (7) there were inserted the provision in subsection (2).

(2) That provision is—

"(8) A person who is a beneficiary of a settlement is connected with—

(a) a person in the capacity as trustee of the settlement, and
(b) the settlor in relation to the settlement.

(9) For the purposes of this section—

(a) a man and woman living together as husband and wife are treated as if they were husband and wife,
(b) two people of the same sex living together as if they were civil partners of each other are treated as if they were civil partners of each other, and
(c) "close company" includes a company that would be a close company if it were resident in the United Kingdom."

809ZR Minor definitions

(1) In this Chapter—

"arrangements" includes any scheme, arrangement or understanding of any kind, whether or not legally enforceable, involving a single transaction or two or more transactions;
"charity" includes a registered club within the meaning of section 658(6) of CTA 2010 (meaning of "community amateur sports club" and "registered club").

(2) In this Chapter, in the case of a charitable trust, references to a charity being entitled to a repayment of, or liable to pay, tax are to be read as references to the trustees of the trust being so entitled or liable."

PART 2

CORPORATION TAX

2 After Part 21B of CTA 2010 (inserted by Schedule 5 to this Act) insert—

"PART 21C

TAINTED CHARITY DONATIONS

Introduction

939A Overview of Part

(1) This Part makes provision for removing entitlement to corporation tax reliefs where a person makes a relievable charity donation which is a tainted donation.

(2) See Chapter 8 of Part 13 of ITA 2007 and section 257A of TCGA 1992 for the removal of entitlement to other reliefs, and the ways in which other income tax advantages are counteracted, where a person makes a relievable charity donation which is a tainted donation.

939B Relievable charity donations

(1) In this Chapter "relievable charity donation" means a gift or other disposal which—

(a) is made by a person to a charity, and
(b) is eligible for tax relief.

(2) A gift or other disposal is eligible for tax relief if one or both of the following apply—

(a) (ignoring the tainted donation provisions) tax relief would be available in respect of it under a relevant relieving provision;
(b) the charity is entitled to claim a repayment of tax in respect of it.

(3) "The tainted donation provisions" are—

(a) this Part,
(b) section 257A of TCGA 1992 (tainted charity donations: disapplication of section 257), and
(c) Chapter 8 of Part 13 of ITA 2007 (tainted charity donations: removal of income tax relief etc).

(4) The following are "relevant relieving provisions"—

(a) section 257 of TCGA 1992 (gifts of chargeable assets),
(b) section 63(2)(a), (aa) and (ab) of CAA 2001 (gifts of plant and machinery),
(c) Part 12 of ITEPA 2003 (payroll giving),
(d) section 108 of ITTOIA 2005 (gifts of trading stock),
(e) Chapters 2 and 3 of Part 8 of ITA 2007 (gift aid and gifts of shares),
(f) section 105 of CTA 2009 (gifts of trading stock), and
(g) Part 6 of this Act (charitable donations relief).

(5) For the purposes of this Part, an amount of income which arises under a UK settlement and to which a charity is entitled under the terms of the settlement is to be regarded as an amount gifted to the charity by the trustees of the settlement.

"UK settlement" has the same meaning as in section 628 of ITTOIA 2005.

Tainted donations

939C Tainted donations

(1) For the purposes of this Part, a relievable charity donation is a tainted donation if (and only if) Conditions A, B and C are met.

(2) Condition A is that—

(a) a linked person enters into arrangements (whether before or after the donation is made), and
(b) it is reasonable to assume from either or both of—
  (i) the likely effects of the donation and the arrangements, and
  (ii) the circumstances in which the donation is made and the circumstances in which the arrangements are entered into,

that the donation would not have been made and the arrangements would not have been entered into independently of one another.

(3) "Linked person" means—

(a) the person who made the donation ("the donor"), or
(b) a person who is connected with the donor at a relevant time.

(4) In subsection (3) "relevant time" means a time during the period which begins with the earliest, and ends with the latest, of the following times—

(a) the time when the arrangements are entered into as mentioned in subsection (2);

(b) the time when the relievable charity donation is made;
(c) the time when the arrangements are first materially implemented.

(5) Condition B is that the main purpose, or one of the main purposes, of the linked person in entering into the arrangements is to obtain a financial advantage—

(a) directly or indirectly from the charity to which the donation is made or a connected charity,
(b) for one or more linked persons who are not charities (each of whom is referred to in this Part as "a potentially advantaged person").

(6) Condition C is that the donor is not—

(a) a qualifying charity-owned company, or
(b) a relevant housing provider linked with the charity to which the donation is made.

(7) For the purposes of subsection (6)(b) a relevant housing provider is linked with the charity if (and only if)—

(a) one is wholly owned, or subject to control, by the other, or
(b) both are wholly owned, or subject to control, by the same person.

(8) In this section—

"qualifying charity-owned company", in relation to a relievable charity donation, means a company which—

(a) is wholly owned by one or more charities, at least one of which is the charity to which the donation is made or a connected charity, and
(b) has not previously been under the control of, and does not carry on a trade or business previously carried on by, one or more of the following—

(i) a potentially advantaged person;
(ii) a person (other than a charity) who, at any time within the period of 4 years ending with the day on which paragraph (a) was first satisfied, was connected with a person who is a potentially advantaged person;

"relevant housing provider" means a body which is—

(a) a non-profit registered provider of social housing, or
(b) entered on a register maintained under section 1 of the Housing Act 1996, section 20 of the Housing (Scotland) Act 2010 (asp 17) or Article 14 of the Housing (Northern Ireland) Order 1992 (SI 1992/1725 (N.I. 15)).

(9) Section 200 (company wholly owned by a charity) applies for the purposes of subsection (8), and for those purposes references in that section to "charity" include a registered club within the meaning of section 658(6).

(10) This section is subject to section 939E (certain financial advantages to be ignored).

939D Circumstances in which financial advantage deemed to be obtained

(1) This section applies for the purposes of Condition B.

(2) Subsection (3) applies where the arrangements entered into by the linked person (as mentioned in Condition A) involve a transaction to which—

(a) that or another linked person ("X"), and
(b) another person ("Y"),

are parties.

(3) X obtains a financial advantage from the charity to which the donation is made or a connected charity if—

(a) the terms of the transaction are less beneficial to Y or more beneficial to X (or both) than those which might reasonably be expected in a transaction concluded between parties dealing at arm's length, or
(b) the transaction is not of a kind which a person dealing at arm's length and in place of Y might reasonably be expected to make.

(4) Nothing in this section is intended to limit the circumstances in which a linked person may be regarded as obtaining a financial advantage for the purposes of section 939C.

(5) In this section—

"Condition A" and "Condition B" have the same meaning as in section 939C;
"linked person" has the meaning given by section 939C(3);
"transaction" includes (for example)—

(a) the sale or letting of property,
(b) the provision of services,
(c) the exchange of property,

(d) the provision of a loan or any other form of financial assistance, and
(e) investment in a business.

939E Certain financial advantages to be ignored

(1) When determining whether a relievable charity donation is a tainted donation, a financial advantage within subsection (2), (3), (4) or (5) is to be ignored.

(2) A financial advantage is within this subsection if the person for whom it is obtained applies the advantage for charitable purposes only.

(3) A financial advantage is within this subsection if (ignoring the tainted donation provisions) it is—

(a) a benefit associated with a gift which is a qualifying donation for the purposes of Chapter 2 of Part 8 of ITA 2007 (gift aid), or
(b) a benefit associated with a payment which is a qualifying payment for the purposes of Chapter 2 of Part 6 (charitable donations relief: payments to charity).

(4) A financial advantage is within this subsection if (ignoring the tainted donation provisions)—

(a) the relievable charity donation is a disposal in respect of which tax relief would be available under Chapter 3 of Part 8 of ITA 2007 (gifts of shares, securities and real property to charities etc) or Chapter 3 of Part 6 (charitable donations: certain disposals to charity), and
(b) the advantage is a benefit the value of which would be taken into account in determining the relievable amount in respect of the disposal for the purposes of the Chapter in question.

(5) A financial advantage is within this subsection if (ignoring the tainted donation provisions)—

(a) the relievable charity donation is a gift in respect of which tax relief would be available under section 108 of ITTOIA 2005 or section 105 of CTA 2009 (gifts of trading stock to charities etc), and
(b) the advantage is a benefit attributable to the making of the gift in respect of which an amount would be brought into account under section 109 of ITTOIA 2005 or section 108 of CTA 2009 (receipt of benefits by donor or connected person).

(6) In this section—

"benefit associated with a gift" has the meaning given by section 417 of ITA 2007;
"benefit associated with a payment" has the meaning given by section 196;
"the tainted donation provisions" has the meaning given by section 939B(3).

Removal of reliefs

939F Removal of corporation tax relief in respect of tainted donations etc

(1) This section applies where a tainted donation is made by a company.

(2) Where (ignoring this Part) corporation tax relief would be available in respect of the tainted donation, that relief is not available.

(3) Where—

(a) (ignoring this Part) corporation tax relief would be available in respect of an associated donation, and
(b) entitlement to that relief is not withdrawn by subsection (2),

that relief is not available.

(4) In this section—

"associated donation", in relation to a tainted donation, means a relievable charity donation made—

(a) in accordance with the relevant arrangements, and
(b) by a person, other than—

(i) a qualifying charity-owned company in relation to that relievable charity donation, or
(ii) a relevant housing provider linked (within the meaning of section 939C(7)) with the charity to which that donation is made;

"corporation tax relief" means relief under—

(a) section 63(2)(a), (aa) or (ab) of CAA 2001 (gifts of plant and machinery), so far as it applies in relation to corporation tax,
(b) section 105 of CTA 2009 (gifts of trading stock), or
(c) Part 6 of CTA 2010 (charitable donations relief);

"qualifying charity-owned company" has the meaning given by section 939C(8) (except that paragraph (b) of that definition does not apply);
"relevant housing provider" has the meaning given by section 939C(8);
"the relevant arrangements", in relation to a tainted donation, means the arrangements by reference to which Conditions A to C in section 939C are met.

Supplementary

939G Connected charities

For the purposes of this Part, a "connected charity" in relation to another charity means a charity which is connected with that other charity in a matter relating to the structure, administration or control of either charity.

939H Connected persons

(1) Section 1122 (meaning of "connected" persons) applies for the purposes of this Part (except section 939G), but subject to the following modification.

(2) Section 1122 has effect as if after subsection (8) there were inserted—

"(9) A person who is a beneficiary of a settlement is connected with—

(a) a person in the capacity as trustee of the settlement, and
(b) the settlor in relation to the settlement.

(10) For the purposes of this section—

(a) a man and woman living together as husband and wife are treated as if they were husband and wife,
(b) two people of the same sex living together as if they were civil partners of each other are treated as if they were civil partners of each other, and
(c) "close company" includes a company that would be a close company if it were resident in the United Kingdom."

939I Minor definitions

(1) In this Part—

"arrangements" includes any scheme, arrangement or understanding of any kind, whether or not legally enforceable, involving a single transaction or two or more transactions;
"charity" includes a registered club within the meaning of section 658(6) (meaning of "community amateur sports club" and "registered club").

(2) In this Part, in the case of a charitable trust, references to a charity being entitled to a repayment of tax are to be read as references to the trustees of the trust being so entitled."

PART 3

CAPITAL GAINS TAX

3 After section 257 of TCGA 1992 insert—

"257A Tainted charity donations

(1) Section 257 does not apply in relation to—

(a) a tainted donation made by a person, or
(b) any associated donation.

(2) For the purposes of this section—

(a) "tainted donation" means a tainted donation within the meaning of Chapter 8 of Part 13 of ITA 2007 (tainted charity donations: removal of income tax reliefs etc) or Part 21C of CTA 2010 (tainted charity donations: removal of corporation tax relief), and
(b) "associated donation" means an associated donation within the meaning of section 809ZM of ITA 2010 or section 939F of CTA 2010."

PART 4

CONSEQUENTIAL AMENDMENTS

Capital Allowances Act 2001

4 In section 63 of CAA 2001 (cases in which disposal value is nil), in subsection (4)—

(a) after "Subsection (2)" insert

"—

(a)

(b) at the end insert

", and

(b) is subject to section 809ZM of ITA 2007 and section 939F of CTA 2010 (removal of tax relief in respect of tainted charity donations etc)."

Income Tax (Employment and Pensions) Act 2003

5 In section 713 of ITEPA 2003 (donations to charity: payroll deduction scheme), after subsection (5) insert—

"(6) This section is subject to section 809ZM of ITA 2007 (removal of income tax relief in respect of tainted charity donations etc)."

Income Tax (Trading and Other Income) Act 2005

6 In section 108 of ITTOIA 2005 (gifts of trading stock to charities etc), in subsection (5)—

(a) after "This section" insert

"—

(a)

(b) at the end insert

", and

(b) is subject to section 809ZM of ITA 2007 (removal of income tax relief in respect of tainted charity donations etc)."

Income Tax Act 2007

7 ITA 2007 is amended as follows.

8 In section 30 (calculation of income tax liability: additional tax)—

(a) in subsection (1) before the entry for section 205 of FA 2004 insert—
"section 809ZN (tainted gift aid donations: charge to tax),
section 809ZO (tainted charity donations by trustees: charge to tax),", and

(b) for subsection (2) substitute—

"(2) If the taxpayer is a trustee, the provisions referred to at Step 7 of the calculation in section 23 are—

section 496 (discretionary payments by trustees: tax pool adjustment),
section 809ZN (tainted gift aid donations: charge to tax), and
section 809ZO (tainted charity donations by trustees: charge to tax)."

9 In section 58 (meaning of "adjusted net income), at the end insert—

"(4) Subsection (6) of section 809ZM (removal of income tax relief in respect of tainted donations etc) excludes certain donations from being deducted at step 2 in subsection (1)."

10 In section 413 (gift aid: overview of Chapter), after subsection (4) insert—

"(4A) This Chapter is subject to section 809ZM (removal of income tax relief in respect of tainted charity donations etc)."

11 In section 431 (gifts of shares, securities and real property to charities etc), after subsection (6) insert—

"(7) This Chapter is subject to section 809ZM (removal of income tax relief in respect of tainted charity donations etc)."

12 In section 543 (meaning of "non-charitable expenditure"), omit subsection (1)(g) and (h).

13 Sections 549 to 557 (substantial donor transactions) are repealed.

14 In Schedule 2 (transitionals and savings), omit paragraphs 105 and 106.

15 In Schedule 4 (index of defined expressions), at the appropriate places insert—

"arrangements (in Chapter 8 of Part 13)	section 809ZR"
"charity (in Chapter 8 of Part 13)	paragraph 1 of Schedule 6 to FA 2010 (and see also section 809ZR)"
"the donor (in Chapter 8 of Part 13)	section 809ZJ(3)"
"potentially advantaged person (in Chapter 8 of Part 13)	section 809ZJ(5)"
"relievable charity donation (in Chapter 8 of Part 13)	section 809ZI(1)"

"tainted donation (in Chapter 8 of Part 13)	section 809ZJ".

Housing and Regeneration Act 2008

16 In Schedule 9 (amendment of enactments: Part 1), omit paragraph 34.

Corporation Tax Act 2009

17 In section 105 of CTA 2009 (gifts of trading stock to charities etc), in subsection (6) after "charity)" insert "and section 939F of that Act (removal of corporation tax relief in respect of tainted charity donations etc)".

18 In Schedule 1 (minor and consequential amendments), omit paragraphs 703 and 704.

Corporation Tax Act 2010

19 CTA 2010 is amended as follows.

20 In section 1 (overview of Act), in subsection (4)—

(a) in the opening words for "21" substitute "21C", and

(b) after paragraph (j) insert

", and

(k) tainted donations made to charities (see Part 21C)."

21 In section 189 (relief for qualifying charitable donations), in subsection (5) for "any" substitute "section 939F and to any other".

22 In section 496 (meaning of "non-charitable expenditure"), omit subsection (1)(e) and (f).

23 Sections 502 to 510 (substantial donor transactions) are repealed.

24 In Schedule 1 (minor and consequential amendments), omit paragraphs 532 to 535.

25 In Schedule 2 (transitionals and savings etc), omit paragraphs 73 to 76.

26 In Schedule 4 (index of defined expressions), at the appropriate places insert—

"arrangements (in Part 21C)	section 939I"
"charity (in Part 21C)	paragraph 1 of Schedule 6 to FA 2010 (and see also section 939I)"
"the donor (in Part 21C)	section 939C(3)"
"potentially advantaged person (in Part 21C)	section 939C(5)"
"relievable charity donation (in Part 21C)	section 939B(1)"
"tainted donation (in Part 21C)	section 939C".

PART 5

COMMENCEMENT AND TRANSITIONAL PROVISION

Commencement

27 (1) Subject to sub-paragraph (2), the amendments made by this Schedule have effect in relation to relievable charity donations made on or after 1 April 2011.

(2) The repeals made by paragraphs 12 to 14, 16, 18 and 22 to 25 have effect in relation to any transaction, other than an excluded transaction, occurring on or after 1 April 2013.

(3) A transaction is "excluded" if it is entered into in pursuance of a contract made before 1 April 2013, other than in pursuance of a variation of the contract made on or after that date.

Treatment of existing arrangements

28 In the amendments made by Parts 1 and 2 of this Schedule, references to arrangements include arrangements made, or made and implemented, before 1 April 2011.

Treatment of substantial donor transactions

29 (1) For the purposes of section 549(2) of ITA 2007 (meaning of substantial donor), relievable gifts (within the meaning of section 550 of that Act) received by a charitable trust on or after 1 April 2011 are to be disregarded.

(2) Sub-paragraphs (3) and (4) apply where—

(a) a substantial donor transaction is entered into before, or on or after 1 April 2011, and

(b) that transaction is not tainted.

(3) Where a payment made on or after 1 April 2011 by a charitable trust to a substantial donor in the course of, or for the purposes of, the substantial donor transaction would (in the absence of this sub-paragraph) be treated under section 551(1) or (5) of ITA 2007 as non-charitable expenditure, that payment is not to be so treated.

(4) Where, as a result of the substantial donor transaction, non-charitable expenditure would (in the absence of this sub-paragraph) be treated as incurred under section 551(2) of that Act on or after 1 April 2011, that expenditure is not to be treated as so incurred.

(5) A substantial donor transaction is "tainted" if (and only if) it is reasonable to assume from—

(a) the likely effects of the relevant relievable gifts and the substantial donor transaction, and

(b) the circumstances in which the relevant relievable gifts were made and the circumstances in which the substantial donor transaction was entered into,

that the relevant relievable gifts (or one or more of them) would not have been made and the transaction would not have been entered into independently of one another.

(6) In this section—

"relevant relievable gifts", in relation to the substantial donor transaction, means the relievable gifts by reason of which a person is a substantial donor and the transaction is a substantial donor transaction;

"relievable gift" has the meaning given by section 550 of ITA 2007;

"substantial donor" and "substantial donor transaction" have the meaning given by section 549 of that Act.

30 (1) For the purposes of section 502(2) of CTA 2010 (meaning of substantial donor), relievable gifts (within the meaning of section 503 of that Act) received by a charitable company on or after 1 April 2011 are to be disregarded.

(2) Sub-paragraphs (3) and (4) apply where—

(a) a substantial donor transaction is entered into before, or on or after, 1 April 2011, and

(b) that transaction is not tainted.

(3) Where a payment made on or after 1 April 2011 by a charitable company to a substantial donor in the course of, or for the purposes of, the substantial donor transaction would (in the absence of this sub-paragraph) be treated under section 504(1) or (5) of CTA 2010 as non-charitable expenditure, that payment is not to be so treated.

(4) Where, as a result of the substantial donor transaction, non-charitable expenditure would (in the absence of this sub-paragraph) be treated as incurred under section 504(2) of that Act on or after 1 April 2011, that expenditure is not to be treated as so incurred.

(5) The substantial donor transaction is "tainted" if (and only if) it is reasonable to assume from—

(a) the likely effects of the relevant relievable gifts and the substantial donor transaction, and

(b) the circumstances in which the relevant relievable gifts were made and the circumstances in which the substantial donor transaction was entered into,

that the relevant relievable gifts (or one or more of them) would not have been made and the transaction would not have been entered into independently of one another.

(6) In this section—

"relevant relievable gifts", in relation to the substantial donor transaction, means the relievable gifts by reason of which a person is a substantial donor and the transaction is a substantial donor transaction;

"relievable gift" has the meaning given by section 503 of CTA 2010;

"substantial donor" and "substantial donor transaction" have the meaning given by section 502 of that Act.

Housing (Scotland) Act 2010 (asp 17)

31 Until such time as section 20 of the Housing (Scotland) Act 2010 is brought into force, the references to that section in the following provisions are to be read as references to section 57 of the Housing (Scotland) Act 2001 (asp 10)—

(a) the definition of "relevant housing provider" in section 809ZJ(8) of ITA 2007;

(b) the definition of "relevant housing provider" in section 939C(8) of CTA 2010.

GENERAL NOTE

Schedule 3 introduces new anti-avoidance legislation to prevent the abuse of tax reliefs available to donors to charity. It applies to donations made on or after 1 April

2011 and, for those donations, replaces the Substantial Donors legislation introduced some years ago for the same purpose. However there are transitional provisions, which mean that the Substantial Donors legislation in ITA2007 ss 549–557 and CTA 2010 ss 502–510 remains in respect of earlier donations, applying to relevant transactions carried out or contracted for until 1 April 2013.

The new sections withdraw tax relief on donations made on or after 1 April 2011 where the donor obtains a financial advantage as a result of arrangements related to the donation, whether the arrangements are made before or after that date.

In all cases, the donor includes a connected person and is referred to in the legislation as a "linked person". For this purpose, the definition of a connected person is extended from the normal definition used in the Taxes Acts. A man and woman living together as husband and wife are treated as husband and wife and two people of the same sex living together as if they were civil partners are treated as civil partners. A company, which would be a close company if resident in the UK, is treated as a close company.

The schedule applies to income tax, capital gains tax and corporation tax reliefs and exemptions for donations to charities by individuals and companies. Because these are contained in ITA 2007 for individuals and CTA 2010 for companies, the legislation in Parts 1 and 2 of this Schedule introduce new sections into both acts which are identical apart from any matters which can only relate exclusively to individuals and trusts or to companies. Part 3 of the schedule dis-applies TCGA 1992 s 257 to prevent relief from capital gains tax on a gift of an asset to a charity where it meets the definition of a tainted donation. Part 4 contains consequential amendments to other legislation and Part 5 deals with the commencement of the new rules and transitional provisions.

The legislation applies to any gift on which tax relief is available to the donor or in respect of which the charity can claim a tax repayment, specifically, gifts of chargeable assets, gifts of plant and machinery, payroll giving, gifts of trading stock, gift aid, gifts of shares and property and donations by companies. In order to be a tainted donation, 3 conditions have to be met:

1. The donor makes arrangements without which it is reasonable to assume the donation would not otherwise have been made and the arrangements not entered into. The arrangements can be made before or after the donation.
2. The main purpose or one of the main purposes of the donor entering into the arrangements is to obtain a financial advantage.
3. The donor is not a company wholly owned by one or more charities or a relevant housing provider. This is to stop the new rules applying to arrangements where charities use their own companies to avoid paying tax on certain income that is intended for the charity's use, such as trading subsidiaries.

Arrangements are very widely defined and include any kind of understanding or agreement between two or more people. It does not have to be a legally enforceable agreement.

A financial advantage is ignored if it is applied for charitable purposes and also if it is already covered by the legislation on gift aid or gifts of shares and property, where financial benefits are already taken into account in calculating the relief available.

A financial advantage for the purposes of the above conditions is where the donor enters into a transaction with someone else and the terms are less beneficial to the other person or more beneficial to the donor than might reasonably be expected in an arm's length transaction. It is also where the transaction is not of a kind that the other person, dealing at arm's length, might reasonably be expected to make. The legislation is therefore very wide and depends on an interpretation of what might reasonably be expected by two parties acting at arm's length. The section specifically states that nothing in it is intended to limit the circumstances in which a financial advantage might be obtained but gives as examples the sale or letting of property, the provision of services, the exchange of property, the making of a loan or giving other financial assistance and investment in a business. The donation then becomes tainted.

Where there is a tainted donation, the tax relief available to the donor is withdrawn and if relief has already been given, a tax charge can be made. Where gift aid has been claimed and a repayment of tax has been made to the charity, this can be recovered, under a joint and several liability, from the donor, each potentially advantaged person, the charity concerned and a charity connected in a matter relating to structure, administration or control. However, recovery of tax can only be made from a charity if it was a party to the arrangements and was aware at the time that the donor was making the arrangements for the main purpose (or one of the main purposes) of obtaining a financial advantage.

These new rules are based on a purpose test which considers why the donor entered into arrangements with a charity and to what extent those arrangements gave the donor a financial advantage. Therefore, only those donors arranging a financial advantage need to consider whether the new rules apply to their donation. The rules can also be ignored if the financial advantage has to be taken into account in calculating the relief available under the rules for gift aid, gifts of shares or property or trading stock.

If a donation is tainted, it is the donor who will normally suffer a tax charge, not the charity (as is the case with the Substantial Donor rules), although a charity may be required to repay a tax repayment it has had on a gift aid donation to the extent that it cannot be recovered from the donor, with whom there is joint and several liability and the charity was aware that the financial advantage being obtained was one of the main purposes of the making the donation.

SCHEDULE 4

AMOUNTS NOT FULLY RECOGNISED FOR ACCOUNTING PURPOSES

Section 28

Loan relationships

1 Part 5 of CTA 2009 (loan relationships) is amended as follows.

2 (1) Section 311 (amounts not fully recognised for accounting purposes) is amended as follows.

(2) In subsection (2)—

(a) at the end of paragraph (a) insert "and", and

(b) for paragraphs (b) and (c) substitute—

"(b) as a result of tax avoidance arrangements to which the company is at any time a party, an amount is (in accordance with generally accepted accounting practice) not fully recognised for the period in respect of the creditor relationship."

(3) Omit subsections (3) to (5A).

(4) In subsection (6)—

(a) in the opening words—

(i) after "section" insert "and section 312", and

(ii) omit ", a contribution to it or securities issued by it", and

(b) in paragraphs (a) and (b), omit ", contribution or securities".

(5) After subsection (6) insert—

"(7) For the purposes of this section arrangements are "tax avoidance arrangements" if the main purpose, or one of the main purposes, of any party to the arrangements, in entering into them, is to obtain a tax advantage.

(8) In subsection (7) "arrangements" includes any arrangements, scheme or understanding of any kind, whether or not legally enforceable, involving a single transaction or two or more transactions.

(9) For the purposes of this section a company is to be treated as a party to a creditor relationship even though it has disposed of its rights under the relationship to another person—

(a) under a repo or stock lending arrangement, or

(b) under a transaction which is treated as not involving any disposal as a result of section 26 of TCGA 1992 (mortgages and charges not to be treated as disposals)."

3 (1) Section 312 (determination of credits and debits where amounts not fully recognised) is amended as follows.

(2) For subsection (1A) substitute—

"(1A) Subsection (1B) applies in a case where—

(a) pursuant to the arrangements mentioned in section 311(2)(b), the company becomes, or is treated as becoming, a party to a debtor relationship, and

(b) an amount is (in accordance with generally accepted accounting practice) not fully recognised for any period in respect of the debtor relationship."

(3) In subsection (1B) omit "by reference to which that condition is met".

(4) In subsection (3) for "But" substitute

"But—

(a) no debits are, as a result of this section, to be brought into account by the company in respect of the creditor relationship mentioned in section 311(2), and

(b)

4 In section 440 (overview of Chapter 15), in subsection (2), omit the "and" at the end of paragraph (e), and after paragraph (f) insert

", and

(g) for rules about debits arising as a result of the derecognition of creditor relationships, see section 455A."

5 After section 455 insert—

"Derecognition

455A Debits arising from derecognition of creditor relationships

(1) This section applies where—

(a) a company is at any time a party to tax avoidance arrangements,

(b) as a result of those arrangements, a creditor relationship to which the company is party, or any part of such a relationship, is (in accordance with generally accepted accounting practice) derecognised by the company, and

(c) the company continues to be a party to the creditor relationship immediately after the transaction or other event giving rise to the derecognition.

(2) No debit that would apart from this section be brought into account by the company for the purposes of this Part as a result of the derecognition is to be so brought into account.

(3) An amount that would be brought into account for the purposes of this Part as respects any matter apart from this section—

(a) is treated for the purposes of section 464(1) (priority of this Part for corporation tax purposes) as if it were so brought into account, and

(b) accordingly, may not be brought into account for any other corporation tax purposes as respects that matter.

(4) For the purposes of this section a company is to be treated as a party to a creditor relationship even though it has disposed of its rights under the relationship to another person—

(a) under a repo or stock lending arrangement, or

(b) under a transaction which is treated as not involving any disposal as a result of section 26 of TCGA 1992 (mortgages and charges not to be treated as disposals).

(5) For the purposes of this section arrangements are "tax avoidance arrangements" if the main purpose, or one of the main purposes, of any party to the arrangements, in entering into them, is to obtain a tax advantage.

(6) In subsection (5) "arrangements" includes any arrangements, scheme or understanding of any kind, whether or not legally enforceable, involving a single transaction or two or more transactions."

6 In section 464 (priority of Part for corporation tax purposes), in subsection (4), omit the "and" at the end of paragraph (a) and after paragraph (b) insert

", and

(c) section 455A(3) (debits arising from derecognition of creditor relationships)."

Derivative contracts

7 Part 7 of CTA 2009 (derivative contracts) is amended as follows.

8 (1) Section 599A (amounts not fully recognised for accounting purposes) is amended as follows.

(2) In subsection (2)—

(a) at the end of paragraph (a) insert "and", and

(b) for paragraphs (b) and (c) substitute—

"(b) as a result of tax avoidance arrangements to which the company is at any time a party, an amount is (in accordance with generally accepted accounting practice) not fully recognised for the period in respect of the contract."

(3) Omit subsections (3) to (5B).

(4) In subsection (6)—

(a) in the opening words, omit ", a contribution to it or securities issued by it", and

(b) in paragraphs (a) and (b), omit ", contribution or securities".

(5) After subsection (6) insert—

"(7) For the purposes of this section arrangements are "tax avoidance arrangements" if the main purpose, or one of the main purposes, of any party to the arrangements, in entering into them, is to obtain a tax advantage.

(8) In subsection (7)—

(a) "arrangements" includes any arrangements, scheme or understanding of any kind, whether or not legally enforceable, involving a single transaction or two or more transactions, and

(b) "tax advantage" has the meaning given by section 1139 of CTA 2010.

(9) For the purposes of this section a company is to be treated as a party to a derivative contract even though it has disposed of its rights and liabilities under the contract to another person—

(a) under a repo or stock lending arrangement, or

(b) under a transaction which is treated as not involving any disposal as a result of section 26 of TCGA 1992 (mortgages and charges not to be treated as disposals)."

9 (1) Section 599B (determination of credits and debits where amounts not fully recognised) is amended as follows.

(2) After subsection (2) insert—

"(2A) But no debits are, as a result of this section, to be brought into account by the company in respect of the derivative contract."

(3) After subsection (3) insert—

"(4) If—

(a) the company is, or is treated as, a party to the contract at the beginning of the period referred to in section 599A(1), and

(b) the fair value of the contract at that time is greater than the carrying value of that contract at that time,

a credit of an amount equal to the difference is to be brought into account for that period for the purposes of this Part in respect of the contract."

10 In section 689 (overview of Chapter 11), in subsection (2), omit the "and" at the end of paragraph (c), and after paragraph (d) insert

", and

(e) for rules about debits arising as a result of the derecognition of derivative contracts, see section 698A."

11 After section 698 insert—

"Derecognition

698A Debits arising from derecognition of derivative contracts

(1) This section applies where—

(a) a company is at any time a party to tax avoidance arrangements,

(b) as a result of those arrangements, a derivative contract to which the company is party, or any part of such a contract, is (in accordance with generally accepted accounting practice) derecognised by the company, and

(c) the company continues to be a party to the derivative contract immediately after the transaction or other event giving rise to the derecognition.

(2) No debit that would apart from this section be brought into account by the company for the purposes of this Part as a result of the derecognition is to be so brought into account.

(3) An amount that would be brought into account for the purposes of this Part as respects any matter apart from this section—

(a) is treated for the purposes of section 699(1) (priority of this Part for corporation tax purposes) as if it were so brought into account, and

(b) accordingly, may not be brought into account for any other corporation tax purposes as respects that matter.

(4) For the purposes of this section a company is to be treated as a party to a derivative contract even though it has disposed of its rights and liabilities under the contract to another person—

(a) under a repo or stock lending arrangement, or

(b) under a transaction which is treated as not involving any disposal as a result of section 26 of TCGA 1992 (mortgages and charges not to be treated as disposals).

(5) For the purposes of this section arrangements are "tax avoidance arrangements" if the main purpose, or one of the main purposes, of any party to the arrangements, in entering into them, is to obtain a tax advantage.

(6) In subsection (5)—

(a) "arrangements" includes any arrangements, scheme or understanding of any kind, whether or not legally enforceable, involving a single transaction or two or more transactions, and

(b) "tax advantage" has the meaning given by section 1139 of CTA 2010."

Consequential repeals

12 In consequence of the amendments made by this Schedule, omit—

(a) in Schedule 30 to FA 2009, paragraph 2(1) to (6), and

(b) in Schedule 5 to F(No2)A 2010, paragraphs 1 and 3.

Commencement

13 (1) The amendments made by this Schedule have effect in relation to periods of account beginning on or after 6 December 2010.

(2) But, for the purposes of sub-paragraph (1), a period of account beginning before, and ending on or after, 6 December 2010 is to be treated as if so much of the period as falls before that date, and so much of the period as falls on or after that date, were separate periods of account.

(3) The following provisions of CTA 2009 do not have effect where they apply by reason of tax avoidance arrangements to which the company became a party before 23 March 2011—

(a) section 312(3)(a) (as inserted by paragraph 3(4) of this Schedule);

(b) section 599B(2A) (as inserted by paragraph 9(2) of this Schedule);

(c) section 599B(4) (as inserted by paragraph 9(3) of this Schedule).

GENERAL NOTE

Schedule 4 makes changes to CTA 2009 s 311 (loan relationships) and s 599A (derivative contracts). These provisions apply where an amount is not fully recognised in a company's accounts in accordance with generally accepted accounting practice in respect of a loan relationship or a derivative contract respectively. Before the changes made by Schedule 4 took effect, the sections applied where prescribed conditions were satisfied. These prescribed conditions have now been replaced by a more general requirement that an amount is not fully recognised in respect of a creditor relationship or a derivative contract respectively as a result of tax avoidance arrangements to which the company is at any time a party. These changes apply for amounts relating to times on or after 6 December 2010 (see sub-paras 13(1), (2)).

Where a company becomes a party to the tax avoidance arrangements on or after 23 March 2011 it will not be permitted to bring any debits into account under CTA 2009 s 312 (in respect of the creditor relationship) or s 599B (in respect of the derivative contract) (see para 13(3)). Payments under a derivative can flow both ways. It is understood that HMRC will be publishing guidance in which they will indicate that relief will only be denied for a net debit arising on a derivative contract in an accounting period under the new CTA 2009 s 599B(2A), rather than for all debits arising on the contract in that period. Further, in the case of a derivative contract, where a company is (or is treated as being) a party to the contract at the start of the first accounting period to which CTA 2009 s 599A applies and the fair value of the contract at that time is greater than its carrying value in the company's accounts, the company will be required to include a credit equal to the difference in computing its derivative contract profits for that period (CTA 2009 s 599B). This change applies where the company became a party to the tax avoidance arrangements on or after 23 March 2011 (para 13(3)).

At the same time new CTA 2009 ss 455A and 698A have been introduced into the loan relationship legislation and the derivative contracts legislation respectively. Under these new sections a company will be denied relief for any debits arising from the derecognition of a creditor relationship or derivative contract respectively in its accounts where the company continues to be a party to the creditor relationship or derivative and the derecognition results from tax avoidance arrangements to which the company is at any time a party. A company is treated as continuing to be a party to a creditor relationship or derivative contract where it disposes of the creditor relationship or derivative under a repo or stock lending transaction, or where the creditor relationship or derivative contract is transferred in order to provide security for a loan. It would be very unusual for a derivative contract to be transferred under a repo or stock loan and the reason for this wording in CTA 2009 s 698A is probably because the draftsman copied the equivalent provisions that are applied in the case of loan relationships. In each case these changes apply for times on or after 6 December 2010 (see sub-paras 13(1), (2)).

SCHEDULE 5

GROUP MISMATCH SCHEMES

Section 30

Insertion of new Part 21B of CTA 2010 and consequential amendments

1 In section 1(4) of CTA 2010 (overview of Act), omit the "and" at the end of paragraph (h), and after paragraph (i) insert—

"(j) group mismatch schemes (see Part 21B)."

2 After Part 21A of that Act insert—

"PART 21B

GROUP MISMATCH SCHEMES

938A Losses and profits from group mismatch schemes to be disregarded

(1) This section applies to a company that—

(a) is (at any time) a party to a group mismatch scheme, and
(b) is a member of the scheme group.

(2) No scheme loss or profit made by the company in any accounting period in relation to the scheme is to be brought into account as a debit or credit for the purposes of Part 5 of CTA 2009 (loan relationships) or Part 7 of that Act (derivative contracts).

(3) An amount that would, apart from this section, be brought into account for the purposes of Part 5 or 7 of that Act as respects any matter—

(a) is treated, for the purposes of section 464(1) or (as the case may be) 699(1) of that Act (priority of Part 5 or 7 for corporation tax purposes) as if it were so brought into account, and
(b) accordingly, may not be brought into account for any other corporation tax purposes as respects that matter.

938B Meaning of "a group mismatch scheme" and "the scheme group"

(1) A scheme is "a group mismatch scheme" if—

(a) the parties to the scheme are, or include, members of the same group, and
(b) condition A or B is met.

(2) Condition A is that, at the time the scheme is entered into, there is no practical likelihood that the scheme will fail to secure a relevant tax advantage of £2 million or more.

(3) The Treasury may by order substitute a higher amount for the amount for the time being specified in subsection (2).

(4) Any such substitution is to have effect in relation to schemes entered into on or after the day on which the order comes into force.

(5) Condition B is that—

(a) the purpose, or one of the main purposes, of any member of the scheme group in entering into the scheme is to obtain the chance of securing a relevant tax advantage (of any amount), and
(b) at the time the scheme is entered into—

(i) there is no chance that the scheme will secure a relevant tax disadvantage, or
(ii) there is such a chance, but the expected value of the scheme is nevertheless a positive amount.

(6) If, at the time the company enters into the scheme, there are chances that the scheme would, if carried out, secure different relevant tax advantages or disadvantages in different circumstances, the amounts and probabilities of each must be taken into account in determining the expected value of the scheme.

(7) In determining whether condition A or B is met, it is to be assumed that the parties to the scheme carry it out.

(8) Where, at the time the scheme is entered into, the length of the scheme period is uncertain, condition A or B is met if it would be met on any reasonable assumption as to the length of the scheme period.

(9) In determining whether condition A or B is met, section 938A (scheme profits and losses to be left out of account) is to be disregarded.

(10) In this Part "the scheme group" means the group mentioned in subsection (1)(a).

938C Meaning of "scheme loss" and "scheme profit"

(1) A loss or profit made by a company in an accounting period is a "scheme loss" or "scheme profit" in relation to a group mismatch scheme if the loss or profit—

(a) arises from a transaction, or series of transactions, that forms part of the scheme,

(b) is, or is comprised in, an amount that is brought into account as a debit or credit for the purposes of Part 5 or 7 of CTA 2009, and

(c) meets the first or second asymmetry condition.

(2) The first asymmetry condition is that the loss or profit affects the amount of any relevant tax advantage secured by the scheme.

(3) Where, at the end of the accounting period—

(a) it is not certain whether the scheme will secure a relevant tax advantage, or

(b) it is not certain what the amount of the relevant tax advantage secured by the scheme will be,

a loss or profit is to be treated as meeting the first asymmetry condition if, at that time, there is a chance that the scheme will secure a relevant tax advantage and that the loss or profit will affect its amount.

(4) Where—

(a) a loss or profit meets the conditions in subsection (1)(a) and (b), and

(b) a part, but not the whole, of the loss or profit meets the first asymmetry condition,

only that part of the loss or profit is a "scheme loss" or "scheme profit".

(5) The second asymmetry condition is that the loss or profit—

(a) does not meet the first asymmetry condition, but

(b) arises from a transaction, or series of transactions, that might (if events had turned out differently) have given rise to a loss or profit that would have done so.

(6) References in this section to a loss or profit include a loss or profit arising in respect of interest or expenses.

(7) In determining whether the condition in subsection (1)(b) or the first or second asymmetry condition is met, section 938A (scheme profits and losses to be left out of account) is to be disregarded.

938D Meaning of "relevant tax advantage" etc and "the scheme period"

(1) In this Part "relevant tax advantage", in relation to a scheme, means an economic profit that—

(a) is made by the scheme group over the scheme period,

(b) meets the condition in subsection (3), and

(c) is not negligible.

(2) In this Part "relevant tax disadvantage", in relation to a scheme, means an economic loss that—

(a) is made by the scheme group over the scheme period,

(b) meets the condition in subsection (3), and

(c) is not negligible.

(3) The condition is that the economic profit or loss arises as a result of asymmetries in the way different members of the scheme group bring, or do not bring, amounts into account as debits and credits for the purposes of Part 5 or 7 of CTA 2009.

(4) A reference in this section to asymmetries includes, in particular—

(a) asymmetries relating to quantification, and

(b) asymmetries relating to timing.

(5) In this section—

(a) a reference to an economic profit includes an increase in an economic profit and a decrease in an economic loss, and

(b) a reference to an economic loss includes an increase in an economic loss and a decrease in an economic profit.

(6) In this Part "the scheme period", in relation to a scheme, means the period during which the scheme has effect.

938E Meaning of "group"

(1) For the purposes of this Part a company ("company A") is a member of a group, in relation to a scheme, if any other company is at any time in the scheme period associated with company A.

(2) The group consists of company A and each company in relation to which the condition in subsection (1) is met.

(3) For the purposes of this section a company ("company B") is associated with company A at a time ("the relevant time") if any of the following five conditions is met.

(4) The first condition is that the financial results of company A and company B, for a period that includes the relevant time, meet the consolidation condition.

(5) The second condition is that there is a connection between company A and company B for the accounting period of company A in which the relevant time falls.

(6) The third condition is that, at the relevant time, company A has a major interest in company B or company B has a major interest in company A.

(7) The fourth condition is that—

(a) the financial results of company A and a third company, for a period that includes the relevant time, meet the consolidation condition, and

(b) at the relevant time the third company has a major interest in company B.

(8) The fifth condition is that—

(a) there is a connection between company A and a third company for the accounting period of company A in which the relevant time falls, and

(b) at the relevant time the third company has a major interest in company B.

(9) In this section, the financial results of any two companies for any period meet "the consolidation condition" if—

(a) they are required to be comprised in group accounts,

(b) they would be required to be comprised in such accounts but for the application of an exemption, or

(c) they are in fact comprised in such accounts.

(10) In subsection (9), "group accounts" means accounts prepared under—

(a) section 399 of the Companies Act 2006, or

(b) any corresponding provision of the law of a territory outside the United Kingdom.

(11) The following provisions apply for the purposes of this section—

sections 466 to 471 of CTA 2009 (companies connected for accounting period), and sections 473 and 474 of CTA 2009 (meaning of "major interest").

938F Meaning of references to economic profits and losses

(1) An economic profit or loss is to be computed for the purposes of this Part taking into account, in particular—

(a) profits and losses made as a result of the operation of the Corporation Tax Acts, and

(b) any adjustments required to reflect the time value of money.

(2) A reference in this Part to an economic profit or loss made by the scheme group over the scheme period is to an economic profit or loss made in that period by the members of the group considered together.

(3) In determining for the purposes of this Part the amount of an economic profit or loss made by the scheme group over the scheme period, profits and losses made by a member of the group are to be taken into account only to the extent that they are attributable to times at which the member is a party to the scheme.

938G Tax capacity assumption

(1) This section applies for the purpose of determining whether a scheme will, or might, secure a relevant tax advantage.

(2) The economic profits and losses made by the scheme group over the scheme period must be calculated on the assumption that each company that is at any time a party to the scheme—

(a) obtains the full tax benefit of any loss made by that company in relation to a loan relationship or a derivative contract during the period, and

(b) incurs the full tax cost of any profit made by that company in relation to a loan relationship or a derivative contract during the period.

(3) The "full tax benefit" of a loss is the reduction in the liability of the company to corporation tax that would result if—

(a) the loss were brought into account as a debit or as a reduction in a credit for the purposes of Part 5 or 7 of CTA 2009, and

(b) the company's profits chargeable to corporation tax, disregarding the loss, were equal to the debit (or the reduction in the credit) determined by reference to the loss.

(4) The "full tax cost" of a profit is the increase in the liability of the company to corporation tax that would result if—

(a) the profit were brought into account as a credit or as a reduction in a debit for the purposes of Part 5 or 7 of CTA 2009, and

(b) the company's profits chargeable to corporation tax, disregarding the profit, were nil.

938H Meaning of "scheme"

In this Part "scheme" includes any scheme, arrangements or understanding of any kind whatever, whether or not legally enforceable, involving a single transaction or two or more transactions.

938I Schemes involving repos or quasi-repos

(1) This section applies where—

(a) a scheme includes an arrangement under which a member of the scheme group has a debtor repo or a debtor quasi-repo, and

(b) the advance under that arrangement is received, directly or indirectly, from a member of the scheme group.

(2) References in this Part to amounts brought into account, or not brought into account, as debits or credits for the purposes of Part 5 of CTA 2009 include amounts brought into account, or not brought into account, for the purposes of any other provision so far as it applies the charge to corporation tax on income to the repayment of the advance.

(3) Sections 548 and 549 of CTA 2009 (meaning of debtor repo and debtor quasi-repo) apply for the purposes of this section.

(4) For the purposes of subsection (2) "the repayment of the advance" means the consideration given on the purchase of securities mentioned in condition D in section 548 or 549 of CTA 2009.

938J Schemes involving finance arrangements

(1) This section applies in relation to a scheme if—

(a) it includes a type 1, 2 or 3 finance arrangement under which a member of the scheme group is the borrower, and

(b) the advance under that arrangement is received, directly or indirectly, from a member of the scheme group.

(2) References in this Part to amounts brought into account, or not brought into account, as debits or credits for the purposes of Part 5 of CTA 2009 include amounts brought into account, or not brought into account, for the purposes of any other provision so far as it applies the charge to corporation tax on income to the repayment of the advance.

(3) Sections 758, 763 and 767 of this Act (meaning of type 1, 2 and 3 finance arrangements) apply for the purposes of this section.

(4) For the purposes of subsection (2) "the repayment of the advance" means the payments mentioned in condition A in section 758, 763 or 767 of this Act.

938K Trading income

References in this Part to amounts brought into account, or not brought into account, as debits or credits for the purposes of Part 5 or 7 of CTA 2009 include amounts brought into account, or not brought into account, as expenses or receipts of a trade by virtue of section 297 or 573 of that Act (trading credits and debits to be brought into account under Part 3).

938L Foreign companies and foreign permanent establishments

(1) References in this Part to a company not bringing amounts into account as debits or credits for the purposes of Part 5 or 7 of CTA 2009 do not include the company not bringing amounts into account by virtue of—

(a) the company being non-UK resident, or

(b) an election under section 18A of CTA 2009 (profits or losses of foreign permanent establishments).

(2) See section 938M for provision about controlled foreign companies.

938M Controlled foreign companies

(1) Paragraph 5(1) of Schedule 24 to ICTA (assumption that a controlled foreign company is not a member of any group for the purposes of any provision of the Tax Acts) does not apply for the purposes of this Part.

(2) References in this Part to a company bringing amounts into account, or not bringing them into account, as debits or credits for the purposes of Part 5 or 7 of CTA 2009 include bringing amounts into account, or not bringing them into account, as debits or credits under that Part in determining the chargeable profits of the company (or in determining that there were no such profits) for the purposes of Chapter 4 of Part 17 of ICTA (controlled foreign companies).

938N Priority

For the purposes of this Part the following provisions are to be treated as of no effect—

(a) section 441 of CTA 2009 (loan relationships for unallowable purposes);
(b) section 690 of that Act (derivative contracts for unallowable purposes);
(c) Part 4 of TIOPA 2010 (transfer pricing);
(d) Part 6 of that Act (tax arbitrage);
(e) Part 7 of that Act (tax treatment of financing costs and income)."

3 (1) Sections 938 to 940 of that Act are renumbered as follows—

(a) section 938 becomes section 940A,
(b) section 939 becomes section 940B, and
(c) section 940 becomes section 940C.

(2) In section 940A (as so renumbered)—

(a) in subsection (2), for "939" substitute "940B",
(b) in subsection (3), for "940" substitute "940C".

4 (1) Schedule 4 to that Act (index of defined expressions) is amended as follows.

(2) In the entry for "the predecessor (in Chapter 1 of Part 24)"—

(a) for "24" substitute "22", and
(b) for "939(4)" substitute "940B(4)".

(3) In the entry for "the successor (in Chapter 1 of Part 22)", for "939(4)" substitute "940B(4)".

(4) In the entry for "trade (in Chapter 1 of Part 22)", for "939(5)" substitute "940B(5)".

(5) In the entry for "transfer of a trade (in Chapter 1 of Part 24)"—

(a) for "24" substitute "22", and
(b) for "939(2)" substitute "940B(2)".

(6) In the entry for "the transferred trade (in Chapter 1 of Part 24)"—

(a) for "24" substitute "22", and
(b) for "939(3)" substitute "940B(3)".

(7) At the appropriate places insert—

"economic loss (in Part 21B)	section 938F"
"economic profit (in Part 21B)	section 938F"
"group (in Part 21B)	section 938E"
"a group mismatch scheme (in Part 21B)	section 938B"
"relevant tax advantage (in Part 21B)	section 938D"
"relevant tax disadvantage (in Part 21B)	section 938D"
"scheme (in Part 21B)	section 938H"
"the scheme group (in Part 21B)	section 938B"
"scheme loss (in Part 21B)	section 938C"
"the scheme period (in Part 21B)	section 938D"
"scheme profit (in Part 21B)	section 938C "

5 (1) In section 147(6) of TIOPA 2010 (transfer pricing: basic rule), omit the "and" at the end of paragraph (e) and at the end of paragraph (f) insert

", and

(g) section 938N of CTA 2010 (this Part treated as of no effect for the purposes of Part 21B of CTA 2010 (group mismatch schemes))."

(2) In section 231 of that Act (tax arbitrage: overview), after subsection (7) insert—

"(8) This Part has effect subject to section 938N of CTA 2010 (this Part treated as of no effect for the purposes of Part 21B of CTA 2010 (group mismatch schemes))."

Commencement of new Part 21B of CTA 2010 and consequential amendments

6 (1) The amendments made by paragraphs 1, 2 and 5 have effect in relation to schemes entered into at any time (including any time before the commencement date).

(2) But section 938A in Part 21B of CTA 2010 (as inserted by paragraph 2) does not apply to—

(a) scheme losses or profits that relate to a time before the commencement date, or

(b) scheme profits that relate to a time on or after that date but are made in relation to a scheme entered into before that date.

(3) In this Schedule "the commencement date" means the day on which this Act is passed.

Repeal of sections 418 to 419 of CTA 2009

7 (1) Omit sections 418 to 419 of CTA 2009 (loan relationships treated differently by connected debtor and creditor).

(2) In consequence of the repeals made by sub-paragraph (1), omit—

(a) in section 748ZA of ICTA (as inserted by paragraph 5 of Schedule 12 to this Act), subsection (5)(a),

(b) in Schedule 30 to FA 2009, paragraph 4,

(c) in section 416 of CTA 2009, subsection (4),

(d) in Schedule 1 to CTA 2010, paragraph 615, and

(e) section 29 of this Act.

(3) The repeals made by this paragraph have effect in relation to loan relationships to which a company is a party (or to which it is treated as a party under section 418(6A) of CTA 2009) on or after the commencement date.

(4) But amounts are to continue to be brought into account for the purposes of Part 5 of CTA 2009 disregarding the repeals made by sub-paragraph (1) if the amounts relate to a time before the commencement date; and the repeals made by sub-paragraph (2) have effect accordingly.

Repeal of section 453 of CTA 2009

8 (1) Omit section 453 of CTA 2009 (connected parties deriving benefit from creditor relationships).

(2) That repeal has effect in relation to loan relationships to which a company is a party on or after the commencement date.

(3) But amounts are to continue to be brought into account for the purposes of Part 5 of CTA 2009 disregarding that repeal if the amounts relate to a time before the commencement date.

GENERAL NOTE

The purpose of s 30 and Sch 5, according to HMRC, is to ensure that groups of companies cannot use loan relationships or derivative contracts to reduce their tax liabilities purely as a result of asymmetries in the way that different members of the group bring amounts into account under CTA 2009 Parts 5 or 7.

The enactment of the legislation follows the publication of consultation documents by HMRC in March and December 2010. HMRC's stated concern is that groups of companies often operate as single economic entities, without regard to the position of the individual companies in the group; but, in contrast, UK tax legislation is generally concerned with the profits and losses of individual companies. This difference presents an arbitrage opportunity. Intra-group transactions may be structured in a way which gives rise to asymmetrical tax treatments, as a result of which a tax deductible loss is recognised by one company in the group but the other member of the group does not recognise an equivalent taxable profit. Since the transaction is intra-group, it will not feature in the group's consolidated accounts, and its main, or possibly only, purpose may be to reduce the group's effective tax rate.

HMRC say that many avoidance schemes of this nature have been notified to them under the FA 2004 disclosure rules. The notified schemes generally involve the use of financial instruments such as loans, arrangements economically equivalent to loans or derivatives to create group mismatches. The examples mentioned by HMRC include the following:

(a) Example 1: Company A and Company B are within the same group. Company A issues a £100 million zero coupon bond to Company B that can be converted into ordinary shares in Company A. Company A accounts for the bond in accordance with International Accounting Standards and bifurcates the bond into an equity element valued at £10 million and a debt element of £90 million. Company B accounts using old UK Generally Accepted Accounting Practice and therefore does not bifurcate the bond for accounting purposes and so accounts for the debt element at £100 million. Company A claims a finance charge of £10 million over the life of the bond whereas Company B brings in no equivalent credits.

(b) Example 2: Company A holds shares in a US subsidiary. Company A is a subsidiary of Company B and both companies account in sterling. Company B hedges the shares by borrowing in US dollars from a third party and on-lends this US dollar amount to Company A. The loan between Company A and Company B is a US dollar loan (meaning that B would normally have to repay the dollars at any exchange rate reflecting the exchange rate at the time of repayment), but B has an option to repay the loan for the sterling equivalent using the exchange rate when the loan was entered into. There are then two alternative outcomes:

    Scenario 1: If the US dollar weakens, the option for the internal loan to be repaid in sterling is not exercised. The loan is therefore repaid in US dollars. Company B makes an exchange gain on the external borrowing and an equivalent loss on the internal loan. Company A's exchange gain on the internal loan is not taxed because it is matched with the shares.

    Scenario 2: If the US dollar strengthens, the option to repay the internal loan in sterling is exercised. Consequently, company B makes an exchange loss on the external loan without a corresponding exchange gain on the internal loan.

There are already a number of statutory provisions which counter specific arrangements of this kind. Indeed, HMRC acknowledge that they could challenge Example 1 under CTA 2009 s 418 and Example 2 under CTA 2009 ss 328A–328H. However, HMRC's stated aim is to counter this area of perceived avoidance using a more generic or principles-based approach.

By way of very broad summary, the legislation is intended to apply where two or more companies that are members of a group are party to a scheme which is practically certain to give rise to a tax advantage arising from asymmetrical tax treatments in respect of a loan or derivative, or the group members enter into a scheme for the main purpose of obtaining the chance of securing such an advantage. Where the legislation applies, its intended effect is that the tax advantage arising from that asymmetry will be countered.

CTA 2010 new ss 938A–938N

New s 938A sets out the basic operative rule, that if a company is party to a "group mismatch scheme" at any time in an accounting period and is a member of the "scheme group", then no "scheme loss" or "scheme profit" arising to the company in that period will be brought into account as a debit or credit under the loan relationships or derivative contracts regimes or under any other corporation tax provision.

New s 938B principally defines a "group mismatch scheme". A "scheme" (see new section 938H below) will be a "group mismatch scheme" essentially if the parties to the scheme include members of the same "group" (see new section 938E below) and either:

- at the time when the scheme is entered into, there is no practical likelihood that the scheme will fail to secure a "relevant tax advantage" of £2 million or more; or
- the purpose, or one of the main purposes, of any member of the group in entering into the scheme is to obtain the chance of securing a "relevant tax advantage" and, at the time when the scheme is entered into, either (a) there is no chance that the scheme will secure a "relevant tax disadvantage" or (b) there is such a chance, but the expected value of the scheme is nevertheless a positive amount.

Both of these conditions are tested at the outset of the scheme, and not with the benefit of hindsight.

New s 938C defines the terms "scheme loss" and "scheme profit". A loss or profit made by a company in an accounting period will be a "scheme loss" or "scheme profit" essentially if it:

— arises from a transaction, or series of transactions, that forms part of a "group mismatch scheme";
— is, or is comprised in, an amount that is brought into account as a debit or credit for the purposes of CTA 2009 Parts 5 or 7; and
— either:
  (a) the loss or profit affects the amount of any "relevant tax advantage" secured by the scheme; or
  (b) the loss or profit arises from a transaction, or series of transactions, that might (if events had turned out differently) have given rise to a loss or profit that would have done so. This condition (b) will be relevant if a scheme is a "group mismatch scheme" in an accounting period because it satisfies condition (a) above, scheme losses arising in that accounting period are disallowed under the legislation, and then in a later accounting period it becomes clear that the scheme will not produce a "relevant tax advantage". This condition (b) ensures that the scheme can remain a "group mismatch scheme" in the later accounting period and any profit arising from the scheme in that accounting period will be exempted from tax under the legislation.

New s 938D principally defines a "relevant tax advantage". This is defined essentially as an "economic profit" that:

(a) is made by the scheme group over the relevant period;
(b) arises as a result of asymmetries in the way that different members of the scheme group bring, or do not bring, amounts into account as debits and credits for the purposes of Part 5 or 7 CTA 2009. This includes "asymmetries" relating to quantification and timing; and
(c) is not negligible.

"Relevant tax disadvantage" is defined in a similar way.

HMRC acknowledge that the requirement in new ss 938C and 938D that the profit or loss must arise from asymmetries of tax treatment means that losses or profits arising from "genuine" third party loans or derivatives that might be part of a scheme cannot be "scheme losses" or "scheme profits", because they do not affect the amount of any "relevant tax disadvantage" arising from the scheme. For example, HMRC say that if a group company brings debits into account in respect of money it has borrowed from an unrelated company (and those debits reduce its liability to corporation tax), the absence of corresponding credits in any other member of the group will not be the consequence of asymmetries in the way that group members bring amounts into account for tax purposes.

New s 938E provides that company A and company B will be members of the same "group" for these purposes essentially if:

— the financial results of the companies are consolidated into group accounts;
— the companies are "connected" (as defined in CTA 2009 s 466);
— company A has a "major interest" (as defined in CTA 2009 ss 473 and 474) in company B;
— the financial results of company A and a third company are consolidated into group accounts, and that third company has a "major interest" in company B; or
— company A and a third company are "connected", and that third company has a "major interest" in company B.

New s 938F provides essentially that an "economic profit" or "economic loss" is to be computed for these purposes taking into account, in particular, profits and losses made as a result of the operation of the Corporation Tax Acts, and any adjustments required to reflect the time value of money.

New s 938G provides essentially that, when determining whether a scheme will or might secure a "relevant tax advantage", it must be assumed that each member of the group will have sufficient "tax capacity" to enable it to obtain the full benefit of any loss arising from the scheme, and will suffer the full tax cost of any taxable profit arising from the scheme.

New s 938H defines a "scheme" as including all arrangements, schemes and understandings of any type, whether or not legally enforceable, and whether involving a single transaction or series of transactions.

New ss 938I and 938J essentially ensure that the "group mismatch" legislation can apply to transactions which are treated as a loan relationship by just one party, namely the borrower under a repo or a "quasi-repo" (CTA 2009 Part 6 Ch 10) or certain arrangements involving transfers of income streams (see CTA 2010 Part 6).

New s 938K clarifies that references to amounts being brought into account, or not brought into account, under CTA 2009 Parts 5 or 7 include cases where credits or debits arising under the loan relationships or derivative contracts regimes are brought into account under CTA 2009 Part 3 as trading items.

New s 938L provides essentially that references in the "group mismatch" legislation to a company not bringing amounts into account as debits or credits for the purposes of CTA 2009 Parts 5 or 7 do not include cases where the company does not bring amounts into account by virtue of its being non-UK resident. The intended effect of this provision is apparently to ensure that non-UK resident companies are outside the scope of the "group mismatch" legislation, unless they enter into the relevant loan relationship or derivative contract through or for the purposes of a trade carried on by a UK permanent establishment.

New s 938M deals with cases where a group company is not resident in the UK but is a Controlled Foreign Company within the scope of ICTA 1988 Part XVII Ch IV, and provides essentially that references in the "group mismatch" legislation to a company bringing amounts into account, or not bringing them into account, as debits or credits for the purposes of CTA 2009 Parts 5 or 7 include bringing amounts into account, or not bringing them into account, as debits or credits in determining the "chargeable profits" of the company for the purposes of the CFC legislation.

New s 938N provides essentially that, when determining whether any amounts would be brought into account apart from the "group mismatch" legislation, certain other anti-avoidance rules are to be disregarded. Those provisions include CTA 2009 s 441 (loan relationships for unallowable purposes), CTA 2009 s 690 (derivative contracts for unallowable purposes), TIOPA 2010 Part 4 (transfer pricing), Part 6 (anti-arbitrage) and Part 7 (worldwide debt cap). This is essentially a "boundary" provision which ensures that the "group mismatch" legislation applies in priority to those provisions.

Schedule 5 continued

Paragraph 5 makes consequential amendments to the transfer pricing and anti-arbitrage rules in TIOPA 2010 Parts 4 and 6.

Paragraph 6 sets out the commencement rules for the "group mismatch" legislation. The legislation will have effect in relation to schemes entered into at any time (whether before or after Royal Assent), but will not apply to:

— scheme losses or profits that relate to a time before the date of Royal Assent; or

— scheme profits that relate to a time on or after the date of Royal Assent but are made in relation to a scheme entered into before that date.

Paragraphs 7 and 8 provide for the repeal of CTA 2009 ss 418 and 419 (loan relationships treated differently by connected debtor and creditor) and s 453 (connected parties deriving benefit from creditor loan relationships), as a result of the enactment of the "group mismatch" legislation.

SCHEDULE 6

LEASING BUSINESSES

Section 32

Businesses carried on by companies alone

1 Chapter 3 of Part 9 of CTA 2010 (sale of lessors: leasing business carried on by a company alone) is amended as follows.

2 (1) Section 387 ("business of leasing plant or machinery") is amended as follows.

(2) In subsection (3), for "qualifying leased plant or machinery" substitute "plant or machinery falling within subsection (7)".

(3) For subsection (5) substitute—

"(5) Condition B is that at least half of the relevant company's income in the past 12 months derives from plant or machinery falling within subsection (7)."

(4) For subsections (7) and (8) substitute—

"(7) Plant or machinery falls within this subsection if—

(a) it is or at any time in the past 12 months has been leased out by the relevant company or a qualifying associate,
(b) the lease under which it is or has been leased out is a plant or machinery lease but not an excluded lease of background plant or machinery for a building (see section 437(3)), and
(c) if the plant or machinery satisfies paragraph (a) only because it is or has been leased out by a qualifying associate, the lessee under the lease is or was someone other than the relevant company.

(8) For the purposes of subsection (7)—

(a) plant or machinery is "leased out" by a person if it is subject to a plant or machinery lease under which that person is a lessor,
(b) "associate" means a person connected with the relevant company (see also subsection (9)), and
(c) a person is a "qualifying associate" if the person is an associate at the start of the relevant day or at any earlier time in the past 12 months (whether or not a time when the plant or machinery was leased out by the person).

(9) If the relevant company is owned by a consortium or is a qualifying 75% subsidiary of a company owned by a consortium, the reference in subsection (8)(b) to a person connected with the relevant company also includes—

(a) any member of the consortium, and
(b) any person connected with such a member.

(10) A reference in this section to the past 12 months is to the period of 12 months ending with the relevant day."

3 In section 389 (provision supplementing section 388), in subsection (5)(b), for "market value" substitute "ascribed value".

4 In section 390 (relevant plant or machinery value where relevant company lessee under long funding lease etc), in subsection (2), for "market value" substitute "ascribed value".

5 In section 391 (relevant company's income for condition B in section 387), in subsection (5), for "qualifying leased plant or machinery" substitute "plant or machinery falling within section 387(7)".

6 (1) Section 398G (transfers into and out of A) is amended as follows.

(2) Omit subsection (2).

(3) For subsection (3) substitute—

"(3) If any event occurs that requires A to bring the disposal value of plant or machinery into account under Part 2 of CAA 2001, that Part has effect as if the disposal value that A is required to bring into account were the higher of—

(a) the disposal value determined in accordance with that Part, and
(b) the ascribed value of the plant or machinery.

(4) Section 265 of CAA 2001 (successions) is subject to this section."

7 In section 401 (provisions supplementing section 400), in subsection (5)(b), for "market value" substitute "ascribed value".

8 In section 402 ("PM" where relevant company lessee under long funding lease etc), in subsection (2), for "market value" substitute "ascribed value".

9 (1) Section 403 ("TWDV" in section 399) is amended as follows.

(2) In subsection (2), for paragraph (b) substitute—

"(b) in calculating the amounts of unrelieved qualifying expenditure mentioned in subsection (1)(a) to (c), any part of those amounts that is relevant new expenditure is to be left out of account."

(3) After that subsection insert—

"(3) Relevant new expenditure" means—

(a) expenditure attributable to plant or machinery acquired by the relevant company on the relevant day except for plant or machinery acquired on that day from an associated company, and
(b) expenditure incurred on the relevant day but attributable to plant or machinery acquired by the relevant company before that day.

(4) In subsection (3)—

(a) "acquired" includes brought into use or made available for use for the first time for the purposes of the business, and
(b) a reference to anything acquired or incurred includes anything treated as acquired or treated as incurred."

Businesses carried on by companies in partnership

10 Chapter 4 of Part 9 of CTA 2010 (sale of lessors: leasing business carried on by a company in partnership) is amended as follows.

11 (1) Section 410 ("business of leasing plant or machinery") is amended as follows.

(2) In subsection (2), for "qualifying leased plant or machinery" substitute "plant or machinery falling within subsection (6)".

(3) For subsection (4) substitute—

"(4) Condition B is that at least half of the partnership's income in the past 12 months derives from plant or machinery falling within subsection (6)."

(4) For subsections (6) and (7) substitute—

"(6) Plant or machinery falls within this subsection if—

(a) it is or at any time in the past 12 months has been leased out by the partnership or a qualifying associate,
(b) the lease under which it is or has been leased out is a plant or machinery lease but not an excluded lease of background plant or machinery for a building (see section 437(3)), and
(c) if the plant or machinery satisfies paragraph (a) only because it is or has been leased out by a qualifying associate, the lessee under the lease is or was someone other than the partnership.

(7) For the purposes of subsection (6)—

(a) plant or machinery is "leased out" by a person if it is subject to a plant or machinery lease under which that person is a lessor,
(b) "associate" means a person who is a partner in the partnership or connected with a partner in the partnership (see also subsection (8)), and
(c) a person is a "qualifying associate" if the person is an associate at the start of the relevant day or at any earlier time in the past 12 months (whether or not a time when the plant or machinery was leased out by the person).

(8) In relation to a corporate partner who is owned by a consortium or is a qualifying 75% subsidiary of a company owned by a consortium, the reference in subsection (7)(b) to a person connected with a partner also includes—

(a) any member of the consortium, and
(b) any person connected with such a member.

(9) A reference in this section to the past 12 months is to the period of 12 months ending with the relevant day."

12 In section 412 (provision supplementing section 411), in subsection (5)(b), for "market value" substitute "ascribed value".

13 In section 413 (relevant plant or machinery value where partnership lessee under long funding lease etc), in subsection (2), for "market value" substitute "ascribed value".

14 In section 414 (partnership's income for condition B in section 410), in subsection (5), for "qualifying leased plant or machinery" substitute "plant or machinery falling within section 410(6)".

15 (1) Section 421 (the amount of the income: the basic amount) is amended as follows.

(2) In subsection (6), for paragraph (b) substitute—

"(b) in calculating the amounts of unrelieved qualifying expenditure mentioned in subsection (5)(a) to (c), any part of those amounts that is relevant new expenditure is to be left out of account."

(3) After that subsection insert—

"(6A) Relevant new expenditure" means—

(a) expenditure attributable to plant or machinery acquired by the partnership on the relevant day except for plant or machinery acquired on that day from a qualifying company, and
(b) expenditure incurred on the relevant day but attributable to plant or machinery acquired by the partnership before that day.

(6B) In subsection (6A)—

(a) "acquired" includes brought into use or made available for use for the first time for the purposes of the business, and
(b) a reference to anything acquired or incurred includes anything treated as acquired or treated as incurred."

Anti-avoidance provisions

16 Chapter 5 of Part 9 of CTA 2010 (sales of lessors: anti-avoidance provisions) is amended as follows.

17 (1) Section 434 (introduction to sections 435 and 436) is amended as follows.

(2) In subsection (2), for "question A or B" substitute "question A, B or C".

(3) After subsection (4) insert—

"(5) Question C is the question of the amount of any disposal value to be substituted by section 398G(3)."

18 (1) Section 435 (disregard of increases or decreases in balance sheet amounts) is amended as follows.

(2) In subsection (1), for paragraph (a) substitute—

"(a) an amount mentioned in subsection (1A) is to be ascertained for the purpose of determining a question as to the application of Chapter 3 or 4,".

(3) After that subsection insert—

"(1A) The amounts are—

(a) the relevant plant or machinery value,

(b) the value of plant or machinery falling within section 387(7) or 410(6),

(c) the relevant company's or partnership's income in the period of 12 months ending with the relevant day,

(d) the amount of PM,

(e) the amount of TWDV,

(f) the amount of any disposal value to be substituted by section 398G(3), and

(g) any underlying amount required to calculate or verify an amount mentioned in any of the preceding paragraphs."

(4) In subsection (2)—

(a) omit "or" at the end of paragraph (b), and

(b) at the end of paragraph (c) insert

", or

(d) the amount of any disposal value to be substituted by section 398G(3) would be reduced."

(5) In subsection (3), for "which falls (or would fall) to be shown in the balance sheet in respect of plant or machinery" substitute "to be ascertained".

(6) Accordingly, in the heading of that section, for "**in balance sheet amounts**" substitute "**in certain amounts**".

19 In section 436 (balance sheet amounts determined on assumption company has no liabilities), after subsection (6) insert—

"(7) Except for subsection (6), this section applies to a partnership as it applies to a company, and references to "company" are to be read accordingly."

General interpretation of sales of lessors Chapters

20 Chapter 6 of Part 9 of CTA 2010 (sales of lessors: general interpretation) is amended as follows.

21 In section 437, omit subsection (9) (definition of "market value").

22 After that section insert—

"437A Determining the ascribed value of plant or machinery

(1) For the purposes of the sales of lessors Chapters, the ascribed value of plant or machinery at any given time ("the relevant time") is the value determined in accordance with this section.

(2) Subsection (3) applies to plant or machinery if—

(a) it is subject to a plant or machinery lease at the relevant time,

(b) the relevant company or partnership is a lessor under the lease, and

(c) subsection (5) does not apply to it.

(3) The ascribed value of plant or machinery to which this subsection applies is the higher of—

(a) the market value of the plant or machinery at the relevant time, and

(b) the present value at that time of the lease referred to in subsection (2).

(4) Subsection (5) applies to plant or machinery if—

(a) it is subject to a plant or machinery lease at the relevant time,

(b) the lease is an equipment lease within the meaning of Chapter 14 of Part 2 of CAA 2001 (fixtures),

(c) the relevant company or partnership is the equipment lessor in respect of the lease (see section 174 of that Act), and

(d) the equipment lessor is treated at that time as the owner of the plant or machinery by virtue of an election made in reliance on section 177(1)(a)(i) of that Act (which permits elections if the conditions in section 178 are met in relation to the lease).

(5) The ascribed value of plant or machinery to which this subsection applies is the present value at the relevant time of the lease referred to in subsection (4).

(6) The ascribed value of plant or machinery to which neither subsection (3) nor subsection (5) applies is the market value of the plant or machinery at the relevant time.

437B Section 437A: supplementary

(1) This section supplements section 437A.

(2) Market value is to be determined on the assumption of a disposal by an absolute owner free from all leases and other encumbrances (including any agreement or arrangement that is or includes a plant or machinery lease).

(3) If plant or machinery is a fixture, its market value is so much of the market value of the relevant land and the fixture together as is attributable to the fixture on a just and reasonable apportionment.

(4) "Relevant land" has the meaning given in section 173(2) of CAA 2001.

437C Present value of a lease

(1) For the purposes of section 437A, the present value of a lease is the present value of the amounts mentioned in subsection (2).

(2) The amounts are—

(a) the amounts payable under the lease after the relevant time, and

(b) any residual amount.

(3) Subsection (2)(a) does not apply to amounts payable by the lessor or to amounts that represent—

(a) charges for services, or

(b) qualifying UK or foreign tax to be paid by the lessor.

(4) Present value is to be calculated by using the interest rate implicit in the lease.

(5) The interest rate implicit in the lease is the interest rate that would apply in accordance with normal commercial criteria, including, in particular, generally accepted accounting practice (where applicable).

(6) But if a rate cannot be determined in accordance with subsection (5), the interest rate implicit in the lease is taken to be 1% above LIBOR.

(7) For this purpose—

(a) LIBOR means the London interbank offered rate on the applicable day for deposits for a term of 12 months in the applicable currency,

(b) the applicable day is the day comprising or including the relevant time (or, if that day is not a business day, the first business day after it), and

(c) the applicable currency is the currency in which payments under the lease are payable.

(8) If—

(a) the lessee has an option to continue the lease for a period after expiry of its initial term, and

(b) it is reasonably certain at the relevant time that the lessee will exercise that option,

references in this section to amounts payable under the lease include amounts payable under the lease as continued for any such period.

(9) If the lease also relates to land or assets that are not plant or machinery, the present value of the lease is so much of the present value of the amounts mentioned in subsection (2) as is attributable to the plant or machinery on a just and reasonable apportionment.

(10) In this section, "qualifying UK or foreign tax" and "residual amount" have the meaning given in section 70YE of CAA 2001."

Consequential amendments

23 In section 267A of CAA 2001 (restriction on effect of election), in subsection (2), for "is qualifying leased plant or machinery" substitute "falls within section 387(7) of CTA

2010 (if the business is carried on otherwise than in partnership) or within section 410(6) of that Act (if the business is carried on in partnership)".

24 In section 948 of CTA 2010 (modified application of CAA 2001), in subsection (6), before paragraph (a) insert—

"(za) section 398G of this Act (sale of lessors: transfers into and out of A after election under section 398A),".

25 (1) Section 950 of CTA 2010 (transfers of trades involving business of leasing plant or machinery) is amended as follows.

(2) In subsection (5), for the words from "its market value" to the end substitute

"the higher of—

(a) its ascribed value immediately before the transfer of the trade, and

(b) the disposal value that the predecessor would be required to bring into account under Part 2 of CAA 2001 in respect of it as a result of the transfer of the trade."

(3) In subsection (6)—

(a) before the definition of "business of leasing plant or machinery" insert—

""ascribed value", in relation to plant or machinery, is to be read in accordance with section 437A (but reading the reference to the relevant company or partnership as a reference to the predecessor);", and

(b) omit the definition of "market value".

26 (1) In Schedule 4 to CTA 2010 (index of defined expressions), omit the entry for "market value (in relation to plant or machinery) (in Chapters 3 to 6 of Part 9)".

(2) In that Schedule, insert the following entry at the appropriate place—

"ascribed value (in relation to plant or machinery) (in Chapters 3 to 6 of Part 9)	section 437A".

Application of new provisions

27 (1) The amendments made by paragraphs 2 to 5 and 7 to 15, and the general paragraphs so far as relevant to those amendments, have effect where the relevant day (as defined for the purposes of the amended provision) falls on or after 23 March 2011.

(2) The amendment made by paragraph 6(3), and the general paragraphs so far as relevant to that amendment, have effect in relation to disposal events taking place on or after 23 March 2011 (including in cases where the election was made before that date).

(3) The amendments made by paragraphs 6(2) and 23 to 25, and the general paragraphs so far as relevant to those amendments, have effect in relation to transfers or successions taking place on or after 23 March 2011 (including, in the case of the amendment made by paragraph 6(2), where the election was made before that date).

(4) The general paragraphs are—

(a) paragraph 1,

(b) paragraphs 16 to 22, and

(c) paragraph 26.

GENERAL NOTE

The provisions of Schedule 6 modify the sale of lessor rules in CTA 2010 Part 9. They are a response to disclosures that showed that taxpayers were still attempting to avoid the application of those rules on sales of lessors.

The concept of "qualifying leased plant and machinery" in CTA 2010 s 387 is to be replaced. This concept is used to determine whether or not a company carries on a business of leasing plant or machinery for the purposes of the sale of lessor rules. It is currently a requirement that the company has or has had an entitlement to capital allowances in respect of the relevant plant or machinery and schemes have been devised to exploit this. This link to capital allowance entitlement is removed. In future, Conditions A and B will fall to be met by reference to any plant or machinery falling within new CTA 2010 sub-s 387(7), being (with limited exceptions) plant or machinery leased out by the relevant company or a qualifying associate under a plant or machinery lease within the past 12 months. There are certain changes consequential on this and an equivalent change to the partnership provisions.

There are various places in CTA 2010 Part 9 Chs 3 and 4 where the "market value" of an asset is required to be used and which are to be replaced with the concept of "ascribed value". "Market value" is determined on the basis of a hypothetical sale by the owner of an asset free of encumbrances. Where an asset is subject to a lease that does not pick up the value of the asset and the lease as a package (though the value of the asset itself may be low, the right to receive future rentals may be valuable). "Ascribed value" is to be the higher of the market value of the leased asset and the present value of the lease. The present value of the lease is calculated as being the present value, calculated using the interest rate implicit in the lease or, failing that, LIBOR +1% of the remaining amounts payable under the lease and the residual amount.

Paragraph 9 is aimed at arrangements that were effected whereby a leasing company would, on the same day as it suffered a change in ownership but after that time, have a trade or part of a trade transferred to it. The deemed income amount is calculated by reference to the PM-TWDV formula, with PM being calculated at the start of the relevant day and TWDV at the end. The intention was to reduce or eliminate the deemed income amount by increasing TWDV without affecting PM. Expenditure attributable to plant and machinery acquired on the relevant day otherwise than from an associated company and expenditure incurred on the relevant day but in relation to plant and machinery acquired before it are to be left out of account in calculating TWDV. There is an equivalent change to the partnership provisions.

Paragraphs 16, 17 and 18 widen the scope of the existing anti-avoidance provisions. It is currently aimed at preventing the manipulation of balance sheet values taken into account in determining whether a leasing business is being carried on or the amount of any deemed income or expense. It will now cover manipulation of any of the seven amounts listed in s 435(1A) and will include manipulation of any such amounts in determining any disposal value to be substituted under s 398G(3).

The amendments outlined above have effect where the relevant day or, as the case may be, the disposal event, falls on or after 23 March, 2011.

SCHEDULE 7

INVESTMENT COMPANIES

Section 34

Amendments of Chapter 4 of Part 2 of CTA 2010

1 (1) Section 6 of CTA 2010 (UK resident company operating in sterling and preparing accounts in another currency) is amended as follows.

(2) In subsection (1), after "company" insert "(other than a UK resident investment company)".

(3) After that subsection insert—

"(1A) This section also applies if, for a period of account, a UK resident investment company—

(a) in accordance with generally accepted accounting practice, prepares its accounts in a currency other than sterling, and

(b) either—

(i) has sterling as its designated currency for that period of account (see sections 9A and 9B), or

(ii) if it does not have a designated currency for that period, in those accounts identifies sterling as its functional currency in accordance with generally accepted accounting practice."

2 (1) Section 7 of that Act (UK resident company operating in currency other than sterling and preparing accounts in another currency) is amended as follows.

(2) In subsection (1), in paragraph (a), after "company" insert "(other than a UK resident investment company)".

(3) After that subsection insert—

"(1A) This section also applies if, for a period of account, a UK resident investment company—

(a) in accordance with generally accepted accounting practice, prepares its accounts in one currency,

(b) either—

(i) has another currency as its designated currency for that period (see sections 9A and 9B), or

(ii) if it does not have a designated currency for that period, in those accounts identifies another currency as its functional currency in accordance with generally accepted accounting practice, and

(c) that other currency is not sterling."

(4) In subsection (2), in step 1, for "functional" substitute "relevant".

(5) In subsection (3) for "functional" substitute "relevant".

(6) After that subsection insert—

"(4) In subsections (2) and (3) "the relevant currency" means the currency other than sterling referred to in subsection (1)(c) or (1A)(c)."

3 After section 9 of that Act insert—

"9A Designated currency of a UK resident investment company

(1) The designated currency of a UK resident investment company is the currency which the company elects as its designated currency.

(2) A company ("X") may elect a currency as its designated currency only if—

(a) at the time the election is made condition A or B is met, or

(b) the election is made in the period (if any) beginning with the company's incorporation and ending immediately before its first accounting period.

(3) But an election made under subsection (2)(b) is void if, at the time X's first accounting period begins, neither condition A nor condition B is met.

(4) Condition A is that a significant proportion of X's assets and liabilities are denominated in the currency.

(5) Condition B is that—

(a) the currency is the functional currency of another company, and

(b) it is reasonable to assume that the two companies will meet the consolidation condition.

(6) X and another company ("Y") meet the consolidation condition at any time if—

(a) for a period which includes that time, the financial results of X are comprised in financial statements of Y's group prepared in accordance with acceptable accounting practice, or

(b) if no financial statements of the group are prepared in accordance with acceptable accounting practice for a period which includes that time, the financial results of X would be comprised in financial statements of Y's group for a period which includes that time if such statements were prepared in accordance with international accounting standards.

(7) In subsection (6)—

"financial statements of the group" means consolidated financial statements of Y and its subsidiaries (within the meaning of section 351 of TIOPA 2010),

"Y's group" means a group of which Y is the ultimate parent (and for this purpose "group" and "ultimate parent" have the same meaning as they have for the purposes of Part 7 of that Act (see sections 338 and 339)), and

"acceptable accounting practice" means—

(a) international accounting standards,

(b) UK generally accepted accounting practice, or

(c) accounting practice which is generally accepted in the country in which Y is resident.

(8) A currency is the designated currency of X for a period of account if the election in respect of that currency has effect throughout that period (see section 9B).

9B Period for which an election under section 9A has effect

(1) An election under section 9A(2)(a) takes effect at the beginning of the day specified in the election as the day on which it takes effect (which must be later than the day on which the election is made).

(2) An election under section 9A(2)(b) is treated as taking effect at the time of X's incorporation.

(3) An election under section 9A(2)(a) may be revoked by notice of the revocation being given to an officer of Revenue and Customs before the election takes effect.

(4) Subject to that, an election has effect until immediately before—

(a) the day on which another election by X takes effect, or

(b) the day on which a revocation event occurs,

(whichever first occurs).

(5) A revocation event occurs in a period of account (other than a period to which subsection (6) applies) if, at any time during that period—

(a) it is not the case that a significant proportion of X's assets and liabilities are denominated in the currency to which the election relates, and

(b) it is not the case that the currency is the functional currency of another company which, with X, met the consolidation condition (within the meaning of section 9A(6)) at any time during the preceding period of account.

(6) Where the election is made under section 9A(2)(b), a revocation event occurs in the period of account in which X's first accounting period begins only if—

(a) Condition A and not Condition B is satisfied at the beginning of that accounting period, and

(b) the condition in subsection (5)(a) is met at any time during the period of account but after the first accounting period begins.

(7) Subsections (8) and (9) apply if a period of account of X ("the straddling period of account") begins before, and ends on or after, the day on which—

(a) an election under section 9A(2)(a) takes effect, or

(b) a revocation event occurs.

(8) It is to be assumed, for the purposes of this Chapter, that the straddling period of account consists of two separate periods of account—

(a) the first beginning with the straddling period of account and ending immediately before that day, and

(b) the second beginning with that day and ending with the straddling period of account,

and X's profits and losses are to be computed accordingly for the purposes of corporation tax.

(9) For those purposes, it is to be assumed—

(a) that X prepares its accounts for each of the two periods in the same currency, and otherwise on the same basis, as it prepares its accounts for the straddling period of account, and

(b) that if the accounts for the straddling period of account, in accordance with generally accepted accounting practice, identify a currency as X's functional currency, the accounts for each of the two periods do likewise.

(10) In this section references to "X" are to be construed in accordance with section 9A."

4 In section 17 of that Act (interpretation of Chapter 4 of Part 2), after subsection (3) insert—

"(3A) In this Chapter "investment company" means a company whose business consists wholly or mainly in the making of investments and the principal part of whose income is derived from those investments."

Amendments of ICTA

5 In Schedule 24 to ICTA (assumptions for calculating chargeable profits, creditable tax and corresponding United Kingdom tax of foreign companies), in paragraph 4 (reliefs under Corporation Tax Acts dependent upon the making of a claim or election), after sub-paragraph (2) insert—

"(2B) For the purposes of sub-paragraph (1) an election under section 9A of CTA 2010 (designated currency of a UK resident investment company) is not to be regarded as an election upon which relief under the Corporation Tax Acts is dependent, and sub-paragraph (2)(b) does not apply in relation to such an election.

(2C) But if, by notice given to an officer of the Board, the United Kingdom resident company which has or, as the case may be, any two or more United Kingdom resident companies which together have, a majority interest in the company so request, the company shall be assumed (subject to section 9A(2) of CTA 2010) to have made an election under section 9A of that Act in the form specified in the notice (and accordingly that section and section 9B of that Act apply to determine the effect (if any) of that election)."

Amendments of CTA 2009

6 (1) Section 328 of CTA 2009 (loan relationships: exchange gains and losses) is amended as follows.

(2) In subsection (2), after "subsections" insert "(2A),".

(3) After that subsection insert—

"(2A) Subsection (1) does not apply to an exchange gain or loss of an investment company (within the meaning of section 17 of CTA 2010) which would not have arisen but for a change in the company's functional currency (within the meaning of section 17(4) of that Act) as between—

(a) the period of account of the company in which the gain or loss arises, and

(b) a period of account of the company ending in the 12 months immediately preceding that period."

7 (1) Section 606 of that Act (derivative contracts: exchange gains and losses) is amended as follows.

(2) In subsection (2), after "subsections" insert "(2A),".

(3) After that subsection insert—

"(2A) Subsection (1) does not apply to an exchange gain or loss of an investment company (within the meaning of section 17 of CTA 2010) which would not have arisen but for a change in the company's functional currency (within the meaning of section 17(4) of that Act) as between—

(a) the period of account of the company in which the gain or loss arises, and

(b) a period of account of the company ending in the 12 months immediately preceding that period."

Commencement

8 (1) The amendments made by this Schedule have effect in relation to periods of account beginning on or after 1 April 2011.

(2) An election may be made or revoked for the purposes of section 9A of CTA 2010 (as inserted by paragraph 3) at any time on or after 9 December 2010.

(3) Where an election made by a company before 27 June 2011 does not specify the day on which it takes effect, the election is to be treated as if it specified the first day of the first period of account of the company beginning after the election was made.

(4) An election made before the day on which this Act is passed must be made by notice in writing to an officer of Revenue and Customs.

(5) Schedule 1A to TMA 1970 does not apply to an election made before the day on which this Act is passed.

GENERAL NOTE

The normal rule is that a company's taxable profits (other than chargeable gains or allowable losses) have to be computed by reference to its functional currency. Where an investment company is a member of a group it will often be required to adopt the group's functional currency as its own functional currency, even though its economic exposure may be to a different currency. For example, X Limited is an investment company that is a member of a wider group. The majority of X's assets and liabilities are in US dollars. As, however, the group's functional currency is sterling, X Limited is required to adopt sterling as its functional currency.

Schedule 7 modifies the rules of CTA 2010 ss 6 and 7, which provide that a company's taxable profits are to be determined by reference to its functional currency, in the case of a UK resident investment company, to permit such a company to elect for its taxable profits (other than chargeable gains or allowable losses) to be computed by reference to a designated currency. The amendments have effect for periods of account beginning on or after 1 April 2011 (para 8(1)). Following Report Stage amendments, an election can take effect at any time (as opposed to the start of the period of account following that in which it was made, as was originally proposed) but not earlier than the day following that on which it is made (CTA 2010 s 9B(1), as inserted by para 3). It was possible for a company to make an election before 1 April 2011 to HMRC to use a particular currency as its designated currency with effect for a period of account beginning on or after 1 April 2011 (para 8(4)).

In the case of a newly incorporated company it is possible for the election to be made after the company's incorporation and before the start of its first accounting period and in which case the election takes effect from the time of the company's incorporation (CTA 2010 ss 9A(2)(b), 9B(2), as inserted by para 3). The election is void if neither Condition A nor Condition B (see below) is satisfied at the time that its first accounting period begins (CTA 2010, s 9A(3), as inserted by para 3).

In order for a company (other than a newly incorporated company) to elect for a particular currency to be treated as its designated currency, at the time that the election is made either:

(a) a significant proportion of the company's assets and liabilities must be denominated in that currency (Condition A); or

b) broadly, the currency must be the functional currency of the ultimate parent company of the group (Condition B) (CTA 2010 s 9A(4)–(7), as inserted by para 3).

If made, such an election continues to have effect until the company makes a further election, or, broadly, the time where the requirements of Condition A or Condition B are no longer satisfied (revocation event). In such cases the election ceases to have effect immediately before the earlier of the day that the revised election takes effect or the revocation event occurs. In determining whether Condition B ceases to be satisfied at any time in a period of account regard is had to whether the designated currency is the functional currency of the company that was the UK resident investment company's ultimate parent company at any time in the preceding period of account (CTA 2010 s 9B(3)–(5), as inserted by para 3). Where a revised election takes effect, or a revocation event occurs, during a period of account the period of account is deemed to be split into two periods with the first ending immediately before the day that the revised election takes effect or the revocation event occurs (see further CTA 2010 s 9B(7)–(10) as inserted by para 3).

In the case of a newly incorporated company a revocation event will occur in its first period of account if a currency is a designated currency because Condition A (and not Condition B) is satisfied at the start of its first accounting period and this condition ceases to be satisfied at any time in that period of account (and after the start of its first accounting period) (CTA 2010 s 9B(6), as inserted by para 3).

The elections discussed above also apply for the purposes of computing the chargeable profits of a CFC and in this case an election can be made by the UK resident company which has, or any two or more UK resident companies which together have, a majority interest in the CFC (see new ICTA 1988 Sch 24 para 4(2B), (2C), as introduced by para 5).

Where a UK resident investment company changes its functional currency with effect for a period of account commencing on or after 1 April 2011 any exchange movements arising as a result of the change to its functional currency will be disregarded in computing its taxable profits (CTA 2009 ss 328(2A), 606(2A), as inserted by paras 6 and 7).

SCHEDULE 8

REDUCTION IN CHILDCARE RELIEF FOR HIGHER EARNERS

Section 35

Introduction

1 ITEPA 2003 is amended as follows.

Childcare vouchers

2 (1) Section 270A (limited exemption for qualifying childcare vouchers) is amended as follows.

(2) In subsection (2), for "C" substitute "D".

(3) After subsection (5B) (inserted by section 36) insert—

"(5C) Condition D is that the employer has, at the required time, made an estimate of the employee's relevant earnings amount for the tax year in respect of which the voucher is provided (see section 270B)."

(4) In paragraph (a) of subsection (6), for "£55" substitute "the appropriate amount".

(5) After that subsection insert—

"(6ZA) In subsection (6)(a) "the appropriate amount", in the case of an employee, means—

(a) if the relevant earnings amount in the case of the employee for the tax year, as estimated in accordance with subsection (5C), exceeds the higher rate limit for the tax year, £22,

(b) if the relevant earnings amount in the case of the employee for the tax year, as so estimated, exceeds the basic rate limit for the tax year but does not exceed the higher rate limit for the tax year, £28, and

(c) otherwise, £55."

(6) In subsection (11)—

(a) for "exempt amount" (in each place) substitute "amounts",
(b) for "(6) above" substitute "(6ZA) above", and
(c) for "318A(6)" substitute "318A(6A)".

3 After section 270A insert—

"270B Meaning of "relevant earnings amount" and "required time"

(1) For the purposes of section 270A, the "relevant earnings amount", in the case of an employee provided with vouchers by an employer for any qualifying week in a tax year, means—

(a) the aggregate of—

(i) the amount of any relevant earnings for the tax year from employment by the employer, and

(ii) any amounts treated under Chapters 2 to 12 of Part 3 as earnings from such employment, less

(b) the aggregate of any excluded amounts.

(2) But if the employee becomes employed by the employer during the tax year, what would otherwise be the amount of the aggregate mentioned in subsection (1)(a) is the relevant multiple of that amount; and the relevant multiple is—

365 / RD

where RD is the number of days in the period beginning with the day on which the employee becomes employed by the employer and ending with the tax year.

(3) In subsection (1)(a) "relevant earnings" means—

(a) salary, wages or fees, and
(b) any other earnings specified in regulations made by the Treasury under this paragraph.

(4) In subsection (1)(b) "excluded amounts" means amounts specified in regulations made by the Treasury under this subsection.

(5) In section 270A "the required time", in the case of an employee, means—

(a) if the employee joins the scheme under which the vouchers are provided at a time during the tax year, that time, and
(b) otherwise, the beginning of the tax year.

(6) For the purposes of subsection (5)(a) the employee is taken to join the scheme as soon as—

(a) the employer has agreed that vouchers will be provided under the scheme for the employee, and
(b) there is a child falling within section 270A(3)(a) or (b) in relation to the employee.

(7) The Treasury may by order amend this section."

Childcare provided otherwise than at employer's premises etc

4 (1) Section 318A (limited exemption for childcare provided otherwise than at employer's premises etc) is amended as follows.

(2) In subsection (1), for "C" substitute "D".

(3) After subsection (5B) (inserted by section 36) insert—

"(5C) Condition D is that the employer has, at the required time, made an estimate of the employee's relevant earnings amount for the tax year in respect of which the care is provided (see section 318AA)."

(4) In subsection (6), for "£55" substitute "the appropriate amount".

(5) After that subsection insert—

"(6A) In subsection (6) "the appropriate amount", in the case of an employee, means—

(a) if the relevant earnings amount in the case of the employee for the tax year, as estimated in accordance with subsection (5C), exceeds the higher rate limit for the tax year, £22,
(b) if the relevant earnings amount in the case of the employee for the tax year, as so estimated, exceeds the basic rate limit for the tax year but does not exceed the higher rate limit for the tax year, £28, and
(c) otherwise, £55."

5 After section 318A insert—

"318AA Meaning of "relevant earnings amount" and "required time"

(1) For the purposes of section 318A, "relevant earnings amount", in the case of an employee provided with care by an employer for any qualifying week in a tax year, means—

(a) the aggregate of—

(i) the amount of any relevant earnings for the tax year from employment by the employer, and

(ii) any amounts treated under Chapters 2 to 12 of Part 3 as earnings from such employment, less

(b) the aggregate of any excluded amounts.

(2) But if the employee becomes employed by the employer during the tax year, what would otherwise be the amount of the aggregate mentioned in subsection (1)(a) is the relevant multiple of that amount; and the relevant multiple is—

365 / RD

where RD is the number of days in the period beginning with the day on which the employee becomes employed by the employer and ending with the tax year.

(3) In subsection (1)—

"relevant earnings" has the same meaning as in subsection (1)(a) of section 270B (see subsection (3) of that section), and

"excluded amounts" has the same meaning as in subsection (1)(b) of section 270B (see subsection (4) of that section).

(4) In section 318A "the required time", in the case of an employee, means—

(a) if the employee joins the scheme under which the care is provided at a time during the tax year, that time, and

(b) otherwise, the beginning of the tax year.

(5) For the purposes of subsection (5)(a) the employee is taken to join the scheme as soon as—

(a) the employer has agreed that care will be provided under the scheme for the employee, and

(b) there is a child falling within section 318A(3)(a) or (b) in relation to the employee.

(6) The Treasury may by order amend this section."

6 In subsection (1) of section 318D (childcare: power to vary exempt amount)—

(a) for "318A(6)" substitute "318A(6A)", and

(b) for "exempt amount) so as to substitute a different sum of money for that" substitute "amounts which are the exempt amount) so as to substitute different sums of money for those";

and, accordingly, in the heading of that section, after "**vary**" insert "**amounts which are the**".

Commencement and transitional provision

7 The amendments made by this Schedule have effect for the tax year 2011–12 and subsequent tax years.

8 (1) But the amendments made by paragraphs 2(2) to (5) and 3 to 5 do not apply for a tax week in the case of an employee and employer and a scheme if—

(a) the employee joined the scheme before 6 April 2011,

(b) the employee has not ceased to be employed by the employer during the period beginning with that date and ending with the tax week, and

(c) during that period there has not been a continuous period of 52 weeks throughout which vouchers were not, or care was not, being provided for the employee under the scheme.

(2) For the purposes of sub-paragraph (1) the employee is taken to join the scheme as soon as—

(a) the employer has agreed that vouchers, or care, will be provided under the scheme for the employee, and

(b) there is a child falling within section 270A(3)(a) or (b), or section 318A(3)(a) or (b), of ITEPA 2003 in relation to the employee.

9 Regulations made under section 270B(3)(b) or (4) of ITEPA 2003 (inserted by paragraph 3) on or before 31 December 2011 may have retrospective effect in relation to the tax year 2011–12.

10 The amendments made by paragraphs 2(6) and 6 do not prevent the making of provision under section 270A(11)(a) or 318D(1) of ITEPA 2003 in relation to sections 270A(6) and 318A(6) of that Act as, by virtue of paragraph 8, they continue to have effect otherwise than as amended by this Schedule.

GENERAL NOTE

As previously announced, tax relief for childcare vouchers and employer-supported childcare is restricted from 6 April 2011 such that new entrants joining employer-supported childcare and childcare voucher schemes on or after that date only receive tax relief at the basic rate of tax on the exempt amount, regardless of their marginal rate of tax. Relief at the higher and additional rates of tax continue to be available to employees who joined an employer-supported childcare or childcare voucher scheme prior to 6 April 2011.

Broadly, effect is given to the restriction in relief for new joiners by amending the exempt amount such that it remains at £55 per week for basic rate taxpayers and those already in a scheme prior on 5 April 2011 but is reduced to £28 per week for higher rate taxpayer and to £22 per week for additional rate taxpayers who join on or after 6 April 2011. The effect is that for those joining a scheme on or after 6 April 2011, the relief is worth £11 per week, regardless of the taxpayer's marginal rate of tax.

Legislative effect is given to the measure via amendments made to ITEPA 2003.

Childcare vouchers

The rules governing the limited exemption for childcare vouchers are set out in ITEPA 2003 s 270A. The provisions are amended to introduce a new condition (set out in new ITEPA 2003 s 270A(5C) which requires the employer to estimate the employee's relevant earnings for the tax year in respect of which the vouchers are provided (para 2(3), (4)). This is to enable the employer to ascertain whether the employee is a basic rate, higher rate or additional rate taxpayer and to apply the appropriate tax exempt amount.

To accommodate the differing exempt limits, the reference in ITEPA 2003 s 270A(6)(a) to £55 per week is replaced with a reference to 'the appropriate amount' (para 2(4)).

The 'appropriate amount' is set in new ITEPA 2003 s 270A(6A) (inserted by para 2(5)) at:

— £22 where the relevant earning exceed the higher rate limit for the tax year (£150,000 for 2011/12);

— £28 where the relevant earnings exceed the basic rate limit for the tax year (£35,000 for 2011/12) ; and

— £55 otherwise.

Consequential amendments are made to ITEPA 2003 s 270A(11) (para 2(6).

As noted above, new condition D requires the employer, at 'the required time' to make an estimate of the employee's 'relevant earnings amount'. New ITEPA 270B (as inserted by para 3) defines 'relevant earnings amount' and 'required time' for these purposes.

The relevant earnings amount is the aggregate of the employee's relevant earnings for the tax year plus any amount treated as earnings by virtue of ITEPA 2003 Pt 3, Ch 2 – 12 (benefits in kind), less the aggregate of any excluded amounts (new ITEPA 2003 s 270B(1)). Where the employee's employment commences during the tax year, the annualised relevant earnings are used instead (new ITEPA 2003 s 270B(2).

For these purposes, 'relevant earnings' comprise salary, wages or fees or any other earnings to which the employee is contractually entitled (new ITEPA 2003 s 270B(3)). Excluded amounts include contributions to a registered pension scheme made under a net pay agreement, payroll giving donations, expense payments covered by a dispensation or included within a PAYE settlement agreement, exempt removal expenses and the personal and any other allowance included within the employee's tax code (new ITEPA 2003 s 270B(4)).

The employer is required to make the estimate of the employee's earnings at 'the required time'. Where the employee is already in the scheme at the start of the tax year, the required time is the beginning of the tax year. Where the employee joins the scheme during the tax year, the required time is the time at which the employee joins the scheme (new ITEPA 2003 s 270A(5)). The employee is regarded as joining the voucher scheme as soon as the employer agrees that vouchers will be provided and the employee has a child or step-child maintained wholly or partly at his or her expenses or a child who resides with the employee for whom the employee has parental responsibility (new ITEPA 2003 s 270B(6)).

The Treasury is given the power to amend new ITEPA 2003 s 270B by order (new ITEPA 2003 s 270B(7)).

Childcare provided other than at the employer's premises etc

The restriction in higher rate relief applies equally to employer-supported childcare provided other than at the employer's premises, such as that provided via a commercial nursery or registered childminder.

Similar changes are made to ITEPA 2003 s 318B (by para 4) in respect of employer-supported childcare as are made to ITEPA 2003 s 270A (by para 2) in relation to childcare vouchers (see above).

A new condition D (set out in new ITEPA 2003 s 318A as inserted by para 4(3)) requires the employer to make an estimate of the employee's relevant earnings amount at the appropriate time.

The reference to £55 (in ITEPA 2003 s 318A(6)) is replaced with a reference to 'the appropriate amount' (para 4(4)). The appropriate amount is defined in new ITEPA 2003 s 318A(6), as inserted by para 4(5) and which mirrors new ITEPA 2003 s 270A(6A) at £22 per week for an additional rate taxpayer, at £28 per week for a higher rate taxpayer and at £55 per week otherwise.

The meaning of 'relevant earnings amount' and 'required time' are set out in new ITEPA 2003 s 318AA, which mirrors new ITEPA 2003 s 270B, the provisions of which are outlined above).

Commencement and transitional provisions

The restriction on higher and additional rate relief apply for 2011/12 and subsequent tax years, but only in relation to those who join and employer supported childcare scheme or a childcare voucher scheme on or after 6 April 2011 (paras 7 and 8).

The restriction in relief does not apply (para 8(1)) for a tax week where:

— an employee joined a scheme before 6 April 2011;
— the employee had not ceased to be employed by the employer during the period beginning on or after 6 April 2011 and ending with the tax week in question; and
— during that period there has not been a continuous period of 52 weeks during which vouchers or care were not provided under the scheme.

The time at which an employee is regarded as joining a scheme mirrors that set out in new ITEPA 2003 s 270B(6) and new s 318AA(6), as outlined above (para 8(2)).

The powers under ITEPA 2003 s 318D to vary by order the exempt amount and qualifying conditions continue to have effect (para 9).

SCHEDULE 9

VALUE SHIFTING

Section 44

Amendments of TCGA 1992

1 In section 30 of TCGA 1992 (tax-free benefits)—

(a) in subsection (1)(a) omit "or a relevant asset",

(b) for subsection (2) substitute—

"(2) But, for the purposes of corporation tax, this section does not have effect if the disposal of the asset is a disposal by a company of shares in, or securities of, another company (as to which see section 31).", and

(c) omit subsection (8).

2 For sections 31 to 34 of TCGA 1992 (which make provision about disposals by companies of shares in or securities of other companies) substitute—

"31 Disposal of shares or securities by a company

(1) For the purposes of corporation tax, subsection (2) has effect as respects the disposal by a company ("the disposing company") of shares in, or securities of, another company if—

(a) arrangements have been made whereby the value of those shares or securities, or any relevant asset, is materially reduced,

(b) the main purpose, or one of the main purposes, of the arrangements is to obtain a tax advantage, and

(c) the arrangements do not consist solely of the making of an exempt distribution.

(2) Any allowable loss or chargeable gain accruing on the disposal is to be calculated as if the consideration for the disposal were increased by such amount as is just and reasonable having regard to—

(a) the arrangements, and

(b) any charge to, or relief from, corporation tax that, in the absence of this section, would arise in consequence of the disposal or the arrangements.

(3) For the purposes of subsection (1)—

(a) an asset is a relevant asset if, at the time of the disposal, it is owned by a company which is a member of the same group as the disposing company, and

(b) it does not matter whether the tax advantage is obtained for the disposing company or any other person.

(4) In relation to a case in which the disposal of the shares or securities precedes their acquisition, the reference in subsection (1)(a) to a reduction is to be read as including a reference to an increase.

(5) Where, but for arrangements to which subsection (6) applies, a transaction would, by virtue of section 29(2), be treated as a disposal of shares by a company, that transaction is to be treated as if it were, by virtue of section 29(2), a disposal of those shares.

(6) The arrangements to which this subsection applies are arrangements—

(a) whereby the value of the shares or securities is materially reduced, and

(b) the main purpose, or one of the main purposes, of which is to obtain a tax advantage (whether for the company or any other person).

(7) In this section—

"arrangements" includes any agreement, understanding, scheme, transaction or series of transactions (whether or not legally enforceable);

"exempt distribution" means a distribution which—

(a) for the purposes of section 931D of CTA 2009 (exemption from charge to tax: distributions received by companies that are not small), falls within an exempt class by virtue of section 931H of that Act (dividends derived from transactions not designed to reduce tax), or

(b) would be within paragraph (a) but for the recipient being a small company (within the meaning of section 931S of that Act) in the accounting period of the recipient in which the distribution was received;

"group" is to be construed in accordance with section 170;

"securities" has the same meaning as in section 132;

"tax advantage" means the avoidance of a liability to corporation tax in respect of chargeable gains."

3 In section 176 of TCGA 1992 (depreciatory transactions within a group), in subsection (1), for "on or after 31st March 1982" substitute "within the period of 6 years ending with the disposal".

4 In section 179 of TCGA 1992 (company ceasing to be member of group), in subsection (9)(b), after "section 30" insert "or 31".

Consequential repeals

5 The following provisions are repealed—

(a) in Schedule 20 to FA 1996, paragraph 47(b) and (c),

(b) Schedule 9 to FA 1999,

(c) in Schedule 29 to FA 2000, paragraph 17,

(d) in Schedule 9 to FA 2002, paragraph 5(2) and (3),

(e) in Schedule 30 to that Act, paragraph 6,

(f) in Schedule 1 to CTA 2009, paragraph 361, and

(g) in Schedule 23 to FA 2009, paragraph 8.

Commencement and transitionals

6 (1) The amendments made by paragraphs 1 to 3 and 5 have effect in relation to disposals of shares or securities by companies made on or after the day on which this Act is passed ("the commencement day").

(2) But nothing in paragraph 1, 2 or 5 prevents section 31A of TCGA 1992 (asset-holding company leaving group), as it had effect immediately before the commencement day, continuing to have effect on or after that day in relation to cases where the section 30 disposal to which that section refers occurred before that day.

(3) The amendment made by paragraph 4 has effect in relation to disposals of shares or securities treated under section 179 of TCGA 1992 as taking place on or after the commencement day.

(4) In this paragraph "securities" has the same meaning as in section 132 of TCGA 1992.

GENERAL NOTE

As part of the overall simplification of the capital gains code for groups of companies, the value shifting rules in respect of the disposal of shares or securities by a company are simplified. It replaces the current complex and mechanical rules with a simpler rule based on whether there is an intention to avoid tax.

Paragraph 2 replaces the existing TCGA 1992 ss 31–34 with a new s 31. The new value shifting a rule applies where there is a disposal of shares in, or securities of, another company and arrangements have been made whereby the value of those shares or securities, or of a relevant asset, have been materially reduced and the main purpose or one of the main purposes of the arrangements was to obtain a tax advantage. A relevant asset is an asset owned by a company which is a member of the same group as the disposing company, and it does not matter if the tax advantage is obtained for the disposing company or any other person.

In cases where the disposal of the shares or securities precedes their acquisition, this provision will apply, instead, where there is a material increase in the value of the shares or securities in respect of the disposal, or other relevant asset, instead of to a material decrease.

The effect of the rule is to increase the consideration for the disposal by an amount that is just and reasonable taking into account both the arrangements and any charge to or relief from corporation tax that would arise absent this new provision.

The provision does not apply if the arrangements consist solely of the making of an exempt distribution. An exempt distribution is a dividend that does not derive from transactions designed to reduce tax (see CTA 2009 Part 9A).

The new rules also make provision in respect of the value shifting rules under TCGA s 29(2). If the value of the shares of the company have been materially reduced, prior to an event to which s 29(2) would apply but for that reduction in value, and the arrangements have the main purpose, or one of their main purposes, as the avoidance of corporation tax, then the new s 31 will apply to the deemed disposal under s 29(2), as well.

Paragraph 3 introduces a time limit to TCGA s 176, depreciatory transactions within a group. The rules for depreciatory transactions apply where there has been a transaction within a group followed by a disposal of shares which creates an allowable capital loss. That loss could be reduced or eliminated at any time after the depreciatory transactions. Paragraph 3 now restricts the application of this provision to a disposal of the shares up to 6 years after the original depreciatory transaction.

Paragraphs 4 and 5 have various consequential amendments and repeals.

The new rules will apply to disposals of shares or securities by companies on or after the date of Royal Assent to FA 2011. Where the relevant disposal is a deemed disposal under the degrouping rules of TCGA 1992 s 179, the amended rule applies to disposals of shares or securities deemed to have taken place on or after the date of Royal Assent.

There is a transitional provision to ensure that latent charges under s 31A, which is otherwise repealed, will continue to apply if an asset-holding company leaves a group following a s 30 disposal that occurred prior to Royal Assent.

SCHEDULE 10

COMPANY CEASING TO BE MEMBER OF GROUP

Section 45

Degrouping

1 In section 139 of TCGA 1992 (reconstruction involving transfer of business), after subsection (1A) insert—

"(1B) Nothing in section 179(3D) prevents the two companies being treated as mentioned in subsection (1)."

2 In section 171A of TCGA 1992 (election to reallocate gain or loss to another member of the group), omit subsection (7).

3 (1) Section 179 of TCGA 1992 (company ceasing to be member of group) is amended as follows.

(2) In subsection (1)(a) for "company B is a member of a group" substitute "company A and company B are members of the same group".

(3) In subsection (1A) omit the words from "For this purpose" to the end.

(4) For subsection (2) substitute—

"(2) Where two companies cease to be members of the group at the same time, subsection (1) does not have effect as respects the acquisition of an asset by one of the companies from the other if condition A or B is met.

(2ZA) Condition A is that the companies—

(a) are both 75 per cent subsidiaries and effective 51 per cent subsidiaries of another company on the date of the acquisition, and

(b) remain both 75 per cent subsidiaries and effective 51 per cent subsidiaries of that other company until immediately after they cease to be members of the group.

(2ZB) Condition B is that one of the companies—

(a) is both a 75 per cent subsidiary and an effective 51 per cent subsidiary of the other on the date of the acquisition, and

(b) remains both a 75 per cent subsidiary and an effective 51 per cent subsidiary of the other until immediately after the companies cease to be members of the group."

(5) For subsection (2A)(a) substitute—

"(a) a company ("company A") acquired an asset from another company ("company B") at a time when both company A and company B were members of the same group ("the first group"),

(aa) company A has ceased to be a member of the first group,".

(6) After subsection (3) insert—

"(3A) Any chargeable gain or allowable loss which would otherwise accrue to company A on the sale referred to in subsection (3) does not so accrue if—

(a) company A ceases to be a member of the group in consequence of—

(i) a disposal of shares in company A or another member of the group made by a member of the group, or

(ii) two or more such disposals,

(b) either—

(i) subsection (3B) applies to the disposal or, if there is more than one disposal, to at least one of them, or

(ii) sub-paragraph (i) does not apply but had subsection (3B) applied to the disposal or, if there is more than one disposal, to each of them, any gain arising on the disposal or disposals would not have been a chargeable gain by virtue of Schedule 7AC, and

(c) in the absence of this subsection, section 535 of CTA 2010 (UK REITS: exemption of gains) would not apply to the chargeable gain or allowable loss which would accrue to company A on the sale.

(3B) This subsection applies to a disposal of shares if—

(a) the company making the disposal is resident in the United Kingdom at the time of the disposal,

(b) the shares are chargeable assets in relation to that company immediately before that time, or

(c) any part of the chargeable gain or allowable loss accruing on the disposal is treated as a gain or loss accruing to a person by virtue of section 13(2) (attribution of gains to members of non-resident companies).

In this section "group disposal" means a disposal within subsection (3A)(a) to which this subsection applies and the company making the disposal is referred to as "the transferor company".

(3C) For the purposes of subsections (3A) and (3B), the question whether there is a disposal is to be determined ignoring section 127 (share reorganisations etc treated as not involving disposal).

(3D) If subsection (3A) applies, any chargeable gain or allowable loss accruing to the transferor company on a group disposal (other than a group disposal to which section 127 applies) is to be calculated—

(a) where a chargeable gain would accrue to company A in the absence of subsection (3A), as if the amount of the consideration for the group disposal were increased by the amount of the gain, and

(b) where an allowable loss would accrue to company A in the absence of subsection (3A), as if an amount equal to the amount of the loss were a sum allowable under section 38 as a deduction in the computation of the gain or loss accruing on the group disposal.

(3E) If subsection (3A) applies, and section 127 applies to a group disposal, any chargeable gain or allowable loss accruing to the transferor company on a disposal of the new holding arising from the group disposal (or any part of that holding) is to be calculated—

(a) where a chargeable gain would accrue to company A in the absence of subsection (3A)—

(i) as if an amount equal to the amount of the gain were excluded from the expenditure allowable as a deduction under section 38 in the computation of the gain or loss accruing on the disposal (but not so as to reduce that expenditure below nil), and

(ii) where (ignoring sub-paragraph (i)) the amount of the gain exceeds the expenditure allowable as such a deduction, as if a gain equal to that excess accrued on the disposal of the new holding (or, if the disposal is of a part of the new holding, a gain equal to the corresponding part of that excess accrued on that disposal), in addition to any gain or loss that actually accrues on the disposal of the new holding or part, and

(b) where an allowable loss would accrue to company A in the absence of subsection (3A), as if an amount equal to the amount of the loss were a sum allowable under section 38 as a deduction in the computation of the gain or loss accruing on the disposal.

In this subsection "new holding" has the meaning given by section 126.

(3F) If there is more than one group disposal, the references in subsections (3D) and (3E) to the amount of the gain or loss which would accrue to company A in the absence of subsection (3A) are to be read, in relation to each disposal, as references to—

(a) such proportion of that amount as the transferor companies in relation to the group disposals jointly elect as the appropriate proportion in relation to the disposal in question, or

(b) where no election is made, the proportion of that amount attributable to that disposal if that amount is divided equally between the group disposals.

(3G) An election under subsection (3F) must—

(a) specify the appropriate proportion in relation to each group disposal, and

(b) be made, by notice to an officer of Revenue and Customs, no later than 2 years after the end of the first accounting period of a company in which any chargeable gain or allowable loss on a group disposal accrues.

(3H) If a group disposal by a company consists of shares of more than one class, then, for the purposes of subsections (3D) and (3E), the company may apportion any increase or deduction to be made between the classes of shares in such manner as it considers appropriate."

(7) For subsection (5) substitute—

"(5) Subsections (6) to (8) apply where—

(a) in the absence of subsection (6), company A would be treated by virtue of subsection (3) as selling an asset at any time, by reason of ceasing to be a member of the group, and

(b) company A ceases to be a member of the group by reason only of the fact that the principal company of that group becomes a member of another group."

(8) In subsection (6)—

(a) for "The company" to "but" substitute "Subsection (3) does not apply to treat company A as selling the asset at that time; but", and

(b) for "the company in question" (in each place) substitute "company A".

(9) In subsection (7) for "the company" (in both places) substitute "company A".

(10) After that subsection insert—

"(7A) Any chargeable gain or allowable loss which would otherwise accrue to company A on the sale referred to in subsection (6) does not so accrue if—

(a) company A ceases at the relevant time to satisfy the conditions in subsection (7) in consequence of—

(i) a disposal of shares in company A, or another member of the other group mentioned in subsection (5)(b), made by a member of that other group, or
(ii) two or more such disposals,

(b) either—

(i) subsection (3B) applies to the disposal or, if there is more than one disposal, to at least one of them, or
(ii) sub-paragraph (i) does not apply but had subsection (3B) applied to the disposal or, if there is more than one disposal, to each of them, any gain arising on the disposal or disposals would not have been a chargeable gain by virtue of Schedule 7AC, and

(c) in the absence of this subsection, section 535 of CTA 2010 (UK REITS: exemption of gains) would not apply to the chargeable gain or allowable loss which would accrue to company A on the sale.

(7B) Where subsection (7A) applies, subsections (3C) to (3H) apply to the calculation of any chargeable gain or allowable loss accruing on a disposal within subsection (7A)(a) to which subsection (3B) applies (a "relevant disposal") with the following modifications—

(a) in subsections (3C) to (3H) for the references to a group disposal substitute references to a relevant disposal, and
(b) in subsections (3C), (3D) and (3E) for the references to subsection (3A) substitute references to subsection (7A)."

(11) In subsection (8) for the words from "the company" to the end substitute "company A on the sale referred to in subsection (6) is to be treated as accruing immediately before the relevant time."

(12) In subsection (10), for paragraph (a) substitute—

"(a) two companies are associated with each other if one is a 75 per cent subsidiary of the other or both are 75 per cent subsidiaries of another company."

(13) After that subsection insert—

"(10A) For the purposes of this section an asset is a "chargeable asset" in relation to a company at any time if any gain accruing to the company on a disposal of the asset by the company at that time—

(a) would be a chargeable gain and would by virtue of section 10B form part of its chargeable profits for corporation tax purposes, or
(b) would, but for Schedule 7AC (exemptions for disposals by companies with substantial shareholdings), be within paragraph (a)."

4 After section 179 of TCGA 1992 insert—

"179ZA Claim for adjustment of calculations under section 179

(1) This section applies where—

(a) a gain accrues to a company ("company A") on a sale referred to in subsection (3) or (6) of section 179, or
(b) a gain would so accrue but for subsection (3A) or (7A) of that section.

(2) If subsection (3D) or (3E) of that section applies in relation to one or more group disposals (within the meaning of that section)—

(a) the company making the disposal, or
(b) if there is more than one disposal, the companies making those disposals acting jointly,

may make a claim for the amount of the gain to be treated for the purposes of the subsection in question as reduced by an amount specified in the claim.

(3) In any other case, company A may make a claim for the amount of the gain to be treated for all purposes of this Act as reduced by an amount specified in the claim.

(4) Where a claim is made under subsection (2) or (3), the gain must be treated, for the purposes mentioned in the subsection in question, as reduced by such amount (if any) as is just and reasonable.

(5) In determining the amount which is just and reasonable regard must be had, in particular, to any transaction as a direct or indirect result of which company A or any associated company (within the meaning of section 179(10)) acquired the asset to which the gain relates.

(6) Where under this section the gain accruing to company A on a sale referred to in subsection (3) or (6) of section 179 is treated as reduced by an amount ("the permitted deduction"), the subsection in question has effect, so far as it provides for

the immediate reacquisition of the asset by company A, as if the reference to market value of the asset were to its market value less the permitted deduction."

5 In TCGA 1992, the following provisions are repealed—

(a) section 179A (reallocation within group of gain or loss accruing under section 179);

(b) section 179B (roll-over of degrouping charge on business assets);

(c) Schedule 7AB (roll-over of degrouping charge: modification of enactments).

Substantial shareholding exemption

6 (1) Schedule 7AC to TCGA 1992 (exemptions for disposals by companies with substantial shareholdings) is amended as follows.

(2) After paragraph 15 insert—

"Effect of transfer of trading assets within a group

15A (1) For the purposes of this Part, the period for which the investing company is treated as holding a substantial shareholding in the company invested in is extended in accordance with sub-paragraph (3) if the following conditions are met.

(2) The conditions are—

(a) that, immediately before the disposal, the investing company holds a substantial shareholding in the company invested in,

(b) that an asset which, at the time of the disposal, is being used for the purposes of a trade carried on by the company invested in was transferred to it by the investing company or another company,

(c) that, at the time of the transfer of the asset, the company invested in, the investing company and, if different, the company which transferred the asset were all members of the same group, and

(d) that the asset was previously used by a member of the group (other than the company invested in) for the purposes of a trade carried on by that member at a time when it was such a member.

(3) The investing company is to be treated as having held the substantial shareholding at any time during the final 12 month period when the asset was used as mentioned in sub-paragraph (2)(d) (if it did not hold a substantial shareholding at that time).

(4) "The final 12 month period" means the period of 12 months ending with the time of the disposal."

(3) In paragraph 19 (requirements relating to the company invested in), after sub-paragraph (2) insert—

"(2A) If the conditions in paragraph 15A(2)(b) to (d) are met, sub-paragraph (2B) applies for the purpose of determining whether the requirement of sub-paragraph (1)(a) is satisfied.

(2B) The company invested in is to be treated as having been a trading company at any time during the final 12 month period when the asset was used as mentioned in paragraph 15A(2)(d) (if it was not a trading company at that time).

(2C) "The final 12 month period" has the meaning given in paragraph 15A(4)."

Intangible fixed assets: degrouping

7 (1) Part 8 of CTA 2009 (intangible fixed assets) is amended as follows.

(2) In section 780 (deemed realisation and reacquisition at market value), in subsection (5)(b) before "associated" insert "certain".

(3) In section 783 (associated companies leaving group at same time), for subsection (1) substitute—

"(1) Where two companies cease to be members of a group at the same time, section 780 does not apply in relation to a transfer by one of the companies to the other if condition A or B is met.

(1A) Condition A is that the companies—

(a) are both 75% subsidiaries and effective 51% subsidiaries of another company on the date of the transfer, and

(b) remain both 75% subsidiaries and effective 51% subsidiaries of that other company until immediately after they cease to be members of the group.

(1B) Condition B is that one of the companies—

(a) is both a 75% subsidiary and an effective 51% subsidiary of the other on the date of the transfer, and

(b) remains both a 75% subsidiary and an effective 51% subsidiary of the other until immediately after the companies cease to be members of the group.",

and, in the section heading, for "*Associated*" substitute "*Certain associated*".

(4) In section 788 (provisions supplementing provisions about degrouping), for subsection (3) substitute—

"(3) For the purposes of those sections and this section two companies are associated with each other if one is a 75% subsidiary of the other or both are 75% subsidiaries of another company."

Consequential repeals

8 In consequence of the repeals made by paragraph 5, the following are also repealed—

(a) in IHTA 1984, section 97(1)(a)(iii) and the "or" before it,
(b) in FA 2002, section 42(1) and (3)(a),
(c) in F(No2)A 2005, in Schedule 4, paragraphs 8 and 10(3), and
(d) in FA 2009, in Schedule 12, paragraph 2.

Commencement

9 (1) The amendments made by paragraphs 1 to 5 and 8 have effect in relation to any disposal of an asset by one company ("company B") to another company ("company A") made at a time when company B is a member of a group, if—

(a) company A ceases to be a member of the group on or after the passing of this Act, or
(b) where company A ceased to be such a member before the passing of this Act in circumstances where section 179(6) to (8) of TCGA 1992 applied, company A ceases to satisfy the conditions in section 179(7) of that Act on or after the passing of this Act.

(2) The amendments made by paragraph 6 have effect in relation to disposals of shares made on or after the passing of this Act.

(3) The amendments made by paragraph 7 have effect in relation to any disposal of an asset by one company ("company B") to another company ("company A") made at a time when company B is a member of a group, if—

(a) company A ceases to be a member of the group on or after the passing of this Act, or
(b) where company A ceased to be such a member before the passing of this Act in circumstances where section 783 of CTA 2009 applied, company A ceases to be a member of another group on or after the passing of this Act.

(4) But where an early commencement election is made in relation to a group—

(a) sub-paragraphs (1) and (3) apply in relation to that group as if the references in those sub-paragraphs to the passing of this Act were references to 1 April 2011, and
(b) sub-paragraph (2) applies in relation to any disposal of shares by a member of that group as if the reference in that sub-paragraph to the passing of this Act were a reference to 1 April 2011.

(5) An early commencement election in relation to a group means an election made for the purposes of this paragraph by the principal company of the group.

(6) If a company ceases to be a member of a group in the period which begins with 1 April 2011 and ends with the passing of this Act, an early commencement election may be made or revoked in relation to the group only with the consent of that company contained in a notice which accompanies the election or revocation.

(7) Where an early commencement election is revoked, the election is treated as never having had effect.

(8) An early commencement election may not be made or revoked after 31 March 2012 (and paragraph 3(1)(b) of Schedule 1A to the Management Act (amendment of elections etc) does not apply in relation to an early commencement election).

GENERAL NOTE

Schedule 10 simplifies and clarifies various aspects of the capital gains degrouping charge.

General background

A degrouping charge arises when a company ceases to be a member of a group while holding an asset that has been transferred to it by another group member. The asset is deemed to be sold and reacquired by the company, using the value of the asset when it was transferred to the company, although the gain is deemed to accrue to the company when the company leaves the group or at the beginning of the accounting period.

Under the new rule, the deemed disposal and reacquisition and the computation of the gain or loss are the same. But in most cases the cost will now fall on the vendor company, not on the company leaving the group.

Commencement

The new rules will generally apply from the date of Royal Assent to FA 2011. However, an 'early commencement election' can be made by the principal company of a group, such that the new rules apply from 1st April 2011. This election must be made by 31st March 2012 and can also be revoked on or before that date, in which case it is treated as never having been made. However, if an election is revoked and a company left the group between 1st April 2011 and the date of Royal Assent to FA 2011, that company must also agree to the revocation of the early commencement election.

The new degrouping rule for share disposals

The new rule applies where a company ceases to be a member of a group by virtue of one or more disposals of shares of the target company of another member of the group. This is referred to as "the group disposal".

Where a company leaves a group without a group disposal, for example, if there is a significant investment by a new shareholder, so that the company is no longer a 75% subsidiary, the chargeable gain or allowable loss will accrue in the company leaving the group, as there is no vendor company in such cases. So for these disposals, there is no change in the basic degrouping charge.

The company making the disposal must either be resident in the United Kingdom or the shares must be chargeable assets of that company immediately before the disposal or the company could be subject to a gain treated as accruing under TCGA 1992 s 13(2).

The effect of the new rule is that, instead of the target company being subject to the chargeable gain arising on the deemed disposal or reacquisition, that gain is added to the consideration for the group disposal by the vendor company, or deducted from it where the result of the computation is a degrouping loss. The major impact of this is that any reliefs or exemptions which apply to the chargeable gain arising on the group disposal will apply to that chargeable gain as augmented (or reduced) by the degrouping element. While the legislation is reasonably complex, this is a practical simplification in that, prior to FA 2011, it was very easy to have a commercial disposal where the main disposal would be exempt under, say, the substantial shareholdings exemption but a degrouping charge would nevertheless apply in the target company in respect of assets previously transferred to it.

The new rule can also apply if the group disposal is outside the scope of UK corporation tax (for example, because the vendor is not UK resident for tax purposes) but a degrouping charge arises in a UK resident target company. If the group disposal would have been exempt under the substantial shareholdings exemption, had the vendor company been within the charge to UK corporation tax, the new rules can also apply to the deemed disposal and reacquisition by the target company, even though the main disposal is outside the scope of UK corporation tax.

Note that this new rule does not apply to degrouping charges arising in respect of intangible fixed assets to which CTA 2009 Part 8 applies.

Companies leaving a second group

A degrouping charge does not generally arise when a principal company of a group becomes a member of another group. However, as a result of such a transaction, a company that is a 75% subsidiary and a 51% effective subsidiary of the first group may not be a 75% subsidiary or a 51% effective subsidiary of the principal company of the second group. Under those circumstances, a degrouping charge does not arise in respect of that company while it remains a 75% subsidiary and an effective 51% subsidiary of at least 1 member of the new group. A degrouping charge will then only arise if, within 6 years of the asset transfer, the relevant company ceases to be a 75% subsidiary and an effective 51% subsidiary of any member of the second group.

The new rule applies so that, if a degrouping charge in respect of the company leaving the second group occurs because of a group disposal, ie because of a disposal of shares, the new rule will impose the deferred degrouping gain on the vendor company and not on the company leaving the group. However, if the company is leaving the group as the result of a transaction other than a disposal of shares, the gain will apply to the company leaving the group.

Multiple Group Disposals

Where the degrouping charge arises as a result of more than one group disposal, the vendor companies can make a joint election to allocate the degrouping charge between them. The election must be made no later than two years after the end of the first accounting period of a company in which any chargeable gain or allowable loss on a group disposal accrues and must specify the appropriate proportion of the gain in respect of each group disposal. If no election is made then the amount is divided equally between the group disposals.

Where the group disposals are of shares of more than one class, then the company may apportion any increase or deduction to the chargeable gains on the group disposal as it chooses.

The election must be made, by notice to an officer of Revenue and Customs, no later than 2 years after the end of the first accounting period of a company in which any chargeable gain or allowable loss on a group disposal accrues. The election must also specify the appropriate proportion in relation to each group disposal.

Interaction with reorganisation provisions

A degrouping charge can arise where a company leaves a group by way of a share-for-share exchange or reconstruction transaction to which TCGA 1992 s 127 would apply, deeming there to have been no disposal for tax purposes. In such a case, the "no disposal" fiction is ignored in deciding whether there is a disposal to which the new rules at TCGA 1992 ss 179(3A) and (3B) might apply.

Where, however, there is a degrouping event and TCGA 1992 s 127 applies to the group disposal, the no disposal fiction means that there will be no chargeable gain to which the degrouping charge can be applied under the new rules. Instead, the degrouping gain is effectively held over and will enhance the chargeable gain on the eventual disposal of the new assets. Where the degrouping charge gives rise to a loss, the relevant amount will, instead, be deducted from the chargeable gain on disposal of the new holding.

Interaction with reconstruction provisions

If a company transfers all or part of its business to another company as part of a scheme of reconstruction, the transfer may be deemed to be at no gain and no loss under TCGA s 139 so long as there is no consideration given for the transfer of business (except for the assumption of debt). Section 139 is amended so that this rule continues to apply even if the transfer of business gives rise to a degrouping charge which would otherwise be deemed to be consideration received by the disposing company in such a reconstruction. In other words, the deemed degrouping consideration is ignored when considering whether a reconstruction transaction has occurred without the payment of any consideration.

Prevention of double charge

FA 2011 introduced a new provision whereby a claim can be made for the adjustment of the degrouping charge in cases where it would be unreasonable for such a charge to apply. The provision, at TCGA 1992 s 179ZA, applies where there is a gain that accrues either to the target company or to one or more vendor companies. The company to which the gain would accrue (either the vendor company or the target company) may make a claim for the gain to be reduced for all purposes of the Act by an amount that must be specified in the claim.

Where a claim is made, HMRC is required to reduce the gain by such amount as is just and reasonable, taking into account, in particular, any transaction whereby the asset holding company or an associated company acquired the asset directly or indirectly. Where a claim is admitted, the gain is treated as reduced for all purposes of the Act and the difference is also applied to the deemed disposal and reacquisition of the asset concerned, so that references to its market value are replaced by references to its market value less the amount deducted under this provision.

Associated companies exception

The degrouping rule has an exception where two companies that are associated (ie form a group together) leave a group at the same time. The associated company exception is now 'clarified', and only applies if one of two conditions is met:

— Condition A is that the companies are both 75% subsidiaries and effective 51% subsidiaries on the date of acquisition and remain so until immediately after they cease to be members of the group

— Condition B is that one of the companies is a 75% subsidiary and an effective 51% subsidiary of the other on the date of acquisition and remains so until immediately after the companies ceased to be members of the group.

This is more restrictive than the original rules. In the past, if an asset transfer occurred while companies were associated, and they were associated when they left the group together, the exception applied. But it was not necessary that they remained associated throughout the intervening period. The new rule requires that the association remain in place throughout the period between acquisition of the asset and the degrouping event.

Associated companies exception and intangible fixed assets

This is the only part of Sch 10 that affects the intangibles regime in CTA 2009 Part 8. The degrouping rule in CTA 2009 s 783 is also amended so that it only applies if one of two conditions is met:

— Condition A is that the companies are both 75% subsidiaries and effective 51% subsidiaries on the date of acquisition and remain so until immediately after they cease to be members of the group

— Condition B is that one of the companies is a 75% subsidiary and an effective 51% subsidiary of the other on the date of acquisition and remains so until immediately after the companies ceased to be members of the group.

Extension to substantial shareholdings exemption

There is an extension to the substantial shareholdings exemption where a company is disposing of a trade or part of a trade and wishes to do so by transferring that trading activity into a new company to sell. Previously, such a transaction would have left the target company (the new trading company) susceptible to a degrouping charge. Under the new rule, this degrouping charge would, instead, be added to the consideration for the disposal of the new company by the vendor. But the substantial shareholdings exemption would not apply, as prima facie the new trading company would not have been owned for long enough and nor would it have been trading for long enough for the exemption to apply.

The extension to the substantial shareholdings exemption is intended to ensure that the disposal of the new company by the vendor will qualify for the substantial shareholdings exemption. The conditions for the extension of the relief are that:

— Immediately before the disposal the vendor company holds a substantial shareholding in the new company

— An asset which, at the time of the disposal is being used for the purposes of a trade carried on by the new company has been transferred to it by the vendor or another company in the group at a time when all the relevant companies were members of the same group and

— The asset was previously used by a member of the group, other than the new company, for the purposes of a trade carried on by that company.

If these conditions are satisfied the vendor company is treated as having held the substantial shareholding in the new company for the period of twelve months ending with the time of the disposal, so long as, during the whole of that period, the relevant asset had been in use for the purposes of a trade carried on by a company in the group. Furthermore, if the conditions are met then the new company is also treated as having been a trading company throughout that twelve month period, again so long as the asset had been in use as a trading asset by a member of the group during that period.

As a result, this relief is available for the "packaging" of trading activities by a vendor company, as both the actual disposal proceeds and any deemed proceeds in respect of the degrouping will qualify for the substantial shareholdings exemption.

Once again, note that this change has no impact on the degrouping rules for chargeable intangible assets under, so that this exemption will not be useful for companies with material value in new goodwill or other intangible assets.

Repeals and other amendments

The result of the main change to the mechanics of the degrouping charge is that s 179A, the facility for a vendor company to elect with the company leaving the group that the gain should remain within vendors group, is no longer required and is repealed.

Nevertheless, companies might wish to allocate a degrouping gain elsewhere within the group using the facility under s 171A. This facility is therefore extended to degrouping charges, which were previously excluded from s 171A.

The facility to roll over a de-grouping gain under s 179B is, however, repealed in its entirety as a "simplification". HMRC's view was that this facility is rarely, if ever, used and its repeal will not, therefore, cause any loss to company tax payers.

SCHEDULE 11

PRE-ENTRY LOSSES

Section 46

TCGA 1992

1 In section 177A of TCGA 1992 (restriction on set-off of pre-entry losses), omit "and losses accruing on assets held by any company at such a time".

2 Schedule 7A to that Act (restriction on set-off of pre-entry losses) is amended as follows.

3 (1) Paragraph 1 (application and construction of Schedule) is amended as follows.

(2) In sub-paragraph (1) for "is or has been" substitute "becomes".

(3) For sub-paragraph (2) substitute—

"(2) In this Schedule "pre-entry loss", in relation to any company, means any allowable loss that accrued to that company at a time before it became a member of the relevant group."

(4) Omit sub-paragraphs (3), (3A), (4) and (5).

(5) In sub-paragraph (6) for "Subject to" to "if" substitute "If".

(6) Omit sub-paragraph (8).

4 Omit paragraphs 2 to 5 (determination of pre-entry proportion of losses on pre-entry assets).

5 (1) Paragraph 6 (restrictions on the deduction of pre-entry losses) is amended as follows.

(2) In sub-paragraph (2)—

(a) omit paragraph (a) (and the "and" after it), and
(b) in paragraph (b), omit "in any other case".

(3) In sub-paragraph (3)—

(a) omit paragraph (a) (and the "and" after it), and
(b) in paragraph (b), omit "in the case of an election under sub-paragraph (2)(b) above,".

6 (1) Paragraph 7 (gains from which pre-entry losses are to be deductible) is amended as follows.

(2) In sub-paragraph (1), for paragraph (c) substitute—

"(c) on the disposal of any asset in respect of which the conditions in sub-paragraph (1A) are met."

(3) After that sub-paragraph insert—

"(1A) The conditions referred to in sub-paragraph (1)(c) are—

(a) that the asset was acquired, on or after the entry date, by—

(i) the company to which the pre-entry loss accrued ("company A"), or
(ii) a company which, at the time of the acquisition, was a group company of company A,

from a person who at the time of the acquisition was not a group company of company A, and

(b) that the asset has not, since its acquisition from that person, been used or held for any purposes other than those of a trade or business which—

(i) was being carried on by company A immediately before the entry date, and

(ii) continued until the disposal to be carried on by company A or a company which, when it carried on the trade or business, was a group company of company A.

(1B) For the purposes of sub-paragraph (1A), a company is a "group company of company A" at any time when it is a member of a group of companies of which company A is also a member.

(1C) Where a company, having become a member of the relevant group, subsequently becomes a member of another group ("the new group")—

(a) sub-paragraph (1) continues to have effect, in relation to any loss which accrued to the company before it became a member of the relevant group, by reference to the date on which it became such a member, and

(b) accordingly, that sub-paragraph does not apply separately in relation to the loss by reason of it also having accrued to the company before it became a member of the new group."

(4) Omit sub-paragraph (2).

(5) In sub-paragraph (3)—

(a) omit ", without prejudice to paragraph 9 below",

(b) omit paragraph (b), and

(c) in paragraph (c), for "sub-paragraphs (1)(c) and (2)(c)" substitute "sub-paragraph (1A)".

(6) For sub-paragraph (4) substitute—

"(4) Sub-paragraphs (4A) and (4B) apply for determining for the purposes of this paragraph whether an asset on the disposal of which a chargeable gain accrues was an asset held by a company immediately before the entry date (a "pre-entry asset").

(4A) Except as provided by sub-paragraph (4B), an asset is not a pre-entry asset if—

(a) the company which held the asset at the entry date is not the company which makes the disposal, and

(b) since the entry date that asset has been disposed of otherwise than by a disposal to which section 171 applies.

(4B) Without prejudice to sub-paragraph (4C), where, on a disposal to which section 171 does not apply—

(a) an asset would cease to be a pre-entry asset by virtue of sub-paragraph (4A), but

(b) the company making the disposal retains an interest in or over the asset in question,

that interest is a pre-entry asset.

(4C) For the purposes of this paragraph—

(a) an asset acquired or held by a company at any time and an asset held at a later time by that company, or by any company which is or has been a member of the same group of companies as that company, is to be treated as the same asset if the value of the second asset is derived in whole or in part from the first asset, and

(b) if—

(i) any asset is treated (whether by virtue of paragraph (a) or otherwise) as the same as an asset held by a company at a later time, and

(ii) the first asset would have been a pre-entry asset in relation to that company,

the second asset is also to be treated as a pre-entry asset in relation to that company;

and paragraph (a) applies, in particular, where the second asset is a freehold and the first asset is a leasehold the lessee of which acquires the reversion."

(7) In sub-paragraph (5) omit "or (2)" (in both places).

(8) In sub-paragraph (6) omit "or (2)".

7 (1) Paragraph 8 (change of a company's nature) is amended as follows.

(2) In sub-paragraph (1)—

(a) after "trade" (in each place) insert "or business",

(b) in paragraph (a) for "carried on by that company" substitute "which was carried on by that company immediately before it became a member of that group", and

(c) for "paragraph 7(1)(c) and (2)(c)" substitute "paragraph 7(1A)".

(3) For sub-paragraph (2) substitute—

"(2) In sub-paragraph (1) "a major change in the nature or conduct of a trade or business" includes—

(a) a major change in the type of property dealt in, or services or facilities provided, in the trade or business,

(b) a major change in customers, markets or outlets of the trade or business, or
(c) in the case of a company with investment business (within the meaning of section 1218 of CTA 2009), a major change in the nature of the investments held;

and this paragraph applies even if the change is the result of a gradual process which began outside the period of three years mentioned in sub-paragraph (1)(a)."

8 Omit paragraph 9 (identification of "the relevant group" and application of Schedule to every connected group).

9 In paragraph 11 (continuity provisions), omit sub-paragraph (3)(b) (and the "and" before it).

Consequential repeals

10 Omit the following provisions (which relate to the provisions repealed by paragraphs 1 to 9)—

(a) in FA 1994, sections 93(8) to (10) and 94;
(b) in FA 1998, section 138;
(c) in FA 2000, in Schedule 29, paragraph 7(2) to (5);
(d) in F(No2)A 2005, section 65(2), (3) and (5).

Commencement

11 (1) The amendments made by this Part of this Schedule have effect on and after commencement in relation to the deduction of any pre-entry loss within paragraph 1(2) of Schedule 7A to TCGA 1992 (as substituted by paragraph 3 of this Schedule) regardless of—

(a) whether the loss accrued before or on or after commencement, and
(b) whether the company which accrued the loss became a member of the relevant group (within the meaning of that Schedule) before or on or after commencement.

(2) In this paragraph "commencement" means the day on which this Act is passed.

Transitional provision

12 (1) Sub-paragraph (2) applies where, immediately before commencement, Schedule 7A to TCGA 1992 had effect, in the case of a company which is or has been a member of a group of companies ("the relevant group") in relation to a loss of that company within paragraph 1(2)(b) of that Schedule (pre-entry proportion of an allowable loss that has accrued to a company on the disposal of a pre-entry asset).

(2) On and after commencement that loss is to be treated, for the purposes of Schedule 7A to TCGA 1992, as if it were a pre-entry loss within the meaning of paragraph 1(2) of that Schedule (as substituted by paragraph 3 of this Schedule) which accrued to that company immediately before it became a member of the relevant group.

(3) In this paragraph "commencement" means the day on which this Act is passed.

GENERAL NOTE

Schedule 11 simplifies the rules on capital loss buying in TCGA 1992 Sch 7A as part of the simplification of the capital gains rules for companies.

Background

Schedule 7A prevents companies that are making chargeable gains from buying capital losses to shelter those gains. Essentially, losses that are bought into a group cannot be used to shelter gains on assets that were already in the group. The restriction applies both to losses that have accrued to a company that was bought in and to the pre-entry proportion of any loss that arose on assets that were held by that company and subsequently sold at a loss.

Use of pre-entry proportion of losses

This second element is now repealed. While pre-entry losses still cannot be used, there is no longer a restriction on the use the pre-entry proportion of losses that arise on the post-entry disposal of an asset held by the target company. While this appears, superficially, to be a relaxation of the rules, the legislation at TCGA s 184A, which also restricts the use of purchased losses where there is a tax avoidance motive, remain unchanged. So the change to Sch 7A does not open the door to tax planning.

Extension of trading exception

There was an exception from the general restriction on the use of pre-entry losses for trading companies. If a trading company with a capital loss was acquired by another group, that company subsequently acquired a trading asset and later disposed of it for a gain, the pre-entry loss could be used against the gain on this post-entry asset, so long as the asset had been used in the trade throughout its period of ownership. This was very restrictive, as it only applied to the company that held the capital loss and only if it was carrying on a trade. This rule is now simplified and relaxed in two ways:

— The legislation now refers to a business, not just to a trade, so that the rule can apply even if the activities of the company do not amount to a trade, so long as they are sufficient to qualify as a business.

— The rule is also relaxed so that it will apply to any company in the group that is now carrying on the relevant business. That is, if the business is transferred to another group company which makes the gain on disposal of an asset that was used in the business, the pre-entry loss can be set against that gain even though the business is being carried on by a different company. There is some anti-avoidance legislation to ensure that this exception will not apply where there has been a major change in the nature or conduct of the business of the company.

Anti-avoidance measures

The rules as to when a loss is pre-entry loss are "clarified" following attempts to circumvent the rules through complex planning involving multiple changes of group.

Commencement

All of the changes apply from Royal Ascent to FA 2011. The commencement provisions are designed to apply to the set off of pre-entry losses from the date of commencement, regardless of when the pre-entry losses accrued or when the company was acquired. There is a transitional provision that applies where a company has joined a group with an asset standing at a loss. Any pre-entry proportion of that loss is treated as if it were an accrued pre-entry loss at the date of commencement of these changes.

SCHEDULE 12

CONTROLLED FOREIGN COMPANIES

Section 47

PART 1

EXEMPTIONS FOR COMPANIES WITH LIMITED UK CONNECTION

1 (1) Section 748 of ICTA (cases where apportionment of chargeable profits and creditable tax under section 747(3) does not apply) is amended as follows.

(2) In subsection (1), in paragraph (b) for "that Schedule" substitute "Schedule 25".

(3) After that paragraph insert—

"(ba) the company is exempt for that period by virtue of Part 2A of that Schedule (exemption for trading companies with limited UK connection); or

(bb) the company is exempt for that period by virtue of Part 2B of that Schedule (exemption for companies exploiting intellectual property with limited UK connection); or".

2 After section 751AA of that Act insert—

"751AB Reduction in chargeable profits: failure to qualify for exemptions

(1) This section applies if—

(a) an apportionment under section 747(3) would fall to be made as regards an accounting period ("the relevant accounting period") of a controlled foreign company,

(b) but for a relevant failure, section 748(1)(ba) or (bb) would have prevented such an apportionment, and

(c) a company resident in the United Kingdom ("the UK resident company") has a relevant interest in the controlled foreign company in that period.

(2) "Relevant failure" means—

(a) in the case of section 748(1)(ba), one or both of the following—

(i) a failure to satisfy the requirement of paragraph 12E of Schedule 25 (requirement as to company's UK connection) in circumstances where the requirement would be satisfied if the reference in sub-paragraph (3)(a) of that paragraph to 10% were a reference to 50%, and

(ii) a failure to satisfy the requirement of paragraph 12F of that Schedule (finance income and relevant IP income) in circumstances where the relevant IP income of the controlled foreign company for the accounting period does not exceed 5% of the company's gross income for that period, and

(b) in the case of section 748(1)(bb), a failure to satisfy the requirement of paragraph 12M of that Schedule (finance income).

(3) The UK resident company may make an application to the Commissioners for Her Majesty's Revenue and Customs for the chargeable profits of the controlled foreign company for the relevant accounting period ("the chargeable profits") to be reduced to an amount specified in the application ("the specified amount").

The specified amount may be nil.

(4) If the Commissioners grant the application—

(a) the chargeable profits are treated as reduced to the specified amount, and

(b) the controlled foreign company's creditable tax (if any) for that period is treated as reduced by so much of that tax as, on a just and reasonable basis, relates to the reduction in the chargeable profits,

for the purpose of applying section 747(3) to (5) for determining the sum (if any) chargeable on the UK resident company under section 747(4)(a) (but for no other purpose).

(5) The Commissioners may grant the application only if—

(a) they are satisfied that the specified amount is not less than the relevant amount, and

(b) they have not previously granted an application made by the UK resident company in respect of the relevant accounting period under section 751A or 751AC.

(6) "The relevant amount" means—

(a) if the relevant failure is within subsection (2)(a), the sum of—

(i) the excess finance and IP income (if any) for the relevant accounting period, and

(ii) in a case where there is a failure specified in subsection (2)(a)(i), so much (if any) of the net chargeable profits for that period as are not excluded by subsection (8), and

(b) if the relevant failure is within subsection (2)(b)—

(i) the amount (if any) by which the controlled foreign company's finance income for the relevant accounting period exceeds 5% of its gross income for that period, or

(ii) if that amount is a negligible amount, nil.

(7) "The excess finance and IP income" for the relevant accounting period means—

(a) the amount (if any) by which the total of the controlled foreign company's finance income and relevant IP income for that period exceeds 5% of its gross income for that period, or

(b) if that amount is a negligible amount, nil.

(8) Net chargeable profits are excluded by this subsection if, and to the extent that, they can reasonably be regarded—

(a) as representing the net economic value which—

(i) arises to the appropriate body of persons (taken as a whole), and

(ii) is created directly by qualifying work, or

(b) as not being wholly or partly attributable, directly or indirectly, to transactions with persons within the charge to United Kingdom tax.

(9) In subsection (8)(a) "qualifying work" means work which—

(a) is done in the territory in which the controlled foreign company is resident, and

(b) is done in that territory by individuals working for the controlled foreign company there.

(10) A transaction with a company which is within the charge to United Kingdom tax only because it carries on a trade in the United Kingdom through a permanent

establishment there is within subsection (8)(b) only if the transaction is attributable to activities carried on through that establishment.

(11) For the purposes of subsections (8) and (9)—

(a) section 751A(5), (6) and (9) applies as it applies for the purposes of the equivalent provisions of section 751A, and

(b) paragraph 5(2) to (5) of Schedule 25 (residence of controlled foreign company) applies as it applies in relation to Part 2 of that Schedule.

(12) In this section—

"finance income" has the meaning given by paragraph 12F(3) of Schedule 25 (with references to C read as references to the controlled foreign company);

"relevant IP income" has the meaning given by paragraph 12F(4) of that Schedule;

"net chargeable profits" means chargeable profits excluding so much of those profits as is directly attributable to the finance income or relevant IP income of the controlled foreign company;

"UK-connected gross income" has the same meaning as in paragraph 12E of Schedule 25;

"United Kingdom tax" means corporation tax or income tax;

and paragraph 12G of that Schedule (gross income) applies for the purposes of this section as it applies for the purposes of Part 2A of that Schedule (with references to C read as references to the controlled foreign company)."

3 In Schedule 25 to that Act (cases where section 747(3) does not apply), after Part 2 insert—

"PART 2A

TRADING COMPANIES WITH LIMITED UK CONNECTION

Introductory

12B (1) For the purposes of section 748(1)(ba), a controlled foreign company ("C") is exempt for an accounting period if the requirements of this Part of this Schedule are satisfied.

(2) The requirements are those imposed as to C's—

(a) business establishment (see paragraph 12C),

(b) business activities (see paragraph 12D),

(c) UK connection (see paragraph 12E), and

(d) finance income and relevant IP income (see paragraph 12F).

Business establishment

12C (1) The requirement of this paragraph is that throughout the accounting period C has a business establishment in the territory in which it is resident.

(2) For the purposes of sub-paragraph (1)—

(a) paragraph 5(2) to (5) (special rules about residence of the company) applies as it applies for the purposes of Part 2 of this Schedule, and

(b) paragraph 7 (meaning of "business establishment") applies as it applies for the purposes of paragraph 6(1)(a).

Business activities

12D (1) The requirement of this paragraph is that—

(a) C's business does not, at any time during the accounting period, include to a substantial extent non-exempt activities, or

(b) if C is wholly engaged in business falling within paragraph 11(1)(c) (banking etc), C's business does not, at any time during the accounting period, include to a substantial extent non-exempt activities which do not constitute investment business.

(2) For this purpose—

"non-exempt activities" means—

(a) the holding or managing of shares or securities,

(b) the holding of intellectual property,

(c) dealing in securities, other than in the capacity of a broker,

(d) the leasing of any description of property or rights,

(e) the investment in any manner of funds which would otherwise be available, directly or indirectly, for investment by or on behalf of any person (whether resident in the United Kingdom or not) who has, or is connected or associated with a person who has, control, either alone or together with other persons, of C, and

(f) if C is not a member of an insurance group throughout the accounting period, the effecting or carrying out of contracts of insurance between C and persons related to C;

"investment business" means activities within paragraphs (a) to (d) of paragraph 9(1).

(3) For the purposes of sub-paragraph (2)(f), a person is "related" to C if—

(a) the person is connected or associated with C,

(b) the person has a 25 per cent assessable interest in C in the case of the accounting period in question (within the meaning of paragraph 6(4C)), or

(c) if C is a controlled foreign company in that accounting period by virtue of subsection (1A) of section 747, the person is connected or associated with either or both of the two persons mentioned in that subsection.

(4) In sub-paragraph (2)—

"broker" includes any person offering to sell securities to, or purchase securities from, members of the public generally;

"contract of insurance" has the meaning given by Article 3(1) of the Financial Services and Markets Act 2000 (Regulated Activities) Order 2001;

"insurance group" has the meaning given by paragraph 11A(4);

"intellectual property" is to be construed in accordance with paragraph 9(1A);

"member of an insurance group" has the meaning given by paragraph 11A(6).

UK connection

12E (1) The requirement of this paragraph is that C does not have a significant connection with the United Kingdom during the accounting period.

(2) C has a significant connection with the United Kingdom during the accounting period if Condition A or B is met.

(3) Condition A is that—

(a) the UK-connected gross income of C's business for that period exceeds 10% of the gross income of that business for that period, and

(b) sub-paragraph (4) does not apply.

(4) This sub-paragraph applies if—

(a) at all times in the accounting period there are sufficient individuals working for C in the territory in which it is resident, or in any other territory outside of the United Kingdom, who have the competence and authority to undertake all, or substantially all, of C's business,

(b) C's relevant profits for the accounting period do not exceed 10% of C's relevant operating expenses for that period, and

(c) the UK-connected gross income of C's business for that period does not exceed 50% of the gross income of that business for that period.

(5) Condition B is that—

(a) the UK-connected related-party business expenditure of C's business for that period exceeds 50% of the total related-party business expenditure of C's business for that period, and

(b) during the accounting period C has been involved in a scheme where the main purpose, or one of the main purposes, of any party to the scheme in entering into the scheme is to achieve a reduction in corporation tax or any tax chargeable as if it were corporation tax.

(6) For the purposes of sub-paragraph (4)(a), individuals are not to be regarded as working for C in any territory unless—

(a) they are employed by C in the territory, or

(b) they are otherwise directed by C to perform duties on its behalf in the territory.

(7) In this paragraph—

"related-party business expenditure" means any expenditure, other than capital expenditure, which gives rise, directly or indirectly, to income of a person related to C;

"relevant profits", for an accounting period, means the total profits of C for that period calculated in accordance with generally accepted accounting practice (disregarding any capital gains or losses), but before any deduction for interest or tax;

"relevant operating expenses" of C means operating expenses of C other than—

(a) the cost of goods sold, and

(b) related-party business expenditure;

"scheme" means any scheme, arrangements or understanding of any kind whatever, whether or not legally enforceable, involving one or more transactions;

"UK-connected gross income" means the gross income derived, directly or indirectly, from persons who are within the charge to United Kingdom tax for all or part of the accounting period;

"UK-connected related-party business expenditure" means related-party business expenditure which gives rise, directly or indirectly, to income of a person within the charge to United Kingdom tax in respect of that income;

"United Kingdom tax" means income tax or corporation tax;

and paragraph 12D(3) (persons "related" to C) applies for the purposes of this paragraph as it applies for the purposes of paragraph 12D(2)(f).

(8) In the case of a company which is within the charge to United Kingdom tax only because it carries on a trade in the United Kingdom through a permanent establishment there, for the purposes of sub-paragraph (7)—

(a) the gross income derived from that company is so much of the gross income as is attributable to that establishment, and

(b) the income received by that company is such of its income as is attributable to that establishment.

Finance income and relevant IP income

12F (1) The requirement of this paragraph is that not more than 5% of C's gross income for the accounting period falls within sub-paragraph (2).

(2) Gross income falls within this sub-paragraph to the extent that it is—

(a) finance income, or

(b) relevant IP income.

(3) "Finance income" means—

(a) any amount which in accordance with UK generally accepted accounting practice falls to be recognised as arising from a financial asset, and

(b) any return, in relation to an amount, which—

(i) is produced for C by an arrangement to which C is party, and

(ii) is economically equivalent to interest,

except to the extent that the return is taken into account in determining an amount within paragraph (a).

(4) "Relevant IP income" means royalties and receipts of a similar nature arising from intellectual property.

(5) For the purposes of sub-paragraph (3)(b), the amount of a return is the amount which by virtue of the return would, in calculating C's chargeable profits, be treated under section 486B of CTA 2009 (disguised interest to be regarded as profit from loan relationship) as a profit arising to C from a loan relationship.

(6) But, in calculating that profit for the purposes of sub-paragraph (5), sections 486B(7) and 486C to 486E of CTA 2009 are to be ignored.

(7) In this paragraph—

"economically equivalent to interest" is to be construed in accordance with section 486B(2) and (3) of CTA 2009;

"financial asset" means a financial asset as defined for the purposes of UK generally accepted accounting practice or international accounting standards;

"intellectual property" is to be construed in accordance with paragraph 9(1A).

Gross income

12G (1) References in this Part of this Schedule to C's gross income are to be construed in accordance with this paragraph.

(2) C's gross income for an accounting period does not include—

(a) any distribution that would not be included in C's chargeable profits by reason of it being exempt for the purposes of Part 9A of CTA 2009 (see section 931A of that Act), or

(b) any amount that would be taken into account in computing chargeable gains if C were within the charge to corporation tax.

(3) C's gross income for an accounting period includes—

(a) any income which accrues during that period to the trustees of a settlement in relation to which C is a settlor or a beneficiary, and

(b) any income which accrues during that period to a partnership of which C is a partner, apportioned between C and the other partners on a just and reasonable basis.

(4) Where there is more than one settlor or beneficiary in relation to the settlement mentioned in sub-paragraph (3)(a), the income is to be apportioned between C and the other settlors or beneficiaries on a just and reasonable basis.

(5) In this paragraph—

"distribution" has the same meaning as in the Corporation Tax Acts (see Part 23 of CTA 2010);

"partnership" includes an entity established under the law of a country or territory outside the United Kingdom of a similar character to a partnership; and "partner" is to be read accordingly.

PART 2B

COMPANIES EXPLOITING INTELLECTUAL PROPERTY WITH LIMITED UK CONNECTION

Introductory

12H (1) For the purposes of section 748(1)(bb), a company ("C") is exempt for an accounting period if the requirements of this Part of this Schedule are satisfied.

(2) The requirements are those imposed as to C's—

(a) business establishment (see paragraph 12I),
(b) intellectual property business (see paragraph 12J),
(c) other business activities (see paragraph 12K),
(d) UK connection (see paragraph 12L), and
(e) finance income (see paragraph 12M).

Business establishment

12I (1) The requirement of this paragraph is that throughout the accounting period C has a business establishment in the territory in which it is resident.

(2) For the purposes of sub-paragraph (1)—

(a) paragraph 5(2) to (5) (special rules about residence of the company) applies as it applies for the purposes of Part 2 of this Schedule, and

(b) paragraph 7 (meaning of "business establishment") applies as it applies for the purposes of paragraph 6(1)(a).

Intellectual property business

12J (1) The requirement of this paragraph is that C's main business, throughout the accounting period, consists of the exploitation of intellectual property which does not have a relevant UK connection.

(2) For the purposes of sub-paragraph (1), if any part of C's main business consists of the exploitation of intellectual property which has a relevant UK connection, that part is to be ignored if it is an insignificant part of C's main business.

(3) Intellectual property has a relevant UK connection if—

(a) at any time during the accounting period or the 6 years immediately preceding that period, it has been held by a person resident in the United Kingdom, or

(b) activities relating to the creation, maintenance or enhancement of the intellectual property (other than activities of an incidental or insignificant nature) have been carried on by a person who for some or all of the period—

(i) beginning when the activities were first carried on by the person, and
(ii) ending at the end of the accounting period,

was related to C and within the charge to United Kingdom tax.

Other business activities

12K (1) The requirement of this paragraph is that—

(a) C does not, at any time during the accounting period, carry on any activities otherwise than in the course of its main business, or

(b) if it carries on any such activities ("secondary activities"), the secondary activities condition is met.

(2) The secondary activities condition is that either—

(a) the secondary activities do not, at any time during the accounting period, constitute a substantial part of the activities of C's business taken as a whole, or
(b) section 748(1)(b) or (ba) would apply to prevent an apportionment under section 747(3) falling to be made as regards that period, if C's business consisted only of the secondary activities carried on by it during the accounting period.

UK connection

12L (1) The requirement of this paragraph is that C does not have a significant connection with the United Kingdom during the accounting period.

(2) C has a significant connection with the United Kingdom during the accounting period if—

(a) all or a substantial proportion of C's gross income for that period consists of income from the exploitation of intellectual property which derives from persons within the charge to United Kingdom tax, or
(b) during that period C incurs expenditure (other than expenditure of an incidental or insignificant nature) on—
(i) R&D sub-contractor payments, or
(ii) the creation, development or maintenance of relevant intellectual property,

and that expenditure forms part of the income of a person who for some or all of that period is related to C and within the charge to United Kingdom tax.

(3) In this paragraph—

"R&D sub-contractor payment" means a payment made by C to another person in respect of research and development contracted out by C to that person;
"relevant intellectual property" means intellectual property which does not have a relevant UK connection (see paragraph 12J(3)) and which C exploits in the course of its main business.

Finance income

12M The requirement of this paragraph is that not more than 5% of C's gross income for the accounting period consists of finance income (within the meaning of paragraph 12F(3)).

Interpretation of Part 2B

12N (1) For the purpose of this Part of this Schedule—

"intellectual property" is to be construed in accordance with paragraph 9(1A);
"United Kingdom tax" means corporation tax or income tax;

and paragraph 12G (meaning of "gross income") applies as it applies for the purposes of Part 2A of this Schedule.

(2) For the purposes of this Part of this Schedule a person is "related" to C at a particular time if at that time—

(a) the person is connected or associated with C,
(b) the person has a 25 per cent assessable interest in C in the case of the accounting period of C in which that time falls (within the meaning of paragraph 6(4C)), or
(c) if C is a controlled foreign company in the accounting period in which that time falls by virtue of subsection (1A) of section 747, the person is connected or associated with either or both of the two persons mentioned in that subsection.

(3) In the case of a company which is within the charge to United Kingdom tax only because it carries on a trade in the United Kingdom through a permanent establishment there—

(a) for the purposes of paragraph 12J(3)(b), the activities carried on by the company are such of the activities as are carried on through that establishment,
(b) for the purposes of paragraph 12L(2)(a), the income derived from that company is such of the income so derived as is attributable to that establishment, and
(c) for the purposes of paragraph 12L(2)(b), the income of that company is such of its income as is attributable to that establishment."

PART 2

AMENDMENT OF SMALL CHARGEABLE PROFITS EXEMPTION

4 (1) Section 748 of ICTA (cases where apportionment of chargeable profits and creditable tax under section 747(3) does not apply) is amended as follows.

(2) In subsection (1), after paragraph (d) insert—

"(da) the relevant profits for the accounting period, after any adjustment required by subsection (3C), do not exceed—

(i) £200,000, or

(ii) if the accounting period is less than 12 months, a proportionately reduced amount; or".

(3) After subsection (3) insert—

"(3A) The reference in subsection (1)(da) to the relevant profits for an accounting period are to the sum of—

(a) the profits of the company for that period calculated in accordance with generally accepted accounting practice (disregarding any exempt distributions and any capital gains or losses), before any adjustment required or authorised by law in calculating chargeable profits,

(b) any amount which accrues during that period to the trustees of a settlement in relation to which the company is a settlor or a beneficiary, and

(c) the company's share of any income which accrues during that period to a partnership of which the company is a partner.

(3B) For the purposes of subsection (3A)—

(a) "exempt distribution" means a distribution (within the meaning of Part 23 of CTA 2010) which would be excluded from the company's chargeable profits by reason of it being exempt for the purposes of Part 9A of CTA 2009 (company distributions),

(b) where there is more than one settlor or beneficiary in relation to the settlement mentioned in subsection (3A)(b), the income is to be apportioned between the company and the other settlors or beneficiaries on a just and reasonable basis, and

(c) the company's share of any income which accrues to a partnership as mentioned in subsection (3A)(c) is to be determined by apportioning that income between the company and the other partners on a just and reasonable basis;

and in subsection (3A) and this subsection "partnership" includes an entity established under the law of a country or territory outside the United Kingdom of a similar character to a partnership; and "partner" is to be read accordingly.

(3C) For the purposes of subsection (1)(da), Part 4 of TIOPA 2010 (transfer pricing) applies in relation to the calculation of the relevant profits for the accounting period as it applies in relation to the calculation of the chargeable profits for that period.

(3D) But where the difference made in the amount of the relevant profits for the period as a result of the application of subsection (3C) would (disregarding this subsection) not exceed £50,000, no adjustment under that subsection is to be made."

(4) In subsection (6) for "section" substitute "sections 748ZA and".

5 After that section insert—

"748ZA Exclusion of small profits exemptions

(1) Nothing in section 748(1)(da) prevents an apportionment falling to be made as regards an accounting period ("the relevant accounting period") of a controlled foreign company ("X") if condition A, B or C is met.

(2) Condition A is that at any time before the end of the relevant accounting period a scheme is entered into and—

(a) in the absence of this subsection, in consequence of the scheme, section 748(1)(da) would apply to prevent an apportionment falling to be made as regards the relevant accounting period of X, and

(b) the main purpose, or one of the main purposes, of any party to the scheme in entering into the scheme is to secure that section 748(1)(da) prevents an apportionment falling to be made as regards that period, or that period and one or more other accounting periods of X.

(3) Condition B is that at any time before the end of the relevant accounting period a scheme is entered into and—

(a) in consequence of the scheme profits are shifted to X from another company ("Y"),

(b) the main purpose or one of the main purposes of any party to the scheme in entering into the scheme is to ensure that section 748(1)(da) prevents an apportionment falling to be made as regards the chargeable profits of one or more controlled foreign companies for one or more accounting periods, and

(c) the relevant accounting period of X falls wholly or partly within that accounting period or those accounting periods.

(4) For the purposes of subsection (3), profits are shifted to X from Y if it is reasonable to suppose that in the absence of the scheme, and any similar scheme, the whole or a part of the income which is reflected in X's profits would have been reflected in Y's profits.

(5) Condition C is that, in determining X's chargeable profits for the relevant accounting period—

(a) section 418(5) of CTA 2009 (loan relationships involving connected debtor and creditor where debits exceed credits) has effect so as to treat X, for the purposes of Part 5 of that Act, as bringing into account for that period credits in respect of a loan relationship, or

(b) Part 21B of CTA 2010 (group mismatch schemes) has effect so as to exclude an amount from being brought into account as a debit or credit for the purposes of Part 5 of CTA 2009 (loan relationships) or Part 7 of that Act (derivative contracts).

(6) For the purposes of this section—

"apportionment" means an apportionment under section 747(3);

"scheme" means any scheme, arrangements or understanding of any kind whatever, whether or not legally enforceable, involving one or more transactions."

PART 3

TEMPORARY EXEMPTION FOLLOWING REORGANISATION ETC

6 (1) Section 748 of ICTA (cases where section 747(3) does not apply) is amended as follows.

(2) After subsection (1)(e) insert

"; or

(f) the accounting period ends during an exempt period in relation to the company (see Part 3A of Schedule 25)."

(3) In subsection (3) for "(e)" substitute "(f)".

7 After section 751AB of that Act (inserted by paragraph 2 of this Schedule) insert—

"751AC Reduction in chargeable profits following an exempt period

(1) This section applies if—

(a) an exempt period in relation to a controlled foreign company ends in accordance with paragraph 15F(2) of Schedule 25 (time exempt period ends if there is an early termination event), other than by reason of an early termination event within paragraph 15F(3)(b),

(b) an accounting period ("the relevant accounting period") of the company ends after that exempt period but before the time the exempt period would have ended had paragraph 15F(2) of that Schedule not applied,

(c) an apportionment under section 747(3) would fall to be made as regards the relevant accounting period, and

(d) a company resident in the United Kingdom ("the UK resident company") has a relevant interest in the controlled foreign company in that period.

(2) The UK resident company may make an application to the Commissioners for Her Majesty's Revenue and Customs for the chargeable profits of the controlled foreign company for that accounting period ("the chargeable profits") to be reduced to an amount ("the specified amount") specified in the application (which may be nil).

(3) If the Commissioners grant the application—

(a) the chargeable profits are treated as reduced to the specified amount, and

(b) the controlled foreign company's creditable tax (if any) for that period is treated as reduced by so much of that tax as, on a just and reasonable basis, relates to the reduction in the chargeable profits,

for the purpose of applying section 747(3) to (5) for determining the sum (if any) chargeable on the UK resident company under section 747(4)(a) (but for no other purpose).

(4) The Commissioners may grant the application only if—

(a) they are satisfied that the specified amount is not less than the relevant amount, and

(b) they have not previously granted an application made by the UK resident company in respect of the relevant accounting period under section 751A or 751AB.

(5) "The relevant amount" means the amount (if any) equal to so much of the chargeable profits as it is just and reasonable to regard as referable to—

(a) the relevant transaction which triggered the end of the exempt period, or

(b) any later relevant transaction occurring before the time the exempt period would have ended had paragraph 15F(2) of Schedule 25 not applied.

(6) "Relevant transaction" has the meaning given by paragraph 15E of Schedule 25 (and it does not matter if the transaction occurs pursuant to an agreement entered into by the controlled foreign company before the relevant time (within the meaning of paragraph 15G of that Schedule))."

8 In Schedule 25 to that Act (cases where section 747(3) does not apply), before Part 4 of that Schedule insert—

"PART 3A

EXEMPT PERIODS

Introductory

15A The provisions of this Part of this Schedule have effect for the purposes of section 748(1)(f).

Beginning of exempt period

15B (1) An exempt period begins in relation to a company ("X") at a time ("the relevant time") when—

(a) X is resident outside the United Kingdom,

(b) X is controlled by persons resident in the United Kingdom,

(c) there is at least one relevant UK corporate investor in X, and

(d) the requirements of paragraph 15C or 15D are met.

(2) There is a "relevant UK corporate investor in X" at a particular time if, at that time, there is a company which—

(a) is resident in the United Kingdom, and

(b) would, on the assumptions set out in sub-paragraph (3), be a company to which an apportionment of X's chargeable profits for the relevant accounting period would fall to be made in circumstances where section 747(5) would not prevent tax being chargeable on the company under section 747(4).

(3) The assumptions are—

(a) X has chargeable profits for the relevant accounting period,

(b) an apportionment of those profits falls to be made under section 747(3) for that period, and

(c) no reduction of those profits arises under section 751A, 751AA or 751AB.

(4) "The relevant accounting period" means the accounting period of X in which the time mentioned in sub-paragraph (2) falls.

15C (1) The requirements of this paragraph are that—

(a) no company was, at any time before the relevant time, a relevant UK corporate investor in X,

(b) no asset owned by X, or part of the business carried on by X, at the relevant time was previously owned, or carried on, by a company which—

(i) was under the control of persons resident in the United Kingdom at any time it owned the asset or carried on the part of the business, and

(ii) is or has been related to X,

(c) condition A, B, C or D is met, and

(d) no disqualifying relevant transaction occurs (see paragraph 15E).

(2) Condition A is that, immediately before the relevant time, X—

(a) was in existence, but

(b) was not a member of the same group of companies as any person who, at the relevant time, was a controlling UK person.

(3) Condition B is that—

(a) at the relevant time X is controlled by a company which is resident in the United Kingdom, and

(b) immediately before that time, X was controlled by that same company but that company was not then resident in the United Kingdom.

(4) Condition C is that—

(a) at the relevant time—

(i) X is controlled by a company which is resident in the United Kingdom ("the intermediate parent"), and

(ii) the intermediate parent is controlled by a company which is not resident in the United Kingdom ("the parent"), and

(b) immediately before that time X was controlled by the parent but not the intermediate parent.

(5) Condition D is that X—

(a) is a controlled foreign company at the time it is formed, and

(b) is formed by one or more persons for the purpose of controlling one or more companies in circumstances where it is expected that an exempt period will begin in relation to one or more of those companies at the time when X begins to control the company or companies.

(6) In this paragraph "controlling UK person" means a person resident in the United Kingdom who alone, or together with other such persons, controls X.

15D (1) The requirements of this paragraph are that—

(a) the relevant time falls after 23 March 2011,

(b) X has an accounting period during which 23 March 2011 falls,

(c) no company was, at any time during that accounting period, a relevant UK corporate investor in X,

(d) no company was, immediately before the relevant time, a relevant UK corporate investor in X,

(e) at the relevant time X is controlled by a company which—

(i) is resident in the United Kingdom, and

(ii) is not under the control of another body corporate, or two or more other bodies corporate taken together, and

(f) no disqualifying relevant transaction occurs (see paragraph 15E).

(2) In determining for the purposes of sub-paragraph (1)(e)(ii) whether a company is under the control of two or more bodies corporate taken together, a body corporate which holds less than 10% of the issued ordinary shares of that company is to be disregarded.

(3) For the purposes of sub-paragraph (2), a body corporate is treated as holding any shares held by persons who are connected or associated with the body corporate.

Disqualifying relevant transactions

15E (1) This paragraph applies for the purposes of paragraph 15C and 15D.

(2) A disqualifying relevant transaction occurs if—

(a) a relevant transaction occurs at the relevant time (whether or not the transaction occurs pursuant to an agreement entered into by X before that time), or

(b) a relevant transaction occurs on or after 9 December 2010 but before the relevant time and that transaction forms part of an avoidance scheme.

(3) "Relevant transaction" means—

(a) the making by X of a loan or advance of an amount (other than a negligible amount) to a person who, at the time it is made, is related to X and subject to United Kingdom tax,

(b) an increase (other than an increase of a negligible amount) in the amount of an existing loan or advance made by X to a person who, at the time of the increase, is related to X and subject to United Kingdom tax,

(c) a change in the terms or conditions of an existing loan or advance made by X where—

(i) the loan or advance is to a person who, at the time the change is made, is related to X and subject to United Kingdom tax, and

(ii) the change has an effect (other than a negligible effect) on the amount of interest payable, or

(d) a transaction to which sub-paragraph (4) applies.

(4) This sub-paragraph applies to a transaction if—

(a) it is referable to an activity carried on by X as part, or the whole, of any non-exempt activities carried on by X,

(b) the results of the transaction are reflected in the profits arising in an accounting period of X and are not negligible in value, and

(c) the results of the transaction alone, or together with the results of one or more other transactions, achieves a reduction in United Kingdom tax.

(5) A transaction achieves, or two or more transactions together achieve, a reduction in United Kingdom tax if, had the transaction or transactions not been effected, any person—

(a) would have been liable for any such tax or for a greater amount of any such tax, or

(b) would not have been entitled to a relief from or repayment of any such tax or would have been entitled to a smaller relief from or repayment of any such tax.

(6) In this paragraph—

"avoidance scheme" means a scheme the main purpose, or one of the main purposes, of any party to which in entering into the scheme is to secure that section 748(1)(f) prevents an apportionment falling to be made under section 747(3) as regards an accounting period, or accounting periods, of X;

"non-exempt activities" has the meaning given by paragraph 12D(2);

"scheme" means any scheme, arrangements or understanding of any kind whatever, whether or not legally enforceable, involving one or more transactions;

"United Kingdom tax" means corporation tax (or any tax chargeable as if it were corporation tax) or income tax.

Ending of exempt period

15F (1) An exempt period ends on the expiry of the period of 24 months which begins immediately after the first accounting period of X to end after the relevant time, unless sub-paragraph (2) applies.

(2) If an early termination event occurs after the relevant time but before the time the exempt period would end under sub-paragraph (1), the exempt period ends immediately before that event.

(3) An early termination event occurs if and when—

(a) a relevant transaction occurs, whether or not the transaction occurs pursuant to an agreement entered into by X before that time, or

(b) where the exempt period began because Condition D was met, X's business does not consist wholly in the holding of shares of companies which X controls, together with activities incidental to the holding of such shares.

Interpretation of Part 3A

15G (1) In this Part of this Schedule—

"group" means a company and any other companies it controls;

"the relevant time" has the meaning given by paragraph 15B;

"relevant transaction" has the meaning given by paragraph 15E;

"relevant UK corporate investor in X" has the meaning given by paragraph 15B(2);

"X" is to be construed in accordance with paragraph 15B.

(2) For the purposes of this Part of this Schedule a person is "related" to X at a particular time if—

(a) the person is connected or associated with X at that time,

(b) the person has a 25 per cent assessable interest in X in the case of the accounting period in which that time falls (within the meaning of paragraph 6(4C)), or

(c) if X is a controlled foreign company in the accounting period in which that time falls by virtue of subsection (1A) of section 747, the person is connected or associated with either or both of the two persons mentioned in that subsection."

PART 4

HOLDING COMPANIES: EXTENSION OF TRANSITIONAL PROVISION

9 (1) Part 2 of Schedule 16 to FA 2009 (controlled foreign companies: amendment of exempt activities exemption) is amended as follows.

(2) In paragraph 12 (commencement), in sub-paragraph (2)(b) for "2011" substitute "2012".

(3) In paragraph 15 (qualifying holding companies: periods straddling 1 July 2011)—

(a) in sub-paragraph (1)(a) for "2011" substitute "2012",

(b) in sub-paragraph (2)(a) for "2011" substitute "2012", and

(c) accordingly, in the heading for "*2011*" substitute "*2012*".

(4) In paragraph 16 (qualifying holding companies: definition of "relevant accounting period"), in paragraph (b) for "2011" substitute "2012".

(5) In the italic heading before paragraph 17 for "*two years before 1 July 2011*" substitute "*three years before 1 July 2012*".

PART 5

MINOR AND CONSEQUENTIAL AMENDMENTS

10 In the following provisions of ICTA, for "or 751AA" substitute ", 751AA, 751AB or 751AC"—

(a) section 747(3A) and (5A) (imputation of chargeable profits and creditable tax of controlled foreign companies),

(b) section 749(10) (residence),

(c) section 749A(9) (elections and designations under section 749: supplementary provisions), and

(d) section 750(3)(ab) (territories with a lower level of taxation).

11 In section 751A of that Act (reduction in chargeable profits for certain activities of EEA business establishments), for subsection (4) substitute—

"(4) The Commissioners may grant the application only if—

(a) they are satisfied that the specified amount does not exceed the amount (if any) equal to so much of those chargeable profits as can reasonably be regarded as representing the net economic value which—

(i) arises to the appropriate body of persons (taken as a whole), and

(ii) is created directly by qualifying work, and

(b) they have not previously granted an application made by the UK resident company in respect of the relevant accounting period under section 751AB or 751AC."

12 (1) Section 751B of that Act (sections 751A and 751AA: supplementary) is amended as follows.

(2) For "or 751AA" in subsections (1), (2), (3) (in each place) and (5) substitute ", 751AA, 751AB or 751AC".

(3) In subsection (2), for paragraph (a) substitute—

"(a) may be made at any time before the end of the application period, and"

(4) In subsection (8), omit the "and" before paragraph (b), and after that paragraph insert—

"(c) in the case of an appeal in respect of the refusal of an application under section 751AB, has the meaning given by subsection (6) of that section, and

(d) in the case of an appeal in respect of the refusal of an application under section 751AC, has the meaning given by subsection (5) of that section."

(5) For subsection (10) substitute—

"(10) In this section—

"the application period" means—

(a) the period within which an amendment to the relevant company tax return may be made by virtue of paragraph 15(4) of Schedule 18 to the Finance Act 1998 (disregarding any extension of that period provided by subsections (3) and (4) of this section or any other enactment), or

(b) if the relevant company tax return is amended under paragraph 34(2)(b) or (2A) of that Schedule as a consequence of the application of this Chapter—

(i) the period of 30 days beginning when the amendment was notified to the company, or

(ii) if an appeal is brought against such an amendment, the period of 30 days beginning when that appeal is finally determined;

"relevant company tax return", in relation to a company, means the return for the accounting period for which—

(a) any sum is chargeable on the company under section 747(4)(a), or

(b) any sum would be so chargeable but for section 751A, 751AA, 751AB or 751AC,

in respect of the chargeable profits of the company for the accounting period mentioned in section 751A, 751AA, 751AB or 751AC."

(6) In the heading for "**and 751AA**" substitute "**to 751AC**".

13 Omit the following provisions—

(a) in Schedule 17 to FA 1998, paragraph 3(7), and

(b) in Schedule 16 to FA 2009, paragraphs 22 and 24(3) and (5).

PART 6

COMMENCEMENT AND TRANSITIONAL PROVISION

14 (1) The amendments made by paragraph 9 are treated as always having had effect.

(2) The other amendments made by this Schedule have effect in relation to accounting periods of controlled foreign companies beginning on or after 1 January 2011.

GENERAL NOTE

Part 1

Part 1 to Sch 12 makes significant changes to ICTA 1988 s 748(1), by introducing two new scenarios under which a charge to tax under the CFC charging provisions will not apply.

The trading CFC with limited UK connection–new case exemption

The first new case exempts a trading CFC from the charging provisions where it is party to certain intra-group transactions (eg the provision of intra-group goods and services) but where there are limited business connections with the UK. The requirements of the CFC to meet the exemption are stipulated in new ICTA 1988 Sch 25 Part 2A.

The first requirement is that the CFC must have a business establishment in the territory in which it is resident (Part 2A para 12C). The second requirement is that the CFC's business does not included to a substantial extent non-exempt activities (para 12D) Non-exempt activities are defined in new para 12D(2).

The trading CFC will be held to have a significant UK connection (and will therefore fail the requirements for the exemption) if either of conditions A or B are met.

Condition A (para 12E(3)) states that the CFC will have a significant UK connection, and therefore fall outside of the exemption, if more than 10 percent of its gross income in the period is UK-connected (where 'UK-connected gross income' is defined (in para 12E(7)) as gross income derived, directly or indirectly, from transactions with persons who are within the charge to UK tax). This condition effectively brings trading subsidiaries into the CFC rules where there is a markup of more than ten percent of cost, which for some industries might be perfectly acceptable from a transfer pricing perspective.

New para 12E(4) however, stipulates that Condition A will not apply where the trading CFC has sufficient staff based outside of the UK to manage its business; its profits do not exceed 10 percent of relevant operating expenses, and its UK-connected gross income for the period does not exceed more than half of its gross income.

New para 12E(5) sets out Condition B , which will be met if it is shown that, in the relevant period, more than 50 percent of the trading CFC's related-party business expenditure is UK-connected, and the CFC has engaged in a scheme or arrangement which has the main purpose or one of the main purposes of any party of either reducing UK corporation tax, or reducing a CFC tax charge. 'Related-party business expenditure' is defined (in para 12E(7))as non-capital expenditure which gives rise, directly or indirectly, to the receipt of income by a person related to the CFC. If Condition B is met, then the CFC will fall outside of the exemption

New para 12F sets out the final requirement for the exemption and specifies that the sum of its 'finance income' and relevant intellectual property (IP) income' cannot exceed more than 5 percent of its gross income.

'Finance income' is defined as income arising from a financial asset, according to UK generally accepted accounting practice plus any amounts which would fall to be recognised as income under the loan relationship disguised interest legislation.

'Relevant IP income' is defined as royalties and receipts of a similar nature arising from intellectual property.

New para 12G defines 'Gross income' as excluding amounts which would be exempt under the UK dividend exemption legislation (per CTA 2009 Part 9A) and chargeable gains but includes settlement income where the company is a settlor or beneficiary or a proportion of the income accruing to a partnership where the CFC is a partner.

The new provisions provide clear quantitative guidance as to when a trading CFC will be deemed to have a significant UK connection. If the new exemption is to be complied with, there is a clear emphasis upon the CFC successfully demonstrating a degree of independence from the UK, both in respect of income and expenditure. The CFC also needs to have operational substance within its governing jurisdiction, a key indicator of this being the actual employment of individuals whom are resident outside of the UK and are actively engaged in the management of the CFC's business.

The CFC exploiting intellectual property with limited UK connection–new case exemption

The second scenario exempts the application of CFC charging provisions where the CFC's business relates to intellectual property (IP) exploitation. For this exemption to apply, both the CFC and the IP it is exploiting need to be shown not to have a relevant connection with the UK. The requirements of this new case exemption are detailed in ICTA 1988 Sch 25 new Part 2B.

New para 12H details the five requirements to be met if this exemption is to apply. The requirements relate to the CFC's:

— Business establishment (para 12I)

— IP business (para 12J)

— Other business activities (para 12K)

— UK connection (para 12L), and

— Finance income (para 12M)

The IP business requirement is failed if the IP business has a relevant UK connection. New para 12J explains that IP is held to have a relevant UK connection in two circumstances. The first determines that the IP will be UK-connected if at any time during the accounting period, or during the preceding six years, it has been held by a person resident in the UK. The second circumstance, broadly, identifies a UK connection where activities are undertaken(disregarding those of an incidental or insignificant nature) in terms of the IP being created, maintained or enhanced by a person related to the CFC, who is within the scope of charge to UK tax. This test is applied from when the activities were first carried on by the person to the end of the current accounting period.

The requirements for the exemption will not be met if the CFC has a significant UK connection. The CFC company itself will have a significant UK connection if all, or a substantial proportion, of its gross income is obtained via the exploitation of IP, where the IP is created by individuals or companies within the charge to UK income or corporation tax. Alternatively, a significant UK connection would be established during a period where the CFC exploiting the IP incurs significant expenditure, such as R&D sub-contractor payments or IP development and related costs, and the recipient(s) of the income are similarly within the charge to UK taxation (new para 12L).

For the CFC case exemption to apply, IP exploiting companies clearly need to develop and own IP within their own tax jurisdiction. Profits derived by CFCs from IP that has a connection with the UK, either as the place of its initial creation or ongoing maintenance and development, may well fall within the CFC charging provisions.

Consequential amendments as a result of the new exemptions

The introduction of the new exemptions leads to consequential legislative amendments at ICTA 1988 new s 751AB. This section, provides scope for the reduction of a CFC charge where the conditions of the new exemptions are only partially complied with.

An application to reduce the CFC apportionment will only be accepted by the Commissioners of HM Revenue and Customs (HMRC) if the quantitative measures of new s 751AB(2), relating to the level of connected UK income or finance and IP income as a proportion of total income of the CFC, are met.

Subsections 3–5 of s 751AB provide detail as to the application process, with the CFC being required to specify the reduced apportionment of profit they deem reasonable (which may include a specified reduction to nil). Where the Commissioners accept the application, and agree the specified amount of apportioned profits, any creditable tax paid by the CFC will be proportionately reduced, on a just and reasonable basis. One would presume a proportional reduction of apportioned profits and creditable tax, would apply.

Subsections 6–10 provide the basis for calculating the 'relevant amount' of apportioned CFC profits that will be subject to the charging provisions. These subsections are relevant in establishing the net chargeable profits to be excluded from the 'relevant amount'. Profits attributable to work carried on within the CFC's own country of residence and from transactions with non-UK companies (i e companies outside the charge to UK corporation tax) do not form part of the profits ultimately liable to

CFC charging provisions. This is an equitable provision, giving due recognition to economic value added by the CFC through its non-UK connections.

Summary

The introduction of two new exemptions reflects the Government's willingness to increase the competitiveness of the existing CFC legislation. The Government has acknowledged the need to recognise the global nature of many companies' commercial activities and the extension of the range of exempting cases provides further opportunity for structured international growth and a reduction in potentially negative UK tax consequences.

Disappointingly, the introduction of Condition A (para 12E(3)) effectively leaves trading subsidiaries into the CFC rules where they would otherwise qualify for the new exemption but where there is a markup of more than ten percent of cost. For some industries this might be perfectly acceptable from a transfer pricing perspective but given that the UK has a robust transfer pricing regime in operation, such a test in the CFC rules appears excessive and against the spirit of making the UK an attractive place to do business.

Furthermore, the rules concerning an application for reduction in the CFC apportionment where the conditions are only partially complied with, while fair, will be complex to administer.

Part 2

An important change has been made to ICTA s 748, in respect of the exemption of CFCs with low levels of profits, from the charging provisions stipulated at s 747(3).

Currently, CFC's with chargeable profits of less than £50,000 are exempt from apportionment tax charges. This will continue to be the case, but new s 748(1)(DA) provides a further de minimis exemption level for CFCs with accounting profits of less than £200,000 per annum (proportionately reduced for shorter accounting periods).

The new profits exemption level applies to accounting periods commencing on or after 1 January 2011. The existing de minimis limit of £50,000 will continue to apply. Disappointingly, the £50,000 limit has not been increased at the same time. The £50,000 limit has applied since 1 July 1999 when it was increased by FA 1998 from £20,000.

Given that the new de minimis exemption focuses on accounting profits rather than chargeable profits computed in accordance with UK tax rules, various consequential amendments have been made to s 748, all predominantly focusing upon anti-avoidance considerations with respect to the computation of the 'relevant profits' of a CFC.

New s 748(3A) states that the relevant profits of a CFC are to be calculated in accordance with generally accepted accounting practice (GAAP), excluding exempt company distributions (per CTA 2009 Part 9) and capital gains or losses, but including trust and partnership income, to establish consistency with the wider CFC regime.

New s 748(3C) confirms the need for transfer pricing adjustments to be considered with regard to the £200,000 de minimis threshold. Any transfer pricing adjustments required to accounting profits of the CFC should be made in accordance with the rules stated in TIOPA 2010 Part 4. A transfer pricing adjustment will not be so required if the resulting adjustment is less than £50,000 (new s 748(3D)).

Further anti-avoidance provisions in relation to the new de minimis exemption are stated at new s 748(ZA). Here, the focus is on the activities of group companies and seeks to prevent the distortion of a CFC's relevant profits by the implementation of tax planning arrangements, such as profit fragmentation. The de minimis exemption stated at new s 748(1)(DA) will not apply where a CFC is shown to have been party to such a scheme that meets any one of three exclusionary conditions, A, B or C.

Condition A states that the de minimis exemption will not apply where the CFC has taken part in a scheme where the main purpose or one of the main purposes of any party was to ensure that the new de minimis exemption applies. Condition B prevents the splitting of profits between group companies, where the main purpose or one of the main purposes of any party is to ensure that the de minimis exemption applies to one or more CFCs of the group for one or more accounting periods. Condition C targets the distortion of the relevant profits of a CFC via intra-group loan relationships involving connected debtors and creditors where debits exceed credits, or group mismatch schemes.

The new de minimis profits exemption threshold will be gratefully received by UK companies with foreign subsidiaries subject to the CFC provisions. It allows for a greater level of profitable activity by a CFC, without the need for profit apportionment and CFC tax charging provisions.

Part 3

The temporary improvements to the CFC rules include an important formalisation of the period of grace that is extended to companies who come under UK control for the first time, as a result of an acquisition or corporate reorganisation. ICTA 1988 s 748 is amended to include a temporary period of exemption for companies that potentially fall within the CFC charging provisions (new s 748(1)(f)).

Further details of the temporary period of exemption are contained within a new ICTA 1988 Sch 25 Part 3A. The new provisions provide for the accounting periods of CFCs to be exempted from the rules if they end within a stipulated exempt period. The temporary exempt period commences at "the relevant time", here defined as the point in time where the overseas company is controlled from the UK, has at least one "relevant UK corporate investor" and meets the requirements of new paras 15C or 15D (new para 15B). For the purposes of the legislation, a "relevant UK corporate investor" is defined as a UK resident company which would be subject to the CFC charging provisions as a result of their interest in the overseas company (in accordance with ICTA 1988 s 747(3)), with no exemptions or reductions available under ss 751A, 751AA and 751AB.

The temporary period of exemption from the CFC rules will end upon the expiration of 24 months from the end of the overseas company's first exempt accounting period, or earlier if certain arrangements are entered into by the company ('early termination events'). In practice therefore, there is an exempt period of up to three years.

The temporary period of exemption will, however, only apply if the CFC meets one of four of the conditions contained within new para 15C. Broadly, Paragraph 15C states that no UK resident company should have formerly been a relevant UK corporate investor in the CFC; no part of its business or assets should previously have been carried on or owned by a UK controlled company which is or has been related to the CFC, and the CFC needs to be shown to meet one of four conditions (A to D) stated at para 15C(1)(c), without the occurrence of any "disqualifying relevant transactions"(here, "disqualifying relevant transactions" refers to upstream loans and variations to the amount or terms thereof, and other transactions achieving reductions in UK tax which occur at the 'relevant time', or occurring on or after 9 December 2010 where that transaction is part of a scheme designed to take advantage of the new exemption).

Conditions A to D of para 15C cover scenarios where companies were not members of UK controlled groups before the 'relevant time' i e when it becomes a CFC; where companies are controlled by a UK resident company at the 'relevant time' but that controlling company was not UK resident before then; where companies remain in the same group but control passes from a non-UK resident parent company to an UK-resident intermediate holding company and where the company is a CFC at its formation but is so formed to control one or more companies where an exempt period is anticipated to commence in respect of any of the companies when the CFC starts to control one or more of those companies.

New para 15D sets out alternative requirements of a CFC to benefit from the temporary period of exemption, where the 'relevant time' occurs after 23 March 2011. Paragraph 15D provides that the company will qualify for the temporary exempt period if it was not a CFC during its period of account spanning 23 March 2011; the company was not under UK control immediately before becoming a CFC, and where, upon becoming under the control of a UK resident company, the controlling company is the group's ultimate parent. Once again, for the temporary period of exemption to apply, no disqualifying relevant transactions must occur. For the purposes of determining whether or not an overseas company is under the control of two or more bodies corporate taken together (in accordance with para 15D(e)(ii)), a body corporate holding less than ten percent of the issued shares of the company will be disregarded.

The temporary exemption will be applied on a company by company basis. A change in the main business or activities of a CFC will only affect the application of the exemption where there is deemed to be an erosion to the UK tax base. Here, the CFC would have the opportunity to apply to HMRC for a reasonable apportionment of profits, giving specific reference to profits that have arisen as a result of the change.

The formalisation of a temporary exempt period will certainly be welcomed by companies considering the acquisition of foreign companies and/or the reorganisation of groups which include UK controlled overseas subsidiaries.

Part 4

FA 2009 Sch 16 Part 2 has been amended to extend the transitional holding company provision. The extension of the transitional rules means that superior and non-local holding companies can be certain that they will continue to qualify under the exempt activities test until 1 July 2012, by which time, the Government hopes to have completed its programme of CFC reforms.

Part 6

The extension of the transitional provision for holding companies is to be treated as if it had always had effect. It is intended that all other amendments to the CFC provisions contained in Sch 12 will apply to the accounting periods of CFCs commencing on or after 1 January 2011.

SCHEDULE 13

PROFITS OF FOREIGN PERMANENT ESTABLISHMENTS ETC

Section 48

PART 1

AMENDMENTS OF CTA 2009

1 CTA 2009 is amended as follows.

2 In section 1(1)(c) (overview of Act), for "Chapter 4" substitute "Chapters 3A and 4".

3 In section 5(1) (territorial scope), insert at the end "(but see Chapter 3A for an exemption from charge in respect of profits of foreign permanent establishments)".

4 After section 18 insert—

"CHAPTER 3A

UK RESIDENT COMPANIES: PROFITS OF FOREIGN PERMANENT ESTABLISHMENTS

Exemption

18A Exemption for profits or losses of foreign permanent establishments

(1) If a UK resident company makes an election under this section, exemption adjustments are to be made at the appropriate stages in calculating the taxable total profits of the company for each relevant accounting period.

(2) For that purpose "exemption adjustments" means any such adjustments as are appropriate to secure that there are left out of account any profits and losses taken into account in arriving at the foreign permanent establishments amount in relation to any relevant accounting period.

(3) In this Chapter "relevant accounting period", in relation to a company by which an election is made under this section, means an accounting period of the company to which the election applies (as to which see section 18F).

(4) For the purposes of this Chapter the "foreign permanent establishments amount", in relation to an accounting period of a company, is—

(a) the aggregate of the relevant profits amount in the case of each relevant foreign territory in relation to which there is a relevant profits amount for the accounting period, less

(b) the aggregate of the relevant losses amount in the case of each relevant foreign territory in relation to which there is a relevant losses amount for the accounting period.

(5) In this Chapter "relevant foreign territory", in relation to a company, means a territory outside the United Kingdom in which the company carries on, or has carried on, business through a permanent establishment.

(6) For the purposes of this Chapter "relevant profits amount", in relation to a relevant foreign territory and an accounting period of a company, means—

(a) in the case of a full treaty territory, profits which would be taken to be attributable to the permanent establishment of the company in the territory for the purpose of ascertaining the amount of any credit to be allowed under TIOPA 2010 (in respect of tax paid under the law of the relevant foreign territory) against corporation tax if the company were to be liable to corporation tax for the accounting period (apart from this Chapter), or

(b) in the case of any other territory, profits which would be taken to be so attributable for that purpose if the territory were a full treaty territory and the double taxation arrangements having effect in relation to the territory were in the terms of the OECD model.

(7) For the purposes of this Chapter "relevant losses amount", in relation to a relevant foreign territory and an accounting period of a company, means—

(a) in the case of a full treaty territory, any losses which would be taken to be attributable to the permanent establishment of the company in the territory on the application of the same rules and principles as fall to be applied under subsection (6)(a), and

(b) in the case of any other territory, any losses which would be taken to be so attributable on that basis if it were a full treaty territory and the double taxation arrangements having effect in relation to the relevant foreign territory were in the terms of the OECD model.

(8) Subsection (9) applies if the amount of any credit to be allowed under TIOPA 2010 in relation to a company in the case of a full treaty territory does not depend on the profits taken to be attributable to the permanent establishment of the company in the territory because tax under the law of the territory is charged, pursuant to the double taxation arrangements having effect in relation to the territory, otherwise than by reference to such profits (as an alternative to a charge by reference to such profits).

(9) The reference in subsection (6)(a) to profits which would be taken to be attributable to the permanent establishment of the company in the territory is to the profits that would be so taken if tax under the law of the territory were charged by reference to such profits; and subsection (7)(a) is to be construed accordingly.

(10) For the purposes of subsections (6) and (7) if double taxation arrangements having effect in relation to a relevant foreign territory do not include provision for the credit to be allowed against tax to be computed by reference to the same profits as those by reference to which the tax was computed under the law of the relevant foreign territory, they are to be assumed to do so.

(11) This section is subject to the following provisions of this Chapter.

18B Chargeable gains etc

(1) The exemption adjustments required to be made by section 18A(1) include, in the case of any gains or losses on the disposal or realisation of assets which are relevant in the calculation of the taxable total profits of a company for a relevant accounting period, adjustments to remove the effect of any gains or losses relating to the assets taken into account in computing the foreign permanent establishments amount in relation to any relevant accounting period (so that, in appropriate cases, a gain may be increased to reflect a loss so taken into account or a loss increased to reflect a gain so taken into account).

(2) The references in section 18A(6) to profits which would be taken to be attributable to the permanent establishment of a company in a territory include any gains in respect of immoveable property which has been used for the purposes of the business carried on by the company through the permanent establishment in the territory (to such extent as is appropriate having regard to the extent to which it has been so used); and the references to losses in section 18A(7) are to be construed accordingly.

(3) The references in section 18A(6) to profits which would be taken, in the case of a company in relation to which an election under section 18A has effect, to be attributable to the permanent establishment of the company in a territory (including as extended by subsection (2)) do not include any gains which would be taken to be so attributable for the purposes of ascertaining credit to be allowed in respect of tax payable under the law of the territory before the election has effect; and the references to losses in section 18A(7) are to be construed accordingly.

18C Capital allowances etc

(1) Any allowance under Part 2 of CAA 2001 which, but for section 18A and for section 15(2A)(b) of CAA 2001, could be claimed under section 3(1) of that Act in respect of assets provided for the purposes of a permanent establishment in a territory outside the United Kingdom through which business is or has been carried

on by a company in relation to which an election under section 18A has effect (and any charge in connection with any such allowance) is to be made automatically and reflected in any calculation for any relevant accounting period of the company of the profits or losses attributable to business carried on by the company through such a permanent establishment.

(2) In the application of section 13 of CAA 2001 by virtue of subsection (1) on the taking effect of the election under section 18A, references to "market value" have effect as references to "transition value" within the meaning of section 62A of that Act in relation to any plant or machinery in the case of which that is the disposal value under section 61 of that Act.

(3) In determining any relevant profits amount or relevant losses amount under section 18A(6) or (7) in relation to a company there are to be left out of account any profits or losses arising from a plant or machinery lease under which the company is a lessor if an allowance under CAA 2001 has been made to the company or a connected company in respect of expenditure on the provision of any plant or machinery subject to the lease (otherwise than in accordance with this section).

(4) Section 70K of that Act (meaning of "plant or machinery lease" and "lessor") applies for the purposes of subsection (3).

(5) In determining for the purposes of section 18A the amount of any credit to be allowed under TIOPA 2010 in respect of tax under the law of a relevant foreign territory in the case of a company, it is to be assumed that the company made any claim or election (other than a claim for allowances under Part 2 of CAA 2001) which would reduce any relevant profits amount, or increase the relevant losses amount, by any means, and within any time limit, applicable to it.

18D Payments subject to deduction

(1) In determining any relevant profits amount or relevant losses amount under section 18A(6) or (7) in relation to a company there are to be left out of account profits or losses referable to any transaction between a person who is UK resident and a permanent establishment in a territory outside the United Kingdom through which the company carries on, or has carried on, business ("the foreign territory in question") if the condition in subsection (2) is met.

(2) That condition is that the UK resident would be obliged under Part 15 of ITA 2007 to deduct income tax that is not repayable from payments in respect of the transaction if the payments were made to a company resident in the foreign territory in question (taking account of any double taxation arrangements having effect in relation to the foreign territory in question).

(3) But subsection (1) does not apply if the company is a bank unless the transaction forms part of arrangements the main purpose, or one of the main purposes, of which is the avoidance of an obligation under Part 15 of ITA 2007 to deduct income tax from any payments.

(4) Section 1120 of CTA 2010 (meaning of "bank") applies for the purposes of subsection (3).

18E Employee share acquisitions

(1) Any relief which would be given under Chapter 2 or 3 of Part 12 is to be taken into account in determining any relevant profits amount or relevant losses amount in the case of a company under section 18A(6) or (7) in relation to a relevant foreign territory in so far as it is linked to the business carried on by the company through a permanent establishment in the territory.

(2) The extent to which any such relief is so linked is to be determined on a just and reasonable basis having regard to the extent to which the work of the employees concerned contributes to the purposes of the business so carried on.

18F Effect of election

(1) An election made by a company under section 18A—

(a) (subject to subsection (6)) is irrevocable, and

(b) applies to all accounting periods of the company beginning on or after the relevant day.

(2) "The relevant day" is the day on which, at the time of the election, the accounting period following that in which the election is made is expected to begin.

(3) Subsection (4) applies if an accounting period of the company ("the straddling period") begins before, and ends on or after, the relevant day.

(4) It is to be assumed, for the purposes of the Corporation Tax Acts, that the straddling period consists of two separate accounting periods—

(a) the first beginning with the straddling period and ending immediately before the relevant day, and

(b) the second beginning with that day and ending with the straddling period.

(5) Where for those purposes it is necessary to apportion the profits and losses for the straddling period to different parts of the period, that apportionment is to be made on a just and reasonable basis.

(6) The election can be revoked at any time before the relevant day.

Anti-diversion rule

18G Anti-diversion rule

(1) This section applies for the purposes of this Chapter if the lower level of tax test is met for any relevant accounting period of a company in relation to any permanent establishment through which the company carries on, or has carried on, business in a territory outside the United Kingdom.

(2) If there is an adjusted relevant profits amount in relation to the territory for the relevant accounting period, that amount is to be taken to be nil (but this is subject to section 18I).

(3) For the purposes of this Chapter "adjusted", in relation to a relevant profits amount, is what the relevant profits amount would be if it were determined without reference to gains and losses which are chargeable gains or allowable losses for the purposes of corporation tax.

(4) The lower level of tax test is met for a relevant accounting period in relation to a permanent establishment in a territory if—

(a) the amount of tax paid under the law of that territory in respect of the adjusted relevant profits amount in accordance with a relevant treaty provision, is less than

(b) 75% of the amount of corporation tax that would be payable in respect of that amount if it were subject in full to corporation tax, ignoring any credit which would be allowed against it under section 18(3) of TIOPA 2010 and assuming, where there is more than one rate of corporation tax applicable to the relevant accounting period, that it were chargeable at the average rate over the accounting period.

(5) In subsection (4)(a) "a relevant treaty provision" means—

(a) provision in double taxation arrangements having effect in relation to the territory, or

(b) if no double taxation arrangements have effect in relation to the territory, provision in the terms of the OECD model.

(6) This section does not apply if—

(a) the adjusted relevant profits amount in relation to the territory for the relevant accounting period would (apart from subsection (2)) be less than the entry limit (as to which see subsection (7)), or

(b) the motive test is met (as to which see section 18H).

(7) "The entry limit" is—

(a) £200,000, or

(b) if the relevant accounting period is less than 12 months, a proportionately reduced amount.

18H The motive test

(1) The motive test is met if conditions A and B are met.

(2) Condition A is that in so far as any relevant transaction, or two or more transactions at least one of which was a relevant transaction (taken together), achieved a reduction in United Kingdom tax either—

(a) the reduction was minimal, or

(b) it was not the main purpose, or one of the main purposes, of the transaction, or of those transactions taken together, to achieve the reduction.

(3) In subsection (2) "relevant transaction" means a transaction the results of which are reflected in such of the company's profits in the accounting period as are attributable to the permanent establishment.

(4) For the purposes of subsection (2) a transaction achieves (or transactions achieve) a reduction in United Kingdom tax if, had the transaction (or transactions) not been effected, any person—

(a) would (disregarding section 18G(2)) have been liable for United Kingdom tax or for a greater amount of United Kingdom tax, or

(b) would (disregarding that provision) not have been entitled to a relief from, or repayment of, United Kingdom tax or would have been entitled to a smaller relief from, or repayment of, United Kingdom tax.

(5) For the purposes of subsection (2) it is the main purpose, or one of the main purposes, of a transaction (or of transactions taken together) to achieve a reduction in United Kingdom tax if that is the main purpose, or one of the main purposes, of—

(a) the company, or

(b) a person who has an interest in the company at any time during the relevant accounting period;

and section 749B of ICTA (persons who have an interest in a company) applies for the purposes of paragraph (b) as for the purposes of Chapter 4 of Part 17 of that Act.

(6) Condition B is that it was not the main reason, or one of the main reasons, for the company carrying on business through the permanent establishment to achieve a reduction in United Kingdom tax by a diversion of profits from the United Kingdom.

(7) For the purposes of subsection (6) the fact that the company carries on the business through the permanent establishment achieves a reduction in United Kingdom tax by a diversion of profits from the United Kingdom if it is reasonable to make the supposition in subsection (8).

(8) That supposition is that, if the company did not carry on business through any permanent establishment and there were no related companies—

(a) the whole or a substantial part of the receipts which are reflected in the profits attributable to the permanent establishment would have been received by the company otherwise than through the permanent establishment or by another UK resident company which is a non-electing company or an individual resident in the United Kingdom, and

(b) the company, that other UK resident company, that individual resident in the United Kingdom or any other person resident in the United Kingdom either—

(i) would (disregarding section 18G(2)) have been liable for United Kingdom tax or for a greater amount of United Kingdom tax, or

(ii) would (disregarding that provision) not have been entitled to a relief from, or repayment of, United Kingdom tax or would have been entitled to a smaller relief from, or repayment of, United Kingdom tax.

(9) For the purposes of subsection (8) a company is "related" to the company if—

(a) either it is a UK resident company in relation to which an election under section 18A has effect or it is not a UK resident company,

(b) it is connected with, or is an associate of, the company, and

(c) it fulfils or could fulfil, directly or indirectly, the same functions as those of the permanent establishment.

(10) Companies are associates for the purposes of subsection (9) if they are associated for the purposes of Chapter 4 of Part 19 of CTA 2010 (see section 882).

(11) References in subsection (8) to a UK resident company include a company which it is reasonable to assume would have been established if the permanent establishment did not exist.

(12) For the purposes of subsection (8) a UK resident company is a non-electing company if no election under section 18A has effect in relation to the company.

(13) In this section "United Kingdom tax" means corporation tax, income tax or capital gains tax.

18I Proportionate reduction in certain cases

(1) This section applies if—

(a) condition A in section 18H is not met, but

(b) condition B in that section is met.

(2) If there is an adjusted relevant profits amount in relation to the territory for the relevant accounting period, section 18G(2) has effect to cause it to be reduced by only any such amount as it is just and reasonable to regard as referable to tainted relevant transactions.

(3) In subsection (2) "tainted relevant transactions" means relevant transactions which achieve a reduction in United Kingdom tax, other than any in relation to which the condition in section 18H(2)(b) is met.

Companies with total opening negative amount

18J Companies with total opening negative amount

(1) The following sections make provision about a company in relation to which an election under section 18A has effect if there is a total opening negative amount in the case of the company at the beginning of the company's first relevant accounting period.

(2) To determine for the purposes of this Chapter whether there is a total opening negative amount at the beginning of the company's first relevant accounting period, take the following steps.

Step 1

Take the adjusted foreign permanent establishments amount in relation to the earliest affected prior accounting period in relation to which that amount is negative.

Step 2

Add to the amount arrived at under step 1 the adjusted foreign permanent establishments amount in relation to the next affected prior accounting period (but not so as to cause the result to exceed nil).

Step 3

Add to the amount arrived at under step 2 the adjusted foreign permanent establishments amount in relation to each remaining affected prior accounting period, starting with the earliest (but not so as to cause the result to exceed nil).

If after the application of the preceding steps there is a negative amount for the last affected prior accounting period there is a total opening negative amount at the beginning of the company's first relevant accounting period of an amount equal to that negative amount.

(3) In subsection (2) "affected prior accounting period" means—

(a) the accounting period of the company in which the election under section 18A is made, and

(b) any earlier accounting period of the company ending less than 6 years before the end of that accounting period.

(4) For the purposes of subsection (2) the "adjusted" foreign permanent establishments amount is what the foreign permanent establishments amount would be if it were determined without reference to gains or losses which are chargeable gains or allowable losses for the purposes of corporation tax.

18K Total opening negative amount: "matching"

(1) At the end of each relevant accounting period of the company (starting with the first) the total opening negative amount is to be reduced (or further reduced) by the amount of any aggregate relevant profits amount of the company for the accounting period (but not to below nil).

(2) In any relevant accounting period of the company for which there is a reduction under subsection (1), section 18A(1) does not apply in relation to the aggregate relevant profits amount of the company for the accounting period.

(3) But in the case of the last relevant accounting period of the company for which there is a reduction under subsection (1), section 18A(1) is disapplied by subsection (2) only in relation to so much of the aggregate relevant profits amount of the company for the accounting period as is equal to the total opening negative amount of the company at the beginning of the accounting period.

(4) The company may, in its company tax return for that relevant accounting period, specify to which part of the aggregate relevant profits amount of the company for the accounting period section 18A(1) is to apply by virtue of subsection (3).

(5) In this Chapter "aggregate relevant profits amount", in relation to an accounting period, means the aggregate of the relevant profits amount in the case of each relevant foreign territory in relation to which there is a relevant profits amount for the accounting period.

(6) This section is subject to section 18L.

18L Streaming

(1) If a streaming election has effect in relation to the company sections 18M and 18N apply (instead of section 18K).

(2) For the purposes of this section "streaming election" means an election, made at the same time as the company's election under section 18A, which—

(a) states that sections 18M and 18N are to have effect in relation to the company (instead of section 18K), and

(b) specifies which of the territories that are relevant foreign territories in relation to the company are to be streamed territories for the purposes of the operation of sections 18M and 18N in relation to the company.

(3) Subject to subsection (4), a streaming election is irrevocable.

(4) A streaming election can be revoked at any time before the first relevant accounting period of the company.

(5) A streaming election does not have effect unless the company, in the company tax return for the first relevant accounting period of the company, specifies how much of the amount eligible to be streamed to each streamed territory is to constitute for the purposes of sections 18M and 18N the streamed opening negative amount at the beginning of that relevant accounting period.

(6) For the purposes of subsection (5) the amount eligible to be streamed to a territory by the company is the amount that would be the total opening negative amount of the company at the beginning of the first relevant accounting period of the company if at all material times the territory were the only relevant foreign territory in relation to the company.

18M Streamed opening negative amounts: "matching"

(1) At the end of each relevant accounting period of the company (starting with the first) the streamed opening negative amount in relation to a territory is to be reduced (or further reduced) by the amount of any relevant profits amount of the company for the territory for the accounting period (but not to below nil).

(2) In any relevant accounting period of the company for which there is a reduction under subsection (1) in relation to a territory, section 18A(1) does not apply in relation to the relevant profits amount of the company for the territory for the accounting period.

(3) But in the case of the last relevant accounting period of the company for which there is a reduction under subsection (1) in relation to a territory, section 18A(1) is disapplied by subsection (2) only in relation to so much of the relevant profits amount of the company for the territory for the accounting period as is equal to the streamed opening negative amount in relation to the territory at the beginning of the accounting period.

(4) The company may, in its company tax return for that relevant accounting period, specify to which part of the relevant profits amount of the company for the territory for the accounting period section 18A(1) is to apply by virtue of subsection (3).

18N Residual opening negative amount: "matching"

(1) At the end of each relevant accounting period of the company (starting with the first) the residual opening negative amount is to be reduced (or further reduced) by the amount of any residual aggregate relevant profits amount of the company for the accounting period (but not to below nil).

(2) For the purposes of this section the "residual opening negative amount", at the beginning of the company's first relevant accounting period, is—

(a) the total opening negative amount of the company at that time, less

(b) the aggregate of the streamed opening negative amounts of the company at that time.

(3) For the purposes of this section the "residual aggregate relevant profits amount", in relation to an accounting period, means the amount (if any) by which—

(a) the aggregate relevant profits amount of the company for the accounting period, exceeds

(b) the aggregate of so much of any relevant profits amounts of the company for the accounting period as has effect to bring about a reduction under section 18M(1) for the accounting period.

(4) In any relevant accounting period of the company for which there is a reduction under subsection (1), section 18A(1) does not apply in relation to the residual aggregate relevant profits amount of the company for the accounting period.

(5) But in the case of the last relevant accounting period of the company for which there is a reduction under subsection (1), section 18A(1) is disapplied by subsection (4) only in relation to so much of the residual aggregate relevant profits amount of the company for the accounting period as is equal to the residual opening negative amount of the company at the beginning of the accounting period.

(6) The company may, in its company tax return for that relevant accounting period, specify to which of the amounts forming part of the residual aggregate relevant profits amount of the company for the accounting period section 18A(1) is to apply by virtue of subsection (4).

18O Transfers of foreign permanent establishment business

(1) This section applies if—

(a) business carried on by a company ("the transferor") through a permanent establishment in a territory outside the United Kingdom is transferred to a connected company that is (or later becomes) a UK resident company ("the transferee"), and

(b) there is a transferred total opening negative amount in relation to the business transferred.

(2) In a case where the transferor had not made an election under section 18A before the transfer took place, or such an election had not had effect before that time, the "transferred total opening negative amount" is the amount that would have been the total opening negative amount in the case of the transferor at the beginning of the transferor's first relevant accounting period if—

(a) the only business carried on by the transferor was the business transferred,

(b) the transfer had not taken place,

(c) the transferor's first relevant accounting period had begun on the day after the transfer day, and

(d) any reference in section 18J(3) to the accounting period in which the election is made were a reference to the period beginning with the accounting period in which the transfer took place and ending with the transfer day.

(3) In a case where an election made by the transferor under section 18A had effect before the transfer took place, the "transferred total opening negative amount" is—

(a) the amount that would have been the total opening negative amount in the case of the transferor on the transfer day if the accounting period in which the transfer took place had ended on that day (the "remaining total opening negative amount"), less

(b) the amount that would have been the remaining total opening negative amount if the transferor had never carried on the business transferred.

But the transferred total opening negative amount cannot be below nil.

(4) In a case where—

(a) an election made by the transferee under section 18A first has effect after the transfer takes place, and

(b) the accounting period of the transferee in which the transfer took place is an affected prior accounting period for the purposes of section 18J(2),

there is to be added to the adjusted foreign permanent establishments amount in relation to that accounting period a negative amount equal to so much (if any) of the transferred total opening negative amount as is attributable to profits or losses arising after the beginning of the earliest affected prior accounting period of the transferee.

(5) In a case where an election made by the transferee under section 18A had effect before the transfer took place, sections 18K to 18N have effect in relation to the transferee and the transferred total opening negative amount as if—

(a) any reference to the total opening negative amount were a reference to the transferred total opening negative amount,

(b) any reference to the first relevant accounting period were a reference to the period beginning with the day after the transfer day and ending immediately before the start of the next accounting period of the transferee, and

(c) the requirement in section 18L(2) that a streaming election be made at the same time as the company's election under section 18A did not apply.

(6) Where for the purposes of this section it is necessary to apportion the profits and losses for any accounting period to different parts of that period, that apportionment is to be made on a just and reasonable basis.

(7) Any amount included in a transferred total opening negative amount is to be disregarded in the application of sections 18J to 18N in the case of the transferor after the transfer day.

(8) In this section "the transfer day" means the day on which the transfer of the business takes place.

Special cases

18P Exclusions

(1) If a company is a small company at any time during a relevant accounting period, there is for that relevant accounting period no relevant profits amount or relevant losses amount for the purposes of this Chapter in relation to any relevant foreign territory that is not a full treaty territory.

(2) If a company is a close company at any time during a relevant accounting period, so much of the profits of the company for the relevant accounting period as derives from gains which are chargeable gains for the purposes of corporation tax is not to be regarded as forming part of a relevant profits amount or relevant losses amount of the company for the purposes of this Chapter.

18Q Insurance companies

(1) So much of the profits or losses of a company as consists of profits or losses arising from basic life assurance and general annuity business (as defined in section 431(2) of ICTA) is not to be regarded as forming part of a relevant profits amount or relevant losses amount of the company for the purposes of this Chapter.

(2) In determining what part of any items brought into account as mentioned in section 83(2)(a), (b), (c) or (d) of FA 1989 (receipts to be taken into account) as profits attributable to a permanent establishment in a territory outside the United Kingdom through which the company carries on business are referable to life assurance business or gross roll-up business, section 432E of ICTA (apportionment: participating funds) has effect as if—

(a) references in that section to the surplus of the relevant business were to the surplus of the business carried on through the permanent establishment, and

(b) subsections (3) to (4A) of that section and section 432F of that Act were omitted.

(3) No amount which, by virtue of any enactment, is to be regarded as being brought into account by a company as an increase in the value of non-linked assets is to be regarded for the purposes of this Chapter as being attributable to a permanent establishment in a territory outside the United Kingdom through which the company carries on business.

(4) Any election under section 107(4) of FA 2000 (general insurance: adjustment for technical provision) is to be ignored for the purposes of this Chapter.

Interpretation

18R Meaning of "full treaty territory"

(1) For the purposes of this Chapter a territory is a "full treaty territory" if—

(a) double taxation arrangements have been made in relation to the territory, and

(b) the arrangements contain a relevant non-discrimination provision.

(2) "Relevant non-discrimination provision" means a provision to the effect that the taxation on a permanent establishment of an enterprise of a state which is party to the arrangements (a "contracting state") is not to be less favourably levied in any other contracting state than the taxation levied on enterprises of that other contracting state carrying on the same activities.

18S Other interpretation

In this Chapter—

"company tax return" has the same meaning as in Schedule 18 to FA 1998 (see paragraph 3(1));

"double taxation arrangements" means arrangements that have effect under section 2(1) of TIOPA 2010;

"the OECD model" means the Model Tax Convention on Income and on Capital published by the Organisation for Economic Co-operation and Development in July 2010 ("the OECD") or such other document published by the OECD in place of it as is designated from time to time by order made by the Treasury;

"small company" means a micro or small enterprise, as defined in the Annex to Commission Recommendation 2003/361/EC of 6 May 2003."

5 In section 775(4) (intangible fixed assets: cases where transfers within group provisions do not apply), omit the "or" at the end of paragraph (a) and insert at the end

", or

(c) an election under section 18A has effect in relation to the transferor and the asset has at any time been held by the transferor wholly or partly for the purposes of a permanent establishment in a territory outside the United Kingdom through which the transferor carries on business."

6 In section 803(b) (assets held for non-taxable activities excluded from Part 10), insert at the end ", otherwise than as a result of Chapter 3A of Part 2."

7 In section 845(4) (exceptions to rule that transfer between company and related party treated as being at market value)—

(a) omit the "and" at the end of paragraph (c), and

(b) after that paragraph insert—

"(ca) section 848A (assets held for purposes of exempt foreign permanent establishments), and".

8 After section 848 insert—

"848A Assets held for purposes of exempt foreign permanent establishments

(1) This section applies if—

(a) subsection (1) of section 775 (transfers within a group) would apply in relation to the transfer but for paragraph (c) of subsection (4) of that section, and

(b) the asset has not at all times when the election under section 18A had effect been held by the transferor wholly for the purposes of a permanent establishment such as is mentioned in that paragraph.

(2) The transfer is treated for the purposes of this Part as being at the following value—

WDV + FPEA

where—

WDV is the tax written-down value of the asset, and

FPEA is the amount which, for the purposes of Chapter 3A of Part 2, would in the case of the transferor be the foreign permanent establishments amount attributable to the transfer for the accounting period in which it took place if the transfer were at market value."

9 In section 1007(2)(b) (relief if employee etc acquires shares), insert at the end "or would be but for section 18A."

10 In section 1015(2)(b) (relief if employee etc obtains share option), insert at the end "or would be but for section 18A."

11 In Schedule 4 to that Act (index of defined expressions), insert at the appropriate places—

"adjusted (in relation to a relevant profits amount) (in Chapter 3A of Part 2)	section 18G(3)"
"aggregate relevant profits amount (in Chapter 3A of Part 2)	section 18K(5)"
"company tax return (in Chapter 3A of Part 2)	section 18S"
"double taxation arrangements (in Chapter 3A of Part 2)	section 18S"
"foreign permanent establishments amount (in Chapter 3A of Part 2)	section 18A(4)"
"full treaty territory (in Chapter 3A of Part 2)	section 18R"
"the OECD model (in Chapter 3A of Part 2)	section 18S"
"relevant accounting period (in Chapter 3A of Part 2)	section 18A(3)"
"relevant foreign territory (in Chapter 3A of Part 2)	section 18A(5)"
"relevant losses amount (in Chapter 3A of Part 2)	section 18A(7)"
"relevant profits amount (in Chapter 3A of Part 2)	section 18A(6)"
"small company (in Chapter 3A of Part 2)	section 18S"
"total opening negative amount" (in Chapter 3A of Part 2)	section 18J(2)"

PART 2

AMENDMENTS OF OTHER ACTS

ICTA

12 In paragraph 4(1) of Schedule 24 to ICTA (assumptions for calculating chargeable profits etc of foreign companies: election or claim to give maximum relief assumed to be made), insert at the end ", except that the company shall be assumed not to have made an election under section 18A of CTA 2009."

TCGA 1992

13 In TCGA 1992, after section 276 insert—

"276A No gain/no loss: foreign permanent establishment exemption

(1) On a no gain/no loss disposal by a company in relation to which an election under section 18A of CTA 2009 (exemption for profits or losses of foreign permanent establishments) has effect, the amount of the consideration which would secure that neither a gain nor a loss would accrue to the company on the disposal is to be arrived at after taking account of the operation of the provisions of Chapter 3A of Part 2 of that Act (with the result that that amount includes the amount which for the purposes of that Chapter would in the case of the company be the foreign permanent establishments amount attributable to the disposal for the accounting period in which it was made if the disposal were not a no gain/no loss disposal).

(2) For the purposes of this section a no gain/no loss disposal is one on which by virtue of section 152 or any of the no gain/no loss provisions neither a gain nor a loss accrues to the company making the disposal."

CAA 2001

14 CAA 2001 is amended as follows.

15 In section 15 (plant and machinery allowances: qualifying activities), after subsection (2) insert—

"(2A) A business carried on through one or more permanent establishments outside the United Kingdom by a company in relation to which an election under section 18A of CTA 2009 has effect—

(a) is an activity separate from any other activity of the company, and

(b) is to be regarded as an activity all the profits and gains from which are not, or (if there were any) would not be, chargeable to tax."

16 In the Table in section 61 (disposal events and disposal values), after item 6 insert—

"6A Disposal event to which section 62A applies.	The relevant transition value (see section 62A)."

and in column 1 of item 7, for "6" substitute "6A".

17 After section 62 insert—

"62A Cases in which disposal value is transition value

(1) Subject as follows, this section applies where an election under section 18A of CTA 2009 has effect in relation to a company and the operation of section 15(2A) brings about a disposal event consisting of plant or machinery beginning to be used for purposes other than those of a qualifying activity.

(2) Where this section applies to a disposal event, the disposal value is the transition value.

(3) The transition value is such amount as gives rise to neither a balancing allowance nor a balancing charge.

(4) This section does not apply if—

(a) the qualifying expenditure in respect of the plant or machinery, or of the group of assets of which it forms part at any time during a relevant accounting period, exceeds £5 million, and

(b) the company has used the plant or machinery otherwise than for the purposes of a permanent establishment in a territory outside the United Kingdom at any time during a relevant preceding accounting period.

(5) For the purposes of subsection (4)(a) plant or machinery used together constitutes a group of assets.

(6) In subsection (4) "relevant preceding accounting period" means the accounting period in which the election under section 18A is made or an earlier accounting period ending less than 6 years before the end of that accounting period."

ITA 2007

18 ITA 2007 is amended as follows.

19 In section 879(1) (interest paid on advances from banks), insert at the end "or is a bank that would be within the charge to corporation tax as respects the interest apart from section 18A of CTA 2009."

20 (1) Section 918 (manufactured dividends on UK shares: REITs) is amended as follows.

(2) After subsection (3) insert—

"(3A) But subsection (3) does not apply if—

(a) the manufactured dividend is paid by a UK resident company in the course of a trade carried on through a permanent establishment in a territory outside the United Kingdom, and

(b) section 18A of CTA 2009 has effect in relation to the company for the accounting period in which it is paid."

(3) In subsection (4), for paragraphs (a) and (b) substitute—

"(a) is non-UK resident and pays the manufactured dividend otherwise than in the course of a trade carried on through a branch or agency in the United Kingdom, or

(b) is a UK resident company and pays the manufactured dividend in the course of a trade carried on through a permanent establishment in a territory outside the United Kingdom and section 18A of CTA 2009 has effect in relation to the company for the accounting period in which it is paid,".

(4) After subsection (5) insert—

"(5A) But a UK resident is not a United Kingdom recipient if—

(a) it is a UK resident company which receives the manufactured dividend for the purposes of a trade carried on by the recipient through a permanent establishment in a territory outside the United Kingdom, and

(b) section 18A of CTA 2009 has effect in relation to the company for the accounting period in which it is received."

21 In section 919 (manufactured interest on UK securities: payments by UK residents etc), after subsection (1) insert—

"(1A) But this section does not apply if—

(a) the manufactured interest is paid by a UK resident company in the course of a trade carried on through a permanent establishment in a territory outside the United Kingdom, and

(b) section 18A of CTA 2009 has effect in relation to the company for the accounting period in which it is paid."

22 (1) Section 920 (foreign payers of manufactured interest: the reverse charge) is amended as follows.

(2) After subsection (1) insert—

"(1A) This section also applies if—

(a) a UK resident company pays manufactured interest in the course of a trade carried on through a permanent establishment in a territory outside the United Kingdom, and

(b) section 18A of CTA 2009 has effect in relation to the company for the accounting period in which it is paid."

(3) After subsection (2) insert—

"(2A) But this section does not apply if—

(a) the recipient is a UK resident company which receives the manufactured interest for the purposes of a trade carried on by the recipient through a permanent establishment in a territory outside the United Kingdom, and

(b) section 18A of CTA 2009 has effect in relation to the company for the accounting period in which it is received."

(4) In subsection (3), insert at the end "and section 919(1A) did not apply".

23 In section 922 (manufactured overseas dividends: payments by UK residents etc), after subsection (1) insert—

"(1A) But this section does not apply if—

(a) the manufactured overseas dividend is paid by a UK resident company in the course of a trade carried on through a permanent establishment in a territory outside the United Kingdom, and

(b) section 18A of CTA 2009 has effect in relation to the company for the accounting period in which it is paid."

24 (1) Section 923 (foreign payers of manufactured overseas dividends: the reverse charge) is amended as follows.

(2) After subsection (1) insert—

"(1A) This section also applies if—

(a) a UK resident company pays a manufactured overseas dividend in the course of a trade carried on through a permanent establishment in a territory outside the United Kingdom, and

(b) section 18A of CTA 2009 has effect in relation to the company for the accounting period in which it is paid."

(3) After subsection (2) insert—

"(2A) But this section does not apply if—

(a) the recipient is a UK resident company which receives the manufactured overseas dividend for the purposes of a trade carried on by the recipient through a permanent establishment in a territory outside the United Kingdom, and

(b) section 18A of CTA 2009 has effect in relation to the company for the accounting period in which it is received."

(4) In subsection (3), insert at the end "and section 922(1A) did not apply."

TIOPA 2010

25 TIOPA 2010 is amended as follows.

26 In section 18 (entitlement to credit for foreign tax reduces UK tax by amount of credit), after subsection (3) insert—

"(3A) References in subsection (3) to tax payable under the law of a territory outside the United Kingdom do not include tax paid by a company in relation to which an election under section 18A of CTA 2009 (exemption for profits or losses of overseas permanent establishments) has effect in respect of a relevant profits amount or relevant losses amount within the meaning of that section."

27 For section 43 substitute—

"43 Profits attributable to permanent establishments for purposes of section 42(2)

(1) This section applies in determining for the purposes of section 42(2) the amount of the profits of a UK resident company on which corporation tax is or would be chargeable that is attributable to a permanent establishment of the company in a territory outside the United Kingdom.

(2) The amount of the profits of the company that is attributable to the permanent establishment is the amount that the permanent establishment would have made if it were a distinct and separate enterprise which—

(a) engaged in the same or similar activities under the same or similar conditions, and

(b) dealt wholly independently with the company.

(3) In applying subsection (2) assume that—

(a) the permanent establishment has the same credit rating as the company, and

(b) (subject to subsection (5)) the permanent establishment has such equity and loan capital as it could reasonably be expected to have if the equity and loan capital of the company were allocated in accordance with subsection (4).

(4) The allocation is one made on a just and equitable basis between the permanent establishments in territories outside the United Kingdom through which the company carries on business and the entity that the company would consist of if each such permanent establishment were an entity distinct and separate from the company.

(5) If the permanent establishment is in a full treaty territory (within the meaning of Chapter 3A of Part 2 of CTA 2009) subsection (3)(b) has effect subject to the double taxation arrangements having effect in relation to the territory.

(6) Subsections (3)(b) to (5) prevail over any allotment of equity or loan capital to the permanent establishment made by the company.

(7) If the company is an insurance company (within the meaning given by section 431(2) of ICTA), in applying subsection (2) assume that the permanent establishment has such free assets as it would have in the circumstances described in that subsection.

(8) The Commissioners for Her Majesty's Revenue and Customs may by regulations make provision as to the meaning of "free assets" in subsection (7)."

28 (1) Section 78 (meaning of "overseas permanent establishment") is amended as follows.

(2) In subsection (2)—

(a) in paragraph (a), for "and define the expression" substitute "which contain a relevant non-discrimination provision", and

(b) in paragraph (b)—

(i) for "but do not define the expression" substitute "which do not contain a relevant non-discrimination provision", and

(ii) for "is to be read in accordance with Chapter 2 of Part 24 of CTA 2010." substitute "has the meaning given by the Model Tax Convention on Income and on Capital published by the Organisation for Economic Co-operation and Development in July 2010 ("the OECD") or such other document published by the OECD in place of it as is designated from time to time by order made by the Treasury."

(3) After that subsection insert—

"(3) In subsection (2) "relevant non-discrimination provision" means a provision to the effect that the taxation on a permanent establishment of an enterprise of a state which is party to the arrangements (a "contracting state") is not to be less favourably levied in any other contracting state than the taxation levied on enterprises of that other contracting state carrying on the same activities."

29 In section 263 (tax treatment of financing costs and income: net debt of a company), after subsection (4) insert—

"(4A) For the purposes of subsections (3) and (4), if the company is one in relation to which an election under section 18A of CTA 2009 has effect anything that would otherwise form part of the company's relevant liabilities or relevant assets does not do so if and to the extent that amounts in respect of it are left out of account under that section."

30 After section 317 insert—

"317A Companies with permanent establishments profits election

(1) This section applies if, apart from this section, an amount is a financing expense amount or a financing income amount of a company in relation to which an election under section 18A of CTA 2009 has effect.

(2) It is treated as not being a financing expense amount or a financing income amount of the company if and to the extent that it is left out of account under that section."

PART 3

COMMENCEMENT AND TRANSITIONAL PROVISION

Commencement

31 The amendments made by this Schedule come into force on the day on which this Act is passed.

Condition B of motive test

32 (1) This paragraph applies in relation to a company carrying on business through a permanent establishment in an accounting period which is the first relevant accounting period or an accounting period beginning less than 12 months after the beginning of the first relevant accounting period (an "affected relevant accounting period") if the company carried on the business through the permanent establishment throughout the period of 12 months ending with the day before that on which this Act is passed ("the pre-commencement year").

(2) Condition B in section 18H of CTA 2009 (as inserted by this Schedule) is assumed to be met in relation to an affected relevant accounting period if—

(a) the gross income attributable to the permanent establishment for the affected relevant accounting period does not exceed by more than 10% the gross income attributable to the permanent establishment for the period of 12 months ending immediately before the beginning of the first relevant accounting period (or, if the affected relevant accounting period is less than 12 months, such proportion of that gross income as the length of the affected relevant accounting period bears to 12 months),

(b) there has been no major change in the nature or conduct of the business carried on through the permanent establishment in the period ("the relevant period") beginning with the pre-commencement year and ending with the end of the affected relevant accounting period, and

(c) no asset attributable to the permanent establishment was previously owned, and no part of the business carried on through the permanent establishment in the affected relevant accounting period was previously carried on, by a company whose chargeable profits and creditable tax (if any) for any accounting period ending within the relevant period were (or, but for an agreement made or undertaking given, would have been) apportioned under section 747(3) of ICTA.

(3) For the purposes of sub-paragraph (2) "major change in the nature or conduct of the business" includes—

(a) a major change in the type of property dealt in, or services or facilities provided, in the business, and

(b) a major change in customers, outlets or markets of the business.

(4) A reference in sub-paragraph (3) to a change includes a change which is achieved gradually as a result of a series of transfers.

33 (1) This paragraph applies in relation to a company ("company A") carrying on business through a permanent establishment in an accounting period which is the first relevant accounting period or an accounting period beginning less than 12 months after the beginning of the first relevant accounting period (an "affected relevant accounting period") if a company which—

(a) was a non-UK resident company, and

(b) was controlled by company A,

("company B") carried on the business throughout the period of 12 months ending with the day before that on which this Act is passed ("the pre-commencement year").

(2) Condition B in section 18H of CTA 2009 (as inserted by this Schedule) is assumed to be met in relation to an affected relevant accounting period if—

(a) the gross income attributable to the permanent establishment for the affected relevant accounting period does not exceed by more than 10% the gross income of the business for the period of 12 months ending immediately before the beginning of the first relevant accounting period of the company (or, if the affected relevant accounting period is less than 12 months, such proportion of that gross income as the length of the affected relevant accounting period bears to 12 months),

(b) there has been no major change in the nature or conduct of the business carried on through the permanent establishment in the period ("the relevant period") beginning with the pre-commencement year and ending with the end of the affected relevant accounting period,

(c) company B was not a company whose chargeable profits and creditable tax (if any) for any accounting period ending within the relevant period were (or, but for an agreement made or undertaking given, would have been) apportioned under section 747(3) of ICTA, and

(d) no asset attributable to the permanent establishment was previously owned, and no part of the business carried on through the permanent establishment in the affected relevant accounting period was previously carried on, by such a company.

(3) Sub-paragraphs (3) and (4) of paragraph 32 apply for the purposes of sub-paragraph (2).

(4) Section 1124 of CTA 2010 (meaning of "control") applies for the purposes of this paragraph.

Large pre-commencement losses

34 (1) This paragraph applies if—

(a) there is a relevant losses amount exceeding £50 million in the case of a company in relation to any relevant foreign territory for any accounting period beginning within the period of 6 years ending with the day before that on which this Act is passed, and

(b) (apart from this paragraph) the accounting period would not be an affected prior accounting period for the purposes of section 18J(2) of CTA 2009 (as inserted by this Schedule).

(2) The accounting period, and every later accounting period of the company before the first relevant accounting period of the company which would not otherwise be an affected prior accounting period for those purposes, is an affected prior accounting period for those purposes.

35 (1) This paragraph applies if—

(a) section 18O of CTA 2009 (as inserted by this Schedule) applies in relation to a transfer of business, and

(b) (apart from this paragraph) the effect of subsection (4) of that section would be that a relevant losses amount falling within paragraph 34(1)(a) would be ignored for the purposes of section 18J(2) of that Act.

(2) There is to be added to the adjusted foreign permanent establishments amount in relation to the accounting period of the transferee in which the transfer took place a negative amount equal to that relevant losses amount.

Section 62A of CAA 2001

36 For the purposes of section 62A of CAA 2001 (as inserted by this Schedule)—

(a) where the qualifying expenditure in respect of the plant or machinery, or of the group of assets of which it forms part, in question does not exceed £50 million, an accounting period ending more than 12 months before the day on which this Act is passed is not a relevant preceding accounting period, and

(b) where it does, any accounting period beginning within the period of 6 years ending with the day before that on which this Act is passed which (apart from this paragraph) would not be a relevant preceding accounting period is such a period.

Section 43(8) of TIOPA 2010: free assets

37 Until provision made under subsection (8) of section 43 of TIOPA 2010 (as substituted by this Schedule) has effect, "free assets" in subsection (7) of that section has the meaning given by regulation 3 of the Non-resident Insurance Companies Regulations 2003 (SI 2003/2714).

GENERAL NOTE

Prior to the enactment of the FA 2011, UK resident companies were liable to UK corporation tax on all of their profits, regardless of the jurisdiction within which they arose and including those of any foreign permanent establishments.

To avoid double taxation, credit is normally given for any foreign taxes incurred by a branch company, in accordance with prevailing UK Double Taxation Agreements (DTA). Where no DTA is in place, relief for foreign taxes suffered is given by means of unilateral relief.

This measure introduces an optional exemption from UK corporation tax for profits and losses of foreign permanent establishments.

A UK company has a permanent establishment in another state when it trades there through a branch or other fixed place of business, or through an agent (other than an independent agent), as defined in CTA 2009 s 1141.

Part 1–Amendments of CTA 2009

A new Chapter 3A has been inserted into CTA 2009 Part 2, immediately following s 18. New s 18A contains significant changes to the treatment of profits realised by the foreign permanent establishments of UK resident companies. It states that the profits or losses of a foreign permanent establishment are to be left out of account in computing the chargeable profits of a UK company, where a company elects for s 18A to apply.

In order to determine the chargeable UK profits of a company who have foreign permanent establishments, and have elected for the new s 18A to apply, 'exemption adjustments' will need to be made (new s 18A(2)). The exemption adjustments refer to the process of ensuring that profits or losses accounted for in computing the exempted profits of a foreign permanent establishment are not then taken into account when computing the chargeable profits of a UK resident company.

A relevant accounting period of a foreign permanent establishment, for the purposes of identifying exempted permanent establishment profits, is defined as any accounting period to which the election will apply s 18A(3)). New s 18F identifies the first relevant accounting period as the period immediately following the one in which the election under new s 18A is made.

The election is irrevocable, and applies to all accounting periods subsequent to the one in which the election is made (sub-ss 18F(1)(a) and (b)). If the election is to be revoked, the applicant company needs to notify HMRC before the commencement of the first accounting period to which s 18A would apply (s 18F(2)).

It will be necessary for companies to compute a 'Foreign Permanent Establishments Amount' (FPEA), which will equate to the aggregate sum of profits and losses realised by all foreign permanent establishments in their respective foreign territories (new s 18A(4)). For the purposes of the provisions, a 'relevant foreign territory' is defined at new s 18A(5) as a foreign territory where the company is or has carried on a trade through a permanent establishment.

In order to calculate the aggregated FPEA, the 'relevant profits amount' of each foreign permanent establishment needs to be determined at the territory level. Where the territory has a full treaty with the UK the relevant profits of the permanent establishment are to be calculated in accordance with the terms of the treaty (new s 18A(6)(a)). This would be consistent with the existing practice for computing the taxable profits of a foreign permanent establishment for the purposes of determining any creditable foreign tax paid (per TIOPA 2010).

For the purposes of the provisions, a 'full treaty' is defined as a UK Double Taxation Agreement (DTA) that includes a relevant non-discrimination clause (new s 18R).

Where the foreign permanent establishment is resident in a territory with which the UK does not have a full DTA, the profits of the permanent establishment for the purposes of the exemption are to be calculated with reference to the 2010 version of the Organisation for Economic Co-operation and Development (OECD) Model Convention (new s 18S). Here, the profits are computed in accordance with the conventional treaty framework, as if a full treaty were in place and the associated double taxation arrangements applied (new s 18A(6)(b)).

The same methodology for the computation of foreign permanent establishments profits is applied to the calculation of losses. Where a full treaty is in place the accounting loss for the period is calculated by giving reference to the terms of the treaty between the UK and the foreign territory. Where no such agreement exists, the principles of the OECD model will again be referred to, and will be applied on the basis that a full treaty was in place (new s 18A(7)).

New sub-ss 18A(8) and (9) apply where some full treaties in force provide for taxation by the foreign territory in respect of certain profits, without the requirement that said profits are attributable to a permanent establishment in that territory. When computing the 'relevant profits' of the territory for the purposes of the permanent establishment profit exemption however, only those profits that are attributable to the permanent establishment are included.

New s 18A(10) provides that where there are differences in the attribution profits to a permanent establishment for the purposes of calculating credit relief when comparing the UK and territorial treatment, relevant profits and losses should be calculated as if there were no such disparity.

Section 18B–Chargeable gains etc

New s 18B of CTA 2009 outlines the treatment of chargeable gains arising within a foreign permanent establishment. New s 18B(1) provides that the exemption adjustments of a foreign permanent establishment, where an exemption election has been made under new s 18A, must remove the impact of any gains or losses taken into account when calculating the FPEA. This will have the effect of increasing a gain where the FPEA includes a loss or increasing a loss where the FPEA includes a gain.

New s 18B(2) addresses the issue of chargeable gains realised upon immoveable property, in the context of computing the exempt profits of a foreign permanent establishment. In many cases prevailing tax treaties contain a protectionist clause to ensure that any gains realised upon the sale of immoveable property in either territory remain within the scope of charge to tax in the jurisdiction in which the property is situated. This can mean that there is no attribution of such gains to the profits of a permanent establishment, and as such, foreign tax credit relief may not apply. This is addressed by s 18B(2) by allowing any gains realised upon immoveable property to form part of the relevant profits or losses of a foreign permanent establishment, where the immoveable property forms part of the business of the permanent establishment.

The realisation of chargeable gains (or losses) by a permanent establishment in prior accounting periods may be taken into account for the purposes of the profits exemption election (new s 18A). New s 18B(3) allows for earlier gains to be included in computing the relevant profits (or losses) of a permanent establishment, but only where the tax so payable is paid in an accounting period to which the profits exemption election applies. This effectively prevents the application of new s 18A to chargeable gains or losses arising in accounting periods prior to the exemption taking effect for a company. However, where foreign tax has been suffered on those amounts, credit relief should be available, as was previously the case.

Section 18C–Capital allowances etc

New s 18C of CTA 2009 outlines how plant and machinery allowances and associated elections are to be made in relation to the new s 18A profits exemption.

New s 18C(1) provides that, for accounting periods to which the profits exemption election under s 18A applies, notional plant and machinery allowances and charges shall automatically be taken into account in computing the relevant profits of the foreign permanent establishment.

New s 15(2A)(a) of CAA 2001 has been inserted to apply as if the activity of the foreign permanent establishment is a qualifying activity for the purposes of the Capital Allowances Act (CAA 2001), provided that it would be so considered but for the effect of an election made under new s 18A CTA 2009 and new s 15(2A)(b) of CAA 2001. Notional capital allowance computations will therefore need to be completed in determining the relevant profits of a foreign permanent establishment.

Where a capital allowances disposal event occurs as a result of a company making an election under new s 18A of CTA 2009, the proceeds value to be taken into account for the purposes of computing any balancing allowance or charge arising is the tax written down value of the asset (new s 18C(2)). Here, the tax written down value is to be known as the 'transition value', as stated in new s 62A of CAA 2001. To ensure reasonable treatment, the expenditure so taken into account by the foreign permanent establishment for the purposes of computing future allowances is to be the same transition value under new s 15(2A)(a) CAA 2001.

A further provision relating to the interaction of CAA 2001 and the new profits exemption election under new s 18A refers to the exclusion of profits or losses on plant and machinery leases when computing the relevant profits of the foreign permanent establishment (new s 18C(3)).

When determining the relevant profits of the foreign permanent establishment, for the purposes of identifying the exempt amount under s 18A, it is to be assumed that all available plant and machinery claims and elections have been made, reducing the relevant profits of the foreign permanent establishment accordingly (new s 18C(5)). This is an important consideration in determining whether or not foreign territory tax paid will be creditable for UK tax purposes (in accordance with the provisions stipulated in TIOPA 2010). In general, foreign tax suffered upon relevant profits of the permanent establishment (calculated in accordance with new s 18A) will be creditable against UK corporation tax.

Section 18D–Payments subject to deduction

New s 18D of CTA 2009 refers to the treatment of profits or losses arising on transactions between UK resident persons and a permanent establishment in a territory outside of the UK. For the purposes of computing the relevant profits or losses of the permanent establishment (per new ss 18A(6)&(7)), profits or losses realised on transactions that are subject to the deduction of tax in the UK that are not repayable (taking account of the relevant tax treaty) will not form part of the relevant profits of the permanent establishment (new ss 18D(1) and 18D(2)). If the payments in question are not liable to the deduction of tax in the UK then any profits or losses arising will form part of the exempt profits of the permanent establishment.

Subsequently, new s 18D(3) asserts that the exclusion of payments subject to the deduction of tax will not apply if the recipient company is a bank (as defined within s 1120 of CTA 2010), unless the transaction is entered in to for the purposes of avoiding the deduction of tax on the payment.

Section 18E–Employee share acquisitions

The costs associated with employee share acquisitions are to be taken into account when calculating the relevant profits or losses of a foreign permanent establishment.

New ss 18E(1) and 18E(2) of CTA 2009 determine that the costs of employee share acquisitions are to be deductible in determining the amount of relevant profits of an exempt foreign permanent establishment, to the extent that the work of the employees contributes to the business carried on in the foreign territory. A just and reasonable apportionment of costs should therefore be made.

Section 18G–Anti-diversion rule

New s 18G focuses predominantly upon anti-avoidance considerations with respect to the exemption of a permanent establishment's profits or losses. In certain circumstances, the profits of a foreign permanent establishment will not qualify for exemption under new s 18A. New s 18G looks to prevent the artificial diversion of profits to exempt permanent establishments.

The circumstances in which the profits exemption will not apply are stipulated at new s 18G(1). Broadly, the exemption will not apply if the 'lower level of tax test' is met in relation to the territory of permanent establishment. Here, the emphasis of the provisions are along the lines of the Controlled Foreign Company (CFC) rules and try to ensure that companies are not able to use the permanent establishment profits exemption to divert profits to lower tax jurisdictions.

New s 18G(2) asserts that where a foreign permanent establishment has relevant profits, but the 'lower level of tax test' is failed, the exempt profits for the purposes of new s 18A will be taken to be nil. Therefore, the profits of the foreign permanent establishment would not be exempted and would fall within the scope of charge to UK tax.

Section 18G(3) sets out how to calculate the adjusted profits amount ie by disregarding chargeable gains and allowable losses

The 'lower level of tax' test is failed with respect to the permanent establishment if the foreign territory tax due upon those profits is less than 75 percent of the corresponding UK tax that would be due (new s 18G(4)). Here, any credit given for foreign tax paid by the permanent establishment is ignored. Similarly, for the purposes of the lower level of tax test, the adjusted profits of the permanent establishment are computed without reference to available losses or group relief.

The anti-diversion provisions contained at new s 18G will not apply in two specified circumstances. The first circumstance is explained at new s 18G(6), asserting that the lower level of tax principles will not be applied where the adjusted relevant profits of the foreign permanent establishment are less than the 'entry limit'. The entry limit has been set at £200,000 (proportionately reduced for periods of less than 12 months), in accordance with new s 18G(7). The second circumstance where the anti-diversion provisions will not apply is where the 'motive test', as defined at new s 18H, is met.

Section 18H–The motive test

The motive test in respect of the foreign permanent establishment will be met if both conditions A and B of new s 18H are met.

Condition A will be met if it can be shown that any reduction in UK tax arising from a 'relevant transaction' is minimal, or the achievement of the reduction was not the main purpose, or one of the main purposes, of the transaction (new s 18H(2)). For the purposes of this section, a 'relevant transaction' is one which forms part of the permanent establishment's profits in a given accounting period (new s 18H(3)).

When determining whether there has been a 'reduction in UK tax', it has to be shown that had a relevant transaction (or transactions) not taken place, a person in the UK would have been liable to UK tax, or would not have been entitled to a relief from, or a repayment of, UK tax (new s 18H(4)(a)&(b)).

The main purpose of a transaction (for the purposes of new s 18H(2)) will be a matter of fact. Where it is clear that the intention of those undertaking the transaction (namely the company, or a person that has an interest in the company) was to achieve a reduction in UK tax, the intended purpose will be established and the anti-diversion provisions will apply (new s 18H(5)).

Condition B represents an overriding principle that has to be complied with if the anti-diversion rules under new s 18G are not to apply. This condition will be met if it can be shown that the use of a foreign permanent establishment is not predetermined with the aim of achieving a reduction in UK tax via the diversion of profits to a foreign permanent establishment (new s 18H(6)).

In determining whether or not the use of a foreign permanent establishment is motivated by a potential reduction in UK tax, new ss 18H(7)&(8) outline the circumstances in which HMRC could make a reasoned supposition that this is the case.

Broadly, condition B will not be met if it can be shown that, were the foreign establishment not in existence and there was no related company relationship, permanent establishment profits would arise directly to a UK resident company or individual, who would then be subject to higher levels of tax in the UK then those suffered in the territory of the permanent establishment.

Similarly, a fair supposition of artificial profit diversion could be made if it can be shown that a UK resident company or individual benefits from greater relief from, or a larger repayment of, UK tax as a result of the existence of the foreign permanent establishment.

Consequential amendments (new sub-ss 18H(9–13) define various terms used in new s 18H. Making reference to new s 18H(8), companies are deemed to be related to one another if any of the conditions stated at new s 18H(9) are met. New s 18H(13) asserts that for the purposes of the section, UK tax is held to mean UK income tax, corporation tax or capital gains tax.

One would expect that the level of business activity within the territory of the permanent establishment would be a major factor in determining whether or not the existence of the permanent establishment is motivated by the scope for UK tax avoidance. The choice of jurisdictional residence for the permanent establishment will also be important; where a known tax haven is chosen it is highly likely that anti-diversion provisions will apply.

Section 18I–Proportionate reduction in certain cases

Where it is shown that a foreign permanent establishment complies with condition B of new s 18H, but fails to comply with condition A (as stated at new s 18H(2)), a proportionate reduction to the exempt permanent establishment's profits will apply, rather than a reduction to nil as stated at new s 18G(2).

New s 18I(1) would apply if, for example, a relevant transaction gave rise to a significant reduction in UK tax (were the same profits to arise to an equivalent UK company rather than a foreign permanent establishment), but the main reason for the transaction (or transactions) was not to achieve a reduction in tax by the diversion of profits to a foreign permanent establishment.

Subsequently, new s 18I(2) states that where sub-s 1 applies, the proportionate reduction to the profits of a foreign permanent establishment would be made on a just and reasonable basis, with the relevant transactions being referred to as 'tainted relevant transactions'. Tainted relevant transactions are those which achieve a reduction in UK tax (as stated above), but this was not their main purpose (new s 18I(3)).

Section 18J–Companies with total opening negative amount

New s 18J provides the basis for which a permanent establishment can ascertain whether or not they have an opening negative amount at the start of the first accounting period to which the election under new s 18A applies. Here, an opening negative amount is equivalent to the unrelieved brought forward losses of a permanent establishment in the six years prior to the election.

Section 18J(2) outlines the method by which the opening negative amount should be calculated, known here as the adjusted FPEA (where applicable). The process is broken down into three steps; the first requires that the earliest negative adjusted FPEA, arising in an 'affected prior accounting period', be identified. For the purposes of this new section, 'affected prior accounting period' refers to the accounting period in which a s 18A election is made, and all preceding accounting periods ending in the six years before the end of that accounting period (new s 18J(3)).

The second step sees the adjusted negative FPEA carried forward to a subsequent accounting period, which should also fall within the affected prior accounting period. Here, effectively, a loss realised by a foreign permanent establishment is carried forward and aggregated with any profits or losses of the subsequent accounting period. The aggregation of profits should in no circumstance see the adjusted negative FPEA exceed nil.

The third step requires the aggregation of profits against all subsequent accounting periods of the permanent establishment, where they end within the affected prior accounting period (ie the opening negative FPEA amount is chronologically matched to accounting periods ending in the six years preceding the end of the accounting period in which the election under new s 18A is made). Once again, the aggregation with profits should not see the negative FPEA exceed nil.

The 'adjusted' FPEA is what the foreign permanent establishment's profits would be, when determined without reference to chargeable gains or allowable losses for the purposes of corporation tax (new s 18J(4)).

Section 18K–Total opening amount: "matching"

Where there is a negative opening balance, and in subsequent periods, aggregated relevant permanent establishment profits, the matching provisions will apply until the opening negative balance is reduced to nil. It is after this point that the new foreign permanent establishment profits exemption under the new s 18A will apply.

New s 18K explains that an opening negative amount is to be aggregated against the relevant profits (if any) of a foreign permanent establishment for each accounting period following the one in which an election under new s 18A is made. Where an opening negative amount completely extinguishes the relevant profits of a subsequent accounting period, the foreign permanent establishment's profits of the period will not be exempt (new s 18K(2)).

The negative opening balance is reduced on a year by year basis (where applicable), until the amount is reduced to nil. For the purposes of the accounting period during which it is reduced to nil, the permanent establishment profits exemption will partially apply (new s 18K(3)). The company should specify in its tax return that the opening negative balance has been reduced to nil, and stipulate to what portion of aggregate profits of the period the new permanent establishment exemption will apply (new s 18K(4)).

'Aggregate relevant profits' of the foreign permanent establishment refers to the aggregate sum of relevant profits of each foreign territory for which there is a relevant profits amount for the period. Therefore, the relevant profits and losses of each foreign permanent establishment within a given accounting period are aggregated to provide the aggregated relevant permanent establishment profits (new s 18K(5)).

The new provisions stipulate that the matching process will apply, subject to the streaming provisions at new s 18L (new s 18K(6)).

Section 18L–Streaming

The provisions of new s 18K provide for the aggregation of the relevant profits of all foreign permanent establishments in a given accounting period. Under new s 18L the company is provided with an alternative option of streaming the negative opening amount of a particular territory. The purpose of new s 18L is to give companies the option of applying the foreign permanent establishment profit exemption to certain territories immediately (e g for those territories to which an opening negative amount would not apply).

New s 18L(1) asserts that where a streaming election is made, new ss 18M and 18N will have effect instead of new s 18K.

The provisions state that an election made under new s 18L needs to be made at the same time as the election under new s 18A for the foreign permanent establishment profits exemption to apply (new s 18L(2)). The election should state that ss 18M and 18N are to apply to the company rather than s 18K. It should also specify the territories to which the streaming provisions will apply.

The streaming election becomes irrevocable at the start of the first exempt period (new s 18L(3)).

The election can however be revoked any time before the first relevant accounting period of the company (new s 18L(4)). The 'first relevant accounting period' of the company is as defined at s 18A(3).

The amount eligible to be streamed in the chosen streaming territories is calculated at the territory level as if the territory was the only foreign permanent establishment of the company (new s 18L(6)).

Section 18M–Streamed opening negative amounts: "matching"

New s 18M governs the matching of the opening negative amounts of streamed territories (here, 'streamed territory' refers to a territory chosen for streaming in accordance with new s 18L). New s 18N governs the matching of any residual opening negative amounts of territories not subject to the streaming provisions (un-streamed territories), if applicable.

The opening negative amount of a streamed territory is reduced by the matching of any relevant profits arising within a relevant accounting period (new s 18M(1)). The first accounting period in which matching may apply is the period immediately following the one in which elections under new s 18A (foreign permanent establishment profits exemption) and new s 18L (election for streaming to apply in respect of certain territories) are made. The matching of negative opening amounts occurs in subsequent accounting periods until the opening territory loss figure is reduced to nil.

The foreign permanent establishment profits exemption under new s 18A will not apply to the relevant profits of a foreign permanent establishment territory until the opening negative amount has been reduced to nil (new s 18M(2)).

When the opening negative amount has been exhausted, the company will need to stipulate in the relevant tax return the opening negative amount at the beginning of the accounting period, and the proportion of profits to which the profits exemption under new s 18A are to apply (new ss 18L(3)&(4)).

Section 18N–Residual opening negative amount: "matching"

The matching of opening negative amounts of territories not chosen for streaming is governed by new s 18N, where applicable. The aggregated opening negative amounts of unstreamed territories is known for the purposes of the provisions as the 'residual opening negative amount'.

The residual opening negative amount of unstreamed territories is reduced by the residual aggregate relevant profits of all of the unstreamed territories in relevant accounting periods. The matching of residual aggregate relevant profits will first occur in the accounting period immediately following the period in which elections under new ss 18A (foreign permanent establishment profits election) and 18L (territory streaming election) have been made. The matching continues in subsequent periods until the aggregated opening negative amount is reduced to nil (new s 18N(1)).

New s 18N(2) makes it clear that the aggregated opening negative amount is computed by calculating the aggregated negative amount of all permanent establishments of the company, less the opening negative amounts of the territories chosen for streaming. Similarly, the aggregated residual relevant profits of unstreamed territories is calculated by reducing them by any profits of the streamed territories (new s 18N(3)).

Consistent with the provisions stipulated at new s 18M(4) with respect to the matching of the opening negative amount of streamed territories, new s 18A will not apply to aggregated residual profits of the unstreamed territories until the residual opening negative amount has been reduced to nil through the matching process (new s 18N(4)).

Once the residual opening amount of the unstreamed territories has been extinguished through the matching process, the election for the exemption of foreign permanent establishment profits will apply. Here again, the company needs to notify HMRC of the residual opening negative amount at the beginning of the final accounting period in which matching takes place and must also stipulate the profits against which new s 18A is to apply (new ss 18N(5) and (6)).

Section 18O–Transfers of foreign permanent establishments

New s 18O will apply in certain circumstances where the foreign permanent establishment of a company is transferred to a connected company's foreign permanent establishment. In this context, the section looks to address the operation of the transitional provisions set out at new ss 18K–18N.

Section 18O will apply where the transfer of one foreign permanent establishment to another foreign permanent establishment lessens the effect of transitional provisions 18K to 18N on the disapplication of new s 18A–i e the opening negative amount of the combined permanent establishments is less than it would have been if the business had been so combined at all material times (new s 18O(1)). Here, 'all material times' refers to the periods stipulated in new ss 18K–18N.

This provision is in place to negate the possibility of foreign permanent establishments being transferred and/or consolidated with the aim of accelerating the application of new s 18A to the profits of foreign permanent establishments, therefore obtaining a UK tax advantage.

Section 18P–Exclusions

If a company is a small company, the foreign permanent establishment profits exemption (new s 18A) will not apply to a foreign permanent establishment that is resident in a territory with which the UK does not have a full double taxation treaty (new s 18P(1)). Here, a 'small company' is determined in accordance with the European Commission Recommendation 2003/361/EC of May 2003 as defined in new s 18S.

New s 18P(2) provides that chargeable gains arising to a close company should not, for the purposes of Chapter 3A, be considered when computing the relevant profits or losses of a foreign permanent establishment. The profits or losses derived from chargeable gains will not therefore form part of the profits available for exemption from UK tax under new s 18A.

Section 18Q–Insurance companies

New s 18Q contains certain provisions applicable to the calculation of the relevant profits of a foreign permanent establishment, where the foreign permanent establishment concerned is carrying on insurance business.

Section 18Q(1) asserts that, for the purposes of new Chapter 3A, profits or losses derived from basic life assurance policies and general annuity business are to be excluded in the calculation of relevant profits and losses of the foreign permanent establishment. Profits derived from these activities are therefore excluded from the profit exemption stipulated at new s 18A and may fall within the scope of UK tax.

New s 18Q(2) determines that the investment return of a an investment business carried on through a permanent establishment is to be calculated with reference to existing ICTA 1988 s 432E, but the section will only apply to the surplus of the permanent establishment rather than the surplus of the company.

Transfer of intangible fixed assets used by a permanent establishment

Paragraph 5 of Sch 13 amends existing provisions with respect to the transfer of intangible fixed assets between group companies.

New CTA 2009 s 775(c) asserts that the transfer of an intangible fixed asset will not be neutral for tax purposes where new s 18A has effect in respect of the transferring company, and the asset has, at some point during its ownership, been used for the purposes of a foreign permanent establishment.

Partial exemption upon transfer of intangible fixed assets

Subsequently Sch 13 para 6 introduces a new s 776A. The new section will have effect where new s 775(c) applies, but the asset has not been used exclusively for the purposes of a foreign permanent establishment. Here, a partial exemption will apply so as to ensure that the intangible fixed asset is transferred between group companies at a value between the tax neutral value, and its open market value.

Accordingly, where the intangible fixed asset has been used exclusively for the purposes of a foreign permanent establishment, it will transfer between group companies at its open market value.

Other amendments

Subsequently, Sch 13 paras 7–12 identify various legislative amendments arising as a result of the new profits exemption election under s 18A.

Paragraph 6 enables Part 10 to apply when computing the relevant profits and losses of a foreign permanent establishment. Part 10 refers to miscellaneous incomes.

Paragraphs 7 and 8 insert a new exception to the rule that transfers of intangible assets between related parties are at market value.

Paragraphs 9 and 10 provide for statutory deductions to be allowed for the costs of an employee share scheme. Deductions will therefore be allowed in computing the relevant profits and losses of a foreign permanent establishment, even where new s 18A applies.

Part 2–Consequential amendments

Part 2 of Sch 13 identifies various consequential amendments that have been made to other Acts as a result of the new foreign permanent establishment profits exemption.

Amendments to ICTA 1988–amendments to CFC provisions

Paragraph 13 of Part 2 amends ICTA 1988 Sch 24 para 4(1). The amendment refers to existing CFC legislation, and in particular, the method of computing the profits or losses of such an entity.

Paragraph 4(1) asserts that the profits or losses of a foreign company should be computed as if the company was UK resident and all beneficial claims and elections had been made, within the stipulated time limits. Paragraph 4(1) is amended such that the company is not assumed to have made an election under new s 18A.

Were the new s 18A election to be assumed to have been made, all the chargeable profits of the CFC would likely be exempted, therefore avoiding a required charge to UK tax upon realised foreign profits. This is therefore an anti-avoidance provision.

Amendments to TCGA 1992–computation of chargeable gains

Paragraph 12 of Sch 13 includes a new TCGA 1992 s 276A. The new section outlines the computation of a no gain/no loss transfer when the foreign permanent establishment exemption applies. The consideration to be used to achieve a no gain/no loss transfer should take account of the operation of Chapter 3A Part 2.

Amendments to CAA 2001–computation of capital allowances

Schedule 13 para 15 outlines amendments made to CAA 2001. Upon a company making an election under new s 18A, the permanent establishment will be treated as if it is commencing a new, separate trade, with effect from the beginning of the first accounting following the one in which the election is made (new s 15(2A) of CAA 2001).

Application of 'transition value'

For the purposes of plant and machinery allowances, the commencement of a new trade infers the cessation of the previous trade, and as such, balancing adjustments would be expected to arise (in the form of balancing allowances and charges) in capital allowance pools. New s 62A of CAA 2001 ensures that where an election under new s 18A of CTA 2009 is made, any assets qualifying for capital allowances will be deemed to transfer to the permanent establishment's new trade at their tax written down value. This will avoid the realisation of balancing adjustments within the applicable capital allowance pools.

New s 62A of CAA 2001 will only apply where new s 18A has effect. The disposal value of the capital assets subject to plant and machinery allowances is to be known as the 'transition value' (new s 62A(2) of CAA 2001). Here, the transition value is equal to the tax written down value of the asset (new s 62A(3) of CAA 2001).

Section 62A does not apply where the plant and machinery in question has been used other than in the foreign permanent establishment and the expenditure exceeds £5 million in the six years ending with the year in which an election is made for new s 18A to apply. Special commencement provisions also apply.

Amendments to ITA 2007

ITA 2007s 879(1) has been extended to enable the disapplication of the duty to withhold tax on certain interest payments to the foreign permanent establishment of a bank, where an election under new s 18A has been made.

Various amendments have been made to ss 918–923. The legislative amendments determine that where an exempt foreign permanent establishment (i e one that has made an election under new s 18A of CTA 2009) is party to the below payments (paid or received), the withholding and accounting for UK income tax is to apply, as if the payments had been received by a non-UK resident:

— manufactured dividends on UK shares relating to Real Estate Investment Trusts (REIT) (s 918 as amended);
— manufactured interest payments (ss 919 and 920 as amended); and
— manufactured overseas dividends (ss 922 and 923 as amended).

Amendments to TIOPA 2010

Availability of double taxation relief where new s 18A applies

Schedule 13 para 26 provides for an amendment to TIOPA 2010 s 18. With regard to double taxation relief by way of credit, a new sub-s 18(3A) is to be inserted. The new sub-s ensures that a UK company will not receive foreign tax credit relief in respect of the exempted profits of its foreign permanent establishment. This measure is consistent with the government's overriding aim of moving towards a territorial corporation tax system. Foreign permanent establishments of UK companies will pay tax within their given territory, with relevant profits exempted from UK tax where an election under new s 18A has effect. Giving UK foreign tax credit relief for the exempted profits of a foreign permanent establishment would negate the territorial principles of the new provisions, and would potentially see the foreign permanent establishment avoiding a charge to tax in either jurisdiction.

Calculation of the profits of foreign permanent establishments

A further amendment to TIOPA 2010 sees the replacement of s 43. The existing s 43 referred to the calculation of profits of a UK resident company that were attributable to its foreign permanent establishment(s). Section 43 has been repealed and replaced.

New s 43(2) provides for the profits of foreign permanent establishments to be calculated as if they were a separate enterprise carrying on similar activities to, and dealing independently of, the UK company of which they are a permanent establishment.

Further, it is to be assumed that the foreign permanent establishment has the same credit rating as the UK resident company (new s 43(3)). Subsequent sub-s 43(3)(b) determines that foreign permanent establishment(s) should be assumed to have the loan and equity capital as would apply if new s 43(4) were applied. Section 43(4) states that the attribution of equity and loan capital between the UK company and its foreign permanent establishment(s) should be done on a just and equitable basis, calculated on the premise that the UK company and its foreign permanent establishments are distinct, independent entities.

For the assumption at 43(3)(b) to be applied, the UK will need to have a full tax treaty in place with the territory of the permanent establishment (new s 43(5)).

To ensure that the spirit of the new provisions stipulated at new ss 43(3)(b) to (5) are complied with, these provisions override any allocation of equity and loan capital made by the UK company (an obvious anti-avoidance provision).

Profits of foreign permanent establishments–Insurance businesses

If the foreign permanent establishment is an insurance company, new s 43(7) determines that the permanent establishment has such 'free assets' attributed to it as would be reasonable if it were to be treated as a distinct, independent entity (in accordance with new sub-s 43(2)). Here, the 'free assets' of an insurance company can be broadly defined as the surplus value of the company's long-term business, with reference to the value of liabilities, money debts and excess shareholder assets (ICTA 1988 s 431).

TIOPA 2010 s 43(8) of provides for HMRC to be able to make provision as to the meaning of free assets when reviewing the attribution of such to its foreign permanent establishment(s).

Other changes

Paragraph 29 of Sch 13 amends the TIOPA definition of permanent establishment. Section 78 has been updated to give effect to the OECD Model Convention definition of permanent establishment, where the UK does not have a full tax treaty with the territory of the permanent establishment.

World debt-cap calculations and exempt permanent establishment profits

Final amendments to TIOPA 2010 arise for the purposes of calculating the worldwide debt cap of a company. For this purpose, the net debt attributable to a foreign permanent establishment, whose profits or losses are exempt from UK tax under new s 18A CTA 2009, will not be included within the total net debt of the UK company (new s 263(4A)).

A consequential amendment, referring to the debt cap definition, sees the exclusion of any financing expense or income amount that is taken into account when computing the exempt profits or losses of a foreign permanent establishment. Such amounts will therefore not be considered when computing the net debt of a UK company (new s 317A).

Part 3–Commencement provisions

Part 3 of Sch 13 sets out the commencement provisions for the legislation contained within the new CTA 2009 Part 2 Ch 3A.

General provisions

Schedule 13 will take effect from the day in which the Act is passed into law.

Condition B of the motive test

Condition B of the motive test is stipulated at new s 18H(6) of CTA 2009 and refers to the overriding principle of the anti-diversion provisions that profits of a UK company cannot be diverted to a foreign permanent establishment with the predetermined aim of reducing a charge to UK tax.

Paragraphs 33 and 34 of Sch 13 refer to the application of the motive test under Condition B in certain circumstances where the permanent establishment was carried on in the 12 months preceding the Act being passed (known here as the 'pre-commencement year').

Paragraph 33(1) of Part 3 applies to the 'first relevant accounting period' or an accounting period beginning less than 12 months after the beginning of the first relevant accounting period ('affected relevant accounting period'), where the permanent establishment was carried on throughout the pre-commencement year.

Condition B in respect of new s 18H(6) is assumed to be met in relation to an affected accounting period if three conditions are met.

The first condition specifies that the gross income of the foreign permanent establishment does not exceed by more than 10% the gross income received in the 12 months preceding the first relevant accounting period (proportionately adjusted for short accounting periods). Therefore, the provision looks to target any increase in profits realised by a foreign permanent establishment which may be the result of profit diversion for the means of benefiting from the new s 18A foreign permanent establishment profits exemption.

The second condition determines that there should be no major change in the nature or conduct of the business carried on through the permanent establishment in the period spanning the pre-commencement year and affected relevant accounting periods. Here, a major change in the nature or conduct of the business includes a major change in the property dealt in, including services or facilities provided, and a major change in customers, outlets or markets of the business.

The third condition states that for Condition B of the motive test to be met, no asset used in the trade of the permanent establishment should have been owned, and no part of the business should have been previously carried on, by a company that has been subject to the CFC profit apportionment provisions under ICTA 1988 s 747(3). The reference period for the third condition spans the pre-commencement year and the affected relevant accounting periods.

Paragraph 34 of Sch 13 also looks at the application of Condition B of the anti-diversion rules stated at new s 18H. But here, the meeting of the condition is considered in the context of a company ('Company A') who has a foreign permanent establishment in an affected accounting period, which was previous carried on by a non-UK resident company controlled by Company A ('Company B') throughout the period of 12 months before the commencement of the provisions of the Act.

Condition B of the anti-diversion rules will assumed to have been met by Company A if four conditions relating to the permanent establishment are met.

The first condition stipulates that the gross income of the permanent establishment should not exceed by more than 10% the gross income of the business in the 12 months immediately preceding the first relevant accounting period (quantitative gross income measures proportionately reduced for short accounting periods).

The second condition is the same as that stated in para 31, in that the trade in an affected accounting period should not show a major change in the nature or conduct of the business being continued by the permanent establishment. Here, the business carried on in the pre-commencement year will be compared to the business carried on in an affected accounting period.

The third condition states that Company B (the non-UK resident company which was previously controlled by Company A) was not a company to whom the attributed profits provision applied in respect of ICTA 1988 s 747(3) (attribution of chargeable profits provision under the existing CFC rules).

The final condition is similar to the third condition of para 31; no asset attributable to the permanent establishment, and no part of the business continued by it, should have previously been subject to the CFC charging provisions stipulated at s 747(3).

The provisions under para 32 are predominantly anti-avoidance related, targeting the intra-group transfer of a permanent establishment by non-UK resident companies. The provisions aim to prevent the diversion of profits into a new foreign permanent establishment which may benefit from the foreign permanent establishment profit exemption, particularly where the profits of the previously controlled foreign permanent establishment were subject to the CFC charging provisions.

Large pre-commencement losses

Paragraph 35 of Sch 13 extends the 'affected prior accounting period' for the purposes of calculating the opening negative amount where a company has losses in excess of £50 million in relation to any foreign territory for any accounting period beginning with the period of six years ending with the day before the Act is passed. Without this extension, 'affected prior accounting period' refers to the accounting period in which a s 18A election is made, and all preceding accounting periods ending in the six years before the end of that accounting period (new s 18J(3)).

Transfers between related parties and negative amounts

Paragraph 36 introduces an adjustment where a relevant losses amount would otherwise be ignored for the purposes of s 18J(2) by the operation of CTA 2009 s 18O(4).

Capital allowances: prior use of plant and machinery

Upon making an election under new CTA 2009 s 18A, the permanent establishment is deemed to commence a new, distinct trade, independent of the business carried on by the UK company of which it is a foreign permanent establishment. The deemed commencement of a new trade is an occasion of charge for the purposes of capital allowances, and thus, balancing adjustments could arise upon plant and machinery owned at the date an election under new s 18A takes effect.

New CAA 2001 s 62A of has been inserted to provide that, where an election under new s 18A takes effect, plant and machinery is deemed to transfer to the permanent establishment (and the deemed 'new' trade it continues) at its tax written down value, so as to avoid any balancing adjustments. Section 62A does not apply however where the plant and machinery in question has been used other than in the foreign permanent establishment and the expenditure exceeds £5 million in the six years ending with the year in which an election is made for new s 18A to apply.

Paragraph 34 extends the reference period to which the use of the plant and machinery is to be reviewed. For qualifying expenditure of less than £50 million, the reference period (in terms of reviewing the use of the assets) will not include an accounting period ending more than 12 months before the Act is passed.

Where qualifying expenditure on plant and machinery is in excess of £50 million, the reference period is extended to any accounting period beginning within six years before the commencement of the Act.

SCHEDULE 14

FURNISHED HOLIDAY LETTINGS

Section 52

PART 1

INCOME TAX

FA 2004

1 (1) In FA 2004, section 189 (relevant UK individual) is amended as follows.

(2) In subsection (2), omit the "and" at the end of paragraph (ba), and after that paragraph insert—

> "(bb) income which is chargeable under Part 3 of ITTOIA 2005 and is immediately derived from the carrying on of an EEA furnished holiday lettings business (whether individually or as a partner acting personally in a partnership), and".

(3) After subsection (6) insert—

"(6A) EEA furnished holiday lettings business" means an overseas property business so far as consisting of the commercial letting of furnished holiday accommodation (within the meaning of Chapter 6 of Part 3 of ITTOIA 2005) in one or more EEA states.

(6B) If there is a letting of accommodation only part of which is holiday accommodation, just and reasonable apportionments are to be made for the purpose of determining what is comprised in an EEA furnished holiday lettings business."

ITTOIA 2005

2 (1) ITTOIA 2005 is amended as follows.

(2) In section 322 (introduction)—

(a) after subsection (2) insert—

"(2A) It matters whether an overseas property business consists of or includes the commercial letting of furnished holiday accommodation in one or more EEA states for the purposes of—

(a) section 312 (deduction for expenditure on energy-saving items: see section 313(3)),

(b) certain provisions of TCGA 1992 (see section 241A of that Act),

(c) CAA 2001 (see, for example, sections 250 and 250A of that Act),

(d) section 189(2)(bb) of FA 2004 (meaning of "relevant UK earnings" for pension purposes),

(e) Part 4 of ITA 2007 (loss relief: see section 127ZA of that Act), and

(f) section 836(3) of ITA 2007 (jointly held property: see exception DA).",

(b) in subsection (3), for "the above provisions" substitute "the provisions mentioned in subsection (2)", and

(c) after subsection (3) insert—

"(4) This Chapter also supplements the provisions mentioned in subsection (2A) by providing in certain circumstances for the profits of the EEA furnished holiday lettings part of an overseas property business to be calculated separately (see sections 328A and 328B)."

(3) In section 325 (meaning of "qualifying holiday accommodation")—

(a) in subsection (2), for "140 days" substitute "210 days", and

(b) in subsection (3), for "70 days" substitute "105 days".

(4) In section 326 (under-used holiday accommodation)—

(a) in subsection (3), for "70" substitute "105", and

(b) after subsection (6) insert—

"(7) This section is to apply separately in relation to accommodation in the United Kingdom and accommodation in EEA states other than the United Kingdom."

(5) After section 326 insert—

"326A Under-used holiday accommodation: letting condition not met

(1) This section applies if—

(a) during a tax year a person lets qualifying holiday accommodation,

(b) the accommodation is let by the person—

(i) during the next tax year, or

(ii) during the next two tax years,

(c) the accommodation would (apart from this section) not be qualifying holiday accommodation—

(i) during the tax year mentioned in paragraph (b)(i), or

(ii) during both of the tax years mentioned in paragraph (b)(ii),

only because of a failure to meet the letting condition (see section 325(3)), and

(d) there was a genuine intention to meet the letting condition for the tax year within subsection (1)(c)(i) or each of the tax years within subsection (1)(c)(ii) (as the case may be).

(2) If the person makes an election in respect of that accommodation for any tax year in respect of which the failure mentioned in subsection (1)(c) occurs, the accommodation is to be treated as qualifying holiday accommodation for that tax year.

(3) Subsection (2) does not apply for the purposes of section 326 or subsection (1)(a).

(4) If an election is not made for the first of the tax years within subsection (1)(c)(ii), an election may not be made for the second.

(5) An election for a tax year must be made on or before the first anniversary of the normal self-assessment filing date for the tax year.

(6) References in subsection (1)(a) and (c) to qualifying holiday accommodation include accommodation treated as such under section 326."

(6) In section 327 (capital allowances and loss relief), in the heading, for "**relief**" substitute "**relief: UK property business**".

(7) In section 328 (relevant UK earnings for pension purposes), in the heading, for "**purposes**" substitute "**purposes: UK property business**".

(8) After section 328 insert—

"328A Capital allowances and loss relief: overseas property business

(1) If an overseas property business consists of both—

(a) the commercial letting of furnished holiday accommodation in one or more EEA states ("the EEA furnished holiday lettings part"), and

(b) other businesses or transactions ("the other part"),

this section requires separate calculations to be made of the profits of the EEA furnished holiday lettings part and the other part.

(2) The calculations must be made if—

(a) section 250 or 250A of CAA 2001 (giving effect to allowances and charges) applies to the EEA furnished holiday lettings part or the other part, or

(b) any provision of Part 4 of ITA 2007 (loss relief) applies in relation to a loss made in either of those parts.

(3) If there is a letting of accommodation only part of which is holiday accommodation, such apportionments are to be made for the purposes of this section as are just and reasonable.

328B Relevant UK earnings for pension purposes: overseas property business

(1) If an overseas property business consists of both—

(a) the commercial letting of furnished holiday accommodation in one or more EEA states ("the EEA furnished holiday lettings part"), and

(b) other businesses or transactions,

this section requires a separate calculation to be made of the profits of the EEA furnished holiday lettings part.

(2) The calculation must be made if the profits of the EEA furnished holiday lettings part are relevant UK earnings within section 189(2)(bb) of FA 2004.

(3) If there is a letting of accommodation only part of which is holiday accommodation, such apportionments are to be made for the purposes of this section as are just and reasonable."

ITA 2007

3 (1) ITA 2007 is amended as follows.

(2) In section 117 (overview of Chapter), after subsection (2) insert—

"(2A) This Chapter also makes provision for an overseas property business which consists of, or so far as it includes, the commercial letting of furnished holiday accommodation in one or more EEA states to be treated as a trade for the purposes of this Part (see section 127ZA)."

(3) In section 127 (UK furnished holiday lettings business treated as trade), for subsections (4) to (6) substitute—

"(3A) Chapter 2 applies as if sections 64 to 82 and 89 to 95 were omitted."

(4) After section 127 insert—

"127ZA EEA furnished holiday lettings business treated as trade

(1) This section applies if, in a tax year, a person carries on an EEA furnished holiday lettings business.

(2) "EEA furnished holiday lettings business" means an overseas property business which consists of, or so far as it includes, the commercial letting of furnished holiday accommodation (within the meaning of Chapter 6 of Part 3 of ITTOIA 2005) in one or more EEA states.

(3) For the purposes of this Part (but as modified below) the person is treated instead as carrying on in the tax year a single trade—

(a) which consists of every commercial letting of furnished holiday accommodation comprised in the person's EEA furnished holiday lettings business, and
(b) the profits of which are chargeable to income tax.

(4) Chapter 2 applies as if sections 64 to 82 and 89 to 95 were omitted.

(5) If there is a letting of accommodation only part of which is furnished holiday accommodation, just and reasonable apportionments are to be made for the purpose of determining what is comprised in the trade treated as carried on."

(5) In section 836 (jointly held property), in subsection (3), after exception D insert—

"Exception DA

Income arising from an overseas property business which consists of, or so far as it includes, the commercial letting of furnished holiday accommodation (within the meaning of Chapter 6 of Part 3 of ITTOIA 2005) in one or more EEA states."

Commencement

4 Subject to paragraphs 5 and 6, this Part has effect in relation to the tax year 2011–12 and subsequent tax years.

5 Paragraph 2(3) and (4)(a) have effect in relation to the tax year 2012–13 and subsequent tax years (but do not have effect in relation to relevant periods which begin before, and end on or after, 6 April 2012).

6 Paragraph 2(5) has effect where the tax year mentioned in section 326A(1)(a) of ITTOIA 2005 is 2010–11 or a subsequent tax year.

PART 2

CORPORATION TAX

CTA 2009

7 (1) CTA 2009 is amended as follows.

(2) In section 264 (overview of Chapter)—

(a) after subsection (2) insert—

"(2A) It matters whether an overseas property business consists of or includes the commercial letting of furnished holiday accommodation in one or more EEA states for the purposes of—

(a) Chapter 4 of Part 4 of CTA 2010 (relief for property business losses: see section 67A of that Act),
(b) certain provisions of TCGA 1992 (see section 241A of that Act), and
(c) CAA 2001 (see, for example, sections 250 and 250A of that Act).",

(b) in subsection (3), for "the above provisions" substitute "the provisions mentioned in subsection (2)", and
(c) after subsection (3) insert—

"(4) This Chapter also supplements the provisions mentioned in subsection (2A) by providing in certain circumstances for the profits of the EEA furnished holiday lettings part of an overseas property business to be calculated separately (see sections 250 and 250A)."

(3) In section 267 (meaning of "qualifying holiday accommodation")—

(a) in subsection (2), for "140 days" substitute "210 days", and
(b) in subsection (3), for "70 days" substitute "105 days".

(4) In section 268 (under-used holiday accommodation: averaging elections)—

(a) in subsection (3), for "70" substitute "105", and
(b) after subsection (6) insert—

"(7) This section is to apply separately in relation to accommodation in the United Kingdom and accommodation in EEA states other than the United Kingdom."

(5) After section 268 insert—

"268A Under-used holiday accommodation: letting condition not met

(1) This section applies if—

(a) during an accounting period a company lets qualifying holiday accommodation,
(b) the accommodation is let by the company—
  (i) during the next accounting period, or
  (ii) during the next two accounting periods,

(c) the accommodation would (apart from this section) not be qualifying holiday accommodation—

(i) during the accounting period mentioned in paragraph (b)(i), or

(ii) during both of the accounting periods mentioned in paragraph (b)(ii),

only because of a failure to meet the letting condition (see section 267(3)), and

(d) there was a genuine intention to meet the letting condition for the period within subsection (1)(c)(i) or each of the periods within subsection (1)(c)(ii) (as the case may be).

(2) If the company makes an election in respect of that accommodation for any accounting period in respect of which the failure mentioned in subsection (1)(c) occurs, the accommodation is to be treated as qualifying holiday accommodation for that accounting period.

(3) Subsection (2) does not apply for the purposes of section 268 or subsection (1)(a).

(4) If an election is not made for the first of the accounting periods within subsection (1)(c)(ii), an election may not be made for the second.

(5) An election for an accounting period must be made within the period of two years beginning at the end of the accounting period.

(6) References in subsection (1)(a) and (c) to qualifying holiday accommodation include accommodation treated as such under section 268."

(6) In section 269 (capital allowances and loss relief), in the heading, for "**relief**" substitute "**relief: UK property business**".

(7) After section 269 insert—

"269A Capital allowances and loss relief: overseas property business

(1) If an overseas property business consists of both—

(a) the commercial letting of furnished holiday accommodation in one or more EEA states ("the EEA furnished holiday lettings part"), and

(b) other businesses or transactions ("the other part"),

this section requires separate calculations to be made of the profits of the EEA furnished holiday lettings part and the other part.

(2) The calculations must be made if—

(a) section 250 or 250A of CAA 2001 (giving effect to allowances and charges) applies to the EEA furnished holiday lettings part or the other part, or

(b) any provision of Chapter 2, 4 or 6 of Part 4 of CTA 2010 (loss relief) applies in relation to a loss made in either of those parts.

(3) If there is a letting of accommodation only part of which is holiday accommodation, such apportionments are to be made for the purposes of this section as are just and reasonable."

(8) In section 748 (assets held for purposes of property business)—

(a) in subsection (4), for paragraphs (a) to (c) substitute—

"(a) an ordinary UK property business,

(b) a UK furnished holiday lettings business,

(c) an ordinary overseas property business, or

(d) an EEA furnished holiday lettings business.", and

(b) for subsection (5) substitute—

"(5) In this section—

"commercial letting of furnished holiday accommodation" has the meaning given by section 265,

"EEA furnished holiday lettings business" means an overseas property business so far as it consists of the commercial letting of furnished holiday accommodation in one or more EEA states,

"ordinary overseas property business" means an overseas property business except so far as it is an EEA furnished holiday lettings business,

"ordinary UK property business" means a UK property business except so far as it is a UK furnished holiday lettings business, and

"UK furnished holiday lettings business" means a UK property business so far as it consists of the commercial letting of furnished holiday accommodation."

CTA 2010

8 (1) CTA 2010 is amended as follows.

(2) In section 65 (UK furnished holiday lettings business treated as trade)—

(a) in subsection (3), after "Part" insert "(but as modified below)",

(b) in subsection (4), omit "Accordingly", and
(c) after that subsection insert—

"(4A) Chapter 2 applies as if sections 37 to 44 and 48 to 54 were omitted."

(3) After section 67 (overseas property business to be commercial or carried on for statutory functions) insert—

"67A EEA furnished holiday lettings business treated as trade

(1) This section applies if a company carries on an EEA furnished holiday lettings business.

(2) "EEA furnished holiday lettings business" means an overseas property business so far as it consists of the commercial letting of furnished holiday accommodation (within the meaning of Chapter 6 of Part 4 of CTA 2009) in one or more EEA states.

(3) For the purposes of this Part (but as modified below) the company is treated as carrying on a single trade—

(a) which consists of every commercial letting of furnished holiday accommodation comprised in the company's EEA furnished holiday lettings business, and
(b) in relation to which the profits of which are chargeable to corporation tax under Chapter 2 of Part 3 of CTA 2009.

(4) Sections 66 and 67 apply in relation to the company's overseas property business as if the lettings mentioned in subsection (3)(a) were not included in it.

(5) Chapter 2 applies as if sections 37 to 44 and 48 to 54 were omitted.

(6) If there is a letting of accommodation only part of which is furnished holiday accommodation, just and reasonable apportionments are to be made for the purpose of determining what is comprised in the trade treated as carried on."

Commencement

9 Subject to paragraphs 10 and 11, this Part has effect in relation to accounting periods beginning on or after 1 April 2011.

10 Paragraph 7(3) and (4)(a) have effect in relation to accounting periods beginning on or after 1 April 2012 (but do not have effect in relation to relevant periods which begin before, and end on or after, 1 April 2012).

11 Paragraph 7(5) has effect where the accounting period mentioned in section 268A(1)(a) of CTA 2009 begins on or after 1 April 2010.

PART 3

CAPITAL ALLOWANCES

CAA 2001

12 (1) CAA 2001 is amended as follows.

(2) After section 13A (use for other purposes of plant or machinery previously used for long funding lease) insert—

"13B Use for other purposes of plant or machinery: property businesses

(1) This section applies if a person who has been using plant or machinery for the purposes of a relevant qualifying activity—

(a) ceases to use the plant or machinery for that purpose without ceasing to use it for the purposes of another relevant qualifying activity ("the other activity") carried on by the person, and
(b) on the date of the cessation, owns the plant or machinery as a result of having incurred capital expenditure on its provision for the purposes of the other activity.

(2) The person is to be treated—

(a) as having incurred capital expenditure ("notional expenditure") on the provision of the plant or machinery for the purposes of the other activity on the day after the cessation,
(b) as owning the plant or machinery as a result of having incurred that expenditure, and
(c) as if the plant or machinery on or after that day were different plant or machinery from the plant or machinery before that day.

(3) Subject to subsection (4), the amount of the notional expenditure is the market value of the plant or machinery on the date of cessation.

(4) If the market value is greater than the actual expenditure, the amount of the notional expenditure is the amount of the actual expenditure.

(5) "Relevant qualifying activity" means—

(a) ordinary UK property business or UK furnished holiday lettings business, or
(b) ordinary overseas property business or EEA furnished holiday lettings business,

(as the case may be)."

(3) In section 15 (qualifying activities)—

(a) in subsection (1)(b), after "ordinary" insert "UK",
(b) in subsection (1)(c), for "furnished" substitute "UK furnished",
(c) in subsection (1)(d), for "overseas" substitute "ordinary overseas",
(d) after subsection (1)(d) insert—
"(da) an EEA furnished holiday lettings business,",
(e) in subsection (3)(a), after "ordinary" insert "UK", and
(f) in subsection (3)(b), for "overseas" substitute "ordinary overseas".

(4) In section 16 (ordinary property business)—

(a) in the heading, after "**ordinary**" insert "**UK**",
(b) after ""ordinary" insert ""UK", and
(c) for "furnished" substitute "UK furnished".

(5) In section 17 (furnished holiday lettings businesses)—

(a) in the heading, for "**Furnished**" substitute "**UK furnished**",
(b) in subsection (1), for ""furnished" substitute ""UK furnished", and
(c) in subsection (2), after "All" insert "such".

(6) After section 17 insert—

"17A Ordinary overseas property business

In this Part "ordinary overseas property business" means an overseas property business except in so far as it is an EEA furnished holiday lettings business.

17B EEA furnished holiday lettings businesses

(1) In this Part "EEA furnished holiday lettings business" means an overseas property business which consists in, or so far as it consists in, the commercial letting of furnished holiday accommodation in one or more EEA states.

(2) All such commercial lettings of furnished holiday accommodation made by a particular person or partnership or body of persons are to be treated as one qualifying activity.

(3) Subsections (3) and (4) of section 17 are to apply for the purposes of this section as they apply for the purposes of that section."

(7) In section 28(1) and (2) (thermal insulation of buildings)

(a) after "ordinary" insert "UK", and
(b) for "overseas" substitute "ordinary overseas".

(8) In section 33(8) (personal security)—

(a) in paragraph (b), after "ordinary" insert "UK",
(b) in paragraph (c), for "furnished" substitute "UK furnished",
(c) in paragraph (d), for "overseas" substitute "ordinary overseas", and
(d) omit the "or" at the end of paragraph (d), and after that paragraph insert—
"(da) an EEA furnished holiday lettings business, or".

(9) In section 35(1) (expenditure on plant or machinery for use in dwelling-house not qualifying expenditure in certain cases)—

(a) in paragraph (a), after "ordinary" insert "UK", and
(b) in paragraph (b), for "overseas" substitute "ordinary overseas".

(10) In section 63(3) (cases in which disposal value is nil)—

(a) in paragraph (b), after "ordinary" insert "UK",
(b) in paragraph (c), for "furnished" substitute "UK furnished",
(c) in paragraph (d), for "overseas" substitute "ordinary overseas", and
(d) omit the "or" at the end of paragraph (d), and after that paragraph insert—
"(da) an EEA furnished holiday lettings business, or".

(11) In section 248 (ordinary property businesses)—

(a) in the heading, after "**Ordinary**" insert "**UK**", and
(b) after "ordinary" insert "UK".

(12) In section 249 (furnished holiday lettings businesses)—

(a) in the heading, for "**Furnished**" substitute "**UK furnished**", and
(b) in subsection (1), for "furnished" substitute "UK furnished".

(13) In section 250 (overseas property businesses)—

(a) in the heading, for "**Overseas**" substitute "**Ordinary overseas**", and
(b) for "overseas" substitute "ordinary overseas".

(14) After section 250 insert—

"250A EEA furnished holiday lettings businesses

(1) If the qualifying activity of a person who is entitled or liable to an allowance or charge for a chargeable period is an EEA furnished holiday lettings business, the allowance or charge is to be given effect in calculating the profits of that business by treating—

(a) the allowance as an expense of that business, and
(b) the charge as a receipt of that business.

(2) Section 67A of CTA 2010 (letting of EEA furnished holiday accommodation treated as trade for purposes of loss relief rules, etc) applies to profits calculated in accordance with subsection (1)."

(15) In section 536(5)(a) (contributions not made by public bodies and not eligible for tax relief)—

(a) in sub-paragraph (i), after "ordinary" insert "UK",
(b) in sub-paragraph (ii), for "furnished" substitute "UK furnished",
(c) in sub-paragraph (iii), for "overseas" substitute "ordinary overseas", and
(d) after sub-paragraph (iii) insert—

"(iiia) an EEA furnished holiday lettings business;".

(16) In Schedule A1 (first-year tax credits)—

(a) in paragraph 5(1), for "a UK property business other than a furnished holiday lettings business" substitute "an ordinary UK property business or an ordinary overseas property business",
(b) in paragraph 11(1), for "or a furnished holiday lettings business" substitute ", a UK furnished holiday lettings business or an EEA furnished holiday lettings business",
(c) in paragraph 12(1), for "a UK property business other than a furnished holiday lettings business" substitute "an ordinary UK property business or an ordinary overseas property business",
(d) in paragraph 20—

(i) in sub-paragraph (a), for "or a furnished holiday lettings business" substitute ", a UK furnished holiday lettings business or an EEA furnished holiday lettings business", and
(ii) in sub-paragraph (c), for "a UK property business (other than a furnished holiday lettings business)" substitute "an ordinary UK property business or an ordinary overseas property business", and

(e) in paragraph 21(1)—

(i) for "a UK" substitute "an ordinary UK", and
(ii) for "overseas" substitute "ordinary overseas".

(17) In Part 2 of Schedule 1—

(a) omit the entries for "furnished holiday lettings business" and "ordinary property business", and
(b) at the appropriate place insert—

"EEA furnished holiday lettings business	section 17B"
"ordinary UK property business	section 16"
"ordinary overseas property business	section 17A"
"UK furnished holiday lettings business	section 17"

Commencement

13 This Part has effect—

(a) for corporation tax purposes, in relation to chargeable periods beginning on or after 1 April 2011, and
(b) for income tax purposes, in relation to chargeable periods beginning on or after 6 April 2011.

PART 4

CHARGEABLE GAINS

TCGA 1992

14 (1) TCGA 1992 is amended as follows.

(2) In section 241 (furnished holiday lettings)—

(a) in the heading, for "**Furnished**" substitute "**UK furnished**",
(b) in subsection (3A), omit "Schedule 6 (retirement relief etc)", and
(c) in subsection (4), after "furnished holiday accommodation" insert "in the United Kingdom".

(3) After that section insert—

"241A EEA furnished holiday lettings

(1) The following provisions of this section shall have effect with respect to the treatment for the purposes of tax on chargeable gains of the commercial letting of furnished holiday accommodation in EEA states other than the United Kingdom.

(2) For the purposes of this section as it applies to capital gains tax, the "commercial letting of furnished holiday accommodation" has the same meaning as it has for the purposes of Chapter 6 of Part 3 of ITTOIA 2005.

(3) For the purposes of this section as it applies to corporation tax in respect of chargeable gains, the "commercial letting of furnished holiday accommodation" has the same meaning as it has for the purposes of Chapter 6 of Part 4 of CTA 2009.

(4) Subject to subsections (6) to (10) below, for the purposes of the provisions mentioned in subsection (5) below—

(a) any overseas property business which consists of, or so far as it consists of, the commercial letting of furnished holiday accommodation in one or more EEA states shall be treated as a trade, and
(b) all such lettings made by a particular person or partnership or body of persons shall be treated as one trade.

(5) The provisions referred to in subsection (4) above are—

sections 152 to 157 (roll-over relief on replacement of business assets),
section 165 (gifts relief),
section 169S(1) (entrepreneurs' relief),
section 253 (relief for loans to traders), and
Schedule 7AC (exemptions for disposals by companies with substantial shareholdings).

(6) Subject to subsection (7) below, for the purposes of the provisions mentioned in subsection (5) above as they apply by virtue of this section, where in any chargeable period a person makes a commercial letting of furnished holiday accommodation in an EEA state other than the United Kingdom—

(a) the accommodation shall be taken to be used in that period only for the purposes of the trade of making such lettings, and
(b) that trade shall be taken to be carried on throughout that period.

(7) Subsection (6) does not apply to any part of a chargeable period during which the accommodation is neither let commercially nor available to be so let unless it is prevented from being so let or available by any works of construction or repair.

(8) Where—

(a) a gain to which section 222 applies accrues to any individual on the disposal of an asset, and
(b) by virtue of subsection (4) above the amount or value of the consideration for the acquisition of the asset is treated as reduced under section 152 or 153,

the gain to which section 222 applies shall be reduced by the amount of the reduction mentioned in paragraph (b) above.

(9) Where there is a letting of accommodation only part of which is holiday accommodation such apportionments shall be made for the purposes of this section as are just and reasonable.

(10) Where a person has been charged to tax in respect of chargeable gains otherwise than in accordance with the provisions of this section, such assessment, reduction or discharge of an assessment, or, where a claim for repayment is made, such repayment, shall be made as may be necessary to give effect to those provisions.

(11) In this section "overseas property business" means—

(a) an overseas property business within the meaning of the Income Tax Acts (see section 989 of ITA 2007), or
(b) a overseas property business within the meaning of the Corporation Tax Acts (see section 1119 of CTA 2010)."

Commencement etc

15 Subject to paragraph 16, this Part has effect—

(a) for corporation tax purposes, in relation to disposals made in accounting periods beginning on or after 1 April 2011, and

(b) for capital gains tax purposes, in relation to disposals made on or after 6 April 2011.

16 Section 241A of TCGA 1992, so far as it applies for the purposes of section 253 of that Act, has effect—

(a) for corporation tax purposes, in relation claims made on or after 1 April 2011, and

(b) for capital gains tax purposes, in relation to claims made on or after 6 April 2011.

17 (1) In relation to disposals within paragraph 15 and claims within paragraph 16, section 241A of TCGA 1992 is to be treated as having had effect on and after 1 January 1994 in determining, for the purposes of any of the provisions referred to in section 241A(5) of that Act, whether a trade was carried on in any period beginning on or after that date.

(2) Sub-paragraph (3) has effect, for the purposes of sub-paragraph (1), in relation to any expression in section 241A of TCGA 1992 which is defined by reference to any provision of ITTOIA 2005, ITA 2007, CTA 2009 or CTA 2010.

(3) As respects any time before the coming into force of that provision, that expression is to have the meaning that it had under the enactments in force at that time.

GENERAL NOTE

Income from furnished holiday lettings enjoys a tax-privileged status as compared to other property income. Although, income from furnished holiday lettings is income from property, where certain conditions are met, commercial letting of furnished holiday accommodation qualifies for certain specified tax treatments that apply to trades. This includes more generous loss relief than that available under the income from property rules, the availability of capital allowance and entitlement to certain capital gains tax reliefs (including business asset rollover relief, entrepreneur's relief, relief for gifts of business assets, relief for loans to traders and exemptions for disposals of shares by companies with a substantial shareholding). Income from furnished holiday lettings also counts as relevant UK earnings when calculating the maximum relief due in respect of an individual's pension contributions.

The furnished holiday letting rules originally applied only to lettings carried out in the UK. Following concerns that this limitation did not comply with EU law, the government announced in 2009 that the furnished holiday letting rules would be applied to all properties in the EEA as an interim measure but that the rules would then be abolished from 2010/11.

However, it was announced in the June 2010 Budget that the furnished holiday letting rules would not be abolished from 2010/11 as originally planned because of the adverse effect that it would have UK businesses and UK tourism. Instead, the rules continued to apply to the 2010/11 tax year while a consultation exercise was undertaken. In summer 2010, the Government published a consultation paper setting out proposed changes to the furnished holiday lettings rules. Following consultation, changes were made to the proposals and legislation is introduced which:

- extends the special rules to the commercial letting of furnished holiday accommodation outside the UK but within the EEA;
- removes the income tax relief for losses against general income and for terminal losses and the corporation tax relief for losses against total profits; and
- increase by 50 per cent the periods of time for which a property must be available to let and actually let if it is to qualify for holiday accommodation.

The first two changes are introduced from 2011/12 for income tax and for accounting periods beginning on or after 1 April 2011 for corporation. The changes to the letting and availability conditions apply for income tax purposes from 2012/13 and for accounting periods beginning on or after 1 April 2012 for corporation tax purposes.

A period of grace is granted for satisfying the new rules on availability for letting and actual letting, thereby effectively allowing furnished holiday letting businesses time to comply with the tighter conditions applying from 2012/13 for income tax and from 1 April 2012 for corporation tax.

Income tax

Changes are made to FA 2004 s 189 to provide that income from an EEA furnished holiday letting business (as defined in new FA 2004 s 189(6A), as inserted by para 1(3)) is relevant UK earnings for pension tax relief purposes (para 1).

Various changes are made to the furnished holiday lettings provisions contained within ITTOIA 2005 Pt 3 Ch 6.

The introductory provisions (in ITTOIA 2005 s 322) are amended to extend their application to the commercial letting of furnished holiday accommodation in one or more EEA states (new ITTOIA 2005 s 322(2A), (4) as inserted by para 2(2)).

Changes are made to the period for which accommodation must be available for letting and actually to let in order to qualify for the furnished holiday lettings treatment. From 2012/13, the property must be available for letting (the availability condition) for at least 210 days in the tax year (rather than 140 as at present) and actually let (the letting condition) for at least 105 days (rather than for 70 as at present) (ITTOIA 2005 s 325(2), (3), as amended by para 2(3)).

Where in a tax year, a person lets both accommodation that meets the conditions for qualifying holiday accommodation and accommodation that would be qualifying holiday accommodation were the letting condition met, an election can be made to average the numbers of days for which the properties were actually let. As long as the average let meets the letting condition, the under-let properties are treated as qualifying holiday accommodation. From 2012/13, minimum average let is increased from 70 to 105 days (ITTOIA 2005 s 326(3), as amended by para 2(4)(a)). New ITTOIA s 326(7) (as inserted by para 2(4)(b)) which applies from 2011/12, makes it clear that that averaging must be applied separately in relation to UK properties and to EEA properties.

A period of grace is granted by new ITTOIA s 326A (as inserted by para 2(4)(5)), which allows a property owner to elect that once a property has qualified as furnished holiday accommodation, it can be treated as continuing to qualify for up to two later years despite the fact that the letting condition is not met in the later year or years. The election can be made where a property is let as qualifying holiday accommodation in 2010/11 or a subsequent tax year and is let during the next tax year or next two tax years during which the letting condition is not met. However, there must be a genuine intention to meet the letting condition. The election can only be made if an averaging election is has not been made for the same year and must be made for the first year in which the letting condition is not met. The election must be made on or before the first anniversary of the normal self-assessment filing date. The election provides for a period of adjustment in which to comply with the new more stringent letting condition of 105 let days applying from 2012/13.

Where a person's UK property business comprises the commercial letting of furnished holiday accommodation and of other businesses and transactions, separate profit calculations are required for each part for capital allowances and loss relief purposes (ITTOIA 2005 s 327) and also for determining relevant UK earnings for pension purposes (ITTOIA 2005 s 328). These provisions are amended to restrict their application to the UK property business (para 2(6), (7) respectively) and new sections, ITTOIA 2005 s 328A and 328B are introduced (by para 2(8)), replicating the provisions for overseas property businesses and requiring, where the overseas property business comprises the commercial letting of furnished holiday accommodation in one or more EEA states and other business or transactions, separate profit calculations for the EEA furnished holiday lettings and the other parts for capital allowance and loss relief purposes (new ITTOIA 2005 s 328A) and for determining relevant UK earnings for pension purposes (new ITTOIA 2005 s 328B).

Various changes are made to ITA 2007 to reflect the new rules on relief of losses for losses and to make provision for an overseas property business which consists of or includes the commercial letting of furnished holiday accommodation in one or more EEA states to be treated as a trade for the purposes ITA 2007 Pt 4 (loss relief).

One of the main changes to the furnished holiday lettings rules is the restriction in loss relief. From 2011/12 losses from a UK furnished holiday business can only be set against profits from the same UK furnished holiday letting business. It is no longer possible to apply the trading loss provisions to set the loss against general income, use any used parts of that loss as an allowable loss for capital gains tax purposes or to claim terminal loss relief. The restriction in loss relief from 2011/12 is given statutory effect in relation to UK furnished holiday lettings businesses by restricting the application of the trade loss provisions in ITA 2007 Pt 4 Ch 2 such that ss 64 to 82 and 89 to 95 are disapplied (ITA 2007 s 127 as amended by para 3(3)). The provisions (as amended) are replicated for the purposes of EEA furnished holiday lettings business in new ITA 2007 s 127ZA (as inserted by para 3(4)).

As a general rule, income arising from property held jointly by married couple's or civil partners living together is treated as arising in equal shares. However, this rule does not apply to income from furnished holiday lettings in the UK (ITA 2007 s 836(3)

Exception D). A new exception (Exception DA) is introduced in relation to the commercial letting of furnished holiday accommodation in one or more EEA states (ITA 2007 s 836(3) Exception DA, as inserted by para 3(5)).

Corporation tax

The rules governing the corporation tax treatments commercial letting of furnished holiday accommodation are contained in CTA 2009 Pt 4 Ch 6. Existing CTA 2009 s 264 (overview) makes it clear that it matters for the purposes of relief for property business losses, certain provisions of TCGA 1992 and for capital allowances purposes whether a UK property business consists of or includes the commercial letting of furnished holiday accommodation (CTA 2009 s 264(2)). This is replicated for an overseas property business to make it clear for these purposes that it matters whether the overseas property business consists of or includes the commercial letting of furnished holiday accommodation in one or more EEA states (new CTA 2009 s 264(2A), as inserted by para 7(2)(a)). Existing CTA 2009 s 264(3) provides that in certain circumstances for the profits of the furnished holiday lettings part of a UK property business to be calculated separately from other parts of the property business. This is replicated for the EEA furnished lettings part of an overseas property business by new CTA 2009 s 264(4) (as inserted by para 7(2)(c)).

Statutory effect is given to the change in the meaning of qualifying holiday accommodation (taking effect for corporation tax purposes from 1 April 2012) by amending the availability condition in CTA 2009 s 267(2) such that from that date the property must be available for letting for at least 210 days (previously at least 140 days) and by amending the letting condition in CTA 2007 s 267(3) such that from that date the property must actually be let for at least 105 days (previously at least 70 days) (para 7(3)).

Where in an accounting period a company lets qualifying holiday accommodation and accommodation that would be qualifying holiday accommodation but for the fact that the letting condition is not met, it is possible to elect within two years from the end of the accounting period for the actual lettings of all properties to be averaged. Where an election is made, for the properties to qualify as furnished holiday lettings, the average let is increased from 70 to 105 days for accounting periods beginning on or after 1 April 2012 (CTA 2009 s 268(3) as amended by para 7(4)(a)). Averaging elections must be made separately in relation to accommodation in the UK and accommodation in other EEA states (new CTA 2009 s 268(7), as inserted by para 7(4)(b)).

As for income tax purposes (see above) a period of grace is introduced to enable under-used holiday accommodation to continue to qualify as holiday accommodation for up to two years. Where a property has qualified as holiday accommodation in an accounting periods beginning on or after 1 April 2011, the company can elect for the property to continue to qualify as holiday accommodation in the following or next two years if in that year or years the letting condition is not met (new CTA 2009 s 268A as inserted by para 7(5)). The election can only be made if an averaging election (under CTA 2009 s 268) has not been made in respect of the same year and must be made for the first accounting period in which the letting condition is not met. The election allows for a period of adjustment in which to meet the new more stringent letting condition apply for accounting periods beginning on or after 1 April 2012.

Where a UK property business comprises both the commercial letting of furnished holiday accommodation and other businesses or transactions, existing provisions (in CA 2009 s 269) require separate calculations of the profits of each part for capital allowances and loss relief purposes. The requirements are mirrored for overseas property businesses which comprise the commercial letting of furnished holiday accommodation in one or more EEA states and other businesses or transactions in new CA 2009 s 269A (as inserted by para 7(7)). The heading to existing s 269 is amended to make it clear that it applies to UK property businesses (para. 7(6)).

Consequential changes are made to CTA 2009 s 748, amending the definition of 'property business' and introducing new defined terms to reflect the extension of the furnished holiday lettings regime to lets in other EEA states (para 7(8)).

A UK furnished holiday business is treated as a trade for the purposes of corporation tax loss relief by virtue of CTA 2010 s 65. For accounting periods beginning on or after 1 April 2011 it is no longer possible to set losses against total profits. From that date relief for losses is restricted to set-off against profits of the same UK furnished holiday lettings business (CTA 2010 s 65 as amended by para 8(2)).

The corporation tax loss relief provisions are mirrored for a EEA furnished holiday lettings business, which is treated as a trade by virtue of new CTA 2010 s 67A (as inserted by para 8(3)).

The changes to the letting and availability conditions apply in relation to accounting periods beginning on or after 1 April 2012. Other changes apply in relation to accounting periods beginning on or after 1 April 2011 (para 9, 10).

Capital allowances

The list of qualifying activities for the purposes of plant and machinery capital allowances is amended to reflect the extension of the furnished holiday letting regime to EEA furnished holiday lets and to distinguish between UK and overseas property business and between a UK furnished holiday lettings business and an EEA furnished holiday lettings business (CAA 2001 s 15, as amended by para 12(3)).

A new rule is introduced to deal with the situation where a person carrying on any of the qualifying property businesses, namely a UK property business, a UK furnished holiday lettings business, an overseas property business or an EEA furnished holiday lettings business, uses plant and machinery in rotation between the different types of business (new CAA 2001 s 13B, as inserted by para 12(2)). Under the new rule, where use of plant and machinery is rotated between the different types of property business whilst ownership is retained, the owner is treated as if the plant and machinery was first acquired on the date that it started to be re-used for the first property business after ceasing to be used in the second property business. The amount of qualifying expenditure is the lower of the amount of the original expenditure and the market value on the date it ceased to be used in the second property business.

Consequential amendments are made to CAA 2001 s 16, 17, 28, 33 35, 63, 248, 249, 250, 536, Sch A1, 1; definitions of 'ordinary overseas property business (new CAA 2001 s 17A) and 'EEA furnished holiday lettings business' (new CAA 2001 s 17B) are inserted and provisions are introduced (new CAA 2001 s 250A) setting out the rules for giving effect the allowances and charges where the qualifying activity is an EEA furnished holiday lettings business (para 12(4) – 17).

The amendments made to CAA 2001 apply for income tax purposes in relation to chargeable periods beginning on or after 6 April 2011 and for corporation tax periods for chargeable periods beginning on or after 1 April 2011 (para 13).

Chargeable gains

The rules governing the treatment for the purposes of tax on chargeable gains on the commercial letting of furnished holiday letting accommodation are set out in TCGA 1992 s 241. This provision is amended so as to restrict its application to a UK furnished holiday lettings business and an obsolete reference to retirement relief is removed (para 14(2)). Equivalent rules are introduced for EEA furnished holiday lettings in new TCGA 1992 s 241A, as inserted by para 14(3)). In so far as it applies for the purposes of TCGA 1992 s 253 (relief for loans to traders) new s 241A applies for corporation tax purposes in relation to claims made on or after 1 April 2011 and for capital gains tax purposes in relation to claims made on or after 6 April 2011. To ensure that maximum capital gains tax relief is available, new TCGA 1992 s 241A is treated as having had effect on or after 1 January 1994 for the purposes of determining whether, for the provisions specified in new TCGA 1992 s 241A(5), a trade was carried on in any period beginning on or after that date. Other amendments to TCGA 1992 have effect for corporation tax purposes in relation to disposals made on or after 6 April 2011 and for capital gains tax purposes in relation to disposals made on or after 6 April 2011 (para 15–17).

SCHEDULE 15

CHARGEABLE GAINS: OIL ACTIVITIES

Section 64

PART 1

LICENCE SWAPS

1 In section 195A of TCGA 1992 (oil licence swaps), in subsection (1), for "195E" substitute "195F".

2 After section 195E of that Act (company that gives mixed consideration) insert—

"195F Reimbursed expenditure

(1) This section applies if—

(a) expenditure is incurred by company A or company B (see section 195A) on a licence disposed of by it under a licence-consideration swap or mixed-consideration swap,

(b) the expenditure is incurred before the disposal,

(c) the expenditure falls within section 38(1)(b), and

(d) the expenditure is reimbursed or effectively reimbursed (whether by way of adjustment of the non-licence consideration (if any) or otherwise) by the company ("the other company") to whom the disposal is made (whether before, on or after the date of the disposal).

(2) The expenditure is to be treated for the purposes of this Act as expenditure—

(a) incurred by the other company on the licence immediately after the disposal, and

(b) which falls within section 38(1)(b)."

3 (1) Section 196 of that Act (interpretation of sections 194 to 195E) is amended as follows.

(2) In the heading, for "**195E**" substitute "**195F**".

(3) In subsection (1B), for "195E" substitute "195F".

(4) In subsection (5)—

(a) for "195E" substitute "195F", and

(b) in the definition of "non-licence consideration", omit "as determined at the time the swap arrangements are entered into".

(5) For subsection (5B) substitute—

"(5B) Subsections (5C) to (5F) apply for the purposes of sections 195A to 195F.

(5C) Any determination—

(a) of the consideration given for disposal A or disposal B,

(b) of the non-licence consideration, or

(c) of the value of a licence comprised in disposal A or disposal B,

is to be made as at the time the swap arrangements are entered into.

But this is subject to subsections (5D) to (5F).

(5D) Subsections (5E) and (5F) apply if, under the swap arrangements, economic benefits and liabilities under the licences concerned are treated as passing at a time ("the effective time") which falls before or after the day on which the arrangements are entered into.

(5E) Any determination—

(a) of the consideration given for disposal A or disposal B,

(b) of the non-licence consideration, or

(c) of the value of a licence comprised in disposal A or disposal B,

is to be made as at the effective time.

(5F) But if the swap arrangements make provision for an increase in the non-licence consideration to reflect the period between the effective time and the time it is payable, the non-licence consideration is to be treated as if it were the amount found by making a corresponding increase in the amount determined under subsection (5E)."

4 The amendments made by this Part of this Schedule have effect in relation to disposals made on or after 23 March 2011.

PART 2

REINVESTMENT OF RING FENCE ASSETS

5 After section 198H of TCGA 1992 (acquisition by member of same group) insert—

"198I Exploration, appraisal and development expenditure

(1) The incurring of exploration, appraisal and development expenditure in the course of a ring fence trade is to be treated for the purposes of sections 198A to 198H as the acquisition of assets—

(a) which are the new assets mentioned in section 152,

(b) which are taken into use, and used only, for the purposes of the ring fence trade,

(c) which are oil assets, and
(d) which fall within the classes of assets listed in section 155.

(2) The reference in subsection (1) to sections 198A to 198H includes sections 152, 153, 175 and 198(1) so far as they apply for the purpose of determining whether a disposal and acquisition qualifies for roll-over relief or section 153 relief (within the meaning given in section 198F or 198G).

(3) Section 198C has effect in relation to expenditure within subsection (1) of this section as if subsection (5) of that section were omitted.

(4) References in this section to exploration, appraisal and development expenditure are to expenditure on oil and gas exploration, appraisal and development activities which is treated as such under generally accepted accounting practice.

(5) Nothing in this section affects sections 152, 153, 175 and 198(1) so far as they apply otherwise than for the purposes of sections 198A to 198H.

(6) In this section—

"oil asset" has the meaning given in section 198E(5);
"ring fence trade" has the meaning given in section 198."

6 The amendment made by this Part of this Schedule has effect in relation to disposals made on or after 24 March 2010 (whether the deemed acquisition takes place before, on or after that date).

GENERAL NOTE

Schedule 15 brings in changes to two provisions which were introduced in 2009 to provide for a) swaps of developed licence interests to only be taxed to the extent of the net cash consideration paid, and b) an exemption for capital gains on the sale of certain UK oil and gas interests to the extent the proceeds are reinvested in certain "ring fence" expenditures within a specified period (reinvestment relief).

Swap rules

Under the original FA 2009 provisions, where there was a swap of oil and gas licences, at least one of which had a development consent, only the cash differential would be brought into charge for capital gains tax purposes. However to qualify for this treatment cash could only pass in one direction.

Following oil industry lobbying, which pointed out that in almost every such deal involving producing interests there would be cash adjustments to the original agreed consideration in respect of both interests, such that these rules would never apply, the rules have been changed, by the introduction of new s 196 (5C)–(5E). The measure of cash consideration is now to be looked at either at the date a) the swap agreement is entered into, or b) if there is a different, economic effective date for the deal, which will normally be the case, that date.

A further change, achieved by the introduction of new TCGA 1992 s 195F, is that if a party to the swap reimburses expenditure incurred between the economic date and completion, that reimbursement will be treated a CGT base cost of the licence interest acquired.

If the requirements to fall within these provisions are met it is only the net cash differential that is brought into account. However new s 196(5F) provides that if the agreement requires that this cash amount is to be adjusted, by way of additional notional interest, this adjustment is also brought into account.

It is thought that these changes will enable the swap rules to operate as originally intended but, while the changes are welcome, it is thought likely that in most cases the taxpayers will try to ensure that any such transactions fall within the reinvestment relief rules, making these provisions superfluous.

Reinvestment relief rules

The classes of expenditure in which the reinvestment could be made under the original rules largely followed the allowable costs for PRT purposes, but did not include exploration or drilling costs. For disposals after March 23rd 2010 the list of qualifying reinvestment spend has been increased to cover all exploration, appraisal and development expenditure. This is achieved by introducing a new TCGA 1992 s 198I.

Subsection 1, 2, and 3 operate to deem exploration, appraisal and development expenditure to be expenditure on assets which meet the necessary tests for reinvestment relief to apply.

Subsection 4 defines exploration, appraisal and development expenditure to be any expenditure which is treated as such for GAAP. There is no such definition in UK GAAP although there is a definition of exploration and development expenditure which includes appraisal expenditure. It is understood the HMRC accept that all exploration, appraisal and development expenditure falls within this definition.

Subsection 5 provides that the deeming provisions set out in this section only apply for reinvestment relief purposes, and not for other provisions of the Taxes Acts.

SCHEDULE 16

BENEFITS UNDER PENSION SCHEMES

Section 65

PART 1

CHANGES TO BENEFITS AVAILABLE UNDER PENSION SCHEMES ETC

Unsecured and alternatively secured pension to be replaced by drawdown pension

1 (1) In Part 4 of FA 2004 (pension schemes etc), section 165 (pension rules) is amended as follows.

(2) In subsection (1)—

(a) in pension rule 4—

(i) for "If the member has not reached the age of 75, no payment of pension" substitute "No payment of pension", and

(ii) for paragraph (c) substitute—

"(c) drawdown pension,";

(b) for pension rule 5 substitute—

"Pension rule 5

The total amount of drawdown pension paid in each drawdown pension year in respect of a money purchase arrangement must not exceed 100% of the basis amount for the drawdown pension year.";

(c) omit pension rules 6 and 7.

(3) After subsection (3) insert—

"(3A) This subsection applies to an arrangement if—

(a) the member meets the flexible drawdown conditions,

(b) the member makes a valid declaration to the scheme administrator to that effect, and

(c) the declaration is accepted by the scheme administrator.

(3B) The member meets the flexible drawdown conditions if—

(a) the member satisfied the minimum income requirement on the relevant day,

(b) no relevant contributions are paid under any money purchase arrangement (other than a cash balance arrangement) relating to the member under a registered pension scheme in the tax year in which the declaration is made, and

(c) at the time of the declaration the member is not an active member of any registered pension scheme under which there is a defined benefits or cash balance arrangement relating to the member."

Meaning of "drawdown pension"

2 Part 1 of Schedule 28 to FA 2004 (pension rules) is amended as follows.

3 (1) In paragraph 4 (meaning of "unsecured pension"), for ""Unsecured pension"" substitute ""Drawdown pension"".

(2) The heading before paragraph 4 becomes "*Drawdown pension*".

4 In paragraph 6 (short-term annuity), in sub-paragraph (1)—

(a) in paragraph (a), for "member's unsecured pension fund" substitute "member's drawdown pension fund";

(b) in paragraph (d), omit "and ends before the member reaches the age of 75".

5 For paragraph 7 (meaning of "income withdrawal") substitute—

"7 Income withdrawal" means an amount (other than an annuity) which the member is entitled to be paid from the member's drawdown pension fund in respect of an arrangement."

Member's drawdown pension fund

6 (1) In Part 1 of Schedule 28 to FA 2004, paragraph 8 (member's unsecured pension fund) is amended as follows.

(2) In sub-paragraph (1), for "member's unsecured pension fund" substitute "member's drawdown pension fund".

(3) In sub-paragraph (1A)(a), for "unsecured pension" substitute "drawdown pension".

(4) Omit sub-paragraphs (2) and (3).

(5) In sub-paragraph (4), for "unsecured pension fund" (in each place) substitute "drawdown pension fund".

(6) The heading before paragraph 8 becomes "*Member's drawdown pension fund*".

Drawdown pension year and basis amount for drawdown pension year

7 (1) In Part 1 of Schedule 28 to FA 2004, paragraph 9 (unsecured pension year) is amended as follows.

(2) In sub-paragraph (1)—

(a) for ""Unsecured pension year"" substitute ""Drawdown pension year"";
(b) in paragraph (a), for "unsecured pension" substitute "drawdown pension";
(c) at the end insert—

"This is subject to paragraph 10B."

(3) For sub-paragraph (2) substitute—

"(2) The drawdown pension year in which the member dies is the last drawdown pension year and ends immediately before the member's death."

(4) The heading before paragraph 9 becomes "*Drawdown pension year and basis amount for drawdown pension year*".

8 (1) Paragraph 10 of that Schedule (basis amount) is amended as follows.

(2) For sub-paragraph (1) substitute—

"(A1) This paragraph applies in relation to drawdown pension years beginning on or before the member's 75th birthday.

(1) Subject as follows, the period of three drawdown pension years beginning with the first drawdown pension year, and each succeeding period of three drawdown pension years, is a "reference period".

(1ZA) But the reference period in which the member reaches the age of 75 ends with the drawdown pension year in which the member reaches that age."

(3) In sub-paragraph (1B)(b)—

(a) after "subject to" insert "sub-paragraph (1ZA) and";
(b) for "five unsecured pension years" (in both places) substitute "three drawdown pension years".

(4) In sub-paragraphs (2) and (4)—

(a) for "unsecured pension year" substitute "drawdown pension year";
(b) for "member's unsecured pension fund" substitute "member's drawdown pension fund".

(5) In sub-paragraph (5)—

(a) for "an unsecured pension year" substitute "a drawdown pension year";
(b) for "that unsecured pension year" substitute "that drawdown pension year".

(6) In sub-paragraph (6)—

(a) for "unsecured pension year" substitute "drawdown pension year";
(b) for "member's unsecured pension fund" substitute "member's drawdown pension fund".

(7) After sub-paragraph (6) insert—

"(6A) But sub-paragraph (5) does not apply where the operation of that sub-paragraph in relation to an additional fund designation during a drawdown pension year would reduce the basis amount for that drawdown pension year."

(8) In sub-paragraph (7), for "member's unsecured pension fund" substitute "member's drawdown pension fund".

(9) In sub-paragraph (8), for "unsecured pension" substitute "drawdown pension".

(10) In sub-paragraph (8A), for "member's unsecured pension fund" substitute "member's drawdown pension fund".

(11) In sub-paragraph (9)(b), for "unsecured pension year" substitute "drawdown pension year".

(12) After sub-paragraph (10) insert—

"(11) Nothing in this paragraph applies in respect of an arrangement to which section 165(3A) applies."

9 After paragraph 10 of that Schedule insert—

"**10A** (1) This paragraph applies in relation to drawdown pension years beginning after the member's 75th birthday.

(2) For the first drawdown pension year beginning after the member reached the age of 75, and each succeeding drawdown pension year, the basis amount is the annual amount of the relevant annuity which could have been purchased by the application of the sums and assets representing the member's drawdown pension fund on the nominated date.

(3) In a case where the member first becomes entitled to drawdown pension in respect of the arrangement after reaching the age of 75, "the nominated date", in relation to the first drawdown pension year in respect of the arrangement, is the first day of that year.

(4) In any other case, "the nominated date", in relation to the first drawdown pension year beginning after the member reached the age of 75, is—

(a) if the member and the scheme administrator so agree, the day immediately before the member's 75th birthday, or

(b) if they do not so agree, such day within the period of 60 days ending with the first day of the drawdown pension year as is nominated by the scheme administrator (or, if no day is nominated by the scheme administrator, the first day of that year).

(5) "The nominated date", in relation to each other drawdown pension year, is such day within the period of 60 days ending with the first day of the drawdown pension year as is nominated by the scheme administrator (or, if no day is nominated by the scheme administrator, is the first day of that year).

(6) On the occasion of each additional fund designation during a drawdown pension year, the basis amount of that drawdown pension year is to be recalculated in accordance with sub-paragraph (7).

(7) The basis amount for the drawdown pension year is the annual amount of the relevant annuity which could have been purchased by the application of the sums and assets representing the member's drawdown pension fund immediately after the additional fund designation.

(8) But sub-paragraph (6) does not apply where the operation of that sub-paragraph in relation to an additional fund designation during a drawdown pension year would reduce the basis amount for that drawdown pension year.

(9) "Additional fund designation" has the meaning given by paragraph 10(8).

(10) Paragraph 14 defines "relevant annuity".

(11) Nothing in this paragraph applies in respect of an arrangement to which section 165(3A) applies.

10B (1) This paragraph applies if the member has reached the age of 75.

(2) Sub-paragraph (3) applies if, at any time during a drawdown pension year in respect of an arrangement ("the current drawdown pension year"), the member notifies the scheme administrator that the member wishes the drawdown pension year following the current drawdown pension year to begin on the day on which the next drawdown pension year in respect of another arrangement relating to the member under the pension scheme (including any arrangement relating to that person as a dependant) will begin.

(3) The scheme administrator may determine—

(a) that the current drawdown pension year is to end immediately before that day, and

(b) that the period of 12 months beginning with that day, and each succeeding period of 12 months, is a drawdown pension year in respect of the arrangement.

(4) The scheme administrator may not make a determination under this paragraph more than once in relation to the same arrangement."

Flexible drawdown: minimum income requirement etc

10 In Part 1 of Schedule 28 to FA 2004, after paragraph 14 insert—

"Minimum income requirement

14A (1) The member satisfies the minimum income requirement at any time in a tax year if the amount of relevant income payable to the member for that tax year is not less than the minimum income threshold.

(2) The minimum income threshold is £20,000.

(3) "Relevant income" means any of the following kinds of income—

(a) payments of a scheme pension or dependants' scheme pension provided by a registered pension scheme;

(b) payments of a lifetime annuity or dependants' annuity made by a registered pension scheme;

(c) payments under an overseas pension scheme which, if the scheme were a registered pension scheme, would fall within paragraph (a) or (b);

(d) payments of a social security pension;

(e) payments under the financial assistance scheme which are payable until the member's death;

(f) payments made under that scheme in anticipation of, and on account of, payments falling within paragraph (e).

(4) But "relevant income" does not include—

(a) drawdown pension or dependants' drawdown pension, or

(b) any payments under an overseas pension scheme which, if the scheme were a registered pension scheme, would be drawdown pension or dependants' drawdown pension.

(5) A payment of any pension or annuity within sub-paragraph (3), or a payment under the financial assistance scheme, is not to be regarded as relevant income unless the member has, at any time before the time mentioned in sub-paragraph (1), already received a payment of that pension or annuity or (as the case may be) a payment under that scheme.

(6) For the purposes of sub-paragraph (1), the amount of any relevant income payable in a currency other than sterling is to be taken to be the equivalent amount in sterling, calculated by reference to an appropriate spot rate of exchange prevailing on the relevant day.

(7) In this paragraph—

"financial assistance scheme" means the scheme provided for by regulations under section 286 of the Pensions Act 2004;

"social security pension" means—

(a) any pension, benefit or allowance to which section 577 of ITEPA 2003 applies, and

(b) any pension, benefit or allowance which—

(i) is payable under the law of a country or territory outside the United Kingdom, and

(ii) is substantially similar in character to a pension, benefit or allowance to which that section applies.

(8) Any regulations made under paragraph 7 of Schedule 34 (application of Part 4 of this Act in relation to relevant non-UK schemes) have effect for the purposes of sub-paragraphs (3)(c) and (4)(b) of this paragraph as they have effect for the purposes of that Schedule.

14B (1) The Treasury may by order amend paragraph 14A(2) so as to substitute a different amount for the amount for the time being specified as the minimum income threshold.

(2) The Treasury may by regulations—

(a) amend paragraph 14A so as to add, vary or remove descriptions of payments which are relevant income;

(b) provide that in prescribed circumstances the whole or part of any relevant payment, or any relevant payment of a prescribed description, is not to be regarded as relevant income.

(3) In this paragraph—

"prescribed" means prescribed in regulations made by the Treasury;

"relevant payment" means a payment falling within paragraph 14A(3).

The relevant day

14C "The relevant day" means—

(a) in a case where subsection (3A) of section 165 has not previously applied to an arrangement relating to the member, the day on which the declaration referred to in paragraph (b) of that subsection is made, and

(b) in a case where subsection (3A) of that section has previously applied to such an arrangement, the day on which that subsection first so applied.

Relevant contributions

14D "Relevant contributions" means—

(a) relievable pension contributions paid by or on behalf of the member, or

(b) contributions paid in respect of the member by an employer of the member.

Valid and accepted declarations

14E (1) A declaration is "valid" if it complies with such requirements as may be prescribed by regulations made by the Commissioners for Her Majesty's Revenue and Customs.

(2) A declaration is accepted by the scheme administrator of a registered pension scheme if, as a result of the making of the declaration, the member becomes eligible to receive payments of drawdown pension in respect of an arrangement under the scheme which, but for the application of section 165(3A), would be unauthorised member payments."

Dependants' drawdown pension

11 (1) In Part 4 of FA 2004, section 167 (pension death benefit rules) is amended as follows.

(2) In subsection (1)—

(a) in pension death benefit rule 3—

(i) for "If a dependant has not reached the age of 75, no payment of pension death benefit to the dependant" substitute "No payment of pension death benefit",

(ii) for paragraph (c) substitute—

"(c) dependants' drawdown pension,", and

(iii) for "the dependant" substitute "a dependant";

(b) for pension death benefit rule 4 substitute—

"Pension death benefit rule 4

The total amount of dependants' drawdown pension paid to a dependant in each drawdown pension year in respect of a money purchase arrangement must not exceed 100% of the basis amount for the drawdown pension year.

But this limit does not apply in relation to an arrangement to which subsection (2A) applies.";

(c) omit pension death benefit rules 5 and 6.

(3) After subsection (2) insert—

"(2A) This subsection applies to an arrangement if—

(a) the dependant meets the flexible drawdown conditions,

(b) the dependant makes a valid declaration to the scheme administrator to that effect, and

(c) the declaration is accepted by the scheme administrator.

(2B) The dependant meets the flexible drawdown conditions if—

(a) the dependant satisfied the minimum income requirement on the relevant day,

(b) no relevant contributions are paid under any money purchase arrangement (other than a cash balance arrangement) relating to the dependant under a registered pension scheme in the tax year in which the declaration is made, and

(c) at the time of the declaration the dependant is not an active member of any registered pension scheme under which there is a defined benefits or cash balance arrangement relating to the dependant."

Meaning of "dependants' drawdown pension"

12 Part 2 of Schedule 28 to FA 2004 (pension death benefit rules) is amended as follows.

13 (1) In paragraph 18 (meaning of "dependants' unsecured pension"), for ""Dependants' unsecured pension"" substitute ""Dependants' drawdown pension"".

(2) The heading before paragraph 18 becomes "*Dependants' drawdown pension*".

14 In paragraph 20 (dependants' short-term annuity), in sub-paragraph (1)—

(a) in paragraph (a), for "dependant's unsecured pension fund" substitute "dependant's drawdown pension fund";

(b) in paragraph (d), omit the words "reaches the age of 75 or".

15 For paragraph 21 (meaning of "dependants' income withdrawal") substitute—

"**21** Dependants' income withdrawal" means an amount (other than an annuity) which the dependant is entitled to be paid from the dependant's drawdown pension fund in respect of an arrangement."

Dependant's drawdown pension fund

16 (1) In Part 2 of Schedule 28 to FA 2004, paragraph 22 (dependant's unsecured pension fund) is amended as follows.

(2) In sub-paragraph (1), for "dependant's unsecured pension fund" substitute "dependant's drawdown pension fund".

(3) In sub-paragraph (2)(a), for "dependant's unsecured pension" substitute "dependants' drawdown pension".

(4) In sub-paragraph (3)—

(a) for "dependant's unsecured pension fund" (in both places) substitute "dependant's drawdown pension fund";

(b) in paragraph (a), for "an unsecured pension fund" substitute "a drawdown pension fund".

(5) The heading before paragraph 22 becomes "*Dependant's drawdown pension fund*".

Drawdown pension year and basis amount for drawdown pension year

17 (1) In Part 2 of Schedule 28 to FA 2004, paragraph 23 (unsecured pension year) is amended as follows.

(2) In sub-paragraph (1)—

(a) for ""Unsecured pension year"" substitute ""Drawdown pension year"";

(b) in paragraph (a), for "dependants' unsecured pension" substitute "dependants' drawdown pension";

(c) at the end insert—

"This is subject to paragraph 24B."

(3) For sub-paragraph (2) substitute—

"(2) The drawdown pension year in which the dependant dies is the last drawdown pension year and ends immediately before the dependant's death."

(4) The heading before paragraph 23 becomes "*Drawdown pension year and basis amount for drawdown pension year*".

18 (1) Paragraph 24 of that Schedule (basis amount) is amended as follows.

(2) For sub-paragraph (1) substitute—

"(A1) This paragraph applies in relation to drawdown pension years beginning on or before the dependant's 75th birthday.

(1) Subject as follows, the period of three drawdown pension years beginning with the first drawdown pension year, and each succeeding period of three drawdown pension years, is a "reference period".

(1ZA) But the reference period in which the dependant reaches the age of 75 ends with the drawdown pension year in which the dependant reaches that age."

(3) In sub-paragraph (1B)(b)—

(a) after "subject to" insert "sub-paragraph (1ZA) and";

(b) for "five unsecured pension years" (in both places) substitute "three drawdown pension years".

(4) In sub-paragraphs (2) and (4)—

(a) for "unsecured pension year" substitute "drawdown pension year";

(b) for "dependant's unsecured pension fund" substitute "dependant's drawdown pension fund".

(5) In sub-paragraph (5)—

(a) for "an unsecured pension year" substitute "a drawdown pension year";

(b) for "that unsecured pension year" substitute "that drawdown pension year".

(6) In sub-paragraph (6)—

(a) for "unsecured pension year" substitute "drawdown pension year";

(b) for "dependant's unsecured pension fund" substitute "dependant's drawdown pension fund".

(7) After sub-paragraph (6) insert—

"(6A) But sub-paragraph (5) does not apply where the operation of that sub-paragraph in relation to an additional fund designation during a drawdown pension year would reduce the basis amount for that drawdown pension year."

(8) In sub-paragraph (7), for "dependant's unsecured pension fund" substitute "dependant's drawdown pension fund".

(9) In sub-paragraph (8)—

(a) for "sums and assets" substitute "sums or assets";

(b) for "unsecured dependants' pension" substitute "dependants' drawdown pension".

(10) In sub-paragraph (8A), for "dependant's unsecured pension fund" substitute "dependant's drawdown pension fund".

(11) In sub-paragraph (9)(b), for "unsecured pension year" substitute "drawdown pension year".

(12) After sub-paragraph (10) insert—

"(11) Nothing in this paragraph applies in respect of an arrangement to which section 167(2A) applies."

19 After paragraph 24 of that Schedule insert—

"24A (1) This paragraph applies in relation to drawdown pension years beginning after the dependant's 75th birthday.

(2) For each drawdown pension year beginning after the dependant reached the age of 75, the basis amount is the annual amount of the relevant annuity which could have been purchased by the application of the sums and assets representing the dependant's drawdown pension fund on the nominated date.

(3) "The nominated date" is such day within the period of 60 days ending with the first day of the drawdown pension year as is nominated by the scheme administrator (or, if no day is nominated by the scheme administrator, is the first day of that year).

(4) On the occasion of each additional fund designation during a drawdown pension year, the basis amount of that drawdown pension year is to be recalculated in accordance with sub-paragraph (5).

(5) The basis amount for the drawdown pension year is the annual amount of the relevant annuity which could have been purchased by the application of the sums and assets representing the dependant's drawdown pension fund immediately after the additional fund designation.

(6) But sub-paragraph (4) does not apply where the operation of that sub-paragraph in relation to an additional fund designation during a drawdown pension year would reduce the basis amount for that drawdown pension year.

(7) "Additional fund designation" has the meaning given by paragraph 24(8).

(8) Paragraph 14 defines "relevant annuity".

(9) Nothing in this paragraph applies in respect of an arrangement to which section 167(2A) applies.

24B (1) This paragraph applies if the dependant has reached the age of 75.

(2) Sub-paragraph (3) applies if, at any time during a drawdown pension year in respect of an arrangement ("the current drawdown pension year"), the dependant notifies the scheme administrator that the dependant wishes the drawdown pension year following the current drawdown pension year to begin on the day on which the next drawdown pension year in respect of another arrangement relating to the dependant under the pension scheme (including any arrangement relating to that person as a member of the scheme) will begin.

(3) The scheme administrator may determine—

(a) that the current drawdown pension year is to end immediately before that day, and

(b) that the period of 12 months beginning with that day, and each succeeding period of 12 months, is a drawdown pension year in respect of the arrangement.

(4) The scheme administrator may not make a determination under this paragraph more than once in relation to the same arrangement."

Flexible drawdown: minimum income requirement etc

20 In Part 2 of Schedule 28 to FA 2004, after paragraph 24B insert—

"Minimum income requirement

24C (1) The dependant satisfies the minimum income requirement at any time in a tax year if the amount of relevant income payable to the dependant for that tax year is not less than the minimum income threshold.

(2) The minimum income threshold is £20,000.

(3) "Relevant income" means any of the following kinds of income—

(a) payments of a scheme pension or dependants' scheme pension provided by a registered pension scheme;

(b) payments of a lifetime annuity or dependants' annuity made by a registered pension scheme;

(c) payments under an overseas pension scheme which, if the scheme were a registered pension scheme, would fall within paragraph (a) or (b);

(d) payments of a social security pension;

(e) payments under the financial assistance scheme which are payable until the dependant's death;

(f) payments made under that scheme in anticipation of, and on account of, payments falling within paragraph (e).

(4) But "relevant income" does not include—

(a) drawdown pension or dependants' drawdown pension, or

(b) any payments under an overseas pension scheme which, if the scheme were a registered pension scheme, would be drawdown pension or dependants' drawdown pension.

(5) A payment of any pension or annuity within sub-paragraph (3), or a payment under the financial assistance scheme, is not to be regarded as relevant income unless the dependant has, at any time before the time mentioned in sub-paragraph (1), already received a payment of that pension or annuity or (as the case may be) a payment under that scheme.

(6) For the purposes of sub-paragraph (1), the amount of any relevant income payable in a currency other than sterling is to be taken to be the equivalent amount in sterling, calculated by reference to an appropriate spot rate of exchange prevailing on the relevant day.

(7) In this paragraph—

"financial assistance scheme" means the scheme provided for by regulations under section 286 of the Pensions Act 2004;

"social security pension" means—

(a) any pension, benefit or allowance to which section 577 of ITEPA 2003 applies, and

(b) any pension, benefit or allowance which—

(i) is payable under the law of a country or territory outside the United Kingdom, and

(ii) is substantially similar in character to a pension, benefit or allowance to which that section applies.

(8) Any regulations made under paragraph 7 of Schedule 34 (application of Part 4 of this Act in relation to relevant non-UK schemes) have effect for the purposes of sub-paragraphs (3)(c) and (4)(b) of this paragraph as they have effect for the purposes of that Schedule.

24D (1) The Treasury may by order amend paragraph 24C(2) so as to substitute a different amount for the amount for the time being specified as the minimum income threshold.

(2) The Treasury may by regulations—

(a) amend paragraph 24C so as to add, vary or remove descriptions of payments which are relevant income;

(b) provide that in prescribed circumstances the whole or part of any relevant payment, or any relevant payment of a prescribed description, is not to be regarded as relevant income.

(3) In this paragraph—

"prescribed" means prescribed in regulations made by the Treasury;

"relevant payment" means a payment falling within paragraph 24C(3).

The relevant day

24E "The relevant day" means—

(a) in a case where subsection (2A) of section 167 has not previously applied to an arrangement relating to the dependant, the day on which the declaration referred to in paragraph (b) of that subsection is made, and

(b) in a case where subsection (2A) of that section has previously applied to such an arrangement, the day on which that subsection first so applied.

Relevant contributions

24F "Relevant contributions" means—

(a) relievable pension contributions paid by or on behalf of the dependant, or

(b) contributions paid in respect of the dependant by an employer of the dependant.

Valid and accepted declarations

24G (1) A declaration is "valid" if it complies with such requirements as may be prescribed by regulations made by the Commissioners for Her Majesty's Revenue and Customs.

(2) A declaration is accepted by the scheme administrator of a registered pension scheme if, as a result of the making of the declaration, the dependant becomes eligible to receive payments of dependants' drawdown pension in respect of an arrangement under the scheme which, but for the application of section 167(2A), would be unauthorised member payments."

Foreign pensions: temporary non-residents

21 (1) In Part 9 of ITEPA 2003 (pension income), Chapter 4 (foreign pensions: general rules) is amended as follows.

(2) In section 574 ("pension": interpretation)—

(a) for subsection (1) substitute—

"(1) For the purposes of this Chapter "pension" includes—

(a) an annuity under, or purchased with sums or assets held for the purposes of, or representing acquired rights under, a relevant non-UK scheme or an overseas pension scheme,

(b) an amount paid under a relevant non-UK scheme or an overseas pension scheme which, if the scheme were a registered pension scheme, would be income withdrawal or dependants' income withdrawal (within the meaning of paragraphs 7 and 21 of Schedule 28 to FA 2004), and

(c) if conditions A and B are met, a pension which is paid voluntarily or is capable of being discontinued.";

(b) for subsection (4) substitute—

"(4) In this section—

"office" includes in particular any position which has an existence independent of the person who holds it and may be filled by successive holders;

"overseas pension scheme" has the same meaning as in Part 4 of FA 2004 (see section 150(7) of that Act);

"relevant non-UK scheme" is to be read in accordance with paragraph 1(5) of Schedule 34 to FA 2004."

(3) In section 575(1) (taxable pension income), at the end insert "and section 576A".

(4) After section 576 insert—

"576A Temporary non-residents

(1) If this section applies in relation to a tax year, any relevant non-UK income withdrawal under a relevant non-UK scheme which—

(a) is paid to a person in respect of a flexible drawdown arrangement relating to the person under the scheme,

(b) is paid in a year of non-residence, and

(c) would not, apart from this section, be chargeable to tax under this Part,

is to be treated for the purposes of section 575 as if it arose in that tax year.

(2) This section applies in relation to a tax year if—

(a) the person satisfies the residence requirements for the tax year ("the year of return"),

(b) the person did not satisfy those requirements for one or more tax years immediately before the year of return but did satisfy those requirements for an earlier tax year,

(c) there are fewer than 5 tax years between—

(i) the last tax year before the year of return for which the person satisfied those requirements ("the year of departure"), and

(ii) the year of return, and

(d) the person satisfied those requirements for at least 4 out of the 7 tax years immediately before the year of departure.

(3) For the purposes of this section—

(a) a person satisfies the residence requirements for a tax year if the person—

(i) is resident in the United Kingdom during that year, and
(ii) is not Treaty non-resident at any time in that year;

(b) a person is Treaty non-resident at any time if, at that time, the person falls to be regarded as resident in a territory outside the United Kingdom for the purposes of double taxation relief arrangements having effect at that time.

(4) If—

(a) section 809B, 809D or 809E of ITA 2007 (remittance basis) applies to the person for the year of return, and
(b) the person—
(i) is not domiciled in the United Kingdom in that year, or
(ii) is not ordinarily resident in the United Kingdom in that year,

any amounts of relevant non-UK income withdrawal falling within subsection (1) which were remitted in a year of non-residence are treated as remitted in the year of return.

(5) This section does not apply to any relevant non-UK income withdrawal paid to or in respect of a relieved member of a relevant non-UK scheme unless the payment is referable to the member's UK tax-relieved fund under the scheme.

(6) This section does not apply to any relevant non-UK income withdrawal paid to or in respect of a transfer member of a relevant non-UK scheme unless the payment is referable to the member's relevant transfer fund under the scheme.

(7) Nothing in any double taxation relief arrangements is to be read as preventing the person from being chargeable to income tax in respect of any relevant non-UK income withdrawal treated by virtue of this section as arising in the year of return (or as preventing a charge to that tax from arising as a result).

(8) In this section—

"double taxation relief arrangements" means arrangements that have effect under section 2(1) of TIOPA 2010;

"flexible drawdown arrangement" means an arrangement to which section 165(3A) or 167(2A) of FA 2004 applies;

"member's relevant transfer fund" has the same meaning as in Schedule 34 to FA 2004 (see paragraph 4(2) of that Schedule);

"member's UK tax-relieved fund" has the same meaning as in that Schedule (see paragraph 3(2));

"relevant non-UK income withdrawal", in relation to a relevant non-UK scheme, means an amount paid under the scheme which, if the scheme were a registered pension scheme, would be income withdrawal or dependants' income withdrawal (within the meaning of paragraphs 7 and 21 of Schedule 28 to FA 2004);

"relevant non-UK scheme" is to be read in accordance with paragraph 1(5) of Schedule 34 to FA 2004;

"relieved member" and "transfer member" have the same meaning as in that Schedule (see paragraph 1(7) and (8));

"year of non-residence" means any tax year which falls between the year of departure and the year of return."

Pensions under registered pension schemes: temporary non-residents

22 (1) In Part 9 of ITEPA 2003 (pension income), Chapter 5A (pensions under registered pension schemes) is amended as follows.

(2) In section 579B (taxable pension income), at the end insert—

"This is subject to section 579CA."

(3) After section 579C insert—

"579CA Temporary non-residents

(1) If this section applies in relation to a tax year, any income withdrawal or dependants' income withdrawal under the registered pension scheme which—

(a) is paid to a person in respect of a flexible drawdown arrangement relating to the person under the scheme,
(b) is paid in a year of non-residence, and
(c) would not, apart from this section, be chargeable to tax under this Part,

is to be treated for the purposes of section 579B as if it accrued in that tax year.

(2) This section applies in relation to a tax year if—

(a) the person satisfies the residence requirements for the tax year ("the year of return"),

(b) the person did not satisfy those requirements for one or more tax years immediately before the year of return but did satisfy those requirements for an earlier tax year,

(c) there are fewer than 5 tax years between—

(i) the last tax year before the year of return for which the person satisfied those requirements ("the year of departure"), and

(ii) the year of return, and

(d) the person satisfied those requirements for at least 4 out of the 7 tax years immediately before the year of departure.

(3) For the purposes of this section—

(a) a person satisfies the residence requirements for a tax year if the person—

(i) is resident in the United Kingdom during that year, and

(ii) is not Treaty non-resident at any time in that year;

(b) a person is Treaty non-resident at any time if, at that time, the person falls to be regarded as resident in a territory outside the United Kingdom for the purposes of double taxation relief arrangements having effect at that time.

(4) Nothing in any double taxation relief arrangements is to be read as preventing the person from being chargeable to income tax in respect of any income withdrawal or dependants' income withdrawal treated by virtue of this section as accruing in the year of return (or as preventing a charge to that tax from arising as a result).

(5) In this section—

"double taxation relief arrangements" means arrangements that have effect under section 2(1) of TIOPA 2010;

"flexible drawdown arrangement" means an arrangement to which section 165(3A) or 167(2A) of FA 2004 applies;

"year of non-residence" means any tax year which falls between the year of departure and the year of return."

(4) For section 579D (interpretation) substitute—

"579D Interpretation

In this Chapter—

"dependants' income withdrawal" has the meaning given by paragraph 21 of Schedule 28 to FA 2004;

"income withdrawal" has the meaning given by paragraph 7 of that Schedule;

"pension under a registered pension scheme" includes—

(a) an annuity under, or purchased with sums or assets held for the purposes of, or representing acquired rights under, a registered pension scheme, and

(b) income withdrawal or dependants' income withdrawal under a registered pension scheme."

Lump sums to be payable to persons aged 75 or over

23 Part 1 of Schedule 29 to FA 2004 (lump sum rule) is amended as follows.

24 (1) Paragraph 1 (pension commencement lump sum) is amended as follows.

(2) In sub-paragraph (1)—

(a) omit paragraph (a);

(b) in paragraph (b), after "available" insert "(but see sub-paragraph (3A))".

(3) After sub-paragraph (3) insert—

"(3A) In a case where—

(a) the member becomes entitled to a lump sum before reaching the age of 75, but

(b) it is not paid to the member until after the member has reached that age,

the reference in sub-paragraph (1)(b) to the lump sum being paid is to be read as a reference to the member becoming entitled to it."

(4) In sub-paragraph (6), for the words from "even though" to the end substitute "even though the condition in sub-paragraph (1)(c) is not met."

25 In paragraph 2 (pension commencement lump sum: calculation of permitted maximum), after sub-paragraph (7) insert—

"(7A) For the purposes of determining the available portion of the member's lump sum allowance—

(a) the fact that benefit crystallisation event 5 or benefit crystallisation event 5B has occurred in relation to the member is to be disregarded, and

(b) anything which, but for paragraph 2 or 15A of Schedule 32, would have been a benefit crystallisation event is to be treated as if it were such an event."

26 In paragraph 3 (pension commencement lump sum: calculation of applicable amount), in sub-paragraph (7), for the definition of "AC" substitute—

"AC is—

(a) in a case where the member becomes entitled to the pension before reaching the age of 75, the amount crystallised by reason of the member becoming entitled to the pension, disregarding paragraph 3 of Schedule 32, and

(b) in a case where the member becomes entitled to the pension after reaching that age, the amount that would have been so crystallised (disregarding that paragraph) but for paragraph 2 of that Schedule."

27 (1) Paragraph 3A (recycling of pension commencement lump sums) is amended as follows.

(2) In sub-paragraph (2), for "sub-paragraphs (3) and (4)" substitute "sub-paragraphs (3) to (4A)".

(3) After sub-paragraph (4) insert—

"(4A) This paragraph does not apply if—

(a) the member has reached the age of 75 when the contributions are paid as mentioned in sub-paragraph (2)(a), and

(b) the contributions are not paid by an employer of the member."

(4) For sub-paragraph (5) substitute—

"(5) The appropriate amount" is—

(a) where the member becomes entitled to the lump sum before reaching the age of 75, so much of the amount crystallised by the benefit crystallisation event constituted by its payment (or the amount that would have been so crystallised but for paragraph 15A of Schedule 32) as does not exceed the amount of the member's lifetime allowance which is available on it;

(b) where the member becomes entitled to the lump sum after reaching that age, the amount of the lump sum."

28 (1) Paragraph 4 (serious ill-health lump sum) is amended as follows.

(2) In sub-paragraph (1)—

(a) at the end of paragraph (c) insert "and";

(b) omit paragraph (e) (and the "and" before it).

(3) After sub-paragraph (2) insert—

"(3) For the purposes of sub-paragraph (2)—

(a) the fact that benefit crystallisation event 5 or benefit crystallisation event 5B has occurred in relation to the member is to be disregarded, and

(b) anything which, but for paragraph 2 of Schedule 32, would have been a benefit crystallisation event is to be treated as if it were such an event."

29 In paragraph 7 (trivial commutation lump sum), in sub-paragraph (1)(e), omit "but has not reached the age of 75".

30 In paragraph 10(1) (winding-up lump sum)—

(a) at the end of paragraph (d) insert "and";

(b) omit paragraph (f) (and the "and" before it).

31 In paragraph 12 (interpretation of Part 1), after sub-paragraph (1) insert—

"(1A) For the purposes of determining whether all or part of the member's lifetime allowance is available—

(a) the fact that benefit crystallisation event 5 or benefit crystallisation event 5B has occurred in relation to the member is to be disregarded, and

(b) anything which, but for paragraph 2 or 15A of Schedule 32, would have been a benefit crystallisation event is to be treated as if it were such an event."

Lump sum death benefits to be payable to persons aged 75 or over

32 Part 2 of Schedule 29 to FA 2004 (lump sum death benefit rule) is amended as follows.

33 (1) Paragraph 13 (defined benefits lump sum death benefit) is amended as follows.

(2) The existing text becomes sub-paragraph (1).

(3) In that sub-paragraph—

(a) omit paragraph (a);

(b) omit paragraph (c) (but not the "and" after it);

(c) at the end insert—

"But, in a case where the member had not reached the age of 75 at the date of the member's death, a lump sum death benefit is a defined benefits lump sum death benefit only if it is paid before the end of the relevant two-year period."

(4) After that sub-paragraph insert—

"(2) The relevant two-year period" means the period of two years beginning with the earlier of the day on which the scheme administrator first knew of the member's death and the day on which the scheme administrator could first reasonably be expected to have known of it."

34 (1) Paragraph 14 (pension protection lump sum death benefit) is amended as follows.

(2) In sub-paragraph (1), omit paragraph (a).

(3) In sub-paragraph (3), for the definition of "AC" substitute—

"AC is—

(a) in a case where the member became entitled to the pension before reaching the age of 75, the amount crystallised by reason of the member becoming entitled to the pension, and

(b) in a case where the member became entitled to the pension after having reached that age, the amount that would have been so crystallised but for paragraph 2 of Schedule 32,".

35 (1) Paragraph 15 (uncrystallised funds lump sum death benefit) is amended as follows.

(2) In sub-paragraph (1)—

(a) omit paragraphs (a) and (c);

(b) at the end of paragraph (d) insert

", and

(e) it is not a charity lump sum death benefit.";

(c) at the end insert—

"But, in a case where the member had not reached the age of 75 at the date of the member's death, a lump sum death benefit is an uncrystallised funds lump sum death benefit only if it is paid before the end of the relevant two-year period."

(3) After that sub-paragraph insert—

"(1A) The relevant two-year period" means the period of two years beginning with the earlier of the day on which the scheme administrator first knew of the member's death and the day on which the scheme administrator could first reasonably be expected to have known of it."

36 (1) Paragraph 16 (annuity protection lump sum death benefit) is amended as follows.

(2) In sub-paragraph (1), omit paragraph (a).

(3) In sub-paragraph (3), for the definition of "AC" substitute—

"AC is—

(a) in a case where the member became entitled to the pension or annuity before reaching the age of 75, the amount crystallised by reason of the member becoming entitled to the pension or annuity, disregarding paragraphs 3 and 4 of Schedule 32, and

(b) in a case where the member became entitled to the pension or annuity after having reached that age, the amount that would have been so crystallised (disregarding those paragraphs) but for paragraph 2 of that Schedule,".

37 (1) Paragraph 17 (unsecured pension fund lump sum death benefit) is amended as follows.

(2) For sub-paragraph (1) substitute—

"(1) For the purposes of this Part a lump sum death benefit is a drawdown pension fund lump sum death benefit if—

(a) it is paid in respect of income withdrawal to which the member was entitled under an arrangement at the date of the member's death, and

(b) it is not a charity lump sum death benefit."

(3) In sub-paragraph (2)—

(a) for "an unsecured pension fund lump sum death benefit" substitute "a drawdown pension fund lump sum death benefit";

(b) omit paragraph (b);

(c) at the end of paragraph (c) insert

", and

(d) it is not a charity lump sum death benefit."

(4) In sub-paragraph (3), for "an unsecured pension fund lump sum death benefit" substitute "a drawdown pension fund lump sum death benefit".

(5) In sub-paragraph (4), for "unsecured pension fund" substitute "drawdown pension fund".

(6) The heading before paragraph 17 becomes "*Drawdown pension fund lump sum death benefit*".

38 (1) Paragraph 18 (charity lump sum death benefit) is amended as follows.

(2) In sub-paragraph (1)—

(a) omit paragraph (a);

(b) in paragraph (c), for the words from "in respect of" to "Schedule 28)" substitute "in respect of the member's drawdown pension fund";

(c) in paragraph (d), omit from "(or, if the member" to the end.

(3) After sub-paragraph (1) insert—

"(1A) A lump sum death benefit is also a charity lump sum death benefit if—

(a) the member had reached the age of 75 at the date of the member's death,

(b) there are no dependants of the member,

(c) it is paid in respect of relevant uncrystallised funds in respect of a money purchase arrangement at the date of the member's death, and

(d) it is paid to a charity nominated by the member.

(1B) "Relevant uncrystallised funds" has the meaning given by paragraph 15(2)."

(4) In sub-paragraph (2)—

(a) omit paragraph (b);

(b) in paragraph (d), for "the dependant's alternatively secured pension fund" substitute "the dependant's drawdown pension fund";

(c) in paragraph (e), omit from "(or, if neither the member" to the end.

(5) In sub-paragraph (4), for the words from "representing" to "pension fund" substitute "representing what is the member's or dependant's drawdown pension fund".

39 In paragraph 20(1) (trivial commutation lump sum death benefit), omit—

(a) paragraph (a), and

(b) paragraph (c) (but not the "and" after it).

Serious ill-health lump sum charge

40 In Part 4 of FA 2004 (pension schemes etc), after section 205 insert—

"205A Serious ill-health lump sum charge

(1) A charge to income tax, to be known as the serious ill-health lump sum charge, arises where a serious ill-health lump sum is paid by a registered pension scheme to a member who has reached the age of 75.

(2) The person liable to the serious ill-health lump sum charge is the scheme administrator.

(3) The scheme administrator is liable to the serious ill-health lump sum charge whether or not—

(a) the scheme administrator, and

(b) the person to whom the serious ill-health lump sum is paid,

are resident, ordinarily resident or domiciled in the United Kingdom.

(4) The rate of the charge is 55% in respect of the lump sum.

(5) The Treasury may by order increase or decrease the rate for the time being specified in subsection (4).

(6) Tax under this section is to be charged on the amount of the lump sum paid or, if the rules of the pension scheme permit the scheme administrator to deduct the tax before payment, on the amount of the lump sum before deduction of tax.

(7) A serious ill-health lump sum paid to a member who has reached the age of 75 is not to be treated as income for any purpose of the Tax Acts."

Special lump sum death benefits charge

41 (1) In Part 4 of FA 2004, section 206 (special lump sum death benefits charge) is amended as follows.

(2) In subsection (1), for paragraph (c) substitute—

"(c) a drawdown pension fund lump sum death benefit,".

(3) After that subsection insert—

"(1A) The special lump sum death benefits charge also arises where—

(a) a defined benefits lump sum death benefit, or

(b) an uncrystallised funds lump sum death benefit,

is paid by a registered pension scheme in respect of a member who had reached the age of 75 at the date of the member's death."

(4) In subsection (4), for "35%" substitute "55%".

(5) For subsection (7) substitute—

"(7) None of the following is to be treated as income for any purpose of the Tax Acts—

(a) any lump sum death benefit mentioned in subsection (1);

(b) a defined benefits lump sum death benefit or uncrystallised funds lump sum death benefit paid in respect of a member who had reached the age of 75 at the date of the member's death."

Exemption from income tax of certain lump sums and lump sum death benefits

42 (1) Section 636A of ITEPA 2003 (exemption for certain lump sums under registered pension schemes) is amended as follows.

(2) In subsection (1)—

(a) in paragraph (b), after "serious ill-health lump sum" insert "paid to a member who has not reached the age of 75";

(b) in paragraph (d), after "defined benefits lump sum death benefit" insert "paid in respect of a member who had not reached the age of 75 at the date of the member's death";

(c) in paragraph (e), after "uncrystallised funds lump sum death benefit" insert "paid in respect of such a member".

(3) After subsection (3) insert—

"(3A) A serious ill-health lump sum which is paid under a registered pension scheme to a member who has reached the age of 75 is subject to income tax in accordance with section 205A of FA 2004 (charge to tax on scheme administrator in respect of such a lump sum) but not otherwise."

(4) In subsection (4)—

(a) before paragraph (a) insert—

"(za) a defined benefits lump sum death benefit paid in respect of a member who had reached the age of 75 at the date of the member's death,";

(b) after paragraph (a) insert—

"(aa) an uncrystallised funds lump sum death benefit paid in respect of a member who had reached the age of 75 at the date of the member's death,";

(c) for paragraph (c) substitute—

"(c) a drawdown pension fund lump sum death benefit,".

(5) In subsection (7)—

(a) after ""defined benefits lump sum death benefit"," insert—

""drawdown pension fund lump sum death benefit",";

(b) after ""pension protection lump sum death benefit"," insert "and";

(c) omit ""unsecured pension fund lump sum death benefit"," (and the "and" before it).

Lifetime allowance charge: benefit crystallisation events

43 In section 216 of FA 2004 (benefit crystallisation events and amounts crystallised), in the table in subsection (1), after the entry for benefit crystallisation event 5A insert—

"5B The individual reaching the age of 75 when there is a money purchase arrangement relating to the individual under any of the relevant pension schemes	The amount of any remaining unused funds".

44 (1) Schedule 32 to FA 2004 (benefit crystallisation events: supplementary) is amended as follows.

(2) After paragraph 14 insert—

"Benefit crystallisation event 5B: meaning of "remaining unused funds"

14A For the purposes of benefit crystallisation event 5B "remaining unused funds" means—

(a) in relation to a cash balance arrangement, a sum equal to what would, on the valuation assumption in section 277(a), be available for the provision of benefits to or in respect of the member if the member became entitled to them on reaching the age of 75, and

(b) in relation to any other arrangement, such of the sums and assets held for the purposes of the arrangement as are not member-designated funds and have not been applied towards the provision of a scheme pension or a dependants' scheme pension."

(3) After paragraph 15 insert—

"Benefit crystallisation event 6: prevention of overlap with other events

15A Benefit crystallisation event 6 does not apply in relation to a pension commencement lump sum paid in respect of a money purchase arrangement if—

(a) the individual becomes entitled to it before reaching the age of 75, but

(b) it is not paid to the individual until after the individual has reached that age."

Annual allowance charge: persons meeting flexible drawdown conditions

45 (1) In section 227 of FA 2004 (annual allowance charge), at the end of subsection (4) insert—

"But see section 227A (individuals who meet flexible drawdown conditions)."

(2) After section 227 insert—

"227A Individuals who meet flexible drawdown conditions

(1) This section applies in the case of an individual in relation to whom there is or has been a flexible drawdown arrangement under a pension scheme.

In this section "flexible drawdown arrangement" means an arrangement to which section 165(3A) or 167(2A) applies.

(2) For each tax year following the first tax year in which there was a flexible drawdown arrangement in relation to the individual, section 227 applies to the individual as if the reference in subsection (4) of that section to the amount by which the total pension input amount exceeds the amount of the annual allowance were a reference to the amount in subsection (3) of this section.

(3) The amount referred to in subsection (2) is—

TPIA–RPIA

where—

TPIA is the total pension input amount for the tax year, and

RPIA is so much of the aggregate of the pension input amounts in respect of each defined benefits or cash balance arrangement relating to the individual under any registered pension scheme of which the individual is not an active member as does not exceed the annual allowance.

(4) For the tax year following the first tax year in which there was a flexible drawdown arrangement in relation to the individual, the reference in subsection (3) to a registered pension scheme of which the individual is not an active member includes, in a case where the individual was an active member of a registered pension scheme at any time during that first tax year but has not been such a member since the relevant time, a reference to that registered pension scheme.

(5) In subsection (4) the "relevant time" is the time at which there first began to be a flexible drawdown arrangement in relation to the individual."

Removal of certain charges to inheritance tax in respect of pension schemes

46 IHTA 1984 is amended as follows.

47 (1) Section 12 (dispositions allowable for income tax or conferring benefits under pension scheme) is amended as follows.

(2) After subsection (2) insert—

"(2ZA) Where a person who is a member of a registered pension scheme, a qualifying non-UK pension scheme or a section 615(3) scheme omits to exercise pension rights under the pension scheme, section 3(3) above does not apply in relation to the omission."

(3) Omit subsections (2A) to (2E).

48 Omit the following provisions—

(a) section 151A (person dying with alternatively secured pension fund);

(b) section 151B (relevant dependant with pension fund inherited from member over 75);

(c) section 151BA (rate or rates of charge under section 151B);
(d) section 151C (dependant dying with other pension fund);
(e) section 151D (unauthorised payment where person dies over 75 with pension or annuity);
(f) section 151E (rate or rates of charge under section 151D).

PART 2
CONSEQUENTIAL AMENDMENTS

Inheritance Tax Act 1984

49 IHTA 1984 is amended as follows.

50 (1) Section 12 (dispositions allowable for income tax or conferring benefits under pension scheme) is amended as follows.

(2) In subsection (2F), omit paragraph (b) (and the "and" before it).

(3) In subsection (2G)—

(a) omit the definitions of "lump sum death benefit", "pension death benefit" and "relevant dependant";
(b) in the definition of "pension", for "that Part" substitute "Part 4".

51 In section 151 (treatment of pension rights, etc), in subsection (2), for "Subject to sections 151A and 151C below, an interest" substitute "An interest".

52 In section 200 (transfer on death)—

(a) in subsection (1), omit "(subject to subsection (1A) below)";
(b) omit subsection (1A).

53 In section 210 (pension rights, etc), omit subsections (2) and (3).

54 (1) Section 216 (delivery of accounts) is amended as follows.

(2) In subsection (1), omit paragraph (bca).

(3) In subsection (3)(a), omit "(or would do apart from section 151A(3)(b) or 151C(3)(b) above)".

(4) In subsection (4), omit "(or would be apart from section 151A(3)(b), 151C(3)(b) or 151B(4) above)".

(5) In subsection (6), omit paragraph (ac).

(6) In subsection (7), for ", 126 or 151D" substitute "or 126".

55 In section 226 (payment: general rules), in subsection (4)—

(a) for ", 126, 151B or 151D" substitute "or 126";
(b) omit from ", or under section 151A" to "that section,".

56 In section 233 (interest on unpaid tax), in subsection (1)(c)—

(a) for ", 126, 151B or 151D" substitute "or 126";
(b) omit from ", or under section 151A" to "that section,".

57 In section 272 (general interpretation), omit the definition of "scheme administrator".

Pension Schemes Act 1993

58 Until such time as the repeal of section 28A of the Pension Schemes Act 1993 (requirements for interim arrangements) by paragraph 11 of Schedule 4 to the Pensions Act 2007 has effect for all purposes, subsection (3) of that section has effect with the following amendments—

(a) in paragraph (a)—

(i) for "unsecured pension year" substitute "drawdown pension year",
(ii) after "twelve months" insert "(disregarding the second sentence of pension rule 5)", and
(iii) for "where the member has not reached the age of 75," substitute "or";

(b) in paragraph (c)—

(i) for "unsecured pension year" substitute "drawdown pension year",
(ii) after "twelve months" insert "(disregarding the second sentence of pension death benefit rule 4)", and
(iii) omit "and the member's widow, widower or surviving civil partner has not reached the age of 75, or";

(c) omit paragraphs (b) and (d).

Pension Schemes (Northern Ireland) Act 1993

59 Until such time as the repeal of section 24A of the Pension Schemes (Northern Ireland) Act 1993 (requirements for interim arrangements) by paragraph 11 of Schedule 4 to the Pensions Act (Northern Ireland) 2008 has effect for all purposes, subsection (3) of that section has effect with the following amendments—

(a) in paragraph (a)—

(i) for "unsecured pension year" substitute "drawdown pension year",

(ii) after "twelve months" insert "(disregarding the second sentence of pension rule 5)", and

(iii) for "where the member has not reached the age of 75," substitute "or";

(b) in paragraph (c)—

(i) for "unsecured pension year" substitute "drawdown pension year",

(ii) after "twelve months" insert "(disregarding the second sentence of pension death benefit rule 4)", and

(iii) omit "and the member's widow, widower or surviving civil partner has not reached the age of 75, or";

(c) omit paragraphs (b) and (d).

Income Tax (Earnings and Pensions) Act 2003

60 (1) Section 683 of ITEPA 2003 (PAYE income) is amended as follows.

(2) In subsection (3), for "subsections (3A) and (4)" substitute "subsections (3A) and (3B)".

(3) After subsection (3A) insert—

"(3B) PAYE pension income" for a tax year does not include any taxable pension income which is treated as accruing in that tax year by section 579CA (temporary non-residents)."

61 In Part 2 of Schedule 1 to ITEPA 2003 (index of defined expressions), at the appropriate place insert—

"dependants' income withdrawal (in Chapter 5A of Part 9)	section 579D";
"income withdrawal (in Chapter 5A of Part 9)	section 579D".

Finance Act 2004

62 Part 4 of FA 2004 (pension schemes etc) is amended as follows.

63 In section 164 (authorised member payments), in subsection (2)(b), after "the short service refund lump sum charge" insert ", the serious ill-health lump sum charge".

64 In section 165 (pension rules), in subsection (3)(a), for "unsecured pension" substitute "drawdown pension".

65 In section 168(1) (lump sum death benefit rule), for paragraph (e) substitute—

"(e) a drawdown pension fund lump sum death benefit,".

66 In section 169 (recognised transfers), in subsection (1D)—

(a) in paragraph (a), for "person's unsecured pension fund or dependant's unsecured pension fund" substitute "member's drawdown pension fund or dependant's drawdown pension fund";

(b) omit paragraph (b) (and the "or" before it).

67 (1) Section 172B (increase in rights of connected person on death) is amended as follows.

(2) In subsection (2)(b), for "member's unsecured pension fund or dependant's unsecured pension fund" substitute "member's drawdown pension fund or dependant's drawdown pension fund".

(3) In subsection (7A)—

(a) in paragraph (a), for "dependants' unsecured pension fund or dependants' alternatively secured pension fund" substitute "dependant's drawdown pension fund";

(b) in paragraph (b), for "dependants' unsecured pension fund" substitute "dependant's drawdown pension fund".

(4) Omit subsection (8A).

68 Omit section 172BA (increase in rights on death arising from alternatively secured pension fund etc).

69 Omit section 181A (minimum level of payment of alternatively secured pensions).

70 (1) Section 182 (unauthorised borrowing: money purchase arrangements) is amended as follows.

(2) In subsection (3)—

(a) in paragraph (a), for "member's unsecured pension fund or alternatively secured pension fund" substitute "member's drawdown pension fund";

(b) in paragraph (b), for "dependants' unsecured pension funds or alternatively secured pension funds" substitute "dependants' drawdown pension funds".

(3) In subsection (5), for "unsecured pension fund or alternatively secured pension fund" substitute "drawdown pension fund".

71 In section 211 (surchargeable unauthorised member payments: valuation of crystallised rights), in subsection (1)(b), for "member's unsecured pension fund or alternatively secured pension fund" substitute "member's drawdown pension fund".

72 In section 212 (surchargeable unauthorised member payments: valuation of uncrystallised rights), in subsection (2), for "member's unsecured pension fund or alternatively secured pension fund" substitute "member's drawdown pension fund".

73 (1) In section 216 (benefit crystallisation events and amounts crystallised), the table in subsection (1) is amended as follows.

(2) In the entry for benefit crystallisation event 1, for "unsecured pension" substitute "drawdown pension".

(3) In the entry for benefit crystallisation event 5A—

(a) for "unsecured pension" substitute "drawdown pension";

(b) for "individual's unsecured pension fund" substitute "individual's drawdown pension fund".

74 In section 241(1) (scheme chargeable payment), omit paragraph (aa) (and the "and" after it).

75 In section 268 (unauthorised payments surcharge and scheme sanction charge), in subsection (6), omit—

(a) "172BA,", and

(b) "or arises under section 181A".

76 In section 273A (insurance company liable as scheme administrator), in subsection (1), for paragraph (c) substitute—

"(c) a drawdown pension fund lump sum death benefit,".

77 (1) Section 280(2) (general index) is amended as follows.

(2) Omit the entries relating to "dependant's alternatively secured pension fund" and "member's alternatively secured pension fund".

(3) Omit the entries relating to "dependant's unsecured pension fund" and "member's unsecured pension fund" and at the appropriate place insert—

"dependant's drawdown pension fund	paragraph 22 of Schedule 28";
"member's drawdown pension fund	paragraph 8 of Schedule 28".

(4) At the appropriate place insert—

"serious ill-health lump sum charge	section 205A(1)".

(5) Omit the entry relating to "unsecured pension fund lump sum death benefit" and at the appropriate place insert—

"drawdown pension fund lump sum death benefit	paragraph 17 of Schedule 29".

78 In Schedule 28 (pension rules), omit the following provisions—

(a) paragraph 5 (meaning of "alternatively secured pension");

(b) paragraphs 11 to 13 (member's alternatively secured pension fund etc);

(c) paragraph 19 (meaning of "dependants' alternatively secured pension");

(d) paragraphs 25 to 27 (dependant's alternatively secured pension fund etc).

79 (1) Schedule 29 (authorised lump sums) is amended as follows.

(2) In paragraph 1 (pension commencement lump sum), in sub-paragraph (3)(b), omit ", otherwise than by virtue of the operation of paragraph 8(2) of Schedule 28,".

(3) In paragraph 3 (pension commencement lump sum: calculation of applicable amount)—

(a) in sub-paragraph (1)(a), for "unsecured pension" substitute "drawdown pension";

(b) in sub-paragraph (5)(a), for "member's unsecured pension fund" substitute "member's drawdown pension fund";

(c) in sub-paragraph (8)(a), for "member's unsecured pension fund" substitute "member's drawdown pension fund".

(4) In paragraph 15 (uncrystallised funds lump sum death benefit), in sub-paragraph (2)(b), for "unsecured pension" substitute "drawdown pension".

80 (1) Schedule 32 (benefit crystallisation events: supplementary) is amended as follows.

(2) In paragraph 3 (benefit crystallisation events 1 and 2: prevention of overlap)—

(a) in sub-paragraph (1), for "unsecured pension fund" substitute "drawdown pension fund";
(b) in sub-paragraph (2), for "unsecured pension" substitute "drawdown pension".

(3) In paragraph 4 (benefit crystallisation events 1 and 4: prevention of overlap)—

(a) in sub-paragraph (1), for "unsecured pension fund" substitute "drawdown pension fund";
(b) in sub-paragraph (2), for "unsecured pension" substitute "drawdown pension".

(4) In paragraph 5 (benefit crystallisation events 1 and 5: hybrid arrangements), in sub-paragraph (2), omit the words from "(with the effect that" to the end.

(5) In paragraph 17 (benefit crystallisation event 8: prevention of overlap with other events), in sub-paragraph (2)—

(a) for "unsecured pension fund" substitute "drawdown pension fund";
(b) for "unsecured pension" substitute "drawdown pension".

81 (1) Schedule 34 (non-UK schemes: application of certain charges) is amended as follows.

(2) In paragraph 1(3) (member payment charges), after paragraph (c) insert—

"(ca) the serious ill-health lump sum charge,".

(3) After paragraph 4 insert—

"**4A** (1) For the purposes of determining whether a person meets the flexible drawdown conditions in section 165(3A) or 167(2A)—

(a) any reference in paragraph 14A or 24C of Schedule 28 (minimum income requirement) to payments made to or in respect of a member of a registered pension scheme includes a reference to payments made to or in respect of a relieved member or transfer member of a relevant non-UK scheme,
(b) any tax-relieved contributions made under a relevant non-UK scheme by or on behalf of, or in respect of, a member of the scheme are to be treated as if they were relevant contributions paid under a registered pension scheme,
(c) any tax-exempt provision made under a relevant non-UK scheme in relation to a member of the scheme is to be treated as if it was a relevant contribution paid under a registered pension scheme, and
(d) a person who is an active member of a relevant non-UK scheme is to be treated as if the person were an active member of a registered pension scheme.

(2) In this paragraph—

"relevant contributions" has the meaning given by paragraph 14D or 24F of Schedule 28;
"tax-exempt contributions" and "tax-exempt provision" have the same meaning as in paragraph 3 of this Schedule."

(4) In paragraph 5—

(a) for "Sections 205 and 206" substitute "Sections 205 to 206";
(b) after "short service refund lump sum charge" insert ", serious ill-health lump sum charge".

(5) Omit paragraph 7ZA (unauthorised payment charge: alternatively secured pension etc).

82 (1) Schedule 36 (transitional provisions and savings) is amended as follows.

(2) In paragraph 20 (amount of lifetime allowance available to person who had right to payment of pension on 5 April 2006), for sub-paragraph (4) substitute—

"(4) In the case of drawdown pension, ARP is—

(a) the maximum amount that may be paid in the drawdown pension year in which the time falls in accordance with pension rule 5 (see section 165), or
(b) in the case of an arrangement to which subsection (3A) of section 165 applies, the maximum amount that could have been paid in accordance with that rule in the drawdown pension year in which that subsection first applied to the arrangement if it had not so applied."

(3) In paragraph 28 (lump sum rights for members with enhanced protection), in sub-paragraph (3), for "sub-paragraphs (5) to (7)" substitute "sub-paragraphs (5) to (7A)".

(4) In paragraph 29 (lump sum rights for members with enhanced protection)—

(a) in sub-paragraph (2), in the text treated as substituted for sub-paragraphs (1) to (3) of paragraph 3 of Schedule 29, for "unsecured pension" (in both places) substitute "drawdown pension";

(b) in sub-paragraph (3), in the text treated as substituted for sub-paragraphs (5) to (7A) of that paragraph—

(i) for "member's unsecured pension fund" substitute "member's drawdown pension fund", and

(ii) for the definition of "AC" substitute—

"AC is—

(a) in a case where the member becomes entitled to the pension before reaching the age of 75, the amount crystallised by reason of the member becoming entitled to the pension, and

(b) in a case where the member becomes entitled to the pension after reaching that age, the amount that would have been so crystallised but for paragraph 2 of Schedule 32."

(5) In paragraph 34 (entitlement to lump sums exceeding 25% of uncrystallised rights), in sub-paragraph (2), in the text treated as substituted for sub-paragraphs (5) to (8) of paragraph 2 of Schedule 29, for the definition of "AC" substitute—

"AC is—

(a) in a case where the member becomes entitled to the pension in connection with which the lump sum is paid before reaching the age of 75, the amount crystallised by reason of the member becoming entitled to the pension, and

(b) in a case where the member becomes entitled to that pension after reaching that age, the amount that would have been so crystallised but for paragraph 2 of Schedule 32,

(but this is subject to sub-paragraphs (7AA) and (7B)),".

(6) In paragraph 36 (right to payment of lump sum death benefit)—

(a) in sub-paragraph (3)—

(i) after paragraph (a) insert "and", and

(ii) omit paragraph (c) (and the "and" before it);

(b) omit sub-paragraphs (4) and (8);

(c) in sub-paragraph (9)—

(i) for ", annuity protection lump sum death benefit or unsecured pension fund lump sum death benefit" substitute "or annuity protection lump sum death benefit", and

(ii) for "sub-paragraphs (3) to (8)" substitute "sub-paragraphs (3) to (7)";

(d) in sub-paragraph (10)(a), for ", annuity protection lump sum death benefit or unsecured pension fund lump sum death benefit" substitute "or annuity protection lump sum death benefit";

(e) in sub-paragraph (11), in the definition of "TPLS", for ", annuity protection lump sum death benefit or unsecured pension fund lump sum death benefit" substitute "or annuity protection lump sum death benefit".

Income Tax Act 2007

83 In section 30(1) of ITA 2007 (additional tax), after the entry relating to section 205 of FA 2004 insert—

"section 205A of FA 2004 (pension schemes: the serious ill-health lump sum charge),".

Consequential repeals

84 In consequence of the amendments made by this Schedule, omit the following provisions—

(a) in Schedule 10 to FA 2005, paragraphs 18(4), 20, 23 and 25(3);

(b) in FA 2006—

(i) in Schedule 22, paragraphs 3 to 9, 10(3) and 12, and

(ii) in Schedule 23, paragraph 29;

(c) in FA 2007—

(i) in Schedule 19, paragraphs 2(3), 4, 11, 12(2) and (5), 13 to 15, 16(2) to (4) and (6), 18(4), 20 to 26 and 29(2), (4) and (5), and
(ii) in Schedule 20, paragraphs 11(3) and 13;
(d) in FA 2008—
(i) in Schedule 4, paragraphs 4 and 9(2),
(ii) in Schedule 28, paragraphs 6 to 14, and
(iii) in Schedule 29, paragraph 16;
(e) in F(No2)A 2010—
(i) section 6, and
(ii) Schedule 3.

PART 3
COMMENCEMENT AND TRANSITIONAL PROVISION

General

85 Subject to the provisions of this Part, the amendments made by this Schedule have effect for the tax year 2011–12 and subsequent tax years.

Entitlement to unsecured or alternatively secured pension on 5 April 2011

86 Any person who, immediately before 6 April 2011, was entitled to unsecured pension or alternatively secured pension is to be treated, on and after that date, as entitled to drawdown pension.

87 Paragraph 6 of Schedule 28 to FA 2004 (short-term annuity) has effect on and after 6 April 2011 as if the reference to an annuity purchased by the application of sums or assets representing the whole or any part of the member's drawdown pension fund in respect of an arrangement included a reference to an annuity purchased before that date by the application of sums or assets representing the whole or any part of the member's unsecured pension fund in respect of the arrangement.

Member's unsecured or alternatively secured pension fund existing on 5 April 2011

88 Paragraph 8(1A) of Schedule 28 to FA 2004 (member's drawdown pension fund) has effect on and after 6 April 2011 as if any reference to sums or assets having been designated as available for the payment of drawdown pension included a reference to sums or assets having been designated, before that date, as available for the payment of unsecured pension or alternatively secured pension.

Current unsecured pension year to become drawdown pension year

89 (1) This paragraph applies in the case of a person who, immediately before 6 April 2011, was entitled to unsecured pension.

(2) Where the last unsecured pension year began on or after 7 April 2010, the reference in paragraph 9(1)(a) of Schedule 28 to FA 2004 (drawdown pension year) to the day on which the member first becomes entitled to drawdown pension is to be read as a reference to the day on which that unsecured pension year began.

(3) Accordingly, any unsecured pension year which began on or after 7 April 2010 is to be regarded, on and after 6 April 2011, as a drawdown pension year.

(4) In this paragraph and paragraphs 90 and 91 "the last unsecured pension year" means the unsecured pension year in which 5 April 2011 fell.

Previous limit on amount of pension payable in year to apply for limited period

90 (1) This paragraph applies in the case of a person who, immediately before 6 April 2011—
(a) was entitled to unsecured pension, and
(b) had not reached the age of 75.

(2) Where, immediately before 6 April 2011, the last reference period to begin before that date has not ended—
(a) pension rule 5 in section 165 of FA 2004 has effect in relation to every drawdown pension year ending on or before the relevant date as if for "100%" there were substituted "120%", and
(b) paragraph 10 of Schedule 28 to FA 2004 has effect with the following modifications—

(i) the reference in sub-paragraph (1) to the first drawdown pension year is to be read as a reference to the first drawdown pension year beginning after the relevant date;

(ii) any reference in sub-paragraphs (1ZA) to (1C) to a reference period is to be read as including a reference to the current reference period.

(3) The "relevant date" is the earlier of the following—

(a) the day on which the current reference period ends, and

(b) if a transfer within sub-paragraph (5) occurs in relation to the person, the day on which the drawdown pension year in which the transfer takes place ends.

(4) Subject to the operation of paragraph 10(1ZA) and (1B) of Schedule 28 to FA 2004, "the current reference period" is the period of 5 years beginning before 6 April 2011 and comprising—

(a) the drawdown pension year in which that date falls,

(b) any unsecured pension years which—

(i) began after the end of the last reference period ending before that date, and

(ii) ended before that date,

and

(c) if the sum of the years falling within paragraphs (a) and (b) is less than five, one or more drawdown pension years beginning after that date.

(5) A transfer is within this sub-paragraph if—

(a) it takes place on or after 6 April 2011, and

(b) it is a recognised transfer for the purposes of Part 4 of FA 2004 (see section 169 of that Act).

(6) For the purposes of pension rule 5 in section 165 of FA 2004, the amount which, immediately before 6 April 2011, was by virtue of paragraph 10 of Schedule 28 to FA 2004 the basis amount for the last unsecured pension year continues, on and after that date, to be the basis amount for every drawdown pension year ending on or before the relevant date.

(7) Paragraph 10(4) of Schedule 28 to FA 2004 has effect for drawdown pension years beginning on or after 6 April 2011 and ending on or before the relevant date as it has effect for drawdown pension years falling within any reference period beginning after the relevant date, but as if—

(a) paragraph (a) were omitted,

(b) in paragraph (b), for "otherwise" there were substituted "if there has been a recent annuity, recent additional fund designation or recent pension sharing event", and

(c) in paragraph 10(9) of that Schedule—

(i) the reference to the reference date were a reference to the day on which the last unsecured pension year began, and

(ii) the reference to the immediately preceding drawdown pension year included, in the case of a drawdown pension year beginning on 6 April 2011, a reference to the last unsecured pension year.

(8) In paragraph 10(7) to (8A) of that Schedule any reference to drawdown pension or the member's drawdown pension fund is to be read as including, in relation to anything occurring before 6 April 2011, a reference to unsecured pension or the member's unsecured pension fund.

91 (1) This paragraph applies in the case of a person who—

(a) reached the age of 75 on or after 22 June 2010 and before 6 April 2011, and

(b) immediately before 6 April 2011, was entitled to unsecured pension.

(2) Where the last unsecured pension year began on or after 7 April 2010—

(a) pension rule 5 in section 165 of FA 2004 has effect in relation to that year as if for "100%" there were substituted "120%", and

(b) for the purposes of that pension rule, the amount which, immediately before 6 April 2011, was the basis amount for that year by virtue of paragraph 10 of Schedule 28 to FA 2004 continues, on and after that date, to be the basis amount for that year.

(3) The amendments made by paragraph 9 of this Schedule have effect in relation to drawdown pension years beginning on or after 6 April 2011.

Drawdown pension year and basis amount where person's whereabouts unknown at age 75

92 (1) This paragraph applies in the case of a person who—

(a) reached the age of 75 before 22 June 2010, and

(b) immediately before 6 April 2011, had a member's unsecured pension fund by virtue of paragraph 11(6) and (7) of Schedule 28 to FA 2004 (cases where member's whereabouts are unknown at age 75).

(2) In a case where—

(a) the scheme administrator was unable to ascertain the person's whereabouts during the relevant period, but

(b) the person's whereabouts are ascertained by the scheme administrator after the end of that period,

the reference in paragraph 9(1)(a) of Schedule 28 to FA 2004 (drawdown pension year) to the day on which the member first becomes entitled to drawdown pension is to be read as a reference to the day on which the person's whereabouts are so ascertained.

(3) The "relevant period" is the period beginning with the person's 75th birthday and ending with 5 April 2011.

(4) In a case where the person's whereabouts have been ascertained by the scheme administrator within the period of 6 months ending on 6 April 2011, the reference in paragraph 9(1)(a) of that Schedule to the day on which the member first becomes entitled to drawdown pension is to be read as a reference to 6 April 2011.

Current alternatively secured pension year to become drawdown pension year

93 (1) This paragraph applies in the case of a person who, immediately before 6 April 2011, was entitled to alternatively secured pension.

(2) Where the last alternatively secured pension year began on or after 7 April 2010, the reference in paragraph 9(1)(a) of Schedule 28 to FA 2004 (drawdown pension year) to the day on which the member first becomes entitled to drawdown pension is to be read as a reference to the day on which that alternatively secured pension year began.

(3) Accordingly, any alternatively secured pension year which began on or after 7 April 2010 is to be regarded, on and after 6 April 2011, as a drawdown pension year.

(4) For the purposes of pension rule 5 in section 165 of FA 2004, the amount which, immediately before 6 April 2011, was the basis amount for that alternatively secured pension year by virtue of paragraph 13 of Schedule 28 to FA 2004 continues, on and after that date, to be the basis amount for that year.

(5) In this paragraph "the last alternatively secured pension year" means the alternatively secured pension year in which 5 April 2011 fell.

Entitlement to dependants' unsecured or alternatively secured pension on 5 April 2011

94 Any person who, immediately before 6 April 2011, was entitled to dependants' unsecured pension or dependants' alternatively secured pension is to be treated, on and after that date, as entitled to dependants' drawdown pension.

95 Paragraph 20 of Schedule 28 to FA 2004 (short-term annuity) has effect on and after 6 April 2011 as if the reference to an annuity purchased by the application of sums or assets representing the whole or any part of the dependant's drawdown pension fund in respect of an arrangement included a reference to an annuity purchased before that date by the application of sums or assets representing the whole or any part of the dependant's unsecured pension fund in respect of the arrangement.

Dependant's unsecured or alternatively secured pension fund existing on 5 April 2011

96 Paragraph 22(2) of Schedule 28 to FA 2004 (dependant's drawdown pension fund) has effect on and after 6 April 2011 as if any reference to sums or assets having been designated as available for the payment of dependants' drawdown pension included a reference to sums or assets having been designated, before that date, as available for the payment of dependants' unsecured pension or dependants' alternatively secured pension.

Current unsecured pension year to become drawdown pension year

97 (1) This paragraph applies in the case of a person who, immediately before 6 April 2011, was entitled to dependants' unsecured pension.

(2) Where the last unsecured pension year began on or after 7 April 2010, the reference in paragraph 23(1)(a) of Schedule 28 to FA 2004 (drawdown pension year) to the day on which the dependant first becomes entitled to dependants' drawdown pension is to be read as a reference to the day on which that unsecured pension year began.

(3) Accordingly, any unsecured pension year which began on or after 7 April 2010 is to be regarded, on and after 6 April 2011, as a drawdown pension year.

(4) In this paragraph and paragraphs 98 and 99 "the last unsecured pension year" means the unsecured pension year in which 5 April 2011 fell.

Previous limit on amount of pension payable in year to apply for limited period

98 (1) This paragraph applies in the case of a person who, immediately before 6 April 2011—

(a) was entitled to dependants' unsecured pension, and

(b) had not reached the age of 75.

(2) Where, immediately before 6 April 2011, the last reference period to begin before that date has not ended—

(a) pension death benefit rule 4 in section 167 of FA 2004 has effect in relation to every drawdown pension year ending on or before the relevant date as if for "100%" there were substituted "120%", and

(b) paragraph 24 of Schedule 28 to FA 2004 has effect with the following modifications—

(i) the reference in sub-paragraph (1) to the first drawdown pension year is to be read as a reference to the first drawdown pension year beginning after the relevant date;

(ii) any reference in sub-paragraphs (1ZA) to (1C) to a reference period is to be read as including a reference to the current reference period.

(3) The "relevant date" is the earlier of the following—

(a) the day on which the current reference period ends, and

(b) if a transfer within sub-paragraph (5) occurs in relation to the person, the day on which the drawdown pension year in which the transfer takes place ends.

(4) Subject to the operation of paragraph 24(1ZA) and (1B) of Schedule 28 to FA 2004, "the current reference period" is the period of 5 years beginning before 6 April 2011 and comprising—

(a) the drawdown pension year in which that date falls,

(b) any unsecured pension years that—

(i) began after the end of the last reference period ending before that date, and

(ii) ended before that date,

and

(c) if the sum of the years falling within paragraphs (a) and (b) is less than five, one or more drawdown pension years beginning after that date.

(5) A transfer is within this sub-paragraph if—

(a) it takes place on or after 6 April 2011, and

(b) it is a recognised transfer for the purposes of Part 4 of FA 2004 (see section 169 of that Act).

(6) For the purposes of pension death benefit rule 4 in section 167 of FA 2004, the amount which, immediately before 6 April 2011, was by virtue of paragraph 24 of Schedule 28 to FA 2004 the basis amount for the last unsecured pension year continues, on and after that date, to be the basis amount for every drawdown pension year ending on or before the relevant date.

(7) Paragraph 24(4) of Schedule 28 to FA 2004 has effect for drawdown pension years beginning after 6 April 2011 and ending on or before the relevant date as it has effect for drawdown pension years falling within any reference period beginning after the relevant date, but as if—

(a) paragraph (a) were omitted,

(b) in paragraph (b), for "otherwise" there were substituted "if there has been a recent annuity, recent additional fund designation or recent pension sharing event", and

(c) in paragraph 24(9) of that Schedule—

(i) the reference to the reference date were a reference to the day on which the last unsecured pension year began, and

(ii) the reference to the immediately preceding drawdown pension year included, in the case of a drawdown pension year beginning on 6 April 2011, a reference to the last unsecured pension year.

(8) In paragraph 24(7) to (8A) of that Schedule any reference to dependants' drawdown pension or the dependant's drawdown pension fund is to be read as including, in relation to anything occurring before 6 April 2011, a reference to dependants' unsecured pension or the dependant's unsecured pension fund.

99 (1) This paragraph applies in the case of a person who—

(a) reached the age of 75 on or after 22 June 2010 and before 6 April 2011, and

(b) immediately before 6 April 2011, was entitled to dependants' unsecured pension.

(2) Where the last unsecured pension year began on or after 7 April 2010—

(a) pension death benefit rule 4 in section 167 of FA 2004 has effect in relation to that year as if for "100%" there were substituted "120%", and

(b) for the purposes of that pension death benefit rule, the amount which, immediately before 6 April 2011, was the basis amount for that year by virtue of paragraph 24 of Schedule 28 to FA 2004 continues, on and after that date, to be the basis amount for that year.

(3) The amendments made by paragraph 19 of this Schedule have effect in relation to drawdown pension years beginning on or after 6 April 2011.

Current alternatively secured pension year to become drawdown pension year

100 (1) This paragraph applies in the case of a person who, immediately before 6 April 2011, was entitled to dependants' alternatively secured pension.

(2) Where the last alternatively secured pension year began on or after 7 April 2010, the reference in paragraph 23(1)(a) of Schedule 28 to FA 2004 (drawdown pension year) to the day on which the dependant first becomes entitled to drawdown pension is to be read as a reference to the day on which that alternatively secured pension year began.

(3) Accordingly, any alternatively secured pension year which began on or after 7 April 2010 is to be regarded, on and after 6 April 2011, as a drawdown pension year.

(4) For the purposes of pension death benefit rule 4 in section 167 of FA 2004, the amount which, immediately before 6 April 2011, was the basis amount for that alternatively secured pension year by virtue of paragraph 27 of Schedule 28 to FA 2004 continues, on and after that date, to be the basis amount for that year.

(5) In this paragraph "the last alternatively secured pension year" means the alternatively secured pension year in which 5 April 2011 fell.

Lump sums and lump sum death benefits

101 The amendments made by paragraphs 24 to 26, 31 and 79(2) and (3) have effect in relation to any lump sum to which a person becomes entitled for the purposes of Part 4 of FA 2004 on or after 6 April 2011.

102 The amendments made by paragraphs 27 to 30, 40, 42(2)(a) and (3), 63, 77(4), 81(2) and (4), 82(3) to (5) and 83 have effect in relation to lump sums paid on or after 6 April 2011.

103 The amendments made by paragraphs 33 to 39, 41, 42(2)(b) and (c), (4) and (5), 65, 67, 68, 75(a), 76, 77(5), 79(4) and 82(6) have effect in relation to deaths occurring on or after 6 April 2011.

Lifetime allowance charge

104 (1) The amendments made by paragraphs 43, 44, 73, 80 and 82(2) have effect in relation to benefit crystallisation events occurring on or after 6 April 2011.

(2) Any reference in a provision within sub-paragraph (3) to an amount previously crystallised on the designation of sums or assets as available for the payment of drawdown pension includes a reference to an amount crystallised before 6 April 2011 on the designation of sums or assets as available for the payment of unsecured pension.

(3) The provisions are—

(a) paragraph 3(2) of Schedule 32 to FA 2004 (benefit crystallisation events 1 and 2: prevention of overlap);

(b) paragraph 4(2) of that Schedule (benefit crystallisation events 1 and 4: prevention of overlap);

(c) paragraph 17(2) of that Schedule (benefit crystallisation event 8: prevention of overlap with other events).

Inheritance tax

105 The amendments made by paragraphs 47 and 50 have effect in relation to dispositions made (or treated as made) on or after 6 April 2011.

106 The amendments made by paragraphs 48 and 51 to 57 have effect in relation to deaths occurring on or after 6 April 2011.

Consequential repeals

107 Any repeal in paragraph 84 has effect to the same extent as the provision of this Schedule to which the repeal relates.

Power to make retrospective provision in orders and regulations under Part 4 of FA 2004

108 (1) This paragraph applies to any order or regulations under Part 4 of FA 2004 which—

(a) are made in the tax year beginning on 6 April 2011, and

(b) are made in consequence of, or for the purposes of, or for giving full effect to, the amendments of that Part made by this Schedule.

(2) Section 282 of that Act (orders and regulations) has effect in relation to any order or regulations to which this paragraph applies as if in subsection (A1) the words "if that provision does not increase any person's liability to tax" were omitted.

Application of rules of pension schemes

109 (1) The trustees or managers of a registered pension scheme may make any payment under the scheme which, by virtue of the amendments made by this Schedule, is an authorised member payment (within the meaning of section 164 of FA 2004), despite any provision of the rules of the pension scheme (however framed) prohibiting the making of such a payment.

(2) In the case of a personal pension scheme within the meaning of section 1 of the Pension Schemes Act 1993, nothing in subsection (1) of section 28 of that Act (ways of giving effect to protected rights) is to be taken to prevent the trustees or managers of the scheme from giving effect to the protected rights of a member of the scheme in the way provided for by subsection (1A) of that section.

(3) In the case of a personal pension scheme within the meaning of section 1 of the Pension Schemes (Northern Ireland) Act 1993, nothing in subsection (1) of section 24 of that Act (ways of giving effect to protected rights) is to be taken to prevent the trustees or managers of the scheme from giving effect to the protected rights of a member of the scheme in the way provided for by subsection (1A) of that section.

GENERAL NOTE

For many years HM Treasury had insisted, despite considerable lobbying, that in money purchase pension schemes there must be a rule requiring members to purchase an annuity from a life office securing their retirement benefits by age 75. This measure was ostensibly required to obviate problems arising where pension schemes ran out of money from which to pay pensions for the remainder of an individual's lifetime and to prevent tax-free cash lump sum abuse. It was particularly aimed at small self-administered pension schemes with one or two members and personal pensions. When the current pensions tax regime was being considered before 6 April 2006 it was decided to drop this requirement where there was security of income, eg where there was a large self-administered or wholly insured pension scheme. Changes were made to the unauthorised payments rules to prevent any lump sum abuse and at the same time member protection in small schemes was assured by Department for Work and Pensions legislation on scheme funding and the establishment of the Pension Protection Fund. So from 6 April 2006 when the current pensions tax regime commenced, an annuity has not had to be purchased for a member of a money purchase pension scheme from a life office until age 75 or an alternatively secured pension payable after age 75 is offered. Between retirement and age 75 an unsecured pension, commonly referred to as income drawdown, could be paid. Pension schemes could however retain the rule requiring members to purchase an annuity by age 75.

On 22 June 2010 the new Government announced that it would end this effective requirement for members of registered pension schemes to purchase an annuity by age 75 starting in 2011–12. It consulted widely on the detail of the change following the publication on 15 July 2010 of its consultation document, Removing the requirement to annuitise by age 75, and completed its consultation on 10 September 2010. Thereafter the Government announced that from 6 April 2011 the requirement to buy annuity by age 75 was to be abolished and the alternatively secured pension rules repealed. The legislation is contained in schedule 16.

The concepts of unsecured pensions and alternatively secured pensions will disappear with the legislation allowing individuals to leave their pension fund invested in a drawdown arrangement and to make withdrawals throughout their retirement subject to an annual cap. The maximum income withdrawal that can be made from most drawdown funds on reaching the minimum pension age of 55 will be capped at 100 per cent of the equivalent annuity that could have been purchased with the fund value. The maximum capped amount is to be determined at least every three years until the end of the year in which members reach age 75 following which such reviews are to be carried out annually.

Where an individual can demonstrate that they have a secure pension income for life of at least £20,000pa they will have full access to their drawdown funds with no annual cap. All withdrawals from drawdown funds will be subject to tax as pension income as at present. Where an individual makes a withdrawal from a drawdown pension fund when they are resident outside the UK for a period of less than five full tax years, they will be liable to UK income tax on that withdrawal for the tax year in which they again become UK resident.

Any new pension savings by an individual after they have demonstrated their secure pension lifetime income is at least £20,000 per annum will be liable to the annual allowance tax charge on all pension input amounts. Most of the rules that prevent registered pension schemes from paying lump sum benefits after members reach age 75 are being removed. All lump sum death benefits will be taxed at 55 per cent except death benefits for those who die before age 75 and who have not taken a pension. Such latter payments will remain tax-free.

Inheritance tax (IHT) will not apply with effect from 6 April 2011 to drawdown pension funds remaining under a registered pension scheme including when the member dies after reaching age 75. The IHT anti-avoidance charges applicable to registered pension schemes and qualifying non-UK pension schemes where the scheme member omits to take their retirement entitlements, eg fails to purchase an annuity, will be abolished from 6 April 2011. These changes also apply to superannuation funds that are occupational pension schemes by virtue of ICTA 1988 s 615(3).

PART 1

Paragraph 1 makes the amendments necessary to FA 2004 s 165 enabling unsecured and alternatively secured pensions to be replaced by drawdown pension with effect from 6 April 2011. Paragraph 1(2) amends the pension rules to remove the distinction between the types of pension that can be paid before and after reaching age 75. The amendments also replace the concepts of unsecured and alternatively secured pensions with the concept of a drawdown pension and limit the amount that can be paid as a drawdown pension to 100 per cent of the equivalent annuity that could have been purchased with the fund value unless the conditions in FA 2004 s 165(3A) inserted by para 1(3) are met. These conditions are that members must make a declaration to the pension scheme administrator that they meet the flexible drawdown conditions and the administrator accepts the declaration. Paragraph 1(3) also amends FA 2004 s 165 regarding the flexible drawdown conditions that must be met. These are that members must have a minimum pension income (see para 10) for the tax year, no contributions must be paid into their money purchase arrangement under a registered pension scheme during the tax year and, where members have a defined benefits (final salary) or cash balance arrangement under the pension scheme, they must have ceased being active members before making the declaration.

Paragraph 2 introduces the amendments made to Part 1 FA 2004 Sch 28 regarding the meaning of drawdown pension.

Paragraph 3 amends FA 2004 Sch 28 para 4 by replacing the definition of unsecured pension with a definition of drawdown pension.

Paragraph 4 amends FA 2004 Sch 28 para 6 in respect of the definition of short term annuity which is a form of drawdown pension. The amendments ensure that payments under a short term annuity need not end when members reach age 75 and make other consequential changes to the definition so it refers to drawdown pension instead of unsecured pension.

The definition of income withdrawal is amended in FA 2004 Sch 28 para 7 by para 5 so it refers to drawdown pension instead of unsecured or alternatively secured pensions.

Paragraph 6 amends FA 2004 Sch 28 para 8 by replacing the definition of an unsecured pension fund with the definition of a drawdown pension fund. Paragraph 6(4) specifically omits the rule requiring relevant uncrystallised funds to be treated as having been designated as available for payment of a drawdown pension immediately before age 75.

The provisions of FA 2004 Sch 28 para 9 are amended by para 7 by replacing the definition of unsecured pension year with a definition of drawdown pension year. The amendment in para 7(3) provides that a drawdown pension may continue after a member reaches age 75 and makes it clear that when a member dies, the drawdown pension year ends immediately before the member's death and is the last drawdown pension year.

Paragraph 8 amends FA 2004 Sch 28 para 10 by defining how the basis amount of drawdown pension is to be determined for a member who has not yet reached age 75. This is necessary to calculate the amount of drawdown pension to be paid in each drawdown pension year in accordance with the substituted pension rule 5 in FA 2004 s 165. The maximum amount a member may withdraw in accordance with pension rule 5 is determined at least every three years. To allow for a fall in the fund value which determines the basis amount despite there having been an additional fund designation in the drawdown pension year, para 8(7) provides that the reduction in the maximum amount the member may withdraw in accordance with pension rule 5 is not applied until the following pension drawdown year. Paragraph 8(12) provides that none of the rules relating to the basis amount for a drawdown pension year apply to a drawdown pension arrangement to which the cap on withdrawal as imposed by pension rule 5 does not apply because FA 2004 s 165(3A) applies (see para 1 above).

Paragraph 9 amends FA 2004 Sch 28 by inserting paras 10A and 10B. Paragraph 10A applies if the drawdown pension year begins after the member has reached age 75. The legislation provides how the basis amount is determined for calculating the amount of drawdown pension payable in each drawdown pension year. It also provides how to determine the date on which the sums and assets held for the purposes of the drawdown pension arrangement are valued in order to calculate the basis amount. The legislation goes on to provide how and when the basis amount is re-calculated if members add more sums and assets to their drawdown pension fund. Finally, para 10A provides that none of the rules relating to the basis amount for a drawdown pension year apply to a drawdown pension arrangement to which the cap on withdrawals imposed by pension rule 5 does not apply because FA 2004 s 165(3A) applies (see para 1 above).

Paragraph 10B of FA 2004 Sch 28 applies to members who have reached age 75. The legislation provides a right for members to notify the pension scheme administrator that they wish the pension drawdown year for one of their drawdown pension arrangements under the scheme to start on the same day as another of their drawdown pension arrangements under that scheme. This includes when the other arrangement is a dependant's drawdown pension arrangement relating to the member. The scheme administrator has discretion to comply with the member's wish and, if they do, the drawdown pension year brought to an end prematurely is treated as if it were a drawdown pension year for the purposes of operating pension rule 5 in FA 2004 s 165. The next year begins on the following day and the drawdown pension year for that arrangement will begin on the anniversary of when the next year began. The scheme administrator is prevented from bringing to an end prematurely a drawdown pension year at the wish of a member more than once per drawdown pension arrangement.

Paragraph 10 amends FA 2004 Sch 28 by inserting paras 14A to 14E defining how and when the minimum income requirement is satisfied. Paragraph 14A provides that members meet the minimum income requirement when they have at least £20,000 of relevant income which for these purposes is defined as scheme pensions from UK registered pension schemes or the equivalent from overseas schemes, lifetime annuities and social security pensions. Drawdown pensions from UK registered pension schemes and from overseas schemes do not count as relevant income for these purposes.

Paragraph 14B of FA 2004 Sch 28 provides HM Treasury with the power to vary the amount of the minimum income threshold by Treasury Order. It also provides the power for HM Treasury to make regulations to change the description of payments counting towards the minimum income threshold and to provide that certain types of payment are not taken into account when determining whether the minimum income threshold is met.

Paragraph 14C defines relevant day for the purposes of FA 2004 s 165(3B)(a), (see para 1 above). If no previous declaration has been made, the relevant day is when the member makes that first declaration. If a previous declaration has been made, the relevant day is when the member first actually became eligible to receive flexible withdrawals from a drawdown pension fund.

Paragraph 14D defines relevant contributions for the purposes of FA 2004 s 165(3B)(b), (see para 1 above), as tax relievable pension contributions paid by the member or on their behalf, or pension contributions paid by an employer in respect of the member.

Paragraph 14E provides for the requirements of a valid declaration by the member to meet the flexible drawdown conditions to be set out in regulations. This declaration is acceptable for the purposes of FA 2004 s 165(3A)(c), (see para 1 above), if the pension scheme administrator is satisfied that the person meets the flexible drawdown condition.

Paragraph 11 amends FA 2004 s 167 by changing the pension death benefit rules 3 and 4 and deleting rules 5 and 6 in relation to dependants' drawdown pension. The distinction between the type of pension death benefits that can be paid before and after age 75 is removed. The amendments also replace the concepts of dependants' unsecured and dependants' alternatively secured pensions with dependants' drawdown pension and cap the amount payable out of a dependants' drawdown pension at 100 per cent of the equivalent annuity that could have been purchased with the fund value. Paragraph 11(3) inserts FA 2004 s 167 sub-ss (2A) and (2B) setting out the rules for when the 100 per cent cap on a dependant's drawdown pension arrangement does not need to be applied. These rules are the same as for members' drawdown pensions as in para 1 in that members must make a declaration to the pension scheme administrator that they meet the flexible drawdown conditions and the administrator accepts the declaration. Paragraph 11(3) also amends FA 2004 s 167 regarding the flexible drawdown conditions that must be met. These are that members must have a minimum pension income (see para 20) for the tax year, no contributions must be paid into their money purchase arrangement under a registered pension scheme during the tax year and, where dependants have a defined benefits (final salary) or cash balance arrangement under the pension scheme, they must have ceased being active members before making the declaration.

Paragraph 12 introduces the amendments made to Part 2 FA 2004 Sch 28 regarding the meaning of dependants' drawdown pension.

Paragraph 13 amends a number of definitions in FA 2004 Sch 28 so they refer to dependants' drawdown pension instead of dependants' unsecured pension.

Paragraph 14 amends the definition of dependants' short term annuity which is a form of drawdown pension. The amendments ensure that payments under a short term annuity need not end when dependants reach age 75.

The definition of dependants' income withdrawal in FA 2004 Sch 28 para 20 is amended by para 15 so it refers to dependants' drawdown pension instead of dependants' unsecured or dependants' alternatively secured pension.

Paragraph 16 amends FA 2004 Sch 28 para 22 by replacing the definition of a dependant's unsecured pension fund with the definition of a dependant's drawdown pension fund.

The provisions of FA 2004 Sch 28 para 23 are amended by para 17 by replacing the definition of unsecured pension year with a definition of drawdown pension year. The amendment in para 17(3) provides that a dependant's drawdown pension may continue after a dependant reaches age 75 and makes it clear that when a dependant dies, the drawdown pension year ends immediately before the dependant's death and is the last drawdown pension year.

Paragraph 18 amends FA 2004 Sch 28 para 24 by defining how the basis amount of drawdown pension is to be determined for a dependant who has not yet reached age 75. This is necessary to calculate the amount of drawdown pension to be paid in each drawdown pension year in accordance with the substituted pension rule 5 in FA 2004 s 167. The maximum amount a dependant may withdraw in accordance with pension rule 5 is determined at least every three years. To allow for a fall in the fund value which determines the basis amount despite there having been an additional fund designation in the drawdown pension year, para 18(7) provides that the reduction in the maximum amount the dependant may withdraw in accordance with pension rule 5 is not applied until the following pension drawdown year. Paragraph 18(12) provides that none of the rules relating to the basis amount for a drawdown pension year apply to a drawdown pension arrangement to which the cap on withdrawal as imposed by pension rule 5 does not apply because FA 2004 s 167(2A) applies (see para 11 above).

Paragraph 19 amends FA 2004 Sch 28 by inserting paras 24A and 24B. Paragraph 24A applies if the drawdown pension year begins after the dependant has reached age 75. The legislation provides how the basis amount is determined for calculating the amount of the dependant's drawdown pension payable in each drawdown pension year. It also provides how to determine the date on which the sums and assets held for the purposes of the drawdown pension arrangement are valued in order to calculate the basis amount. The legislation goes on to provide how and when the basis amount is re-calculated if dependants add more sums and assets to their drawdown pension fund. Paragraph 24A also provides that none of the rules relating to the basis amount for a drawdown pension year apply to a drawdown pension arrangement to which the cap on withdrawals imposed by pension rule 5 does not apply because FA 2004 s 167(2A) applies (see para 11 above).

Paragraph 24B of FA 2004 Sch 28 applies to dependants who have reached age 75. The legislation provides a right for dependants to notify the pension scheme administrator that they wish the pension drawdown year for one of their pension drawdown arrangements under the scheme to start on the same day as another of their drawdown pension arrangements under that scheme. This includes when the other arrangement is a dependant's drawdown pension arrangement relating to the dependant. The scheme administrator has discretion to comply with the dependant's wish and, if they do, the drawdown pension year brought to an end prematurely is treated as if it were a drawdown pension year for the purposes of operating pension rule 5 in FA 2004 s 167. The next year begins on the following day and the drawdown pension year for that arrangement will begin on the anniversary of when the next year began. The scheme administrator is prevented from bringing to an end prematurely a drawdown pension year at the wish of a dependant more than once per drawdown pension arrangement.

Paragraph 20 amends FA 2004 Sch 28 by inserting paras 24C to 24G defining how and when the minimum income requirement is satisfied for dependants. Paragraph 24C provides that dependants meet the minimum income requirement when they have at least £20,000 of relevant income which for these purposes is defined as scheme pensions from UK registered pension schemes or the equivalent from overseas schemes, lifetime annuities and social security pensions. Drawdown pensions from UK registered pension schemes or the equivalent from overseas schemes do not count as relevant income for these purposes.

Paragraph 24D of FA 2004 Sch 28 provides HM Treasury with the power to vary the amount of the minimum income threshold by Treasury Order. It also provides the power for HM Treasury to make regulations to change the description of payments counting towards the minimum income threshold and to provide that certain types of payment are not taken into account when determining whether the minimum income threshold is met.

Paragraph 24E defines relevant day for the purposes of FA 2004 s 167(2A), (see para 11 above). If no previous declaration has been made, the relevant day is when the dependant makes that first declaration. If a previous declaration has been made, the relevant day is when the dependant first actually became eligible to receive flexible withdrawals from a dependant's drawdown pension fund.

Paragraph 24F defines relevant contributions for the purposes of FA 2004 s 167(2A), (see para 11 above), as tax relievable pension contributions paid by the dependant or on their behalf, or pension contributions paid by an employer in respect of the dependant.

Paragraph 24G provides for the requirements of a valid declaration by the dependant to meet the flexible drawdown conditions to be set out in regulations. This declaration is acceptable for the purposes of FA 2004 s 167(2A), (see para 11 above), if the pension scheme administrator is satisfied that the person meets the flexible drawdown condition.

Paragraph 21(1) introduces amendments to ITEPA 2003 Part 9 which imposes tax charges on pension income. Paragraph 21(2) amends ITEPA 2003 s 574 by providing that foreign pensions include annuities and income withdrawals under overseas pension schemes. Paragraph 21(3) makes a consequential change to ITEPA 2003 s 575(1). Paragraph 21(4) amends ITEPA 2003 s 576 by inserting s 576A regarding members who are temporarily non-residents. The legislation provides that a withdrawal from a flexible drawdown pension fund under a relevant non-UK pension scheme during a year of non-residence in the UK is to be treated as pension income for the tax year in which the individual returns to the UK. Section 576A only applies when the individual did not satisfy the residence requirements for a temporary period and prescribes what counts as temporary non-residence. The residence requirements are set out in s 576A(3). Where an individual is chargeable to tax on the remittance basis under ITEPA 2003 ss 809B, 809D or 809E, and they withdraw an amount from a flexible drawdown pension fund and remit this to the UK during a period of temporary non-residence, the remittance is treated as if it were actually remitted in the year in which the individual returns to the UK. The provisions of s 576A do not apply unless the withdrawal from a flexible drawdown pension fund is referable to either the individual's UK tax-relieved fund created by the accumulation of pension rights supported by UK tax relief or their relevant transfer fund created by the transfer to the relevant non-UK pension scheme from a registered pension scheme or from another relevant non-UK scheme. No double taxation relief arrangements will prevent a charge to tax under ITEPA 2003 s 575 from arising under s 576A. Section 576A(8) provides various definitions for the purposes of this section.

Paragraph 22(1) introduces amendments to ITEPA 2003 Ch 5A Part 9 regarding pensions under registered pension schemes. Paragraph 22(2) makes a consequential amendment to ITEPA s 579B regarding taxable pension income. Paragraph 22(3) amends ITEPA 2003 s 579 by inserting s 579CA regarding temporary non-residents. The legislation provides that any income withdrawal or dependants' income withdrawal from a flexible drawdown pension fund under a relevant non-UK pension scheme during a year of non-residence in the UK is to be treated as pension income in the tax year in which the individual returns to the UK. Section 579CA only applies when the individual did not satisfy the residence requirements for a temporary period and prescribes what counts as temporary non-residence. The residence requirements are set out in s 579CA(3). No double taxation relief arrangements will prevent a charge to tax under ITEPA 2003 s 575 from arising under s 579CA. Section 579CA(5) provides definitions for the purposes of this section. Paragraph 22(4) amends ITEPA 2003 s 579D by providing new definitions.

Paragraph 23 introduces amendments to FA 2004 Sch 29 Part 1 regarding the commencement lump sum and other lump sum rules.

Paragraph 24 amends FA 2004 Sch 29 para 1 by providing that a pension commencement lump sum may be paid when members become entitled to it when aged 75 or over. Members are treated as becoming entitled to a pension commencement lump sum when they become entitled to the relevant pension in connection with which the lump sum is paid. The amendment has the effect when a member becomes entitled to a pension commencement lump sum before reaching age 75, but the lump sum is not paid until after reaching that age. In these circumstances only the requirement in FA 2004 Sch 29 para 1(1)(b) that the member has not used up all of their lifetime allowance is modified so that it is applied when the member became entitled to the lump sum, not when it is paid. The member can thus receive a tax-free pension commencement lump sum before reaching age 75 even if all their lifetime allowance has subsequently been exhausted.

Paragraph 25 amends FA 2004 Sch 29 para 2 to provide that one of the two calculations (to determine the available portion) needed to determine the maximum tax-free pension commencement lump sum payable is determined without reference to any lifetime allowance used up by a new benefit crystallisation event 5B (inserted in FA 2004 s 216 by para 43 of this schedule), but takes into account events which would have been benefit crystallisation events if the event or payment had occurred before the member reached age 75. The concept of the available portion broadly limits the value of tax-free lump sums that an individual may receive over a lifetime to one quarter of the lifetime allowance.

The calculation in FA 2004 Sch 29 para 3 is amended by para 26 to provide how the applicable amount is determined when members become entitled to a relevant pension after reaching age 75. The applicable amount limits the tax-free pension commencement lump sum to an amount that is broadly no more than one quarter of the value of an individual's pension rights. The amendment expresses the value of the pension rights in terms of the amount crystallised by the rights to the pension and lump sum for the purposes of the lifetime allowance. Once a member reaches age 75 the lifetime allowance is no longer relevant so FA 2004 Sch 29 para 3 is amended to provide that the applicable amount is determined by reference to the amount that would have been crystallised by that event were it to have been a benefit crystallisation event, but was not because the member was aged 75 or over. The maximum pension commencement lump sum permitted is the lower of the available portion and the applicable amount per FA 2004 Sch 29 para 2(5).

Paragraph 27 amends FA 2004 Sch 29 para 3A regarding the recycling of pension commencement lump sums. The amendment ensures that the provisions of para 3A do not apply in respect of pension commencement lump sums recycled into contributions paid on or after the member reaching age 75. Such contributions are not relievable contributions under FA 2004 s 188. The amendment in para 27(4) confirms that where the entitlement to the pension commencement lump sum arises when the member is aged 75 or more, the appropriate amount is the lump sum paid.

Paragraph 28 amends FA 2004 Sch 29 para 4 to allow for a serious ill-health lump sum to be paid when a member is aged 75 or more.

Paragraph 29 amends FA 2004 Sch 29 para 7(1)(e) so that a trivial commutation lump sum may be paid when a member is aged 75 or more.

Paragraph 30 amends FA 2004 Sch 29 para 10(1) so that a winding-up lump sum may be paid when a member is aged 75 or more.

Paragraph 31 amends FA 2004 Sch 29 para 12(1) to provide that none of the specific lifetime allowance charge rules affecting a member on reaching age 75 affect when a member, who has reached that age, is treated as having lifetime allowance available for the purposes of the commencement lump sum, the serious ill-health lump sum, the trivial commutation lump sum or the winding-up lump sum.

Paragraph 32 introduces amendments to FA 2004 Sch 29 Part 2 regarding the lump sum death benefit rules.

Paragraph 33 amends FA 2003 Sch 29 para 13 so that in a final salary pension scheme a lump sum may be paid when the member is aged 75 or over and on the member's death after age 75 the amendment removes the condition that the lump sum has to be paid within two years of the pension scheme administrator learning of the member's death.

FA 2004 Sch 29 para 14 is amended by para 34 regarding pension protection lump sum benefits so that a lump sum death benefit may be paid from a final salary pension scheme when the member is aged 75 or more. Paragraph 34(3) sets out how the pension protection limit is determined when the pension or annuity relating to a pension protection lump sum is paid. This is by deducting the pension payments from the value of the pension rights when the member became entitled to it. The value of the pension rights is expressed in terms of the amount crystallised by the rights to the pension and lump sum for the purposes of the lifetime allowance. Once a member reaches age 75 the lifetime allowance is no longer relevant so FA 2004 Sch 29 para 14 is amended to provide that the pension protection limit is determined by reference to the amount that would have been crystallised by the member becoming entitled to the pension were it to have been a benefit crystallisation event, but was not because the member was aged 75 or over. The pension protection limit is the maximum amount that may be paid as a pension protection lump sum death benefit. It is liable to the special lump sum death benefits tax charge under FA 2004 s 206.

Paragraph 35 amends FA 2004 Sch 29 para 15 regarding the uncrystallised funds lump sum death benefit so that this benefit may be paid when a member is aged 75 or more. On a member's death after age 75 the amendment removes the condition that the lump sum has to be paid within two years of the pension scheme administrator learning of the member's death.

Paragraph 36 amends FA 2004 Sch 29 para 16 regarding the annuity protection lump sum death benefit that may be paid when the member is aged 75 or over. The amendment in para 36(2) ensures that an annuity protection lump sum death benefit may be paid when a member is aged 75 or more. The amendment in para 36(3) provides how the annuity protection limit is determined when a member became entitled at age 75 or more to the pension or annuity in respect of which an annuity protection lump sum is paid. This limit is determined by deducting the pension payments made from the value of the pension rights when the member became entitled to it. The value of the pension rights is expressed in terms of the amount crystallised by the rights to a pension for the purposes of the lifetime allowance. However, once a member has reached the age of 75 the lifetime allowance is no longer relevant, so the amendment in para 36(3) provides that the annuity protection limit is to be determined by reference to the amount that would have been crystallised by the member becoming entitled to the pension or annuity were it to have been a benefit crystallisation event, but was not because at the time the member was aged 75 or more. The annuity protection limit is the maximum amount that may be paid as an annuity protection lump sum death benefit. It is liable to the special lump sum death benefits tax charge under FA 2004 s 206.

FA 2004 Sch 29 para 17 is amended by para 37 regarding the unsecured pension fund lump sum death benefit so that a drawdown pension fund lump sum death benefit may be paid instead of an unsecured pension fund lump sum death benefit.

Paragraph 38 amends FA 2004 Sch 29 para 18 regarding the charity lump sum death benefit so that a charity lump sum death benefit may be paid tax-free from a drawdown pension fund whether or not a member has reached age 75. The payment can only be paid when members have no dependants and it is paid to a charity nominated by them. The amendment permits a charity lump sum death benefit to be paid in these circumstances without some or all of the fund to provide a pension. Similar provisions apply to a dependant's drawdown pension fund where the dependant dies whether or not they had reached age 75. In this event the payment can only be made where there are no other dependants of the original member and the payment is made to a charity nominated by either the original member or dependant. Paragraph 37(5) places a cap on the amount of the charity lump sum death benefit at the value of the sums and assets in the drawdown pension fund immediately before the payment is made.

Paragraph 39 amends FA 2004 Sch 29 para 20(1) regarding the trivial commutation lump sum death benefit so that it may be paid when a member is aged 75 or more.

Paragraph 40 amends FA 2004 s 205 by providing for a serious ill-health lump sum tax charge. Serious ill-health lump sums are defined in FA 2004 Sch 29 para 4 and are tax-free when paid to a member who has not yet reached age 75. A tax charge will arise from 6 April 2011 where a serious ill-health lump sum is paid to a member aged 75 or over. The pension scheme administrator will be liable to the tax charge at a rate of 55 per cent on the gross amount of the lump sum.

FA 2004 s 206 is amended by para 41 regarding the special lump sum death benefits tax charge so that it covers a drawdown pension fund instead of an unsecured pension fund. The amendment ensures that the special lump sum death benefits charge now arises where a final salary pension scheme lump sum death benefit or an uncrystallised funds lump sum death benefit is paid by a registered pension scheme in respect of a member who has reached age 75 at their date of death. The rate of the tax charge is increased from 35 to 55 per cent. Paragraph 41(5) ensures that any lump sum death benefit paid under FA 2004 s 206 is not to be treated as income for the purposes of the Taxes Acts.

Paragraph 42 makes consequential amendments to ITEPA 2003 s 636A regarding serious ill-health lump sums, defined benefits (final salary) lump sum death benefits and uncrystallised funds lump sum death benefits which terms are respectively defined in FA 2004 Sch 29 paras 4, 13 and 15.

Paragraph 43 amends FA 2004 s 216 to provide for a new benefit crystallisation event 5B covering the situation when a member, with remaining unused funds held for the purposes of a money purchase arrangement relating to the member, reaches age 75.

Paragraph 44(1) introduces amendments to FA 2004 Sch 32 regarding supplementary provision in connection with benefit crystallisation events and the lifetime allowance charge. Paragraph 44(2) amends FA 2004 Sch 32 para 14 to define remaining unused funds for the purposes of benefit crystallisation event 5B in FA 2004 s 216 (see para 43 above). Paragraph 44(3) amends FA 2004 Sch 32 para 15 to provide that where a member becomes entitled to a pension commencement lump sum in respect of a money purchase arrangement before age 75, but it is not paid until later, it is not treated as a benefit crystallisation event 6.

Paragraph 45 amends FA 2004 s 227 regarding the annual allowance charge. The amendments provide that where a member enters flexible drawdown any subsequent pension input amounts in respect of a registered pension scheme of which they are an active member are subject to the annual allowance charge in full without the benefit of the annual allowance. A formula for calculating the pension input amount in these circumstances is provided.

Paragraph 46 makes provision for amendments to IHTA 1984 regarding the removal of certain charges to IHT in respect of pension schemes.

Paragraph 47 amends IHT Act 1984 s 12 regarding dispositions allowable for income tax or conferring benefits under a pension scheme. The amendment in para 47(2) provides that the IHT charges for omissions such as the failure to purchase an annuity in relation to registered pension schemes, qualifying non-UK pensions as defined in IHTA 1984 s 271A and superannuation schemes within ICTA 1988 s 615(3) no longer apply. The amendment in para 47(3) removes IHTA 1984 ss 12(2A) to (2E) which currently provide for IHT charges in the event of omissions by members of the pension schemes mentioned or prevents a double charge arising under IHTA 1984 ss 3(1) or 3(3) and 151A to 154E. As the latter charges are being removed by the amendments, the charge under IHTA 1984 s 3(1) is re-instated.

Paragraph 48 provides for the removal of IHTA 1984 ss 151A to 151E. This removes the IHT charge that currently applies to alternatively secured pensions.

PART 2

Paragraph 49 introduces consequential amendments to IHTA 1984.

Paragraph 50 amends IHTA 1984 s 12 regarding dispositions allowable for income tax or conferring benefits under pension schemes. The amendments in para 50(2) provide for the removal of the term "registered" from IHTA 1984 s 12(2F)(b). The amendments in para 50(3) remove terms from IHTA 1984 s 12(2G) which are currently contained in IHTA 1984 ss 12(2A) to 12(2E), but which are removed by para 47(3) above.

Paragraph 51 amends IHTA 1984 s 151 by removing any references to sections which are removed by para 50 above.

Paragraph 52 removes IHTA 1984 s 200(1A) and any reference thereto in IHTA 1984 s 200(1) regarding transfers on death as this legislation currently makes pension scheme administrators liable for the tax chargeable under IHTA 1984 ss 151A to 151C.

Paragraph 53 removes IHTA 1984 s 210(2) and (3) as this legislation currently sets out who is liable for charges under IHTA 1984 ss 151B and 151 D which are removed by para 48 above.

Paragraph 54 amends IHTA 1984 s 216 by providing for the IHT rules governing the delivery of accounts to reflect the removal of charges by Sch 16.

Paragraph 55 amends IHTA 1984 s 226(4) to provide for the current IHT rules governing the due date and payment to reflect the removal of charges by Sch 16.

Paragraph 56 amends IHTA 1984 s 233(1)(c) to provide for the current IHT rules governing interest due on amounts brought into charge to reflect the removal of charges by Sch 16.

Paragraph 57 amends IHTA 1984 s 272 to provide for the removal of the definition of the term "scheme administrator", the necessity for which is removed by virtue of Sch 16.

Paragraph 58 amends Pension Schemes Act 1993 s 28A(3) because of the consequential changes required to apply the limit on withdrawals from a drawdown pension fund insofar as the sums and assets in the fund represent Protected Rights under Social Security legislation. The limits on withdrawals imposed by pension rule 5 in FA 2004 s 165 and by pension death benefit rule 4 in FA 2004 s 167 cannot be disapplied in relation to Protected Rights.

Paragraph 59 amends Pension Schemes (Northern Ireland) Act 1993 s 24A(3) for the same reasons and in the same manner as the amendments in paragraph 58 above.

Paragraph 60 amends ITEPA 2003 s 683(3) to prevent an obligation on a registered pension scheme to operate PAYE on pension income that is taxable in the year of return to the UK by a temporary non-resident by virtue of ITEPA 2003 s 579CA.

Paragraph 61 amends Part 2 ITEPA 2003 Sch 1 to make consequential changes to definitions.

Paragraph 62 introduces consequential changes to Part 4 FA 2004.

Paragraph 63 amends FA 2004 s 164(2)(b) to extend the regulation making power as provision may be made in regulations that payments prescribed as authorised payments using this power may be subject to the ill-health lump sum charge (see para 40 above).

Paragraph 64 amends FA 2004 s 165 by replacing a reference to unsecured pension with a reference to drawdown pension.

FA 2004 s 168(1)(e) is amended by para 65 to provide for a drawdown pension fund lump sum death benefit to be a specified category of authorised lump sum death benefit.

Paragraph 66 amends FA 2004 s 169(1D) by providing a power to make regulations enabling transfers of sums or assets made out of a drawdown pension fund to a new arrangement to be treated as if they were sums or assets held under the old arrangement to the extent provided for. The amendment also replaces references to unsecured and alternatively secured pensions with references to drawdown pensions.

Paragraph 67 amends FA 2004 s 172B regarding increases in rights of connected persons on death by removing references to unsecured and alternatively secured pension funds and substituting references to drawdown pension funds.

Paragraph 68 removes FA 2004 s 172BA so that the rules on increases in rights on death arising from alternatively secured pension funds cease to have effect.

Paragraph 69 removes FA 2004 s 181A so that the rules setting minimum levels of payments out of alternatively secured pension funds cease to have effect.

Paragraph 70 amends FA 2004 s 182 regarding unauthorised borrowing by money purchase pension schemes by removing references to unsecured an alternatively unsecured pension funds and substituting references to drawdown pension funds.

Paragraph 71 amends FA 2004 s 211 regarding surchargeable unauthorised member payments by removing references to unsecured and alternatively secured pension funds and substituting references to drawdown pension funds.

Paragraph 72 amends FA 2004 s 212 regarding surchargeable unauthorised member payments by removing references to unsecured and alternatively secured pension funds and substituting references to drawdown pension funds.

Paragraph 73 amends FA 2004 s 216(1) regarding benefit crystallisation events and amounts crystallised by replacing references to unsecured pension with references to drawdown pension.

Paragraph 74 removes the cross-reference in FA 2004 s 241(1) to FA 2004 s 181A concerning minimum withdrawals from alternatively secured pensions.

Paragraph 75 deletes the cross-references in FA 2004 s 268(6) to FA 2004 ss 172BA and 181A.

Paragraph 76 amends FA 2004 s 273A(1) by removing the reference to the liability of insurance companies to pay the special lump sum death benefits tax charge relating to an unsecured pension fund lump sum death benefit and substituting a reference to a drawdown pension lump sum death benefit.

Paragraph 77 amends the general index in FA 2004 s 280(2) to reflect the changes provided for in schedule 16.

Paragraph 78 repeals certain provisions from FA 2004 Sch 28 paras 5, 11 to 13, 19, and 25 to 27.

Paragraph 29 makes consequential amendments to FA 2004 Sch 29 paras 1, 3 and 15 regarding authorised lump sums.

This paragraph replaces references to unsecured pension in FA 2004 Sch 32 paras 3, 4, 5 and 17 with references to drawdown pension.

Paragraph 81(1) introduces consequential amendments to FA 2004 Sch 34 regarding the application of certain charges to non-UK pension schemes. Paras 81(2) and (4) provide that the serious ill-health lump sum charge is one of the member payment charges applying to members of relevant non-UK pension schemes by virtue of FA 2004 Sch 34 and that the member of the relevant non-UK scheme is the person liable for the tax arising on such lump sums. The amendments in para 81(3) modify certain of the provisions inserted or revised by schedule 16 for the purposes of determining whether a member or their dependant of a relevant non-UK pension scheme meets the flexible drawdown conditions for members and their dependants in FA 2004 ss 165(3A) and 176(2A), (see paras 1 and 11 above). Paragraph 81(5) repeals the provisions in FA 2004 Sch 34 para 7ZA relating to alternatively secured pension arrangements under a relevant non-UK pension scheme.

Paragraph 82(1) introduces amendments to FA 2004 Sch 36 regarding transitional provisions and savings. Paragraph 82(2) amends FA 2004 Sch 36 para 20 to provide how to determine the value of a person's pre-commencement rights regarding a flexible drawdown arrangement. This is necessary to determine the lifetime allowance treated as used up by pension rights existing before 6 April 2006, when the current pensions tax regime commenced, and to ascertain whether there is any liability to the lifetime allowance charge due to a benefit crystallisation event after that date. Paragraph 82(3) makes a consequential amendment to FA 2004 Sch 36 para 28(3). Paragraph 82(4) amends FA 2004 Sch 36 para 29 regarding transitionally protected rights receiving a pension commencement lump sum of more than £375,000. The amendment addresses the conversion of unsecured pension funds into drawdown pension funds on 6 April 2011 and also the removal of the rule preventing pension commencement lump sums from being paid to members who have reached age 75. Paragraph 82(5) amends FA 2004 Sch 36 para 34(2) regarding transitionally protected rights to receive a lump sum worth more than 25 per cent of the total rights under the pension scheme to deal with cases where members become entitled to the pension after they reach age 75. Paragraph 82(6) makes consequential amendments to FA 2004 Sch 36 para 36 regarding the right to payment of lump sum death benefits.

Paragraph 83 makes a consequential change to ITA 2007 s 30(1) regarding additional tax in respect of the serious ill-health lump sum charge.

Paragraph 84 makes various consequential repeals of legislation that no longer applies.

PART 3

Paragraph 85 provides for the new rules in schedule 16 to take effect on and after 6 April 2011.

Paragraph 86 provides for a person who immediately before 6 April 2011 was entitled to an unsecured or alternatively secured pension to be treated from this date as entitled to drawdown pension.

Paragraph 87 provides that FA 2004 Sch 28 para 6 has the effect that where a short term annuity has to be purchased out of the assets in a drawdown pension fund this includes annuities purchased out of assets in an unsecured pension fund before 6 April 2011.

Paragraph 88 provides that where FA 2004 Sch 28 para 8(1A) stipulates that sums or assets have been designated as available for payment out of the funds of a drawdown pension, this includes sums or assets designated as available for an unsecured or alternatively secured pension fund before 6 April 2011.

Paragraph 89 provides that where a member was entitled to an unsecured pension, the start of the next pension year for their drawdown pension is the anniversary of the start of the unsecured pension year which includes 6 April 2011 and that the unsecured pension year in which 5 April 2011 falls is called the last unsecured pension year.

Paragraph 90 provides rules for working out the maximum amount that members, who had unsecured pension fund arrangements and who were under age 75 before 6 April 2011, can draw from a drawdown pension fund. The paragraph provides that the current withdrawal limits for members under pension rule 5 FA 2004 s 165 are preserved until the first pension drawdown year to start after the relevant date, as is the ability to re-determine the basis amount only every five years before age 75. The relevant date is the earlier of the date on which the last reference period to begin before 6 April 20011 ends in accordance with the rules in FA 2004 Sch 28 disregarding any amendments made by schedule 16 and the end of the drawdown pension year in which there is a recognised transfer to another pension scheme.

Paragraph 91 sets out the rules for working out the maximum amount that members, who had unsecured pension fund arrangements and who reached age 75 on or after 22 June 2010 (the date of the Chancellor's announcement of this measure) and before 6 April 2011, can draw from a drawdown pension fund in the drawdown pension year which includes 6 April 2011. The transitional rules affecting these members in F (No. 2) A 2010 s 6 and Sch 3 are repealed by para 84(e) above.

Paragraph 92 sets out the rules for individuals who reached age 75 before 22 June 2010 and who immediately before 6 April 2011 had an unsecured pension because their whereabouts were unknown to the pension scheme administrator. This paragraph provides that in such circumstances there is a new drawdown pension year. This year starts either on 6 April 2011 if the scheme administrator ascertained their whereabouts before that date, but the six months period of grace has not yet elapsed, and the sums and assets have not all been used to provide an annuity or scheme pension and so remain held for the purposes of the unsecured pension fund on 5 April 2011, or on the date on which the scheme administrator ascertains their whereabouts after 5 April 2011. Annual reviews and withdrawals capped at 100 per cent of the basis amount apply to these formerly untraceable members from the first day of the start of this drawdown pension year on or after 6 April 2011.

Paragraph 93 applies to members who immediately before 6 April 2011 were entitled to an alternatively secured pension. A member's first drawdown pension year is treated as having commenced on the first day of an alternatively secured pension scheme year which began on or after 7 April 2010. As a result a member may take income withdrawals for that year up to 100 per cent of the basis amount at the start of the year in accordance with pension rule 5 of FA 2004 s 165 as amended by schedule 16. The minimum level of payment from an alternatively secured pension under FA 2004 s 181A will not apply as it is repealed by para 69 above.

Paragraph 94 provides for a person who immediately before 6 April 2011 was entitled to a dependant's unsecured or alternatively unsecured pension to be treated from this date as entitled to a dependant's drawdown pension.

Paragraph 95 provides that FA 2004 Sch 28 para 20 has the effect that where a short term annuity is to be purchased out of the assets in a dependant's drawdown pension fund, this includes annuities purchased out of assets in a dependant's unsecured pension fund before 6 April 2011.

Paragraph 96 provides that where FA 2004 Sch 28 para 22(2) stipulates that sums or assets have been designated as available for payment out of the funds of a dependant's drawdown pension, this includes sums or assets designated as available from a dependant's unsecured or alternatively secured pension fund before 6 April 2011.

Paragraph 97 provides that where a person was entitled to a dependant's unsecured pension, the start of the next pension year for their dependant's drawdown pension is the anniversary of the start of the unsecured pension year which includes 6 April 2011 and that the unsecured pension year in which 5 April 2011 falls is called the last unsecured pension year.

Paragraph 98 provides rules for working out the maximum amount that persons, who had dependants' unsecured pension fund arrangements and who were under age 75 before 6 April 2011, can draw from a dependant's drawdown pension fund. The paragraph provides that the current withdrawal limits under pension rule 4 in FA 2004 s 167 are preserved until the first pension drawdown year to start after the relevant date, as is the ability to re-determine the basis amount only every five years before age 75. The relevant date is the earlier of the date on which the last reference period to begin before 6 April 2011 ends in accordance with the rules in FA 2004 Sch 28 disregarding any amendments made by schedule 16 and the end of the drawdown pension year in which there is a recognised transfer to another pension scheme.

Paragraph 99 sets out the rules for working out the maximum amount that a dependant, who had a dependant's unsecured pension fund arrangement and who reached age 75 on or after 22 June 2010 (the date of the Chancellor's announcement of this measure) and before 6 April 2011, can draw from a dependant's drawdown pension fund in the drawdown pension year which includes 6 April 2011. The transitional rules affecting such dependants in F (No. 2) A 2010 s 6 and Sch 3 are repealed by para 84(e) above.

Paragraph 100 applies to members who immediately before 6 April 2011 were entitled to a dependant's alternatively secured pension. A dependant's first drawdown pension year is treated as having commenced on the first day of an alternatively secured pension scheme year which began on or after 7 April 2010. As a result a dependant may take income withdrawals for that year up to 100 per cent of the basis amount at the start of the year in accordance with pension rule 4 in FA 2004 s 167 as amended by schedule 16. The minimum level of payment from a dependant's alternatively secured pension under FA 2004 s 181A will not apply as it is repealed by para 69 above.

Paragraph 101 provides that the amendments made by schedule 16 in relation to pension commencement lump sums apply to lump sums to which members became entitled on or after 6 April 2011.

Paragraph 102 provides that the amendments made by schedule 16 regarding lump sums other than pension commencement lump sums and lump sum death benefits apply to lump sums paid on or after 6 April 2011.

Paragraph 103 provides that the amendments to lump sum death benefit rules apply to lump sums paid in respect of deaths on or after 6 April 2011.

Paragraph 104 provides that the changes made in schedule 16 to the benefit crystallisation event rules apply to benefit crystallisation events occurring on or after 6 April 2011.

Paragraph 105 provides that the amendments made by paras 47 and 50 to IHTA 1984 s 12 have effect in respect of dispositions made or treated as being made on or after 6 April 2011.

Paragraph 106 provides that the amendments made by paras 48 and 51 to 57 to IHTA 1984 s 151 and the related administrative arrangements have effect in relation to deaths occurring on or after 6 April 2011.

Paragraph 107 makes provision for how the consequential repeals in para 84 are to have effect.

Paragraph 108 extends the regulation making power in FA 2004 s 282 to provide that regulations made during the tax year 2011–12 relating to amendments made by schedule 16 may have retrospective effect even if they increase an individual's liability to tax.

Finally, para 109 provides that payments may be made by registered pension schemes that are authorised member payments under schedule 16 even if the pension scheme rules prohibit such a payment. This includes the payment of Protected Rights under Social Security legislation.

SCHEDULE 17
ANNUAL ALLOWANCE CHARGE

Section 66

PART 1
AMENDMENTS

1 Part 4 of FA 2004 (pension schemes etc) is amended as follows.

2 In section 172D(4)(b) (limit on increase in benefits), for "236" substitute "236A".

3 (1) Section 227 (annual allowance charge) is amended as follows.

(2) Omit subsections (2) and (3).

(3) In subsection (4), for "rate of 40%" substitute "appropriate rate".

(4) After that subsection insert—

"(4A) The appropriate rate is—

(a) the basic rate in relation to so much (if any) of the excess as, when added to the individual's reduced net income for the tax year, does not exceed the basic rate limit for the tax year,

(b) the higher rate in relation to so much (if any) of the excess as, when so added, exceeds the basic rate limit for the tax year but does not exceed the higher rate limit for the tax year, and

(c) the additional rate in relation to so much (if any) of the excess as, when so added, exceeds the higher rate limit for the tax year.

(4B) The individual's reduced net income for the tax year is the amount after taking Step 3 in section 23 of ITA 2007 in the case of the individual for the tax year.

(4C) Where the basic rate limit or the higher rate limit for the tax year is (in accordance with section 192 of this Act or section 414 of ITA 2007) increased in the case of the individual, the references to the limit in subsection (4A) are to the limit as so increased."

(5) Omit subsections (5A) and (5B).

(6) In subsection (6), after the entry relating to sections 230 to 237 (before the "and") insert—

"sections 237A to 237F (persons liable to charge),".

4 For section 228 substitute—

"228 Annual allowance

(1) The annual allowance for the tax year 2011–12 and, subject to subsection (2), each subsequent tax year is £50,000.

(2) The Treasury may by order provide that the annual allowance for any tax year subsequent to the tax year 2011–12 is such amount as is specified in the order."

5 After that section insert—

"228A Carry forward of unused annual allowance

(1) This section applies if the individual has unused annual allowance available for the tax year ("the current tax year").

(2) The annual allowance for the current tax year in the case of the individual is to be treated as increased by the amount of the unused annual allowance available for the current tax year.

(3) The individual has unused annual allowance available for the current tax year if—

(a) the amount of the annual allowance (before any increase under this section) for the immediately preceding tax year exceeded the total pension input amount in the case of the individual for that tax year, or

(b) the amount of the annual allowance (before any such increase) for either or both of the two tax years immediately preceding that immediately preceding tax year exceeded the total pension input amount in the case of the individual for the tax year concerned and the excess (or, where there is an excess for both of those tax years, the excess for both tax years) has not been used up,

or both.

(4) Subsection (3)—

(a) does not apply in relation to a tax year preceding the current tax year unless the individual was a member of a registered pension scheme at some time during that tax year, but

(b) subject to that, applies in relation to such a tax year even if the total pension input amount in the case of the individual for that tax year was nil (in which case the excess within paragraph (a) or (b) of that subsection is the whole amount of the annual allowance before any increase under this section).

(5) The amount of the unused annual allowance available for the current tax year is the aggregate of—

(a) any excess within subsection (3)(a), and

(b) so much of any excess within subsection (3)(b) as has not been used up.

(6) An amount of an excess within subsection (3)(b) for a tax year has been "used up" if—

(a) for a tax year falling between that tax year and the current tax year (an "intervening tax year"), the total pension input amount in the case of the individual exceeded the annual allowance (apart from any increase under this section), and

(b) the amount of the excess had effect by virtue of this section to reduce (or eliminate) the annual allowance charge for the intervening tax year in the case of the individual.

(7) In calculating for the purposes of subsection (6) the amount of which of the excesses for different tax years had effect to reduce or eliminate the annual allowance charge for an intervening tax year, an amount of the excess for an earlier tax year is to be taken to have done so before that for a later tax year."

6 (1) Section 229 (total pension input amount) is amended as follows.

(2) In subsection (2)(c), for "236" substitute "236A".

(3) In subsection (3), for paragraph (a) substitute—

"(a) satisfies the severe ill-health condition, or".

(4) After that subsection insert—

"(4) For the purposes of subsection (3)(a) the individual satisfies the severe ill-health condition if the individual—

(a) becomes entitled to all the benefits to which the individual is entitled under the arrangement in consequence of the scheme administrator having received evidence from a registered medical practitioner that the individual is suffering from ill-health which makes the individual unlikely to be able (otherwise than to an insignificant extent) to undertake gainful work (in any capacity) before reaching pensionable age,

(b) becomes entitled to a serious ill-health lump sum under the arrangement, or

(c) is a member of the armed forces of the Crown who becomes entitled under the arrangement to a benefit on which no liability to income tax arises by virtue of section 641(1) of ITEPA 2003."

7 (1) Section 230 (cash balance arrangements) is amended as follows.

(2) In subsection (4), for "beginning of the pension input period" substitute "end of the immediately preceding pension input period (or is nil if the pension input period is the first pension input period of the arrangement)".

(3) After subsection (5) insert—

"(5A) If, during the pension input period, minimum payments are made under—

(a) section 8 of the Pension Schemes Act 1993, or

(b) section 4 of the Pension Schemes (Northern Ireland) Act 1993,

in relation to the individual in connection with the arrangement, their amount is to be subtracted from what would otherwise be the pension input amount in the case of the individual in respect of the arrangement.

(5B) The pension input amount in respect of the arrangement is nil if—

(a) the individual is a deferred member of the pension scheme under which it is an arrangement (or would be if it were the only arrangement under the pension scheme relating to the individual) throughout the pension input period or is (or would be) such a deferred member for part of the pension input period and a pensioner member for the rest of it, and

(b) the value of the relevant rights of the individual does not increase during the pension input period by more than the relevant percentage.

(5C) In this section—

"guaranteed minimum pension" has the meaning given by—

(a) section 8(2) of the Pension Schemes Act 1993, or

(b) section 4(2) of the Pension Schemes (Northern Ireland) Act 1993;

"predecessor arrangement", in relation to an arrangement, means another arrangement (under the same or another registered pension scheme) from which some or all of the sums or assets held for the purposes of the arrangement directly or indirectly derive;

"predecessor registered pension scheme", in relation to a pension scheme, means another registered pension scheme from which some or all of the sums or assets held for the purposes of the arrangement under the pension scheme directly or indirectly derive;

"the relevant percentage"—

(a) where throughout the pension input period the arrangement (or a predecessor arrangement) includes provision for the value of the relevant rights of the individual to increase at an annual rate specified in the rules of the pension scheme (or a predecessor registered pension scheme) on 14 October 2010, that percentage, and

(b) otherwise, the percentage by which the consumer prices index for a month falling within the pension input period and nominated by the scheme administrator is higher than it was for the same month in the previous period of 12 months (or nil per cent if it is not higher);

"the relevant rights of the individual" means rights of the individual under the arrangement, other than any rights to a guaranteed minimum pension;

"specified", in relation to an annual rate, means specified as a percentage figure or as a percentage produced by movement in an index (or a combination of the two) but does not include a percentage produced by the exercise of a discretion by any person."

8 In section 231 (cash balance arrangements: uprating of opening value), for subsection (3) substitute—

"(3) The appropriate percentage is the percentage (if any) by which the consumer prices index for the September before the start of the tax year is higher than it was for the previous September."

9 (1) Section 232 (cash balance arrangements: adjustments of closing value) is amended as follows.

(2) In subsection (2), for "the debit" substitute "the reduction".

(3) In subsection (3), for "the credit" substitute "the increase".

(4) In subsection (4)—

(a) for "Subsection (5) applies if" substitute "If",

(b) for "virtue of a transfer of any sum or asset" substitute "reason of a transfer relating to the individual of any sums or assets",

(c) omit "other", and

(d) insert at the end (not as part of paragraph (b)) "the amount of the reduction is to be added."

(5) Omit subsection (5).

(6) In subsection (6)—

(a) for "Subsection (7) applies if" substitute "If",

(b) for "virtue of a transfer" substitute "reason of a transfer relating to the individual", and

(c) insert at the end ", the amount of the increase is to be subtracted."

(7) Omit subsection (7).

(8) For subsection (8) substitute—

"(8) If, during the pension input period, the rights of the individual under the arrangement have been reduced by any surrender made, or similar action taken, pursuant to an option available to the individual under the arrangement, the amount of the reduction is to be added.

(8A) If, during the pension input period—

(a) benefit crystallisation event 1, 2 or 4 occurs in relation to the individual and the arrangement,

(b) benefit crystallisation event 3 occurs in relation to the individual and the arrangement otherwise than by reason of a provision contained in, or made under, any enactment,

(c) benefit crystallisation event 6 occurs or, but for paragraph 15A of Schedule 32, would occur in relation to the individual and the arrangement by virtue of the individual becoming entitled to a pension commencement lump sum or a lifetime allowance excess lump sum, or

(d) there is an allocation of rights of the individual under the arrangement (not falling within paragraph (a)),

the relevant amount is to be added.

(8B) In subsection (8A) "the relevant amount" is—

(a) in the case of benefit crystallisation event 2, what the annual rate of the pension would be on the valuation assumptions,
(b) in the case of benefit crystallisation event 3, the increase in the annual rate of the pension,
(c) in the case of benefit crystallisation event 6, the amount of the lump sum, and
(d) in any other case, the amount of the reduction in the amount of the rights available for the provision of benefits to or in respect of the individual occurring by reason of the benefit crystallisation event or allocation.

(8C) If, during the pension input period, an adjustment to the individual's rights under the arrangement is made in consequence of the scheme administrator satisfying a liability under section 237B in respect of the individual, if and to the extent that the adjustment is reflected in the closing amount the amount of the adjustment is to be added to the closing amount.

(8D) But no amount is to be added under subsection (8C) by reason of an adjustment made in consequence of the scheme administrator satisfying a liability under section 237B in a case where subsection (6) of that section applied."

(9) Omit subsection (9).

10 (1) Section 234 (defined benefits arrangements) is amended as follows.

(2) In subsection (4)—

(a) for "10" substitute "16",
(b) in the definition of PB, for "beginning of the pension input period" substitute "end of the immediately preceding pension input period (or is nil if the pension input period is the first pension input period of the arrangement)", and
(c) in the definition of LSB, for "that time" substitute "the end of the immediately preceding pension input period (or is nil if the pension input period is the first pension input period of the arrangement)".

(3) In subsection (5), for "10" substitute "16".

(4) After that subsection insert—

"(5A) If, during the pension input period, minimum payments are made under—

(a) section 8 of the Pension Schemes Act 1993, or
(b) section 4 of the Pension Schemes (Northern Ireland) Act 1993,

in relation to the individual in connection with the arrangement, their amount is to be subtracted from what would otherwise be the pension input amount in the case of the individual in respect of the arrangement.

(5B) The pension input amount in respect of the arrangement is nil if—

(a) the individual is a deferred member of the pension scheme under which it is an arrangement (or would be if it were the only arrangement under the pension scheme relating to the individual) throughout the pension input period or is (or would be) such a deferred member for part of the pension input period and a pensioner member for the rest of it, and
(b) the value of the relevant rights of the individual does not increase during the pension input period by more than the relevant percentage.

(5C) In this section—

"guaranteed minimum pension" has the meaning given by—

(a) section 8(2) of the Pension Schemes Act 1993, or
(b) section 4(2) of the Pension Schemes (Northern Ireland) Act 1993;

"predecessor arrangement", in relation to an arrangement, means another arrangement (under the same or another registered pension scheme) from which some or all of the sums or assets held for the purposes of the arrangement directly or indirectly derive;

"predecessor registered pension scheme", in relation to a pension scheme, means another registered pension scheme from which some or all of the sums or assets held for the purposes of the arrangement under the pension scheme directly or indirectly derive;

"the relevant percentage"—

(a) where throughout the pension input period the arrangement (or a predecessor arrangement) includes provision for the value of the relevant rights of the individual to increase at an annual rate specified in the rules of the pension scheme (or a predecessor registered pension scheme) on 14 October 2010, that percentage, and

(b) otherwise, the percentage by which the consumer prices index for a month falling within the pension input period and nominated by the scheme administrator is higher than it was for the same month in the previous period of 12 months (or nil per cent if it is not higher);

"the relevant rights of the individual" means rights of the individual under the arrangement, other than any rights to a guaranteed minimum pension;

"specified", in relation to an annual rate, means specified as a percentage figure or as a percentage produced by movement in an index (or a combination of the two) but does not include a percentage produced by the exercise of a discretion by any person."

(5) In subsection (6), for "and section 236 (adjustments of closing value)" substitute ", section 236 (adjustments of closing value) and section 236A (post-entitlement enhancements)".

11 (1) Section 235 (defined benefits arrangements: uprating of opening value) is amended as follows.

(2) In subsection (1), omit "in a case where rights do not accrue to the individual under the arrangement during the pension input period".

(3) For subsection (3) substitute—

"(3) The appropriate percentage is the percentage (if any) by which the consumer prices index for the September before the start of the tax year is higher than it was for the previous September."

12 (1) Section 236 (defined benefits arrangements: adjustments of closing value) is amended as follows.

(2) In subsection (1), for "the closing value of the individual's rights as calculated" substitute "PE and LSE".

(3) In subsection (2)—

(a) for "rights of the individual under the arrangement have" substitute "annual rate of the pension, or the amount of the lump sum, to which the individual would be entitled under the arrangement has",
(b) for "the debit" substitute "the reduction", and
(c) insert at the end "to PE or LSE".

(4) In subsection (3)—

(a) for "rights of the individual under the arrangement have" substitute "annual rate of the pension, or the amount of the lump sum, to which the individual would be entitled under the arrangement has",
(b) for "the credit" substitute "the increase", and
(c) insert at the end "from PE or LSE".

(5) For subsections (4) to (7) substitute—

"(4) If, during the pension input period, the annual rate of the pension, or the amount of the lump sum, to which the individual would be entitled under the arrangement has been reduced by reason of a transfer relating to the individual of any sums or assets held for the purposes of, or representing accrued rights under, the arrangement so as to become held for the purposes of, or to represent rights under, any pension scheme that is—

(a) a registered pension scheme, or
(b) a qualifying recognised overseas pension scheme,

the amount of the reduction is to be added to PE or LSE.

(5) If, during the pension input period, the annual rate of the pension, or the amount of the lump sum, to which the individual would be entitled under the arrangement has been increased by reason of a transfer relating to the individual of any sums or assets held for the purposes of, or representing accrued rights under, any pension scheme so as to become held for the purposes of, or to represent rights under, the arrangement, the amount of the increase is to be subtracted from PE or LSE."

(6) For subsection (8) substitute—

"(8) If, during the pension input period, the annual rate of the pension, or the amount of the lump sum, to which the individual would be entitled under the arrangement has been reduced by any surrender made in return for any other entitlement, any allocation made, or any similar action taken, pursuant to an option available to the individual under the arrangement, the amount of the reduction (to the extent that it is not reflected in an amount added under subsection (8A)) is to be added to PE or LSE.

(8A) If, during the pension input period—

(a) benefit crystallisation event 2 occurs in relation to the individual and the arrangement,

(b) benefit crystallisation event 3 occurs in relation to the individual and the arrangement otherwise than by reason of a provision contained in, or made under, any enactment, or

(c) benefit crystallisation event 6 occurs in relation to the individual and the arrangement by virtue of the individual becoming entitled to a pension commencement lump sum or a lifetime allowance excess lump sum,

the relevant amount is to be added to PE or LSE.

(8B) In subsection (8A) "the relevant amount" is—

(a) in the case of benefit crystallisation event 2, the annual rate of the pension to which the individual became entitled,

(b) in the case of benefit crystallisation event 3, the increase in the annual rate of the pension, and

(c) in the case of benefit crystallisation event 6, the amount of the lump sum.

(8C) If, during the pension input period, an adjustment to the annual rate of the pension, or the amount of the lump sum, to which the individual would be entitled under the arrangement has been made in consequence of the scheme administrator satisfying a liability under section 237B in respect of the individual, if and to the extent that the adjustment is reflected in PE or LSE the amount of the adjustment is to be added to PE or LSE.

(8D) But no amount is to be added under subsection (8C) by reason of an adjustment made in consequence of the scheme administrator satisfying a liability under section 237B in a case where subsection (6) of that section applied."

(7) Omit subsection (9).

13 After section 236 insert—

"236A Post-entitlement enhancements

(1) This section applies in relation to the arrangement if, during the pension input period ("the affected pension input period"), the individual enters into a scheme for the making of an avoidance-inspired post-entitlement enhancement.

(2) A "post-entitlement enhancement" is an increase in the annual rate of a scheme pension under the arrangement, at a time after the member has become entitled to the scheme pension.

(3) A post-entitlement enhancement is "avoidance-inspired" if the main purpose, or one of the main purposes, of the individual in entering into the scheme was to avoid or reduce a liability to the annual allowance charge.

(4) This Part has effect in relation to the arrangement and the individual, as respects the affected pension input period and all subsequent pension input periods, as if—

(a) section 234 were modified in accordance with subsection (5), and

(b) sections 235 and 236 were omitted.

(5) The modifications of section 234 are that—

(a) in subsection (4), for the words after "the arrangement is" there are substituted "such amount as, applying normal actuarial practice, is the expected cost of giving effect to the individual's rights under the arrangement at the end of the immediately preceding pension input period (or is nil if the pension input period is the first pension input period of the arrangement).",

(b) in subsection (5), for the words after "the arrangement is" there are substituted "such amount as, applying normal actuarial practice, is the expected cost of giving effect to the individual's rights under the arrangement at the end of the pension input period.", and

(c) subsection (6) is omitted.

(6) In this section "scheme" includes any arrangements, agreement, understanding, transaction or series of transactions (whether or not legally enforceable)."

14 In subsection (5) of section 237 (hybrid arrangements), for "236" substitute "236A".

15 After that section insert—

"237A Liability of individual

(1) The individual is liable to the annual allowance charge.

(2) The individual is liable to the annual allowance charge whether or not—

(a) the individual, and

(b) the scheme administrator of the pension scheme or pension schemes concerned,

are resident, ordinarily resident or domiciled in the United Kingdom.

237B Liability of scheme administrator

(1) This section applies if—

(a) the amount of the individual's liability to the annual allowance charge for a tax year exceeds £2,000, and

(b) the pension scheme input amount in the case of the individual in relation to a registered pension scheme for the tax year exceeds the amount of the annual allowance specified in section 228(1) for the tax year.

(2) The pension scheme input amount in the case of the individual in relation to a pension scheme for a tax year is the aggregate of the pension input amounts for the tax year in respect of arrangements relating to the individual under the pension scheme.

(3) The individual may give a notice to the scheme administrator of the pension scheme specifying that the individual and the scheme administrator are to be jointly and severally liable in respect of so much of the annual allowance charge arising in the case of the individual as—

(a) does not exceed the amount of the annual allowance charge which would be chargeable on the excess mentioned in subsection (1)(b) if it were charged at the relevant rate, and

(b) is specified in the notice,

("the joint liability amount").

(4) In subsection (3)(a) "the relevant rate" means—

(a) in relation to so much of the excess as does not exceed the amount (if any) on which tax is chargeable in the case of the individual for the tax year at the additional rate by virtue of paragraph (c) of subsection (4A) of section 227, the additional rate,

(b) in relation to so much of the excess as is not within paragraph (a) and does not exceed the amount (if any) on which tax is so chargeable at the higher rate by virtue of paragraph (b) of that subsection, the higher rate, and

(c) in relation to any remaining part of the excess, the basic rate.

(5) The notice—

(a) must be given not later than 31 July in the year following that in which the tax year ends (but subject to subsection (6)),

(b) must be made in such manner and form, and contain such particulars, as may be prescribed by regulations made by the Commissioners for Her Majesty's Revenue and Customs, and

(c) may be amended by giving the scheme administrator notice in accordance with provision made by regulations made by the Commissioners for Her Majesty's Revenue and Customs but may not be revoked.

(6) In a case in which the individual becomes actually entitled to all of the individual's benefits under the pension scheme in the tax year or benefit crystallisation event 5, 5A or 5B occurs in the tax year in relation to the individual and the pension scheme, the notice must be given before the date on which the individual becomes so entitled or the benefit crystallisation event occurs.

(7) On receipt by the scheme administrator of the notice the scheme administrator and the individual become jointly and severally liable to pay the joint liability amount, but subject to sections 237C and 237D and to any amendment made to the notice in accordance with regulations under subsection (5)(c).

(8) The scheme administrator is liable under subsection (7) whether or not—

(a) the individual, and

(b) the scheme administrator,

are resident, ordinarily resident or domiciled in the United Kingdom.

(9) Where (but for this subsection) a notice could be given to a scheme administrator of a pension scheme but, before it is given, there is a transfer of all of the sums or assets—

(a) held for the purposes of, or
(b) representing accrued rights under,

the pension scheme so as to become held for the purposes of, or to represent rights under, another registered pension scheme, the notice may not be given to that scheme administrator but may instead be given to the scheme administrator of that other pension scheme.

(10) The Treasury may by regulations make provision modifying the operation of this section in other cases in which there is a transfer of any of the sums or assets—

(a) held for the purposes of, or
(b) representing accrued rights under,

the pension scheme so as to become held for the purposes of, or to represent rights under, another registered pension scheme.

(11) The Treasury may by order amend paragraph (a) of subsection (1) so as to increase the sum for the time being specified in that paragraph.

237C Exceptions

(1) The scheme administrator of a pension scheme does not become liable under section 237B if the time when the scheme administrator would become liable is during an assessment period in relation to the pension scheme; and if an assessment period in relation to a pension scheme begins at a time when the scheme administrator is already so liable (but has not satisfied the liability), the liability ceases when the assessment period begins.

References to an assessment period are to be construed in accordance with sections 132 and 159 of the Pensions Act 2004 and articles 116 and 143 of the Pensions (Northern Ireland) Order 2005 (SI 2005/255 (NI 1)).

(2) The scheme administrator of a pension scheme is not liable under section 237B in respect of any amount if there is no power to make a consequential adjustment to the entitlement of the individual concerned to benefits under the pension scheme in respect of the amount because of section 237E(2) (inalienability of guaranteed minimum pension etc).

(3) The Treasury may by regulations prescribe other circumstances in which a scheme administrator of a pension scheme does not become, or ceases to be, liable under section 237B.

237D Discharge of scheme administrator's liability

(1) If the scheme administrator of a pension scheme is liable under section 237B, the scheme administrator may apply to an officer of Revenue and Customs for the discharge of the scheme administrator's liability on either of the following grounds.

(2) The grounds are—

(a) that paying the amount to which the scheme administrator is liable would be to the substantial detriment of the interests of the members of the pension scheme, and

(b) that in all the circumstances of the case it would not be just and reasonable for the scheme administrator to be liable to that amount.

(3) On receiving an application under subsection (1), an officer of Revenue and Customs must decide whether to discharge the scheme administrator's liability.

(4) An officer of Revenue and Customs must notify the scheme administrator of the decision on the application.

(5) The discharge of the scheme administrator's liability does not affect the liability of any other person in respect of the same amount.

(6) The Treasury may by regulations amend this section so as to alter the grounds on which an application under subsection (1) may be made.

(7) Regulations made by the Commissioners for Her Majesty's Revenue and Customs may make provision supplementing this section; and the regulations may in particular make provision as to the time limits for the making of an application.

237E Consequential benefit adjustments to be reasonable etc

(1) Where the scheme administrator of a pension scheme satisfies a liability under section 237B in respect of the individual, consequential adjustment must be made to the entitlement of the individual to benefits under the pension scheme on a basis that is just and reasonable having regard to normal actuarial practice.

(2) Any power to make such consequential adjustment is subject to section 159 of the Pension Schemes Act 1993 or section 155 of the Pension Schemes (Northern Ireland) Act 1993 (inalienability of guaranteed minimum pension etc).

237F Power to modify rules

The Commissioners for Her Majesty's Revenue and Customs may by regulations make any modification of the rules of registered pension schemes that appear appropriate to facilitate the operation of sections 237A to 237E."

16 (1) Section 238 (pension input period) is amended as follows.

(2) In subsection (1)(a), for the words after "ending with" substitute

"—

(i) a nominated date falling before the anniversary of the relevant commencement date, or

(ii) if there is not such a nominated date, the first 5 April after the relevant commencement date (or, if the relevant commencement date is itself 5 April, that date), and"

(3) After subsection (4) insert—

"(4A) A date nominated for the purposes of subsection (3) must not be a date before that on which the nomination is made."

(4) In subsection (6)—

(a) omit "the earlier of",

(b) for "and" substitute "or", and

(c) insert at the beginning of paragraph (b) "if there is not such a nominated date,".

(5) In subsection (7), for "to be treated as having ended when" substitute "that in which".

17 After that section insert—

"238A Power to make orders about charge

(1) The Treasury may by order make provision about the annual allowance charge.

(2) The provision may include modifications of any of sections 227 to 238.

(3) The provision may include provision consequential on, or supplementary or incidental to, the provision made by those sections and transitional provisions (including provision making modifications of enactments).

(4) "Modifications" includes amendments."

18 In section 254 (accounting for tax by scheme administrators), after subsection (7) insert—

"(7A) Where a scheme administrator is liable under section 237B in respect of the annual allowance charge for a tax year, for the purposes of subsection (2) the tax is to be taken to be charged on the scheme administrator in the period ending with 31 December in the year following that in which that tax year ended (or such earlier period as the scheme administrator may elect in a return for that earlier period).

(7B) But if the notice which gave rise to the liability is amended in accordance with regulations under section 237B(5)(c), any additional tax to which the scheme administrator becomes liable is to be taken for the purposes of subsection (2) to be charged in the later of the period in which it is taken to be charged by virtue of subsection (7A) and the period in which the scheme administrator receives notice of the amendment."

19 In section 255(1) (assessments), after paragraph (c) insert—

"(ca) liability to the annual allowance charge by virtue of section 237B,".

20 In section 269(1)(a) (appeal against discharge of liability), after "under" insert "section 237D (discharge of scheme administrator's liability to annual allowance charge),".

21 In section 279(1) (other definitions), insert at the appropriate places—

""consumer prices index" means—

(a) the general index for consumer prices published by the Statistics Board, or

(b) if that index is not published for a relevant month, any substituted index or index figures published by the Statistics Board,", and

""pensionable age" has the meaning given by the rules in paragraph 1 of Schedule 4 to the Pensions Act 1995 or paragraph 1 of Schedule 2 to the Pensions (Northern Ireland) Order 1995,".

22 In section 280(2) (general index), insert at the appropriate places—

"consumer prices index	section 279(1)", and
"pensionable age	section 279(1)".

23 In section 282(1A) (orders and regulations subject to Commons-only draft affirmative procedure)—

(a) for "227(5A)," substitute "237B(11),", and

(b) after "242(5)" insert ", no order may be made under section 228(2) which specifies an amount for any tax year less than the annual allowance for the immediately preceding tax year and no order may be made under section 238A which increases any person's liability to tax".

24 (1) Schedule 34 (currently-relieved non-UK pension schemes etc) is amended as follows.

(2) In paragraph 8(1), after "a currently-relieved non-UK pension scheme" insert "and its scheme manager".

(3) After paragraph 9 insert—

"**9A** (1) This paragraph applies where an individual—

(a) is a currently-relieved member of a currently-relieved non-UK pension scheme in relation to a tax year, but

(b) was a member, but not a currently-relieved member, of the currently-relieved non-UK pension scheme in relation to any one or more of the 3 immediately preceding tax years (a "relevant tax year").

(2) Section 228A has effect in relation to the individual for the tax year as it would if the individual had been a currently-relieved member of the pension scheme for the relevant tax year (or each of the relevant tax years) and paragraphs 10 and 11 of this Schedule were omitted.

9B (1) This paragraph applies where an individual—

(a) is a member of a registered pension scheme in relation to a tax year, and

(b) was a currently-relieved member of a currently-relieved non-UK pension scheme in relation to any one or more of the 3 immediately preceding tax years (a "relevant tax year").

(2) Section 228A has effect in relation to the individual for the tax year as it would if the currently-relieved non-UK pension scheme had been a registered pension scheme for the relevant tax year (or each of the relevant tax years)."

(4) In paragraph 12(1), after "a currently-relieved non-UK pension scheme" insert "and its scheme manager".

25 In Schedule 36 (transitional provision etc), omit paragraph 49 (disapplication of annual allowance charge for individuals with enhanced protection) and the heading before it.

26 (1) In FA 2009—

(a) in Schedule 2, omit paragraph 15, and

(b) in Schedule 35, omit paragraph 22.

(2) In the Registered Pension Schemes (Standard Lifetime and Annual Allowances) Order 2010 (SI 2010/922), omit article 3.

PART 2

COMMENCEMENT AND TRANSITIONAL PROVISION

27 (1) The amendments made by Part 1 have effect for the tax year 2011–12 and subsequent tax years.

(2) Apart from the amendments made by paragraph 16(2) and (4), such of the amendments as apply in relation to pension input periods have effect in relation to pension input periods ending in the tax year 2011–12 but beginning earlier (as well as those beginning in that tax year).

28 (1) This paragraph applies where—

(a) the pension input period in respect of any arrangement relating to the individual which ends in the tax year 2011–12 begins before 14 October 2010 (a "straddling pension input period"), and

(b) the total pension input amount in the case of the individual for that tax year exceeds £50,000.

(2) The following provisions apply for arriving at the amount in respect of which the annual allowance charge is charged for that tax year (instead of the charge being in respect of the amount by which the total pension input amount exceeds the amount of the annual allowance).

(3) Treat each straddling pension input period as if it were 2 separate pension input periods—

(a) one beginning when the straddling pension input period begins and ending with 13 October 2010 (a "pre-announcement period"), and

(b) the other beginning with 14 October 2010 and ending when the straddling pension input period ends (a "post-announcement period").

And treat any pension input period in respect of any arrangement relating to the individual which ends in the tax year 2011–12 which is not a straddling pension input period as if it were a post-announcement period.

(4) Arrive at the pension input amount in respect of each post-announcement period (as if it were a pension input period ending in the tax year 2011–12) and aggregate those amounts.

(5) Deduct £50,000 from that aggregate.

(6) Arrive at the pension input amount in respect of each pre-announcement period (as if it were a pension input period ending in the tax year 2011–12) and aggregate those amounts.

(7) Deduct from that aggregate the difference between £255,000 and the lesser of—

(a) £50,000, and

(b) the aggregate arrived at under sub-paragraph (4).

The result (or, if a negative amount, nil) is the pre-announcement periods total.

(8) Aggregate the post-announcement periods total and the pre-announcement periods total.

(9) Deduct any amount by which (apart from this paragraph) the annual allowance in the case of the individual for the tax year would have been increased by virtue of section 228A of FA 2004 or, if less, by so much of any such amount as equals that aggregate.

(10) Any result is the amount in respect of which the annual allowance charge is charged for the tax year 2011–12.

29 Where paragraph 28 applies in the case of the individual, section 228A of FA 2004 has effect in the case of the individual for tax years subsequent to the tax year 2011–12—

(a) as if the references in subsections (3)(a) and (b) of that section to the amount of the annual allowance for that tax year were to £50,000, and

(b) as if any amount deducted under sub-paragraph (9) of that paragraph had been "used-up" within the meaning of that section.

30 (1) This paragraph has effect in relation to the application of section 228A of FA 2004 for the tax years 2011–12, 2012–13 and 2013–14.

(2) The assumptions in sub-paragraph (3) are to be made in determining—

(a) whether the amount of the annual allowance for the tax years 2008–09, 2009–10 and 2010–11 exceeded the total pension input amount in the case of the individual for the tax year, and

(b) whether any excess of the annual allowance over the total pension input amount in the case of the individual for any of those tax years has been used up.

(3) The assumptions are—

(a) that the annual allowance for each of the tax years 2008–09, 2009–10 and 2010–11 was £50,000, and

(b) that the provisions of Part 4 of FA 2004 apply in relation to pension input periods in respect of arrangements relating to the individual that end in any of those tax years subject to the amendments made by this Schedule (including that inserting section 228A).

31 In determining under section 233 of FA 2004 the pension input amount in respect of an arrangement relating to an individual for a pension input period of the arrangement that ends in the tax year 2009–10, 2010–11 or 2011–12, there is to be deducted from what would otherwise be the pension input amount so much of any contributions refund lump sum (within the meaning of paragraph 15 of Schedule 35 to FA 2009) paid to the individual (or the personal representatives of the individual) as is attributable to contributions paid under the arrangement in the pension input period.

32 Section 237B has effect in relation to the tax year 2011–12 as if the reference in subsection (5)(a) of that section to 31 July in the year following that in which the tax year ends were to 31 December 2013.

33 Section 254(7A) has effect in relation to the tax year 2011–12 as if the reference in that provision to 31 December in the year following that in which the tax year ends were to 31 March 2014.

34 Expressions used in this Part of this Schedule and Part 4 of FA 2004 have the same meaning in this Part of this Schedule as in that Part of that Act.

GENERAL NOTE

The previous Chancellor's Pre Budget Report of 9 December 2009 indicated that the restrictions on tax relief at the higher rate for the tax year 2011–12 in respect of contributions to pension schemes should apply as fairly as possible between individuals in different types of pension schemes and employment, and with different remuneration arrangements, whilst remaining targeted on those on the highest incomes. The former Government announced that the restrictions would apply to those with gross incomes over £150,000 where gross income incorporated all pension contributions, including the value of any pension benefit funded by an individual's employer. This would be subject to an income floor such that those with pre-tax incomes, excluding the value of any employer contributions, of less than £130,000 would be unaffected. Individuals with incomes at or above this level would need to establish the value of the pension benefit funded by their employer. A taper would apply for those on gross incomes between £150,000 and £180,000 gradually reducing tax relief on pension contributions until it was restricted to the basic rate. The restriction on relief on pension contributions would be set at a rate determined according to where individuals lay on the taper.

The former Government consulted on its proposed changes and in particular on the valuation method to be used for employers' contributions to final salary pension schemes to ensure consistent treatment in restricting tax relief for individuals across money purchase and final salary schemes. Following this consultation FA 2010 s 23 introduced legislation in Sch 2 to restrict tax relief given at above the basic rate on pension contributions for 2011–12 et seq by high income individuals. This legislation was subject to widespread criticism because it was extremely complicated, lengthy (it was accompanied by over 80 pages of guidelines) and difficult to understand. In his Emergency Budget of 22 June 2010 the current Chancellor stated that the approach legislated for in FA 2010 could have unwelcome consequences for pension saving, bring significant complexity to the tax system and damage UK business and competitiveness. He suggested an alternative approach involving reform of the existing annual allowance, perhaps significantly reduced, might better meet the new Government's objectives. The new Government conducted a review of the legislation in FA 2010 Sch 2 in consultation with employers, pension schemes, experts and other interested parties to determine the best design of a regime for raising the same tax revenue by simpler means. Meanwhile F (No. 2) A 2010 s 5 contained provisions to repeal the legislation in FA 2010 Sch 2 should the new Government later consider it appropriate. The review was completed in October 2010 and draft legislation published thereafter for further comment. Following more refinement the legislation now appears in Sch 17 and the repeal of FA 2020 s 6 and Sch 2 has been confirmed by Treasury Order on 10 December 2010. The key features of the new rules for restricting tax relief on pension contributions from 6 April 2011 are the reduction of the annual allowance for 2011–12 from £255,000 to £50,000, the anti-forestalling rules to minimise tax relief that were introduced in April 2009 will still apply for 2010–11, any unused annual allowance from the three previous years can be carried forward to offset provision in the current tax year, and although tax relief on contributions will be at the individual's highest marginal rate an annual allowance tax charge will recover the full marginal rate received. From 2011–12 the annual allowance charge will apply in the year in which pension benefits are drawn except where the benefits are in the form of a serious or severe ill-health lump sum and will also apply to those individuals who have enhanced protection under FA 2004 Sch 36 para 12.

Additionally, in October 2010 the Government announced it was considering options to enable individuals to meet the annual allowance charge out of their pension benefits rather than current income. In November 2010 the Government published a discussion document on the subject, Options to meet high annual allowance charges from pension benefits: a discussion document, inviting views on two broad options:

payment from pension benefits at the point the charge arises; or payment at the point the pension benefit crystallises. The main purpose of this exercise was to establish which of the two broad options better met the Government's objectives and how it would work in practice. Consultation on this concluded on 7 January 2011. As a result schedule 17 contains legislation that from 6 April 2011 will allow individuals to elect for their pension scheme to pay their annual allowance charge out of their pension benefits. This election will be subject to certain qualifying conditions and exceptions.

PART 1

Paragraph 1 introduces the amendments in schedule 17 to Part 4 FA 2004 regarding the changes to the annual allowance charge.

Paragraph 2 amends FA 2004 s 172D(4)(b) to refer to FA 2004 s 236A introduced by para 13 below.

Paragraph 3 amends FA 2004 s 227 by deleting s 227(2) and (3), which deals with an individual's liability to the annual allowance charge, and providing that the charge is to be met at the appropriate rate instead of 40 per cent. The amendments in para 3(4) set out how to calculate the appropriate rate and link the rate of the annual allowance charge to the top slice of an individual's income to reflect the rate of tax relief that was given on the pension saving. The amendments also define reduced net income as used in working out the appropriate rate to be used for the annual allowance charge and provide that where the basic and higher rate bands are increased, the new increased band applies for the purposes of working out the appropriate rate. Paragraph 3(5) removes FA 2004 s 227(5A) and (5B) which provides a power to make orders to vary the rate of the annual allowance charge and for there to be different rates in different circumstances. Paragraph 3(6) makes an amendment to refer to FA 2004 ss 237A to 237F introduced by para 15 below regarding persons liable to the annual allowance charge.

Paragraph 4 replaces FA 2004 s 228 by setting the level of the annual allowance for 2011–12 and subsequent years at £50,000. The amendment also provides the power to amend the annual allowance in future years by Treasury Order.

Paragraph 5 inserts new FA 2004 s 228A. This provides for any unused annual allowance for the three tax years preceding the current tax year to be added to the annual allowance for the current tax year to determine whether an annual allowance charge applies for the current year. Unused annual allowances are only available for carry forward where they arise during a tax year in which an individual is a member of a registered pension scheme, but applies to a tax year even if the pension input amount for that year is nil. The earlier year's unused allowance is to be set off against the current year before that of the later year.

Paragraph 6 amends FA 2004 s 229 regarding the total pension input amount. The amendments provide for the pension input amount to be treated as nil under an arrangement in a tax year where the individual satisfies the severe ill-health condition. This condition is that the individual is unable to work again in any gainful capacity before reaching pensionable age except to an insufficient extent or becomes entitled to a serious ill-health lump sum under the arrangement or to a tax-free benefit provided as compensation to a member of the armed forces by reason of illness or injury.

Paragraph 7 amends FA 2004 s 230 regarding cash balance arrangements. The amendments provide for the measure of the opening right of such an arrangement to be by reference to the previous closing value of the individual's rights under the arrangement for the previous pension input period. The pension input amount relating to a cash balance arrangement does not include minimum payments or amounts recovered under Pension Schemes Act 1993 s 8 or Pension Schemes (Northern Ireland) Act 1993 s 4. The pension input amount is treated as nil in a tax year where the individual is a deferred member or a deferred member for part of the year and a pensioner member for the remainder and the value of their relevant rights in that arrangement does not increase by more than the relevant percentage. Definitions are provided for the various terms introduced by the new legislation inserted in FA 2004 s 230 by these amendments.

Paragraph 8 amends FA 2004 s 231(3) so that the opening value of an individual's rights under a cash balance arrangement is increased by the annual percentage increase in the consumer prices index for September in the previous tax year.

Paragraph 9 amends FA 2004 s 232 regarding adjustments to the closing value of cash balance arrangements. The amount of any adjustment is calculated by reference to the amount of the annual rate of the pension that has been reduced or increased by a transfer in or out, a reduction or increase in pension, a surrender of rights or a benefit crystallisation event. Any consequential adjustment made to an individual's rights because the scheme pays the individual's annual allowance charge is added to the closing value of the individual's pension savings. This ensures that members of final salary or cash balance and money purchase schemes are treated fairly in comparison with one another.

FA 2004 s 234 is amended by para 10 regarding final salary arrangements. Paragraph 10(2) provides for the opening value of a final salary arrangement to be adjusted by a factor of 16, instead of 10 as previously, when calculating the pension input amount. It also provides for the opening value of an individual's rights under the arrangement to be measured by reference to the previous closing value of those rights for the previous pension input period. Paragraph 10(3) provides for the closing value of a final salary arrangement to be adjusted also by a factor of 16, instead of 10 as previously, when calculating the pension input amount. The amendments in para 10(4) ensure that the pension input amount relating to a final salary pension scheme does not include minimum payments or amounts recovered under Pension Schemes Act 1993 s 8 or Pension Schemes (Northern Ireland) Act 1993 s 4. The pension input amount is treated as nil in a tax year where the individual is a deferred member or a deferred member for part of the year and a pensioner member for the remainder and the value of their relevant rights in the arrangement does not increase by more than the relevant percentage. Definitions are provided for the various terms introduced by the legislation inserted into FA 2004 s 234 by the amendments. Paragraph 10(5) inserts a reference into FA 2004 s 234(6) regarding new s 236A so that it supplements FA 2004 s 234.

Paragraph 11 amends FA 2004 s 235 regarding the uprating of opening values in final salary arrangements. The amendments provide for the opening value of an individual's rights under a final salary arrangement to be increased by the annual percentage increase in the consumer prices index for September in the previous tax year.

Paragraph 12 amends FA 2004 s 236 regarding adjustments to the closing value of final salary arrangements. The amendments provide for the closing value of an individual's rights under a final salary arrangement to be adjusted. The adjustment is calculated by reference to the annual rate of the pension that has been reduced or increased by a transfer in or out, a pension reduction, a surrender made in return for any other entitlement, or a benefit crystallisation event. Any consequential adjustment made to an individual's rights because the pension scheme pays the individual's annual allowance charge must be added to the closing value of the individual's pension savings. This ensures that members of final salary or cash balance and money purchase schemes are treated fairly in comparison with one another.

Paragraph 13 inserts FA 2004 s 236A regarding post-entitlement enhancements. This is a counter-measure which provides that the opening and closing values of an individual's annual rights in an arrangement are to be based on the cash equivalent value where they enter into a scheme for making a post-entitlement enhancement the main purpose of which is to avoid or reduce a liability to the annual allowance charge.

Paragraph 14 amends FA 2004 s 237(5) by substituting the reference to FA 2004 s 236 with a reference to FA 2004 s 236A so the new s is taken into account in calculating the pension input amount regarding hybrid arrangements.

Paragraph 15 inserts FA 2004 ss 237A–237E regarding liability to pay the annual allowance charge. Section 237A provides for an individual's liability to the annual allowance charge. Section 237B sets out the conditions that apply where the pension scheme administrator is liable to pay the annual allowance charge. Here an individual gives notice to the scheme administrator that the individual's annual allowance charge calculated by reference to their marginal rate of tax, defined in s 237(B4) as the relevant rate, is to be paid from their pension benefits. This is permitted provided the individual has an annual allowance charge of more than £2,000 and the total of the individual's pension input amounts for arrangements within that pension scheme exceeds the annual allowance. The individual can only give notice for the scheme administrator to pay an amount up to the amount by which their total pension input amount exceeds the annual allowance for that pension scheme. The notice must be given by the individual by 31 July of the year following the end of the tax year in which the annual allowance tax charge arises. So where an individual exceeds the annual allowance in the tax year 2012–13 the notice must be given by 31 July 2013. (This does not provide much opportunity for individuals to calculate their marginal rate of tax for the previous tax year as their self-assessment tax return does not have to be sent to HMRC until the following 31 January). The notice has to be given in the manner and form to be prescribed by regulations. It can be amended in accordance with provisions made by regulations, but not revoked. Any notice given in the year in which an individual becomes entitled to all the remaining benefits under the pension scheme or in relation to whom benefit crystallisation events 5, 5A or 5B occurred, has to be given before the date on which the individual becomes entitled to those benefits or the benefit crystallisation event occurred. Once the notice is received by the pension scheme administrator, the administrator and the individual are jointly and severally liable to pay the amount of the annual allowance charge specified in the notice whether or not they are both resident, ordinarily resident or domiciled in the UK, but subject to the exceptions in sections 237C and 237D (see below) and any amendments made to the notice. Individuals who transfer all their pension benefits to another pension scheme and who exceed the annual allowance in the transferring pension scheme, must give notice to the receiving scheme to meet their annual allowance charge. HM Treasury is given power to make regulations in the situation where there is a transfer of sums and assets from the pension scheme to another registered pension scheme. It is also empowered to make an Order increasing the £2,000 limit.

Section 237C of FA 2004 provides an exception for the pension scheme administrator to pay the annual allowance charge where the pension scheme concerned has already entered an assessment period for the Pension Protection Fund or does so after the individual has given notice, but before the pension scheme has been able to process the payment. Section 237C also provides that the scheme administrator is not liable to pay the annual allowance charge if it would result in a reduction to the benefits of the individual concerned below the amount of the statutory Guaranteed Minimum Pension. HM Treasury is given power to make regulations specifying other circumstances where the pension scheme administrator is not jointly and severally liable to pay the amount of the annual allowance charge specified in the notice.

Section 237D provides for the scheme administrator to apply to HMRC for the discharge of their liability to pay the annual allowance charge from an individual's pension benefits. The administrator has to demonstrate that to do so would be to the substantial detriment of the interests of the pension scheme's members or it would not be just and reasonable for the administrator to do so. HMRC has then to decide whether or not to discharge the scheme administrator's liability and must notify the administrator of their decision. If there is such a discharge, the individual remains liable for the amount of the annual allowance charge which is the subject of the notice. HM Treasury is given power to make regulations altering the grounds on which an application for the discharge of the scheme administrator's liability can be made and supplementing s 237D and setting time limits for making any application.

Section 237E provides that where the pension scheme administrator pays the annual allowance charge relating to an individual, consequential adjustment must be made to the individual's entitlement to benefits under the scheme on a just and reasonable basis. Such an adjustment cannot reduce an individual's pension rights below the amount that would provide the individual with their Guaranteed Minimum Pension under Pension Schemes Act 1993 s 159 or Pension Schemes (Northern Ireland) Act 1993 s 155.

Section 237F givers power to HMRC to make regulations modifying the rules of registered pension schemes as appropriate to facilitate the operation of sections 237A–237E.

FA 2004 s 238 is amended by para 16 regarding the pension input period. The amendments provide for the first pension input period to end on a nominated date before the anniversary of the commencement date. If there is no nominated date, the first pension input period ends on the first 5 April following the anniversary of the commencement date or 5 April if that is the commencement date. The nominated date cannot be before the date on which the nomination is made. Paragraph 16(4) provides for pension input periods other than the first pension input period to end on the anniversary of the date on which that period ended. Paragraph 16(5) provides that the final pension input period for an arrangement is the pension input period in which an individual becomes entitled to all the benefits to which they are entitled under the arrangement.

Paragraph 17 inserts s 238A into FA 2004 providing power for HM Treasury to make an Order about the annual allowance charge including modifications to FA 2004 ss 227 to 238.

Paragraph 18 amends FA 2004 s 254(7) regarding accounting for tax by pension scheme administrators. The amendments require scheme administrators to return the annual allowance charge specified in a notice given by an individual in the return from for the quarter ending 31 December of the year following the end of the tax year in which the annual allowance charge arises. So where an individual exceeds the annual allowance charge in 2012–13, the scheme administrator must account for the annual allowance charge in the return for the quarter ending 31 December 2013. If the notice has been amended, any additional tax to which the scheme administrator becomes liable is to be charged in the later of the period specified in FA 2004 s 237A and the period in which the scheme administrator receives notice of amendment.

Paragraph 19 amends FA 2004 s 255(1) by inserting a reference to liability to the annual allowance charge which contains a regulation-making power enabling provision to be made regarding assessments.

Paragraph 20 amends FA 2004 s 269(1)(a) to apply the appeal provisions in that s to decisions taken by HMRC in relation to discharging the pension scheme administrator's liability in accordance with FA 2004 s 237D (see para 15 above).

Paragraph 21 amends FA 2004 s 279(1) by inserting definitions of the consumer price index and pensionable age.

Paragraph 22 amends FA 2004 s 280(2) by inserting definitions of the consumer prices index and pensionable age into the general index covering the pensions tax regime legislation.

Paragraph 23 amends FA 2004 s 282(1A) which lists orders that must be made using the House of Commons affirmative procedure. The reference to the power to make orders varying the rate of the annual allowance in FA 2004 s 227(5A) is removed. Instead there is now a reference to the power contained in FA 2004 s 237B(11) to increase the £2,000 threshold for giving the pension scheme administrator a notice under that section. References to FA 2004 ss 228(2) and 238A are inserted so an order modifying the provisions relating to the annual allowance or varying the annual allowance, which has the effect of increasing a person's liability, must be made under the affirmative procedure.

FA 2004 Sch 34 is amended by para 24 regarding currently-relieved non-UK pension schemes. Paragraph 24(2) and (4) enables the application of joint liability to the annual allowance charge to apply to non-UK pension schemes. The amendments in para 24(3) provide for the carry forward of unused annual allowances by members of overseas pension schemes from years in which they were members of currently-relieved non-UK pension schemes whether or not they were resident in the UK at the time the contributions were made or benefit accrual arose. They also provide for the carry forward of unused annual allowances by members of registered pension schemes for years in which they were members of currently-relieved non-UK pension schemes whether or not they were resident in the UK at the time the contributions were made or the benefits arose.

Paragraph 25 deletes FA 2004 Sch 36 para 49 which disapplies the annual allowance charge for individuals with enhanced protection.

Paragraph 26 removes material which becomes redundant as the rules which it introduced are repealed.

PART 2

Paragraph 27 provides that Sch17 has effect from 2011–12 and for pension input periods that end in 2011–12.

Paragraph 28 provides for transitional provisions to apply in arriving at the amount of the annual allowance charge for 2011–12, where a pension input period ends in 2011–12 and begins before 14 October 2010 (the date when the changes were announced) and the total input amount for that tax year exceeds £50,000. There will be two separate pension input periods for 2011–12, a pre-announcement and post-announcement period, where the pension input period ends in 2011–12 and begins before 14 October 2010. Any other pension input period which ends in 2011–12 is a post-announcement period. To determine an individual's pre-announcement periods' total, the aggregate pension input amount for each pre-announcement period is taken with the value of any rights under a final salary arrangement calculated using a factor of 10 (see para 10 above). From this is deducted the difference between £255,000 and the lesser of £50,000 and the aggregate of the pension input periods for each post-announcement period. The amount of the annual allowance charge is calculated next by totalling the post- and pre-announcement periods totals and deducting the annual allowance for the tax year as increased by any carry forward of unused allowance under FA 2004 s 228A.

Paragraph 29 provides that where the transitional provisions in para 28 apply to the pension input amount for 2011–12, the carry forward amount for that year under FA 2004 s 228A (see para 5 above) is to be calculated as if the annual allowance for that year were £50,000.

Paragraph 30 provides for para 28 above to have effect in determining the amount of unused annual allowance available for carry forward to the years 2011–12 to 2013–14. Certain assumptions are to be made when applying FA 2004 s 228A (see para 5 above) to the years 2011–12 to 2013–14. These assumptions are that the annual allowance for 2008–08 to 2010–11 was £50,000 and the amendments made by schedule 17 apply.

Paragraph 31 provides for contributions paid during 2009–10 and 2010–11, which are repaid as a contributions lump sum under the anti-forestalling rules in FA 2009 Sch 35 para 15, to be deducted when determining the pension input amount for the annual allowance for the arrangement in respect of those years.

Paragraph 32 provides that any notice given by an individual to a pension scheme administrator regarding an annual allowance charge for 2011–12 must be made by 31 December 2013.

Paragraph 33 requires the pension scheme administrator to return any annual allowance charge for 2011–12 in the return form for the period ending 31 March 2014.

Paragraph 34 provides for expressions used in Part 2 of Sch 17 to have the same meaning as the same expressions used in Part 4 FA 2004.

SCHEDULE 18

LIFETIME ALLOWANCE CHARGE

Section 67

PART 1

AMENDMENTS

1 Part 4 of FA 2004 (pension schemes etc) is amended as follows.

2 (1) Section 218 (individual's lifetime allowance and standard lifetime allowance) is amended as follows.

(2) For subsections (2) and (3) substitute—

"(2) The standard lifetime allowance for the tax year 2012–13 and, subject to subsection (3), subsequent tax years is £1,500,000.

(3) The Treasury may by order provide that the standard lifetime allowance for any tax year subsequent to the tax year 2012–13 is such amount, not being less than the standard lifetime allowance for the immediately preceding tax year, as is specified in the order."

(3) After subsection (5) insert—

"(5A) Where the operation of a lifetime allowance enhancement factor is provided for by any of sections 220, 222, 223 and 224 and the time mentioned in the definition of SLA in the section concerned was before 6 April 2012, subsection (4) has effect as if the amount to be multiplied by LAEF were £1,800,000 (the standard lifetime allowance for the tax year 2011–12) if that is greater than SLA.

(5B) Where the operation of a lifetime allowance enhancement factor is provided for by paragraph 7 of Schedule 36, subsection (4) has effect as if SLA were £1,800,000 (the standard lifetime allowance for the tax year 2011–12) if that is greater than SLA.

(5C) Where benefit crystallisation event 7 occurs on or after 6 April 2012 by reason of the payment of a relevant lump sum death benefit in respect of the death of the individual before that date, the standard lifetime allowance at the time of the benefit crystallisation event is £1,800,000 (the standard lifetime allowance for the tax year 2011–12)."

3 Schedule 29 (authorised lump sums) is amended as follows.

4 (1) Paragraph 7 (trivial commutation lump sum) is amended as follows.

(2) In sub-paragraph (4), for "1% of the standard lifetime allowance on the nominated date." substitute "£18,000."

(3) After that sub-paragraph insert—

"(4A) The Treasury may by order substitute for the amount for the time being specified in sub-paragraph (4) such larger amount as is specified in the order."

5 (1) Paragraph 10 (winding-up lump sum) is amended as follows.

(2) In sub-paragraph (2), for "1% of the standard lifetime allowance when the lump sum is paid," substitute "£18,000,".

(3) After that sub-paragraph insert—

"(2A) The Treasury may by order substitute for the amount for the time being specified in sub-paragraph (2) such larger amount as is specified in the order."

6 (1) Paragraph 20 (trivial commutation lump sum death benefit) is amended as follows.

(2) In sub-paragraph (2), for "1% of the standard lifetime allowance on the date the lump sum is paid," substitute "£18,000,".

(3) After that sub-paragraph insert—

"(3) The Treasury may by order substitute for the amount for the time being specified in sub-paragraph (2) such larger amount as is specified in the order."

7 (1) Paragraph 21 (winding-up lump sum death benefit) is amended as follows.

(2) In sub-paragraph (2), for "1% of the standard lifetime allowance on the date the lump sum is paid," substitute "£18,000,".

(3) After that sub-paragraph insert—

"(3) The Treasury may by order substitute for the amount for the time being specified in sub-paragraph (2) such larger amount as is specified in the order."

8 Schedule 36 (transitional provision) is amended as follows.

9 In paragraph 16(3), for "standard lifetime allowance when the first relevant event occurs." substitute "underpinned lifetime allowance when the first relevant event occurs; and "the underpinned lifetime allowance" is the greater of the current standard lifetime allowance and £1,800,000 (the standard lifetime allowance for the tax year 2011–12)."

10 (1) Paragraph 28(3) is amended as follows.

(2) In the sub-paragraphs (6A) and (7) treated as substituted—

(a) in the formula, for "CSLA" substitute "ULA", and

(b) for the definition of CSLA substitute—

"ULA is the underpinned lifetime allowance, and".

(3) After the sub-paragraph (7) treated as substituted insert—

"(7A) The underpinned lifetime allowance" is the greater of the current standard lifetime allowance and £1,800,000 (the standard lifetime allowance for the tax year 2011–12)."

11 (1) Paragraph 34(2) is amended as follows.

(2) In the sub-paragraph (5) treated as substituted, for "CSLA" substitute "ULA".

(3) In the sub-paragraph (7) treated as substituted, for the definition of CSLA substitute—

"ULA is the underpinned lifetime allowance,".

(4) After the sub-paragraph (7A) treated as substituted insert—

"(7AZA) The underpinned lifetime allowance" is the greater of the current standard lifetime allowance and £1,800,000 (the standard lifetime allowance for the tax year 2011–12)."

12 In the Registered Pension Schemes (Standard Lifetime and Annual Allowances) Order 2010 (SI 2010/922), omit article 2.

PART 2

COMMENCEMENT AND TRANSITIONAL PROVISION

13 The amendments made by Part 1 have effect for the tax year 2012–13 and subsequent tax years.

14 (1) This paragraph applies on and after 6 April 2012 in the case of an individual—

(a) who has one or more arrangements under a registered pension scheme on that date,

(b) in relation to whom paragraph 7 of Schedule 36 to FA 2004 (primary protection) does not make provision for a lifetime allowance enhancement factor, and

(c) in relation to whom paragraph 12 of that Schedule (enhanced protection) does not apply on that date,

if notice of intention to rely on it is given to an officer of Revenue and Customs.

(2) The Commissioners for Her Majesty's Revenue and Customs may make regulations specifying how notice is to be given.

(3) Part 4 of FA 2004 has effect in relation to the individual as if the standard lifetime allowance were the greater of the standard lifetime allowance and £1,800,000 (the standard lifetime allowance for the tax year 2011–12).

(4) But this paragraph ceases to apply if on or after 6 April 2012—

(a) there is benefit accrual in relation to the individual under an arrangement under a registered pension scheme,

(b) there is an impermissible transfer into any arrangement under a registered pension scheme relating to the individual,

(c) a transfer of sums or assets held for the purposes of, or representing accrued rights under, any such arrangement is made that is not a permitted transfer, or

(d) an arrangement relating to the individual is made under a registered pension scheme otherwise than in permitted circumstances.

(5) For the purposes of sub-paragraph (4)(a) there is benefit accrual in relation to the individual under an arrangement—

(a) in the case of a money purchase arrangement that is not a cash balance arrangement, if a relevant contribution is paid under the arrangement on or after 6 April 2012,

(b) in the case of a cash balance arrangement or a defined benefits arrangement, if there is an increase in the value of the individual's rights under the arrangement at any time on or after that date (but subject to sub-paragraph (12)), and

(c) in the case of a hybrid arrangement—

(i) where the benefits that may be provided to or in respect of the individual under the arrangement include money purchase benefits other than cash balance benefits, if a relevant contribution is paid under the arrangement on or after 6 April 2012, and

(ii) in any case, if there is an increase in the value of the individual's rights under the arrangement at any time on or after that date (but subject to sub-paragraph (12)).

(6) For the purposes of sub-paragraphs (5)(b) and (c)(ii) and (12) whether there is an increase in the value of the individual's rights under the arrangement (and its amount if there is) is to be determined—

(a) in the case of a cash balance arrangement (or a hybrid arrangement under which cash balance benefits may be provided to or in respect of the individual under the arrangement), by reference to whether there is an increase in the amount that would, on the valuation assumptions, be available for the provision of benefits to or in respect of the member (and, if there is, the amount of the increase), and

(b) in the case of a defined benefits arrangement (or a hybrid arrangement under which defined benefits may be provided to or in respect of the individual under the arrangement), by reference to whether there is an increase in the benefits amount.

(7) For the purposes of sub-paragraph (6)(b) "the benefits amount" is—

$(P \times RVF) + LS$

where—

LS is the annual rate of the lump sum to which the individual would, on the valuation assumptions, be entitled under the arrangement (otherwise than by commutation of pension);

P is the annual rate of the pension which would, on the valuation assumptions, be payable to the individual under the arrangement;

RVF is the relevant valuation factor.

(8) Paragraph 17A of Schedule 36 to FA 2004 (impermissible transfers) applies for the purposes of sub-paragraph (4)(b) but as if the references to a relevant existing arrangement were to the arrangement and the reference in sub-paragraph (2) to 5 April 2006 were to 5 April 2012.

(9) Sub-paragraphs (7) to (8B) of paragraph 12 of Schedule 36 to FA 2004 (when there is a permitted transfer) apply for the purposes of sub-paragraph (4)(c); and where there is a permitted transfer—

(a) if it is a permitted transfer by virtue of sub-paragraph (8)(a) of paragraph 12, this paragraph applies in relation to the arrangement to which the transfer is made,

(b) if it is a permitted transfer by virtue of sub-paragraph (8)(b) of that paragraph, this paragraph applies in relation to the arrangement to which the transfer is made as if it were the same as that from which it is made, and

(c) if it is a permitted transfer by virtue of sub-paragraph (8)(c) of that paragraph, this paragraph applies in relation to the arrangement to which the transfer is made as if it were the same as that from which it is made and (if the employment is transferred) as if the employment with the transferee were the employment with the transferor.

(10) Sub-paragraphs (2A) to (2C) of paragraph 12 of Schedule 36 to FA 2004 ("permitted circumstances") apply for the purposes of sub-paragraph (4)(d).

(11) Paragraph 14 of Schedule 36 to FA 2004 (when a relevant contribution is paid under an arrangement) applies for the purposes of sub-paragraph (5)(a).

(12) Increases in the value of the individual's rights under an arrangement are to be ignored for the purposes of sub-paragraph (5)(b) or (c)(ii) if in no tax year do they exceed the relevant percentage.

(13) The relevant percentage, in relation to a tax year, means—

(a) where the arrangement (or a predecessor arrangement) includes provision for the value of the rights of the individual to increase during the tax year at an annual rate specified in the rules of the pension scheme (or a predecessor registered pension scheme) on 9 December 2010, that percentage (or, where more than one arrangement does so the higher or highest of the percentages so specified), and

(b) otherwise, the percentage by which the consumer prices index for the month of September in the previous tax year is higher than it was for the same month in the period of 12 months (or nil per cent if it is not higher).

(14) In sub-paragraph (13)(a)—

"predecessor arrangement", in relation to an arrangement, means another arrangement (under the same or another registered pension scheme) from which some or all of the sums or assets held for the purposes of the arrangement directly or indirectly derive;

"predecessor registered pension scheme", in relation to a pension scheme, means another registered pension scheme from which some or all of the sums or assets held for the purposes of the arrangement under the pension scheme directly or indirectly derive.

(15) Regulations under sub-paragraph (2) may include supplementary or incidental provision.

(16) The power to make regulations under sub-paragraph (2) is exercisable by statutory instrument.

(17) A statutory instrument containing regulations under sub-paragraph (2) is subject to annulment in pursuance of a resolution of the House of Commons.

(18) Expressions used in this paragraph and Part 4 of FA 2004 have the same meaning in this paragraph as in that Part.

GENERAL NOTE

PART 1

Just as the annual allowance has been reduced to restrict tax relief on pension contributions in Sch 17, the lifetime allowance provided for in FA 2004 s 218, which limits the total amount of tax relief given on an individual's pension savings, is also to be reduced to restrict tax relief for pension savings. The lifetime allowance for determining whether the lifetime allowance charge is applicable is to be reduced from £1,800,000 to £1,500,000 from 6 April 2012. The legislation effecting this change is in schedule 18. The lifetime allowance tax charge will remain unchanged. The legislation introduces transitional provisions providing protection from the lifetime allowance charge for those individuals who may already have built up pension savings on the expectation that the lifetime allowance would remain at the current level of £1,800,000. Because of the reduction to the lifetime allowance the trivial commutation and winding-up lump sum limits will cease to be linked to the lifetime allowance.

Paragraph 1 introduces the amendments in FA 2004 Part 4 Sch 18 regarding the changes to the lifetime allowance charge.

Paragraph 2 amends FA 2004 s 218 regarding the lifetime allowance and the standard lifetime allowance. Paragraph 2(2) provides for the lifetime allowance to be £1,500,000 for the tax year 2012–13 onwards instead of £1,800,000 and gives power to HM Treasury to increase the lifetime allowance in future tax years by Treasury Order. Paragraph 2(3) provides for the standard lifetime allowance to be substituted by a figure of £1,800,000 when calculating the enhancement factor where an individual is relying on protection under FA 2004 ss 220, 222, 223 or 224, which apply a lifetime enhancement factor in respect of pension credits, relevant overseas individuals and transfers from recognised overseas pension schemes. This substitution relates only to events taking place before 6 April 2012. Where an individual is relying on primary protection under FA 2004 Sch 36 para 7, the references to the standard lifetime allowance in FA 2004 s 218(4) are also substituted by a figure of £1,800,000. Where a benefit crystallisation event 7 occurs on or after 6 April 2012 because of the payment of a lump sum death benefit in respect of the death of an individual before 6 April 2012, the reference to the standard lifetime allowance is also substituted by a figure of £1,800,000.

Paragraph 3 provides for FA 2004 Sch 29 to be amended by paras 4–7 regarding authorised lump sums.

Paragraph 4 amends FA 2004 Sch 29 para 7 setting the quantum of a trivial commutation lump sum at £18,000 instead of 1 per cent of the standard lifetime allowance and providing power to HM Treasury to increase the amount of the lump sum in future years by Treasury Order.

Paragraph 5 amends FA 2004 Sch 29 para 10 setting the quantum of a winding-up lump sum at £18,000 instead of 1 per cent of the standard lifetime allowance and providing power to HM Treasury to increase the amount of the lump sum in future years by Treasury Order.

Paragraph 6 amends FA 2004 Sch 29 para 20 setting the quantum of a trivial commutation lump sum death benefit at £18,000 instead of 1 per cent of the standard lifetime allowance and providing power to HM Treasury to increase the amount of the lump sum in future years by Treasury Order.

Paragraph 7 amends FA 2004 Sch 29 para 21 setting the quantum of a winding-up lump sum death benefit at £18,000 instead of 1 per cent of the standard lifetime allowance and providing power to HM Treasury to increase the amount of the lump sum in future years by Treasury Order.

Paragraph 8 provides for FA 2004 Sch 36 to be amended by paras 9–11 regarding the transitional provisions.

Paragraph 9 amends FA 2004 Sch 36 para 16(3) by substituting the underpinned lifetime allowance for the standard lifetime allowance when determining the post-commencement earnings limit used in calculating the relevant benefit accrual for individuals relying on enhanced protection. The underpinned lifetime allowance is the greater of the standard lifetime allowance and £1,800,000.

Paragraph 10 amends FA 2004 Sch 36 para 28(3) so the enhancement factor for individuals relying on primary protection is determined using the underpinned lifetime allowance in FA 2004 Sch 36 para 16(3), (see para 9 above).

Paragraph 11 amends FA 2004 Sch 36 para 34(2) so the enhancement factor for those individuals entitled to a lump sum in excess of 25 per cent of the value of their fund at 5 April 2006, but who do not have enhanced or primary protection, is calculated using the underpinned lifetime allowance in FA 2004 Sch 36 para 16(3), (see para 9 above).

Paragraph 12 removes article 2 from SI 2010/922 which had the effect of freezing the lifetime allowance at £1,800,000 for the tax years 2011–12 to 2015–16.

PART 2

Paragraph 13 provides that Part 1 of Sch 18 has effect for the tax year 2012–13 onwards.

Paragraph 14(1) provides for transitional protection against the lifetime allowance charge from 6 April 2012 for individuals who do not have either primary or enhanced protection. Paragraph 14(2) gives HMRC power to make regulations specifying how a notice of intention to rely on transitional protection should be given. Paragraph 14(3) provides for the underpinned lifetime allowance (see para 9 above) instead of the standard lifetime allowance to be used for individuals relying on the new transitional protection when applying the provisions of Part 4 FA 2004. However, under para 14(4) the transitional protection is lost where there is a benefit accrual, an impermissible transfer, a transfer of sums and assets that is not a permitted transfer or a new arrangement relating to the individual is made otherwise than in permitted circumstances. For the purposes of para 14(4)(a), para 14(5) sets out when benefit accrual occurs for a money purchase arrangement other than a cash balance arrangement, for a cash balance or final salary arrangement, and a hybrid arrangement. For the purposes of paras 5(b) and (c), and 12 (see below), para 6 provides how to determine the increase in the value of an individual's rights under a cash balance or final salary arrangement and hybrid arrangement. Paragraph 7 similarly provides how to determine the increase in the value of an individual's rights for the purposes of para 6(b) under which final salary scheme benefits may be provided. Paras 8 to 11 provide definitions of impermissible transfers, permitted transfers, permitted circumstances and relevant contributions for the purposes of para 14(4). Paragraph 14(12) provides for benefit accrual not to be taken into account in respect of cash balance and final salary arrangements if the accrual is less than the relevant percentage. The definition of a relevant percentage is provided in para 14(13) as the annual rate of increase specified in the pension scheme rules, or predecessor scheme rules if this is more favourable, as at 9 December 2010, if there is one, or the annual percentage increase in the consumer prices index for September in the previous year. Definitions of predecessor arrangement and predecessor registered pension scheme are provided in para 14(14). Paragraph 14(15) provides that regulations made under para 14(2) specifying how the notice of intention to rely on transitional protection is to be given, may include supplementary or incidental provision. Paras 14(16) and (17) provide that regulations under para 14(2) in respect of transitional protection are to be made under statutory instrument and subject to the House of Commons negative resolution procedure. Paragraph 14(18) provides for expressions used in para 14 to have the same meaning as the same expressions in Part 4 FA 2004.

SCHEDULE 19

THE BANK LEVY

Section 73

PART 1

INTRODUCTION

1 There is to be a tax called "the bank levy".

2 The bank levy is charged on certain types of equity and liabilities of certain groups of entities and individual entities as set out in Part 2 of this Schedule.

3 In this Schedule—

Part 3 contains provision defining the different types of groups of entities in relation to which the bank levy is charged;
Part 4 contains provision defining the equity and liabilities on which the bank levy is charged;
Part 5 contains supplementary provision;
Part 6 deals with the collection and management of the bank levy;
Part 7 deals with double taxation relief;
Part 8 contains definitions;
Part 9 confers a power to make changes to this Schedule in specified circumstances.

PART 2

CHARGING OF BANK LEVY

Bank levy to be charged in relation to certain groups of entities

4 (1) The bank levy is charged if, as at the end of a period of account ("the chargeable period") of an entity ("the parent entity")—

(a) the parent entity is a parent and is not a subsidiary of any other entity, and
(b) the group ("the relevant group") for which the parent entity is the parent is a group within sub-paragraph (2).

(2) The groups within this sub-paragraph are—

(a) a UK banking group,
(b) a building society group,
(c) a foreign banking group, or
(d) a relevant non-banking group.

See Part 3 of this Schedule for the definitions of these groups.

(3) "Group", "parent" and "subsidiary" have the meaning given by those provisions of international accounting standards relating to the preparation of consolidated financial statements (whether or not the parent entity prepares financial statements under those standards).

(4) Accordingly, for the purposes of this Schedule the members of the relevant group are—

(a) the parent entity, and
(b) any other entity which, as at the end of the chargeable period, is a member of the group for the purposes of the provisions mentioned in sub-paragraph (3).

(5) Sub-paragraphs (3) and (4) are subject to what follows.

(6) Sub-paragraph (7) applies if—

(a) as at the end of the chargeable period—
(i) the parent entity is resident in a territory outside the United Kingdom,

(ii) generally accepted accounting practice for entities resident in that territory is or includes US GAAP, and

(iii) the parent entity is a parent for the purposes of those provisions of US GAAP which relate to the preparation of consolidated financial statements (as well as being a parent for the purposes of the provisions mentioned in sub-paragraph (3)), and

(b) the parent entity prepares consolidated financial statements for the chargeable period under US GAAP.

(7) The relevant group is the group for which the parent entity is the parent for the purposes of the provisions of US GAAP mentioned in sub-paragraph (6)(a)(iii) (instead of the provisions mentioned in sub-paragraph (3)) and, accordingly, for the purposes of this Schedule the members of the relevant group are—

(a) the parent entity, and

(b) any other entity which, as at the end of the chargeable period, is a member of the group for the purposes of the provisions of US GAAP mentioned in sub-paragraph (6)(a)(iii).

(8) This paragraph applies in relation to periods of account ending on or after 1 January 2011.

Bank levy to be charged in relation to certain entities which are not members of groups

5 (1) The bank levy is charged if, as at the end of a period of account ("the chargeable period") of an entity ("the relevant entity"), the relevant entity—

(a) is a UK resident bank, a building society or a relevant foreign bank, and

(b) does not fall within sub-paragraph (2) or (3).

(2) An entity falls within this sub-paragraph if it is an entity in relation to which paragraph 4(1) applies as at the end of the chargeable period.

(3) An entity ("A") falls within this sub-paragraph if—

(a) there is another entity ("B") in relation to which paragraph 4(1) applies as at the end of the chargeable period (or in relation to which paragraph 4(1) would apply if B had a period of account ending at the same time as the chargeable period), and

(b) A is (or would be) a member of the relevant group.

(4) This paragraph applies in relation to periods of account ending on or after 1 January 2011.

Steps for determining the amount of the bank levy

6 (1) This paragraph applies where the bank levy is charged as provided for by paragraph 4 or 5.

(2) Here are the steps to be taken to determine the amount of the bank levy.

Step 1

In accordance with Part 4 of this Schedule, determine the amount of the chargeable equity and liabilities of the relevant group or the relevant entity (as the case may be).

Step 2

If the amount of the chargeable equity and liabilities is not more than £20,000,000,000, the amount of the bank levy is nil and no further steps are taken.

If the amount of the chargeable equity and liabilities is more than £20,000,000,000, go to Step 3.

Step 3

Determine how much of the chargeable equity and liabilities are long term equity and liabilities and how much are short term liabilities.

Step 4

Determine the proportion ("A%") of the chargeable equity and liabilities which is long term equity and liabilities and the proportion ("B%") of the chargeable equity and liabilities which is short term liabilities.

Step 5

Reduce the amount of the long term chargeable equity and liabilities by an amount equal to A% of £20,000,000,000 and the amount of the short term chargeable liabilities by an amount equal to B% of £20,000,000,000.

Step 6

If the chargeable period is 12 months, go straight to Step 7.

If not, adjust the amount of the long term chargeable equity and liabilities and the amount of the short term chargeable liabilities as follows.

Divide the amount by 365 and then multiply the result by the number of days in the chargeable period.

Step 7

Charge the amount of the long term chargeable equity and liabilities at the rate of 0.039%.
Charge the amount of the short term chargeable liabilities at the rate of 0.078%.

(3) The bank levy is to be paid as provided for by Part 6 of this Schedule.

Special provision for chargeable periods falling wholly or partly before 1 January 2012

7 (1) Paragraph 6(2) applies subject to this paragraph if some or all of the chargeable period falls before 1 January 2012.

(2) For Step 7 there is substituted—

"Step 7
Determine the proportion ("X%") of the chargeable period (if any) falling in the period from 1 January 2011 to 28 February 2011.
Determine the proportion ("Y%") of the chargeable period (if any) falling in the period from 1 March 2011 to 30 April 2011.
Determine the proportion ("Z%") of the chargeable period (if any) falling in the period from 1 May 2011 to 31 December 2011.
Charge X% of the amount of the long term chargeable equity and liabilities at the rate of 0.025%, Y% of that amount at the rate of 0.05%, Z% of that amount at the rate of 0.0375% and the balance (if any) at the rate of 0.039%.
Charge X% of the amount of the short term chargeable liabilities at the rate of 0.05%, Y% of that amount at the rate of 0.1%, Z% of that amount at the rate of 0.075% and the balance (if any) at the rate of 0.078%.
Add these results together to give the amount of the bank levy."

(3) If the chargeable period starts before 1 January 2011, for the purposes of Step 6 and Step 7 (as substituted by sub-paragraph (2)) the part of the period falling before 1 January 2011 is ignored and, accordingly, the period is treated as having started on 1 January 2011.

PART 3

GROUPS COVERED BY THE BANK LEVY

Definitions of "UK banking group", "building society group", "foreign banking group" and "relevant non-banking group"

8 The relevant group is a "UK banking group" if—

(a) the group is a banking group (see paragraph 12), and
(b) the parent entity is a UK resident entity.

9 The relevant group is a "building society group" if the parent entity is a building society.

10 The relevant group is a "foreign banking group" if—

(a) the group is a banking group (see paragraph 12), and
(b) the parent entity is a non-UK resident entity.

11 The relevant group is a "relevant non-banking group" if—

(a) the members of the group include at least one UK resident bank or relevant foreign bank, and
(b) the group is neither a banking group nor a building society group.

Definition of "banking group"

12 (1) The relevant group is a "banking group" if—

(a) condition A, B, C or D is met, and
(b) the exempt activities condition is not met (see paragraph 13).

(2) Condition A is that the parent entity is a UK resident bank (see paragraph 80) or a relevant foreign bank (see paragraph 78).

(3) Condition B is that—

(a) the parent entity is an investment entity, and
(b) the members of the relevant group include at least one UK resident bank to which sub-paragraph (6) applies or relevant foreign bank to which that sub-paragraph applies.

(4) Condition C is that—

(a) the parent entity is a non-UK resident entity to which sub-paragraph (8) applies, and
(b) the members of the relevant group include at least one UK resident bank or relevant foreign bank.

(5) Condition D is that—

(a) the parent entity is an investment entity,

(b) the members of the relevant group include at least one non-UK resident entity to which both sub-paragraphs (6) and (8) apply, and

(c) those members also include at least one UK resident bank or relevant foreign bank.

(6) This sub-paragraph applies to an entity ("E") if, for the purposes of the applicable accounting provisions, E is not a subsidiary of any other entity apart from investment entities.

(7) "The applicable accounting provisions" means—

(a) the provisions mentioned in paragraph 4(3), or

(b) if the members of the relevant group are determined under paragraph 4(7), the provisions of US GAAP mentioned in paragraph 4(6)(a)(iii).

(8) This sub-paragraph applies to an entity ("F") if—

(a) F would be a UK resident bank if—

(i) F were a UK resident entity,

(ii) it carried on its activities in the United Kingdom,

(iii) where it would be required to be an authorised person for the purposes of FISMA 2000 in order to carry on those activities in the United Kingdom, it were an authorised person with permission to carry on those activities, and

(iv) where those activities consist wholly or mainly of any of the relevant activities described in the provisions mentioned in paragraph 79(b) to (f), as a result of carrying on those activities and having such permission it would be a BIPRU 730k firm and a full scope BIPRU investment firm, or

(b) F is a member of a partnership which is a non-UK resident entity and F would be a UK resident bank if—

(i) both F and the partnership were UK resident entities,

(ii) the partnership carried on its activities in the United Kingdom,

(iii) where the partnership would be required to be an authorised person for the purposes of FISMA 2000 in order to carry on those activities in the United Kingdom, the partnership were an authorised person with permission to carry on those activities, and

(iv) where those activities consist wholly or mainly of any of the relevant activities described in the provisions mentioned in paragraph 79(b) to (f), as a result of carrying on those activities and having such permission the partnership would be a BIPRU 730k firm and a full scope BIPRU investment firm.

(9) "Investment entity"—

(a) means an entity the business of which consists wholly or mainly of, and the principal part of the income of which is derived from, the making of investments, and

(b) also includes any savings bank or other bank for savings.

13 (1) The exempt activities condition is met for the purposes of paragraph 12(1)(b) if—

(a) at least 90% of the trading income of the relevant group for the chargeable period derives from exempt activities, or

(b) at least 50% of the trading income of the relevant group for the chargeable period derives from non-financial trading activities.

(2) For this purpose, the trading income of the relevant group for the chargeable period—

(a) consists of the items mentioned in sub-paragraph (3), and

(b) is to be determined by reference to—

(i) the amounts recognised in the group's consolidated financial statements for the chargeable period as prepared under the applicable accounting standards, or

(ii) if no such financial statements are prepared, the amounts which would have been so recognised had consolidated financial statements for the group been prepared for the chargeable period under international accounting standards.

(3) The items referred to in sub-paragraph (2)(a) are—

(a) the group's gross income for the chargeable period arising from its activities (other than net-basis activities) without taking account of any deductions (whether for expenses or otherwise), and

(b) the group's net income for the chargeable period arising from its net-basis activities.

(4) In this paragraph—

"activities" includes buying, holding, managing and selling assets;

"the applicable accounting standards" means—

(a) international accounting standards, or

(b) US GAAP if the members of the relevant group are determined under paragraph 4(7);

"dealing on own account" has the same meaning as in Directive 2004/39/EC of the European Parliament and of the Council of 21 April 2004 on markets in financial instruments (see Article 4(1)(6));

"deposit" has the meaning given by article 5(2) of the Financial Services and Markets Act 2000 (Regulated Activities) Order 2001 (SI 2001/544) but ignoring the exclusions in articles 6 to 9AB;

"exempt activities" means—

(a) insurance activities, asset management activities and related activities, and

(b) non-financial trading activities;

"financial trading entity" means an entity which—

(a) is an authorised person for the purposes of FISMA 2000 (see section 31 of that Act),

(b) is not UK resident, but if it were and it carried on its activities in the United Kingdom, would be required to be an authorised person, or

(c) is not within paragraph (a) or (b) but carries on a trade consisting wholly or partly in dealing in securities;

"insurance activities" means—

(a) the effecting or carrying out of contracts of insurance by a regulated insurer, and

(b) investment business that arises directly from activities falling within paragraph (a);

"lending activities" means—

(a) acceptance of deposits or other repayable funds,

(b) lending of money, including consumer credit, mortgage credit, factoring (with or without recourse) and financing of commercial transactions (including forfeiting),

(c) finance leasing (as lessor),

(d) issuing and administering means of payment,

(e) provision of guarantees or commitments to provide money,

(f) money transmission services,

(g) provision of alternative finance arrangements, and

(h) other activities carried on in connection with activities falling within any of paragraphs (a) to (g);

"net-basis activities" means activities normally reported on a net basis in consolidated financial statements prepared under the applicable accounting standards;

"non-financial trading activities" means activities carried on by an entity which is not a financial trading entity, other than—

(a) lending activities, and

(b) dealing on own account, with the exception of any hedging transactions in relation to activities which (disregarding this exception) are non-financial trading activities;

"regulated insurer", in relation to the relevant group, means a member of the group which—

(a) is authorised under the law of any territory to carry on insurance business, or

(b) is a member of a body or organisation which is so authorised;

"related activities" means—

(a) activities which are ancillary to insurance activities or asset management activities of any entity which is a member of the relevant group (whether or not the entity carrying on the insurance activities or asset management activities), and

(b) activities which would not be carried on but for such insurance activities or asset management activities being carried on,

but does not include dealing on own account;

"securities" includes—

(a) shares,

(b) rights of unit holders in unit trust schemes to which TCGA 1992 applies as a result of section 99 of that Act, and

(c) in the case of a company with no share capital, interests in the company possessed by members of the company.

PART 4

CHARGEABLE EQUITY AND LIABILITIES

Definition of "assets", "equity" and "liabilities"

14 (1) For the purposes of this Schedule, "assets", "equity" and "liabilities" have the same meaning as they have for the purposes of international accounting standards.

(2) Sub-paragraph (1) is without prejudice to any provision of this Schedule which requires anything to be determined by reference to amounts which are recognised, or amounts which would have been recognised, in consolidated financial statements or financial statements prepared under UK GAAP.

Chargeable equity and liabilities of a UK banking group or a building society group

15 (1) This paragraph applies if the relevant group is a UK banking group or a building society group.

(2) To determine the amount of the relevant group's chargeable equity and liabilities—

(a) determine the amount of the group's equity and liabilities (other than excluded equity and liabilities) as at the end of the chargeable period,

(b) adjust that amount in accordance with paragraphs 16 and 44 (so far as applicable), and

(c) finally, reduce that amount (but not below nil) by—

(i) the amount of the group's high quality liquid assets as at the end of that period, other than any asset which for the purposes of an adjustment under paragraph (b) is an asset to which paragraph 16(4) applies, and

(ii) where sub-paragraph (4) applies, the amount determined under that sub-paragraph.

(3) Sub-paragraph (4) applies where—

(a) as at the end of the chargeable period, the assets of the group include a financial asset in respect of an advance of cash made by a member of the group,

(b) that financial asset is not an asset which, for the purposes of an adjustment under sub-paragraph (2)(b), is an asset to which paragraph 16(4) applies, and

(c) underlying that asset, as collateral, is an item ("the collateral") owned by that member which would form part of the group's high quality liquid assets as at the end of that period were the collateral, rather than the financial asset, an asset of the group.

(4) The amount within sub-paragraph (2)(c)(ii) is—

(a) the amount of the financial asset as at the end of that period or, if lower, an amount equal to the fair value of the collateral as at that time, or

(b) if this sub-paragraph applies in relation to more than one financial asset, the total of the amounts determined under paragraph (a) in respect of each of those assets.

(5) For the purposes of this paragraph and paragraph 16 the relevant group's assets, equity and liabilities are to be determined by reference to—

(a) the amounts recognised in the group's consolidated financial statements for the chargeable period as prepared under international accounting standards or UK GAAP, or

(b) if no such financial statements are prepared, the amounts which would have been so recognised had consolidated financial statements for the group been prepared for the chargeable period under international accounting standards.

(6) In reducing the amount of any equity or liabilities under sub-paragraph (2)(c), long term equity and liabilities are to be reduced before short term liabilities.

16 (1) This paragraph applies for the purposes of paragraph 15(2) if—

(a) a member ("M") of the relevant group has liabilities to an entity ("N") which is not a member of the group and N has assets which correspond to those liabilities ("M's liabilities"),

(b) M, or another member of the relevant group, has assets which correspond to liabilities which N, or another entity which is not a member of the group, has to M or (as the case may be) that other member ("N's liabilities"),

(c) there is in place an agreement which makes provision for there to be a single net settlement of all M's liabilities, and liabilities of other members of the group to N or another entity which is not a member of the group, (so far as covered by the provision) and all N's liabilities (so far as covered by the provision) if the netting event occurs, and

(d) the provision mentioned in paragraph (c) is legally effective and enforceable.

(2) For the purposes of sub-paragraph (1)—

(a) "agreement" includes an agreement which forms part of a multi-lateral agreement, arrangement or trading facility,
(b) references to assets of one party which correspond to liabilities of another party are to amounts receivable by that first party which correspond to amounts due from that other party,
(c) a liability which M has to N to which sub-paragraph (3) applies is to be treated as a liability to which an asset of N corresponds, and
(d) "the netting event occurs" if the insolvency or bankruptcy of—

(i) M, or another member of the relevant group which has assets which correspond to a liability covered by the provision mentioned in sub-paragraph (1)(c), or
(ii) N, or another entity which is not a member of the group and which has such a liability,

gives rise to the termination of any arrangements under which such a liability arises.

(3) This sub-paragraph applies to a liability which M has to N if—

(a) as at the end of the chargeable period, the assets of the relevant group include a financial asset in respect of an advance of cash made by M to N,
(b) underlying that asset, as collateral, are securities which have been transferred by M to another person,
(c) the liability is a financial liability in respect of M's obligation to return the securities or similar securities to N, and
(d) the provision mentioned in sub-paragraph (1)(c) covers both the financial asset mentioned in paragraph (a) and that financial liability.

Section 556 of CTA 2009 (meaning of securities and similar securities) applies for the purposes of this sub-paragraph as it applies for the purposes of Chapter 10 of Part 6 of that Act.

(4) The amount of M's net settlement liabilities is to be reduced (but not below nil) by the amount of M's net settlement assets.

(5) "M's net settlement liabilities" means M's liabilities so far as they—

(a) are covered by the provision mentioned in sub-paragraph (1)(c), and
(b) are not excluded liabilities.

(6) "M's net settlement assets" means the assets of M, or of another member of the relevant group, so far as corresponding to N's net settlement liabilities.

(7) But if this paragraph applies in relation to more than one member of the relevant group, no part of an asset may be included in the net settlement assets of more than one such member.

(8) "N's net settlement liabilities" means N's liabilities so far as they are covered by the provision mentioned in sub-paragraph (1)(c).

(9) If M's net settlement liabilities exceed M's net settlement assets, and a proportion (A%) of those liabilities is long term liabilities and a proportion (B%) of those liabilities is short term liabilities, under sub-paragraph (4)—

(a) the long term liabilities are reduced by A% of M's net settlement assets, and
(b) the short term liabilities are reduced by B% of those assets.

Chargeable equity and liabilities of a foreign banking group

17 (1) This paragraph applies if the relevant group is a foreign banking group.

(2) The amount of the chargeable equity and liabilities of the relevant group is the sum of all type A, type B, type C and type D equity and liabilities.

(3) Type A equity and liabilities are the chargeable equity and liabilities of any relevant UK sub-group.

(4) "UK sub-group" means a group of entities—

(a) which is a group for the purposes of those provisions of international accounting standards or UK GAAP which relate to the preparation of consolidated financial statements,
(b) which has as its parent or parent undertaking for the purposes of those provisions an entity which is a UK resident entity, and
(c) the members of which for the purposes of those provisions are all members of the relevant group.

(5) A UK sub-group is "relevant" if—

(a) consolidated financial statements for the chargeable period are prepared for it under international accounting standards or UK GAAP, and
(b) its members are not members of any larger UK sub-group for which such financial statements are prepared.

(6) To determine the amount of the chargeable equity and liabilities of a relevant UK sub-group—

(a) determine the amount of the sub-group's equity and liabilities (other than excluded equity and liabilities) as at the end of the chargeable period,

(b) adjust that amount in accordance with paragraphs 18 and 44 (so far as applicable), and

(c) finally, reduce that amount (but not below nil) by—

(i) the amount of the sub-group's high quality liquid assets as at the end of that period, other than any asset which for the purposes of an adjustment under paragraph (b) is an asset to which paragraph 18(12) applies, and

(ii) where sub-paragraph (8) applies, the amount determined under that sub-paragraph.

(7) Sub-paragraph (8) applies where—

(a) as at the end of the chargeable period, the assets of the relevant UK sub-group include a financial asset in respect of an advance of cash made by a member of that sub-group,

(b) that financial asset is not an asset which, for the purposes of an adjustment under sub-paragraph (6)(b), is an asset to which paragraph 18(12) applies, and

(c) underlying that asset, as collateral, is an item ("the collateral") owned by that member which would form part of the sub-group's high quality liquid assets as at the end of that period were the collateral, rather than the financial asset, an asset of the sub-group.

(8) The amount within sub-paragraph (6)(c)(ii) is—

(a) the amount of the financial asset as at the end of that period or, if lower, an amount equal to the fair value of the collateral as at that time, or

(b) if this sub-paragraph applies in relation to more than one financial asset, the total of the amounts determined under paragraph (a) in respect of each of those assets.

(9) For the purposes of this paragraph and paragraph 18, the assets, equity and liabilities of a relevant UK sub-group are to be determined by reference to the amounts recognised in its consolidated financial statements for the chargeable period.

(10) Type B equity and liabilities are the chargeable equity and liabilities of any UK resident entity which—

(a) is a member of the relevant group, but

(b) is not a member of a relevant UK sub-group.

(11) Type C equity and liabilities are the chargeable equity and liabilities of any non-UK resident entity which—

(a) is a member of the relevant group, and

(b) is a member of a UK sub-group but is not a member of a relevant UK sub-group.

(12) To determine the amount of the chargeable equity and liabilities of an entity covered by sub-paragraph (10) or (11)—

(a) determine the amount of the entity's equity and liabilities (other than excluded equity and liabilities) as at the end of the chargeable period,

(b) adjust that amount in accordance with paragraphs 18 and 44 (so far as applicable), and

(c) finally, reduce that amount (but not below nil) by—

(i) the amount of the entity's high quality liquid assets as at the end of that period, other than any asset which for the purposes of an adjustment under paragraph (b) is an asset to which paragraph 18(12) applies, and

(ii) where sub-paragraph (14) applies, the amount determined under that sub-paragraph.

(13) Sub-paragraph (14) applies where—

(a) as at the end of the chargeable period, the assets of the entity include a financial asset in respect of an advance of cash made by the entity,

(b) that financial asset is not an asset which, for the purposes of an adjustment under sub-paragraph (12)(b), is an asset to which paragraph 18(12) applies, and

(c) underlying that asset, as collateral, is an item ("the collateral") owned by that entity which would form part of the entity's high quality liquid assets as at the end of that period were the collateral, rather than the financial asset, an asset of the entity.

(14) The amount within sub-paragraph (12)(c)(ii) is—

(a) the amount of the financial asset as at the end of the chargeable period or, if lower, an amount equal to the fair value of the collateral as at that time, or

(b) if this sub-paragraph applies in relation to more than one financial asset, the total of the amounts determined under paragraph (a) in respect of each of those assets.

(15) For the purposes of this paragraph and paragraph 18 the assets, equity and liabilities of an entity covered by sub-paragraph (10) or (11) are to be determined by reference to—

(a) the amounts recognised in the entity's financial statements for the chargeable period as prepared under international accounting standards or UK GAAP, or

(b) if no such financial statements are prepared, the amounts which would have been so recognised had such financial statements been prepared—

(i) under international accounting standards, or

(ii) under UK GAAP if that is what the entity prepares its financial statements under.

(16) In reducing the amount of any equity or liabilities under sub-paragraph (6)(c) or (12)(c), long term equity and liabilities are to be reduced before short term liabilities.

(17) Type D equity and liabilities are the UK allocated equity and liabilities (see paragraph 24) as at the end of the chargeable period of any relevant foreign bank which—

(a) is a member of the relevant group, but

(b) is not a member of a UK sub-group.

(18) If—

(a) the amount of the equity and liabilities, as at the end of the chargeable period, of a relevant UK sub-group or an entity covered by sub-paragraph (10) or (11), or

(b) the amount of the UK allocated equity and liabilities, as at the end of that period, of a relevant foreign bank covered by sub-paragraph (17),

is less than £50,000,000, the equity and liabilities, or UK allocated equity and liabilities, may be ignored for the purposes of this paragraph and paragraph 18.

(19) But the total amount of equity and liabilities which may be ignored under sub-paragraph (18) may not exceed £200,000,000.

18 (1) This paragraph applies for the purposes of paragraph 17(6) and (12).

(2) In this paragraph "relevant member" means—

(a) a relevant UK sub-group,

(b) a UK resident entity covered by paragraph 17(10), or

(c) a non-UK resident entity covered by paragraph 17(11).

(3) Sub-paragraph (4) applies if the members of a relevant UK sub-group are also members of one or more larger UK sub-groups.

(4) Any equity of the relevant UK sub-group is to be left out so far as it would have been eliminated under normal consolidation procedures had consolidated financial statements for the chargeable period been prepared for the larger or largest UK sub-group—

(a) under international accounting standards, or

(b) under UK GAAP if the entity which is the parent or parent undertaking for the larger or largest UK sub-group prepares its financial statements under UK GAAP.

(5) Sub-paragraph (6) applies if a relevant member within sub-paragraph (2)(b) or (c) is a member of one or more UK sub-groups.

(6) Any equity of the relevant member is to be left out so far as it would have been eliminated under normal consolidation procedures had consolidated financial statements for the chargeable period been prepared for the UK sub-group or the largest UK sub-group—

(a) under international accounting standards, or

(b) under UK GAAP if the entity which is the parent or parent undertaking for the UK sub-group or the largest UK sub-group prepares its financial statements under UK GAAP.

(7) The following liabilities of a relevant member are to be left out—

(a) liabilities to other relevant members, and

(b) liabilities to a relevant foreign bank covered by paragraph 17(17) so far as the bank's assets corresponding to the liabilities are assets of the permanent establishment through which the bank carries on a trade in the United Kingdom as determined at Step 2 in paragraph 24(1).

(8) Sub-paragraph (12) applies if—

(a) an entity ("M") within sub-paragraph (9) has liabilities to another entity ("N") not within that sub-paragraph, and N has assets which correspond to those liabilities ("M's liabilities"),

(b) M, or another entity within sub-paragraph (9), has assets which correspond to liabilities which N, or another entity not within that sub-paragraph, has to M or (as the case may be) to that other entity within that sub-paragraph ("N's liabilities"),

(c) there is in place an agreement which makes provision for there to be a single net settlement of all M's liabilities, and liabilities of other entities within sub-paragraph (9) to N or another entity which is not within that sub-paragraph, (so far as covered by the provision) and all N's liabilities (so far as covered by the provision) if the netting event occurs, and

(d) the provision mentioned in paragraph (c) is legally effective and enforceable.

(9) An entity is within this sub-paragraph if it is—

(a) a member of a relevant UK sub-group, or

(b) a relevant member within sub-paragraph (2)(b) or (c).

(10) For the purposes of sub-paragraph (8)—

(a) "agreement" includes an agreement which forms part of a multi-lateral agreement, arrangement or trading facility,

(b) if N is a relevant foreign bank covered by paragraph 17(17), liabilities of M to N are to be ignored so far as N's assets corresponding to those liabilities are assets of the permanent establishment through which N carries on a trade in the United Kingdom as determined at Step 2 in paragraph 24(1),

(c) references to assets of one party which correspond to liabilities of another party are to amounts receivable by that first party which correspond to amounts due from that other party,

(d) a liability which M has to N to which sub-paragraph (11) applies is to be treated as a liability to which an asset of N corresponds, and

(e) "the netting event occurs" if the insolvency or bankruptcy of—

(i) M, or another entity within sub-paragraph (9) which has assets which correspond to a liability covered by the provision mentioned in sub-paragraph (8)(c), or

(ii) N, or another entity not within sub-paragraph (9) which has such a liability,

gives rise to the termination of any arrangements under which such a liability arises.

(11) This sub-paragraph applies to a liability which M has to N if—

(a) as at the end of the chargeable period, the assets of M include a financial asset in respect of an advance of cash made by M to N,

(b) underlying that asset, as collateral, are securities which have been transferred by M to another person,

(c) the liability is a financial liability in respect of M's obligation to return the securities or similar securities to N, and

(d) the provision mentioned in sub-paragraph (8)(c) covers both the financial asset mentioned in paragraph (a) and that financial liability.

Section 556 of CTA 2009 (meaning of securities and similar securities) applies for the purposes of this sub-paragraph as it applies for the purposes of Chapter 10 of Part 6 of that Act.

(12) The amount of M's net settlement liabilities is to be reduced (but not below nil) by the amount of M's net settlement assets.

(13) "M's net settlement liabilities" means M's liabilities so far as they—

(a) are covered by the provision mentioned in sub-paragraph (8)(c), and

(b) are not excluded liabilities.

(14) "M's net settlement assets" means the assets of M, or of another entity within sub-paragraph (9), so far as corresponding to N's net settlement liabilities.

(15) But—

(a) if N's net settlement liabilities include liabilities of a relevant foreign bank covered by paragraph 17(17), X% (as determined at Step 2 in paragraph 24(1)) of the assets corresponding to the liabilities of the relevant foreign bank are to be disregarded for the purposes of sub-paragraph (14), and

(b) if sub-paragraph (12) applies in relation to more than one entity within sub-paragraph (9), no part of an asset may be included in the net settlement assets of more than one such entity.

(16) "N's net settlement liabilities" means N's liabilities so far as they are covered by the provision mentioned in sub-paragraph (8)(c).

(17) If M's net settlement liabilities exceed M's net settlement assets, and a proportion (A%) of those liabilities is long term liabilities and a proportion (B%) of those liabilities is short term liabilities, under sub-paragraph (12)—

(a) the long term liabilities are reduced by A% of M's net settlement assets, and

(b) the short term liabilities are reduced by B% of those assets.

Chargeable equity and liabilities of a relevant non-banking group

19 (1) This paragraph applies if the relevant group is a relevant non-banking group.

(2) The amount of the chargeable equity and liabilities of the relevant group is the sum of all type A, type B, type C and type D equity and liabilities.

(3) Type A equity and liabilities are the chargeable equity and liabilities of any relevant UK banking sub-group.

(4) "UK banking sub-group" means a group of entities—

(a) which is a group for the purposes of those provisions of international accounting standards or UK GAAP which relate to the preparation of consolidated financial statements,
(b) which has as its parent or parent undertaking for the purposes of those provisions an entity which is a UK resident bank, and
(c) the members of which are all members of the relevant group.

(5) A UK banking sub-group is "relevant" if—

(a) consolidated financial statements for the chargeable period are prepared for it under international accounting standards or UK GAAP, and
(b) its members are not members of any larger UK banking sub-group for which such financial statements are prepared.

(6) To determine the amount of the chargeable equity and liabilities of a relevant UK banking sub-group—

(a) determine the amount of the sub-group's equity and liabilities (other than excluded equity and liabilities) as at the end of the chargeable period,
(b) adjust the amount in accordance with paragraphs 20 and 44 (so far as applicable), and
(c) finally, reduce the amount (but not below nil) by—

(i) the amount of the sub-group's high quality liquid assets as at the end of that period, other than any asset which for the purposes of an adjustment under paragraph (b) is an asset to which paragraph 20(12) applies, and
(ii) where sub-paragraph (8) applies, the amount determined under that sub-paragraph.

(7) Sub-paragraph (8) applies where—

(a) as at the end of the chargeable period, the assets of the relevant UK banking sub-group include a financial asset in respect of an advance of cash made by a member of the sub-group,
(b) that financial asset is not an asset which, for the purposes of an adjustment under sub-paragraph (6)(b), is an asset to which paragraph 20(12) applies, and
(c) underlying that asset, as collateral, is an item ("the collateral") owned by that member which would form part of the sub-group's high quality liquid assets as at the end of that period were the collateral, rather than the financial asset, an asset of the sub-group.

(8) The amount within sub-paragraph (6)(c)(ii) is—

(a) the amount of the financial asset as at the end of that period or, if lower, an amount equal to the fair value of the collateral as at that time, or
(b) if this sub-paragraph applies in relation to more than one financial asset, the total of the amounts determined under paragraph (a) in respect of each of those assets.

(9) For the purposes of this paragraph and paragraph 20 the assets, equity and liabilities of a relevant UK banking sub-group are to be determined by reference to the amounts recognised in its consolidated financial statements for the chargeable period.

(10) Type B equity and liabilities are the chargeable equity and liabilities of any UK resident bank which—

(a) is a member of the relevant group, but
(b) is not a member of a relevant UK banking sub-group.

(11) Type C equity and liabilities are the chargeable equity and liabilities of any entity (apart from a UK resident bank) which—

(a) is a member of the relevant group, and
(b) is a member of a UK banking sub-group but is not a member of a relevant UK banking sub-group.

(12) To determine the amount of the chargeable equity and liabilities of an entity covered by sub-paragraph (10) or (11)—

(a) determine the amount of the entity's equity and liabilities (other than excluded equity and liabilities) as at the end of the chargeable period,
(b) adjust the amount in accordance with paragraphs 20 and 44 (so far as applicable), and
(c) finally, reduce the amount (but not below nil) by—

(i) the amount of the entity's high quality liquid assets as at the end of that period, other than any asset which for the purposes of an adjustment under paragraph (b) is an asset to which paragraph 20(12) applies, and

(ii) where sub-paragraph (14) applies, the amount determined under that sub-paragraph.

(13) Sub-paragraph (14) applies where—

(a) as at the end of the chargeable period, the assets of the entity include a financial asset in respect of an advance of cash made by the entity,

(b) that financial asset is not an asset which, for the purposes of an adjustment under sub-paragraph (12)(b), is an asset to which paragraph 20(12) applies, and

(c) underlying that asset, as collateral, is an item ("the collateral") owned by that entity which would form part of the entity's high quality liquid assets as at the end of that period were the collateral, rather than the financial asset, an asset of the entity.

(14) The amount within sub-paragraph (12)(c)(ii) is—

(a) the amount of the financial asset as at the end of that period or, if lower, an amount equal to the fair value of the collateral as at that time, or

(b) if this sub-paragraph applies in relation to more than one financial asset, the total of the amounts determined under paragraph (a) in respect of each of those assets.

(15) For the purposes of this paragraph and paragraph 20 the assets, equity and liabilities of an entity covered by sub-paragraph (10) or (11) are to be determined by reference to—

(a) the amounts recognised in the entity's financial statements for the chargeable period as prepared under international accounting standards or UK GAAP, or

(b) if no such financial statements are prepared, the amounts which would have been so recognised had such financial statements been prepared—

(i) under international accounting standards, or

(ii) under UK GAAP if that is what the entity prepares its financial statements under.

(16) In reducing the amount of any equity or liabilities under sub-paragraph (6)(c) or (12)(c), long term equity and liabilities are to be reduced before short term liabilities.

(17) Type D equity and liabilities are the UK allocated equity and liabilities (see paragraph 24) as at the end of the chargeable period of any relevant foreign bank which—

(a) is a member of the relevant group, but

(b) is not a member of a UK banking sub-group.

(18) If—

(a) the amount of the equity and liabilities, as at the end of the chargeable period, of a relevant UK banking sub-group or an entity covered by sub-paragraph (10) or (11), or

(b) the amount of the UK allocated equity and liabilities, as at the end of that period, of a relevant foreign bank covered by sub-paragraph (17),

is less than £50,000,000, the equity and liabilities, or UK allocated equity and liabilities, may be ignored for the purposes of this paragraph and paragraph 20.

(19) But the total amount of equity and liabilities which may be ignored under sub-paragraph (18) may not exceed £200,000,000.

20 (1) This paragraph applies for the purposes of paragraph 19(6) and (12).

(2) In this paragraph "relevant member" means—

(a) a relevant UK banking sub-group,

(b) a UK resident bank covered by paragraph 19(10), or

(c) an entity covered by paragraph 19(11).

(3) Sub-paragraph (4) applies if the members of a relevant UK banking sub-group are also members of one or more larger UK banking sub-groups.

(4) Any equity of the relevant UK banking sub-group is to be left out so far as it would have been eliminated under normal consolidation procedures had consolidated financial statements for the chargeable period been prepared for the larger or largest UK banking sub-group—

(a) under international accounting standards, or

(b) under UK GAAP if the entity which is the parent or parent undertaking for the larger or largest UK banking sub-group prepares its financial statements under UK GAAP.

(5) Sub-paragraph (6) applies if a relevant member within sub-paragraph (2)(b) or (c) is a member of one or more UK banking sub-groups.

(6) Any equity of the relevant member is to be left out so far as it would have been eliminated under normal consolidation procedures had consolidated financial statements for the chargeable period been prepared for the UK banking sub-group or the largest UK banking sub-group—

(a) under international accounting standards, or

(b) under UK GAAP if the entity which is the parent or parent undertaking for the UK banking sub-group or the largest UK banking sub-group prepares its financial statements under UK GAAP.

(7) The following liabilities of a relevant member are to be left out—

(a) liabilities to other relevant members, and

(b) liabilities to a relevant foreign bank covered by paragraph 19(17) so far as the bank's assets corresponding to the liabilities are assets of the permanent establishment through which the bank carries on a trade in the United Kingdom as determined at Step 2 in paragraph 24(1).

(8) Sub-paragraph (12) applies if—

(a) an entity ("M") within sub-paragraph (9) has liabilities to another entity ("N") not within that sub-paragraph, and N has assets which correspond to those liabilities ("M's liabilities"),

(b) M, or another entity within sub-paragraph (9), has assets which correspond to liabilities which N, or another entity not within that sub-paragraph, has to M or, as the case may be, to that other entity within that sub-paragraph ("N's liabilities"),

(c) there is in place an agreement which makes provision for there to be a single net settlement of all M's liabilities, and liabilities of other entities within sub-paragraph (9) to N or another entity which is not within that sub-paragraph, (so far as covered by the provision) and all N's liabilities (so far as covered by the provision) if the netting event occurs, and

(d) the provision mentioned in paragraph (c) is legally effective and enforceable.

(9) An entity is within this sub-paragraph if it is—

(a) a member of a relevant UK banking sub-group, or

(b) a relevant member within sub-paragraph (2)(b) or (c).

(10) For the purposes of sub-paragraph (8)—

(a) "agreement" includes an agreement which forms part of a multi-lateral agreement, arrangement or trading facility,

(b) if N is a relevant foreign bank covered by paragraph 19(17), liabilities of M to N are to be ignored so far as N's assets corresponding to those liabilities are assets of the permanent establishment through which N carries on a trade in the United Kingdom as determined at Step 2 in paragraph 24(1),

(c) references to assets of one party which correspond to liabilities of another party are to amounts receivable by that first party which correspond to amounts due from that other party,

(d) a liability which M has to N to which sub-paragraph (11) applies is to be treated as a liability to which an asset of N corresponds, and

(e) "the netting event occurs" if the insolvency or bankruptcy of—

(i) M, or another entity within sub-paragraph (9) which has assets which correspond to a liability covered by the provision mentioned in sub-paragraph (8)(c), or

(ii) N, or another entity not within sub-paragraph (9) which has such a liability,

gives rise to the termination of any arrangements under which such a liability arises.

(11) This sub-paragraph applies to a liability which M has to N if—

(a) as at the end of the chargeable period, the assets of M include a financial asset in respect of an advance of cash made by M to N,

(b) underlying that asset, as collateral, are securities which have been transferred by M to another person,

(c) the liability is a financial liability in respect of M's obligation to return the securities or similar securities to N, and

(d) the provision mentioned in sub-paragraph (8)(c) covers both the financial asset mentioned in paragraph (a) and that financial liability.

Section 556 of CTA 2009 (meaning of securities and similar securities) applies for the purposes of this sub-paragraph as it applies for the purposes of Chapter 10 of Part 6 of that Act.

(12) The amount of M's net settlement liabilities is to be reduced (but not below nil) by the amount of M's net settlement assets.

(13) "M's net settlement liabilities" means M's liabilities so far as they—

(a) are covered by the provision mentioned in sub-paragraph (8)(c), and

(b) are not excluded liabilities.

(14) "M's net settlement assets" means the assets of M, or of another entity within sub-paragraph (9), so far as corresponding to N's net settlement liabilities.

(15) But—

(a) if N's net settlement liabilities include liabilities of a relevant foreign bank covered by paragraph 19(17), X% (as determined at Step 2 in paragraph 24(1)) of the assets corresponding to the liabilities of the relevant foreign bank are to be disregarded for the purposes of sub-paragraph (14), and

(b) if sub-paragraph (12) applies in relation to more than one entity within sub-paragraph (9), no part of an asset may be included in the net settlement assets of more than one such entity.

(16) "N's net settlement liabilities" means N's liabilities so far as they are covered by the provision mentioned in sub-paragraph (8)(c).

(17) If M's net settlement liabilities exceed M's net settlement assets, and a proportion (A%) of those liabilities is long term liabilities and a proportion (B%) of those liabilities is short term liabilities, under sub-paragraph (12)—

(a) the long term liabilities are reduced by A% of M's net settlement assets, and

(b) the short term liabilities are reduced by B% of those assets.

Chargeable equity and liabilities of UK resident banks and building societies which are not members of groups

21 (1) This paragraph applies where the bank levy is charged as provided for by paragraph 5 and the relevant entity is a UK resident bank or a building society.

(2) To determine the amount of the relevant entity's chargeable equity and liabilities—

(a) determine the amount of the entity's equity and liabilities (other than excluded equity and liabilities) as at the end of the chargeable period,

(b) adjust that amount in accordance with paragraphs 22 and 44 (so far as applicable), and

(c) finally, reduce that amount (but not below nil) by—

(i) the amount of the entity's high quality liquid assets as at the end of that period, other than any asset which for the purposes of an adjustment under paragraph (b) is an asset to which paragraph 22(4) applies, and

(ii) where sub-paragraph (4) applies, the amount determined under that sub-paragraph.

(3) Sub-paragraph (4) applies where—

(a) as at the end of the chargeable period, the assets of the relevant entity include a financial asset in respect of an advance of cash made by the entity,

(b) that financial asset is not an asset which, for the purposes of an adjustment under sub-paragraph (2)(b), is an asset to which paragraph 22(4) applies, and

(c) underlying that asset, as collateral, is an item ("the collateral") owned by the entity which would form part of the entity's high quality liquid assets as at the end of that period were the collateral, rather than the financial asset, an asset of the entity.

(4) The amount within sub-paragraph (2)(c)(ii) is—

(a) the amount of the financial asset as at the end of that period or, if lower, an amount equal to the fair value of the collateral as at that time, or

(b) if this sub-paragraph applies in relation to more than one financial asset, the total of the amounts determined under paragraph (a) in respect of each of those assets.

(5) For the purposes of this paragraph and paragraph 22 the relevant entity's assets, equity and liabilities are to be determined by reference to the amounts recognised in the entity's financial statements for the chargeable period as prepared under international accounting standards or UK GAAP.

(6) In reducing the amount of any equity or liabilities under sub-paragraph (2)(c), long term equity and liabilities are to be reduced before short term liabilities.

22 (1) This paragraph applies for the purposes of paragraph 21(2) if—

(a) the relevant entity has liabilities to another entity ("N") and N has assets which correspond to those liabilities ("the relevant entity's liabilities"),

(b) the relevant entity also has assets which correspond to liabilities which N has to the relevant entity ("N's liabilities"),

(c) there is in place an agreement between the relevant entity and N which makes provision for there to be a single net settlement of all the relevant entity's liabilities (so far as covered by the provision) and all N's liabilities (so far as covered by the provision) if the netting event occurs, and

(d) the provision mentioned in paragraph (c) is legally effective and enforceable.

(2) For the purposes of sub-paragraph (1)—

(a) "agreement" includes an agreement which forms part of a multi-lateral agreement, arrangement or trading facility,

(b) references to assets of one party which correspond to liabilities of another party are to amounts receivable by that first party which correspond to amounts due from that other party,

(c) a liability which the relevant entity has to N to which sub-paragraph (3) applies is to be treated as a liability to which an asset of N corresponds, and

(d) "the netting event occurs" if the insolvency or bankruptcy of the relevant entity or N gives rise to the termination of any arrangements under which any liability covered by the provisions mentioned in sub-paragraph (1)(c) arises.

(3) This sub-paragraph applies to a liability which the relevant entity has to N if—

(a) as at the end of the chargeable period, the assets of the relevant entity include a financial asset in respect of an advance of cash made by the relevant entity to N,

(b) underlying that asset, as collateral, are securities which have been transferred by the relevant entity to another person,

(c) the liability is a financial liability in respect of the relevant entity's obligation to return the securities or similar securities to N, and

(d) the provision mentioned in sub-paragraph (1)(c) covers both the financial asset mentioned in paragraph (a) and that financial liability.

Section 556 of CTA 2009 (meaning of securities and similar securities) applies for the purposes of this sub-paragraph as it applies for the purposes of Chapter 10 of Part 6 of that Act.

(4) The amount of the relevant entity's net settlement liabilities is to be reduced (but not below nil) by the amount of the relevant entity's net settlement assets.

(5) The relevant entity's "net settlement liabilities" are the relevant entity's liabilities so far as they—

(a) are covered by the provision mentioned in sub-paragraph (1)(c), and

(b) are not excluded liabilities.

(6) The relevant entity's "net settlement assets" are its assets so far as corresponding to N's net settlement liabilities.

(7) "N's net settlement liabilities" means N's liabilities so far as they are covered by the provision mentioned in sub-paragraph (1)(c).

(8) If the relevant entity's net settlement liabilities exceed the entity's net settlement assets, and a proportion (A%) of those liabilities is long term liabilities and a proportion (B%) of those liabilities is short term liabilities, under sub-paragraph (4)—

(a) the long term liabilities are reduced by A% of the entity's net settlement assets, and

(b) the short term liabilities are reduced by B% of those assets.

Chargeable equity and liabilities of relevant foreign banks which are not members of groups

23 (1) This paragraph applies where the bank levy is charged as provided for by paragraph 5 and the relevant entity is a relevant foreign bank.

(2) The chargeable equity and liabilities of the relevant entity is the amount of its UK allocated equity and liabilities (see paragraph 24) as at the end of the chargeable period.

Definition of "UK allocated equity and liabilities"

24 (1) Take Steps 1 to 4 to determine the amount of the UK allocated equity and liabilities of a relevant foreign bank as at the end of the chargeable period.

Take Steps 5 and 6 to determine how much of that amount is to be treated as long term equity and liabilities and how much as short term liabilities for the purposes of Step 3 in paragraph 6(2).

Step 1

Determine the amount ("A") of the bank's assets as at the end of the chargeable period (subject to any adjustment under paragraph 25(5)).

Step 2

In accordance with paragraph 26, determine the amount ("B") of the assets, as at the end of the chargeable period, of the permanent establishment through which the bank carries on a trade in the United Kingdom (subject to any adjustment under paragraph 25(6)).

The proportion which B is of A is "X%".

Step 3

In accordance with paragraph 27, determine the amount ("C") of the bank's chargeable equity and liabilities.

Step 4

The amount of the UK allocated equity and liabilities is X% of C.

Step 5

Determine the proportion ("Y%") of C which is long term equity and liabilities.

Step 6

For the purposes of Step 3 in paragraph 6(2), treat Y% of the amount of the UK allocated equity and liabilities as long term equity and liabilities and the rest as short term liabilities.

(2) For the purposes of this paragraph and paragraphs 25 to 27, assets, equity and liabilities of a relevant foreign bank or the permanent establishment through which it carries on a trade in the United Kingdom are to be determined by reference to—

(a) the amounts recognised in the bank's financial statements for the chargeable period as prepared under international accounting standards or UK GAAP, or

(b) if no such financial statements are prepared, the amounts which would have been so recognised had such financial statements been prepared—

(i) under international accounting standards, or

(ii) under UK GAAP if that is what the bank prepares its financial statements under.

25 (1) This paragraph applies if—

(a) the relevant foreign bank has liabilities to another entity ("N") (subject to sub-paragraph (2)), and N has assets which correspond to those liabilities ("the bank's liabilities"),

(b) the bank also has assets which correspond to liabilities which N has to the bank ("N's liabilities"),

(c) there is in place an agreement between the bank and N which makes provision for there to be a single net settlement of all the bank's liabilities (so far as covered by the provision) and all N's liabilities (so far as covered by the provision) if the netting event occurs, and

(d) the provision mentioned in paragraph (c) is legally effective and enforceable.

(2) If the UK allocated equity and liabilities of the bank are being determined for the purposes of paragraph 17(17) or 19(17), this paragraph does not apply if N is—

(a) an entity within paragraph 18(9) or 20(9) (as the case may be), or

(b) another relevant foreign bank covered by paragraph 17(17) or 19(17) (as the case may be).

(3) For the purposes of sub-paragraph (1)—

(a) "agreement" includes an agreement which forms part of a multi-lateral agreement, arrangement or trading facility,

(b) references to assets of one party which correspond to liabilities of another party are to amounts receivable by that first party which correspond to amounts due from that other party,

(c) a liability which the relevant foreign bank has to N to which sub-paragraph (4) applies is to be treated as a liability to which an asset of N corresponds, and

(d) "the netting event occurs" if the insolvency or bankruptcy of the relevant foreign bank or N gives rise to the termination of any arrangements under which any liability covered by the provision mentioned in sub-paragraph (1)(c) arises.

(4) This sub-paragraph applies to a liability which the relevant foreign bank has to N if—

(a) as at the end of the chargeable period, the assets of the relevant foreign bank include a financial asset in respect of an advance of cash made by the relevant foreign bank to N,

(b) underlying that asset, as collateral, are securities which have been transferred by the bank to another person,

(c) the liability is a financial liability in respect of the bank's obligation to return the securities or similar securities to N, and

(d) the provision mentioned in sub-paragraph (1)(c) covers both the financial asset mentioned in paragraph (a) and that financial liability.

Section 556 of CTA 2009 (meaning of securities and similar securities) applies for the purposes of this sub-paragraph as it applies for the purposes of Chapter 10 of Part 6 of that Act.

(5) In determining the amount of the bank's assets at Step 1 in paragraph 24(1), the amount of the bank's net settlement assets is to be reduced (but not below nil) by the amount of the bank's net settlement liabilities.

(6) In determining the amount of the permanent establishment's assets at Step 2 in paragraph 24(1)—

(a) the reduction in the bank's assets under sub-paragraph (5) is to be ignored, but

(b) the amount of the permanent establishment's net settlement assets is to be reduced by Z%.

(7) For this purpose, "Z%" is the proportion by which the bank's net settlement assets are reduced under sub-paragraph (5).

(8) In determining the amount of the bank's chargeable equity and liabilities at Step 3 in paragraph 24(1), the amount of the bank's net settlement liabilities is to be reduced (but not below nil) by the amount of the bank's net settlement assets (ignoring the reduction under sub-paragraph (5)).

(9) The bank's "net settlement liabilities" are the bank's liabilities so far as they—

(a) are covered by the provision mentioned in sub-paragraph (1)(c), and

(b) are not excluded liabilities.

(10) The bank's "net settlement assets" are its assets so far as corresponding to N's net settlement liabilities.

(11) "N's net settlement liabilities" means N's liabilities so far as they are covered by the provision mentioned in sub-paragraph (1)(c).

(12) The permanent establishment's "net settlement assets" are its assets so far as they are part of the bank's net settlement assets.

(13) If the bank's net settlement liabilities exceed the bank's net settlement assets (ignoring the reduction under sub-paragraph (5)), and a proportion (A%) of those liabilities is long term liabilities and a proportion (B%) of those liabilities is short term liabilities, under sub-paragraph (8)—

(a) the long term liabilities are reduced by A% of the bank's net settlement assets, and

(b) the short term liabilities are reduced by B% of those assets.

26 (1) This paragraph applies for the purposes of Step 2 in paragraph 24(1).

(2) The assets of the permanent establishment are those which it would have were it a distinct and separate enterprise which—

(a) engaged in the same or similar activities under the same or similar conditions, and

(b) dealt wholly independently with the relevant foreign bank.

(3) For this purpose, any relevant provisions of sections 21 to 28 of CTA 2009 are to be applied as they would be applied in determining profits attributable to the permanent establishment for corporation tax purposes.

(4) But where paragraph 24(1) is being applied in determining the UK allocated equity and liabilities of a relevant foreign bank for the purposes of paragraph 17(17) or 19(17), any assets within sub-paragraph (5) are to be left out.

(5) The assets within this sub-paragraph are any assets of the permanent establishment (as otherwise determined under this paragraph) representing an excluded loan relationship.

(6) A loan relationship is "excluded" if—

(a) the relevant foreign bank is the creditor,

(b) the debtor ("D") is a UK resident bank or another relevant foreign bank—

(i) which is a member of the relevant group, and

(ii) whose activities include the relevant regulated activity described in the provision mentioned in paragraph 79(a),

(c) the money which is the subject of the transaction giving rise to D's debt is money borrowed by the relevant foreign bank from another entity, and

(d) in borrowing that money the relevant foreign bank was acting as the agent or intermediary of D.

(7) Section 302(1) of CTA 2009 (definition of "loan relationship") applies for the purposes of sub-paragraphs (5) and (6) as it applies for corporation tax purposes.

27 (1) This paragraph applies for the purposes of Step 3 in paragraph 24(1).

(2) To determine the amount of the relevant foreign bank's chargeable equity and liabilities—

(a) determine the amount of the bank's equity and liabilities (other than excluded equity and liabilities) as at the end of the chargeable period,

(b) adjust that amount in accordance with sub-paragraph (5) and paragraphs 25(8) and 44 (so far as applicable), and

(c) finally, reduce that amount (but not below nil) by—

(i) the amount of the entity's high quality liquid assets as the end of that period, other than any asset which for the purposes of an adjustment under paragraph (b) is an asset to which paragraph 25(8) applies, and

(ii) where sub-paragraph (4) applies, the amount determined under that sub-paragraph.

(3) Sub-paragraph (4) applies where—

(a) as at the end of the chargeable period, the assets of the relevant foreign bank include a financial asset in respect of an advance of cash made by the bank,

(b) that financial asset is not an asset which, for the purposes of an adjustment under sub-paragraph (2)(b), is an asset to which paragraph 25(8) applies, and

(c) underlying that asset, as collateral, is an item ("the collateral") owned by the bank which would form part of the bank's high quality liquid assets as at the end of that period were the collateral, rather than the financial asset, an asset of the bank.

(4) The amount within sub-paragraph (2)(c)(ii) is—

(a) the amount of the financial asset as at the end of that period or, if lower, an amount equal to the fair value of the collateral as at that time, or

(b) if this sub-paragraph applies in relation to more than one financial asset, the total of the amounts determined under paragraph (a) in respect of each of those assets.

(5) Where paragraph 24(1) is being applied in determining the UK allocated equity and liabilities of a relevant foreign bank for the purposes of paragraph 17(17) or 19(17), the following liabilities are to be left out—

(a) any liabilities to a relevant member as defined in paragraph 18(2) or 20(2) (as the case may be), or

(b) any liabilities to another relevant foreign bank covered by paragraph 17(17) or 19(17) (as the case may be) so far as the other bank's assets corresponding to the liabilities are assets of the permanent establishment through which the other bank carries on a trade in the United Kingdom as determined at Step 2 in paragraph 24(1).

(6) In reducing any amount of equity or liabilities under sub-paragraph (2)(c), long term equity and liabilities are to be reduced before short term liabilities.

"Excluded" equity and liabilities

28 (1) Equity or liabilities are "excluded" so far as they consist of equity or liabilities which are specified to be excluded—

(a) by any of paragraphs 29 to 39, or
(b) by an order made by the Treasury.

(2) The Treasury may also by order add to, repeal or otherwise amend any of paragraphs 29 to 39.

(3) An order under this paragraph may make consequential amendments of paragraph 76 ("long term" liabilities: non-protected deposits).

(4) An order under this paragraph may have retrospective effect in relation to—

(a) any chargeable period in which the order is made, or
(b) in the case of an order made on or before 31 December 2011, any chargeable period ending on or after 1 January 2011.

(5) Orders under this paragraph are to be made by statutory instrument.

(6) A statutory instrument containing an order under this paragraph may not be made unless a draft has been laid before, and approved by a resolution of, the House of Commons.

29 (1) Liabilities representing protected deposits are excluded.

(2) A deposit is "protected" so far as it is covered by the Financial Services Compensation Scheme under section 213 of FISMA 2000 ("the FSCS").

(3) A deposit is "protected" so far as it is covered by a scheme which—

(a) operates outside the United Kingdom, and
(b) is comparable to the FSCS.

(4) Sub-paragraph (5) applies for the purposes of sub-paragraphs (2) and (3) if—

(a) the entity holding the deposit ("the relevant deposit") is required to pay, in relation to the scheme, levies for purposes mentioned in section 213(3)(b) of FISMA 2000 or purposes comparable to those purposes,
(b) those levies are calculated—

(i) by reference to a proportion ("X%") of the total amount of all deposits held by the entity or all deposits held by the entity within a specified class within which the relevant deposit falls, or

(ii) by reference to another amount which is a proportion ("Y%") of the total amount of all the scheme deposits held by the entity, and

(c) X% or (as the case may be) Y% exceeds the proportion ("Z%") of the relevant deposit covered by the scheme.

(5) The scheme is treated—

(a) in a case within sub-paragraph (4)(b)(i), as covering X% of the relevant deposit (instead of Z%), and

(b) in a case within (4)(b)(ii), as covering Y% or, if smaller, 100% of the relevant deposit (instead of Z%).

(6) In sub-paragraph (4) "scheme deposit" means a deposit the whole or part of which is covered by the scheme (disregarding sub-paragraph (5)).

(7) A deposit is "protected" so far as it is covered by a guarantee—

(a) which is given explicitly by a national government (other than the government of the United Kingdom), and

(b) under which the government guarantees to compensate depositors for losses on their deposits.

(8) In sub-paragraph (2), and sub-paragraphs (4), (5) and (6) so far as relating to a scheme within sub-paragraph (2), "deposit" has the meaning given by article 5(2) of the Financial Services and Markets Act 2000 (Regulated Activities) Order 2001 (SI 2001/544).

(9) In sub-paragraphs (3) and (7), and sub-paragraphs (4), (5) and (6) so far as relating to a scheme within sub-paragraph (3), "deposit" has the meaning given by article 5(2) of that Order but ignoring the exclusions in articles 6 to 9AB.

(10) If two or all of sub-paragraphs (2), (3) and (7) apply to a deposit, the amount of the deposit "protected" is the highest amount which results from any one of those sub-paragraphs.

30 (1) Equity and liabilities which are "tier one capital equity and liabilities" are excluded.

(2) "Tier one capital equity and liabilities" means, in relation to an entity or a group of entities, so much of the entity or group's equity and liabilities as—

(a) is tier one capital before deductions for the purposes of the FSA Handbook, or

(b) would be treated as tier one capital before deductions for those purposes were the tier one capital before deductions of the entity or group as at the end of the chargeable period to be determined under that Handbook.

31 (1) Sovereign repo liabilities are excluded.

(2) "Sovereign repo liability" means a liability of a person ("A") which represents a sum of money or other asset received by A from another person ("B") under an arrangement where—

(a) under the arrangement A sells high quality securities at any time to B,

(b) the arrangement makes provision conferring a right or imposing an obligation on A to buy those or similar securities at any subsequent time, and

(c) the subsequent buying of those or similar securities would extinguish the liability.

(3) Section 556 of CTA 2009 (meaning of securities and similar securities) applies for the purposes of sub-paragraph (2) as it applies for the purposes of Chapter 10 of Part 6 of that Act.

(4) Securities are "high quality" if—

(a) they are debt securities issued by entities within section BIPRU 12.7.3(1) or (2) of the FSA Handbook which meet the requirements of section BIPRU 12.7.4(1) and (2), or

(b) they are issued by a designated multilateral development bank.

"Debt securities" has the same meaning as that term has in section BIPRU 12.7.3 of the FSA Handbook.

32 (1) Sovereign stock-lending liabilities are excluded.

(2) "Sovereign stock-lending liabilities" means liabilities of the lender to redeliver equivalent cash collateral under a stock lending arrangement in respect of high quality securities.

(3) Section 805 of CTA 2010 ("stock lending arrangement") applies for the purposes of sub-paragraph (2) as it applies for the purposes of Chapter 5 of Part 17 of that Act, and the reference in sub-paragraph (2) to "the lender" is to be construed accordingly.

(4) Paragraph 31(3) and (4) apply for the purposes of this paragraph.

33 (1) Relevant insurance liabilities are excluded.

(2) "Relevant insurance liabilities" means liabilities of a regulated insurer carrying on an insurance business which are—

(a) liabilities to policyholders under contracts of general insurance or contracts of long-term insurance, including such contracts effected or carried out outside the United Kingdom,

(b) liabilities representing unallocated surpluses, or

(c) liabilities representing participants' interests in collective investment schemes.

(3) The liabilities of a regulated insurer within sub-paragraph (2)(c) include a liability which would be a liability of the insurer within that provision if the insurer prepared consolidated financial statements.

(4) In this paragraph—

"collective investment scheme" has the same meaning as in Part 17 of FISMA 2000 (see sections 235 and 237 of that Act);

"contract of general insurance" means a contract of a type described in Part 1 of Schedule 1 to the Financial Services and Markets Act 2000 (Regulated Activities) Order 2001 (SI 2001/544);

"contract of long-term insurance" means a contract of a type described in Part 2 of that Schedule;

"regulated insurer" means an entity which—

(a) is authorised under the law of any territory to carry on insurance business, or

(b) is a member of a body or organisation which is so authorised;

"unallocated surplus" means the fund for future appropriations shown in line 15 of Form 3 of a return deposited with the Financial Services Authority under section 9.6 of the Interim Prudential Sourcebook for Insurers made by that Authority under FISMA 2000.

34 (1) Relevant property, plant and equipment reserves are excluded.

(2) "Relevant property, plant and equipment reserves" means equity amounts representing revaluation reserves relating to the revaluation of property, plant and equipment under International Accounting Standard 16 or Financial Reporting Standard 15.

(3) "Property, plant and equipment" has the meaning given, for the time being, by International Accounting Standard 16.

35 (1) Relevant tax liabilities are excluded.

(2) In relation to liabilities to be determined by reference to amounts recognised, or which would have been recognised, in consolidated financial statements or financial statements prepared under international accounting standards, "relevant tax liabilities" means liabilities representing—

(a) current tax or deferred tax liabilities within the meaning, for the time being, of International Accounting Standard 12, or

(b) an amount of the bank levy.

(3) In relation to liabilities to be determined by reference to amounts recognised, or which would have been recognised, in consolidated financial statements or financial statements prepared under UK GAAP, "relevant tax liabilities" means liabilities representing—

(a) current tax or deferred tax within the meaning, for the time being, of Financial Reporting Standard 16 or 19, or

(b) an amount of the bank levy.

36 (1) Relevant retirement benefit liabilities are excluded.

(2) In relation to liabilities to be determined by reference to amounts recognised, or which would have been recognised, in consolidated financial statements or financial statements prepared under international accounting standards, "relevant retirement benefit liabilities" means liabilities under defined benefit plans within the meaning, for the time being, of International Accounting Standard 19.

(3) In relation to liabilities to be determined by reference to amounts recognised, or which would have been recognised, in consolidated financial statements or financial statements prepared under UK GAAP, "relevant retirement benefit liabilities" means liabilities under defined benefit schemes within the meaning, for the time being, of Financial Reporting Standard 17.

37 (1) Financial services compensation scheme liabilities are excluded.

(2) "Financial services compensation scheme liabilities" means liabilities representing—

(a) levies payable by virtue of section 213(2)(b) of FISMA 2000, or

(b) levies payable for purposes comparable with those mentioned in section 213(2)(b) of that Act in relation to a scheme which—

(i) operates outside the United Kingdom, and

(ii) is comparable to the Financial Services Compensation Scheme under section 213 of that Act.

38 (1) Liabilities representing clients' money held by an authorised person are excluded.

(2) "Authorised person" means an entity which—

(a) is an authorised person for the purposes of FISMA 2000 (see section 31 of that Act), or

(b) would be required to be such an authorised person if it were a UK resident entity which carried on its activities in the United Kingdom.

(3) "Clients' money"—

(a) in relation to an authorised person within sub-paragraph (2)(a), has the meaning given by section 139(1) of FISMA 2000 (rules relating to handling of money), and

(b) in relation to an authorised person within sub-paragraph (2)(b), means any money held by the person outside the United Kingdom where the holding of that money is subject to rules comparable with rules made under section 139 of that Act,

but does not include a deposit within the meaning of article 5(2) of the Financial Services and Markets Act 2000 (Regulated Activities) Order 2001 (SI 2001/544) ignoring the exclusions in articles 6 to 9AB.

39 (1) Currency liabilities are excluded.

(2) "Currency liabilities" means liabilities of an entity or a group of entities representing notes issued by the entity or a member of the group as currency.

PART 5

SUPPLEMENTARY PROVISION

Netting agreements

40 (1) The Treasury may by order add to, repeal or otherwise amend any of paragraphs 16, 18(8) to (17), 20(8) to (17), 22 and 25.

(2) An order under this paragraph may make consequential amendments of this Schedule.

(3) An order under this paragraph may have retrospective effect in relation to—

(a) any chargeable period in which the order is made, or

(b) in the case of an order made on or before 31 December 2011, any chargeable period ending on or after 1 January 2011.

(4) Orders under this paragraph are to be made by statutory instrument.

(5) A statutory instrument containing an order under this paragraph may not be made unless a draft has been laid before, and approved by a resolution of, the House of Commons.

Chargeable periods: entities which do not prepare financial statements

41 (1) This paragraph applies where an entity does not prepare financial statements (consolidated or otherwise) for a period ("the relevant period").

(2) If the relevant period is 12 months or less, this Schedule (apart from this paragraph) applies as if that period were a period of account of the entity.

(3) If the relevant period is more than 12 months, this Schedule (apart from this paragraph) applies as if each period to which sub-paragraph (4) applies were a period of account of the entity.

(4) This sub-paragraph applies to a period if—

(a) it is the first period of 12 months falling within the relevant period, or

(b) it begins immediately after the end of the period mentioned in paragraph (a) and ends at the end of the relevant period.

(5) Sub-paragraph (6) applies if, at the end of a period of 36 months beginning with a relevant date, an entity has not prepared financial statements for a period which begins with that date.

(6) The entity is to be treated for the purposes of this paragraph as not having prepared financial statements for that period or, if that period exceeds 24 months, for the first 24 months of that period.

(7) "Relevant date" means—

(a) 1 January 2011,

(b) the first day after a period, ending on or after that date, for which the entity has prepared financial statements, or

(c) the first day after a period for which the company is treated under sub-paragraph (6) as not having prepared financial statements.

Financial statements etc

42 (1) This paragraph applies for the purposes of this Schedule.

(2) References to consolidated financial statements for a period include references to a consolidated balance sheet (or consolidated statement of financial position) as at the last day of the period.

(3) References to financial statements for a period include references to a balance sheet (or statement of financial position) as at the last day of the period.

(4) References to amounts recognised in consolidated financial statements or financial statements include references to an amount comprised in an amount so recognised.

(5) Sub-paragraph (6) applies if an amount for the chargeable period, or as at the last day of the chargeable period, is so recognised in a currency other than sterling.

(6) The amount is to be translated into its sterling equivalent by reference to the spot rate of exchange for the last day of the chargeable period.

(7) If consolidated financial statements or financial statements for the chargeable period are not prepared in a way which complies with the relevant accounting framework under which the statements are prepared, the statements are to be adjusted as necessary to ensure that they comply.

(8) In sub-paragraph (7) "relevant accounting framework" means—

(a) international accounting standards,

(b) US GAAP, or

(c) UK GAAP.

(9) In relation to the preparation of consolidated financial statements or financial statements under UK GAAP, Financial Reporting Standard 23 and Financial Reporting Standard 26 are to be treated as if they were mandatory for all entities.

(10) Accordingly, if any statements are prepared under UK GAAP without one or both of those Standards being applied, the statements are to be treated as not complying with UK GAAP and adjusted under sub-paragraph (7) accordingly.

Joint ventures

43 (1) This paragraph applies if—

(a) the relevant group is a foreign banking group or a relevant non-banking group,

(b) a member of the relevant group has an interest ("the relevant interest") in a joint venture for the purposes of those provisions of the applicable accounting standards which relate to joint ventures,

(c) the amounts recognised in the relevant consolidated financial statements include amounts representing the liabilities ("the JV liabilities") of the joint venture so far as determined by the relevant interest,

(d) the joint venture is a UK resident entity or, if the relevant group is a relevant non-banking group, a UK resident bank, and

(e) none of the liabilities of a relevant UK sub-group, a relevant UK banking sub-group or any entity for the purposes of (as the case may be) paragraph 17(6)(a) or (12)(a), 19(6)(a) or (12)(a) or 27(2)(a) include the JV liabilities.

(2) For the purpose of determining the chargeable equity and liabilities of the relevant group the joint venture is to be treated as if it were (as the case may be) a UK resident entity covered by paragraph 17(10) or a UK resident bank covered by paragraph 19(10)—

(a) the liabilities of which consist of the JV liabilities, and

(b) the assets of which consist of the assets of the joint venture so far as determined by the relevant interest.

(3) In this paragraph references to the amounts recognised in the relevant consolidated financial statements are to—

(a) the amounts recognised in the relevant group's consolidated financial statements for the chargeable period as prepared under the applicable accounting standards, or

(b) if no such financial statements are prepared, the amounts which would have been so recognised had consolidated financial statements for the relevant group been prepared for the chargeable period under international accounting standards.

(4) "The applicable accounting standards" means—

(a) international accounting standards, or

(b) US GAAP if the members of the relevant group are determined under paragraph 4(7).

44 (1) This paragraph applies for the purpose of determining the chargeable equity and liabilities of the relevant group or the relevant entity if, as at the end of the chargeable period—

(a) the parent entity or the relevant entity is a joint venture for the purposes of a JV standard, and

(b) the liabilities of the parent entity or the relevant entity include liabilities ("the JV liabilities") which are subject to a double charge.

(2) The JV liabilities are to be left out for the purpose of determining the chargeable equity and liabilities.

(3) In sub-paragraph (1)(b) the reference to the liabilities of the parent entity includes any liabilities which, in the absence of this paragraph, would form part of the chargeable equity and liabilities of the relevant group.

(4) The JV liabilities are subject to a double charge if conditions A and B are met.

(5) Condition A is that an entity ("V") which has an interest in the joint venture for the purposes of the JV standard—

(a) is an entity in relation to which paragraph 4(1) or 5(1) applies as at the end of the chargeable period (or in relation to which paragraph 4(1) or 5(1) would apply if V had a period of account ending at the same time as the chargeable period), or

(b) falls within sub-paragraph (6).

(6) V falls within this sub-paragraph if—

(a) there is another entity ("A") in relation to which paragraph 4(1) applies as at the end of the chargeable period (or in relation to which paragraph 4(1) would apply if A had a period of account ending at the same time as the chargeable period), and

(b) V is (or would be) a member of the relevant group of which A is (or would be) the parent entity.

(7) Condition B is that—

(a) in the circumstances mentioned in sub-paragraph (5)(a) or sub-paragraph (5)(b) (when read with sub-paragraph (6)), the bank levy is charged (or would be charged), and

(b) in determining the amount of the bank levy, the JV liabilities are (or would be) liabilities for the purposes of paragraph 15(2)(a), 17(6)(a) or (12)(a), 19(6)(a) or (12)(a), 21(2)(a) or 27(2)(a) by virtue of V having an interest in the joint venture.

(8) "JV standard" means those provisions of international accounting standards or UK GAAP which relate to joint ventures.

Residence

45 For the purposes of this Schedule—

(a) the territory in which a company is resident is to be determined as for corporation tax purposes, and

(b) the territory in which a partnership is resident is the territory in which the control and management of the partnership's trade and investment activities take place.

Bank levy to be ignored for other tax purposes

46 In calculating profits or losses for the purposes of income tax or corporation tax—

(a) no deduction is allowed in respect of the bank levy, and

(b) no account is to be taken of any amount which is paid by a member of the relevant group to another member of the group for the purposes of meeting or reimbursing the cost of the bank levy charged in relation to the group.

Anti-avoidance

47 (1) This paragraph applies if—

(a) arrangements are entered into by one or more entities, and

(b) the main purpose, or one of the main purposes, of the entity, or any of the entities, in entering into the arrangements or any part of them is to avoid or reduce a charge or assessment to the bank levy.

(2) In this paragraph "the relevant arrangements"—

(a) means the arrangements or the part of them referred to in sub-paragraph (1)(b), and

(b) includes any part of those arrangements or of that part.

(3) Sub-paragraph (4) applies if an effect of the relevant arrangements is that the bank levy is not charged or assessed as it would have been in the absence of the relevant arrangements.

(4) The bank levy is charged or assessed as it would have been ignoring that effect.

(5) The cases covered by sub-paragraph (3) include (in particular) cases in which the bank levy is charged or assessed but an effect of the relevant arrangements is that the amount of the bank levy charged or assessed—

(a) is nil, or
(b) is otherwise less than it would have been in the absence of the relevant arrangements.

(6) In sub-paragraphs (3) and (5) references to the relevant arrangements do not include those arrangements to the extent to which any of the following sub-paragraphs applies to them.

(7) This sub-paragraph applies to the relevant arrangements so far as their effect is to increase, on an ongoing basis, the excluded equity and liabilities of the relevant group or the relevant entity.

(8) This sub-paragraph applies to the relevant arrangements so far as their effect is to increase, on an ongoing basis, the long term equity and liabilities of the relevant group or the relevant entity.

(9) This sub-paragraph applies to the relevant arrangements so far as—

(a) their effect is to reduce, on an ongoing basis, the short term liabilities of the relevant group or the relevant entity, and
(b) there is no corresponding increase, on an ongoing basis or otherwise, in the amount of the funding, or the size of the financial obligations, of the relevant group or the relevant entity which is not, or are not, excluded equity and liabilities or long term equity and liabilities (it being immaterial for this purpose whether or not any such funding or obligation is recognised in the financial statements of the group or entity).

(10) This sub-paragraph applies to the relevant arrangements so far as—

(a) their effect is to reduce, on an ongoing basis, the long term equity and liabilities of the relevant group or the relevant entity, and
(b) there is no corresponding increase, on an ongoing basis or otherwise, in the amount of the funding, or the size of the financial obligations, of the relevant group or the relevant entity which is not, or are not, excluded equity and liabilities (it being immaterial for this purpose whether or not any such funding or obligation is recognised in the financial statements of the group or entity).

(11) This sub-paragraph applies to the relevant arrangements so far as they are an agreement within paragraph 16(1)(c) and (d), 18(8)(c) and (d), 20(8)(c) and (d), 22(1)(c) and (d) or 25(1)(c) and (d).

(12) This sub-paragraph applies to the relevant arrangements so far as their effect is to increase, on an ongoing basis, the amount of the high quality liquid assets of the relevant group or the relevant entity.

(13) If the relevant group is a foreign banking group or a relevant non-banking group, in the sub-paragraphs above references to the relevant group are to be read as references to the members of the group, collectively, which are relevant members.

(14) In sub-paragraph (13) "relevant member"—

(a) has the same meaning as in paragraph 18 or 20 (as the case may be), and
(b) includes a relevant foreign bank covered by paragraph 17(17) or 19(17) (as the case may be).

48 (1) Section 1139 of CTA 2010 (definition of "tax advantage") is amended as follows.

(2) In subsection (2)—

(a) omit the "or" after paragraph (c), and
(b) after paragraph (d) insert
", or
(e) the avoidance or reduction of a charge or assessment to the bank levy under Schedule 19 to FA 2011 (the bank levy)."

(3) After subsection (3) insert—

"(3A) The avoidance or reduction of a charge or assessment to the bank levy as a result of arrangements to which paragraph 47 of Schedule 19 to FA 2011 (bank levy: anti-avoidance) applies is to be ignored for the purposes of subsection (2)(e) to the extent that it results from arrangements, or part of arrangements, to which any of paragraph 47(7) to (12) of that Schedule applies."

PART 6
COLLECTION AND MANAGEMENT

Responsibility for collection and management

49 (1) The Commissioners for Her Majesty's Revenue and Customs are responsible for the collection and management of the bank levy.

(2) In this Part of this Schedule "HMRC" means Her Majesty's Revenue and Customs.

Payment of the bank levy through the corporation tax system

50 (1) This paragraph applies where the bank levy is charged as provided for by paragraph 4.

(2) The bank levy is to be treated as if it were an amount of corporation tax chargeable on the relevant group's responsible member (see paragraph 54) for the accounting period or periods determined in accordance with the following sub-paragraphs.

(3) Subject to what follows, the accounting period for which the bank levy is to be treated as if it were an amount of corporation tax chargeable is to be—

(a) the responsible member's accounting period which ends at the same time as the chargeable period, or

(b) if it does not have an accounting period which ends at that time, its accounting period during which the chargeable period ends.

(4) If a proportion ("X%") of the chargeable period falls in any other accounting period of the responsible member, X% of the bank levy is to be treated as if it were an amount of corporation tax chargeable for that other accounting period.

51 (1) This paragraph applies where the bank levy is charged as provided for by paragraph 5.

(2) The bank levy is to be treated as if it were an amount of corporation tax chargeable on the relevant entity for the accounting period or periods determined in accordance with the following sub-paragraphs.

(3) Subject to what follows, the accounting period for which the bank levy is to be treated as if it were an amount of corporation tax chargeable is to be—

(a) the relevant entity's accounting period which ends at the same time as the chargeable period, or

(b) if it does not have an accounting period which ends at that time, its accounting period during which the chargeable period ends.

(4) If a proportion ("X%") of the chargeable period falls in any other accounting period of the relevant entity, X% of the bank levy is to be treated as if it were an amount of corporation tax chargeable for that other accounting period.

52 (1) Paragraphs 50(2) and 51(2) are to be taken as applying all enactments applying generally to corporation tax.

(2) This is subject to—

(a) any provisions of the Taxes Acts (within the meaning of TMA 1970),

(b) any necessary modifications, and

(c) sub-paragraph (5).

(3) The enactments mentioned in sub-paragraph (1) include—

(a) those relating to returns of information and the supply of accounts, statements and reports,

(b) those relating to the assessing, collecting and receiving of corporation tax,

(c) those conferring or regulating a right of appeal, and

(d) those concerning administration, penalties, interest on unpaid tax and priority of tax in cases of insolvency under the law in any part of the United Kingdom.

(4) Accordingly—

(a) TMA 1970 is to have effect as if any reference to corporation tax included the bank levy where it is treated by paragraph 50(2) or 51(2) as an amount of corporation tax chargeable on an entity, and

(b) in particular, where the bank levy is so treated, it is due and payable as an amount of corporation tax in accordance with section 59D of TMA 1970, subject to section 59E of that Act.

(5) Nothing in section 53 of this Act (leases and changes to accounting standards) has effect in relation to the bank levy or any provision of this Schedule.

Joint and several liability

53 (1) This paragraph applies where the bank levy is charged as provided for by paragraph 4.

(2) The entities within sub-paragraph (3) are jointly and severally liable for the bank levy liability of the relevant group's responsible member (see paragraph 54) for an accounting period; and HMRC may enforce that liability against any of those entities accordingly.

(3) The entities within this sub-paragraph are—

(a) if the relevant group is a relevant non-banking group, all relevant members of the relevant group within the charge to corporation tax as at the end of the chargeable period, or

(b) otherwise, all members of the relevant group within the charge to corporation tax as at the end of the chargeable period.

(4) In sub-paragraph (3)(a) "relevant member" means a member of the relevant group which—

(a) is a member of a relevant UK banking sub-group,
(b) is a UK resident bank covered by paragraph 19(10),
(c) is an entity covered by paragraph 19(11), or
(d) is a relevant foreign bank covered by paragraph 19(17).

(5) An entity's liability by virtue of sub-paragraph (2) is not affected if, after the end of the chargeable period, it ceases to be within the charge to corporation tax.

(6) An entity is not within sub-paragraph (3) if, as at the end of the chargeable period, it is—

(a) a securitisation company,
(b) a covered bond vehicle, or
(c) an entity of a kind prescribed by an order made by the Treasury.

(7) In sub-paragraph (6)—

"capital market arrangement" has the same meaning as in section 72B(1) of the Insolvency Act 1986 (see paragraph 1 of Schedule 2A to that Act);

"covered bond vehicle" means a limited liability partnership—

(a) which is a party to a capital market arrangement, or a transaction in pursuance of a capital market arrangement,

(b) whose trade or business (ignoring any incidental activities) consists wholly of one or both of the following—

(i) providing guarantees, and

(ii) acquiring, owning and managing assets directly or indirectly forming the whole or part of the security for the capital market arrangement, and

(c) which is within the charge to corporation tax;

"limited liability partnership" includes an entity established under the law of a territory outside the United Kingdom of a similar character to a limited liability partnership;

"securitisation company" means a company of the kind mentioned in paragraphs (a) to (e) of section 83(2) of FA 2005 or paragraphs (a) to (e) of regulation 4(2) of the Taxation of Securitisation Companies Regulations 2006 (SI 2006/3296).

(8) The responsible member's "bank levy liability" for an accounting period—

(a) is the member's liability for corporation tax for that period as calculated in accordance with paragraph 8 of Schedule 18 to FA 1998 so far as the tax calculated consists of the bank levy by virtue of paragraph 50(2) of this Schedule, and

(b) includes any interest or penalties payable in relation to that tax so far as it consists of the bank levy.

(9) An order under sub-paragraph (6) may have retrospective effect in relation to—

(a) any chargeable period in which the order is made, or

(b) in the case of an order made on or before 31 December 2011, any chargeable period ending on or after 1 January 2011.

(10) Orders under sub-paragraph (6) are to be made by statutory instrument.

(11) A statutory instrument containing an order under sub-paragraph (6) is subject to annulment in pursuance of a resolution of the House of Commons.

Meaning of "the responsible member"

54 (1) This paragraph applies where the bank levy is charged as provided for by paragraph 4.

(2) In this paragraph and paragraph 55 "chargeable member" means a member of the relevant group within paragraph 53(3).

(3) The relevant group's responsible member is the entity ("E") in relation to which the following requirements are met—

(a) E is a chargeable member of the relevant group,

(b) E has an accounting period for corporation tax purposes which is the same as the chargeable period,

(c) during the chargeable period but no later than 45 days after it started, the parent entity, or another entity acting on behalf of the parent entity, nominated E to HMRC to be the responsible member, and

(d) HMRC did not reject E's nomination.

See paragraph 55 for further provision about nominations.

(4) If—

(a) no entity meets the requirements in sub-paragraph (3) and the relevant group is a UK banking group or a building society group, and

(b) the parent entity is a chargeable member of the relevant group,

the responsible member is the parent entity.

(5) If no entity meets the requirements in sub-paragraph (3) and the relevant group is a foreign banking group or a relevant non-banking group, the responsible member is the entity in relation to which the following requirements are met—

(a) it is a chargeable member of the relevant group,

(b) it has an accounting period for corporation tax purposes which is the same as the chargeable period, and

(c) it is—

(i) the relevant member with the largest amount of chargeable equity and liabilities, or

(ii) if the relevant member with the largest amount of chargeable equity and liabilities is a relevant UK sub-group or a relevant UK banking sub-group (as the case may be), the entity which is the parent or parent undertaking for that sub-group.

(6) In sub-paragraph (5)(c) "relevant member"—

(a) has the same meaning as in paragraph 18 or 20 (as the case may be), and

(b) includes a relevant foreign bank covered by paragraph 17(17) or 19(17) (as the case may be).

(7) If no entity meets the requirements of sub-paragraph (3) or sub-paragraph (4) or (5) (as the case may be), the responsible member is the member of the relevant group determined by HMRC within the period of 30 days after the end of the chargeable period.

(8) HMRC must give written notice of a determination under sub-paragraph (7) to the member concerned within that period.

(9) HMRC cannot determine as the responsible member under sub-paragraph (7)—

(a) an entity within paragraph 53(6)(a) or (b), or

(b) an entity of a kind prescribed by an order under paragraph 53(6)(c).

(10) In relation to chargeable periods arising by virtue of paragraph 41 (chargeable periods: entities which do not prepare financial statements), the Treasury may by order modify the time limit applying to determinations under sub-paragraph (7) (including determinations in cases to which paragraph 65(3) applies).

(11) An order under sub-paragraph (10) may amend paragraphs 41 to 44 of Schedule 18 to FA 1998 (discovery assessments and determinations) in relation to any bank levy charged by virtue of paragraph 41 of this Schedule.

(12) Orders under sub-paragraph (10) are to be made by statutory instrument.

(13) A statutory instrument containing an order under sub-paragraph (10) is subject to annulment in pursuance of a resolution of the House of Commons.

(14) An order under sub-paragraph (10) may have retrospective effect in relation to—

(a) any chargeable period in which the order is made, or

(b) in the case of an order made on or before 31 December 2011, any chargeable period ending on or after 1 January 2011.

55 (1) This paragraph applies for the purposes of paragraph 54(3).

(2) Only one nomination may be made during the chargeable period.

(3) A nominator may nominate itself.

(4) HMRC may from time to time publish requirements as to the information to be included with a nomination.

(5) HMRC may reject a nomination within the period of 30 days starting with the day on which it receives the nomination.

(6) HMRC may reject a nomination only if—

(a) the nomination contravenes sub-paragraph (2),

(b) information required under sub-paragraph (4) is missing from the nomination, or

(c) HMRC has reason to believe that the nominee will turn out—

(i) not to be a chargeable member of the relevant group,

(ii) not to have an accounting period for corporation tax purposes which is the same as the chargeable period, or

(iii) not to have sufficient resources itself to pay the bank levy.

Consequential amendment to section 1 of PCTA 1968

56 In section 1 of the Provisional Collection of Taxes Act 1968 (temporary statutory effect of House of Commons resolutions affecting certain taxes), in subsection (1) after "corporation tax" insert ", the bank levy".

Consequential amendments to TMA 1970

57 TMA 1970 is amended as follows.

58 (1) Section 59E (provision about when corporation tax is due and payable) is amended as follows.

(2) In subsection (11), after paragraph (c) insert—

"(d) to the bank levy where treated as an amount of corporation tax chargeable on a company by paragraph 50 or 51 of Schedule 19 to the Finance Act 2011 (the bank levy)."

(3) After that subsection insert—

"(12) Without prejudice to the generality of any provision above—

(a) in relation to cases where the bank levy is treated as an amount of corporation tax chargeable on a company, regulations under this section may make provision—

(i) for amounts of the bank levy to be treated as becoming due and payable on dates which fall within the chargeable period (within the meaning of Schedule 19 to the Finance Act 2011);

(ii) for payments in respect of any such amounts of the bank levy as are mentioned in sub-paragraph (i) to become due and payable on dates which fall within that period;

(b) in relation to cases where a company on which the bank levy is treated as an amount of corporation tax chargeable for an accounting period has made payments in respect of corporation tax for that period, regulations under this section may make provision for or in connection with determining the extent to which those payments are to be treated as being payments of the bank levy;

(c) in relation to cases where a company ("the relevant company") has made payments in respect of corporation tax for an accounting period wholly or partly on the assumption that the bank levy will be treated as an amount of corporation tax chargeable on the relevant company for that period, regulations under this section may make provision for or in connection with treating those payments (wholly or partly) to have been made by another company if it turns out that the bank levy is not to be treated as an amount of corporation tax chargeable on the relevant company for that period;

(d) where regulations under this section impose a requirement within subsection (2)(j) above to furnish information for purposes related to the bank levy, the regulations may make provision for or in connection with applying Part 7 of Schedule 36 to the Finance Act 2008 in whole or in part (with or without modification) as if the requirement to furnish the information were contained in an information notice within the meaning of that Schedule."

59 At the end of section 59F(6) (provision for paying corporation tax on behalf of group members) insert

", and

(c) the bank levy where treated as an amount of corporation tax chargeable on a company by paragraph 50 or 51 of Schedule 19 to the Finance Act 2011 (the bank levy)."

Consequential amendments to Schedule 18 to FA 1998

60 Schedule 18 to FA 1998 (company tax returns) is amended as follows.

61 At the end of paragraph 1 insert

", and

paragraphs 50 and 51 of Schedule 19 to the Finance Act 2011 (the bank levy)."

62 After paragraph 3 insert—

"3A (1) Her Majesty's Revenue and Customs may from time to time publish requirements as to the information, accounts, statements and reports which a company must deliver as part of its company tax return where the company has a tax liability by virtue of paragraph 50 or 51 of Schedule 19 to the Finance Act 2011 (the bank levy); and such information, accounts, statements and reports must be delivered as if the notice to the company under paragraph 3(1) had required them to be delivered (and paragraph 4 is to be read accordingly).

(2) The publication of any requirements under sub-paragraph (1) does not stop a notice under paragraph 3(1) requiring the delivery of any additional information, accounts, statements and reports as part of a company tax return."

63 (1) Paragraph 8 is amended as follows.

(2) At the end of the "Third step" in sub-paragraph (1) insert—

"3 Any amount of the bank levy chargeable by virtue of paragraph 50 or 51 of Schedule 19 to the Finance Act 2011 (the bank levy)."

(3) After sub-paragraph (1) insert—

"(1A) Sub-paragraph (1B) applies if an amount of the bank levy chargeable by virtue of paragraph 50 or 51 of Schedule 19 to the Finance Act 2011 (the bank levy) is added at the third step.

(1B) Any deductions made at the fourth step are to be treated as made from all other amounts before being made from the amount of the bank levy."

64 (1) Paragraph 11 is amended as follows.

(2) The existing provision becomes sub-paragraph (1).

(3) After that sub-paragraph insert—

"(2) Sub-paragraph (1) does not affect—

(a) the power to require the delivery of accounts, information or documents in relation to a company's tax liability by virtue of paragraph 50 or 51 of Schedule 19 to the Finance Act 2011 (the bank levy), or

(b) the requirements which may be imposed under paragraph 3A."

Transitional provision

65 (1) Sub-paragraphs (2) to (6) apply if the chargeable period starts on or before the day on which this Act is passed (whether or not it ends on or before that day).

(2) Paragraph 54(3)(c) has effect as if for the words "during the chargeable period but no later than 45 days after it started" there were substituted "within the period of 7 days starting with the day on which this Act is passed".

(3) Paragraph 54(7) has effect as if for the words "30 days after the end of the chargeable period" there were substituted "15 days starting with the day on which this Act is passed".

(4) Paragraph 55(5) has effect as if for "30" there were substituted "7".

(5) Sub-paragraph (6) applies if, before the passing of this Act—

(a) HMRC published a statement stating that it was ready to receive nominations for responsible members,

(b) an entity made a nomination in accordance with HMRC's statement, and

(c) the nomination included all information required by HMRC's statement.

(6) For the purposes of paragraphs 54(3)(c) and 55(5) (as modified above) the nomination is to be treated as if it were made by the entity and received by HMRC immediately after the passing of this Act.

(7) The requirements covered by paragraph 55(4) include any requirements published by HMRC before the passing of this Act which are stated to apply for the purposes of nominations for responsible members.

(8) But such requirements are to apply only to nominations made during 2011.

(9) Regulations under section 59E of TMA 1970, in relation to amounts within subsection (11)(d) of that section (amounts of bank levy), made on or before 31 December 2011 may have effect in relation to amounts of bank levy which—

(a) are payable in respect of chargeable periods ending on or before that day, or

(b) are treated as amounts of corporation tax for accounting periods ending on or before that day.

PART 7

DOUBLE TAXATION RELIEF

Arrangements affording double taxation relief

66 (1) If the Treasury by order declares—

(a) that arrangements specified in the order have been made in relation to any foreign territory with a view to affording relief from double taxation in relation to the bank levy and any equivalent foreign levy, and

(b) that it is expedient that those arrangements should have effect,

those arrangements ("double taxation arrangements") have effect so far as they provide for relief from the bank levy.

(2) In this Part of this Schedule—

"equivalent foreign levy", in relation to a foreign territory, means any tax imposed by the law of that territory which corresponds to the bank levy;

"foreign territory" means a territory outside the United Kingdom.

(3) For the purposes of sub-paragraph (2), tax may correspond to the bank levy even though—

(a) the tax is payable under the law of a province, state or other part of a country,

(b) it is levied by or on behalf of a municipality or other local body, or

(c) its proceeds form a fund used for a particular purpose.

(4) Double taxation arrangements have effect under sub-paragraph (1)—

(a) subject to the following provisions of this paragraph, and

(b) despite anything in any other enactment.

(5) This paragraph gives effect to arrangements even if they provide for relief from the bank levy for periods before the making of the arrangements or before the passing of this Act.

(6) Relief under this paragraph requires a claim.

(7) An order under this paragraph revoking an earlier order may contain transitional provisions that appear to the Treasury to be necessary or expedient.

(8) The Treasury may by regulations make provision—

(a) generally for carrying out the provisions of this paragraph or double taxation arrangements;

(b) for removing, or reducing the amount of, relief obtained by virtue of double taxation arrangements in circumstances where a scheme or arrangement of a specified description has been made or in other specified circumstances;

(c) for restricting the amount of relief allowed against an entity's liability for the bank levy for a chargeable period to an amount calculated in a specified manner.

(9) Regulations under sub-paragraph (8)(a) may, in particular, provide that where, under double taxation arrangements, the Commissioners for Her Majesty's Revenue and Customs arrive at a solution to a case, or make a mutual agreement with an authority in another territory for the resolution of a case—

(a) the Commissioners are to give effect to the solution or mutual agreement despite anything in any enactment, and

(b) any adjustment as is appropriate in consequence may be made.

(10) Regulations under this paragraph may—

(a) amend any provision made by or under an Act whenever passed or made (including this Act), and

(b) contain transitional provisions that appear to the Treasury to be necessary or expedient.

(11) Orders or regulations under this paragraph are to be made by statutory instrument.

(12) A statutory instrument containing an order or regulations under this paragraph is subject to annulment in pursuance of a resolution of the House of Commons.

Power to provide for double taxation relief

67 (1) The Treasury may by regulations make provision for relief from the bank levy for the purpose of affording relief from double taxation in relation to the bank levy and any equivalent foreign levy imposed by the law of a foreign territory.

(2) Regulations under this paragraph must specify the equivalent foreign levy or levies in respect of which they are made.

(3) Regulations under this paragraph may, in particular—

(a) provide for relief from the bank levy for periods before the making of the regulations or before the passing of this Act;

(b) make provision for removing, or reducing the amount of, relief obtained in circumstances where a scheme or arrangement of a specified description has been made or in other specified circumstances;

(c) make provision for restricting the amount of relief allowed against an entity's liability for the bank levy for a chargeable period to an amount calculated in a specified manner.

(4) Regulations under this paragraph may—

(a) make different provision for different purposes, cases or circumstances,

(b) amend any provision made by or under an Act whenever passed or made (including this Act), and

(c) contain transitional provisions that appear to the Treasury to be necessary or expedient.

(5) Regulations under this paragraph are to be made by statutory instrument.

(6) A statutory instrument containing regulations under this paragraph—

(a) in a case where the reciprocity condition is met, are subject to annulment in pursuance of a resolution of the House of Commons, and

(b) in any other case, may not be made unless a draft has been laid before and approved by a resolution of that House.

(7) The reciprocity condition is met if the Treasury is satisfied that in relation to the foreign territory or each of the foreign territories concerned—

(a) appropriate provision has been made under the law of the territory for relief from double taxation in relation to the bank levy and the equivalent foreign levy under the law of that territory to which the regulations apply, or

(b) such provision will be made as a result of an agreement which has been entered into in relation to the territory.

Disclosure of information to foreign tax authorities

68 (1) Sub-paragraph (2) applies if the law of a foreign territory makes provision allowing, in respect of payments of the bank levy, relief from an equivalent foreign levy payable under that law.

(2) No obligation as to secrecy or other restriction on the disclosure of information prevents the Commissioners for Her Majesty's Revenue and Customs, or an officer of Revenue and Customs, from disclosing to the authorised officer of the authorities of the territory such facts as may be necessary to enable the proper relief to be given under the law of the territory.

Consequential amendment to the Constitutional Reform and Governance Act 2010

69 In section 23 of the Constitutional Reform and Governance Act 2010 (which excepts certain treaties from the requirements imposed by section 20 of that Act as to the laying of treaties before Parliament), after subsection (2) insert—

> "(2A) Section 20 does not apply to a treaty in relation to which an order may be made under paragraph 66 of Schedule 19 to the Finance Act 2011 (bank levy: arrangements affording double taxation relief)."

PART 8

DEFINITIONS

General

70 (1) In this Schedule—

"arrangements" includes any agreement, understanding, scheme, transaction or series of transactions (whether or not it is legally enforceable);

"asset management activities" is defined in paragraph 71;

"assets" is defined in paragraph 14;

"banking group" is defined in paragraph 12;

"the bank levy" is defined in paragraph 1;

"building society" means a building society within the meaning of the Building Societies Act 1986;

"building society group" is defined in paragraph 9;

"capital resources condition" is defined in paragraph 72;

"the chargeable period" is defined in paragraph 4(1) or 5(1) (as the case may be);

"company" has the meaning given by section 1121(1) of CTA 2010;

"contract of insurance" has the meaning given by article 3(1) of the Financial Services and Markets Act 2000 (Regulated Activities) Order 2001 (SI 2001/544);
"entity" includes a company, a partnership or a joint venture, but not—

(a) the Crown,
(b) a Minister of the Crown,
(c) a government department,
(d) a Northern Ireland department,
(e) a foreign sovereign power, or
(f) an international organisation;

"equity" is defined in paragraph 14;
"excluded", in relation to equity and liabilities, is defined in paragraph 28;
"excluded entity" is defined in paragraph 73;
"exempt activities condition" is defined in paragraph 13;
"fair value", in relation to an item, means the amount for which the item could be exchanged between knowledgeable, willing parties in an arm's length transaction;
"foreign banking group" is defined in paragraph 10;
"the FSA Handbook" means the Handbook of Rules and Guidance made by the Financial Services Authority (as that Handbook has effect from time to time);
"high quality liquid asset", in relation to an entity or group of entities, means an asset (within the meaning of this Schedule) within section BIPRU 12.7.2(1) to (4) of the FSA Handbook (whether or not it is held by an ILAS BIPRU firm), but see sub-paragraph (4);
"international accounting standards" has the meaning given by section 1127(5) of CTA 2010, including any modifications mentioned in section 1127(6);
"international organisation" means an organisation of which—

(a) two or more sovereign powers are members, or
(b) the governments of two or more sovereign powers are members,

(see also sub-paragraph (5));
"liabilities" is defined in paragraph 14;
"long term", in relation to equity and liabilities, is defined in paragraphs 74 to 77;
"the parent entity" is defined in paragraph 4(1);
"partnership" includes—

(a) a limited liability partnership, and
(b) an entity established under the law of a territory outside the United Kingdom of a similar character to a partnership,

and "member", in relation to a partnership, is to be read accordingly;
"period of account", in relation to an entity, means a period for which the entity prepares financial statements (consolidated or otherwise), (see also paragraph 41);
"permanent establishment" is to be read in accordance with Chapter 2 of Part 24 of CTA 2010;
"the relevant entity" is defined in paragraph 5(1);
"relevant foreign bank" is defined in paragraph 78;
"the relevant group" is defined in paragraph 4(1);
"relevant non-banking group" is defined in paragraph 11;
"relevant regulated activity" is defined in paragraph 79;
"relevant UK banking sub-group" is defined in paragraph 19(5);
"relevant UK sub-group" is defined in paragraph 17(5);
"short term", in relation to liabilities, means any liabilities which are not long term;
"UK allocated equity and liabilities" is defined in paragraph 24;
"UK banking sub-group" is defined in paragraph 19(4);
"UK GAAP" means UK generally accepted accounting practice as defined in section 1127(2) of CTA 2010 (subject to paragraph 42(9));
"UK resident bank" is defined in paragraph 80;
"UK resident entity" means an entity which is resident in the United Kingdom (see paragraph 45) and "non-UK resident entity" is to be read accordingly;
"UK sub-group" is defined in paragraph 17(4);
"US GAAP" means United States Generally Accepted Accounting Principles.

(2) In this Schedule the following terms have the meaning given in the FSA Handbook—

"authorised corporate director";
"BIPRU 730k firm";
"capital resources requirement";
"contracts for differences";
"discretionary investment manager";
"exempt BIPRU commodities firm";
"full scope BIPRU investment firm";

"ILAS BIPRU firm";
"designated multilateral development bank";
"pension scheme";
"principal";
"retail client".

(3) A entity which would be a BIPRU 730k firm and a full scope BIPRU investment firm by virtue of activities carried on in the United Kingdom but for the fact that its registered office (or, if it does not have a registered office, its head office) is not in the United Kingdom is to be treated as being one.

(4) The definition of "high quality liquid assets" has effect, in relation to a particular entity or group of entities, subject to any direction made in relation to that entity or group under section 148 of FISMA 2000 (modification or waiver of rules).

(5) If, in any proceedings, any question arises whether a person is an international organisation for the purposes of the definition of "entity" in sub-paragraph (1), a certificate issued by or under the authority of the Secretary of State stating any fact relevant to that question is conclusive evidence of that fact.

"Asset management activities"

71 (1) "Asset management activities" means activities which consist (or, if they were carried on in the United Kingdom, would consist) of any or all of the following—

(a) acting as the operator of a collective investment scheme (within the meaning of Part 17 of FISMA 2000: see sections 235 and 237 of that Act),

(b) acting as a discretionary investment manager for clients none of which is a linked entity, and

(c) acting as an authorised corporate director.

(2) In sub-paragraph (1), "linked entity", in relation to an entity ("E"), means—

(a) a member of the same group as E,

(b) a company in which a company which is a member of the same group as E has a major interest (within the meaning of Part 5 of CTA 2009: see section 473 of that Act), or

(c) a partnership the members of which include an entity—

(i) which is a member of the same group as E, and

(ii) whose share of the profits or losses of a trade carried on by the partnership for an accounting period of the partnership any part of which falls within the chargeable period is at least a 40% share (see Part 17 of CTA 2009 for provisions about shares of partnership profits and losses).

(3) In sub-paragraph (2) "group" means a group for the purposes of—

(a) the provisions mentioned in paragraph 4(3), or

(b) the provisions of US GAAP mentioned in paragraph 4(6)(a)(iii).

"Capital resources condition"

72 (1) "The capital resources condition" is that the entity has a capital resources requirement of at least £100,000,000.

(2) But if the entity is a member of a group, "the capital resources condition" is that the entity and—

(a) any other entities which—

(i) are members of the group,

(ii) meet either of the conditions in sub-paragraph (3),

(iii) are not excluded entities, and

(iv) are not members of any partnership within paragraph (b), and

(b) any partnership—

(i) the members of which are or include one or more entities which are members of the group and not excluded entities, and

(ii) which meets either of the conditions in sub-paragraph (3),

have (in aggregate) capital resources requirements of at least £100,000,000.

(3) The conditions referred to in sub-paragraph (2) are that the entity or partnership—

(a) is both a BIPRU 730k firm and a full scope BIPRU investment firm, or

(b) is an entity or partnership which carries on in the United Kingdom activities including the relevant regulated activity described in the provision mentioned in paragraph 79(a).

(4) In determining whether the entity is a UK resident bank or a relevant foreign bank by virtue of paragraph 78(2) or 80(2), the references in sub-paragraph (1) to the entity are to the partnership.

(5) If any entity whose capital resources may be material for the purposes of sub-paragraph (1) or (2) prepares its accounts in a currency other than sterling, the amount of its capital resources at the end of the chargeable period is to be translated into its sterling equivalent by reference to the spot rate of exchange on the last day of the chargeable period.

(6) If any entity whose capital resources may be material for the purposes of sub-paragraph (1) or (2) carries on a trade in the United Kingdom through a permanent establishment in the United Kingdom, its capital resources are to be determined as they would be for corporation tax purposes (see Chapter 4 of Part 2 of CTA 2009).

(7) In sub-paragraph (2) "group" means a group for the purposes of—

(a) the provisions mentioned in paragraph 4(3), or

(b) the provisions of US GAAP mentioned in paragraph 4(6)(a)(iii).

"Excluded entity"

73 (1) "Excluded entity" means an entity which is—

(a) an insurance company or an insurance special purpose vehicle,

(b) an entity which is a member of a group and does not carry on any relevant regulated activities otherwise than on behalf of an insurance company or insurance special purpose vehicle which is a member of the group,

(c) an entity which does not carry on any relevant regulated activities otherwise than as the manager of a pension scheme,

(d) an investment trust (within the meaning given by section 1158 of CTA 2010),

(e) an entity which does not carry on any relevant regulated activities other than asset management activities,

(f) an exempt BIPRU commodities firm,

(g) an entity which does not carry on any relevant regulated activities otherwise than for the purpose of trading in commodities or commodity derivatives,

(h) an entity which does not carry on any relevant regulated activities otherwise than for the purpose of dealing in contracts for differences—

(i) as principal with persons all or all but an insignificant proportion of whom are retail clients, or

(ii) with another person to enable the entity or other person to deal in contracts for differences as principal with persons all or all but an insignificant proportion of whom are retail clients,

(i) a society incorporated under the Friendly Societies Act 1992,

(j) a society registered as a credit union under the Industrial and Provident Societies Act 1965 or the Credit Unions (Northern Ireland) Order 1985 (SI 1985/1205 (N.I. 12)), or

(k) a building society.

(2) In sub-paragraph (1)(a) and (b) "insurance company" and "insurance special purpose vehicle" have the meaning given by section 431(2) of ICTA.

(3) In sub-paragraph (1)(b) "group" means a group for the purposes of—

(a) the provisions mentioned in paragraph 4(3), or

(b) the provisions of US GAAP mentioned in paragraph 4(6)(a)(iii).

"Long term" equity and liabilities

74 All equity is "long term".

75 (1) Liabilities are "long term" to the extent that—

(a) as at the end of the chargeable period, the liabilities are not required, and cannot be required, to be repaid or otherwise met during the 12 month period starting with the last day of the chargeable period, and

(b) in the case of liabilities of one member of the relevant group to another member of the relevant group, an officer of Revenue and Customs is satisfied that the following condition is also met in relation to the liabilities.

(2) The condition is that, as at the end of the chargeable period, the liabilities are funded by the relevant group through—

(a) equity,

(b) excluded liabilities to persons who are not members of the relevant group, or

(c) liabilities to such persons which are not required, and cannot be required, to be repaid or otherwise met during the 12 month period starting with the last day of the chargeable period.

76 (1) Liabilities are also "long term" so far as they consist of non-protected deposits.

(2) But sub-paragraph (1) does not apply to a deposit if the depositor is—

(a) an authorised person for the purposes of FISMA 2000 (see section 31 of that Act), or

(b) an entity which if it were a UK resident entity which carried on its activities in the United Kingdom would be required to be an authorised person.

(3) A deposit is "non-protected" so far as it is not a protected deposit for the purposes of paragraph 29.

(4) For the purposes of this paragraph—

(a) "deposit" has the meaning given by article 5(2) of the Financial Services and Markets Act 2000 (Regulated Activities) Order 2001 (SI 2001/544), and

(b) in relation to a deposit held in a territory outside the United Kingdom, the exclusions in articles 6 to 9AB of that Order apply with whatever modifications are appropriate to achieve the following purpose.

(5) The purpose is that the exclusions are to cover, essentially, the same matters in relation to the territory concerned as they cover in relation to the United Kingdom.

77 Paragraphs 74 to 76 are subject to Step 6 in paragraph 24(1).

"Relevant foreign bank"

78 (1) "Relevant foreign bank" means an entity which—

(a) is a non-UK resident entity,

(b) is an authorised person for the purposes of FISMA 2000 (see section 31 of that Act),

(c) is an entity which carries on a trade in the United Kingdom through a permanent establishment in the United Kingdom and—

(i) whose activities include the relevant regulated activity described in the provision mentioned in paragraph 79(a), or

(ii) which is both a BIPRU 730k firm and a full scope BIPRU investment firm, whose activities consist wholly or mainly of any of the relevant regulated activities described in the provisions mentioned in paragraph 79(b) to (f),

(d) carries on that relevant regulated activity, or those relevant regulated activities, wholly or mainly in the course of that trade,

(e) meets the capital resources condition, and

(f) is not an excluded entity.

(2) "Relevant foreign bank" also includes an entity which—

(a) meets the conditions in sub-paragraph (1)(a) and (f), and

(b) is a member of a partnership which meets the conditions in paragraph 80(1)(b) to (e).

"Relevant regulated activity"

79 "Relevant regulated activity" means an activity which is a regulated activity for the purposes of FISMA 2000 by virtue of any of the following provisions of the Financial Services and Markets Act 2000 (Regulated Activities) Order 2001 (SI 2001/544)—

(a) article 5 (accepting deposits),

(b) article 14 (dealing in investments as principal),

(c) article 21 (dealing in investments as agent),

(d) article 25 (arranging deals in investments),

(e) article 40 (safeguarding and administering investments), and

(f) article 61 (entering into regulated mortgage contracts).

"UK resident bank"

80 (1) "UK resident bank" means an entity which—

(a) is a UK resident entity,

(b) is an authorised person for the purposes of FISMA 2000 (see section 31 of that Act),

(c) is an entity—

(i) whose activities include the relevant regulated activity described in the provision mentioned in paragraph 79(a), or

(ii) which is both a BIPRU 730k firm and a full scope BIPRU investment firm, whose activities consist wholly or mainly of any of the relevant regulated activities described in the provisions mentioned in paragraph 79(b) to (f),

(d) carries on that relevant regulated activity, or those relevant regulated activities, wholly or mainly in the course of trade,

(e) meets the capital resources condition, and

(f) is not an excluded entity.

(2) "UK resident bank" also includes an entity which—

(a) meets the conditions in sub-paragraph (1)(a) and (f), and

(b) is a member of a partnership which meets the conditions in sub-paragraph (1)(b) to (e).

PART 9

POWER TO MAKE CONSEQUENTIAL CHANGES

81 (1) The Treasury may, by order made by statutory instrument, make such amendments of this Schedule as they consider appropriate in consequence of—

(a) any change made to or replacement of the Financial Services and Markets Act 2000 (Regulated Activities) Order 2001 (SI 2001/544) (or any replacement),

(b) any change made to the FSA Handbook, or

(c) any change in international accounting standards, UK GAAP or US GAAP.

(2) An order under this paragraph may have retrospective effect in relation to—

(a) any chargeable period in which the order is made, or

(b) in the case of an order made on or before 31 December 2011, any chargeable period ending on or after 1 January 2011.

(3) A statutory instrument containing an order under this paragraph is subject to annulment in pursuance of a resolution of the House of Commons.

GENERAL NOTE

Paragraph 1 introduces the bank levy, and makes clear that it is a tax.

Paragraph 2 introduces the calculation concept for the bank levy, namely that it is charged on certain types of equity and liabilities of banks and groups subject to the bank levy.

Paragraph 3 provides an overview of the contents of Sch 19 Parts 3–9.

Paragraph 4 sets out the basis on which the bank levy will be applied to certain groups, namely a UK banking group, a building society group, a foreign banking group or a relevant non-banking group.

Paragraph 5

The bank levy is also chargeable on individual entities which are not members of groups if the entity is a UK resident bank, a building society or a relevant foreign bank. It is noteworthy that both paras 4 and 5 impose a charge on an "entity", rather than the narrower term "company". The definitions in para 69 include a definition of "entity" which makes it clear that the term includes a partnership. Paragraph 44 defines residence for the purposes of the bank levy.

Paragraph 6 sets out a series of seven calculation steps for the bank levy, by comparing the amount of chargeable equity and liabilities with a £20 billion threshold. Banks, building societies and other groups with chargeable equity and liabilities of less than £20 billon will not be subject to the bank levy. Differential rates of levy are charged according to whether equity and liabilities are long term (as defined in paras 73–76) or short term.

The rates of bank levy have changed twice since the new tax was originally announced. The rates for future periods (i e those falling in periods beginning on or after 1 May 2011) will be 0.078% for long term chargeable equity and liabilities and 0.039% for short term equity and liabilities. More detail on rates is given in para 7.

Paragraph 7

For 2011 differing rates of bank levy apply according to which part(s) of 2011 fall within the chargeable period. This reflects the fact that bank levy rates for 2011 were originally intended to be lower than for 2012 and subsequent years, but were then increased in the 2011 budget announcement to compensate for the reduction in the corporation tax rate.

Paragraph 8

Four separate categories of group will be covered by the bank levy. The legislation defines different types of group because the calculation of chargeable equity and liabilities will vary between these different categories. The first of these categories is a "UK banking group". This will be a banking group with a UK resident parent entity.

Paragraph 9

The second category of group to be covered is a building society group, i e a group where the parent entity is a building society.

Paragraph 10

The third category of group to be covered is a foreign banking group, ie a banking group where the parent is a non-resident entity.

Paragraph 11

The fourth and final category of group to be covered by the bank levy is a "relevant non-banking group".

Paragraph 12

The term "banking group", which is relevant for the definitions of a UK banking group and a foreign banking group respectively, relies in turn on four separate definitions. Thus if any of Conditions A to D in para 12 is satisfied (and the exempt activities condition is not met – see commentary on para 13 below) then a group will be a banking group.

Condition A is that the parent entity of the group is a bank (being either a UK resident bank or a relevant foreign bank).

Condition B is that the parent entity of the group is an investment entity, that there is at least one UK resident bank in the group, and that all of the entities in the ownership chain above this UK resident bank are investment entities.

Condition C is that the parent entity would be a UK resident bank if it were resident in the UK and had the relevant regulatory permissions and that there is at least one UK resident bank or relevant foreign bank in the group.

Condition D is that the parent entity is an investment entity, with a subsidiary that would be a UK resident bank if it were resident and regulated in the UK, and that in addition there is a UK resident bank or relevant foreign bank in the same group.

Paragraph 13

If one of the above four conditions is satisfied then it is also necessary to consider whether the exempt activities condition is met – if not then the group will be a banking group for the purposes of the levy.

There are two separate parts of the exempt activities condition, and meeting either part of the condition will mean that a group is not a banking group. In such a case, however, any UK resident bank or relevant foreign bank in the group may well be subject to the bank levy on a stand-alone basis.

The first part of the condition is aimed at financial services groups which are primarily focused on activities other than banking. Thus if at least 90% of the trading income of the relevant group derives from exempt activities (meaning insurance, asset management and related activities, plus non-financial trading activities) then the condition will be met.

The second part of condition is aimed at non-financial services groups (such as supermarket groups) which may own a bank. Here if at least 50% of the trading income of the relevant group for the chargeable period derives from non-financial trading activities then the condition will be met.

Paragraph 14 makes clear that the terms "assets", "equity" and "liabilities" are to be defined by reference to international accounting standards.

Paragraph 15 sets out rules for calculating the chargeable equity and liabilities of a UK banking group or building society group. The steps in performing this calculation are:

1. Deduct excluded equity and liabilities
2. Adjust the remaining equity and liabilities to take account of any amounts that may be netted under netting arrangements
3. Adjust for any joint venture liabilities
4. Reduce the remaining equity and liabilities (but not below nil) by the amount of the group's relevant high quality liquid assets

The broad intention behind the netting provisions for these groups and for the other groups and stand-alone entities to which the levy applies is that where liabilities are matched by corresponding assets on an entity's balance sheet, and there is a legally effective and enforceable netting mechanism in place, then the balance sheet liabilities can be reduced accordingly when computing liability to the bank levy.

The reduction in respect of high quality liquid assets is to be taken against long-term equity and liabilities before short-term equity and liabilities. This is an unfavourable treatment for taxpayers given that the former are subject to bank levy at the lower rate, and especially so if the high quality liquid assets in question are funded by short-term liabilities.

The intention of the legislation is to avoid double relief being given in respect of high quality liquid assets, i e a deduction for such assets should be restricted in cases where relief is available either under the netting rules or the removal of joint venture liabilities.

Paragraph 16 sets out the situations in which netting relief will be available in reducing a taxpayer's liabilities for the purposes of the bank levy.

Paragraph 17 sets out further complex rules for computing the chargeable equity and liabilities of a foreign banking group. The intention is to aggregate the chargeable equity and liabilities of UK subsidiaries and UK branches of the foreign banking group. Again relief is available for excluded equity and liabilities and for high quality liquid assets. In addition, if the amount of equity and liabilities of a particular sub-group or entity is below certain de minimis limits then such amounts can be excluded from the calculation of chargeable equity and liabilities.

Paragraph 18 contains provisions to eliminate certain equity and liabilities of UK members of a foreign banking group which would have been eliminated on consolidation if the entities concerned had produced consolidated financial statements.

Paragraph 19 sets out rules for calculating the chargeable equity and liabilities of a relevant non-banking group, by focusing on any banking operations (i e UK resident banks, relevant foreign banks and banking sub-groups) that form part of the group. Once again relief is available in respect of excluded equity and liabilities, netting, joint ventures and high quality liquid assets.

Paragraph 20 contains provisions to eliminate certain equity and liabilities of a relevant non-banking group which would have been eliminated on consolidation if the entities concerned had produced consolidated financial statements.

Paragraph 21 sets out rules for calculating the chargeable equity and liabilities of stand-alone UK resident banks and building societies.

Paragraph 22 contains netting rules for stand-alone UK resident banks and building societies.

Paragraph 23 introduces the rules (set out in para 24) for calculating the chargeable equity and liabilities of stand-alone relevant foreign banks, based on their UK branches.

Paragraph 24

There are four steps to be followed in determining the equity and liabilities to be allocated to the UK in respect of a relevant foreign bank.

Step 1 is to determine the total (i e world-wide) assets of the bank at the end of the period in question.

Step 2 is to determine (in accordance with para 26) the amount of these assets that are attributable to the UK permanent establishment of the relevant foreign bank.

Step 3 is to determine the total amount of the bank's chargeable equity and liabilities.

Step 4 is to pro-rate the chargeable equity and liabilities to the UK permanent establishment in accordance with the assets figures determined in Steps 1 and 2.

Two additional calculation steps then determine how this total figure for chargeable equity and liabilities is to be split between long-term and short-term equity and liabilities.

Paragraph 25 contains netting rules for the relevant foreign bank.

Paragraph 26 sets out rules for determining the assets of UK permanent establishment of a relevant foreign bank for the purposes of the Step 2 calculation referred to in para 24. In broad terms these mirror the provisions for attributing profits attributable to a permanent establishment for corporation tax purposes , with some modifications. In particular assets representing loans on-lent to other members of the group which are within the scope of the bank levy are to be excluded in determining the UK allocated equity and liabilities of the relevant foreign bank.

Paragraph 27 contains rules for determining the total amount of the relevant foreign bank's chargeable equity ad liabilities.

Paragraph 28 introduces paras 29–39 which identify various categories of excluded equity or liabilities, i e forms of balance sheet funding on which the bank levy will not be charged. It also provides considerable flexibility to HM Treasury to add additional categories of excluded equity and liabilities, and/ or to amend or repeal the existing exclusions. To date (11 May 2011) no orders have been issued by HM Treasury under the powers conferred by this paragraph.

Paragraph 29

"Protected" deposits, ie retail deposits which are subject to a suitable form of depositor protection scheme, will be treated as excluded liabilities. In a UK context this means retail deposits covered by the Financial Services Compensation Scheme, for which the maximum amount of protection per depositor per authorised institution is currently £85,000. Deposits protected by comparable schemes outside the UK will also be treated as excluded liabilities.

Typically deposit takers who operate within a depositor protection scheme will be required to pay levies to support the operation of the scheme. Where a depositor protection scheme calculates liabilities by reference to a proportion of all of the entity's total deposit base, or a specified class within that deposit base, and this proportion is higher than the relevant deposit base covered by the scheme, then the higher percentage figure may be used to determine the amount of deposits which can be treated as excluded liabilities.

Paragraph 30

Tier 1 capital (ie amounts which are or would be treated as such for the purposes of the FSA Handbook) are excluded.

Paragraph 31

Sovereign repo liabilities (ie repo liabilities based on an obligation to repurchase certain sovereign and supranational debt) are excluded, on the basis that the securities that would be acquired under the repurchase arrangement would supposedly be of high quality.

Paragraph 32

Sovereign stock-lending liabilities (ie liabilities to redeliver cash collateral under a stock lending arrangement in respect of high quality securities) are excluded.

Paragraph 33

Certain insurance liabilities are excluded, namely liabilities of a regulated insurer which are either policyholder liabilities, unallocated surpluses or liabilities representing participants' interests in collective investment schemes.

Paragraph 34

Property, plant and equipment can be re-valued in accordance with IAS 16 or FRS 15, with any surplus on revaluation being held within equity as a revaluation reserve. In such a case this reserve can be excluded from chargeable equity and liabilities.

Paragraph 35

Relevant tax liabilities are to be excluded – these being current or deferred tax liabilities within the meaning of IAS 12 (or FRS 16 or FRS 19), together with liabilities in respect of the bank levy itself. This latter exclusion is particularly welcome as without it every increase in amounts provided in respect of the bank levy would have a circular effect of further increasing a taxpayer's liability to the levy.

Paragraph 36

Certain retirement benefit liabilities (ie liabilities recognised in respect of defined benefit pension schemes) are to be excluded. Relevant liabilities for this purpose are to be determined in accordance with IAS 19 and FRS 17 respectively.

Paragraph 37

Liabilities representing amounts due under the Financial services compensation scheme and comparable overseas schemes are to be excluded.

Paragraph 38

Liabilities representing clients' money are to be excluded, whether such liabilities are in the UK under FISMA 2000 or under comparable overseas rules. This exclusion applies to segregated client money only, and not to ordinary retail deposits which are subject to separate rules and will only be excluded to the extent that they are protected deposits (as per para 29).

Paragraph 39

Liabilities relating to currency notes in issue are to be excluded where such liabilities are not eligible for a deduction in respect of high quality liquid assets.

Paragraph 40 sets out rules for determining periods of account for bank levy purposes where an entity does not prepare financial statements.

Paragraph 41

This paragraph contains various provisions aimed at confirming that the focus for the bank levy will be the balance sheet of the entity or group as at the last day of the period. Amounts stated in currencies other than sterling are to be converted at the spot rate on the last day of the period. UK GAAP (incorporating FRS 23 and FRS 26), international accounting standards and US GAAP will be acceptable accounting frameworks.

Paragraph 42

Interests in banking joint ventures held by UK banks and building societies (and banking and building society groups) will already be included in the balance sheet calculations of those taxpayers for bank levy purposes. Paragraph 42 contains provisions to ensure that relevant joint venture interests held by foreign banking groups or relevant non-banking groups are also brought within the scope of the bank levy.

Paragraph 43 contains further provisions on the amount of chargeable equity and liabilities to be brought into account for bank levy purposes in accordance with para 42.

Paragraph 44 sets out residence rules for the purposes of the bank levy. A company's residence is to be determined in accordance with corporation tax rules; for a partnership the rules will focus on the place of control and management of its trade and investment activities.

Paragraph 45

The legislation expressly states that bank levy will not be deductible for income tax or corporation tax purposes. Rather more helpfully, the legislation also states that charges in respect of the bank levy will not be taken into account for the purposes of these taxes. Among other things this should mean that if a UK banking group charges its overseas subsidiaries for the bank levy then such recharges should not be taxable.

There is no express restriction on obtaining a deduction in respect of bank levies and similar charges imposed by other jurisdictions, should such levies be deductible under general principles.

Paragraph 46 contains a general anti-avoidance rule whereby taxpayers will be assessed to the bank levy on the basis that any transactions with a main purpose of avoiding or reducing the bank levy charge will be ignored.

HMRC guidance (at BLM641000 in the draft bank levy manual) states that the bank levy legislation seeks to encourage banks to adopt lower risk funding strategies. It goes on to say that arrangements with this intention should not be caught by the anti-avoidance rule, and this is the basis for the carve-outs from the application of the rule contain in sub-paras 46(7)–(12).

Informal guidance from HMRC has also suggested that the anti-avoidance rules will be applied with a light touch; time will tell whether or not this is the case.

Paragraph 47

CTA 2010 s 1139 contains a definition of the term "tax advantage" for the purposes of the Corporation Tax Acts. Paragraph 47 of the bank levy legislation widens this definition to include a tax advantage in respect of the bank levy.

Paragraph 48 makes clear that responsibility for collection and management of the bank levy rests with HMRC.

Paragraph 49 relates to groups which are affected by the bank levy (as opposed to stand-alone banks and building societies, for which see para 50). In order to simplify payment arrangements for the bank levy in such cases, it is to be treated as an amount of corporation tax payable by the responsible member (the responsible member being responsible for a group's bank levy liabilities in accordance with para 53). Therefore the liability will need to be disclosed on the form CT600 of whichever company is determined to be the responsible member, and form CT600 will be re-designed for that purpose.

Payments of bank levy will be due quarterly in the same way as corporation tax is payable quarterly.

Paragraph 50

The bank levy is to be treated as an amount of corporation tax for stand-alone banks and building societies and is thus payable in quarterly instalments.

Paragraph 51 makes clear that all enactments applying generally to corporation tax will likewise apply to the bank levy, such as legislation on information to be supplied, assessment and collection of tax, rights of appeal, administration, penalties and interest.

This should mean in turn that the Senior Accounting Officer legislation contained in CTA 2009 Sch 46 is relevant to accounting records maintained for the purposes of the bank levy.

Paragraph 52

Notwithstanding the fact that groups affected by the bank levy will have to nominate a responsible payment, most members of the group within the charge to corporation tax will remain jointly and severally liable for the bank levy liability of that responsible member.

Paragraphs 53 and 54

Groups subject to the bank levy are able to nominate a member of the group as "responsible member" for the purposes of the bank levy, with that entity then being responsible for payment of the bank levy on a quarterly basis, and also for all administrative matters with regard to the bank levy. HMRC has some limited scope to reject such nominations for various reasons, including if HMRC has reason to believe that the entity nominated will not have sufficient resources itself to pay the bank levy.

Paragraph 55 makes a consequential amendment to the Provisional Collection of Taxes Act 1968.

Paragraphs 56–58

These paragraphs contain certain consequential amendments to TMA 1970.

Paragraphs 59–63

These paragraphs contain certain consequential amendments to FA 1998 Sch 18.

Paragraph 64 contains transitional provisions with regard to the nomination of a responsible member. Very little time is given to affected groups to nominate a responsible member once the Finance Bill becomes law, but provision is made for the identity of the responsible member to be agreed with HMRC pending passing of the legislation.

Paragraph 65 provides a framework for double tax relief with respect to the bank levy and similar levies that may be imposed by foreign territories. Existing double tax treaties will not provide relief for such levies. Where arrangements made with a view to affording relief from double taxation in relation to the bank levy and any equivalent foreign levy then such arrangements can take effect where the Treasury makes an order for them to do so.

Provision is made for regulations which could include removing or reducing the amount of double taxation relief in cases where a scheme is in place.

No such regulations have yet been formally issued but arrangements with respect to double tax relief are expected to be concluded with France and Germany in particular.

Paragraph 66 contains a further and separate provision for double taxation. Rather than envisaging bilateral arrangements with regard to the bank levy and similar overseas levies it provides scope for regulations to be issued unilaterally by the UK to allow for relief. A distinction is drawn between situations where reciprocity is in place (i e where the Treasury is satisfied that the foreign territory in question has itself made appropriate provision for double taxation relief) and where it is not. In the former case the Treasury has scope to introduce regulations without reference to Parliament (but subject to annulment by the House of Commons). In the latter case the regulations must be laid before the House of Commons in draft and approved by a resolution of the House.

Paragraph 67 gives authority to HMRC to disclose information to overseas tax authorities in connection with claims for relief under the law of the territory concerned.

Paragraph 68 makes a consequential amendment to the Constitutional Reform and Governance Act 2010.

Paragraph 69 contains definitions applying for the purposes of the bank levy legislation.

Paragraph 70 defines the term "asset management activities" which is in turn relevant for the definition of an excluded entity in para 72. It relies in part on definitions in FISMA 2000.

Paragraph 71 defines the term "Capital resources condition" which is in turn relevant for the definitions of a relevant foreign bank in para 77 and a UK resident bank in para 79. The threshold for the capital resources condition is set at £100 million (aggregated across the entity in question and certain other regulated entities in the group, i e where this threshold is not met then the entity in question should not be a relevant foreign bank or a UK resident bank.

Paragraph 72

This paragraph defines the term "Excluded entity" which is in turn relevant for the definitions of a relevant foreign bank in para 77 and a UK resident bank in para 79.

Certain regulated entities which might otherwise fall within the scope of these terms are excluded. In particular insurance companies, insurance special purpose vehicles, certain entities which are members of insurance groups, pension scheme managers, investment trusts, entities carrying on asset management activities, exempt BIPRU commodities firms, certain commodities traders and dealers in CFDs, Friendly Societies, credit unions and building societies. (Building societies are brought within the scope of the bank levy legislation separately, ie not as UK resident banks or relevant foreign banks.)

The inclusion of dealers in CFDs primarily for retail clients within the definition of "Excluded entity" is intended to take spread betting businesses out of the scope of the bank levy.

Paragraph 73

As per para 6, the bank levy is imposed at differential rates according to whether the equity and liabilities are long term.

Paragraph 73 makes clear that all equity is to be treated as long term.

Paragraph 74 contains rules for determining whether or not liabilities should be treated as long term. Where liabilities are not required to be repaid or otherwise met during the 12 month period starting with the last day of the chargeable period then they will be treated as long term.

HMRC guidance makes clear (at BLM810000) that where a liability such as a loan agreement contains provisions that could trigger early repayment, such as in the case of a default or breach of covenants) then these provisions will not prevent the liability being treated as long term provided that the provisions have not been triggered at the end of the chargeable period.

For intra-group liabilities there is an additional requirement that HMRC must be satisfied that the liabilities must be funded at group level by equity or excluded liabilities or long-term liabilities. In practice it may be difficult to demonstrate this point.

Paragraph 75 provides that non-protected deposits are to be treated as long-term, provided that they are not from other financial institutions.

Paragraph 76 makes clear that these rules on determining long-term liabilities are subject to the rules in para 24 on allocating equity and liabilities to a relevant foreign bank.

Paragraph 77 defines a "relevant foreign bank". The definition is made by reference to certain definitions in FISMA 2000 and (via para 78) in the Financial Services and Markets Act 2000 (regulated Activities) order (SI 2001/544). In broad terms the definition encompasses non-UK resident entities carrying on a trade through a UK permanent establishment, where that trade either includes deposit taking or where the entity is both a BIPRU 730k firm and a full scope BIPRU investment firm and carries on certain regulated activities.

In addition the entity must meet the capital resources condition (see para 71) and not be an excluded entity (see para 72).

Paragraph 78 defines the term "relevant regulated activity" by reference to the Financial Services and Markets Act 2000 (Regulated Activities) Order 2001.

Paragraph 79 defines a "UK resident bank". The definition is very similar to that for a relevant foreign bank except that the focus is on entities resident in the UK.

Paragraph 80

Because the bank levy legislation relies on definitions which are outside the scope of tax law and which may well be subject to changes beyond HMRC's control (in particular to accounting standards and regulatory rules) the Treasury maintains the power to make consequential changes to the legislation accordingly. Such changes may have retrospective effect.

SCHEDULE 20

SUPPLIES OF COMMODITIES TO BE USED IN PRODUCING ELECTRICITY

Section 78

1 Schedule 6 to FA 2000 (climate change levy) is amended as follows.

2 In paragraph 6 (supplies of gas), after sub-paragraph (1) insert—

"(1A) In relation to a supply which is within sub-paragraph (1B) but not sub-paragraph (1C)—

(a) in sub-paragraph (1)(a) the reference to a gas utility is to be read as including a reference to an unregulated gas supplier (within the meaning of paragraph 151), and

(b) in relation to a supply made by an unregulated gas supplier—

(i) sub-paragraph (1) has effect as if paragraph (b)(ii) were omitted, and

(ii) in paragraph 40(2)(b) the reference to a utility is to be read as including a reference to an unregulated gas supplier.

(1B) A supply is within this sub-paragraph if it is a supply of any gas to a person to be used by that person in producing electricity.

(1C) A supply is within this sub-paragraph if it is a supply of any gas to a person who intends to cause the gas to be used in—

(a) a fully exempt combined heat and power station, or

(b) a partly exempt combined heat and power station,

in producing any outputs of the station."

3 (1) Paragraph 14 (exemption: supplies (other than self-supplies) to electricity producers) is amended as follows.

(2) In sub-paragraph (1), for "a taxable commodity" substitute "electricity".

(3) In sub-paragraphs (1)(a), (2)(b) and (3)(b), for "commodity" substitute "electricity".

4 In paragraph 21 (regulations to avoid double charges to levy), after sub-paragraph (2) insert—

"(2A) In sub-paragraph (2)(b) "taxable supply" does not include a taxable supply subject to the carbon price support rates (see paragraph 42A)."

5 In paragraph 42 (amount payable by way of levy), before sub-paragraph (2) insert—

"(1B) Sub-paragraph (1) does not apply to a taxable supply subject to the carbon price support rates (see paragraph 42A)."

6 After paragraph 42 insert—

"**42A** (1) This paragraph applies if a taxable supply is subject to the carbon price support rates.

(2) A supply is subject to the carbon price support rates if—

(a) it is a supply of a taxable commodity, apart from electricity, to a person to be used by that person in producing electricity, and

(b) it is not within sub-paragraph (3).

(3) A supply is within this sub-paragraph if it is a supply of a taxable commodity to a person who intends to cause the commodity to be used in—

(a) a fully exempt combined heat and power station, or

(b) a partly exempt combined heat and power station,

in producing any outputs of the station.

(4) The amount payable by way of levy on the taxable supply is the amount ascertained by applying the relevant carbon price support rate; and the levy payable on a fraction of a quantity of a commodity is that fraction of the levy payable on that quantity of the commodity.

(5) The carbon price support rates are as follows.

Taxable commodity supplied	*Carbon price support rate*
Gas supplied by a gas utility or any gas supplied in a gaseous state that is of a kind supplied by a gas utility	£0.00091 per kilowatt hour
Any petroleum gas, or other gaseous hydrocarbon, supplied in a liquid state	£0.01460 per kilogram
Any other taxable commodity (apart from electricity)	£0.01188 per kilogram

(6) The Commissioners may by regulations make provision for giving effect to this paragraph.

(7) Regulations under sub-paragraph (6) may, in particular, include provision for determining whether or not a taxable supply is subject to the carbon price support rates."

7 In paragraph 101 (civil penalties: incorrect certificates), in sub-paragraph (2)(a)—

(a) omit the "or" after sub-paragraph (ii), and

(b) omit the "and" at the end of sub-paragraph (iv) and after that sub-paragraph insert

"or

(v) a taxable supply (or taxable supplies) subject to the carbon price support rates, and".

8 (1) Subject to what follows, the amendments made by paragraphs 1 to 7 above have effect in relation to supplies treated as taking place on or after 1 April 2013.

(2) Sub-paragraph (3) applies to a supply to a person ("the customer") which—

(a) is of the description mentioned in paragraph 26(1)(b) of Schedule 6 to FA 2000 (gas in gaseous state), and

(b) is not treated as taking place before 23 March 2011.

(3) The amendments made by paragraphs 1 to 7 above have effect in relation to the gas supplied so far as it is actually supplied to the customer on or after 1 April 2013.

9 (1) This paragraph applies for the purposes of Schedule 6 to FA 2000 if—

(a) an invoice is issued, or a payment is received, before 1 April 2013 in respect of the supply to a person ("the customer") of a taxable commodity,

(b) the supply is not of the description mentioned in paragraph 26(1)(b) of Schedule 6 (gas in gaseous state),

(c) if the supply were to be treated as taking place on 1 April 2013, it would be a taxable supply subject to the carbon price support rates (see paragraph 42A of Schedule 6 as inserted by paragraph 6 above),

(d) a quantity of the taxable commodity is not delivered to the customer before 1 April 2013, and

(e) the invoicing or payment in advance of delivery is not acceptable normal practice.

(It does not matter whether the invoice mentioned in paragraph (a) is, or is not, a climate change levy accounting document.)

(2) If the supply would otherwise be treated as taking place before 1 April 2013, and not be a taxable supply, the supply is treated as taking place on that date.

(3) The quantity of the taxable commodity treated as supplied on 1 April 2013 is the quantity to which sub-paragraph (1)(d) applies.

(4) For the purposes of this paragraph invoicing or payment in advance of delivery is "acceptable normal practice" if—

(a) the supply is of a kind in the case of which it is normal practice for invoices to be issued, or payments to be made, in respect of taxable commodities before they are delivered to the person ("the customer") to whom they are being supplied,

(b) the practice does not involve issuing invoices, or making payments, more than 15 weeks in advance of the taxable commodities, in respect of which the invoice is issued or payment is made, being delivered to the customer, and

(c) the advance invoicing or payment is in accordance with that practice.

(5) This paragraph does not apply in relation to supplies treated as taking place before 23 March 2011.

GENERAL NOTE

Climate change levy (CCL) is a tax on the supply of certain energy products for business and public sector use. FA 2000 Sch 6 para 14 exempts supplies of CCL-taxable products to electricity generators. The Government consulted on the introduction of a carbon price floor in 2010/11, which it hopes will encourage additional investment in low-carbon power generation by providing greater support and certainty to the carbon price. To achieve this, a 'carbon price support rate' (CPSR) of CCL will be applied to supplies of fossil fuels used to generate electricity. The CPSR is due to be introduced from 1 April 2013.

Schedule 20 sets out changes to the existing CCL primary legislation required to introduce the CPSR:

— Paragraph 2 inserts three new sub-paragraphs into FA 2000 Sch 6 para 6, to ensure that all gas supplies used for the generation of electricity are brought within the scope of CCL (and thus CPSR).

— Paragraph 3 amends FA 2000 Sch 6 para 14 to restrict the exemption from CCL for taxable products used for electricity generation to electricity alone.

— Paragraph 4 inserts FA 2000 Sch 6 para 21(2A). As CPSR might otherwise be considered a double charge to CCL this paragraph removes CPSR from being considered as double-taxation.
— Paragraph 5 inserts FA 2000 Sch 6 para 42(1B) to ensure that CPSR is not charged at existing rates, or reduced rates, of CCL.
— Paragraph 6 inserts FA 2000 Sch 6 para 42A, setting out the circumstances when CPSR will apply and the rates to be charged. It also allows for regulations to bring the CPSR into force.
— Paragraph 7 amends FA 2000 Sch 6 para 101 to ensure CPSR is brought within the penalty regime for incorrect claiming of relief from CCL.
— Paragraph 8/9 time of supply measures to ensure CPSR becomes chargeable from 1 April 2013. Including anti-forestalling measures, effective from 23 March 2011, to prevent avoidance of CPSR by advance invoicing or payment for supplies to be received from 1 April 2013, when not 'acceptable normal practice' as defined.

SCHEDULE 21

PREVENTION OF SDLT AVOIDANCE

Section 82

Introduction

1 Part 4 of FA 2003 (stamp duty land tax) is amended as follows.

Alternative property finance

2 In section 45 (contract and conveyance: effect of transfer of rights), in subsection (3) for the words from "subsection (3)" to the end substitute "any of sections 71A to 73 (which relate to alternative property finance)."

3 (1) Omit sections 71A(8), 72(7), 72A(8) and 73(5)(a) (which contain definitions of "financial institution" for the purposes of provisions relating to alternative property finance).

(2) After section 73B insert—

"Meaning of "financial institution"

73BA (1) In sections 71A to 73B "financial institution" has the meaning given by section 564B of the Income Tax Act 2007.

(2) For this purpose section 564B(1) applies as if paragraph (d) were omitted."

Exchanges

4 (1) Paragraph 5 of Schedule 4 (chargeable consideration: exchanges) is amended as follows.

(2) In sub-paragraph (3)—

(a) for paragraph (a)(i) and (ii) substitute—

"(i) the amount determined under sub-paragraph (3A) in respect of the acquisition, or

(ii) if greater, the amount which would be the chargeable consideration for the acquisition ignoring paragraph 5;", and

(b) for paragraph (b)(i) and (ii) substitute—

"(i) the amount determined under sub-paragraph (3A) in respect of that acquisition, or

(ii) if greater, the amount which would be the chargeable consideration for that acquisition ignoring paragraph 5;".

(3) After that sub-paragraph insert—

"(3A) The amount mentioned in sub-paragraph (3)(a)(i) and (b)(i) is—

(a) the market value of the subject-matter of the acquisition, and
(b) if the acquisition is the grant of a lease at a rent, that rent."

Commencement

5 (1) Subject to what follows, the amendments made by paragraphs 2 and 4 have effect in relation to any transaction the effective date of which is on or after 24 March 2011.

(2) The amendments do not have effect in relation to any transaction (other than a notional transaction under section 75A of FA 2003)—

(a) which is effected in pursuance of a contract entered into and substantially performed before 24 March 2011, or
(b) which is effected in pursuance of a contract entered into before 24 March 2011 and which is not excluded by sub-paragraph (4).

(3) The amendments do not have effect in relation to any notional transaction under section 75A of FA 2003 if any scheme transaction—

(a) is completed before 24 March 2011,
(b) is effected in pursuance of a contract entered into and substantially performed before 24 March 2011, or
(c) is effected in pursuance of a contract entered into before 24 March 2011 and is not excluded by sub-paragraph (4).

(4) A transaction effected in pursuance of a contract entered into before 24 March 2011 is excluded by this sub-paragraph if—

(a) there is any variation of the contract, or assignment of rights under the contract, on or after 24 March 2011,
(b) the transaction is effected in consequence of the exercise on or after 24 March 2011 of any option, right of pre-emption or similar right, or
(c) on or after 24 March 2011, there is an assignment, sub-sale or other transaction relating to the whole or part of the subject-matter of the contract as a result of which a person other than the purchaser under the contract becomes entitled to call for a conveyance.

(5) Terms used in this paragraph have the same meaning as in Part 4 of FA 2003.

6 (1) The amendments made by paragraph 3 are treated as having come into force on 24 March 2011.

(2) But those amendments—

(a) do not have effect for the purposes of any of sections 71A to 73B of FA 2003 (other than those provisions mentioned in paragraph (b) below) if the arrangements referred to in section 71A(1), 72(1), 72A(1) or 73(1) (as the case may be) were entered into before 24 March 2011, and
(b) do not have effect for the purposes of section 71A(2)(b), 72(2)(b), 72A(2)(b) or 73(2)(b) of that Act if the arrangements referred to there were entered into before 24 March 2011.

GENERAL NOTE

Paragraph 2 amends FA 2003 s 45 (SDLT sub-sale etc relief) so that relief from SDLT on the first chargeable transaction is not available where the second transaction benefits from any of the exemptions provided for in FA 2003 ss 71A–73 on transactions involving alternative finance (ie so called "sharia compliant" transactions). Currently s 45 relief is only precluded from being combined with exemption under the alternative finance reliefs where the transaction in question benefits from exemption under s 73.

Paragraph 3(1) removes the SDLT specific definition of a "financial institution" used in the alternative finance exemptions contained in ss 71A–73. Paragraph 3(2) substitutes via the insertion of a new FA 2003 s 73BA a cross-reference to the definition used in ITA 2007 s 564B but removing the reference in that definition to persons holding consumer credit licences under the CCA 1974. Increasingly purchasers had been obtaining licences which they did not intend to use, entering into sale and leaseback transactions which fell within FA 2003 s 71A and then claiming exemption from SDLT. For SDLT purposes eligible institutions are now limited to banks, building societies and wholly owned subsidiaries of either type of institution.

Paragraph 4 amends the computational provisions of FA 2003 Sch 4 para 5 (exchanges) so that instead of calculating SDLT on the market value of the major interests in land in question, SDLT is calculated on the higher of the consideration that would be taken for SDLT purposes absent Sch 4 para 5 and the market value. This is achieved by amending paras 5(3)(a) and (b), and inserting a new para 5(3A) into Sch 4.

Commencement

As a general rule para 5(1) provides for the changes made by paras 2 and 4 to take effect for chargeable transactions the effective date of which was after Budget Day ie from 24 March 2011 except where the transaction was effected either:

(a) pursuant to a contract entered into and substantially performed on or before Budget Day, or

(b) pursuant to a contract entered into on or before Budget Day even if substantially performed after that day so long as it is not varied, assigned, results from the exercise of an option or right of pre-emption, or is the subject of a sub-sale in any case after 23 March 2011: see paras 5(2) and (4).

In the case of transactions potentially affected by FA 2003 s 75A (where SDLT is calculated by reference to a notional transaction and the actual or "scheme" transactions are ignored for certain purposes), para 5(3) provides for these changes not to apply where any scheme transaction is completed before 24 March 2011, is effected after 23 March 2011 but pursuant to a contract entered into and substantially performed on or before that date, or effected pursuant to a pre-24 March contract that is not affected by para 5(4) restrictions.

As regards the revised definition of "financial institution" relevant to the exemption for alternative finance arrangements, para 6(1) provides that the changes do not apply where the arrangements were entered into before 24 March 2011, and where exemption is sought on a sale by one financial institution to another (see for example s 71A(2)(b)) para 6(2) provides that the changes do not apply to limit the scope of "financial institution" on a sale by that first institution provided the arrangements involving that institution were entered into on or before Budget Day.

SCHEDULE 22

TRANSFERS INVOLVING MULTIPLE DWELLINGS

Section 83

New relief

1 Part 4 of FA 2003 (stamp duty land tax) is amended as follows.

2 After section 58C insert—

"58D Transfers involving multiple dwellings

(1) Schedule 6B provides for relief in the case of transfers involving multiple dwellings.

(2) Any relief under that Schedule must be claimed in a land transaction return or an amendment of such a return."

3 After Schedule 6A insert—

"SCHEDULE 6B

TRANSFERS INVOLVING MULTIPLE DWELLINGS

Section 58D

Introduction

1 This Schedule is arranged as follows—

(a) paragraph 2 identifies the transactions to which this Schedule applies,

(b) paragraph 3 defines key terms,

(c) paragraphs 4 and 5 describe the relief available if a claim is made,

(d) paragraph 6 provides for adjustments if circumstances change after a claim is made, and

(e) paragraph 7 contains rules for determining what counts as a dwelling.

Transactions to which this Schedule applies

2 (1) This Schedule applies to a chargeable transaction that is—

(a) within sub-paragraph (2) or sub-paragraph (3), and

(b) not excluded by sub-paragraph (4).

(2) A transaction is within this sub-paragraph if its main subject- matter consists of—

(a) an interest in at least two dwellings, or

(b) an interest in at least two dwellings and other property.

(3) A transaction is within this sub-paragraph if—

(a) its main subject-matter consists of—

(i) an interest in a single dwelling, or

(ii) an interest in a single dwelling and other property,

(b) it is one of a number of linked transactions, and

(c) the main subject-matter of at least one of the other linked transactions consists of—

(i) an interest in some other dwelling or dwellings, or

(ii) an interest in some other dwelling or dwellings and other property.

(4) A transaction is excluded by this sub-paragraph if—

(a) section 74 or 75 applies to it, or

(b) relief under Schedule 7 or Schedule 8 is available for it or would be available for it on the making of a claim or has been withdrawn from it.

(5) A reference in this Schedule to an interest in a dwelling is to any chargeable interest in or over a dwelling.

(6) But, in the case of a dwelling subject to a lease granted for an initial term of more than 21 years, any interest that is a superior interest in relation to the lease is to be ignored in determining whether a transaction is a relevant transaction.

Key terms

3 (1) A chargeable transaction to which this Schedule applies is referred to in this Schedule as a "relevant transaction".

(2) A relevant transaction is a "single dwelling transaction" if its main subject-matter consists of—

(a) an interest in a single dwelling, or

(b) an interest in a single dwelling and other property.

(3) In relation to such a transaction, the single dwelling is referred to as "the dwelling".

(4) A relevant transaction is a "multiple dwelling transaction" if its main subject-matter consists of—

(a) an interest in at least two dwellings, or

(b) an interest in at least two dwellings and other property.

(5) In relation to such a transaction, those dwellings are referred to as "the dwellings".

The relief

4 (1) If relief under this Schedule is claimed for a relevant transaction, the amount of tax chargeable in respect of the transaction is—

(a) a percentage of the consideration attributable to dwellings, plus

(b) a percentage of the remaining consideration (if any).

(2) "The consideration attributable to dwellings" is—

(a) for a single dwelling transaction, so much of the chargeable consideration for the transaction as is attributable to the dwelling,

(b) for a multiple dwelling transaction, so much of the chargeable consideration for the transaction as is attributable to the dwellings in total.

(3) "The remaining consideration" is the chargeable consideration for the transaction less the consideration attributable to dwellings.

(4) The percentages are determined in accordance with paragraph 5.

(5) If the whole or part of the chargeable consideration for a relevant transaction is rent, sub-paragraph (1) has effect subject to section 56 and Schedule 5.

(6) "Attributable" means attributable on a just and reasonable basis.

The percentages

5 (1) For the purposes of paragraph 4(1)(a), the percentage is the percentage that would be applied under section 55 if—

(a) the relevant land consisted entirely of residential property, and

(b) the relevant consideration were the fraction produced by dividing total dwellings consideration by total dwellings.

(2) But if that percentage turns out to be 0%, the percentage for the purposes of paragraph 4(1)(a) is 1%.

(3) For a transaction that is not one of a number of linked transactions, "total dwellings consideration" is the consideration attributable to dwellings for that transaction (see paragraph 4(2)).

(4) For one of a number of linked transactions, "total dwellings consideration" is—

(a) the total of the consideration attributable to dwellings for that transaction and all the other linked transactions that are relevant transactions, plus

(b) so much of the chargeable consideration for any of the linked transactions (whether or not relevant transactions) as is not included in the calculation under paragraph (a) but is attributable to the same dwellings by reference to which that calculation is made.

(5) "Total dwellings" is the total number of dwellings by reference to which total dwellings consideration is calculated.

(6) In the application of sub-paragraph (1), no account is to be taken of—

(a) section 116(7), or
(b) paragraph 9A(4) of Schedule 5.

(7) For the purposes of paragraph 4(1)(b), the percentage is the percentage that (but for this Schedule) would be applied under section 55 to the chargeable consideration for the transaction.

Adjustment for change of circumstances

6 (1) This paragraph applies if—

(a) relief under this Schedule is claimed for a relevant transaction,
(b) an event occurs in the relevant period, and
(c) had the event occurred immediately before the effective date of the transaction—

(i) the transaction would not have been a relevant transaction or the percentage applied by virtue of paragraph 4(1)(a) would have been higher, and
(ii) more tax would have been payable in respect of the transaction as a result.

(2) If this paragraph applies, tax is chargeable on the transaction as if the event had occurred immediately before the effective date of the transaction.

(3) In that case—

(a) the purchaser must make a return to Her Majesty's Revenue and Customs before the end of the period of 30 days beginning with the date of the event,
(b) the return must contain a self-assessment of the tax chargeable in respect of the transaction on the basis of the information contained in the return,
(c) the tax so chargeable is to be calculated by reference to the rates in force at the effective date of the transaction, and
(d) the additional tax payable must be paid not later than the filing date for the return.

(4) The provisions of section 78A and Schedule 10 apply to a return under this paragraph as they apply to a return under section 76, but with references in Schedule 10 to the effective date of the transaction being read as references to the date of the event.

(5) "The relevant period" means the shorter of—

(a) the period of 3 years beginning with the effective date of the transaction, and
(b) the period beginning with the effective date of the transaction and ending with the date on which the purchaser disposes of the dwelling, or the dwellings, to a person who is not connected with the purchaser.

(6) In relation to a transaction effected on completion of a contract that was substantially performed before completion, sub-paragraph (5) applies as if references to the effective date of the transaction were to the date on which the contract was substantially performed.

(7) In this paragraph—

"completion" has the same meaning as in section 44;
"contract" includes any agreement (including, in the case of Scotland, missives of let not constituting a lease);
"event" includes any change of circumstance or change of plan;
"substantially performed" has the same meaning as in section 44.

(8) Section 1122 of the Corporation Tax Act 2010 (connected persons) has effect for the purposes of this paragraph.

What counts as a dwelling

7 (1) This paragraph sets out rules for determining what counts as a dwelling for the purposes of this Schedule.

(2) A building or part of a building counts as a dwelling if—

(a) it is used or suitable for use as a single dwelling, or
(b) it is in the process of being constructed or adapted for such use.

(3) Land that is, or is to be, occupied or enjoyed with a dwelling as a garden or grounds (including any building or structure on such land) is taken to be part of that dwelling.

(4) Land that subsists, or is to subsist, for the benefit of a dwelling is taken to be part of that dwelling.

(5) The main subject-matter of a transaction is also taken to consist of or include an interest in a dwelling if—

(a) substantial performance of a contract constitutes the effective date of that transaction by virtue of a relevant deeming provision,

(b) the main subject-matter of the transaction consists of or includes an interest in a building, or a part of a building, that is to be constructed or adapted under the contract for use as a single dwelling, and

(c) construction or adaptation of the building, or the part of a building, has not begun by the time the contract is substantially performed.

(6) In sub-paragraph (5)—

"contract" includes any agreement (including, in the case of Scotland, missives of let not constituting a lease);

"relevant deeming provision" means any of sections 44 to 45A or paragraph 12A or 19(3) of Schedule 17A;

"substantially performed" has the same meaning as in section 44.

(7) Subsections (2) to (5) of section 116 apply for the purposes of this paragraph as they apply for the purposes of subsection (1)(a) of that section."

Other amendments of Part 4 of FA 2003

4 In section 57 of FA 2003 (disadvantaged areas relief), insert at the end—

"(3) Relief is not available under that Schedule in the case of any transaction for which relief under Schedule 6B is claimed."

5 In section 87(3) of that Act (interest on unpaid tax), after paragraph (a) insert—

"(aza) in the case of an amount payable by virtue of paragraph 6 of Schedule 6B (adjustment for change of circumstances), the date of the event;".

6 In paragraph 9 of Schedule 5 to that Act (amount of tax chargeable: rent)—

(a) in sub-paragraph (4), after "section 55" insert "or Schedule 6B", and

(b) in sub-paragraph (5), after "section" insert "or Schedule".

7 In paragraph 12(2A) of Schedule 10 to that Act (notice of enquiry into return), for "or 81A (return or further return in consequence of later linked transaction)" substitute ", 81A (return or further return in consequence of later linked transaction) or paragraph 6 of Schedule 6B (adjustment for change of circumstances)".

8 In paragraphs 11(2C) and 19(2C) of Schedule 15 to that Act (partnerships), in the substituted sub-paragraph (4), for "as it has" substitute "or Schedule 6B as they have".

Commencement

9 (1) The amendments made by this Schedule have effect in relation to relevant transactions that—

(a) have an effective date on or after the day on which this Act is passed ("the commencement day"), and

(b) satisfy sub-paragraph (2).

(2) A relevant transaction satisfies this sub-paragraph if—

(a) it is not linked to a land transaction with an effective date before the commencement day (a "pre-commencement transaction"), or

(b) the only pre-commencement transaction to which it is linked is—

(i) an option binding the grantor to enter into the relevant transaction, or

(ii) a right of pre-emption restricting the right of the grantor to enter into it.

GENERAL NOTE

Paragraph 2 introduces the new FA 2003 s 58D which refers to new FA 2003 Sch 6B (to be inserted by para 3) and provides that relief has to be claimed in a land transaction return. Paragraph 4 prevents the application of disadvantaged area relief (see FA 2003 s 57) where relief is claimed under new Sch 6B.

Paragraphs 5 and 7 make consequential amendments to FA 2003 s 87(3) (interest on tax) and Sch 10 para 12A (notices of enquiry) where an adjustment to the amount of tax due arises as a result of the operation of Sch 6B para 6.

Paragraph 6 makes amendments to Sch 5 para 9 consequent upon the introduction of Sch 6B (consideration other than rent on leases) and para 8 makes similar consequential changes to Sch 15 paras 11(2C) and 19(2C) (partnerships).

As for the new Schedule 6B itself, para 2 provides that it applies where a transaction involves the acquisition of any form of chargeable interest (see para 2(5)) in at least two dwellings (defined in para 7), or an interest in either a single dwelling or a single dwelling and other property which is part of a linked transaction the subject matter of which involves the acquisition of an interest in one or more other dwellings (whether or not in conjunction with other property); see paras 2(2) and (3). However relief is not available where relief is available also under FA 2003 s 74 (collective enfranchisement of flats) or s 75 (rights to buy in crofting communities): see para 2(4)(a). Relief under Sch 6B is also unavailable if relief is available, could be available if a claim was made or had been available but has been withdrawn, under either Sch 7 (group relief etc) or Sch 8 (charities relief): see para 2(4)(b). If the interest in a dwelling is subject to a lease the term of which was greater than 21 years on grant (irrespective of the term remaining), that does not count in determining whether relief is available under Sch 6B: see para 2(6). This precludes relief where there is an acquisition of let properties e g to obtain a stream of ground rents. HMRC guidance supports the view that where a property contains flats let on long leases and other flats which are untenanted, the untenanted flats can count as dwellings.

Schedule 6B para 3 provides a definition of "single dwelling transaction" and "multiple dwelling transaction", and definitions of "dwelling" and "dwellings" germane to the calculation of relief under paras 4 and 5.

Schedule 6B para 4 essentially provides for the relief to be limited to the proportion of the aggregate consideration that is attributable on a just and reasonable apportionment (see para 4(6)) to the dwelling or dwellings (and consequently for the rate of tax on that part of the consideration attributable to any other property to be unaltered): see para 4(1)(b) and para 5(7). Where any part of the consideration takes the form of rent the relief is applied subject to the rules contained in FA 2003, Sch 5 (see para 4(5)).

Schedule 6B para 5 provides in effect for the rate of tax to be calculated as if the total dwellings consideration (i e that part of the consideration as is referable to the acquisition of the interest in dwellings–as opposed to the acquisition of any other property acquired) was averaged over the total number of dwellings acquired. So for instance the rate of tax on 3 dwellings the consideration for which individually was £501,000, £115,000 and £134,000 would be 1% because the average consideration does not exceed £250,000. Note, too, that the rate of tax calculated in accordance with paragraph 5 is not affected by the special rules (in terms of rate of SDLT applicable, see FA 2003 s 55) afforded to the acquisition of interests in 6 or more residential properties contained in FA 2003, s 116(7), nor the rules in para 9(4A) Sch 5: see para 5(6). In addition the rate of tax applicable to the dwellings consideration cannot be below 1% in accordance with para 5(2).

Schedule 6B para 6 provides the framework for what happens if, within the "relevant period", an event occurs which means that a greater amount of tax would have been due had that event occurred immediately before the effective date of the transaction e g the acquisition of one less dwelling or a building intended to be constructed or adapted as a dwelling is not so constructed or adapted. The relevant period is the shorter of 3 years beginning with the effective date of the relieved transaction and the period which ends when the purchaser disposes of the dwelling(s) to an unconnected person (the test of connection being contained in CTA 2010 s 1122 in accordance with para 6(8)): see para 6(5). If the transaction was substantially performed before completion, the 3 year period runs not from completion but the date of substantial performance: see para 6(6). In such an event the additional tax is due from the date of the event – see para 6(2); the purchaser has 30 days from the event to file an additional land transaction return, self-assessing the extra tax due and paying the tax due by the end of that 30 day period – see para 6(3); and the appeals, records and other administrative provisions of Sch 10 apply as if references to the effective date were to the date of the event giving rise to the additional tax – see para 6(4). Paragraph 6(7) provides appropriate cross-references, and defines "event".

Schedule 6B para 7 contains the all-important definition of "dwelling", and includes buildings under construction or intended to be adapted for use as a single dwelling as well as existing buildings, to cover "off plan" purchases–see paras 7(2)(b) and 7(5), in the latter case so long as the contract for the acquisition of the interest has been substantially performed even where construction or adaptation has not commenced by the date of substantial performance. The provisions of FA 2003 s 116(2)–(5), which set out circumstances in which a building can be regarded as used or suitable for use as a dwelling, also apply for the purposes of para 7 (see para 7(7)).

Commencement

The relief is available for transactions of which the effective date is on or after Royal Assent so long as the transaction in question is not linked to a transaction which has a pre Royal Assent effective date (except where that pre-Royal Assent transaction is an option or right of pre-emption affecting or limiting the rights of the grantor) (see Sch 22 para 9).

SCHEDULE 23
DATA-GATHERING POWERS

Section 86(1)

PART 1
POWER TO OBTAIN DATA

Power to give notice

1 (1) An officer of Revenue and Customs may by notice in writing require a relevant data-holder to provide relevant data.

(2) Part 2 of this Schedule sets out who is a relevant data-holder.

(3) In relation to a relevant data-holder, "relevant data" means data of a kind specified for that type of data-holder in regulations made by the Treasury.

(4) The data that a relevant data-holder may be required to provide—

(a) may be general data or data relating to particular persons or matters, and
(b) may include personal data (such as names and addresses of individuals).

(5) A notice under this paragraph is referred to as a data-holder notice.

Purpose of power

2 (1) The power in paragraph 1(1) is exercisable to assist with the efficient and effective discharge of HMRC's tax functions—

(a) whether a particular function or more generally, and
(b) whether involving a particular taxpayer or taxpayers generally.

(2) It is additional to and is not limited by other powers that HMRC may have to obtain data (for example, in Schedule 36 to FA 2008).

(3) But it may not be used (in place of the power in paragraph 1 of that Schedule) to obtain data required for the purpose of checking the relevant data-holder's own tax position.

(4) Sub-paragraph (3) does not prevent use of the power in paragraph 1(1) of this Schedule to obtain data about a matter mentioned in paragraph 14(3)(a) (beneficial ownership of certain payments etc).

(5) Nothing in this paragraph limits the use that may be made of data that have been obtained under this Schedule (see section 17(1) of CRCA 2005).

Specifying relevant data

3 (1) A data-holder notice must specify the relevant data to be provided.

(2) Relevant data may not be specified in a data-holder notice unless an officer of Revenue and Customs has reason to believe that the data could have a bearing on chargeable or other periods ending on or after the applicable day.

(3) The applicable day is the first day of the period of 4 years ending with the day on which the notice is given.

Compliance

4 (1) Relevant data specified in a data-holder notice must be provided by such means and in such form as is reasonably specified in the notice.

(2) If the notice specifies that the data are to be provided by sending them somewhere, the data must be sent to such address and within such period as is reasonably specified in the notice.

(3) If the notice specifies that the data are to be provided by making documents available for inspection somewhere, the documents must be made available for inspection at such place and time as is—

(a) reasonably specified in the notice, or

(b) agreed between an officer of Revenue and Customs and the data-holder.

(4) A place used solely as a dwelling may not be specified under sub-paragraph (3)(a).

(5) A data-holder notice requiring the provision of specified documents requires the documents to be provided only if they are in the data-holder's possession or power.

(6) A power in this paragraph to specify something in a notice includes power to specify it in a document referred to in the notice.

Approval by tribunal

5 (1) An officer of Revenue and Customs may ask for the approval of the tribunal before giving a data-holder notice.

(2) This does not require an officer to do so (but see paragraph 28(3) for the effect of obtaining approval).

(3) An application for approval under this paragraph may be made without notice (except as required under sub-paragraph (4)).

(4) The tribunal may not approve the giving of a data-holder notice unless—

(a) the application for approval is made by, or with the agreement of, an authorised officer,

(b) the tribunal is satisfied that, in the circumstances, the officer giving the notice is justified in doing so,

(c) the data-holder has been told that the data are to be required and given a reasonable opportunity to make representations to an officer of Revenue and Customs, and

(d) the tribunal has been given a summary of any representations made by the data-holder.

(5) Paragraphs (c) and (d) of sub-paragraph (4) do not apply to the extent that the tribunal is satisfied that taking the action specified in those paragraphs might prejudice any purpose for which the data are required.

(6) A decision by the tribunal under this paragraph is final (despite the provisions of sections 11 and 13 of the Tribunals, Courts and Enforcement Act 2007).

(7) "Authorised officer" means an officer of Revenue and Customs who is, or is a member of a class of officers who are, authorised by the Commissioners for the purposes of this paragraph.

Power to copy documents

6 An officer of Revenue and Customs may take copies of or make extracts from any document provided pursuant to a data-holder notice.

Power to retain documents

7 (1) If an officer of Revenue and Customs thinks it reasonable to do so, HMRC may retain documents provided pursuant to a data-holder notice for a reasonable period.

(2) While a document is being retained, the data-holder may, if the document is reasonably required for any purpose, request a copy of it.

(3) The retention of a document under this paragraph is not to be regarded as breaking any lien claimed on the document.

(4) If a document retained under this paragraph is lost or damaged, the Commissioners are liable to compensate the owner of the document for any expenses reasonably incurred in replacing or repairing the document.

PART 2
RELEVANT DATA-HOLDERS

Introduction

8 (1) This Part of this Schedule sets out who is a relevant data-holder for the purposes of this Schedule.

(2) Descriptions of the various types of data-holder are to be read as including anyone who was previously of such a description.

Salaries, fees, commission etc

9 (1) Each of the following is a relevant data-holder—

(a) an employer,

(b) a person who is concerned in making payments to or in respect of another person's employees with respect to their employment with that other person,

(c) an approved agent within the meaning of section 714 of ITEPA 2003 (which relates to payroll giving), and

(d) a person who carries on a business in connection with which relevant payments are or are likely to be made.

(2) Relevant payments are—

(a) payments for or in connection with services provided by persons who are not employed in the business, or

(b) periodical or lump sum payments in respect of any copyright, public lending right, right in a registered design or design right.

(3) Payments are taken to be made in connection with a business if they are made—

(a) in the course of carrying on the business or a part of it, or

(b) in connection with the formation, acquisition, development or disposal of the business or a part of it.

(4) Sub-paragraph (1)(d) applies to the carrying on of any other kind of activity as it applies to the carrying on of a business, but only if the activity is being carried on by a body of persons (and references in sub-paragraphs (2) and (3) to the business are to be read accordingly).

(5) A reference in this paragraph to the making of payments includes—

(a) the provision of benefits, and

(b) the giving of any other valuable consideration.

10 (1) This paragraph applies if—

(a) services that an individual provides or is obliged to provide under an agency contract are treated under section 44(2) of ITEPA 2003 as the duties of an employment held by the individual with the agency, or

(b) remuneration receivable under or in consequence of arrangements falling within section 45 of that Act is treated as earnings from an employment held by an individual with the agency.

(2) For the purposes of paragraph 9—

(a) the individual is treated as being employed by the agency, and

(b) payments made to the individual under or in consequence of the agency contract, or treated as earnings under section 45 of ITEPA 2003, do not count as "relevant payments".

(3) "Agency contract" and "remuneration" have the same meaning as in Chapter 7 of Part 2 of ITEPA 2003.

11 (1) This paragraph applies if—

(a) a person ("A") performs in the United Kingdom duties of an employment,

(b) the employment is under or with a person resident outside and not resident in the United Kingdom,

(c) the duties performed in the United Kingdom are performed for a continuous period of not less than 30 days, and

(d) those duties are performed for the benefit of a person ("B") resident or carrying on a trade, profession or vocation in the United Kingdom.

(2) For the purposes of paragraph 9—

(a) B is treated as if B were an employer, but

(b) only the name and place of residence of A may be specified for a relevant data-holder of B's type in regulations made under paragraph 1(3).

Interest etc

12 (1) A person by or through whom interest is paid or credited is a relevant data-holder.

(2) For the purposes of this paragraph, the following are to be treated as interest—

(a) a dividend in respect of a share in a building society,

(b) an amount to which a person holding a deeply discounted security is entitled on the redemption of that security,

(c) a foreign dividend, and

(d) an alternative finance return.

(3) In sub-paragraph (2)—

"alternative finance return" means—

(a) an alternative finance return within the meaning of Part 10A of ITA 2007, and

(b) an alternative finance return within the meaning of Part 6 of CTA 2009;

"building society" means a building society within the meaning of the Building Societies Act 1986;
"deeply discounted security" has the same meaning as in Chapter 8 of Part 4 of ITTOIA 2005;
"foreign dividend" means any annual payment, interest or dividend payable out of, or in respect of the funds or securities of—

(a) a body of persons that is not resident in the United Kingdom, or
(b) a government or public or local authority in a country outside the United Kingdom.

Income, assets etc belonging to others

13 A person who (in whatever capacity) is in receipt of money or value of or belonging to another is a relevant data-holder.

Payments derived from securities

14 (1) Each of the following is a relevant data-holder—

(a) a person who is the registered or inscribed holder of securities,
(b) a person who receives a payment derived from securities or would be entitled to do so if a payment were made,
(c) a person who receives a payment treated by the company that makes it as a payment to which section 1033 of CTA 2010 applies (purchase by unquoted trading company of own shares), and
(d) a person who receives a chargeable payment within the meaning of Chapter 5 of Part 23 of CTA 2010 (company distributions: demergers).

(2) But, for a relevant data-holder of a type described in this paragraph, data may only be specified in regulations under paragraph 1(3) if the data concern a matter mentioned in sub-paragraph (3).

(3) The matters are—

(a) whether the relevant data-holder is the beneficial owner (or sole beneficial owner) of the securities or payment in question,
(b) if not—
(i) details of the beneficial owner (or other beneficial owners), and
(ii) if those details are not known or if different, details of the person for whom the securities are held or to whom the payment is or may be paid on, and
(c) if there is more than one beneficial owner or more than one person of the kind mentioned in paragraph (b)(ii), their respective interests in the securities or payment.

(4) "Payment derived from securities" includes in particular—

(a) an amount (whether of income or capital) that is payable out of or in respect of securities or rights attaching to securities, and
(b) a payment that is representative of any such amount.

15 (1) A person who makes a payment derived from securities that has been received from or is paid on behalf of another is a relevant data-holder.

(2) "Payment derived from securities" has the same meaning as in paragraph 14.

Grants and subsidies out of public funds

16 (1) A person by whom a payment out of public funds is made by way of grant or subsidy is a relevant data-holder.

(2) For these purposes, a payment is a payment out of public funds if it is provided directly or indirectly by—

(a) the Crown,
(b) any government, public or local authority whether in the United Kingdom or elsewhere, or
(c) any EU institution.

Licences, approvals etc

17 (1) A person by whom licences or approvals are issued or a register is maintained is a relevant data-holder.

(2) "Register" includes—

(a) any record or list that a local authority maintains, and
(b) any record or list that any other person is required or permitted to maintain by or under an enactment.

Rent and other payments arising from land

18 (1) Each of the following is a relevant data-holder—

(a) a lessee (or successor in title of a lessee),

(b) an occupier of land,

(c) a person having the use of land, and

(d) a person who, as agent, manages land or is in receipt of rent or other payments arising from land.

(2) The reference to a person who manages land includes a person who markets property to potential tenants, searches for tenants or provides similar services.

Dealing etc in securities

19 (1) Each of the following is a relevant data-holder—

(a) a person who effects or is a party to securities transactions wholly or partly on behalf of others (whether as agent or principal),

(b) a person who, in the course of business, acts as registrar or administrator in respect of securities transactions (including a person who manages a clearing house for any terminal market in securities),

(c) a person who makes a payment derived from securities to anyone other than the registered or inscribed holder of the securities,

(d) a person who makes a payment derived from bearer securities, and

(e) an accountable person within the meaning of the Stamp Duty Reserve Tax Regulations 1986 (SI 1986/1711).

(2) "Payment derived from securities" has the same meaning as in paragraph 14 (and "payment derived from bearer securities" is to be read accordingly).

(3) "Securities transactions" means—

(a) transactions in securities,

(b) transactions under which a representative payment has been, is to be or may be made, or

(c) the making or receipt of a representative payment.

(4) In sub-paragraph (3)—

"representative payment" means a payment that is representative of an amount payable out of or in respect of securities or rights attaching to securities;

"transactions in securities" means transactions, of whatever description, relating to securities, and includes in particular—

(a) the purchase, sale or exchange of securities,

(b) issuing or securing the issue of new securities,

(c) applying or subscribing for new securities, and

(d) altering or securing the alteration of rights attached to securities.

Dealing in other property

20 Each of the following is a relevant data-holder—

(a) the committee or other person or body of persons responsible for managing a clearing house for any terminal market in commodities,

(b) an auctioneer,

(c) a person carrying on a business of dealing in any description of tangible movable property, and

(d) a person carrying on a business of acting as an agent or intermediary in dealings in any description of tangible movable property.

Lloyd's

21 A person who is registered as managing agent at Lloyd's in relation to a syndicate of underwriting members of Lloyd's is a relevant data-holder.

Investment plans etc

22 Each of the following is a relevant data-holder—

(a) a plan manager (see section 696 of ITTOIA 2005), and

(b) an account provider in relation to a child trust fund (as defined in section 3 of the Child Trust Funds Act 2004).

Petroleum activities

23 Each of the following is a relevant data-holder—

(a) the holder of a licence granted under Part 1 of the Petroleum Act 1998, and

(b) the responsible person in relation to an oil field (within the meaning of Part 1 of OTA 1975).

Insurance activities

24 Each of the following is a relevant data-holder—

(a) a person who is involved (in any capacity) in an insurance business (as defined for the purposes of Part 3 of FA 1994),

(b) a person who makes arrangements for persons to enter into contracts of insurance, and

(c) a person who is concerned in a business that is not an insurance business and who has been involved in the entering into of a contract of insurance that provides cover for any matter associated with the business.

Environmental activities

25 A person who is involved (in any capacity) in any of the following activities is a relevant data-holder—

(a) subjecting aggregate to exploitation in the United Kingdom (as defined for the purposes of Part 2 of FA 2001) or connected activities,

(b) making or receiving supplies of taxable commodities (as defined for the purposes of Schedule 6 to FA 2000) or connected activities, and

(c) landfill disposal (as defined for the purposes of Part 3 of FA 1996).

Settlements

26 (1) Each of the following is a relevant data-holder—

(a) a person who makes a settlement,

(b) the trustees of a settlement,

(c) a beneficiary under a settlement, and

(d) any other person to whom income is payable under a settlement.

(2) Section 620 of ITTOIA 2005 (meaning of "settlement" etc) applies for the purposes of this paragraph.

Charities

27 A charity is a relevant data-holder.

PART 3

APPEALS AGAINST DATA-HOLDER NOTICES

Right of appeal

28 (1) The data-holder may appeal against a data-holder notice, or any requirement in such a notice, on any of the following grounds—

(a) it is unduly onerous to comply with the notice or requirement,

(b) the data-holder is not a relevant data-holder, or

(c) data specified in the notice are not relevant data.

(2) Sub-paragraph (1)(a) does not apply to a requirement to provide data that form part of the data-holder's statutory records.

(3) Sub-paragraph (1) does not apply if the tribunal approved the giving of the notice in accordance with paragraph 5.

Procedure for appeal

29 (1) Notice of an appeal under paragraph 28 must be given—

(a) in writing,

(b) before the end of the period of 30 days beginning with the date on which the data-holder notice was given, and

(c) to the officer of Revenue and Customs by whom the data-holder notice was given.

(2) It must state the grounds of appeal.

(3) On an appeal that is notified to the tribunal, the tribunal may confirm, vary or set aside the data-holder notice or a requirement in it.

(4) If the tribunal confirms or varies the notice or a requirement in it, the data-holder must comply with the notice or requirement—

(a) within such period as is specified by the tribunal, or

(b) if the tribunal does not specify a period, within such period as is reasonably specified in writing by an officer of Revenue and Customs following the tribunal's decision.

(5) A decision by the tribunal under this Part is final (despite the provisions of sections 11 and 13 of the Tribunals, Courts and Enforcement Act 2007).

(6) Subject to this paragraph, the provisions of Part 5 of TMA 1970 relating to appeals have effect in relation to appeals under paragraph 28 as they have effect in relation to an appeal against an assessment to income tax.

PART 4
PENALTIES

Penalties for failure to comply

30 (1) If the data-holder fails to comply with a data-holder notice, the data-holder is liable to a penalty of £300.

(2) A reference in this Schedule to failing to comply with a data-holder notice includes—

(a) concealing, destroying or otherwise disposing of a material document, or

(b) arranging for any such concealment, destruction or disposal.

(3) A document is a material document if, at the time when the data-holder acts—

(a) the data-holder has received a data-holder notice requiring the data-holder to provide the document or data contained in the document, or

(b) the data-holder has not received such a notice but has been informed by an officer of Revenue and Customs that the data-holder will do so or is likely to do so.

(4) A document is not a material document by virtue of sub-paragraph (3)(a) if the data-holder notice has already been complied with, unless—

(a) the data-holder has been notified in writing by an officer of Revenue and Customs that the data-holder must continue to preserve the document, and

(b) the notification has not been withdrawn.

(5) A document is not a material document by virtue of sub-paragraph (3)(b) if more than 6 months have elapsed since the data-holder was (or was last) informed.

Daily default penalties for failure to comply

31 If—

(a) a penalty under paragraph 30 is assessed, and

(b) the failure in question continues after the data-holder has been notified of the assessment,

the data-holder is liable to a further penalty, for each subsequent day on which the failure continues, of an amount not exceeding £60 for each such day.

Penalties for inaccurate information or documents

32 (1) This paragraph applies if—

(a) in complying with a data-holder notice, the data-holder provides inaccurate data, and

(b) condition A, B or C is met.

(2) Condition A is that the inaccuracy is—

(a) due to a failure by the data-holder to take reasonable care, or

(b) deliberate on the data-holder's part.

(3) Condition B is that the data-holder knows of the inaccuracy at the time the data are provided but does not inform HMRC at that time.

(4) Condition C is that the data-holder—

(a) discovers the inaccuracy some time later, and

(b) fails to take reasonable steps to inform HMRC.

(5) If this paragraph applies, the data-holder is liable to a penalty not exceeding £3,000.

Failure to comply with time limit

33 A failure to do anything required to be done within a limited period of time does not give rise to liability under paragraph 30 or 31 if the thing was done within such further time (if any) as an officer of Revenue and Customs may have allowed.

Reasonable excuse

34 (1) Liability to a penalty under paragraph 30 or 31 does not arise if the data-holder satisfies HMRC or (on an appeal notified to the tribunal) the tribunal that there is a reasonable excuse for the failure.

(2) For the purposes of this paragraph—

(a) an insufficiency of funds is not a reasonable excuse unless attributable to events outside the data-holder's control,

(b) if the data-holder relies on another person to do anything, that is not a reasonable excuse unless the data-holder took reasonable care to avoid the failure,

(c) if the data-holder had a reasonable excuse for the failure but the excuse has ceased, the data-holder is to be treated as having continued to have the excuse if the failure is remedied without unreasonable delay after the excuse ceased.

Assessment of penalties

35 (1) If the data-holder becomes liable to a penalty under paragraph 30, 31 or 32, HMRC may assess the penalty.

(2) If they do so, they must notify the data-holder.

(3) An assessment of a penalty under paragraph 30 or 31 must be made within the period of 12 months beginning with the latest of the following—

(a) the date on which the data-holder became liable to the penalty,

(b) the end of the period in which notice of an appeal against the data-holder notice (or a requirement in it) could have been given, and

(c) if notice of such an appeal is given, the date on which the appeal is determined or withdrawn.

(4) An assessment of a penalty under paragraph 32 must be made—

(a) within the period of 12 months beginning with the date on which the inaccuracy first came to the attention of an officer of Revenue and Customs, and

(b) within the period of 6 years beginning with the date on which the data-holder became liable to the penalty.

Right to appeal against penalty

36 The data-holder may appeal against a decision by an officer of Revenue and Customs—

(a) that a penalty is payable under paragraph 30, 31 or 32, or

(b) as to the amount of such a penalty.

Procedure on appeal against penalty

37 (1) Notice of an appeal under paragraph 36 must be given—

(a) in writing,

(b) before the end of the period of 30 days beginning with the date on which notification under paragraph 35 was given, and

(c) to HMRC.

(2) It must state the grounds of appeal.

(3) On an appeal under paragraph 36(a) that is notified to the tribunal, the tribunal may confirm or cancel the decision.

(4) On an appeal under paragraph 36(b) that is notified to the tribunal, the tribunal may—

(a) confirm the decision, or

(b) substitute for the decision another decision that the officer of Revenue and Customs had power to make.

(5) Subject to this paragraph and paragraph 40, the provisions of Part 5 of TMA 1970 relating to appeals have effect in relation to appeals under paragraph 36 as they have effect in relation to an appeal against an assessment to income tax.

Increased daily default penalty

38 (1) This paragraph applies if—

(a) a penalty under paragraph 31 is assessed under paragraph 35,

(b) the failure in respect of which that assessment is made continues for more than 30 days beginning with the date on which notification of that assessment is given, and

(c) the data-holder has been told that an application may be made under this paragraph for an increased daily penalty to be imposed.

(2) If this paragraph applies, an officer of Revenue and Customs may make an application to the tribunal for an increased daily penalty to be imposed on the data-holder.

(3) If the tribunal decides that an increased daily penalty should be imposed, then for each applicable day (see paragraph 39) on which the failure continues—

(a) the data-holder is not liable to a penalty under paragraph 31 in respect of the failure, and

(b) the data-holder is liable instead to a penalty under this paragraph of an amount determined by the tribunal.

(4) The tribunal may not determine an amount exceeding £1,000 for each applicable day.

(5) But subject to that, in determining the amount the tribunal must have regard to—

(a) the likely cost to the data-holder of complying with the data-holder notice,

(b) any benefits to the data-holder of not complying with it, and

(c) any benefits to anyone else resulting from the data-holder's non-compliance.

39 (1) If a data-holder becomes liable to a penalty under paragraph 38, HMRC must notify the data-holder.

(2) The notification must specify the day from which the increased penalty is to apply.

(3) That day and any subsequent day is an "applicable day" for the purposes of paragraph 38(3).

Enforcement of penalties

40 (1) A penalty under this Schedule must be paid before the end of the period of 30 days beginning with the date mentioned in sub-paragraph (2).

(2) That date is—

(a) the date on which notification under paragraph 35 or 39 is given in respect of the penalty, or

(b) if (in the case of a penalty under paragraph 30, 31 or 32) a notice of appeal under paragraph 36 is given, the date on which the appeal is finally determined or withdrawn.

(3) A penalty under this Schedule may be enforced as if it were income tax charged in an assessment and due and payable.

Power to change amount of penalties

41 (1) If it appears to the Treasury that there has been a change in the value of money since the last relevant date, they may by regulations substitute for the sums for the time being specified in paragraphs 30(1), 31, 32(5) and 38(4) such other sums as appear to them to be justified by the change.

(2) "Relevant date", in relation to a specified sum, means—

(a) the day on which this Act is passed, and

(b) each date on which the power conferred by sub-paragraph (1) has been exercised in relation to that sum.

(3) Regulations under this paragraph do not apply to—

(a) a failure which began before the date on which they come into force, or

(b) an inaccuracy in any data or document provided to HMRC before that date.

Double jeopardy

42 The data-holder is not liable to a penalty under this Schedule in respect of anything in respect of which the data-holder has been convicted of an offence.

PART 5

MISCELLANEOUS PROVISION AND INTERPRETATION

Application of provisions of TMA 1970

43 Subject to the provisions of this Schedule, the following provisions of TMA 1970 apply for the purposes of this Schedule as they apply for the purposes of the Taxes Acts—

(a) section 108 (responsibility of company officers),

(b) section 114 (want of form), and

(c) section 115 (delivery and service of documents).

Regulations

44 (1) Regulations under this Schedule are to be made by statutory instrument.

(2) The first regulations to be made under paragraph 1(3) may not be made unless the instrument containing them has been laid in draft before, and approved by a resolution of, the House of Commons.

(3) Subject to sub-paragraph (2), a statutory instrument containing regulations under this Schedule is subject to annulment in pursuance of a resolution of the House of Commons.

Tax

45 (1) In this Schedule "tax" means any or all of the following—

(a) income tax,
(b) capital gains tax,
(c) corporation tax,
(d) VAT,
(e) insurance premium tax,
(f) inheritance tax,
(g) stamp duty land tax,
(h) stamp duty reserve tax,
(i) petroleum revenue tax,
(j) aggregates levy,
(k) climate change levy,
(l) landfill tax, and
(m) relevant foreign tax.

(2) "Corporation tax" includes any amount assessable or chargeable as if it were corporation tax.

(3) "VAT" means—

(a) value added tax charged in accordance with VATA 1994, and
(b) value added tax charged in accordance with the law of another member State,

and includes any amount that is recoverable under paragraph 5(2) of Schedule 11 to VATA 1994 (amounts shown on invoices as VAT).

(4) "Relevant foreign tax" means—

(a) a tax of a member State, other than the United Kingdom, which is covered by the provisions for the exchange of information under the Directive of the Council of the European Communities No 77/799/EEC (as amended from time to time), and
(b) any tax or duty which is imposed under the law of a territory in relation to which arrangements having effect by virtue of section 173 of FA 2006 (international tax enforcement arrangements) have been made and which is covered by the arrangements.

Statutory records

46 (1) For the purposes of this Schedule data form part of a data-holder's statutory records if they are data that the data-holder is required to keep and preserve under or by virtue of any enactment relating to tax.

(2) Data cease to form part of a data-holder's statutory records when the period for which the data are required to be preserved under or by virtue of that enactment has expired.

General interpretation

47 In this Schedule—

"address" includes an electronic address;
"body of persons" has the same meaning as in TMA 1970;
"chargeable period" means a tax year, accounting period or other period for which a tax is charged;
"charity" has the meaning given by paragraph 1(1) of Schedule 6 to FA 2010;
"the Commissioners" means the Commissioners for Her Majesty's Revenue and Customs;
"company" has the meaning given by section 288(1) of TCGA 1992;
"data" includes information held in any form;
"the data-holder", in relation to a data-holder notice, means the person to whom the notice is addressed;
"data-holder notice" is defined in paragraph 1;
"dividend" includes any kind of distribution;
"document" includes a copy of a document (see also section 114 of FA 2008);
"employment", "employee" and "employer" have the same meaning as in Parts 2 to 7 of ITEPA 2003 (see, in particular, sections 4 and 5 of that Act);
"HMRC" means Her Majesty's Revenue and Customs;

"local authority" has the meaning given in section 999 of ITA 2007;
"provide" includes make available for inspection;
"specify" includes describe;
"securities" includes—

(a) shares and stock,

(b) debentures, including debenture stock, loan stock, bonds, certificates of deposit and other instruments creating or acknowledging indebtedness, and

(c) warrants or other instruments entitling the holder to subscribe for or otherwise acquire anything within paragraph (a) or (b),

issued by or on behalf of a person resident in, or a government or public or local authority of, any country (including a country outside the United Kingdom);

"shares" is to be construed in accordance with sections 99 and 103A of TCGA 1992;
"tax functions" means functions relating to tax;
"the tribunal" means the First-tier Tribunal or, where determined by or under the Tribunal Procedure Rules, the Upper Tribunal.

48 A reference in this Schedule to providing data includes—

(a) preparing and delivering a return, statement or declaration, and

(b) providing documents.

49 (1) A reference in this Schedule to the carrying on of a business also includes—

(a) the letting of property,

(b) the activities of a charity, and

(c) the activities of a government department, a local authority, a local authority association or any other public authority.

(2) "Local authority association" has the meaning given in section 1000 of ITA 2007.

Crown application

50 This Schedule applies to the Crown but not to Her Majesty in Her private capacity (within the meaning of the Crown Proceedings Act 1947).

PART 6

CONSEQUENTIAL PROVISIONS

TMA 1970

51 (1) TMA 1970 is amended as follows.

(2) Omit—

(a) section 13 (persons in receipt of taxable income belonging to others),

(b) section 14 (return of lodgers and inmates),

(c) section 15 (return of employees' earnings etc),

(d) section 15A (non-resident's staff are UK client's employees for section 15 purposes),

(e) section 16 (fees, commissions etc),

(f) section 16A (agency workers),

(g) section 17 (interest paid or credited by banks, building societies etc without deduction of income tax),

(h) section 18 (interest paid without deduction of income tax),

(i) section 18A (other payments and licences etc),

(j) section 19 (information for purposes of charge on profits of UK property businesses or under Schedule A),

(k) section 21 (stock jobbers' transactions),

(l) section 23 (power to obtain copies of registers of securities),

(m) section 24 (power to obtain information as to income from securities),

(n) section 25 (issuing houses, stockbrokers, auctioneers etc),

(o) section 26 (nominee shareholders),

(p) section 27 (settled property),

(q) section 76 (protection for certain trustees, agents and receivers), and

(r) section 77I (information from petroleum licence-holders).

(3) In the Table in section 98 (special returns etc), omit the entries (so far as they continue to have effect) relating to—

(a) section 77I of TMA 1970,

(b) paragraph 2 of Schedule 15 to FA 1973,

(c) sections 42, 217(4), 226(4) and 768(9) of ICTA,

(d) paragraph 3 of Schedule 12 to FA 1989,

(e) sections 302B and 647 of ITTOIA 2005,

(f) section 241 of CTA 2009, and
(g) sections 728, 1046(5) to (7) and 1097(1) and (2) of CTA 2010.

(4) In that Table—

(a) for the entry relating to section 31 of CTA 2010 substitute the following entry—
"Section 31(3) and (4) of CTA 2010.",
(b) for the entry relating to section 465 of CTA 2010 substitute the following entry—
"Section 465(3) and (4) of CTA 2010.", and
(c) for the entry relating to section 1102 of CTA 2010 substitute the following entry—
"Section 1102(4) and (5) of CTA 2010."

(5) In section 103ZA (disapplication of sections 100 to 103)—

(a) omit "or" at the end of paragraph (d), and
(b) at the end of paragraph (e) insert
", or
(f) Schedule 23 to FA 2011 (data-gathering powers)."

FA 1973

52 In Schedule 15 to FA 1973 (territorial extension of charge to tax: supplementary provisions), omit paragraph 2 so far as it continues to have effect (see section 381 of TIOPA 2010).

FA 1974

53 (1) In section 24 of FA 1974 (returns of persons treated as employees), for the words from "section 15" to the end substitute "any notice given under section 8 of the Taxes Management Act 1970 to the person performing the duties (P) may require a return of P's income to include particulars of any general earnings paid to P."

(2) Sub-paragraph (1) applies so far as section 24 of FA 1974 continues to have effect (see section 381 of TIOPA 2010).

FA 1986

54 In Schedule 18 to FA 1986 (securities: other provisions), omit paragraph 8(4) and (5).

ICTA

55 Omit the following provisions of ICTA so far as they continue to have effect (see section 1184 of CTA 2010 and section 381 of TIOPA 2010)—

(a) section 42(7) (information required to decide whether to give provisional notice of determination),
(b) section 217(4) (information about person for whom chargeable payment is received),
(c) section 226(4) (information about purchase by unquoted trading company of its own shares),
(d) section 768(9) (information about change in ownership of company: disallowance of trading losses), and
(e) section 816(3) (disapplication of bank exemption).

FA 1989

56 In Schedule 12 to FA 1989 (close companies), omit paragraph 3 so far as it continues to have effect (see section 1184 of CTA 2010).

ITTOIA 2005

57 (1) ITTOIA 2005 is amended as follows.

(2) In Chapter 4 of Part 3 (profits of property businesses: lease premiums etc), omit section 302B(3) and (4).

(3) In Chapter 5 of Part 5 (settlements: amounts treated as income of settlor), omit section 647.

FA 2005

58 In Schedule 2 to FA 2005 (alternative finance arrangements: further provisions), omit paragraph 2 so far as it continues to have effect (see section 1329 of CTA 2009).

CRCA 2005

59 In Schedule 2 to CRCA 2005 (functions of Commissioners and officers: restrictions etc), omit paragraph 2.

FA 2008

60 FA 2008 is amended as follows.

61 In section 39 (dormant bank and building society accounts), in subsection (1), omit paragraph (a).

62 (1) Schedule 36 (information and inspection powers) is amended as follows.

(2) Omit paragraph 34A.

(3) In paragraph 61A (involved third parties)—

(a) in sub-paragraph (2), omit ""relevant information",",

(b) in each entry in the second column of the Table, for "Information and documents" substitute "Documents", and

(c) accordingly, in the heading of that column, omit "information and relevant".

CTA 2009

63 In Chapter 4 of Part 4 of CTA 2009 (profits of property businesses: lease premiums etc), omit section 241(3) and (4).

CTA 2010

64 (1) CTA 2010 is amended as follows.

(2) Omit—

(a) section 31(1) (companies with small profits: power to obtain information),

(b) section 465(1) (close companies: power to obtain information),

(c) section 728 (provision of information about ownership of shares etc),

(d) section 1046(5) to (7) (information about purchase by unquoted trading company of its own shares),

(e) section 1097 (information about person for whom chargeable payment is received), and

(f) section 1102(2) (non-qualifying distributions etc: additional information).

(3) In section 1109 (tax credits for certain recipients of exempt qualifying distributions), in subsection (4), for "1102(2)" substitute "1102(3)".

PART 7

APPLICATION OF THIS SCHEDULE

65 (1) This Schedule—

(a) comes into force on 1 April 2012, and

(b) applies from then on to relevant data with a bearing on any period (whether before, on or after that date), subject to paragraph 3(2).

(2) The provisions repealed or otherwise amended by Part 6 of this Schedule continue to have effect in relation to notices given, or requests made, pursuant to any of the repealed provisions before 1 April 2012 as if the repeals and other amendments had not been made.

GENERAL NOTE

Part 1

Paragraph 1 introduces the concept of a 'data-holder notice' which may be issued by an officer of HMRC in writing to the holder (defined in Part 2) of relevant data as specified in regulations made by the Treasury. Such data may be general in nature or relating to particular persons or matters and may include personal data such as names and addresses of individuals.

Paragraph 2 explains the purpose for which the power may be used namely generally for risk assessment purposes or specifically in relation certain tax checks. It cannot be used for checking the tax position of the data-holder except in circumstances where it is not known whether the data-holder is the beneficial owner of securities or payments which are the subject of enquiry.

Paragraph 3 requires that a data-holder notice must specify the relevant data to be provided and the officer must have reason to believe that such data could have a bearing on chargeable or other periods ending on or after the first day of the period of 4 years ending on the day on which the notice is given.

Paragraph 4 enables HMRC to specify the means and form by and in which data is to be provided. The notice may specify the address to which data is to be sent and the reasonable time limit for providing the information. Alternatively, the notice may require the data to be made available for inspection at a time and place, other than a dwelling place, reasonably specified by HMRC or as agreed with the data-holder. Where specific documents are required to be provided, these must be within the data-holder's power or possession.

Paragraph 5 enables HMRC to seek the approval of the Tribunal before issuing a notice the effect of which is that the data-holder may not appeal against the notice. The Tribunal can only give its approval, against which decision there is no right of appeal, if:

— the application is made by, or with the agreement of, an officer of HMRC duly authorised by the Commissioners,

— the Tribunal is satisfied that the officer giving the notice is justified in doing so,

— the data-holder has been told that the data are to be required and has been given reasonable opportunity to make representations to HMRC, and

— the Tribunal has been given a summary of these representations.

But the application may be considered at a hearing without notice being given to the data-holder, if the Tribunal is satisfied that alerting the data-holder might prejudice the purpose for which the data are required.

Paragraph 6 allows HMRC to take copies of or make extracts from any documents provided in response to a notice.

Paragraph 7 says that HMRC are entitled to retain documents for a reasonable period if it is thought reasonable to do so, without this being regarded as breaking any lien claimed on the document, but the data-holder may request a copy. The Commissioners are required to compensate the owners of the documents for any expense reasonably incurred in replacing or repairing documents lost or damaged.

Part 2

Paragraph 8 indicates that the relevant data-holders to whom the Schedule applies are described in paragraphs 9–27 and that the provisions apply to persons who previously fell within a particular category but no longer do so.

Paragraph 9 says:

(1) The following are relevant data-holders:

(a) employers

(b) anyone making a payment to, or in respect of, someone else's employees in relation to their employment by the other party

(c) an approved agent for the purposes of payroll giving, and

(d) anyone carrying on business in connection with which relevant payments are likely to be made.

(2) Relevant payments are:

(a) payments made for, or in connection with, services provided by persons who are not employed in the business, or

(b) periodical or lumps sum payments in respect of any copyright, public lending right, right in a registered design or design right

(3) Payments are to be regarded as made in connection with a business if they are made in the course of carrying on the business or part of it, or in connection with the formation, acquisition, development or disposal of the business or part of it.

(4) Category (1)(d) above applies equally to the carrying on of any other kind of activity as it applies to the carrying on of a business provided the activity is being carried on by a body of persons and other references above to 'business' are to be read accordingly.

(5) Reference to the making of payments includes the provision of benefits and the giving of any other valuable consideration.

Paragraph 10

(1) This paragraph applies if:

(a) the services that an individual provides or is obliged to provide under an agency contract are treated as the duties of an employment held by the individual with an agency, or

(b) remuneration receivable under, or in consequence of, arrangements with an agency is treated as earnings from an employment held by the individual with the agency

(2) For the purposes of paragraph 9 such an individual is treated as being employed by the agency and payments made to that individual do not count as relevant payments.

Paragraph 11

(1) This paragraph applies where:
- (a) a person ("A") performs duties of an employment in the United Kingdom (UK)
- (b) the employer is a person resident outside the UK
- (c) the duties performed in the UK are performed for a continuous period of not less than 30 days, and
- (d) those duties are performed for the benefit of a person ("B") resident or carrying on a trade, profession or vocation in the UK

(2) For the purposes of para 9:
- (a) B is treated as an employer, but
- (b) Only the name and place of residence of A may be specified for a relevant data-holder of B's type in regulations made by the Treasury under paragraph 1

Paragraph 12

(1) A person by or through whom interest is paid or credited is a relevant data-holder

(2) The following are treated as interest:
- (a) a dividend in respect of a share in a building society within the meaning of the Building Societies Act 1986
- (b) an amount to which a person holding a deeply discounted security (as defined in ITTOIA 2005 s 430) is entitled on the redemption of that security
- (c) a foreign dividend, being any annual payment, interest or dividend payable out of, or in respect of the funds or securities of a body of persons not resident in the UK or a government or local authority in a country outside of the UK, and
- (d) an alternative financial return (as defined in ITA 2007 ss 564I–L, and CTA 2009 s 511)

Paragraph 13 says that any person who, in any capacity, receives money or value of or belonging to another person is a relevant data-holder.

Paragraph 14

(1) The following are relevant data-holders:
- (a) the registered or inscribed holder of securities
- (b) a person who receives a payment derived from securities or would be entitled to do so if a payment were made including an amount (whether income or capital) payable out of or in respect of securities or rights attaching to securities and a payment that is representative of any such amount
- (c) a person who receives a payment by a company on the redemption, repayment or purchase of its own shares. and
- (d) a person who receives a chargeable payment on a demerger.

(2) The data which may be required from the data-holders listed in this clause is limited to:
- (a) whether the relevant data holder is the beneficial owner or sole beneficial owner of the securities in question, and if not
- (b) details of the beneficial owner or other beneficial owners, and if these details are not known or if different, details of the person for whom the securities are held or to whom the payment is or may be paid, and
- (c) and if there is more than one beneficial owner or if the securities are held on behalf of more than one person, details of their respective interests in the securities

It should be noted that Banks will no longer enjoy, as they do currently, the limited exemption from providing information in respect of persons not resident in the UK who are beneficially entitled to income from securities.

Paragraph 15 says that a person who makes a payment derived from securities that has been received from or is paid on behalf of another, is also a relevant data-holder.

Paragraph 16 says that a person making a payment out of public funds by way of a grant or subsidy is a relevant data-holder. A payment is treated as being made out of public funds if it is provided directly or indirectly by the Crown, any Government, public or local authority whether in the UK or elsewhere, or by any EU institution.

Paragraph 17 provides that a person by whom licences or approvals are issued or a register or list is maintained, such as a local authority or any other legally authorized person, is a relevant data-holder.

Paragraph 18 treats the following as relevant data-holders:

— a lessee (or successor in title of a lessee)

— an occupier of land

— a person having the use of land

— a person who, as agent (including estate agents) , manages land or is in receipt of rent or other payments arising from land.

Paragraph 19

Each of the following is relevant data-holder:

— a person who effects ,or is party to, securities transactions wholly or partly on behalf of others (whether as agent or principal)

— a person whose business consists of acting as registrar or administrator (including managing a clearing house for any terminal market in securities) in respect of 'securities transactions', which term includes:

— unsurprisingly, transactions in securities. These are transactions of whatever description relating to securities including the purchase or sale or exchange of securities, the issuing , or securing the issue, of new securities, applying or subscribing for new securities and altering, or securing the alteration of, rights attached to securities

— transactions under which a representative payment has been, is to be, or may be made

— the making or receipt of a representative payment–that is a payment representative of an amount payable out of, or in respect of securities, or rights attaching to securities

— a person who makes a payment derived from bearer securities

— an accountable person within the meaning of the SDRT Regulations of 1986.

Paragraph 20 the following are relevant data-holders:

— the committee or other person or body responsible for managing a clearing house for any terminal market in commodities

— an auctioneer

— a person carrying on a business of dealing in any description of tangible movable property or acting as an agent or intermediary in dealings in any description of tangible movable property.

Paragraph 21 a person who is registered as managing agent at Lloyd's in relation to a syndicate of underwriting members of Lloyd's is a relevant data-holder.

Paragraph 22 the following are classified as relevant data-holders:

— an investment plan manager as approved by the Commissioners of HMRC

— an account provider in relation to a Government funded child trust fund set up for a child born after 31 August 2002.

Paragraph 23 deems the following to be relevant data-holders:

— the holder of a licence to search for and recover oil in UK territorial waters and Crown land

— the responsible person in relation to an oil field ,being the partnership or company appointed to deal with tax matters arising in connection with the exploitation of an oil field.

Paragraph 24 lists the following as relevant data-holders:

— a person who is involved in any capacity in an insurance business

— a person who makes arrangements for persons to enter into contracts of insurance

— a person who is concerned in business that is not an insurance business and who has been involved in the entering into of a contract of insurance that provides cover for any matter associated with the business.

Paragraph 25 classifies as a relevant data-holder a person who is involved in any capacity in any of the following activities:

— quarrying rock, gravel or sand and supplying it for use in the construction industry

— making or receiving supplies of commodities such as electricity, coal, gas, or connected activities

— landfill disposal.

Paragraph 26 lists the following as relevant data-holders:

— the settler, trustee and beneficiary of a settlement and any other person to whom income is payable under the settlement, A settlement includes any disposition, trust, covenant, agreement, arrangement or transfer of assets other than a loan to a charity for no consideration.

Paragraph 27

A charity is a relevant data-holder.

Part 3

Paragraph 28

Unless the issue of a notice has been approved by the Tribunal the data-holder may appeal against the notice, or any of its requirements, on any of the following grounds:

— it is unduly onerous to comply (does not apply to the data-holder's statutory records)

— the data-holder is not a relevant data-holder

— the data requested is not relevant data.

Paragraph 29

Notice of appeal, stating the grounds of appeal, must be given in writing within 30 days of the date on which notice is given and must be sent to the officer of HMRC by whom notice has been given. The Tribunal may confirm, vary or set aside the notice or any of its requirements. In which case the data-holder must comply with the notice or requirement within the time specified by the Tribunal or within such period as is reasonably specified in writing by an officer of HMRC following the Tribunal's decision, against which there is no right of appeal. Subject to the foregoing the normal rights of appeal against an assessment to income tax have effect in relation to an appeal under the previous paragraph.

Part 4

Paragraph 30

There is a penalty of £300 for failure to comply with a notice. Failure includes concealing, destroying or otherwise disposing of a document in respect of which, or the data contained in it, a data-holder has received a notice, or arranging for any such concealment, destruction or disposal. This also applies even if the data-holder has not received a notice but has been informed by an officer of HMRC that such a notice will be, or is likely to be, served unless 6 months have elapsed since the data-holder was last so informed. If a notice has been complied with and the data-holder has not been notified in writing that a document must continue to be preserved, and that notification has not been withdrawn, the restrictions contained in this paragraph do not apply.

Paragraph 31

If failure continues after the assessment of a penalty under para 30, the data-holder is liable to a penalty not exceeding £60 for each subsequent day for which the failure continues.

Paragraph 32

A data-holder will be liable to a penalty not exceeding £3000 if inaccurate data is provided and one of the following conditions is met:

— the inaccuracy is due either to a failure by the data-holder to take reasonable care or to a deliberate act on his part

— the data-holder knows of the inaccuracy at the time the data is provided but does not inform HMRC at that time

— the data–holder discovers the inaccuracy some time later and fails to take reasonable steps to inform HMRC.

Paragraph 33

Failure to comply with a time limit does not give rise to a penalty if an extended time limit allowed by an officer of HMRC is complied with.

Paragraph 34

Liability to a penalty under paras 30 or 31 does not arise if the data-holder satisfies HMRC or the Tribunal that there is a reasonable excuse for the failure. For this purpose:

— an insufficiency of funds is not a reasonable excuse unless attributable to events outside the data-holder's control

— if the data-holder relies on another person, that is not a reasonable excuse unless the data-holder took reasonable care to avoid the failure

— if a reasonable excuse for failure has ceased, the data-holder is treated as having continued to have the excuse if the failure is remedied without unreasonable delay after the excuse has ceased.

Paragraph 35

HMRC may assess a penalty to which a data-holder becomes liable under any of the 3 preceding paragraphs and if so they must notify the data-holder. An assessment under paras 30 or 31 must be made within 12 months beginning with the latest of:

— the date on which liability arose

— the end of the period in which notice of appeal could have been given

— the date on which any appeal is determined or withdrawn

An assessment under para 32 must be made:

— within the period of 12 months beginning with the date on which the inaccuracy first came to the attention of an officer of HMRC, and

— within the period of 6 years beginning with the date on which the data-holder became liable to the penalty.

Paragraph 36

There is a right of appeal against a penalty under the 3 preceding paragraphs or against the amount of such a penalty.

Paragraph 37

Notice under para 36 stating the grounds of appeal must be given to HMRC in writing within 30 days of the notification under para 35. On an appeal against a decision that a penalty is payable which is notified to the Tribunal, the Tribunal may confirm or cancel the decision. On an appeal as to the amount of a penalty, the Tribunal may confirm the decision or substitute another decision which HMRC has power to make. Subject to this paragraph and para 40, the provisions relating to appeals against an assessment to income tax apply to appeals under para 36.

Paragraph 38

Where a daily default penalty is assessed and the failure continues for more than 30 days beginning with the date on which the assessment is notified and the data-holder has been told that application may be made for an increased daily penalty, HMRC may apply to the Tribunal for an increased daily penalty to be imposed. If the Tribunal decides that an increased daily penalty should be imposed then for each applicable day (see para 39) the data-holder is liable to a penalty in an amount determined by the Tribunal, not exceeding £1000 for each applicable day, rather than the penalty imposed by HMRC under paragraph 31. In determining the amount of the penalty, the Tribunal must have regard to the likely cost of complying with the notice, any benefit to the data-holder of not complying and any benefit to anyone else resulting from the non-compliance. The data-holder may attend the hearing.

Paragraph 39

HMRC must notify the data-holder if he becomes liable to an increased daily penalty. Such notification must specify the day from which the increased penalty is to apply and that day and any subsequent day is an 'applicable day' for the purpose of para 38.

Paragraph 40

A penalty under this Schedule must be paid before the end of the period of 30 days beginning with the date on which the notification under para 35 or 39 is given or, in the case of an appeal under paragraph 36 against a penalty under para 30, 31 or 32, the date on which the appeal is determined or withdrawn.

Paragraph 41

Where it appears that there has been a change in the value of money since the later of the date on which FA 2011 is passed and each date on which the power under this paragraph has been exercised, the Treasury may by regulations substitute for the penalties under Part 4 such other sums as appear to be justified. Such regulations do not apply to a failure which began before the date on which they come into force or an inaccuracy in any data or document provided to HMRC before that date.

Paragraph 42

The data-holder is not liable to a penalty under this Schedule in respect of anything in respect of which he has been convicted of an offence.

Part 5

Paragraph 43

Subject to the provisions of this Schedule, the following provisions of TMA 1970 apply to this Schedule as they apply for the purposes of the Taxes Acts:

— s 108 (responsibility of company officers)

— s 114 (want of form), and

— s 115 (delivery and service of documents)

Paragraph 44

Regulations under this Schedule may be made by statutory instrument and the regulations specifying the meaning of 'relevant data' may not be made unless the statutory instrument has been laid in draft before, and approved by a resolution of, the House of Commons.

Paragraph 45

In this Schedule, 'tax ' means any or all of income tax, capital gains tax ,corporation tax, VAT, insurance premium tax, inheritance tax, stamp duty land tax, stamp duty reserve tax, petroleum revenue tax, aggregates levy, climate change levy, landfill tax and relevant foreign tax.

Corporation tax includes any amount assessable or chargeable as if it were corporation tax. VAT includes value added tax charged in accordance with the law of another EU member State and any amount t shown on invoices as VAT.

Relevant foreign tax means a tax of an EU member state other than the UK which is covered by the EU exchange of information directive and any tax or duty in relation to which international tax enforcement arrangements have been made.

Paragraph 46

For the purposes of this Schedule data forms part of a data-holder's statutory records only for as long as it is required to be kept and preserved by virtue of any Act relating to tax.

Paragraph 47

In this Schedule-

"address" includes an electronic address

"body of persons" means any body politic, corporate or collegiate, and any company fraternity, fellowship and society of persons, whether corporate or not corporate

"chargeable period" mans a tax year, accounting period or other period for which tax is charged

"charity "means a body of persons or a trust which:

— is established for charitable purposes

— is subject to the control either of the High Court, the Court of Session or the High Court in Northern Ireland in the exercise of their jurisdiction with respect to charities or any other court of another EU member State or a territory specified in regulations made by the Commissioners of HMRC, in the exercise of a corresponding jurisdiction with respect to charities

— meets the relevant registration condition regarding registration under UK charity legislation or the corresponding legislation of territories outside England and Wales

— meets the management condition which requires that the persons in general control of the body or trust are fit and proper persons to be managers of it

"the Commissioners" means the Commissioners of HMRC

"company" means any body corporate or unincorporated association

"data" includes information held in any form

"the data-holder" means the person to whom the notice is addressed

"dividend" includes any kind of distribution

"document" includes a copy of a document and also information held on computer

"employment", "employee" and "employer" have the same meaning as in tax legislation relating to earnings and pensions in particular "employment" includes any employment under a contract of service, a contract of apprenticeship and service of the Crown. The legislation applies equally to offices and office-holders

"local authority" means the various authorities specified in Local Government legislation relating to England & Wales, Scotland and Northern Ireland respectively

"provide" includes make available for inspection

"specify" includes describe

"securities" includes:

— shares and stock,

— debentures, loan stock, bonds, certificates of deposit and other instruments creating or acknowledging indebtedness, and
— warrants or other instruments entitling the holder to subscribe for or acquire shares and debentures

issued by or on behalf of a person resident in, or a government or local authority of, any country (including a government outside the UK)

"shares" applies also to rights in a unit trust resident in the UK and an offshore fund which is not constituted as a company and is not a unit trust

"the Tribunal" means the First-tier Tribunal or the Upper Tribunal

Paragraph 48

Reference to providing data includes preparing and delivering a return statement or declaration and providing documents.

Paragraph 49

Reference to the carrying on of a business includes:

— the letting of property
— the activities of a charity, and
— the activities of a government department, a local authority, a local authority association or any other public authority.

A local authority association is any incorporated or unincorporated association all of whose members are local authorities, groups thereof or local authority associations and whose purpose, or primary purpose, is to protect and further the general interests of local authorities.

Paragraph 50

This Schedule applies to the Crown but not to Her Majesty in Her private capacity.

Part 6

Paragraphs 51–64 repeal and amend various parts of TMA 1970 and other tax legislation relating to the gathering of information.

Part 7

This Schedule comes into force on 1 April 2012 and applies to relevant data with a bearing on any period before, on or after that date subject to the proviso that the period ends on or after the first day of the period of 4 years ending on the day on which the notice is given.

SCHEDULE 24

AMENDMENTS OF SCHEDULE 36 TO FA 2008

Section 86(2)

1 Schedule 36 to FA 2008 (information and inspection powers) is amended as follows.

2 (1) Paragraph 5 (power to obtain information and documents about persons whose identity is not known) is amended as follows.

(2) In sub-paragraph (2), omit "UK".

(3) In sub-paragraph (4)—

(a) in paragraph (b), for the words from "the Taxes Acts" to the end substitute "the law (including the law of a territory outside the United Kingdom) relating to tax,", and

(b) in paragraph (c), omit "UK".

(4) Omit sub-paragraph (5).

(5) The amendments made by this paragraph—

(a) come into force on 1 April 2012, and

(b) apply from then on in relation to tax regardless of when the tax became due (whether before, on or after that date).

3 (1) Paragraph 40A (penalties for inaccurate information and documents) is amended as follows.

(2) In sub-paragraph (1)(b), for "A or B" substitute "A, B or C".

(3) After sub-paragraph (3) insert—

"(3A) Condition B is that the person knows of the inaccuracy at the time the information is provided or the document produced but does not inform HMRC at that time."

(4) In sub-paragraph (4), for "B" substitute "C".

(5) The amendments made by this paragraph have effect in relation to any inaccuracy in information provided, or in documents produced, on or after 1 April 2012.

4 (1) After paragraph 49 insert—

"Increased daily default penalty

49A (1) This paragraph applies if—

(a) a penalty under paragraph 40 is assessed under paragraph 46 in respect of a person's failure to comply with a notice under paragraph 5,

(b) the failure continues for more than 30 days beginning with the date on which notification of that assessment was issued, and

(c) the person has been told that an application may be made under this paragraph for an increased daily penalty to be imposed.

(2) If this paragraph applies, an officer of Revenue and Customs may make an application to the tribunal for an increased daily penalty to be imposed on the person.

(3) If the tribunal decides that an increased daily penalty should be imposed, then for each applicable day (see paragraph 49B) on which the failure continues—

(a) the person is not liable to a penalty under paragraph 40 in respect of the failure, and

(b) the person is liable instead to a penalty under this paragraph of an amount determined by the tribunal.

(4) The tribunal may not determine an amount exceeding £1,000 for each applicable day.

(5) But subject to that, in determining the amount the tribunal must have regard to—

(a) the likely cost to the person of complying with the notice,

(b) any benefits to the person of not complying with it, and

(c) any benefits to anyone else resulting from the person's non-compliance.

(6) Paragraph 41 applies in relation to the sum specified in sub-paragraph (4) as it applies in relation to the sums mentioned in paragraph 41(1).

49B (1) If a person becomes liable to a penalty under paragraph 49A, HMRC must notify the person.

(2) The notification must specify the day from which the increased penalty is to apply.

(3) That day and any subsequent day is an "applicable day" for the purposes of paragraph 49A(3).

49C (1) A penalty under paragraph 49A must be paid before the end of the period of 30 days beginning with the date on which the notification under paragraph 49B is issued.

(2) A penalty under paragraph 49A may be enforced as if it were income tax charged in an assessment and due and payable."

(2) The amendment made by this paragraph has effect in relation to failures to comply with a notice under paragraph 5 that begin on or after 1 April 2012.

5 (1) Paragraph 50 (tax-related penalty) is amended as follows.

(2) In sub-paragraph (1)(d), omit "(within the meaning of paragraph 46)".

(3) After sub-paragraph (6) insert—

"(7) In sub-paragraph (1)(d) "the relevant date" means—

(a) in a case involving an information notice against which a person may appeal, the latest of—

(i) the date on which the person became liable to the penalty under paragraph 39,

(ii) the end of the period in which notice of an appeal against the information notice could have been given, and

(iii) if notice of such an appeal is given, the date on which the appeal is determined or withdrawn, and

(b) in any other case, the date on which the person became liable to the penalty under paragraph 39."

(4) The amendments made by this paragraph have effect where a person becomes liable to a penalty under paragraph 39 of Schedule 36 to FA 2008 on or after the day on which this Act is passed.

6 In paragraph 61A (involved third parties), in the first column of item 11 of the Table, after "receiving" insert "supplies of".

GENERAL NOTE

Paragraph 2 introduces amendments to para 5, which gives HMRC power to obtain information and documents about persons whose identity is not known. It is this power and its predecessor in TMA 1970 s 20 which HMRC have used extensively in recent years in connection with offshore bank accounts. The effect of the amendment is to enable the power to be used to obtain information in relation to relevant foreign tax of a territory outside the UK. Relevant foreign tax means a tax of an EU member state other than the UK which is covered by the EU exchange of information directive and any tax or duty in relation to which international tax enforcement arrangements have been made. The change, which comes into effect on 1 April 2012 and applies regardless of when tax became due, reflects the increasing globalization of tax compliance efforts.

Paragraph 3 amends para 40A to introduce a new category for which a penalty not exceeding £3000 may be charged where a person knowingly provides information containing an inaccuracy but does not notify HMRC at the time. One wonders why it is felt that this was not already caught by Condition A being a deliberate inaccuracy. The change has effect in relation to any inaccuracy in information provided, or in documents produced, on or after 1 April 2012

Paragraph 4 introduces new paras 49A–49C which provide for an increased daily penalty to be charged where a daily default penalty is assessed and the failure to comply continues for more than 30 days beginning with the date on which the assessment is notified. Provided that the data-holder has been told that application may be made for an increased daily penalty, HMRC may apply to the Tribunal for an increased daily penalty to be imposed. If the Tribunal decides that an increased daily penalty should be imposed then for each applicable day (see below) the data-holder is liable to a penalty in an amount determined by the Tribunal, not exceeding £1000 for each applicable day, rather than the penalty imposed by HMRC under para 40. In determining the amount of the penalty, the Tribunal must have regard to the likely cost of complying with the notice, any benefit to the data-holder of not complying and any benefit to anyone else resulting from the non-compliance. The data-holder may attend the hearing.

Where it appears that there has been a change in the value of money since the later of the date on which FA 2011 is passed and each date on which the power under this paragraph has been exercised, the Treasury may by regulations substitute for the penalty under para 49A such other sums as appear to be justified. Such regulations do not apply to a failure which began before the date on which they come into force or an inaccuracy in any information or document provided to HMRC before that date

HMRC must notify the data-holder if he becomes liable to an increased daily penalty. Such notification must specify the day from which the increased penalty is to apply and that day and any subsequent day is an 'applicable day' for the purpose of para 49A.

A penalty under para 49A may be enforced as if it were income tax charged in an assessment which has become due and payable and must be paid before the end of the period of 30 days beginning with the date on which the notification under para 49B is given.

The change has effect in relation to failures to comply with a notice under para 5 that begin on or after 1 April 2012

Paragraph 5 amends the tax-related penalty provision in para 50 so as to clarify the relevant date for the purpose of charging the penalty. Where a person becomes liable to a penalty for failure to comply with a notice or for deliberately obstructing an officer in the course of an inspection of business premises that has been approved by the Tribunal and where the failure or obstruction continues after the imposition of the penalty and the officer has reason to believe that there has been a significant loss of tax as a result, the officer may within 12 months of the 'relevant date' apply to the Upper Tribunal for an additional tax-related penalty to be imposed. The relevant date for this purpose is:

— in a case involving an information notice against which a person may appeal, the latest of:
  — the date on which the person became liable to the penalty under para 39

— the end of the period in which notice of appeal against the information notice could have been given
— if notice of such appeal is given, the date on which the appeal is determined or withdrawn, and

— in any other case, the date on which the person became liable to the penalty under para 39.

This change becomes effective where a person becomes liable to penalty under para 39 on or after the day on which FA 2011 is passed

It is worth recalling that the recipient of a notice may appeal against it or any requirement in it unless the notice requires information or documents which form part of the recipient's statutory records or the tribunal has approved the giving of the notice.

SCHEDULE 25

MUTUAL ASSISTANCE FOR RECOVERY OF TAXES ETC

Section 87

MARD

1 In this Schedule "MARD" means Council Directive 2010/24/EU.

HMRC functions

2 (1) The Commissioners are a competent authority in the United Kingdom for the purposes of all matters under MARD.

(2) HMRC is designated as the central liaison office in the United Kingdom for the purposes of all matters under MARD.

Exchange of information

3 (1) No obligation of secrecy imposed by statute or otherwise precludes a public authority (or anyone acting on behalf of a public authority) from disclosing information if the disclosure is made for the purpose of giving effect, or enabling effect to be given, to MARD or a MARD-related instrument.

(2) Sub-paragraph (1) applies, in particular, to any disclosure (to persons in the United Kingdom or elsewhere) in connection with a request or proposed request by or on behalf of an applicant authority of any member State for assistance in accordance with MARD.

(3) Sub-paragraph (2) is not to be taken to limit sub-paragraph (1).

Onward disclosure of information received from HMRC

4 (1) A public authority commits an offence if—

(a) it discloses relevant information, and
(b) the disclosure is not permitted by sub-paragraph (3).

(2) "Relevant information" is information that—

(a) the public authority has received from HMRC by virtue of paragraph 3, and
(b) relates to a person whose identity is specified in the disclosure or can be deduced from it.

(3) A disclosure is permitted by this sub-paragraph if it is made—

(a) in accordance with paragraph 3,
(b) in accordance with another enactment (or an instrument made under an enactment) permitting the disclosure,
(c) in pursuance of an order of a court,
(d) for the purposes of civil proceedings (whether or not within the United Kingdom),
(e) for the purposes of a criminal investigation or criminal proceedings (whether or not within the United Kingdom),
(f) with the consent of each person to whom the information relates, or
(g) with the consent of the Commissioners.

(4) Sub-paragraph (1) applies to each of the following as it applies to a public authority—

(a) an employee or agent of the public authority;
(b) anyone providing services or exercising functions on behalf of the public authority;
(c) anyone authorised by the public authority to receive information on its behalf.

5 (1) It is a defence for a person charged with an offence under paragraph 4 to prove that the person reasonably believed—

(a) that the disclosure was lawful, or
(b) that the information had already and lawfully been made available to the public.

(2) A person guilty of an offence under paragraph 4 is liable—

(a) on conviction on indictment, to imprisonment for a term not exceeding 2 years or a fine, or both;
(b) on summary conviction, to imprisonment for a term not exceeding 12 months or a fine not exceeding the statutory maximum, or both.

(3) A prosecution for an offence under paragraph 4 may be instituted in England and Wales only—

(a) by the Director of Revenue and Customs Prosecution, or
(b) with the consent of the Director of Public Prosecutions.

(4) A prosecution for an offence under paragraph 4 may be instituted in Northern Ireland only—

(a) by the Commissioners, or
(b) with the consent of the Director of Public Prosecutions for Northern Ireland.

(5) In the application of this paragraph—

(a) in England and Wales, in relation to an offence committed before the commencement of section 154(1) of the Criminal Justice Act 2003, or
(b) in Northern Ireland,

the reference in sub-paragraph (2)(b) to 12 months is to be read as a reference to 6 months.

Enforcement of foreign claims in the UK

6 (1) This paragraph applies if an applicant authority of another member State makes a request in accordance with MARD for the recovery in the United Kingdom of a claim.

(2) The claim in relation to which such a request is made is referred to as "the foreign claim".

(3) Such steps may be taken by or on behalf of the relevant UK authority to enforce the foreign claim as might be taken (whether or not by the relevant UK authority) to enforce a corresponding UK claim.

(4) "Steps" includes any legal or administrative steps, whether by way of legal proceedings, distress, diligence or otherwise.

(5) See paragraphs 7 and 8 for the meaning of "the relevant UK authority" and "corresponding UK claim".

(6) The steps mentioned in sub-paragraph (3) include exercising any powers of set-off that the relevant UK authority would have been entitled to exercise if the foreign claim had been payable to it under an enactment.

(7) Any enactment or rule of law relating to a corresponding UK claim is to apply, with any necessary adaptations, in relation to the foreign claim.

(8) The enactments applied by sub-paragraph (7) include in particular those relating to the recovery of penalties and to the charging and recovery of interest on unpaid amounts.

The relevant UK authority

7 (1) "The relevant UK authority" is—

(a) if the foreign claim relates to anything other than an agricultural levy, the Commissioners;
(b) if the foreign claim relates to an agricultural levy and the steps are ones to be taken in or in relation to England, the Commissioners concurrently with the Secretary of State;
(c) if the foreign claim relates to an agricultural levy and the steps are ones to be taken in or in relation to Wales, the Commissioners concurrently with the Welsh Ministers;
(d) if the foreign claim relates to an agricultural levy and the steps are ones to be taken in or in relation to Scotland, the Commissioners concurrently with the Scottish Ministers;
(e) if the foreign claim relates to an agricultural levy and the steps are ones to be taken in or in relation to Northern Ireland, the Commissioners concurrently with the Department of Agriculture and Rural Development.

(2) A reference in this paragraph to claims relating to an agricultural levy includes claims for penalties, fees, surcharges, interest or costs arising in connection with an agricultural levy.

Corresponding UK claim

8 (1) In relation to a foreign claim, "corresponding UK claim" means a claim in the United Kingdom of a kind that appears to the relevant UK authority to correspond most closely to the kind of foreign claim to which the foreign claim belongs.

(2) But if the relevant UK authority concludes that there is nothing in the United Kingdom of a kind that is similar to that kind of foreign claim, "corresponding UK claim" is taken to mean a claim for income tax charged in an assessment and due and payable.

Application of relevant enactments

9 (1) In relation to any kind of foreign claim, the relevant UK authority may by regulations make provision as to the application, non-application or adaptation of any enactment or rule of law relating to corresponding UK claims.

(2) Paragraph 6(7) is subject to any provision so made.

Power to make further provision

10 The Treasury may by regulations make provision about procedural or other supplementary matters for the purpose of giving effect to MARD and any MARD-related instrument.

Contested claims

11 (1) The taking or continuation of steps against a person under paragraph 6(3) must be suspended if the person shows that relevant proceedings are pending, or about to be instituted, before a court, tribunal or other competent body in the member State in question.

(2) "Relevant proceedings" are proceedings relevant to the person's liability on the foreign claim.

(3) Relevant proceedings are "pending" so long as an appeal may be brought against any decision in the proceedings.

(4) Sub-paragraph (1) does not apply to steps that may be taken or continued against the person by the application (by virtue of paragraphs 6(7) and 9) of an enactment or rule of law that permits such steps to be taken or continued in similar circumstances in the case of a corresponding UK claim.

(5) Sub-paragraph (1) ceases to apply if the relevant proceedings are not prosecuted or instituted with reasonable speed.

Claims determined in taxpayer's favour

12 (1) Steps under paragraph 6(3) must not be taken or continued against a person if a final decision on the foreign claim has been given in the person's favour by a court, tribunal or other competent body in the member State in question.

(2) For this purpose, a final decision is one against which no appeal lies or against which an appeal lies within a period that has expired without an appeal having been brought.

(3) If the person shows that such a decision has been given in respect of part of the foreign claim, steps under paragraph 6(3) must not be taken or continued in relation to that part.

Liability to pay

13 In relation to any steps against a person under paragraph 6(3), no question may be raised as to the person's liability on the foreign claim except as mentioned in paragraph 12.

Presumption of validity

14 For the purposes of any steps under paragraph 6(3), a request made by an applicant authority in another member State is taken to be duly made in accordance with MARD unless the contrary is proved.

Regulations

15 (1) Regulations under this Schedule are to be made by statutory instrument.

(2) A statutory instrument containing regulations under this Schedule is subject to annulment in pursuance of a resolution of the House of Commons.

Interpretation

16 In this Schedule—

"agricultural levy" has the meaning given by section 6 of the European Communities Act 1972;

"applicant authority" has the same meaning as in MARD;

"the Commissioners" means the Commissioners for Her Majesty's Revenue and Customs;

"enactment" includes—

(a) an Act of the Scottish Parliament,

(b) a Measure or Act of the National Assembly for Wales, and

(c) any Northern Ireland legislation as defined by section 24(5) of the Interpretation Act 1978;

"HMRC" means Her Majesty's Revenue and Customs;

"MARD-related instrument" means any EU instrument (including one made after the passing of this Act) that lays down detailed rules for implementing MARD;

"public authority" means a person with functions of a public nature;

"requested authority" has the same meaning as in MARD.

Consequential amendments etc

17 (1) Section 134 of and Schedule 39 to FA 2002 (which concern Council Directive 2008/55/EC) are repealed with effect from 1 January 2012.

(2) Any outstanding request for assistance made in accordance with Council Directive 2008/55/EC before that date is to be treated on and after that date for the purposes of this Schedule as if it had been made in accordance with MARD.

18 (1) Section 322 of FA 2004 (mutual assistance: customs union with the Principality of Andorra) is amended as follows.

(2) In subsection (2), in the definition of "the Mutual Assistance Recovery Directive", after "as" insert "MARD has".

(3) In that subsection, for the definition of "the UK mutual assistance provisions" substitute—

""the UK mutual assistance provisions" means the provisions of section 87 of the Finance Act 2011 (mutual assistance for recovery of taxes etc) and Schedule 25 to that Act."

(4) For subsection (3) substitute—

"(3) In the UK mutual assistance provisions as they have effect in accordance with subsection (1)—

(a) references (except for the one in paragraph 1 of Schedule 25) to MARD are to be read as references to the EC-Andorra Mutual Assistance Recovery Decision,

(b) references to another member State are to be read as references to the Principality of Andorra,

(c) references to an applicant authority of another member State are to be read as references to the competent authority of the Principality of Andorra,

(d) references to a MARD-related instrument are to be disregarded, and

(e) paragraph 10 of Schedule 25 (power to make further provision) is to be treated as omitted."

(5) In subsection (4), for "section 134(6) of the Finance Act 2002 and paragraph 3 of Schedule 39" substitute "section 87(2) of the Finance Act 2011 and paragraph 9 of Schedule 25".

(6) The amendments made by this paragraph have effect from 1 January 2012.

(7) Any regulations made by virtue of subsection (4) of section 322 of FA 2004 and in force immediately before 1 January 2012 are to have effect on and after that date as if made by virtue of that subsection as amended by sub-paragraph (5).

Application

19 This Schedule has effect in relation to the recovery of sums becoming due at any time, whether before or after this Act is passed.

GENERAL NOTE

Section 87 and Sch 25 enable the UK to implement the Mutual Assistance Recovery Directive (MARD) 2010/24/EU agreed by EU Finance Ministers during 2010. This legislation will replace and repeal the existing legislation implementing the current MARD which was originally introduced in 1976 and consolidated in 2008 following a number of revisions. The new Directive has fundamentally modernised and expanded the scope of the existing Directive. The Directive becomes fully applicable on 1 January 2012 and the UK legislation transposing the Directive and setting out the detailed rules will come into force on that date.

Paragraph 2 sets out the functions of HMRC in relation to the Directive, providing that HMRC are competent to deal with all matters under the Directive. It should be noted that amendments to the Finance Bill removed former sub-paras (3) and (4) which would have set out certain excluded matters in relation to devolved taxes.

Paragraph 3 enables public authorities to disclose information for the purposes of the Directive. Paragraph 4 sets out the circumstances when information shared under para 3 can be shared further and creates an offence for the wrongful disclosure of information. Paragraph 5 provides a defence for a person charged under para 4 where that person believed that the disclosure was lawful.

The procedure for claims made by an applicant authority of another member state for recovery in the UK ("foreign claims") is set out in para 6. The relevant UK authority may take such steps to enforce a foreign claim as might be taken to enforce a corresponding UK claim. Definitions of "relevant UK authority" and "corresponding UK claim" are set out in paras 7 and 8.

Paragraph 11 deals with situations where enforcement action must be suspended because legal proceedings are underway (or about to be started) in the member state where the debt arose. This restriction does not apply where enforcement action can continue for a disputed equivalent UK debt, or where the debtor does not begin or progress action to dispute the claim reasonably quickly.

Paragraph 12 states that enforcement action must not be taken or continued if a final decision on the foreign claim has been given in the taxpayer's favour by a court or tribunal in the applicant member state. Where such a decision has been given for part of the foreign claim, enforcement action must not be taken or continued for that part.

Schedule 25 applies to the recovery of sums becoming due at any time, whether before or after Royal Assent to Finance Act 2011.

SCHEDULE 26

REDUNDANT RELIEFS

Section 91

PART 1

INCOME TAX AND CORPORATION TAX

Transitional relief for charities etc on abolition of payment of tax credits on distributions

1 (1) Section 35 of, and Schedule 5 to, F(No2)A 1997 (transitional relief for charities etc and limitations on entitlement to the relief) are repealed.

(2) Accordingly—

(a) in section 231B of ICTA, in subsection (4)—

(i) after paragraph (b) insert "and", and

(ii) omit paragraph (d) (and the "and" before it), and

(b) the following provisions are repealed—

(i) in ITA 2007, paragraph 379 of Schedule 1;

(ii) in FA 2010, paragraph 14 of Schedule 6.

Gifts of money for relief in poor countries ("Millennium Gift Aid")

2 (1) Section 48 of FA 1998 (gifts of money for relief in poor countries etc) is repealed.

(2) Accordingly, the following provisions are repealed—

(a) in FA 1999, sections 56 and 57;

(b) in FA 2000, section 42;

(c) in ITA 2007, paragraph 98 of Schedule 2.

Supplement payable in connection with payroll deduction scheme

3 (1) Section 38 of FA 2000 (supplement payable in connection with payroll deduction scheme) is repealed.

(2) Accordingly, the following provisions are repealed—

(a) in ITEPA 2003, paragraph 243 of Schedule 6;
(b) in FA 2003, section 146;
(c) in ITA 2007, paragraph 390 of Schedule 1.

National Savings Bank ordinary account interest

4 Section 691 of ITTOIA 2005 (National Savings Bank ordinary account interest) is repealed.

PART 2

STAMP DUTY

Exemptions from stamp duty

5 Section 45 of FA 1944 (exemption of certain assignments by seamen from stamp duty) is repealed.

6 Section 31 of FA 1953 (instruments relating to National Savings) is repealed.

7 (1) In Schedule 13 to FA 1999 (stamp duty: instruments chargeable and rates of duty), paragraph 24(b) is repealed (instruments for sale etc of ship or vessel etc).

(2) Accordingly, in that Act—

(a) in section 123(3), in the entry for paragraph 24 of Schedule 13, omit ", (b)", and
(b) in Part V(6) of Schedule 20, in paragraph (d) of the entry for Schedule 13, omit ", (b)".

GENERAL NOTE

This Schedule grew out of the review of reliefs carried out by the Office of Tax Simplification (OTS). The OTS identified 1,042 reliefs and exemptions, and in their March 2011 Review of Tax Reliefs recommended that 47 be abolished.

Seven of these have been included in this Schedule; it is planned that 14 more are to be repealed in 2012, subject to consultation. Legislation abolishing a further 22 is likely to be included in FA 2012, with the date of repeal in particular being subject to consultation.

The seven included in this Schedule are all clearly obsolete, so no consultation was required. Sch 26 opens by abolishing, at paras 1–3, certain out-dated reliefs for charitable donations. These are:

— Transitional relief for charities on distributions received between 1999 and 2004. This was introduced by F(No2)A 1997 Sch 5. The last date for claims under this relief was 5 April 2006.
— Millennium Gift Aid, which was introduced by FA 1998 s 48. It allowed tax relief on gifts to charities for overseas relief work, as long as the gifts were made between July 1998 and 31 December 2000.
— Payroll Giving Supplement, which was introduced by FA 2000 s 38. It granted a 10% top-up to charitable donations made via payroll giving between 6 April 2000 and 5 April 2004.

Schedule 26 para 4 repeals ITTOIA 2005 s 691. This section allowed the first £70 of interest paid on National Savings Ordinary Accounts to be paid tax free. These accounts, however, were withdrawn by National Savings in 2004, and customers were asked to move their money elsewhere. Those who did not do so had the funds transferred to the National Savings Residual Investment account. Ordinary Accounts thus no longer exist, and so there is no requirement for the tax relief.

Finally, three obsolete stamp duty reliefs are abolished:

— that introduced in FA 1944 s 35, which allowed the assignment of wages to bodies representing, or providing assistance to seamen. The OTS review reported that 'the policy rationale is unclear but it is thought that this was an emergency wartime measure.' In any event, stamp duty is no longer chargeable on such assignments, so there is no need for the relief.
— a relief from stamp duty for certain National Savings instruments (FA 1953 s 31). This is no longer needed as such instruments are not chargeable to stamp duty.

— a relief from stamp duty for selling or transferring interests in ships (FA 1999, Sch 13 para 24(b)). Again, these transfers are no longer within the scope of stamp duty, so this relief is not needed.

FINANCE BILL DEBATES

Tuesday 3 May 2011

Committee of the Whole House

Clause 7 — Corporation tax: increase in rate of supplementary charge

(Col 626)

The Economic Secretary (Justine Greening): '… The Government amendments demonstrate that we are engaged with the industry and are listening to its concerns. In fact, as a result of that engagement we wanted to address a technical issue that had arisen

(Col 627)

involving the basis proposed for the apportionment of profits. The Government's amendments seek to address that. The legislation provides for how profits in an accounting period that straddles the date of the rate increase are to be split, so that the two tax rates can be applied to the appropriate amounts of profits. Government amendment 11 provides that a company may elect for a just and reasonable basis to be used where a time apportionment would give an unjust or unreasonable result.

We have proposed amendment 11 to take account of the concerns of industry. The amendment has an Exchequer cost of £40 million in 2011–12 only. We feel that the change is worthwhile because it ensures, for example, that the tax change does not affect the tax liability due in respect of transactions that were wholly completed before the Budget and that should not, therefore, have been affected by the rate change …'

Tuesday 10 May 2011

Public Bill Committee

Clause 8 — CGT: Annual exempt amount

(Col 73)

The Exchequer Secretary (David Gauke): '… the clause makes a technical change to the procedure for indexing the capital gains tax annual exempt amount to ensure clarity in the process, particularly in circumstances when the inflation measure that is used to index the AEA is negative … The AEA is one of the tax allowances that are automatically indexed every year unless Parliament sets a different figure. Indexation works by reference to inflation over the 12 months to September in the previous tax year. In normal years, the Treasury makes an order to set out the exempt amount for the next tax year, following the rules for calculating the increased amount that are laid down in the Taxation of Chargeable Gains Act 1992 …

The 12 months to September 2009, however, were unusual, as inflation was negative. Indexation did not apply in that situation. The exempt amount for the following year, 2010–11, remained the same, and the Treasury made an order to that effect. However, detailed scrutiny of the rules suggested that that may not have been the correct procedure. The changes made by the clause will ensure that there is no doubt in future about what has to happen in such cases. If inflation is positive, the Treasury will continue to make orders, setting out the increased exempt amount for the following year, exactly as it does now. If inflation is zero or negative, the exempt amount for the previous year will be carried forward automatically to the following year. The Treasury will not be required to make an order confirming that there has been no change.

Clause 8 will not change how the increase in the exempt amount is calculated. It only puts right the way in which the indexed amount for the following tax year is fixed. Parliament will still be entitled to overrule indexation and set either a higher or lower figure. Members of the Committee will be aware that in the Budget we announced that indexation will in future be based on the consumer prices index, rather than the retail prices index, as the right hon. Gentleman pointed out. The clause will not make that change. The move to using the CPI will start from 2012–13 and will be included in next year's Finance Bill. For the 2011–12 tax year, the clause sets the exempt amount at £10,600. That represents an increase from £10,100 in the preceding year, and the new figure is the normal indexation amount based on the RPI.

As for why we have not moved to indexation using the CPI this year, the answer is that we have decided to move to using the CPI for indexing rates and allowances

(Col 74)
from April 2012 for all direct taxes, including capital gains tax.'

Thursday 19 May 2011

Public Bill Committee

Clause 26 and Schedule 2 — Employment income provided through third parties

(Col 282)
The Exchequer Secretary (David Gauke): '... It is important to look behind the headline numbers and focus on what these amendments really involve. As I set out in my letter advising the Committee of the amendments, they fall into eight themes or strands and certainly do not represent 90 substantive new ideas or free-standing changes. A significant number of the amendments are consequential, and all of them result from the consultation carried out by HMRC. It is right to say that most of the amendments relate to relieving provisions. They describe the types of transactions that will not be caught by the schedule. This will give taxpayers clarity about what is not included ...'
(Col 284)
The Exchequer Secretary: '... Schedule 2 will ensure that third-party arrangements used by employers to provide reward to employees cannot be used for tax avoidance. It creates an income tax charge where a third party provides an employee with reward, recognition or a loan in connection with the employment. The tax charge will be based on the full amount of the sum, the money used to deliver value to the employee, or cost or market value—whichever is higher—where an asset is used. The legislation will mean that employees benefiting from such schemes will have to pay more tax, but no more than employees who receive their reward directly from their employer. In addition, regulations will be brought forward to apply a class 1 national insurance contribution charge to amounts taxable under the measure.

Ian Murray (Labour, Edinburgh South): 'What happens if one of the loans is given to an employee and is seen as a salary reward, but an agreement is put in place between a third party and the employee to pay back that loan at 1p a month for the next 640 years? Would that constitute repayment, and therefore not be a benefit?'

The Exchequer Secretary: 'My understanding is that such an arrangement would be caught by the measures we set out in schedule 2. The hon. Gentleman demonstrates the ingenuity that exists in this area. An arrangement that was clearly uncommercial in its repayment terms would not be a means of avoiding the legislation.'

(Col 287)

Nic Dakin (Labour, Scunthorpe): 'While the Minister is dealing with these concerns, I thought it might be useful for him to deal with something highlighted by the Institute of Chartered Accountants. It says that there is a likely problem, in that the employer "can still be a 'third person' if he acts as a trustee. This is not qualified in any way so an employer that is a trust (something which is common in the charitable and voluntary sector) and which gives an employee a season ticket loan would be caught and the loan subject to tax when advanced even though it will be repaid." ...'

The Exchequer Secretary: 'As long as there were no circumstances that cast doubt over the genuine nature of the employment, a trustee that is also an employer would not be viewed as a trustee when acting in their capacity as an employer.'

(Col 288)

The Exchequer Secretary: '... I must press on and say a word or two about the amendments; after all, there are a few of them. The changes have been made in response to the ongoing dialogue with representative bodies, and they will ensure that the legislation is better targeted. The changes will provide greater exclusions, where relevant, or they will clarify the existing position, and we want to do so in a way that retains the target of avoidance and does not increase the risk to the Exchequer. The changes will relax some conditions that excluded a tax charge; expand the definition of a group; ensure that the tax position that follows permanent "unearmarking" is right; and, better allow settlements with HMRC. In relation to pension arrangements, schedule 2 provides an up-front tax charge where employers pay contributions to unregistered pension schemes to avoid the new restrictions on pensions tax relief. We are removing the possibility of unintentionally imposed tax charges, depending on the value of the security provided and not on the value of the contributions the employer was to pay. Such concerns are dealt with by the relevant amendments, ensuring that the tax charge is appropriately focused. There are also amendments that ensure that the legislation does not interfere with the legitimate use of deferred remuneration and share schemes to reward employees. Although there were a number of exclusions within the initial draft legislation, in some cases, those were too narrow. The related amendments mean that the employers can continue to use employee share schemes and pay remuneration in genuine deferred arrangements, without unexpected tax charges.'

(Col 291)

Ian Mearns (Labour, Gateshead): '... When the Bill was originally presented to us, it came with a good set of explanatory notes, and they helped us to understand the implications of the clauses, subsections and schedules. However, the Government amendments do not come with explanatory notes, and that makes it difficult for us as financial lay people ...'

The Exchequer Secretary: 'I actually wanted to intervene on the hon. Member for Gateshead to say that explanatory notes on these amendments were sent to the Committee.'

Clause 31 — Company ceasing to be member of group: availability of relief

(Col 322)

The Exchequer Secretary: '... Briefly, the amendment improves the targeting of the anti-avoidance measure introduced by clause 31. It does so by ensuring that the new rule has no adverse impact on commercial transactions that do not have a main purpose of avoiding corporation tax.'

Clause 32 — Investment companies

(Col 323)

The Exchequer Secretary: '... These amendments make changes to ensure that schedule 7 applies to controlled foreign companies in the same way that it applies to UK investment companies. Schedule 7 allows companies, including CFCs, to elect prospectively to change the currency in which

(Col 324)

they prepare their accounts—their functional currency—for tax purposes. It also stops changes in companies' functional currency having a tax effect until the accounting period following the change. The deferral of a tax effect to the change in functional currency blocks an avoidance scheme that allowed companies retrospectively to crystallise foreign exchange losses for tax purposes. Following the publication of the Bill, it came to HMRC's attention that certain provisions in the CFC code prevent the restriction on the timing of the tax effect of a functional currency election from applying to CFCs. The amendments ensure that UK resident companies with interests in CFCs will not be able to change the functional currency of the CFC with the benefit of hindsight to realise a foreign exchange loss for tax purposes to reduce or avoid a CFC apportionment. The amendment will apply to multinational groups with CFCs and protects tax revenue in the low hundreds of millions per year. Although the amendments may at first sight appear to be pre-empting the wider CFC reform, their effect is to ensure that schedule 7 applies to CFCs in the same way as it applies to UK investment companies. Schedule 7 benefits companies by allowing them to elect prospectively to change their functional currency for tax purposes. The amendment is, therefore, not counter to the direction of CFC reform. The amendments ensure that the avoidance opportunity that the original measure was designed to close is blocked for controlled foreign companies in the same way that it is blocked for UK investment companies ...'

Tuesday 24 May 2011

Public Bill Committee

Schedule 8 — Reduction in childcare relief for higher earners

(Col 331)

The Economic Secretary (Justine Greening): 'I will now briefly set out the purpose of the amendments. As a result of continuing consultation with relevant interested parties on the detailed guidance to support schedule 8, we identified some further practical issues that require an amendment to the legislation as published in March. The aim of amendment 108 is to offer further support to employers who have the responsibility for applying the legislation. It is they who will have to determine the appropriate level of tax relief on employer-supported child care. The amendment removes some of the detail related to the estimate of relevant earnings from the primary legislation. The detailed provisions will instead be replaced with a statutory instrument containing regulations relating to the estimate of relevant earnings for the year. A draft of the regulations will be made available for consideration by interested parties as soon as possible. The regulations will be introduced before 31 December 2011 and will take effect from 6 April 2011...'

Clause 45 and Schedule 10 — Company ceasing to be a member of a group

(Col 407)

The Exchequer Secretary (David Gauke): 'The amendment responds to comments on the Finance Bill clause from numerous corporate groups and their accountants, who asked that the provisions of schedule 10 be made available to companies in respect of transactions undertaken before the passing of the Finance Act. It will allow a group of companies to elect to apply the provisions of the schedule from 1 April 2011...'

Tuesday 7 June 2011

Public Bill Committee

Clause 47 and Schedule 12 — Controlled foreign companies

(Col 430)

The Exchequer Secretary (David Gauke): '... The clause introduces three new exemptions. The first provides more certainty for business by removing certain intra-group trading activities from a potential CFC charge—intra-group service companies, for example—where a risk is not posed to the UK tax base. The second exempts CFCs that derive their profits from foreign intellectual property, where, similarly, a risk is not posed to the UK tax base. Those two exemptions provide certainty to UK multinationals that such commercial overseas operations, which could be caught be the current rules, will be exempt ahead of full CFC reform in 2012. The third exemption provides an exempt period of up to three years for overseas subsidiaries that, as a consequence of a reorganisation or change to UK ownership, come within the scope of the CFC regime. That will provide a group with appropriate time to reorganise its overseas affairs, so that it complies with UK CFC rules. The aim is to make the UK a more attractive location for headquartered companies, and for the UK investment that can arise as a result of that, as well as assisting UK businesses that undertake overseas acquisitions. The third exemption is subject to amendments that correct a technical defect that was included in the original draft legislation, but which has only recently been identified. The defect concerns the conditions that a foreign subsidiary must meet if it is to qualify for the exemption. As drafted, the requirements relating to control of the subsidiary are more tightly drawn than intended, and they could prevent such subsidiaries from benefiting from the exemption in circumstances where they should be free to do so. The amendments address those unwanted restrictions and ensure that the exemption will work as intended ...'

Clause 48 and Schedule 13 — Profits of foreign permanent establishments, etc.

(Col 434)

The Exchequer Secretary: '... The Government are tabling six amendments in three groups to ensure that the legislation functions as intended and to provide certainty to business and protection to the Exchequer. Amendment 123 applies to the anti-diversion rule, which will prevent any branch profits that have been artificially diverted from the UK from becoming exempt. It is designed to be broadly consistent with the CFC rules. The amendment makes it clear that chargeable gains are not within the scope of the anti-diversion rule, consistent with the CFC rules on which it is based. Amending the rules will prevent any loss of tax, while providing business with clarity. Amendments 124 and 128 will ensure that the transitional rules apply to transferred businesses in the same way as any other business that moves into exemption for the first time. The transitional rule protects the Exchequer where loss relief has previously been given to a branch and would not otherwise be clawed back—by taxing subsequent profits—once branch profits become exempt. Branch exemption is an optional regime and the election is made on a company-by-company basis. That gives groups of companies flexibility in their use of exemption, but means that we need to ensure that the transitional rule cannot be side-stepped by intra-group transfers of business. As drafted, the clause does not give the right result in two significant circumstances. First, where the transferor of the business is not UK resident there would be an inappropriate application of the rule to losses for which no corporation tax relief was ever given. That would act as a disincentive to a company looking to invest in the UK by moving its branch headquarters here. It runs counter to the policy aim of creating competitive conditions for businesses wanting to invest in the UK. Secondly, the rule will not be fully effective where the transfer of business is made to another group company, which is exempt before the transfer takes place. As currently drafted, this would enable companies to side-step the transitional rules through transfers of business to companies already in exemption.

Let me turn now to the final group of amendments. There are rules in existing legislation for chargeable gains and for intangible fixed assets that deal with intra-group transfers of assets. Those rules ensure that no tax charge arises on any gain realised in an intra-group transfer. Instead, any charge is deferred until such time as the asset is disposed of from the group. It is necessary for the branch exemption legislation to set aside such rules, otherwise a gain made exempt under branch exemption would re-emerge as a taxable gain when the asset is eventually sold outside the group. To prevent that, there are rules in schedule 13 to ensure that the exemption of a gain and a cancellation of a loss arising on a branch asset are made permanent within the group of companies. Amending the rules in relation to intra-group transfers and replacement of business assets will ensure that they have the intended effects, providing certainty for business

(Col 435)

and preventing risk of tax loss. These amendments ensure that the legislation works as intended …'

Clause 53 — Leases and changes to accounting standards

(Col 451)

The Exchequer Secretary: '… Clause 53 will require businesses that account for lease transactions to treat them, for tax purposes, as if the proposed changes to lease accounting had not taken place. The clause will apply to any business, whether as lessee or lessor or both, that accounts for lease transactions using a lease accounting standard that is newly issued or changed on or after 1 January 2011. The clause is not intended to alter the current tax treatment of leases in any way, and as such is expected to be revenue neutral.

(Col 452)

Amendments 185 and 186 ensure that the clause operates correctly in all cases. The draft legislation was published for consultation in December 2010. No comments were received during the consultation period. As such, the legislation was unaltered when the Finance Bill was published in March. However, it has recently been brought to our attention that in certain limited circumstances, when a business chooses to change from one standard to the other, it would be required to ignore the move for all tax purposes, not just for purposes related to the taxation of leases. That would create not only an administrative burden for the business but also potential avoidance opportunities, as profits might be deferred or removed entirely from the tax net. To prevent this unintended consequence, the amendments will ensure that the generally accepted accounting practice that a business uses for calculating taxable profits is the same as that used in the accounts for all matters except for leasing transactions. The proposed amendment also simplifies the legislation.

Clause 53 is an interim measure. When the dust has settled and we have some certainty regarding the accounting changes, we will review the appropriate way forward for leasing taxation in the light of the new rules. The review will focus on providing stability and certainty for the future, and, of course, any consultation would be carried out under the new tax policy-making framework.'

Clause 64 and Schedule 15 — Chargeable gains: oil activities

(Col 470)

The Economic Secretary (Justine Greening): 'It is probably worth briefly running through clause 64 and schedule 15 to say why they are in the Bill and what we intend them to achieve. They introduce small but important changes to chargeable gains legislation that will apply to oil and gas companies. The changes relate to two areas of the fiscal regime and are intended to encourage further investment in oil and gas fields. The existing oil licence swaps legislation provides that no chargeable gain arises on the swap of oil and gas licences in the UK and the UK continental shelf in some circumstances. That legislation was introduced to encourage and enable the transfer of licences so that they would be held by companies that were likely to invest in them. However, it does not adequately address the circumstances that arise in practice, and in many cases the legislation simply cannot apply. The existing ring fence reinvestment legislation provides that no chargeable gain arises in some circumstances when disposable proceeds are invested in new oil trade assets. One requirement of the legislation is that the disposal and acquisition qualify for roll-over relief. Again, that legislation encourages the disposal of licences and at the same time encourages investment of the proceeds in the UK continental shelf. A lot of such investment comprises expenditure on exploration, appraisal and development, such as the cost of drilling wells, which does not qualify for roll-over relief. The right hon. Member for Delyn asked about the definition of expenditure on exploration, appraisal and development, and the measure uses generally accepted accounting principles. I hope that that provides the clarification he wants. However, as a result, the ring fence reinvestment legislation cannot apply, and that is the situation that we want to remedy. The changes made in the clause and in schedule 15 address those issues and ensure that oil licence swaps legislation applies by reference to the date on which the economic benefits under the licences concerned are treated as passing, rather than by reference to the date on which the swap arrangements are entered into. The right hon. Gentleman also asked about valuation reductions. The point is that the parties want the swaps legislation to apply with reference to the position agreed on the effective date, and that any non-licence consideration should not affect the outcome, whatever way the non-licence consideration payments flow. He raises an interesting point, but in practice the way the legislation is now structured should ultimately have no impact. In fact, the changes in the clause and the schedule should ensure that the technical problems facing us in the existing legislation fall away …'

Clause 66 and Schedule 17 — Annual allowance charge

(Col 479)

The Financial Secretary (**Mark Hoban**): '… As a result of ongoing consultation with the pension industry since the publication of the Finance Bill on 31 March, changes have been indentified that would make the application of legislation simpler, and therefore reduce administrative burdens on the pension industry. Government amendments 129 to 133 ensure that the legislation will work as we intend. Amendment 133 addresses a simple drafting issue. The annual allowance charge operates by reference to pension savings made over a certain period. In changing the dates of when that period begins and ends, the Bill inadvertently provided for, in certain circumstances, a period of 364 rather than 365 days. The amendment corrects that so that the period will be 12 months unless the scheme or, in other circumstances, its members nominate otherwise. Amendments 130 to 132 concern individuals who have high annual allowance charges. The schedule provides for them to nominate to meet their tax charge out of their pension savings. If they so nominate, an offsetting adjustment is made by the pension scheme to reduce the individual's pension savings to reflect the tax paid on their behalf. Schedule 17 provides for the amount of the adjustment to be reflected in the valuation of the individual's savings when determining their annual allowance charge in the year the adjustment is made. Amendments 130 to 132 address an imbalance in carrying out the adjustment between individuals in defined benefit or cash schemes and those in defined contribution schemes. Amendment 129 relates to the year in which a pension comes into payment. In calculating the increase in pension rights, there is a choice between continuing to use a notional valuation and using the actual amount of pension benefits taken. Schedule 17 provides for the notional amount to be used, but representations received since the Bill was published have shown that that is confusing for individuals, who could expect the actual amount of their pension to be taken into account. The representations also show that the practical application of the provision is administratively burdensome for pension schemes. Using a notional value in those circumstances also has the unintended consequence of excluding all enhancements paid to an individual who retires early on grounds of ill health. It was not the intention to preclude ill-health retirements that do not meet the definition of serious or severe ill health from the annual allowance charge. Amendment 129 removes that disjoint and makes a value used in the year of retirement easier to understand for those taking benefits …'

Schedule 19 — The bank levy

(Col 491)

The Financial Secretary: 'I am tempted to talk about the amendments at some length. I am sure that people would be interested in details relating to the application of the netting rules to certain lending transactions called reverse repos or those relating to covered bonds. However, I suspect that the appetite of my hon. Friends is not quite as great as I would have thought. In respect of the amendments, we have sought to ensure that the netting provisions in the schedule operate as originally intended in respect of certain reverse repo transactions where securities received as collateral are sold, and also that the netting rules apply correctly to the UK permanent establishments of foreign banks. The amendments flow from correspondence received after publication of the Bill, questioning whether the legislation was sufficiently clear. We have tried to ensure that the provisions will operate as intended and that the various transactions are within the netting provisions. Amendments 181 and 182 provide for an expanded definition of the trade or business of a covered bond vehicle, increasingly important for the funding of banks. The amendments will ensure that all covered bond

(Col 492)

limited liability partnerships within banking groups are excluded from the levy's joint and several liability provisions, again as was originally intended ...'

Thursday 9 June 2011

Public Bill Committee

Clause 74 — Zero-rating: splitting of supplies

(Col 501)

The Exchequer Secretary (**David Gauke**): 'The changes that it makes will remove zero rating from the supply of printed matter when it is supplied in connection with services and in circumstances in which the printed matter would not have been zero-rated if both had been supplied by a single supplier ... The right hon. Gentleman asked about the point raised by the Institute of Chartered Accountants and others that the measure goes further than necessary. We believe that it has much more limited application than some of the respondents fear. It will apply only when a supply of printed matter by one person is so closely connected with the supply of services by another that the two supplies would properly have been considered to be a single supply for VAT purposes if they had been made by the same person. The clause will have an impact only on businesses that have entered into arrangements that artificially split what would otherwise have been a single supply into two separate supplies. It will not have any impact on businesses that are commercially or economically independent of each other and making supplies that, from the customer's point of view, are separate. Therefore, we do not believe that the measure will catch unwitting or innocent transactions ...'

Clause 85 — Security for payment of PAYE

(Col 541)

The Exchequer Secretary: '... The draft regulations exclude employers who employ personal employees, and those who are care and support employers. These safeguards were welcomed. To ensure that the power remained strictly focused on the seriously non-compliant, HMRC was asked to take all reasonable steps to ensure that taxpayers were aware of time-to-pay arrangements. The Government made it clear at the Budget that time-to-pay arrangements would continue to be available to help taxpayers who genuinely and temporarily could not pay their tax bills, and further changes have been made to the regulations to provide that protection. There was some concern that HMRC might automate the security process and thereby go beyond the seriously non-compliant. This does not occur for VAT securities, which are given case-by-case consideration, and this will continue for PAYE. I hope that this reassures Members that the vast majority of employers will be unaffected by this measure and addresses the concern expressed by the right hon. Member for Delyn about the width of the measures. Only a small number of employers who have been passing their tax liabilities on to the taxpaying population will be negatively affected. HMRC will also expose draft guidance for consultation in good time before the power comes in. The right hon. Gentleman asked about the regulations. They will be introduced in early 2012, and will be subject to the negative procedure. He asked which authorised officers or commissioners would be responsible for issuing securities. Implementation of PAYE and NIC security will follow the current VAT process, which ensures that authorisations to request the security are made at least at higher officer level. He also asked about the right of appeal. A wide right of appeal against the requirement is included in the regulations ...'

New Clause 4 — Foreign pensions of UK residents

(Col 544)

The Exchequer Secretary: '… New clause 4 prevents UK residents with foreign pensions from taking unfair advantage of the UK's tax treaties, and follows an announcement I made on 6 April to take effect from that date. The new clause was published in draft on 24 May. Responses confirmed our view that the new clause achieved the desired outcome in preventing avoidance. The clause ensures that a UK resident cannot take advantage of the provisions of one of the UK's tax treaties to avoid UK tax on a foreign pension or lump sum payment. It applies where pension savings are transferred to a pension scheme established in another country and that country has a tax treaty with the UK that provides for a pension or lump sum to be taxed exclusively where it arises. Where a particular country would not tax a pension or lump sum paid to a UK resident, any UK resident with pension savings would have been able to make arrangements to receive their pension or lump sum entirely tax free from that country. The new clause prevents that sort of tax avoidance. However, we do not intend to tax the pensions of those who are not trying to avoid UK tax, so the clause is carefully targeted. It will apply only where pension savings have been transferred and one of the main purposes of making these arrangements is to secure an income tax advantage. If any tax is payable in the other country on the foreign pension or lump sum, the clause makes explicit provision for tax credit relief to be allowed in the UK in respect of any tax paid. This is a straightforward anti-avoidance measure that will protect tens of millions of pounds …'

Tuesday 5 July 2011

Report Stage

Clause 87 and Schedule 25 — Mutual assistance for recovery of taxes, etc.

(Col 1463)

The Exchequer Secretary (David Gauke): '… The amendments remove the exclusions included in the Bill in relation to Scotland and Northern Ireland. They also make an addition to the explanation of "relevant UK authority" in order to include a claim from another member state to recover an agricultural levy in Scotland … The global forum is currently conducting a peer review of the UK and a specific issue has been identified that we have to address. Schedule 36 to the Finance Act 2008 does not allow HMRC to require information from a third party when it does not know the full identity of the taxpayer but has some information from which their full identity can be ascertained, such as a branch code and a bank account number or a credit card number. At present, unless a serious loss of tax is suspected, HMRC is unable to issue a notice to a third party that can be reasonably expected to know the name and address of the person concerned. In the examples I have given, that would be a bank or credit card issuer. To meet our international commitments, we need to amend schedule 36 to allow a formal notice to be issued in those circumstances. However, we have made a clear commitment to consult on tax changes, so I have asked HMRC to consult over the summer on how best to achieve the changes, with a view to publishing draft provisions in the autumn and legislating next year. I envisage the changes taking effect from Royal Assent in 2012. In conclusion, the amendments to clause 87 and schedule 25 will help to ensure that the new mutual assistance recovery directive is fully transposed into UK law by 31 December 2011.'

Schedule 7 — Investment companies : and Schedule 13 — Profits of foreign permanent health establishments, etc.

(Col 1464)

The Exchequer Secretary: '… The amendments will ensure that clauses 34 and 48 operate as intended when companies make retrospective changes to the dates to which their accounts are drawn up. Schedule 7 allows companies to elect prospectively to change the currency in which they prepare their accounts for tax purposes. That is often referred to as their functional currency. That change must be prospective to prevent companies from changing their functional currency with the benefit of hindsight to realise a foreign exchange loss for tax purposes. Following the Public Bill Committee debate on clause 34, a major accountancy firm disclosed an avoidance scheme that retrospectively creates a short accounting period to circumvent the new rules. The amendments will ensure that clause 34 operates as intended when a company retrospectively changes the date to which its accounts are drawn up.

Clause 48 and schedule 13 implement an optional branch exemption regime. Companies must elect into branch exemption in advance of an accounting period to prevent them from leaving known losses outside of exemption in order to retain loss relief. Retrospective accounting period changes create problems similar to those that arise in connection with clause 34, whereby decisions on election into branch exemption may be made with the benefit of hindsight. The amendments will ensure that clause 48 operates as intended when a company changes its accounting periods. In each case, the date on which an election comes into force will be fixed in advance at the time when the election is made.

The amendments that relate to clause 34 will protect the £60 million yield in the original measure, and together the amendments will protect an estimated £200 million that would otherwise be likely to be lost due to avoidance schemes. They will ensure that clauses 34 and 48 operate as intended when a company uses hindsight to alter its accounting periods.

INDEX

ACADEMY
  refunds of VAT to, s 76
ACCOUNTING STANDARDS
  leasing, changes to, s 53
AGGREGATES LEVY
  rate of,
ALCOHOLIC LIQUOR DUTIES
  beer duty—
    high strength, s 15, Sch 1
    lower strength beer, reduced rate for, s 14
  rates of, s 13
AMUSEMENT MACHINE LICENCES
  duty, rates of, s 18
ANTI-AVOIDANCE
  accounting purposes, amounts not fully recognised for, Sch 4
  group mismatch schemes, Sch 5
  investment companies, Sch 7
  leasing business, Sch 6
  stamp duty land tax, prevention of avoidance, Sch 21
  tainted charity donations—
    amended provisions, Sch 3 Pt 4
    capital gains tax, Sch 3 Pt 3
    commencement and transitional provision, Sch 3 Pt 5
    corporation tax, Sch 3 Pt 2
    income tax, Sch 3 Pt 1
  third parties, employment income provided through, Sch 2

BANK LEVY
  anti-avoidance, Sch 19 paras 47, 48
  charge of, Sch 19 Pt 2
  chargeable equity and liabilities, Sch 19 Pt 4
  chargeable periods, Sch 19 para 41
  collection and management, Sch 19 Pt 6
  consequential changes, power to make, Sch 19 Pt 9
  double taxation relief, Sch 19 Pt 7
  financial statements, Sch 19 para 42
  groups covered by, Sch 19 Pt 3
  interpretation, Sch 19 Pt 8
  introduction of, Sch 19 para 1
  joint ventures, Sch 19 paras 43, 44
  netting agreements, Sch 19 para 40
  other tax purposes, ignored for, Sch 19 para 46
  residence, Sch 19 para 45
BEER
  duty—
    high strength, s 15, Sch 1
    lower strength beer, reduced rate for, s 14
BUSINESS SAMPLES
  value added tax treatment, s 74

CAPITAL ALLOWANCES
  annual investment allowance, s 11
  plant and machinery—
    short life assets, s 12
    writing-down, s 10
  property businesses, Sch 14 Pt 3
  ship leasing, companies within tonnage tax, s 57
  tonnage tax, ships within, s 10(5)
CAPITAL GAINS TAX
  annual exempt amount, s 8
  entrepreneurs' relief, amount of, s 9

CAPITAL GAINS TAX – *contd*
pre-entry losses, amended provisions, Sch 11
tainted charity donations, Sch 3 Pt 3
value shifting, amended provisions, Sch 9

CARS
taxable benefits, appropriate percentage, s 51

CHARGEABLE GAINS
oil activities—
licence swaps, Sch 15 Pt 1
ring fence assets, reinvestment of, Sch 15 Pt 2

CHARITIES
redundant reliefs, Sch 26 Pt 1
tainted donations–
amended provisions, Sch 3 Pt 4
capital gains tax, Sch 3 Pt 3
commencement and transitional provision, Sch 3 Pt 5
corporation tax, Sch 3 Pt 2
income tax, Sch 3 Pt 1

CHILD
individual investment plans, s 40

CHILDCARE
vouchers—
flexible remuneration arrangements, s 36
higher earners, reduction in relief for, Sch 8
low-paid employees, s 36
salary sacrifice arrangements, s 36

CLIMATE CHANGE LEVY
commodities used in producing electricity, amended provisions, Sch 20
Northern Ireland gas supplies, amendment of provisions, s 79
rates of, s 23
supplies used in recycling processes, power to suspend exemption for, s 80

COLLECTIVE INVESTMENTS
interests in scheme, stamp duty reserve tax, s 84
offshore funds, residence of, s 59

COMPANIES
UK resident, foreign permanent establishment of—
amended provisions, Sch 13
chargeable gains, no gain/no loss, Sch 13 para 13
commencement, Sch 12 Pt 3
exempt, assets held for purposes of, Sch 13 para 8
profits attributable to, Sch 13 para 27
profits election, Sch 13 para 30
profits, exemption, Sch 13 para 4
transfers of business, Sch 13 para 4
small profits, with, attribution of rights and powers of associates, s 55

CONTROLLED FOREIGN COMPANIES
holding companies, extension of transitional provision, Sch 12 Pt 4
limited UK connection, with—
exemptions, Sch 12 Pt 1
trading companies, Sch 12 para 3
reorganisations, etc, temporary exemption following, Sch 12 Pt 3
small chargeable profits exemption, amendment of, Sch 12 Pt 2

CORPORATION TAX
charge of, s 5(1)
group mismatch schemes, Sch 5
investment companies, amended provisions, Sch 7
main rate for 2011, s 4
rate of, s 5(2)
redundant reliefs, Sch 26 Pt 1
ring fence trades, increase in rate of supplementary charge, s 7
small profits rate and fractions, s 6

CORPORATION TAX – *contd*
tainted charity donations, Sch 3 Pt 2

DERIVATIVE CONTRACTS
recognition, debit arising from, Sch 5 para 11

ELECTRICITY
commodities used in producing, amended provisions, Sch 20
EMPLOYMENT INCOME
monitoring schemes relating to vulnerable persons, exemption for fees, s 39
third parties, provided through, Sch 2
ENTERPRISE INVESTMENT SCHEME
relief, amount of, s 42
EUROPEAN BANKING AUTHORITY
experts seconded to, allowances, s 38
EUROPEAN MEDICINES AGENCY
experts seconded to, allowances, s 38
EUROPEAN POLICE COLLEGE
experts seconded to, allowances, s 38
EUROPEAN UNION
bodies, allowances for experts seconded to, s 38
mutual assistance directives—
application of, s 87, Sch 25

FINANCE LEASE
long funding—
additional expenditure, allowances, s 33(3)
capital expenditure, amount of, s 33(2)
disposal events and disposal values, s 33(4)
relievable amounts, s 33(2)
FINANCIAL SERVICES
specified investments, amended provisions, s 89
FURNISHED HOLIDAY LETTINGS
amended provisions—
capital allowances, Sch 14 Pt 3
chargeable gains, Sch 14 Pt 4
corporation tax, Sch 14 Pt 2
income tax, Sch 14 Pt 1
EEA business, meaning, Sch 14 para 12
EEA business treated as trade—
chargeable gains, Sch 14 para 14
corporation tax, Sch 14 para 8
income tax, Sch 14 para 3
overseas property business, capital allowances and loss relief, Sch 14 para 7
under-used, letting condition not met for—
corporation tax, Sch 14 para 7
income tax, Sch 14 para 2

GAMING DUTY
rates of, s 17
GIFT AID
total value of benefits associated with gifts, increase of limits, s 41
GILT-EDGED SECURITIES
index-linked, meaning, s 60(1)
relevant prices index, meaning, s 60(1)
GROUP OF COMPANIES
company ceasing to be member of, Sch 10
availability of relief, s 31
degrouping, Sch 10
group mismatch schemes, Sch 5

GROUP OF COMPANIES – *contd*
pre-entry losses, amended provisions, Sch 11

HER MAJESTY'S REVENUE AND CUSTOMS
data-gathering powers—
consequential provisions, Sch 23 Pt 6
interpretation, Sch 23 paras 47–49
notices, appeals against, Sch 23 Pt 3
obtaining data, Sch 23 Pt 1
penalties, Sch 23 Pt 4
regulations, Sch 23 para 44
relevant data-holders, Sch 23 Pt 2
statutory records, Sch 23 para 46
tax, meaning, Sch 23 para 45
information and inspection powers, amendment, Sch 24

HYDROCARBON OIL DUTIES
rates of—
goods vehicle without road-friendly suspension for, s 22
23 March 2011, from, s 19
1 January 2012, from, s 20
rebates—
23 March 2011, from, s 19
1 January 2012, from, s 20

INCOME TAX
additional rate, s 1(2)
basic rate, s 1(2)
basic rate limit for 2011–12., s 2
charge to, s 1(1)
higher rate, s 1(2)
persons under 65, personal allowances, s 3
redundant reliefs, Sch 26 Pt 1
tainted charity donations, Sch 3 Pt 1

INSURANCE COMPANY
amounts brought into account, apportionment of, s 56

INTANGIBLE FIXED ASSETS
degrouping, Sch 10 para 7
oil licences, s 62

INVESTMENT COMPANY
anti-avoidance provisions, Sch 7
UK resident, designated currency of, Sch 7 para 3

INVESTMENT PLANS
children, for, s 40

INVESTMENT TRUST
approval, conditions for, s 49(3)
definition, amendment of, s 49(2)
treatment of transactions, power to make provision for, s 50

LANDFILL TAX
standard rate of, s 25

LEASE
accounting standards, changes to, s 53
present value, Sch 6 para 22

LEASING
anti-avoidance provisions, Sch 6

LEASING COMPANY
withdrawal of election, s 54

LOAN RELATIONSHIPS
accounting purposes, amounts not fully recognised for, Sch 4
connected debtor and creditor, involving, s 29

LOAN RELATIONSHIPS – *contd*
derecognition of creditor relationships, debits arising from, Sch 5 para 5

MACHINE GAMES DUTY
provision for introduction of, s 90
MADE-WINE
rates of duty, s 13(5)
MEMBERS OF PARLIAMENT
accommodation expenses, s 37

NORTHERN IRELAND
gas supplies, climate change levy provisions, s 79
transitional tax credit, s 81

OFFSHORE FUNDS
collective investment undertakings in transferable securities, residence of, s 59
OIL FIELD
areas treated as continuing to be, s 61
new—
meaning, s 63
reduction of supplementary charge, s 63
OIL LICENCE
intangible fixed asset, as, s 62
OIL TAXATION
chargeable gains—
licence swaps, Sch 15 Pt 1
ring fence assets, reinvestment of, Sch 15 Pt 2
ring fence trade—
reinvestment of assets, Sch 15 Pt 2
supplementary charge for, s 7
supplementary charge—
new oil fields, reduction for, s 63
ring fence trades, for, s 7

PAYE
security for payment, s 85
PENSION SCHEME
amended provisions, Sch 16
annual allowance—
charge, amended provisions, Sch 17
post-entitlement enhancements, Sch 17 para 13
unused, carry forward of, Sch 17 para 5
benefits available under, changes to, Sch 16 Pt 1
lifetime allowance charge, amended provisions, Sch 18
Pensions Act 2008 s 67, under—
borrowing by, s 68
further provision, power to make, s 70
tax provision, power to make regulations, s 71
unpaid relevant contributions, exemption from tax on interest, s 69
PENSIONS
foreign, of UK residence, interpretation of tax provisions, s 72
PETROLEUM REVENUE TAX
oil fields, areas treated as continuing to be, s 61
PLANT AND MACHINERY
ascribed value, determining, Sch 6 para 22
leasing, anti-avoidance provisions, Sch 6
property businesses, Sch 14 Pt 3
short life assets, allowances for, s 12
writing-down allowances, s 10
PROPERTY BUSINESS
ordinary overseas, Sch 14 para 12
plant or machinery, use of, Sch 14 para 12

PROVISIONAL COLLECTION OF TAXES
amended provisions, s 88

RECYCLING
supplies used in processes, power to suspend CCL exemption for, s 80
RESEARCH AND DEVELOPMENT
small and medium-sized enterprises, relief for expenditure by, s 43

SMALL AND MEDIUM-SIZED ENTERPRISES
research and development expenditure, relief for, s 43
STAMP DUTY
redundant reliefs, Sch 26 Pt 2
STAMP DUTY LAND TAX
avoidance, prevention of, Sch 21
multiple dwellings, transfers involving, Sch 22
STAMP DUTY RESERVE TAX
collective investment schemes, interests in, s 84

TAX CREDIT
Northern Ireland, in, transitional, s 81
TOBACCO PRODUCTS DUTY
rates of, s 16
TONNAGE TAX
ship leasing, capital allowances, s 57
TRANSFER PRICING
guidelines, s 58(1)
OECD principles, application of, s 58

VALUE ADDED TAX
academies, refund to, s 76
books, splitting of supplies, s 75
business samples, treatment of, s 74
imported low value goods, relief for, s 77
VALUE SHIFTING
amended provisions, Sch 9
shares and securities, disposal of by company, Sch 9 para 2
VEHICLE EXCISE DUTY
rates, table of, s 21
VULNERABLE PERSONS
monitoring schemes relating to, exemption for fees, s 39

WINE
rates of duty, s 13(5)